BRITISH CIVIL AIRCRAFT
1919–59

BRITISH
CIVIL AIRCRAFT
1919—59

VOLUME TWO

A. J. JACKSON

PUTNAM
GREAT RUSSELL STREET
LONDON

First published 1960
© A. J. Jackson 1960

*Made and printed in Great Britain
by Richard Clay and Company, Ltd.,
for the publishers, Putnam & Co. Ltd.,
42 Great Russell Street, London, W.C.1*

TO

EDDIE RIDING

CONTENTS

7

Frontispiece: The important contribution to British civil aviation made by converted military aircraft is typified by one of the Handley Page Harrow tankers of Flight Refuelling Ltd., ministering to the Short S.30 'Cabot' over Hamble Aerodrome on July 1, 1939.

('*Daily Express*' *Photo*).

FOREWORD

Uniform with Volume 1, this book continues the history of all aircraft ever used for civil purposes under British ownership and deals alphabetically with the products of manufacturers in the E–Z range. As defined in Volume 1, a British civil aircraft is not necessarily of British design but must have been issued with a Certificate of Registration by the Ministry of Aviation or its predecessors. The word aircraft is further defined as a powered aerodyne. Balloons, airships and gliders have been excluded. To preserve historical focus, companies which have changed their names have been referred to by the name carried when a particular type was built and within each manufacturer's section, aircraft are listed logically by designation. This, with few exceptions, corresponds to the order in which they went into service.

The small size of Appendix C is a measure of the degree of photographic completeness achieved. Every effort has also been made to reach a correspondingly high degree of accuracy in the specifications, but the measure of disagreement between accepted authorities or works of reference is astonishing and very much to be deplored. Many early records have been lost, destroyed or have fallen victim of enemy action, so that many manufacturers are now without accurate details of their more elderly types. The specifications given in this book are therefore the result of careful study and selection, and items of a dubious nature, and they are many, have been rigidly excluded.

Leigh-on-Sea, February 1960   A. J. J.

NOTES ON THE USE OF THIS BOOK

The main stories, specifications and appendixes should be read in conjunction with the following notes:

1. *Registrations.* A temporary system beginning K-100 and reaching K-175 was used for approximately one month from May 1919, thereafter being supplanted by a system beginning G-EAAA. An international convention in 1928 resulted in the commencement of a new series beginning G-AAAA when G-EBZZ was reached. The letter Q was discontinued after its use on a Fokker F.VIIA G-EBTQ in 1927.
   If therefore reference is made, for example, to K-117/G-EABQ, it is understood that the aircraft concerned flew as K-117 under the temporary system and as G-EABQ later.

2. *Class B Registrations.* An aircraft flies under B conditions for experiment or test; for the purpose of qualifying for Certificate of Airworthiness; for its renewal; or for the approval of modifications. Before the Second World War it carried a manufacturer's registration comprising one letter and one figure separated by a hyphen, each firm having its own letter. Since 1945 Class B registrations have been modified and now comprise the national G followed by a manufacturer's individual number and the aircraft identity, e.g. G-43-7 where 43 indicates Edgar Percival Aircraft Ltd. and 7 the aircraft.

3. *Constructor's Number.* As each airframe leaves the factory the manufacturer allots it a constructor's or airframe serial number. These are quoted in Appendix D and form a convenient means, in conjunction with the dates of issue of Cs. of A. of comparing the ages of two given aircraft. By grouping these numbers it is even possible to determine which aircraft were under construction at the same time and so visualise production at any given period. The c/n is the aircraft's only positive identification, ready to proclaim its former identities, irrespective of the nationality marks carried externally.

4. *Mark Numbers.* Aircraft mark numbers used in this, and the previous volume, are a faithful reproduction of those in use at the period under discussion. Before 1939 Roman numerals were already giving place to Arabic and were finally abandoned in 1948.

5. *Abbreviations.*
   C. of A. Certificate of Airworthiness, renewed annually on aircraft plying for hire or reward; every three years on private aircraft.

13

P. to F. Permit to Fly, usually granted for one flight only to a place
of overhaul.
A. to F. Authorisation to Fly, equivalent to a C. of A. for ultra light
aircraft.

6. *Definitions*

Height. The data given is the agreed figure for the aircraft in question
and is assumed to be measured with the aircraft in rigging position.
There is no means of proving that this is always the case. It is also
affected by variables such as airscrew position, tyre and oleo
pressures, or on large aircraft whether the tanks are full or empty.
Wing Area. Includes the area of the ailerons.
Tare Weight. Interpret as basic operational weight for modern air-
craft.
All-up Weight. Alternatively gross weight.
Cruising Speed or Cruise. Interpret as maximum economical cruis-
ing speed for modern aircraft.
Rate of Climb. Measured at take off power.
Ceiling. In many cases there is considerable doubt as to whether
stated figures refer to Service or Absolute ceiling. The absolute
ceiling is given where possible.
Range. With normal tankage unless otherwise stated.

7. *Illustrations.* Extreme care has been taken to present illustrations of
aircraft actually discussed in the text. Where it has been found
impossible to locate the desired photograph of an aircraft with full
British civil lettering, the *identical aeroplane* is always shown with
previous or subsequent markings. In a very few cases the *correct
airframe* is illustrated without markings.

8. *Cirrus Engines.* Every effort has been made to give correct designations
for these engines. Rapid changes in the style of the manufacturer
brought about a complex situation simplified only by reference to
the following table:

Period	Maker's Title	Engine Designation
1925 to 16.2.27	A.D.C. Aircraft Ltd.	A.D.C. Cirrus
16.2.27 to 2.31	Cirrus Aero Engines Ltd.	Cirrus
2.31 to 2.37	Cirrus-Hermes Engineering Co. Ltd.	Cirrus
2.37 to date	Blackburn Aircraft Ltd.	Blackburn Cirrus

ACKNOWLEDGMENTS

The author again acknowledges with gratitude the advice and encourage-
ment he has received from many individuals and organisations during the
compilation of this Second Volume. He wishes in particular to place on
record the invaluable help given by C. H. Barnes and D. E. Roberts, B.Sc.,
who have not only double checked all technical and historical data but
have assisted materially with proof reading. Thanks are also due to L. E.
Bradford for his careful preparation of the three view drawings.

Valuable assistance has again been received from H. F. King M.B.E.,
Editor of *Flight*; C. A. Sims, Chief Photographer to *The Aeroplane and
Astronautics*; the Editor and Staff of *Air Pictorial*; the Librarians of the
Royal Aeronautical Society and the Royal Aero Club; the Staff of the
Airworthiness Department of the Ministry of Aviation; the photographic
records section of the Imperial War Museum; the Information Division of
the Air Ministry and the following operators and manufacturers: Air Ser-
vice Training Ltd., Aviation Traders Ltd., Blackburn and General Aircraft
Ltd., Bristol Aircraft Ltd., British European Airways Corporation, British
Overseas Airways Corporation, Edgar Percival Aircraft Ltd., The Fairey
Aviation Co. Ltd., Gloster Aircraft Co. Ltd., Handley Page Ltd., Hawker
Aircraft Ltd., Hunting Aircraft Ltd., Kelvin-Hughes Ltd., Lancashire Air-
craft Co. Ltd., Lloyd's List and Shipping Gazette, D. Napier and Son
Ltd., Rollason Aircraft and Engines Ltd., Rolls-Royce Ltd., Saunders-
Roe Ltd., Scottish Aviation Ltd., the Shell Petroleum Co.., Ltd., Short
and Harland Ltd., the Tiger Club, Vickers-Armstrongs (Aircraft) Ltd.
and Westland Aircraft Ltd.

Contributions made by the following have not only added materially to
this book but have also served as a constant check on its accuracy: C. F.
Andrews A.R.Ae.S., C. A. Nepean Bishop A.R.Ae.S., J. M. Bruce M.A.,
C. W. Cain, C. W. Callister, P. T. Capon, J. R. Coates, D. K. Fox, J. S.
Havers, P. R. Keating, W. K. Kilsby, G. C. Kohn, C. H. Latimer-
Needham Dipl.Eng., M.Sc.Eng., F.R.Ae.S., A.F.I.Ae.S., W. T. Larkins,
A. S. C. Lumsden, H. G. Martin, F. K. Mason, L. T. Mason, J. McNulty,
P. W. Moss, P. J. R. Moyes, R. H. Nicholls, H. C. Rayner O.B.E., D.
Reid, H. E Scrope, John Stroud, F. G. Swanborough, J. W. R. Taylor,
Miss A. Tilbury, I. Wallis, J. A. Whittle.

Thanks are also due to Air-Britain for the use of certain Appendix D
information which originated in that organisation's publications.

G-APIA, first of two Edgar Percival E.P.9 aircraft delivered by air to Skyspread Ltd. in Australia, October 1957. (*Photo: R. A. Cole.*)

Edgar Percival E.P.9

E. W. Percival, Australian-born designer, builder and pilot of the world famous Percival Gull series, re-entered the British aircraft industry in 1955 and established a small factory at Stapleford Tawney Aerodrome, Essex. Here was constructed a private-venture single-engined agricultural aircraft known as the Percival P.9, based on ideas formulated during a tour to New Zealand in 1953. The designer piloted the prototype, G-AOFU, on its maiden flight on December 21, 1955, and during subsequent development flying the addition of a curved dorsal fin was the only major modification found necessary.

The unusual pod-and-boom fuselage configuration was dictated both by agricultural and aerodynamic considerations. It permitted an extra deep front fuselage capable of carrying a ton of fertiliser in a special hopper, discharging through a 20 in. slit in the bottom of the fuselage. Two pilots sat high in the front with the perfect view so necessary for low-level flying. Flown as a utility transport without the hopper, the Percival P.9 boasted a cabin with 45 sq. ft. of floor area and sufficient headroom for an adult to stand upright. It would accommodate four passengers, three stretcher cases and attendant, or a variety of rural loads, the side and rear clamshell doors being large enough to take standard wool and straw bales, 45 gallon oil drums or small livestock. Only in a low-slung pod-type fuselage was such a variety of loadings possible without excessive C.G. travel. A high wing layout was chosen to keep the stressed skin, alloy covered mainplane clear of chemical corrosion, while the fuselage was a welded steel tube structure, fabric covered aft but with a light alloy skin over the cabin and cockpit section. Fuel for $4\frac{3}{4}$ hours flying was housed in wing root tanks, and the wing itself was equipped with full span flaps and drooping ailerons to give exceptional low-speed control when operating in and out of farm fields.

To avoid confusion with Hunting Percival products, the designation of the aircraft was changed to Edgar Percival E.P.9 in November 1956, by

16

which time a batch of some 20 production aircraft had been laid down. Several were sold in the Commonwealth, one to the French concern S. A. Fenwick and two were submitted to Boscombe Down in military marks for Army evaluation, but the majority demonstrated their remarkable versatility while operating as British civil aircraft overseas. In March 1957 the third production aircraft, G-AOZY, was delivered to the German concern Ernst Lund A.G. for spraying fruit crops, insecticide from the 170 gallon tank being distributed through orifices in underwing booms to spray a swathe 90 ft. wide at 100 m.p.h. It was destroyed in a flying accident while spraying near Wunsdorf a couple of months later and was replaced by the seventh production aircraft, G-APBF, which in May 1957 had completed a demonstration tour of Sweden. From September 1957 this machine was in continuous daily use on pest-control duties all over Germany until it collided with a tree a year later. The next aircraft, G-APAD, which left the works in April 1957, was fitted with four seats in the cabin, crated and shipped to Australia, where it was demonstrated for six weeks by Beverley Snook. Following this tour, orders were received for four E.P.9s, which all completed the 14,000 mile delivery flight to Australia without incident. First of these, G-APBR, originally shown at the Paris Aero Show in June 1957 and subsequently demonstrated in Spain and North Africa by H. Best-Devereux, was acquired, together with G-APFY, by Super Spread Aviation (Pty.) Ltd. of Melbourne. Carrying miscellaneous freight, including a racing-car engine in each, they were flown out by Messrs Miller and Tadgell in September 1957. A month later, the second pair, the all red G-APIA and 'IB, left Croydon, piloted by Messrs. Oates and Whiteman en route to Skyspread Ltd. of Sydney. A fifth E.P.9, with no British associations, was shipped to Proctor Rural Services Ltd. Three others, G-APCR, 'CS and 'CT, left Croydon in September 1957 on delivery to Bahamas Helicopters (U.K.) Ltd. for light freighting and communications duties in connection with the oil drilling contract in Libya. British domestic use of the E.P.9 was confined to two aircraft, mainly because of import restrictions on American engines for installation in British-owned machines. The prototype, acquired by L. Marmol of Air Ads Ltd., Stapleford, in June 1957 has been intensively employed ever since in its primary role as a crop sprayer and G-APLP, was temporarily employed for a similar purpose by the Bembridge, I.O.W. firm, Crop Culture (Aerial) Ltd.

G-AOZO appeared at most major air displays during 1957, and in April 1958 was flown to Ostersund, Sweden, by L. Marmol for demonstration on skis to the military authorities. Later in the year Edgar Percival Aircraft Ltd. was taken over by Samlesbury Engineering Ltd., together with 'ZO, 'LP, seven unfinished airframes and all the jigs. The company was then renamed the Lancashire Aircraft Co. Ltd. and aircraft with the revised designation Lancashire Prospector Type E.P.9 are now in production at Samlesbury Aerodrome. Lycoming engines of 295 h.p. are now fitted as standard, with Cheetah and Wasp conversions available if required. The first Cheetah engined Prospector was Skyspread's VH-FBZ, formerly G-APIB, converted at Sydney at the end of 1959. Intensive sales drives included spraying and passenger carrying demonstrations by G-AOZO and G-APWX respectively at the Vienna International Trade Fair in March 1960, by 'ZO at Hanover a month later and an African sales tour by 'WX flown by the Earl of Bective.

Manufacturers: The Lancashire Aircraft Co. Ltd., Samlesbury Aerodrome, near Blackburn, Lancs. Original design and production batch by Edgar Percival Aircraft Ltd., Stapleford Tawney Aerodrome, Essex.

Power Plants: (E.P.9)   One 270 h.p. Lycoming GO-480-B1.B.
    (Prospector) One 295 h.p. Lycoming GO-480-G1.A6.
    One 370 h.p. Armstrong Siddeley Cheetah 10.

Dimensions: Span, 43 ft. 6 in. Length, 29 ft. 6 in. Height, 8 ft. 9 in. Wing area, 227·6 sq. ft.

	E.P.9		Prospector	
	Normal	Agricultural	Normal	Agricultural
Tare weight .	2,010 lb.	2,010 lb.	2,072 lb.	2.072 lb.
All-up weight .	3,550 lb.	4,140 lb.	3,700 lb.	4,320 lb.
Maximum speed	146 m.p.h.	144 m.p.h.	146 m.p.h.	144 m.p.h.
Cruising speed .	128 m.p.h.	120 m.p.h.	128 m.p.h.	126 m.p.h.
Initial climb .	1,120 ft./min.	960 ft./min.	960 ft./min.	600 ft./min.
Ceiling . .	17,500 ft.	—	14,000 ft.	—
Range . .	580 miles	—	580 miles	—

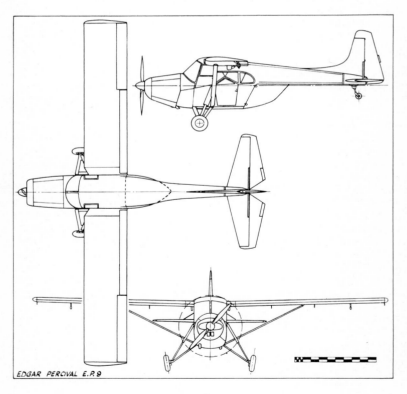

EDGAR PERCIVAL E.P.9

Fairchild Argus 2 G-AJVI in the colours of Cambrian Airways.

Fairchild 24W-41A Argus 2

The Fairchild 24 cabin tourer was first produced at Hagerstown, Maryland, U.S.A., in 1933 as a two seater and continued in production in a variety of developed forms until 1947. It was of fabric-covered composite construction with welded steel tube fuselage and wooden wing with plywood leading edge. The first example imported for British use was a three seat model 24C8-C, G-AECO, which arrived in April 1936 for W. L. S. MacCleod at High Post, exciting much comment on account of its high gloss finish, car-type interior, electric starter and wind-down windows. In November 1937 this aircraft was sold to J. D. Profumo at Leamington Spa, where it was based until impressed by the R.A.F. in October 1940. Three other pre-war Fairchild 24s also achieved British civil status, the first in November 1936, when Lord Willoughby de Broke bought the in-line Ranger engined model 24C8-F G-AEOU. A second aircraft of this type, G-AFFK, was acquired in June 1938 by J. H. Thompson of Heston, joined soon afterwards by an Australian registered, Scarab engined model 24C8-E, VH-AAW, kept at Hatfield by A. S. Van Goës. In October 1938 this became G-AFKW, and early in the following year passed into the hands of J. B. de J. Cleyndest, continuing to fly from Hatfield until R.A.F. impressment also claimed it.

A four seat version, introduced in 1938, was in common use in America before the war both as the radial Warner engined 24W and the in-line Ranger powered 24R. With the coming of war, 161 Fairchild 24W-41 aircraft were supplied to the R.A.F. for communications duties under American Lend-Lease agreements, deliveries commencing in the autumn of 1941. They were allotted the R.A.F. type name Argus 1, many going into service on pilot ferry duties in the United Kingdom with the Air Transport Auxiliary. The Fairchild 24W-41A Argus 2, externally identical, was fitted with a more powerful engine, a 24 volt instead of a 12 volt electrical system, an engine-driven generator and instrument-panel modifications.

The first British owned Fairchild 24C8-C at High Post in 1936. (*Photo courtesy of J. G. Ellison.*)

Some 364, or over half the total production, went into service with the R.A.F. during 1943–44, mainly in the Near and Middle East and were later supplemented by the entire output of 306 Ranger engined Fairchild 24R Argus 3 machines. These were largely employed in the Pacific area, South Africa and the Near East.

When hostilities ceased, large numbers of Argus 2 aircraft (including Argus 1s which had been modified to Mk. 2 standard) were purchased outright from the U.S.A.F. and offered for civilian disposal, not only in the United Kingdom but in almost every part of Europe and the Commonwealth. During the twelve months commencing October 1946, 54 surplus Argus 2s were registered as British civil aeroplanes, which, with few exceptions, were successfully overhauled and flown, becoming a common sight in British skies in the early '50s.

As a civil aeroplane the Argus got away to an ignominious start when the first one, G-AITG, suffered engine failure, and forced landed in the sea, near North House, Silloth, on November 11, 1946, while being flown south by the late F. Bosworth for civil conversion at White Waltham. Firms specialising in Argus overhaul and conversion included Scottish Aviation Ltd. at Prestwick, who delivered G-AIXM to Miss Daphne Miller for joyriding in December 1946 and G-AJFY 'Diana' to Mrs. D. V. Harward for a flight to Kenya in March 1947. They also converted a batch of six, G-AJST-'SY, on behalf of Industrial and Motor Concessions Ltd., two of which, G-AJSU and 'SY, were flown to the Belgian Congo, where the former completed several years of the hardest bush flying in the world. West London Aero Services Ltd. at White Waltham were also much concerned with Argus conversions, which was inevitable in view of White Waltham's close ties with A.T.A. They converted G-AIYO for F. Bosworth, who sold it to the well-known racing pilot W. P. Bowles. It will always be remembered, however, for its years of service as 'Grey Dove' with the Women's Junior Air Corps. Other well-known White Waltham products were J. J. Hofer's G-AJAT and 'SP, H. Holt-Bignell's G-AJDO, the Churchley brothers' G-AJDT, L. D. Hawthorn's G-AJSG and 'SH, Solar Air Services' G-AJSM and G-AKGW, the Hon. B. L. Bathurst's G-AJSN, Pasold Ltd.'s G-AJSR and 'SS, the West London Aero Club's G-AJPI, 'RZ and 'SO and the Denham Aero Club's G-AJXA. Airwork Ltd. at Heston were responsible for a few civilianisations, notably G-AJGW and 'NN for Butlin's holiday camps, which also owned the White Waltham converted G-AJPE and 'JVI. All four were used for joy-riding or carrying the firm's executives to and from the camps, landings being made at Ingoldmells (Skegness), Broomhall (Pwllheli) and else-where. When Butlin's abandoned their aviation interests in 1950 'NN be-came the communications aircraft of Aviation Traders Ltd. at Southend and 'VI went to Cardiff. In Cambrian Airways colours it was the personal aircraft of S. Kenneth Davies for several years.

A most ambitious scheme began in 1947 with the conversion of no less than 10 Argus 2s at Weston-super-Mare. In a standard silver-and-red colour scheme they formed the joint fleet of the Home Counties Aero Club at Willingale Aerodrome, Essex, and of the Weston Aero Club at Weston-super-Mare. Although the low initial cost of the Argus was attractive, many Argus owners and operators soon discovered that a four seater re-quiring 165 h.p. was far from economical by British standards. Thus the Argus was short lived both at Willingale and Weston, the fleet eventually being sold overseas. First to go, G-AJOW, was for several years based at Rome by a B.E.A.C. official, R. MacKisray. Two others, G-AJOX and 'PC, were used for charter work in East Anglia by J. G. Crampton and G. Clifton respectively.

Airtech Ltd. at Thame completed six, including G-AKJA, which eventually passed into the hands of the Air Navigation and Trading Co. Ltd. for joyriding at Squires Gate, where it was joined by G-AJBF and several others. By 1952 the heyday of the Argus in Britain was over and there began an exodus, to taxi firms in the Antipodes and in Finland, and by 1958 only six British owned Argus 2s remained. Two are today based at Elmdon, two at White Waltham, and one each at Gatwick and Darwin, Australia. G-AJSH was used by the well-known racing motorist J. 'Mike' Hawthorn to fly to various appointments with speed, until written off by another pilot at Fairoaks in 1958.

Lord Willoughby de Broke's Fairchild 24C8-F G-AEOU which, in 1938, was based at his private landing ground at Kineton, Warwickshire.

21

Probably the most colourful career was that of G-AIZE, civilianised at Elstree in 1947 for Van Leer Auto Die Castings Ltd. but later sold to B. R. Campanini. After damage in a forced landing at Fiumicino, Italy, on September 5, 1948 it reappeared in the Pan American hangar at London Airport under American ownership as N9996F 'Lil Faster', in which guise it flies regularly at Blackbushe to the present day.

The Ranger engine of the Argus 3 did not qualify for British validation of American C. of A., with the result that three attempts at conversion came to nought. The first, G-AJDD, formerly an R.A.F. aircraft KK512, was overhauled at Bahrein in 1949 by F. Bosworth of the Gulf Aviation Company, but before attempts at certification were fairly under way, it was destroyed by fire on the ground. The second, G-AKPX, formerly HB722, the property of R. L. Whyham at Squires Gate, never flew as a British civil aeroplane. After a year in storage it flew away on June 1, 1950 en route to Finland as OH-FCA, still in its wartime camouflage. A third and final attempt was made by Gulf Aviation Ltd. at Bahrein in 1951 when two local American owned Fairchild 24s, both former R.A.F. aircraft, were acquired. They comprised Argus 2 N79922, which became G-AMAZ, and an Argus 3 N79925, registered as G-AMBA. Although fully painted up in British markings, neither went into service.

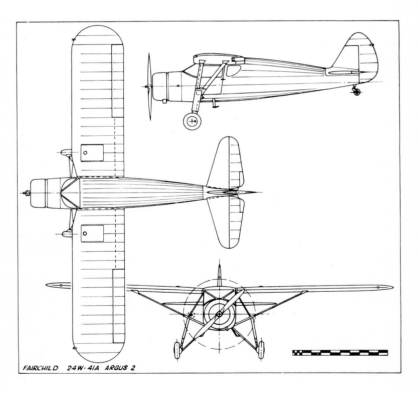

FAIRCHILD 24W-41A ARGUS 2

Manufacturers: Fairchild Aircraft Corporation, Hagerstown, Maryland, U.S.A.
Power Plants: (24C8-C)   145 h.p. Warner Super Scarab SS.210E.
            (24C8-E)   145 h.p. Warner Super Scarab.
            (24C8-F)   150 h.p. Ranger 6-390-D3.
            (24W-41)   145 h.p. Warner Super Scarab 145.
            (24W-41A) 165 h.p. Warner Super Scarab 165.
            (24R)   175 h.p. Ranger 6-440-C2.

	24C8-E	24C8-F	24W-41A	24R
Span . .	36 ft. 4 in.	36 ft. 4 in.	36 ft. 4 in.	36 ft. 4 in.
Length . .	23 ft. 9 in.	24 ft. 10 in.	23 ft. 9 in.	25 ft. 10 in.
Height . .	7 ft. 3 in.	7 ft. 3 in.	7 ft. 7½ in.	7 ft. 8 in.
Wing area . .	186 sq. ft.	186 sq. ft.	173·6 sq. ft.	173·6 sq. ft.
Tare weight .	1,390 lb.	1,577 lb.	1,482 lb.	—
All-up weight .	2,400 lb.	2,400 lb.	2,562 lb.	2,562 lb.
Maximum speed .	133 m.p.h.	130 m.p.h.	124 m.p.h.	132 m.p.h.
Cruising speed .	120 m.p.h.	113 m.p.h.	112 m.p.h.	117 m.p.h.
Initial climb .	700 ft./min.	565 ft./min.	—	—
Ceiling . .	15,500 ft.	14,500 ft.	15,700 ft.	—
Range . .	525 miles	500 miles	720 miles	640 miles

The Fairey III amphibian taxying at Martlesham during the Air Ministry Competitions, September 1920. (*'Flight' Photo.*)

Fairey III to IIIF

The remarkable series of Fairey III variants which spanned two decades stemmed from the two experimental two seat patrol seaplanes built by the Fairey Company in 1917. These bore constructor's numbers F.127 and F.128, and in the easy manner of the period became known as the Fairey F.127 and Fairey F.128 respectively. Their Admiralty serial numbers N9 and N10 were used as an alternative nomenclature. The F.127, intended for shipboard operation, was a sesquiplane powered by a 190 h.p. Rolls-Royce Falcon I water-cooled engine, and after trials at Hamble and the Isle of Grain, carried out early catapault trials on H.M.S. *Slinger*. In 1919 it was repurchased from the Admiralty by the manufacturers and de-militarised as a civil aircraft with the temporary marking K-103, sub-sequently flying as a Fairey III G-EAAJ. It was modified with equal-span wings and Maori engine, and commencing on May 3, Sidney Pickles made a few flights in it from Blackfriars to the Thanet towns, landings being made in and around the Medway estuary to deliver the *Evening News*. The veteran was sold in Norway in May 1920, and thus the ancestor of a line of famous British naval aeroplanes spent the major portion of its life in civil colours in a foreign land. It was heard of in August 1927 at Eids-vold, owned by Bjarne Nielson, and finally went to the scrap heap in February 1929. The fuselage and empennage of the second experimental aircraft, the F.128, N10, were identical with those of the F.127, but it had equal-span folding wings, Fairey Patent Camber Gear, a larger fin, a 260 h.p. Maori engine and side radiators. A more formal designation—Fairey III—was then bestowed upon it, but at the end of 1917 it became a landplane with the radiator placed in the conventional position behind the airscrew. In this form it was known as the Fairey IIIA, and in 1919 was bought back by the makers to become a civil aeroplane G-EALQ. Later it was modified as a single-seat seaplane for entry in the Schneider Trophy Race held at Bournemouth on September 10, 1919. The wing

24

span was reduced from 46 to 28 ft. and a 450 h.p. Napier Lion installed with side radiators, the designation reverting once more to Fairey III. Piloted by Lt.-Col. Vincent Nicholl, D.S.O., 'LQ was the only entry to return to moorings under its own power, but fog eventually caused the event to be declared void. A year later, on September 17, 1920, the same pilot arrived at Martlesham flying the same machine greatly modified for the Air Ministry's commercial amphibian competition. Standard 46 ft. folding wings had been replaced, a cockpit for two passengers side by side was provided behind the pilot and manually retractable, narrow-track wheels were fitted between the floats. Although it performed creditably, making slow-speed runs at 47·25 m.p.h. and completing various sea trials at Felixstowe, no prize was awarded owing to its failure to take off after the 24 hours mooring test on September 26–27. The veteran's useful life came to an end in 1922 after a period on communications duties between Hamble and the Isle of Grain.

Fifty Fairey IIIA naval floatplanes, powered by 260 h.p. Sunbeam Maori engines, built in 1918, saw little service and were put up for disposal. One of these, N2876, was acquired by the Navarro Aviation Company as G-EADZ, but proposals to use it as a landplane for joyriding came to nought. Lt.-Col. G. L. P. Henderson then converted it to approximate Fairey IIIC standard under a new registration G-EAMY, by fitting a 360 h.p. Rolls-Royce Eagle VIII engine before shipment to Sweden in company with the second prototype Fairey IIIC G-EAPV, formerly N2255. The latter made three trans-Baltic proving flights between Stockholm and Helsingfors with passengers and newspapers during the summer of 1920, afterwards doing pleasure flying for the P.O. Flygkompani at Barkaby. Both machines operated on skis during the winter and were modified to carry a passenger beside the pilot and four others in the rear cockpit. Unfortunately 'MY crashed in an inaccessible forest of 50 ft. trees due to the breakage of a rudder control cable.

One of Col. G. L. P. Henderson's Fairey IIIC aircraft on skis in Sweden, 1920. (*Photo : The Fairey Aviation Co. Ltd.*)

25

A Fairey IIIC, G-EARS, built with the main production batch in June 1919, was used as a demonstrator by the manufacturers during 1920, after which it was sold to the Aircraft Disposal Co. Ltd. Two years later, in June 1922, another Fairey IIIC from this batch was civilianised in India by the makers as G-EBDI for the Calcutta–Vancouver section of Major W. T. Blake's proposed World Flight. On August 19, 1922, piloted by Capt. Norman Macmillan and carrying cameraman Geoffrey Malins, it became the first seaplane to take off from the Hoogli River, course being set for Akyab in Assam. An air lock in the fuel system caused a forced landing in a gale near the island of Lukhidia Char in the Bay of Bengal, and eventually 'DI turned turtle with a waterlogged float. Its crew were rescued after six gruelling days afloat on the wreckage, which sank following an attempt to tow it to Chittagong.

The Fairey IIID powered by a 450 h.p. Napier Lion engine and fitted with re-designed fuselage and tail unit had a much improved performance and was in production for the R.A.F. and Fleet Air Arm from 1920 until 1925. One machine, G-EBKE, powered by a 360 h.p. Rolls-Royce Eagle IX was built to the order of Real Daylight Balata Estates Ltd. for ambulance duties in British Guiana. The rear fuselage decking was fitted with portholes and hinged upwards in two sections to admit a stretcher case. After acceptance trials at Hamble in October 1924, it was shipped to Georgetown, where Capt. G. N. Trace flew it regularly for some years, to and from the mining areas 200 miles up-river.

The tropics also claimed the only other British civil Fairey IIID. In December 1926 the North Sea Aerial and General Transport Co. Ltd. inaugurated a mail and passenger service along the Nile between Khartoum and Kisumu with the D.H.50J seaplane G-EBOP 'Pelican'. After only a few flights it struck floating wreckage when taking off, sank and became a total loss. The Air Council thereupon loaned the company a Lion engined Fairey IIID S1076, converted into a four seater G-EBPZ at Aboukir. Its

G-EBKE, the Eagle engined Fairey IIID ambulance (*Photo: The Fairey Aviation Co. Ltd.*)

Sole example of a British civil Fairey IIIF with Lion engine, G-AABY at Mildenhall prior to the race to Australia 1934.

The first of two special Jaguar engined Fairey IIIF survey aircraft. (*Photo: The Fairey Aviation Co. Ltd.*)

first service ex Khartoum was flown by Capt. Boyle on February 2, 1927. In this aircraft the Director of Civil Aviation, Sir Sefton Brancker, and two other passengers were marooned on Lake Victoria Nyanza a few weeks later when altitude and midday heat combined to make take off impossible. On March 13, 1927 the IIID's undercarriage failed after four unsuccessful take off attempts and it sank in Lake Victoria, later to be damaged beyond repair during salvage operations.

By this time the IIID had been replaced in the R.A.F. by the three seat Fairey IIIF. Thus in September 1928 the manufacturers commissioned a standard IIIF G-AABY as a civil demonstrator which figured largely in the proceedings at Heston during the Olympia Aero Show of July 1929.

27

On July 30, 1930 it was flown to Brussels by C. R. McMullin, demonstrated to the Belgian Air Force and later flown to Tatoi, Athens via Vienna and Belgrade, arriving on August 1. During similar demonstration to the Greeks, it was towed to Phaleron Bay and fitted with floats. At a later date the performance was repeated for the military authorities in China, where it met with an accident. In September 1934 'BY reappeared as an entry in the handicap section of the MacRobertson Race to Australia and was rebuilt at North Weald. Starting from Mildenhall on October 20, 1934 piloted by F/O C. G. Davies and Lt.-Com. C. N. Hill, it suffered many vicissitudes, landing south of Paris for fuel and again in Cyprus with minor troubles and eventually retiring from the race. Reaching Australia under its own power, this unique machine eked out the remainder of its useful life in the New Guinea goldfields.

Last civil specimens of a noble line were two Fairey IIIFs G-AASK and 'TT fitted with Jaguar VIC aircooled radials. They were used by the Air Survey Co. Ltd. for mapping the Sudan, 'SK completing its delivery flight to Juba on January 23, 1930. The second IIIF, 'TT, also flown out, left Croydon on February 9, 1930 piloted by R. C. Kemp who made the distance in easy stages, arriving at Juba on February 22, 1930. Although 'TT crashed in October 1930, 'SK had a long and useful career and became an important aeroplane in the annals of aerial photography until retired at the end of 1934.

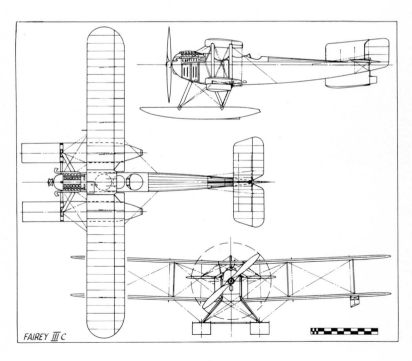

FAIREY III C

Manufacturers: The Fairey Aviation Co. Ltd., Hayes, Mx., and Hamble Aero-drome, near Southampton, Hants.

Power Plants: (Fairey III)   One 450 h.p. Napier Lion.
          (Fairey IIIA) One 260 h.p. Sunbeam Maori II.
          (Fairey IIIC) One 360 h.p. Rolls-Royce Eagle VIII.
          (Fairey IIID) One 360 h.p. Rolls-Royce Eagle IX.
                      One 450 h.p. Napier Lion.
          (Fairey IIIF) One 450 h.p. Napier Lion XI civil.
                      One 490 h.p. Armstrong Siddeley Jaguar VIC.

	Fairey III (Lion) Seaplane	Fairey III Amphibian	Fairey IIIA Landplane
Span	28 ft. 0 in.	46 ft. 1¼ in.	46 ft. 2 in.
Length . .	—	34 ft. 4 in.	31 ft. 0 in.
Height . .	—	12 ft. 0 in.	10 ft. 8 in.
Wing area . .	—	488 sq. ft.	476 sq. ft.
Tare weight .	—	3,771 lb.	2,532 lb.} (1)
All-up weight .	5,000 lb.	5,250 lb.	3,698 lb.}
Maximum speed . .	—	118 m.p.h.	109·5 m.p.h.
Cruising speed .	—	82 m.p.h.	—
Initial climb .	—	—	750 ft./min.
Ceiling . .	—	—	15,000 ft.
Duration . .	—	—	4½ hours

	Fairey IIIC Seaplane	Fairey IIID (Lion) Seaplane	Fairey IIIF (Lion) Landplane
Span	46 ft. 1¼ in.	46 ft. 1¼ in.	45 ft. 9 in.
Length . .	36 ft. 0 in.	36 ft. 0 in.	36 ft. 8⅝ in.
Height . .	12 ft. 1¾ in.	13 ft. 0 in.	14 ft. 2⅜ in.
Wing area . .	476 sq. ft.	500 sq. ft.	438·5 sq. ft.
Tare weight .	3,549 lb.} (2)	—	3,890 lb.} (3)
All-up weight .	5,050 lb.}	—	5,900 lb.}
Maximum speed . .	101 m.p.h.	117 m.p.h.	120 m.p.h.
Cruising speed .	—		
Initial climb .	600 ft./min.	800 ft./min.	900 ft./min.
Ceiling . .	9,100 ft.	19,500 ft.	—
Range/Duration . .	5 hours	530 miles	400 miles

(1) G-EADZ, (2) G-EARS, (3) G-AABY, take off, Australia Race.

The Lynx engined Fokker F.VIIA/3m owned by the Rt. Hon. F. E. Guest from
December 1926 to March 1927.

Fokker F.III to F.XII

Anthony Fokker's immortal transport monoplanes, backbone of European
air lines for almost two decades, were inseparably linked with British aviation. In the earliest days, the majority of K.L.M. Royal Dutch Air Line
pilots were British and the honour of first landing such an aircraft at Croydon fell to W. G. R. Hinchliffe on October 1, 1920. It was a cabin four-
seat Fokker F.II, H-NABD, powered by a 185 h.p. B.M.W. and embodying the welded steel fuselage and one-piece wooden, cantilever, plywood-
covered wing which its larger and better-known successors made famous.
On April 12, 1921 Gordon P. Olley brought from Amsterdam a five seat
Fokker F.III H-NABH powered by a 240 h.p. Siddeley Puma, in which
the single pilot sat, omnibus style, in an open cockpit along the starboard side of the engine. The design matured apace, and by 1925 the
larger Fokker F.VII and F.VIIA monoplanes were in service on the
Amsterdam–Croydon route. They were fitted with the 360 h.p. Rolls-
Royce Eagle IX and the 450 h.p. Gnôme-Rhône Jupiter 9AB engines
respectively, and each accommodated eight passengers and two crew. By
1926 the trimotor Fokker F.VIIA/3m had been devised in order to reduce
the possibility of forced landings through engine failure. Any two of the
Lynx motors were sufficient to maintain height on full load, and the
rugged simplicity of the Fokker design, coupled with an unequalled safety
record, resulted in longevity and their appearance on the second-hand
market. The first British purchaser, the Rt. Hon. F. E. Guest, acquired
two ex K.L.M. aircraft at the end of 1926, a Jupiter powered F.VIIA
G-EBPL and a Lynx engined F.VIIA/3m G-EBPV, both of which carried
out a number of private flights between Croydon and Switzerland.

In August 1927 two further Jupiter engined Fokker F.VIIAs, each of
which had seen two years airline service with K.L.M., were sold to British
owners for the then fashionable occupation of attempting the east–west
crossing of the Atlantic. First of these, G-EBTQ 'St. Raphael', last
British aeroplane to include the letter Q in its registration marks, was
acquired by H.S.H. Princess Alice of Lowenstein-Wertheim, better known

as Lady Anne Savile, Leslie Hamilton's passenger in the D.H.9C
G-EBAX during the 1922 King's Cup Race. After servicing at Filton,
'St. Raphael' took off from Upavon on August 31, 1927 with a crew
consisting of an Imperial Airways pilot Lt.-Col. F. Minchin, Leslie
Hamilton and the owner. The project ended in disaster, 'TQ passed out
over the Irish coast and was never seen again. The other F.VIIA,
acquired by the irrepressible R. H. McIntosh, also an Imperial Airways
pilot, was fitted in the Netherlands with long-range cabin tanks and was
flown to Filton by Maurice Piercey at the beginning of September 1927.
Still in K.L.M. blue and gold and with Dutch markings, it was without
cabin windows and carried the name 'Princess Xenia'. British registered
as G-EBTS and with Commandant J. C. Fitzmaurice of the Irish Free
State Air Corps as co-pilot, 'Princess Xenia' made a start from Baldonnel
on September 16, 1927. When 100 miles out over the Atlantic, a storm of
such violence was encountered that the crew very wisely returned to make
a safe landing at Ballybunnion. R. H. McIntosh then teamed up with
H. J. 'Bert' Hinkler for an attempt to fly 'Princess Xenia' to India, but
after a non-stop flight of 24 hours in almost continuous fog, they were
forced to land in Poland. The aircraft was then sold to a syndicate known
as Air Communications Ltd. and left Lympne on June 10, 1928 in a
second attempt to fly to India. This time it was piloted by C. D. Barnard
and E. H. Alliott and carried the Duchess of Bedford as passenger.
Although Bushire on the Persian Gulf was reached in two days, the flight
was abandoned through an unserviceable engine. Not until a new one had
been shipped out was it possible to fly on to Karachi, reached on August
22. The aircraft then flew back in the record time of $4\frac{1}{2}$ days, after which
it went back to the Fokker factory in the Netherlands for a complete overhaul. A geared Jupiter XI was then installed and the name changed to
'The Spider', symbol of perseverance. With R. Little as co-pilot and navigator, Barnard left Lympne once more at dawn on August 2, 1929. This
time the attack was successful, and $7\frac{1}{2}$ days later Barnard put the Fokker
and a smiling Duchess safely down at Croydon. After an overhaul at
Woodford by A. V. Roe and Co. Ltd. 'The Spider' reappeared with silver

'Princess Xenia' during the abortive India flight of June 1928, showing the ungeared
Jupiter VI engine and small cabin windows above the name. (*Photo: The Bristol
Aeroplane Co. Ltd.*)

31

S. F. 'Timber' Woods of Surrey Flying Services Ltd. taxying the Fokker F.XI Universal at Croydon in 1932.

fuselage and blue lettering in readiness for an attempt on the out-and-home record to the Cape. With the same crew and again carrying the Duchess of Bedford, the veteran Fokker gained fresh long-distance laurels by leaving Lympne on April 10, 1930, covering 19,000 miles and returning to Croydon in record time 21 days later. But for a forced landing, carried out in masterly fashion in the dreaded Dragoman Pass in S.E. Europe, 'The Spider' would have returned one day earlier.

After exhibition for a week at Bush House, Strand, the famous aircraft was taken over by C. D. Barnard Air Tours Ltd. and converted into a 12 seater for joyriding. Airline windows deleted in 1927 were replaced, and to reduce the cabin noise level, the exhaust collector ring, removed before the 1929 India flight, was refitted. Between April 1, 1931 and the final performance at Hanworth on October 11, Barnard's Circus visited 118 towns in all parts of the British Isles, carrying some 40,000 joyriders, most of whom flew in 'The Spider'. In the following year the veteran appeared at Heston in the grey and red colours of the British Air Navigation Co. Ltd. and was put to good use on a luxury service to Le Touquet. For two weeks in July 1932 it was also flown by C. D. Barnard on an experimental service between Whitchurch and Cardiff, operating to a 40 minute schedule. Finally, in May 1935, the machine once more found its way to India, where it flew for a season with C. D. Barnard Air Tours Ltd. and later became the private aeroplane of Sir Dossabhor Hormasje Bhuwandwella, Kt., J.P., at Bombay, until sent to the scrap heap in 1937.

The next Fokker monoplane to appear in British marks was the small, six seat, Wright Whirlwind powered F.XI Universal, G-EBUT, built in America and therefore not of K.L.M. origin. Named 'Miss Africa', it had been based at Nairobi since November 1927 by the pioneer Kenya pilot John Carberry (otherwise Lord Carbery). The machine was later loaned to Sir Piers Mostyn for a flight to Croydon, reached on May 20, 1928. Carberry then flew it back, arriving in Nairobi on December 12, 1928, after which it spent a few weeks as VP-KAB before returning once more to the United Kingdom. From March 1929 until August 1932 it flew in the familiar red colour scheme of Air Taxis Ltd. at Stag Lane, but the most memorable part of its career was spent at Croydon, where, until 1935, it was used for taxi work and joyriding by Surrey Flying Services Ltd. An Australian, Douglas Sheppard, then took it to the Antipodes, where it was eventually destroyed by fire.

Two Lynx engined Fokker F.VIIA/3m trimotors acquired from K.L.M. in 1928, became the personal aircraft of millionaires. The first, G-EBYI, was flown by D. H. Drew, nominal owner on behalf of the Belgian financier Alfred Lowenstein. Carrying a secretary, two typists and a valet, almost daily flights were made between Croydon and Brussels during the early part of 1928, until on July 4 the owner fell out of the machine some 5 miles off the French Coast. In July 1929 the aircraft was chartered to Lt.-Cdr. Glen Kidston for a big-game expedition in Central Africa, during which an airlock in the fuel system caused a forced landing at Tomba, 30 miles from Mongalla, but Donald Drew's masterly handling resulted in damage only to undercarriage and wing. The dismantled aircraft eventually returned to the Fokker works and in 1930 faded from British ownership. The second trimotor, G-EBZJ, property of wealthy Canadian Major A. P. Holt, was delivered from Amsterdam to Croydon in Dutch markings by his personal pilot R. H. McIntosh on June 23, 1928. For two years it flew in and around Europe until sold abroad and was followed to Britain by quite the most remarkable of contemporary Fokker aeroplanes. Starting life as a Jupiter powered F.VIIA H-NADP, this had carried a wealthy American newspaper proprietor Van Lear Black on the first K.L.M. passenger flight ever made to the Dutch East Indies. Rebuilt in 1928 as a Fokker F.VIIB/3m PH-ADP, with three Gnôme Rhône Titan I engines and the new oversize wing of 71 ft. 2¼ in. span, it was again hired by Van Lear Black for a flight from London to the Cape, thence via Persia to the Far East and return. Piloted by K.L.M. Captains Geysendorfer and Scholte, it left Croydon on May 14, 1928, but the flight was abandoned following damage at Khartoum on May 22. After this it was dismantled, shipped back to Holland for repair and fitted with Wright Whirlwind radials. The three view drawing on page 36 shows it in this form. In February 1929 the machine came under British registry as G-AADZ 'Maryland Free State', owned on behalf of Van Lear Black by Sir R. C. Witt, until taken over a few days later by V.L.B. Ltd. Thereafter it became famous as a globe trotter, completing the previously planned round trip from Croydon to the Cape and the Far East between May 31, 1929 and January 22, 1930, leaving again for the same destination on February 8. After this flight it did not return and was sold abroad. A slightly modified Whirlwind powered Fokker F.VIIC/3m G-AATG 'Extra Dry', owned by W.Z. Ltd. of London, was based in Switzerland from February 1930 onwards and was not seen in England until its arrival at Heston in May 1931. After staying a few days, it flew away never to return and was sold abroad four years later.

In 1929 two antique Puma powered Fokker F.III monoplanes were purchased in Denmark by a new firm, British Air Lines Ltd., of Croydon. Their plans were wrecked along with their first aeroplane, G-AALC, when it failed to take off and collided with a house in Plough Lane less than a month after arrival. The other Fokker F.III, G-AARG, remained in a hangar at Heston for several years until sold to G. C. Stead in February

1931. A few flights were made that year, but the veteran was scrapped as soon as its C. of A. expired.

When K.L.M. began replacing its faithful Fokkers with Douglas DC-2s in 1936, four 18 seat Wasp C powered F.XII monoplanes were sold to Crilly Airways Ltd. of Croydon, to which they were no strangers, having flown in and out for several years. Their careers on Crilly cross-Channel services were short because the firm was almost immediately absorbed by British Airways Ltd. The F.XIIs were then stationed at Gatwick, but on August 15, 1936 all flew away to take part in the Spanish Civil War. This catastrophe was also the *raison d'être* for the acquisition by the League of Nations Union of the two elderly F.VIIAs G-AEHE and 'HF. Although nominally registered in June 1936 to Prof. Gilbert Murray, LL.D., D. Litt., as British civil aeroplanes, they never appeared in the United Kingdom and returned to Dutch ownership at the end of the year.

One of the four Crilly Airways Fokker F.XIIs at Croydon in 1936.

One of the twin engined Fokker F.VIIIs used by British Airways Ltd. from 1936 to 1938. They carried twelve passengers and two crew.

34

British Airways Ltd. partially replaced the original F.XIIs with two later models fitted with Wasp T1D1 engines. These became G-AEOS and 'OT, primarily for operating passenger and mail routes between Heston, Gatwick and the Continent. When manoeuvring for a night landing on November 19, 1936, 'OT crashed into a wooded hillside 4½ miles south of Gatwick, Capts. A. P. K. Hattersley and V. J. W. Bredenkamp being killed. To complete the quartet, two twin engined Fokker F.VIIIs G-AEPT and 'PU had also been acquired. These were not only the last of the early Fokker types to assume British nationality but the only specimens of the F.VIII to do so, and flew on the Company's cross-Channel routes for two seasons.

SPECIFICATION

Manufacturers: N. V. Nederlandsche Vliegtuigenfabriek Fokker, Schiphol Aerodrome, Amsterdam, Netherlands.   Fokker F.XI built by The Atlantic Aircraft Corporation, Teterborough, New Jersey, U.S.A.

Power Plants: (F.III)   One 240 h.p. Siddeley Puma.
        (F.VIIA)   One 480 h.p. Bristol Jupiter VI.
                        One 450 h.p. Gnôme-Rhône Jupiter 9AB.
                        One 500 h.p. Bristol Jupiter XI.
        (F.VIIA/3m) Three 215 h.p. Armstrong Siddeley Lynx IVC.
        (F.VIIB/3m) Three 330 h.p. Wright Whirlwind J-6-9.
        (F.VIII)   Two 500 h.p. Pratt and Whitney Wasp T1D1.
        (F.XI)   One 300 h.p. Wright Whirlwind J-6.
        (F.XII)   Three 420 h.p. Pratt and Whitney Wasp C.
                        Three 500 h.p. Pratt and Whitney Wasp T1D1.

	F.III	F.VIIA	F.VIIA/3m	F.VIIB/3m
Span	52 ft. 6 in.	63 ft. 3¾ in.	63 ft. 3¾ in.	71 ft. 2¼ in.
Length	33 ft. 10 in.	47 ft. 10¾ in.	47 ft. 10¾ in.	47 ft. 6¾ in.
Height	10 ft. 6 in.	12 ft. 9 in.	12 ft. 9 in.	12 ft. 9 in.
Wing area	452 sq. ft.	635 sq. ft.	635 sq. ft.	728 sq. ft.
Tare weight	2,645 lb.	4,299 lb.	4,730 lb.	6,724 lb.
All-up weight	4,187 lb.	7,936 lb.	7,920 lb.	11,464 lb.
Maximum speed	105 m.p.h.	115 m.p.h.	125 m.p.h.	128·5 m.p.h.
Cruising speed	—	93 m.p.h.	106 m.p.h.	105 m.p.h.
Initial climb	—	500 ft./min.	800 ft./min.	500 ft./min.
Ceiling	—	10,250 ft.	15,500 ft.	10,180 ft.
Range	—	559 miles	—	528 miles

	F.VIII	F.XI Universal	F.XII
Span	73 ft. 5 in.	53 ft. 9 in.	88 ft. 6 in.
Length	54 ft. 10 in.	36 ft. 5 in.	60 ft. 8 in.
Height	14 ft. 7 in.	10 ft. 0 in.	15 ft. 11 in.
Wing area	893 sq. ft.	382·1 sq. ft.	1,109 sq. ft.
Tare weight	7,400 lb.	2,921 lb.	11,791 lb.
All-up weight	12,800 lb.	4,189 lb.	19,836 lb.
Maximum speed	118 m.p.h.	109 m.p.h.	132 m.p.h.
Cruising speed	96·4 m.p.h.	89 m.p.h.	109 m.p.h.
Initial climb	500 ft./min.	700 ft./min.	500 ft./min.
Ceiling	10,820 ft.	14,435 ft.	14,800 ft.
Range	—	497 miles	700 miles

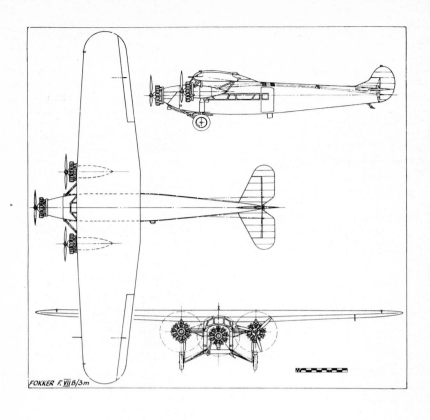

FOKKER F.VII B/3m

G-AFZP, the Fokker F.XXII which survived the war, at Prestwick in full Scottish
Airlines livery, February 1947.

Fokker F.XXII and F.XXXVI

After the Fokker F.XII came the 13 passenger F.XVIII and the 12
passenger F.XX. The single aircraft of the latter type retained the traditional wing but at last abandoned the slab-sided fuselage in favour of a
highly streamlined structure of circular section. In 1934 the time-
honoured system of designation was discontinued and a new one evolved
to indicate seating capacity. The first European-built aircraft so designated was the F.XXXVI, a high-wing monoplane of composite construction with a circular-section fabric-covered fuselage built on similar lines
to that of the successful F.XX trimotor. A standard Fokker-type plywood-
covered wing carried four Wright Cyclone radials along the leading edge,
but unlike the F.XX, its undercarriage did not retract. Only one example,
PH-AJA 'Arend' (Eagle), was constructed and fitted for the carriage of
32 passengers and four crew, flew on K.L.M. daily schedules between
Croydon, Amsterdam and Berlin from 1935 onwards. Four specimens of a
smaller but otherwise similar version, the 22 seat, Wasp powered F.XXII,
were then built. Three registered PH-AJP, 'JQ and 'JR, named 'Pape-
gaai' (Parrot), 'Kwikstaart' (Wagtail) and 'Roerdomp' (Bittern), were
used on K.L.M. European services, and the fourth was sold to A.B.
Aerotransport in Sweden.

'Kwikstaart' was lost in a serious crash at Schiphol during its first summer, but the F.XXXVI and the two surviving F.XXIIs gave trouble-
free service until replaced by Douglas DC-3s in 1939. All three were then
sold to British operators, the first to arrive being the F.XXII PH-AJR,
acquired by British American Air Services Ltd. of Heston and allotted
British markings G-AFXR in August 1939. A month later PH-AJP and
the F.XXXVI were delivered to Scottish Aviation Ltd. at Prestwick,
where they assumed British nationality as G-AFZP and 'ZR respectively.
In the November they were reunited with 'XR, all being converted into
flying classrooms for navigator training and continued to be based at
Prestwick, then a grass aerodrome used by Scottish Aviation Ltd. solely
for the operation of No. 12 E.F.T.S. In the early days of the war all three

37

The Fokker F.XXXVI G-AFZR in civil markings and camouflage at Prestwick in 1940. (*Photo courtesy of C. A. Nepean Bishop.*)

could be seen in the vicinity, fully camouflaged, wearing R.A.F. roundels and small black civil registration letters.

Prior to its development as a trans-Atlantic terminal, Prestwick was hardly large enough for the big Fokkers, and this eventually led to the undoing of the F.XXXVI. In 1940 it overshot while landing, was badly damaged, and without spares this Dutch orphan was reluctantly scrapped. The Fokker F.XXIIs successfully continued their war-time duties until impressed in October 1941. After being picketed for a time at Hendon, the erstwhile G-AFXR, now HM159, and rejoicing in the name 'Brontosaurus', was flown to Harwell and its companion, HM160, went to Abbotsinch in Scotland. At a later date HM159 was also transferred to Abbotsinch, from which station both were continually engaged on training flights over the Atlantic and the North Sea. From one such flight, HM159, then renamed 'Sylvia Scarlet', did not return. It caught fire in the air and fell into West Loch Tarbert on the west side of Kintyre, 40 miles from Abbotsinch.

The survivor returned to Prestwick in 1943, where it remained until acquired by Scottish Aviation Ltd. a year later. Soon after the war it was given a complete overhaul, fitted with Wasp engines and emerged in the orange-and-silver livery of Scottish Airlines, making its first test flight at Prestwick on October 18, 1946. After receiving a renewed C. of A. on December 20, 'ZP operated the Prestwick–Belfast service under charter to British European Airways Corporation until August 10, 1947. Its interim role completed and with spares non-existent, it was then pensioned off in favour of the ubiquitous Dakota and, after occupying valuable hangar space at Prestwick for several years, was pushed outside, broken up and burned in the summer of 1952.

38

Manufacturers: N. V. Nederlandsche Vliegtuigenfabriek, Amsterdam, Netherlands.

Power Plants: (F.XXII) Four 525 h.p. Pratt and Whitney Wasp T1D1.

Four 600 h.p. Pratt and Whitney Wasp R-1340-S3H1-G.

(F.XXXVI) Four 750 h.p. Wright Cyclone SGR-1820-F2.

	Fokker F.XXII	Fokker F.XXXVI
Span	99 ft. 0 in.	108 ft. 2 in.
Length . . .	68 ft. 10 in.	78 ft. 8 in.
Height . . .	15 ft. 1 in.	19 ft. 8 in.
Wing area . . .	1,399 sq. ft.	1,851 sq. ft.
Tare weight . . .	17,475 lb.	22,701 lb.
All-up weight . .	28,600 lb.	36,366 lb.
Maximum speed . .	174 m.p.h.	186 m.p.h.
Cruising speed . .	162 m.p.h.	165 m.p.h.
Initial climb . . .	700 ft./min.	700 ft./min.
Ceiling . . .	13,940 ft.	16,400 ft.
Range . . .	980 miles	960 miles

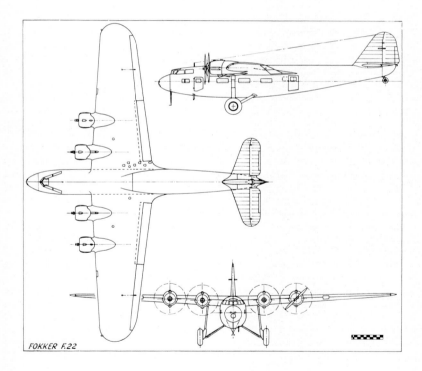

FOKKER F.22

Ford 5AT-C G-ABHF, larger of the original types. (*'Flight' Photo.*)

Ford Trimotors

The all-metal Ford three engined, high-wing transports, loosely referred to as Trimotors, were first produced in America in 1926 after Henry Ford senior, pioneer mass builder of motor cars, assumed control of the Stout Metal Airplane Company. Designed by W. B. 'Bill' Stout, the immensely strong and efficient Ford 4AT and its variants revolutionised American air transport in the mid 'twenties. In their day the Alclad-covered cantilever wing and fuselage were unique, and the resulting freedom from rotting, tearing and warping, not only resulted in long and useful careers but also made them particularly suited for the gruelling task of freighting in remote areas. By 1929, peak sales of the larger 5AT alone reached three per week, and with Ford car factories firmly established in England, the Tri-motors inevitably made their appearance here. The first, an early model 5AT, was exhibited in American markings at Olympia during the Aero Show of July 1929, and afterwards gave demonstration flights at Croydon prior to leaving for a European sales tour.

In October 1930 an 11 seat Ford 4AT-E and a 14 seat Ford 5AT-C were shipped to the United Kingdom, erected and flown at Hooton Park Aerodrome, Cheshire. American publicity techniques figured prominently in the company's attempts to sell the Trimotor. The two demonstrators, respectively registered G-ABEF and 'FF, included Ford's initial 'F' by special arrangement with the Air Ministry. In addition, the old aerodrome at Ford, near Yapton in Sussex, was taken over as a maintenance base. merely because of its appropriate name. There the aircraft were fitted with emergency exits and fireproof engine bulkheads to comply with British airworthiness requirements. After two months an unprecedented piece of manipulation gave the Ford 5AT-C a new registration G-ABHF which included *both* initials of Henry Ford. By happy coincidence the Ford 4AT-E already bore those of Edsel Ford. The two aircraft were demonstrated all over Europe under the nominal ownership of H. S.

Cooper, Ford sales manager in the United Kingdom, and thereafter were very much in evidence at Ford and at Heston.

Only two sales resulted from this considerable effort, the first at the end of 1930, when G-ABHO 'Tanganyika Star' arrived, to become what would now be termed an executive transport, for the Earl of Lovelace. During 1931 it was flown to the owner's estates in Tanganyika for the elephant-hunting season. In the following year G-ACAE, an improved model 5AT-D powered by Wasp C motors, with square cabin door and 8 in. more headroom in the cabin, was supplied to the Hon. A. E. Guinness for his frequent flights between Eastleigh and Castleknock in Ireland. As in the case of several other large private aircraft, 'AE was nominally registered to the owner's personal pilot O. S. Baker. The earlier Ford 'HO was sold in January 1934 to the charter firm BANCO—the British Air Navigation Co. Ltd.—and went into service between Heston, Le Touquet and Deauville, and during a charter flight by Capt. Newman, became the first Ford to visit Sweden. Named 'Voyager' it was also employed as a relief aircraft to the Channel Islands, supplementing the Jersey Airways Rapides during peak holiday periods in 1934. The firm also bought the Ford 4AT-E G-ABEF in July of that year and put it into service with the name 'Vagabond'. Simultaneously with the arrival of 'AE from America, a second-hand model 4AT-E had been imported from Spain, where, since 1930, it had been in service with the Spanish airline CLASSA. On arrival it was repainted as G-ACAK, but saw little service in this country, thereafter spending most of its life in the hangars at Ford. Its two recorded appearances were at Heston and Whitchurch in June 1933.

The Ford 5AT-D G-ACAE continued under Guinness ownership until taken over by No. 271 (Transport) Squadron R.A.F. at Doncaster in April 1940. It then made a number of trips to Norway and saw service during the Dunkirk retreat, finally sustaining fatal damage in Ireland. The remaining four disappeared from British skies at the end of 1934 when they were all shipped by W. S. Shackleton Ltd. to Salamaua, New Guinea, where the two smaller aircraft were sold to Holdens Air Transport Ltd. and the larger to Guinea Airways Ltd. In 1937 all were taken over by Guinea Airways Pty. Ltd. In this inhospitable region their sturdy airframes and ability to fly and climb with full load on two engines made them particularly suited for the haulage of mining equipment, for which purpose large loading hatches were constructed in the top of the fuselage. During the Pacific war, they maintained the vital life-line between Australia and New Guinea until the erstwhile G-ABHF crashed over a 100 ft. cliff at Wau on October 23, 1941 and the ex-Spaniard was destroyed on the ground in New Guinea by the Japanese. The one-time Jersey 'holiday specials' G-ABEF and 'HO were then taken over by the Royal Australian Air Force and went to Townsville on ambulance duties.

Manufacturers: Stout Metal Airplane Co. division of the Ford Motor Company, Dearborn, Michigan, U.S.A.

Power Plants: (Ford 4AT-E) Three 330 h.p. Wright Whirlwind.
     (Ford 5AT-C) Three 425 h.p. Pratt and Whitney Wasp.
     (Ford 5AT-D) Three 425 h.p. Pratt and Whitney Wasp C.

	Ford 4AT-E	Ford 5AT-C	Ford 5AT-D
Span . . .	74 ft. 0 in.	77 ft. 10 in.	77 ft. 10 in.
Length . . .	49 ft. 10 in.	50 ft. 3 in.	50 ft. 3 in.
Height . . .	11 ft. 9 in.	12 ft. 0 in.	12 ft. 8 in.
Wing area . .	785 sq. ft.	835 sq. ft.	835 sq. ft.
Tare weight . .	6,500 lb.	7,600 lb.	7,840 lb.
All-up weight .	10,130 lb.	13,500 lb.	13,500 lb.
Maximum speed .	132 m.p.h.	135 m.p.h.	150 m.p.h.
Cruising speed .	107 m.p.h.	115 m.p.h.	122 m.p.h.
Initial climb . .	920 ft./min.	1,050 ft./min.	1,050 ft./min.
Ceiling . . .	18,600 ft.	20,500 ft.	20,500 ft.
Range . . .	570 miles	560 miles	560 miles

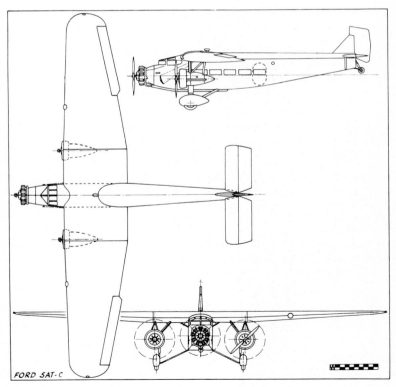

FORD 5AT-C

The first production Wicko G.M.1 at Whitchurch, September 1938, after delivery to the Bristol and Wessex Aeroplane Club. (*Photo courtesy of W. K. Kilsby.*)

Foster Wikner Wicko

The Wicko two-seat, high-wing monoplane originated in 1936 as an attempt by Geoffrey N. Wikner to produce a cabin aircraft at approximately half the price of contemporary light aeroplanes. Mr. Wikner, an Australian, cousin of the other famous designer and pilot, Edgar Wikner Percival, built his first aircraft in 1931. This was the Wicko Sports Monoplane, a single-seat, high-wing cabin type powered by a 60 h.p. Anzani aircooled radial. Two years later he built an open-cockpit variant known as the Wicko Lion, and both aeroplanes bore a remarkable resemblance to the later British-built Wickos and had approximately the same dimensions. His third aircraft, the Wicko Wizard VH-UPW, reminiscent of the D.H.71 Tiger Moth, was a two seat, low-wing monoplane.

Encouraged by the success of his first designs, Mr. Wikner left Australia for England in May 1934 with well-defined ideas on the construction of cheap and efficient aircraft. He enlisted the support of Messrs. V. Foster and J. F. Lusty and formed the Foster Wikner Aircraft Co. Ltd., construction commencing in a corner of Lusty's furniture factory in Colin Street, Bromley-by-Bow. Low initial cost was achieved by fitting a standard Ford V.8 water-cooled engine in place of the more costly aero engine. When fitted with a Pobjoy reduction gear, the Ford V.8 was known as the Wicko F power unit and gave 85 h.p. at 1,500 r.p.m., an aerodynamically clean nose being obtained by fitting a Gallay radiator under the fuselage. The latter was a simple plywood box with a two-spar, fabric-covered mainplane of Clark YH section attached directly to the top longerons and braced by parallel tubular steel struts. On completion in September 1936, the prototype, G-AENU, known as the Wicko F.W.1, was taken by road to Hillman's Aerodrome at Stapleford Abbotts, where its designer carried out the initial test flying. Although the estimated performance was realised, the 450 lb. dead weight of the motor inevitably resulted in an excessive take-off run and poor rate of climb. The aircraft was consequently rebuilt as the Wicko F.W.2 with the Ford V.8 and its attendant plumbing replaced by a 90 h.p. Cirrus Minor I engine. Tare weight was

43

cut from 1,170 lb. to 938 lb., but the price went up from £425 to £650. The Wicko appeared at several flying meetings during the 1937 season, and in the same year the firm took over premises at Eastleigh. There the second aircraft G-AEZZ was completed in time for the King's Cup Race of September 10, 1937, in which it was flown, and forced landed north of Skegness, by F/Lt. H. R. A. Edwards. In common with all subsequent Wickos, 'ZZ had a plywood-covered wing, split trailing edge flaps and full dual control, but was specially fitted with a 150 h.p. Cirrus Major engine for the race, and with this motor was allotted the type number F.W.3. A Gipsy Major engine was installed in 1938, after which the aeroplane was sold to the Cardiff Aeroplane Club. Nine production aircraft were built, all powered by Gipsy Majors and designated G.M.1.

One of the Eastleigh-built Wicko G.M.1s went to New Zealand as ZK-AGN, those built to British order being G-AFAZ for the Bristol and Wessex Aeroplane Club, G-AFJB for the Midland Aero Club and G-AFKU for F. L. Dean of Cardiff. G-AFKS, 'KK and 'VK were demonstrators, the first of which, operated by Nash Aircraft Sales Ltd., was at one time experimentally fitted with skis. Two others had also been completed before the outbreak of war brought an enterprise of great merit to a premature halt. Rolls-Royce Ltd., Hucknall, bought G-AFJB for communications duties in 1939, but like most Wickos, it was eventually impressed into the R.A.F. with the Service type name Warferry. Only 'JB and the eleventh and last aircraft, Warferry HM497, survived R.A.F. service. They reverted to the care of the designer in October 1945, and in the following year 'JB was sold to Miss Philippa Bennett, late of A.T.A., who used it for charter work at Eastleigh. The unused tenth aircraft, stored during the war, was unearthed in 1946 and cannibalised to service HM497, which became G-AGPE and joined Miss Bennett's charter activities. Although 'JB forced landed in bad visibility on Walney Island on September 8, 1946 and fell over an 80 ft. cliff to land upside down in the sea, the occupants were unhurt and the aircraft survived to pass into the possession of M. J. Dible at Denham in 1955. Today it is based on a farm at Arras, Sancton, York, by N. B. Stephenson.

The prototype emerged from wartime storage to receive an overhaul at Rearsby in 1946 and to embark on a wanderer's life. First owned by W. H. Leadbetter at Elmdon, it passed from Lawrence Blackburn at

The unflapped prototype Wicko F.W.1 G-AENU showing the underslung radiator and pointed nose. (*'Flight' Photo.*)

44

Baginton to S/Ldr. J. T. Shaw at Thornaby and in 1950 went to the Air Navigation and Trading Co. Ltd. at Squires Gate. It did little or no flying in post-war years and in 1952 went south, first to W. Stevens at Exeter and finally to L. S. Scali at Plymouth, where it rotted away outside the Embankment Garage and eventually disappeared.

SPECIFICATION

Manufacturers: The Foster Wikner Aircraft Co. Ltd., Southampton Airport, Eastleigh, Hants.
Power Plants: (F.W.1) One 85 h.p. Wicko F modified Ford V.8.
　　　　　　　(F.W.2) One 90 h.p. Blackburn Cirrus Minor I.
　　　　　　　(F.W.3) One 150 h.p. Blackburn Cirrus Major.
　　　　　　　(G.M.1) One 130 h.p. de Havilland Gipsy Major.
Dimensions: Span, 34 ft. 6 in. Length, 23 ft. 3 in. Height, 6 ft. 7 in. Wing area, 153 sq. ft.

	Wicko F.W.1	Wicko F.W.2	Wicko G.M.1
Tare weight . .	1,170 lb.	938 lb.	1,255 lb.
All-up weight .	1,700 lb.	1,500 lb.	2,000 lb.
Maximum speed .	115 m.p.h.	120 m.p.h.	140 m.p.h.
Cruising speed .	98·5 m.p.h.	103 m.p.h.	120 m.p.h.
Initial climb . .	—	—	800 ft./min.
Ceiling . . .	10,000 ft.	15,000 ft.	20,000 ft.
Range . . .	250 miles	450 miles	480 miles

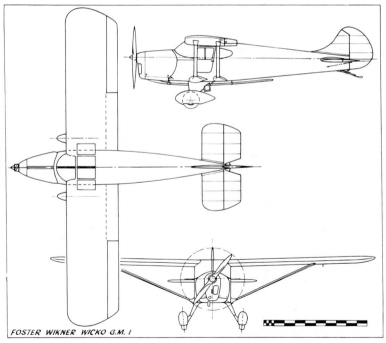

FOSTER WIKNER WICKO G.M. 1

G-ABUZ, prototype ST-4 flying in 1932 with experimental bulged fin. (*'Flight'
Photo.*)

General Aircraft Monospars ST-3 to ST-12

In the 1920s the cantilever monoplane was not only viewed with a super-
stitious distrust dating back to the First World War, but most attempts at
construction, using contemporary materials, had resulted in excessive
structural weight. A typical example was the metal-covered wing of the
three-engined Inflexible monoplane built 1925–27 by Wm. Beardmore and
Co. Ltd. under licence from the German Rohrbach concern. H. J. Stieger,
a Swiss-born engineer working on the Inflexible, brought new thinking to
the subject of weigh/strength ratios of cantilever wings and invented the
'Monospar' system of construction. As the name suggested, his immensely
strong metal wing was built round a single duralumin Warren girder spar
capable of resisting bending and braced by a pyramidal system of tie rods
to take the torsional loads. An experimental wing designated ST-1, fabric
covered in the manner of all subsequent Monospar wings, was then built
to Air Ministry order, exhibited at the Olympia Aero Show of July 1929
and later subjected to strength tests.

When Beardmores closed down all aviation interests, H. J. Stieger
joined forces with F. F. Crocombe, S/Ldr. Rollo de Haga Haig, A. E. L.
Chorlton and C. W. Hayward to form the Monospar Wing Co. Ltd. A
second Air Ministry order was then received, this time for the ST-2, a wing
large enough for, and eventually flight tested on, the Ministry's Fokker
F.VIIB/3m J7986. Work also proceeded on an experimental, twin-
engined, three seat, low-wing, cabin monoplane designated the Monospar
ST-3. Like the Fokker wing, the ST-3 G-AARP was built at Brockworth
by the Gloster Aircraft Co. Ltd. with the Gloster works designation
S.S.1 (Stieger Salmson One) and first flew in 1931. Monospar principles
also featured in the fuselage construction, the main frames being anchored
to a diamond-section Warren girder keel member. Power was supplied
by two 45 h.p. Salmson radials with which the aircraft completed more
than 1,000 hours of manufacturer's and Martlesham trials. These

46

included officially observed terminal velocity dives up to 178 m.p.h. and single-engined take-offs. Much of the development flying was done by S/Ldr. de Haga Haig, who gave a convincing and almost aerobatic demonstration to members of both Houses of Parliament at Hanworth in June 1931.

Success with the ST-3 prompted the formation of a new company, General Aircraft Ltd., to exploit the Monospar Company's patents, one of the former Aircraft Disposal Company hangars at Croydon being acquired for the construction of a Pobjoy powered four seat ST-4. The prototype, G-ABUZ, made its first flight in May 1932, piloted by the Company's test pilot H. M. Schofield, its many novel features including engine starting from the cockpit by cable-operated manual inertia starters. A great deal of its unusually high performance was obtained by a reduction in interference drag, achieved by thinning the mainplane inboard of the engines, the top main spar member continuing through the cabin. The latter was of mixed dural and steel tube riveted construction, and the rear fuselage retained the Monospar features of the ST-3. Orders for five production aircraft G-ABVN to 'VS were placed during the construction of the prototype, and later in 1932 were delivered to Portsmouth, Southsea and I.O.W. Aviation Ltd.; the Maharajah of Patiala; A. C. M. Jackaman, Heston; Capt. O. E. Armstrong, Baldonnel; and a Swiss customer respectively. Capt. Armstrong's ST-4 flew as EI-AAQ, but returned to the United Kingdom as 'VS after a few months. G-ABVN, first flown on the Ryde ferry, was privately owned at the outbreak of war, but no trace of it was found until 1954, when its wingless fuselage came to light among derelict aircraft at Bankstown Aerodrome, Sydney, Australia. A batch of 24 improved ST-4 Mk. IIs followed, externally identifiable by a nose landing light similar to that which had first been experimentally fitted to G-ABVP. Deliveries took place throughout 1933, commencing with G-ACCO for Geoffrey Ambler at Yeadon. It remained his private mount until impressed in 1940, acquiring Pobjoy Niagara III engines during the intervening years. The last machine, G-ACKT, sold to the Duchess of Bedford, was unfortunately short lived and F/Lt. Allen, personal pilot to the Duchess, was killed when it struck high-tension cables in poor light and crashed 4

The prototype ST-3 at the time of its first flight at Brockworth in 1931.

The prototype ST-6 G-ACGI with undercarriage retracted and showing the redesigned nacelles. (*Photo: General Aircraft Ltd.*)

The King's Cup winning ST-10 at Hatfield on the day of its victory July 14, 1934. (*'Flight' Photo.*)

miles from base at Woburn Park. One of the batch, G-ACCP, first de-livered to the Hon. A. E. Guinness, was later sold to the Cambridge Aero Club and in 1939 was flying a regular service between Barnstaple and Lundy Island in the colours of Lundy and Atlantic Coast Air Lines Ltd. Another, G-ACEW 'Inverness', purchased by Highland Airways Ltd., was flown by E. E. Fresson on the first Inverness–Kirkwall service on May 8, 1933. Two others, G-ACJE and 'JF, were operated by Inter-national Airlines Ltd., a newly formed company which inaugurated its Western Air Express between Croydon, Portsmouth, Southampton and Plymouth on August 25, 1933, but went out of business after a few weeks. The ST-4s were then sold to private owners. Six ST-4 Mk. IIs were sold direct to foreign buyers, but a too optimistic view of the order book led to over-production, and several unsold machines stood in the hangar for two years. The last of these, Niagara powered, were acquired by Com-mercial Air Hire Ltd. in June 1935 and registered G-ADIK, 'JP and 'LM for charter work and occasional trips on the Inner Circle Air Line be-tween Croydon and Heston. Their commercial lives ended a year later when two crashed and the survivor, 'JP, was sold to R. K. Dundas Ltd.

ST-12 G-ADBN flying near Hanworth prior to delivery to Sweden in 1935. (*'Flight' Photo.*)

During 1933, technical development went on apace and resulted in the appearance of the ST-6. This was basically an ST-4 but had a manually retracted undercarriage, new engine cowlings and a redesigned nose contour giving enough cabin space to accommodate an occasional fifth passenger. It was the second British commercial aeroplane ever to fly with a retractable undercarriage, being antedated by only a few weeks by the Airspeed Courier, and the allotted markings G-ACGI were a fortuitously happy reminder of its designer's graduation from the City and Guilds (Engineering) College. With a top speed of nearly 140 m.p.h. it was a favourite in the 1933 King's Cup Race, in which, piloted by H. M. Schofield, it carried H. J. Stieger as passenger, but hopes were dashed when it ran out of fuel and retired. Only two other ST-6s existed, G-ACIC built with Pobjoy Niagara engines for R. E. Gardner and G-ACHU, an ST-4 belonging to Robin Cazalet, converted to ST-6 to special order. The prototype finished its peacetime career joyriding at Ipswich Airport six years later; 'IC performed similar duties at the Romford Flying Club, Maylands; and 'HU was kept at Wolverhampton by Murphy Bros.

The Croydon factory closed down at the end of 1933, but in 1934 the company was reorganised financially and larger and better-equipped factory premises were obtained at Hanworth. Here a fresh start was made with the construction of a developed Monospar, the General Aircraft ST-10 first flown as T-5, and later as G-ACTS. This was structurally similar to the earlier models, but fuel was carried under the cabin floor and dual controls of the throw-over spectacle type were provided. The engines were the new 90 h.p. Pobjoy Niagaras which imparted a performance sufficiently impressive for H. M. Schofield to secure a runaway win in the King's Cup Race of July 13–14, 1934 at an average speed of 134·16 m.p.h. The design skill of H. J. Stieger, who rode as passenger, in giving a better streamline shape to the fuselage in spite of increasing its frontal area by 2 sq. ft., and in altering the fore-and-aft attitude of the machine in flight, gave an additional 10 m.p.h. which defeated the handicappers. A. C. M. Jackaman flying his ST-4 G-ABVP 'Peridot V' was eliminated in the heats

49

after averaging 118 m.p.h. and Charles Gardner, who flew his brother's ST-6 G-ACIC into the semi-final at 131·5 m.p.h., suffered a similar fate.

Strangely, the remarkable ST-10 did not go into production, and the prototype passed into the hands of Portsmouth, Southsea and Isle of Wight Aviation Ltd., for service on the Ryde Ferry and the company's route to Heston. One other was built, and together with the two solitary retractable undercarriage versions, designated ST-11, was exported direct to Australia. More success greeted the Gipsy Major powered variant known as the ST-12, four of which appeared in British markings. The first, G-ADBN, was sold to Peter and Niels Jensen and departed to Stockholm for a year, later returning to become a taxi aircraft with Air Dispatch Ltd. at Cardiff. Two others, G-ADDY and 'DZ, both eventually sold abroad, were flown during 1935–36 by racing motorist R. J. B. Seaman and the manufacturers as private and demonstration aircraft respectively. The fourth and last British ST-12, G-ADLL, was fitted with 145 h.p. Gipsy Major high compression engines to the special order of Owen G. E. Marshal Roberts of Hamble. He flew a very good race for the 1935 King's Cup, coming 12th at 166·86 m.p.h. and then took the all-gold ST-12 on a world tour, going as far afield as California. It eventually returned, bedecked with the flags of countries visited and continued in service with the same owner until impressed with other surviving Monospars during the war. None outlived its war service, and the sole post-war memorial in Britain to these early pre-production Monospars was the ST-4 G-ACJF. Owned in 1939 by G. S. Davison at Castle Bromwich, its skeleton could be seen in 1945, up-ended against the fuel pyramid at Heston until destroyed in the gale of March 16, 1947.

SPECIFICATION

Manufacturers: (ST-3)   The Gloster Aircraft Co. Ltd., Hucclecote Aerodrome, Gloucester.

(ST-4 and ST-6)   General Aircraft Ltd., Croydon Aerodrome, Surrey.

(ST-10 and ST-12)   General Aircraft Ltd., Hanworth Air Park, Feltham, Middlesex.

Power Plants: (ST-3)   Two 45 h.p. British Salmson A.D.9.

(ST-4)   Two 85 h.p. Pobjoy R.

(ST-6)   Two 85 h.p. Pobjoy R.

     Two 90 h.p. Pobjoy Niagara I.

(ST-10)   Two 90 h.p. Pobjoy Niagara I.

(ST-12)   Two 130 h.p. de Havilland Gipsy Major.

	ST-3	ST-4	ST-6	ST-10	ST-12
Span	38 ft. 0 in.	40 ft. 2 in.	40 ft. 2 in.	40 ft. 2 in.	40 ft. 2 in.
Length	21 ft. 11½ in.	26 ft. 4 in.	26 ft. 4 in.	26 ft. 4 in.	26 ft. 4 in.
Height	9 ft. 0 in.	7 ft. 0 in.	7 ft. 0 in.	7 ft. 10 in.	7 ft. 10 in.
Wing area	183 sq. ft.	219 sq. ft.	219 sq. ft.	217 sq. ft.	217 sq. ft.
Tare weight	1,057 lb.	1,480 lb.	1,500 lb.	1,470 lb.	1,840 lb.
All-up weight	1,800 lb.	2,550 lb.	2,600 lb.	2,750 lb.	2,875 lb.
Maximum speed	110 m.p.h.	130 m.p.h.	135 m.p.h.	142 m.p.h.	158 m.p.h.
Cruising speed	95 m.p.h.	115 m.p.h.	120 m.p.h.	130 m.p.h.	142 m.p.h.
Initial climb	950 ft./min.	850 ft./min.	850 ft./min.	900 ft./min.	1,233 ft./min.
Ceiling	18,000 ft.	18,000 ft.	18,000 ft.	18,000 ft.	21,000 ft.
Range	—	540 miles	550 miles	585 miles	410 miles

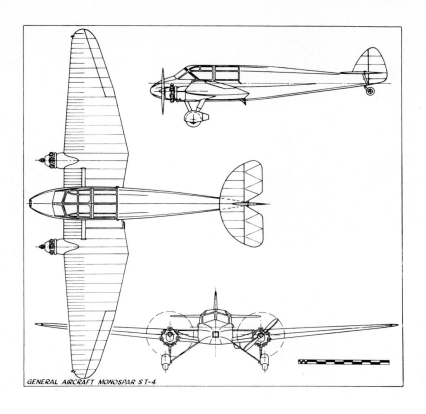

GENERAL AIRCRAFT MONOSPAR ST-4

J. W. Adamson's Monospar ST-25 Universal flying near Hanworth prior to delivery in May 1936. (*Photo: General Aircraft Ltd.*)

General Aircraft Monospar ST-25

The year 1935 saw not only the Silver Jubilee of King George V but also H. J. Stieger's departure from General Aircraft Ltd. Thus Monospar development became the responsibility of F. F. Crocombe as Chief Designer, with D. L. Hollis Williams as Chief Engineer and E. C. Gordon England as Managing Director. At Hanworth, on June 19 of that memorable year, their last basic design made its first public bow in the presence of Lady Shelmerdine, wife of the D.C.A. Substantially the same as an ST-10, it was fitted with a folding seat for an occasional fifth passenger; additional cabin windows were therefore necessary and the radio receiver and homing device was standard fitment. To mark the 25th anniversary of the reign of King George V, type numbers 19–24 were omitted and the new aircraft received both the designation ST-25 and the type name Jubilee. The prototype, G-ADIV, in standard black and yellow and powered by two Niagara II engines, was sold to Radio Transmission Equipment Ltd. for the further development of its specialised radio, but met a watery end in Wigtown Bay a year later. Unlike most small contemporary aircraft, the list price included all instruments, night flying and other primary equipment. The popularity of this idea was such that when production ceased in 1939, 57 had been delivered, all but 19 registered for civil use in the United Kingdom, these including a number ferried abroad.

During 1935–36 Air Commerce Ltd. of Heston employed the fifth ST-25 Jubilee, G-ADLT, on various domestic and continental charters, while at Hanworth G-ADPI became the executive aircraft of the Mobiloil concern under the ownership of Hubert Holliday. The largest 'fleet', three strong, was acquired by Crilly Airways Ltd. in 1935. These aircraft, G-ADPK–'PM, were based at Braunstone, Leicester, and flew on the company's scheduled internal air services to Sywell, Tollerton, Mousehold,

The prototype Monospar ST-25 Jubilee on the occasion of its public presentation, June 19, 1935. (*'Flight 'Photo.*)

Speke and Whitchurch. When Crilly Airways was absorbed by British Airways in 1936, two of the ST-25s were sold to Portsmouth, Southsea and Isle of Wight Aviation Ltd. to join the ST-10. The third, 'PM, went to Stanley Park, Blackpool, to end its days in private ownership with P/O H. S. Ashworth. Albert Bachelor of Ramsgate bought a new ST-25 G-ADVH, but eventually disposed of it to another well-known private owner, F/Lt. G. Shaw at Thornaby. G-ADYN was flown privately at Selsey Bill airfield by Norman E. Holden, while the last Jubilee model, G-AEAT, was acquired by Aerial Sites Ltd. of Hanworth, stripped of furnishings and flown at night for advertising purposes with under-wing neon tubes fed from cabin accumulators.

In 1936 an improved version known as the ST-25 De Luxe made its appearance, powered by Niagara III engines with Rotax electric starters. Controllable trimming tabs were used for the first time on rudder and elevators, and directional stability was improved by increasing the fin area and thereby endowing the new model with its sole recognition feature. The prototype, G-AEDY, made its appearance in March 1936, and once more the R.T.E. homing receiver was standard fitment. Although publicity was given to five basic versions, in fact only one other, the ambulance, was built. The sole aircraft of this type, G-AEGX, had an all-white colour scheme, Red Cross insignia and the appropriate name 'Florence Nightingale'. It was provided with a large door in the starboard side to admit a stretcher with a seat for an attendant situated to port. The De Luxe and the ambulance made their first public appearances together at the Hatfield S.B.A.C. Show of June 28, 1936, thereafter becoming well known at demonstrations in all parts of the British Isles.

The autumn of 1936 found the design staff still not satisfied with directional control with one engine stopped, and G-AEDY was further rebuilt with twin fins and rudders. This proved eminently satisfactory, and no further modifications took place, 26 twin finned production models, designated ST-25 Universal, being sold. Two of the first to appear, standard model G-AESS and ambulance G-AEVN, were exhibited at the garden party of the Royal Aeronautical Society at Heathrow on May 9, 1937, and several other ambulance versions were built, all of which found their way overseas. Models embodying the large starboard hatch but without ambulance interiors were known as Freighters. Seven of these were sold to Eastern Canada Air Lines, the first five, CF-BAH-'AK and 'AO, being named after Canadian cities at Hanworth by Lady Shelmerdine on September 28, 1936. A standard Universal G-ADWI was experimentally fitted with two Cirrus Minor I engines and flew with the designation G.A.L.26. It was the first new type to fly after H. J. Stieger left the company and the last to employ his Monospar wing. In 1937 the ST-25 Universal G-AEJB went to Aden to inaugurate the services of Arabian Airways, afterwards becoming the executive aircraft of a local firm. The Cinque Ports Flying Club at Lympne operated G-AEJV until the club's manager W. E. Davies and three passengers were killed when it crashed in 1938; Lord Londonderry visited all parts of Europe in his private Universal G-AEPG; J. A. M. Henderson raced G-AEPA at the Lympne International Meeting of August 28, 1937; and G-AEGY went to Clifton Aerodrome, York, for use by J. W. Adamson, well known after the war as the operator of Oldstead Aircraft. A trek to the north was undertaken in 1938 by 'PA, which joined H. S. Ashworth's G-ADPM at Stanley Park Aerodrome, Blackpool; by 'DY, christened 'Alcaeus', which went into service with Utility Airways Ltd., Hooton; and by G-ADYN acquired by Williams and Co. of Squires Gate. All three ended their days giving pleasure flights.

When war was declared in 1939, all Monospars fell quickly into the impressment net, but none survived to fly again in peace, although one Universal and one Jubilee later succeeded in functioning for the first time as British civil aeroplanes. CF-BAH, Eastern Canada Air Lines' 'City of Halifax', delivered in 1936, returned in December 1941 to become G-AGDN and in camouflage with yellow undersides, flew throughout the war on communications work for General Aircraft Ltd. It passed to Geoffrey Alington in 1945 and was later scrapped. The other, an equally unusual Monospar, was overhauled by Southern Aircraft (Gatwick) Ltd. in 1946, sold to E. I. H. Ward and later to N. L. Hayman of Fairoaks as G-AHBK. Second of two Jubilees delivered to the R.A.E. for radio development in 1936, it started life as K8308, and although for 10 years a military aeroplane, it flew in civil colours for only a twelvemonth.

G-AEDY, sole example of the Monospar ST-25 de Luxe, showing the enlarged fin.
(*'Flight' Photo.*)

Following a successful forced landing on Barnsley Wold, near Cirencester, in June 1947, the owner had the misfortune to collide with the only large tree in the vicinity and 'BK was consequently destroyed by fire, its engine-less skeleton remaining a feature of the countryside for several years afterwards.

SPECIFICATION

Manufacturers: General Aircraft Ltd., Hanworth Air Park, Feltham, Middlesex.
Power Plants: (Jubilee)   Two 90 h.p. Pobjoy Niagara II.
　　　　　　　 (De Luxe)   Two 95 h.p. Pobjoy Niagara III.
　　　　　　　 (Universal) Two 95 h.p. Pobjoy Niagara III.
Dimensions: Span, 40 ft. 2 in. Height, 7 ft. 10 in. Wing area, 217 sq. ft.

	Jubilee	De Luxe	Universal
Length . . .	26 ft. 4 in.	26 ft. 4 in.	25 ft. 4 in.
Tare weight . .	1,680 lb.	1,758 lb.	1,818 lb.
All-up weight .	2,875 lb.	2,875 lb.	2,875 lb.
Maximum speed .	142 m.p.h.	135 m.p.h.	131 m.p.h.
Cruising speed .	130 m.p.h.	123 m.p.h.	115 m.p.h.
Initial climb . .	800 ft./min.	700 ft./min.	710 ft./min.
Ceiling . . .	16,000 ft.	12,000 ft.	15,300 ft.
Range . . .	585 miles	496 miles	419 miles

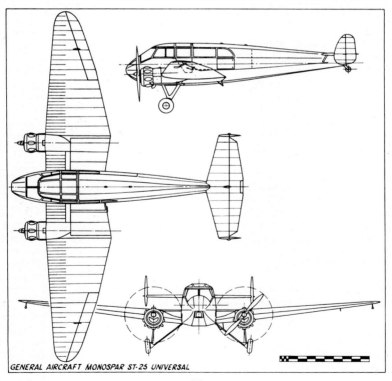

GENERAL AIRCRAFT MONOSPAR ST-25 UNIVERSAL

D. L. Hollis Williams flying the first production G.A.L.42 Cygnet II near Hanworth in July 1939. (*Photo: General Aircraft Ltd.*)

General Aircraft G.A.L.42 Cygnet

The stressed skin, all-metal, two-seat Cygnet side-by-side cabin tourer, initially known as the Cygnet Minor, was designed and built in 1936 by C. R. Chronander and J. I. Waddington, who formed C. W. Aircraft for the purpose. It was an attempt to create a light aircraft more durable and more easily produced in quantity than the usual strut and longeron, plywood and fabric types, and was the first light aeroplane built in the United Kingdom with metal skin on both wing and fuselage. The prototype, G-AEMA, powered by a 90 h.p. Cirrus Minor and built in the firm's workshop at Slough, was noteworthy for its extremely slim semi-monocoque rear fuselage and single, metal-clad fin and unbalanced rudder. It was also fitted with a split trailing edge flap running right under the fuselage, a tailwheel undercarriage and front windscreen panels which raked sharply forward to encourage rapid removal of raindrops by the slipstream.

The prototype was completed in time for exhibition without markings at the Royal Aeronautical Society's Garden Party at Heathrow on May 9, 1937, and made its first flight at Hanworth later in the month. Public demonstration then took place at the Hatfield S.B.A.C. Show of June 27–28 with A. G. M. Wynne Eaton at the controls. Modifications, involving the installation of a Gipsy Major and a rounded windscreen and the removal of the under-fuselage section of the flap, were then carried out in readiness for the King's Cup Race of September 10–11. Redesignated Cygnet Major, it was flown round the Hatfield–Dublin–Hatfield course by Charles Hughesdon, to come 13th at an average speed of 141·3 m.p.h. Flight trials of the revised version continued at Hanworth until March 1938, when the C. W. concern foundered. No orders had been received, and additionally a great deal of money had gone into the twin-engined C. W. Swan project, for which a provisional registration G-AERO had been reserved but not taken up. The Cygnet designs were then sold to General Aircraft Ltd. and the prototype appeared at the R.Ae.S. Garden

Party, at Heathrow on May 8, 1939, bearing the name of its new proprietors. Again piloted by Hughesdon, it competed for the King's Cup, but at an advanced stage of the race and when a very probable winner, retired at Barton through oil shortage.

General Aircraft Ltd. fitted G-AEMA with twin fins and rudders during the autumn of 1938 to obtain increased elevator efficiency, the first of a series of modifications leading to an aircraft which would be viceless and easy to fly. Logically therefore a tricycle undercarriage was added early in 1939, after which the firm went ahead with the construction of the G.A.L.42 Cygnet II. Structurally identical with Chronander and Waddington's much modified prototype, it incorporated the final features necessary for its designed role. It was powered by a 150 h.p. Cirrus Major and the wings were given increased dihedral. Large sliding, instead of standard doors were fitted, and the strutted main undercarriage legs of the rebuilt prototype gave place to cantilever General Aircraft oleo units. It was now virtually a foolproof aeroplane, as D. L. Hollis Williams, the chief engineer and test pilot demonstrated convincingly and amusingly in the few brief months before the outbreak of war. Plans for the construction of an extremely large batch of Cygnet IIs were perforce abandoned, but nine production machines were completed during 1940–41. Three were exported to South America, but the remainder were of British registry and in uncertain war years had chequered careers. Two followed their unregistered brethren to Latin America; one, G-AGAX, non-standard with straight instead of curved runners for the sliding roof, assumed camouflage on its upper surfaces and yellow below, to serve its makers faithfully as a civil communications aircraft throughout the war. The four others were all impressed into the R.A.F. and accompanied the G.A.L. 45 Owlet to 51 O.T.U. to familiarise R.A.F. pilots with tricycle techniques before flying the new Douglas Bostons. Afterwards, they were used for communications, one at least, DG566 alias G-AGAL, seeing service with No. 24 Squadron at Hendon.

In 1946 the four survivors came up for civilian disposal at Kemble,

The original C.W. Cygnet with raked windscreen. (*'Flight' Photo.*)

57

The Cygnet prototype at Hanworth in November 1938 in the interim condition with twin fins and rudders and tail wheel undercarriage. (*Photo: General Aircraft Ltd.*)

Unlike those of production aircraft, the main undercarriage legs of the prototype in tricycle form were strutted. (*Photo: General Aircraft Ltd.*)

where 'VR, 'AU and 'BN were sold to Newman Aircraft Ltd. at Panshanger and 'BA to R. L. Whyham at Squires Gate. Although the last languished untouched until melted down by scrap-metal dealers at Kirby, Lancs., 11 years later, the others became well-known private aeroplanes. G-AGAU was re-engined with a Gipsy Major, afterwards being flown without success by F/Lt. R. Harding in the Folkestone Trophy Race at Lympne on August 30, 1947 and by James Mollison in the Norton Griffiths Race at Elmdon on August 29, 1949. It was at that time owned by Denham Air Services and carried the name 'Dumbo'. During a bombing competition at a Cowes air display in 1949, 'Dumbo' was flown into the ground and destroyed, the wreck afterwards being sold to a local scrap dealer. The war-time communications machine G-AGAX, successively owned by Sir Mark Norman and L. V. D. Scorah, was reconditioned at Ringway in 1955, only to meet an untimely end on the Yorkshire Moors soon afterwards. Today only two remain, the prototype G-AFVR, for 10 years the property of T. F. W. Gunton of King's Lynn, and G-AGBN, kept by Mrs. J. I. Jones on a private landing strip at Munstead Heath, Surrey.

Manufacturers: (C.W. Cygnet)   C. W. Aircraft, Montrose Avenue (removed to Oxford Avenue in 1937), Slough Trading Estate, Slough, Bucks.
(G.A.L.42 Cygnet II) General Aircraft Ltd., Hanworth Air Park, Feltham, Middlesex.
Power Plants: (Cygnet Minor) One 90 h.p. Blackburn Cirrus Minor.
(Cygnet Major) One 130 h.p. de Havilland Gipsy Major.
(Cygnet II)   One 150 h.p. Blackburn Cirrus Major II.

	Cygnet Minor	Cygnet Major	Cygnet II
Span . . .	34 ft. 6 in.	34 ft. 6 in.	34 ft. 6 in.
Length . . .	24 ft. 3 in.	24 ft. 3 in.	23 ft. 3 in.
Height . . .	6 ft. 0 in.	5 ft. 10 in.	7 ft. 0 in.
Wing area .	165 sq. ft.	165 sq. ft.	179 sq. ft.
Tare weight .	1,050 lb.	1,200 lb.	1,475 lb.
All-up weight .	1,600 lb.	1,900 lb.	2,200 lb.
Maximum speed .	125 m.p.h.	150 m.p.h.	135 m.p.h.
Cruising speed .	105 m.p.h.	128 m.p.h.	115 m.p.h.
Initial climb .	750 ft./min.	850 ft./min.	800 ft./min.
Ceiling . . .	20,000 ft.	17,000 ft.	14,000 ft.
Range . . .	500 miles	650 miles	445 miles

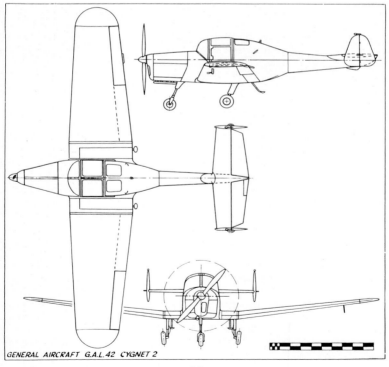

GENERAL AIRCRAFT G.A.L.42 CYGNET 2

A Handley Page O/10 G-EASY. All civil 'Handleys' carried their conversion number on the extreme end of the fuselage. (*Photo: Handley Page Ltd.*)

Handley Page 0/400

Although the distinction of being G-EAAA, the first British civil aeroplane, fell to a de Havilland D.H.9, that of receiving the first British Certificate of Airworthiness went to a Handley Page 0/400. Over 400 of these twin Eagle VIII engined heavy bombers were built during 1918–19 and, retrospectively allotted type number H.P.12, made useful interim civil transports. In spite of their 100 ft. wing span and general immensity, they were structurally simple, the fuselage being a braced box girder of spruce longerons and cross struts, fabric covered, as were the wooden, folding wings. C. of A. No. 1 was issued on May 1, 1919 to Handley Page 0/400 F5414, which on that day became G-EAAF in company with three others, certificated as G-EAAE, 'AG and 'AW respectively. They were the first of 43 civil conversions, a few of which were exported with full C. of A. to the Chinese Government. Thirty-four were of British registry, all were owned by the manufacturers, and none ever suffered a change of ownership. Scheduled services and charter flying were undertaken by a subsidiary concern, Handley Page Air Transport Ltd. under the management of George Woods-Humphery with Lt.-Col. W. F. Sholto Douglas, now Lord Douglas of Kirtleside, chairman of B.E.A.C., as chief pilot. He carried 10 passengers from Cricklewood to Alexandra Park Aerodrome, Manchester, on May 4, 1919 in D8350, not yet painted up as G-EAAE. On the following day he flew North with a 1,500 lb. load of newspapers, which were dropped over Carlisle, Dundee, Aberdeen (where Major Ord-Lees, the 'Guardian Angel' demonstrator, left the aircraft by parachute) and Montrose, a landing being made at Edinburgh. The passengers sat in hastily fitted wicker chairs in a draughty fuselage without soundproofing or windows, only the fortunate, but helmeted, occupants of the front and rear gunners' cockpits being able to view the countryside. Within three months, however, Handley Page Ltd. had produced the 0/7 version, fitted with a properly appointed and windowed cabin for 14 passengers. Apart from

60

the windows, the chief external recognition features were the engine nacelles, lengthened rearward to accommodate the fuel tanks, banished from the fuselage to increase cabin space. Nacelle struts were modified and the oil tanks were repositioned under the upper mainplane. The first o/7 bore no markings other than its conversion number H.P.1, but was, in fact, K-162. The first civil o/400 was also converted to o/7 standard and repainted as G-5414 flew to Amsterdam for exhibition at the First Air Traffic Exhibition of August 1919. A week later, on August 25, the company inaugurated its daily Continental services when Major E. L. Foote carried seven passengers in G-EAAE from Cricklewood to Le Bourget. A month later, on September 22, G-EAAW, flying as G-5417, flew the first Brussels service. Customs clearances took place at Hounslow Heath until the London terminal aerodrome was opened at Plough Lane, Waddon (Croydon), on April 1, 1920, after which Customs were also available at Cricklewood. The aircraft were equipped with the first

One of the seven seat Handley Page O/400s converted for use on the Continental services. These had short nacelles and only four windows.

Marconi R/T, and their pilots included the famous—G. P. Olley, A. S. Wilcockson, F. Dismore, H. H. Perry, W. Rogers, R. Vaughan Fowler, W. L. Hope, H. G. Brackley, E. L. Foote and R. H. McIntosh. In the first nine months of operation nearly 1,500 passengers and 40 tons of freight were carried in eight o/400s and two o/7s G-EAAF and 'MA. The original four o/400s were now joined by 'KF, 'KG and 'LX–'LZ, nil-hour machines, stored since construction by the Metropolitan Wagon Co. Ltd. at Birmingham in the previous year. They were all fitted with windows and furnished cabins for seven passengers, the fuel tanks remaining in the fuselage. Short nacelles were therefore retained, and they continued to be styled o/400s. A windowless o/400 G-EAKE, with seats for 10 passengers was flown to Copenhagen in August 1919 by two R.A.F. officers, one of whom was the Norwegian Tryggve Gran, who became famous on July 30, 1914 by making the first flight across the North Sea in a Bleriot monoplane. His o/400 was unlucky, suffering an accident near Lillisand, Norway on September 6, 1919, followed by a rebuild and a second crash, this time beyond repair, near Stockholm in the following June. An equally unlucky giant was G-EAMC, the *Daily Telegraph* entry for the £10,000 *Daily Mail* prize for the first flight from Cairo to the Cape. With Maj.

The Napier Lion engines of the India flight O/400 being run up at Cricklewood before departure to Croydon.

H. G. Brackley as pilot and Capt. Frederick Tymms navigating, the machine left Cricklewood on January 25, 1920, picked up the sponsor's correspondent Major C. C. Turner at Cairo on February 20 and set off southward. Five days later the flight ended 6 miles north of El Shereik, Sudan, G-EAMC being damaged beyond repair in a crosswind forced landing with jammed controls following severe tail flutter.

An awakening to the possibilities of air transport was at this time taking place overseas, China already possessing at least seven Handley Page 0/7s. Poland also bought them, and the Handley Page Indo Burmese Transport Co. Ltd. was formed to operate the o/7 G-IAAA. In December 1919 a standard o/400 G-EAMD was flown to Poland by E. D. C. Hearne with a long-range fuel tank fitted on top of the fuselage, and a o/7 G-EANV named 'Commando' was flown in South Africa by Major McIntyre, who made pleasure and advertising flights over Cape Town. At the beginning of 1921 these aircraft were followed abroad by three other o/7s G-EAPA, 'PB and 'QZ, all of which had seen a year's service on the London–Paris route.

The company's passenger and freight services were augmented in 1920 by the route to Amsterdam, and two further variants of the o/7 were devised. The first, known as the o/11, carried mixed traffic, two passengers in the bow cockpit, three in a cabin in the rear fuselage and freight in a large hold amidships. Three machines of this type, G-EASL–'SN, were in use until their Cs. of A. expired in March 1921. It was in one of these that R. H. McIntosh inaugurated the company's internal service to Castle Bromwich on December 22, 1920. The freighters were later joined by a fleet of nine aircraft G-EASX, 'SY, 'TG–'TN, fitted for the carriage of 12 passengers and designated the o/10. All were in daily service between Croydon and the Continent by August 1920.

The *Daily Express* had earlier announced a prize of £10,000 for the first flight to India and back, one of the several entries being a special long-range o/400 G-EASO. Named 'Old Carthusian II', it was fitted with

62

Napier Lions and therefore unique. Although machine and crew, Maj. A. Stuart MacLaren and Capt. J. A. Barton, were in readiness at Croydon on May 14, 1920, strained relations with the Arabs compelled the R.A.F. Middle East Command to forbid flights east of Cairo. The competition was therefore abandoned and G-EASO dismantled.

The end of 1920 was a black period for the embryo air transport industry and particularly for Handley Pages. On December 14, 1920, the 0/7 G-EAMA was lost in a disastrous crash at Golders Green, in which the pilot Robert Bager and three others were killed after striking a tree on take off. By the end of the month, intense competition from government-subsidised French airlines had compelled the abandonment of most British services. Handley Pages fought the inevitable until February 1921, when they too ceased operations, one of the 0/10s flying the final service. Following a Government enquiry under the leadership of the late Lord Londonderry, then the Under-Secretary of State for Air, operations were resumed on March 21, 1921, with a subsidised reduction in the Paris fares to the French level of six guineas single and £12 return. Freight did not bear a subsidy, and in the following month not only were the company's surviving 0/11 freighters G-EASM and 'SN scrapped but the 0/10s 'SX–'SZ were sold abroad. On May 27 the landing of a 0/10 at Croydon saw the end of Cricklewood as an air terminal, but it remained the maintenance base, necessitating daily positioning flights. Some difficulty was experienced in taking off from Croydon with full load, and an aircraft was despatched to Martlesham for weighing, after which the all-up weight was reduced from 13,000 to 12,050 lb. by removing all wireless gear, limiting the passengers to 10 and the maximum fuel and oil load to 180 and 12 gallons respectively. Thereafter they gave no trouble, but by 1922 the new Handley Page W8bs were coming into service, and Croydon saw the war-time veterans no more. Last to go to the breaker's yard was G-EATH, which, as late as May 1923, inaugurated a thrice-weekly route from Paris to Basle and Zürich. Although based at Le Bourget it occasionally came to Croydon on Saturday afternoons, and after maintenance left again on Monday mornings. In the following September it

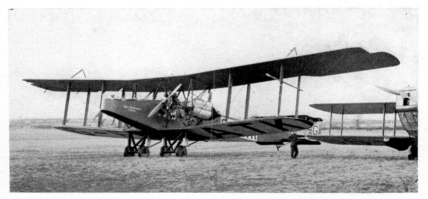

The Jupiter installation of G-EATK, with cowlings removed to show the disposition of the fuel tanks in the rear of the nacelle. (*Photo: The Bristol Aeroplane Co. Ltd.*)

made its last flight, from Zürich to London in the day—surely no mean feat for a 0/10. It was then picketed behind the hangars to fall into dereliction, a sad fate for the last of a worthy line.

During their service careers, two 0/10s were the subject of interesting modifications. During the development of the new Handley Page W8 in 1920, interest in 'hands off' flight quickened to the point where an early automatic pilot, the Aveline Stabiliser, was invented. The prototype was fitted in G-EATN, and during the French Government's Competition in January 1921, was repeatedly flown 'hands off' by H. G. Brackley for periods of over an hour. On January 8 the device brought 'TN from Lympne to London through bad weather, but engine trouble caused a forced landing in a fog-free field at Gravesend. G-EATK was flown to Filton during the winter of 1921, where, in collaboration with the Bristol Aeroplane Co. Ltd., the Eagles were replaced by Jupiter radials in newly designed mountings. A net reduction of 900 lb. was thereby effected in the tare weight. G. P. Olley, who did the test flying, recorded an appreciable increase in the rate of climb and top speed, but with the new Handley Page W8bs in the offing, the proposal to re-engine the whole fleet was shelved.

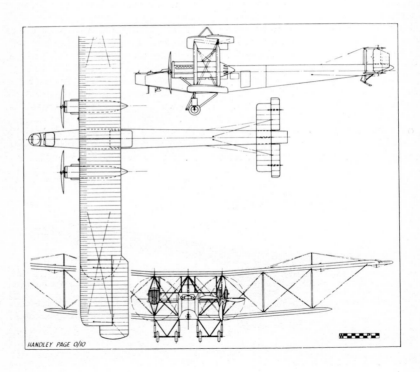

HANDLEY PAGE 0/10

Manufacturers: (1) Handley Page Ltd., Cricklewood, London, N.W.2; (2) The Metropolitan Wagon Co. Ltd., Birmingham; (3) The Birmingham Carriage Co. Ltd., Birmingham. (*The numbers in parentheses form the key to manufacturers in Appendix D.*)

Power Plants: Two 360 h.p. Rolls-Royce Eagle VIII.
Two 436 h.p. Bristol Jupiter IV.
Two 450 h.p. Napier Lion II.

Dimensions: Span, 100 ft. 0 in. Length, 62 ft. 10¼ in. Height, 22 ft. 0 in. Wing area, 1,648 sq. ft.

Weights: Tare weight (Eagle VIII), 8,326 lb. (Jupiter IV), 7,526 lb.
All-up weight (Eagle VIII), 12,050 lb. (Jupiter IV), 12,050 lb.

Performance: (Eagle VIII) Maximum speed, 97·5 m.p.h. Ceiling, 8,500 ft. Duration 7½ hours.
(Jupiter IV) Initial climb, 500 ft./min.

The prototype Handley Page W8 in its original competition form with fuel tanks in elongated nacelles.

Handley Page W8, W9 and W10

As soon as Handley Page Air Transport Ltd. was fairly launched with its fleet of converted 0/400s, work began at Cricklewood on the construction of the firm's first purely civil transport. It accommodated two pilots in an open cockpit forward of a roomy, well-glazed cabin for 15 passengers. Although embodying the well-proven wood and fabric construction of its predecessors, it was cleaner aerodynamically, of lower structural weight and fitted with two Napier Lions, 450 h.p. units renowned for their un-equalled power/weight ratio. First intimation of the existence of the proto-type G-EAPJ came early in 1920, when first flights were made at Crickle-wood. It was obviously an outstanding aeroplane and on May 4, 1920 Capt. (later Professor, of Pterodactyl fame) G. R. T. Hill set up a British Class C.5 record by climbing the machine to 14,000 ft. while carrying a useful load of 3,690 lb. The exact designation of this important aeroplane is complex, being known during its lifetime as the Handley Page W8 with constructor's number W8-1. It also carried on the rear fuselage a factory number HP-15 in the series reserved for converted 0/400s, and in later years was retrospectively allotted a type number H.P.18.

After exhibition at the Olympia Aero Show it was flown to Martlesham on August 3, 1920, by H. G. Brackley for participation in the Air Ministry's heavy commercial aeroplane competition. Not only was there no compar-able aeroplane for comfort and appearance, but it was also supreme in the reliability and handling tests, achieving 118·5 m.p.h., fastest speed of any machine present, to win the highest award of £7,500. In obedience to an Air Ministry ruling, the seating capacity was later reduced to 12, although it had once carried 27. The fuel tanks were also removed from the engine nacelles to reduce fire risk and fitted above the top mainplane. Develop-ment flying continued until October 21, 1921, when H. H. Perry flew the aircraft on its maiden trip to Paris in 2 hours 5 minutes. Although a num-ber of trips were made during which it established a record of 1 hour 44 minutes, 'PJ was essentially a demonstration aircraft and was eventually written off following a forced landing in bad weather. A projected improvement, the W8a G-EAVJ, was never built.

In June 1921 the Air Ministry announced a three year plan for assisting the airlines and was empowered by the Treasury to authorise the construction of a limited number of aircraft for lease to approved firms. Three Handley Page W8b 12 seaters were therefore ordered, which were similar in appearance to the W8. Still known as the H.P.18, they were powered by uncowled Rolls-Royce Eagle VIIIs and consequently more economical to run. In April 1922 the first W8b G-EBBG 'Bombay' went to Martlesham for official trials and on May 16 was renamed 'Princess Mary' at Croydon by the new D.C.A., Sir Sefton Brancker, 'BH at the same time receiving its baptism as 'Prince George'. The third machine 'BI, delivered in the June, became 'Prince Henry'. All three maintained the Paris and Brussels services of the company until absorbed into Imperial Airways Ltd. on April 1, 1924. Although their habits did not change for many years, the W8bs were repainted in the blue and silver of the new owners, returning to the original silver and black when the company's policy changed in 1927.

In an attempt to reduce the possibility of accidents through engine failure, the H.P.26 or W8e was developed with one 360 h.p. Rolls-Royce Eagle IX in the nose and two 240 h.p. Siddeley Pumas in outboard nacelles. The first of the type was sold to the Belgian airline SABENA and five others were later built under licence in Belgium by SABCA. One example of a slightly modified version, the W8f Hamilton, with cabin heating provided by exhaust muffs, was completed for Imperial Airways Ltd. on June 15, 1924, and made its first flight at Cricklewood five days later. This flew for several years on the Continental routes as G-EBIX 'City of Washington', its maiden flight to Paris taking place on November 3, 1924. SABCA subsequently constructed nine Hamiltons for SABENA, but at Cricklewood the three engined theme led to the H.P.27 or W9 Hampstead, a similar aircraft with a bigger power reserve and higher cruising speed, flown by a crew of two and carrying 14 passengers in wicker chairs in a warmed cabin. Only the prototype, G-EBLE, was built, water-cooling

'Princess Mary', first of the three Handley Page W8b passenger aircraft.

being dispensed with in favour of three 385 h.p. Armstrong Siddeley Jaguar IV radials. First flown on October 1, 1925, named 'City of New York' and carrying Mr. (now Sir Frederick) Handley Page among the passengers, it was delivered to Imperial Airways at Croydon by W. G. R. Hinchliffe on October 19, entered scheduled service on November 3 and on March 10, 1926, lowered the London–Paris record to 86 minutes. In April 1926 its Jaguars were replaced by Bristol Jupiters for 250 hours endurance flying under airline conditions. The total cost of the replacement parts needed by the three engines at the end of this period amounted to only 35 shillings! The Jupiters were then retained until its retirement from the Imperial Airways fleet. The change from Jaguars to Jupiters in the W9 is most important historically because it settled the choice of engine for the D.H.66 and H.P.42 fleets. This had remained in the balance since Cobham's flight to the Cape in the Jaguar engined D.H.50 G-EBFO and Minchin's to Cairo in the Jupiter engined Bloodhound G-EBGG had cancelled each other out and shown both engines to be equally reliable under tropical conditions. The choice had then to be made on a basis of maintenance cost, and here the Jupiter (with fewer parts) scored heavily on overhaul, strip and reassembly time. Many people had their first flights in the Hampstead at the Bournemouth and Hamble air pageants, but on June 27 it was seriously damaged when Leslie Minchin forced landed, without injury to the nine passengers, in a small field near Biggin Hill. In March 1929 'LE was dismantled and despatched by sea to Port Moresby, Papua, where it was erected by native labour under G. I. Thompson. He then flew it to Lae, New Guinea, on delivery to the Ellyou Goldfield Development Corporation, in whose service it gave outstanding performance from primitive aerodromes until wrecked on May 31, 1930.

A twin Lion development for 16 passengers, known as the H.P.30 or W10 also appeared in 1925, four aircraft being delivered to Imperial Airways Ltd. These were G-EBMM, 'MR, 'MS and 'MT, allotted City Class names and commissioned on March 30, 1926. They flew on all the regular routes, supplementing earlier brethren, from which they differed by virtue of their rectilineal fins and rudders. The Hamilton G-EBIX was

G-EBIX, the W8f or Hamilton, in the original condition with W8b type fin and rudder. (*Photo: Handley Page Ltd.*)

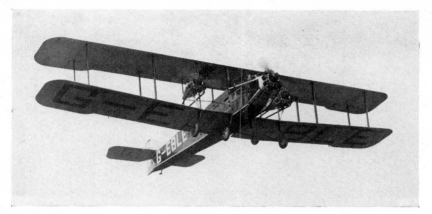

Handley Page W9 Hampstead G-EBLE 'City of New York' flying with Jupiter engines at the Bournemouth Easter Meeting 1927. (*'Flight, Photo.*)

also fitted with this type of tail assembly, and in 1929 lost its central engine and reappeared as the lone W8g with two Eagle IXs.

Although in the 1920s more passenger miles were flown on cross-Channel services by the Handley Page W8 and its offspring than by any other type, they were involved in several serious accidents. With the exception of the Hampstead, none could maintain height with one engine stopped. Thus the comparatively new W10 'City of London' was lost when one engine failed over the Channel on October 21, 1926, Capt. F. Dismore and his 10 passengers being rescued by a trawler. 'City of Ottawa', outward bound for Zürich on June 17, 1929, was less fortunate. An engine failed in mid-Channel, compelling Capt. R. P. D. Brailli to land in the sea 3 miles off Dungeness, the drowning of four of the 11 passengers bringing to an end an unblemished record of 3,900,000 injury-free passenger-miles. 'Princess Mary' was damaged beyond repair in a forced landing at Abbeville while flying from Paris to Croydon on February 15, 1928, but the final accident to the W8g 'City of Washington' was a disaster. Motor stoppage in bad visibility led to its destruction at Neufchatel near Boulogne on October 30, 1930, Capt. J. J. 'Paddy' Flynn being critically injured and three passengers killed. Later, in an attempt to improve single-engine performance, the W10 G-EBMR was temporarily fitted with Rolls-Royce F.XI engines.

With the introduction of the Handley Page H.P.42s in 1931, the aged W series retired from airline service. 'Prince Henry' was hired by E. B. Fielden of Aviation Tours Ltd. and flown by him with the National Aviation Day Displays during 1932. The surviving W10s G-EBMM and 'MR were sold to Sir Alan Cobham for a similar purpose in 1933. In the following year 'MM, renamed 'Youth of New Zealand', was converted into a tanker for refuelling Sir Alan's Airspeed Courier G-ABXN at the start of the attempted non-stop flight to India on September 24, 1934, while G-EBMR stood by in Malta to refuel him over the Mediterranean. As soon as the Courier had been fuelled over the Isle of Wight, 'MM

The Imperial Airways Handley Page W10 'City of Pretoria' (*'Flight' Photo.*)

landed at Ford, where the tanks were removed and in the afternoon left for Whitley to rejoin the Air Display. Near Aston Clinton, failure of a tailplane bracing bolt caused major structural failure and 'MM crashed and burned, with the loss of Capt. C. H. Bremridge and crew. This incident sealed the fate of a single W8e built by SABCA as O-BAHJ in 1924 and later converted to W8b standard with two Eagle VIIIs as OO-AHJ. Bought from SABENA in December 1932 by British Hospitals Air Pageants Ltd., it lay dismantled at Ford during 1933–34 awaiting overhaul for joyriding as G-ACDO. When 'MM crashed, 'MR was sold abroad and the embryo 'DO went to the scrap heap.

SPECIFICATION

Manufacturers: Handley Page Ltd., Cricklewood, London, N.W.2.
Power Plants: (W8)   Two 450 h.p. Napier Lion.
          (W8b) Two 360 h.p. Rolls-Royce Eagle VIII.
          (W8f) One 360 h.p. Rolls-Royce Eagle IX and two 240 h.p. Siddeley Puma.
          (W8g) Two 360 h.p. Rolls-Royce Eagle IX.
          (W9)   Three 385 h.p. Armstrong Siddeley Jaguar IV.
                    Three 420 h.p. Bristol Jupiter VI.
          (W10) Two 450 h.p. Napier Lion.
                    Two 480 h.p. Rolls-Royce F.XI.

	W8	W8b	W8f Hamilton	W9 Hampstead	W10
Span . . .	75 ft. 0 in.	75 ft. 0 in.	75 ft. 2 in.	79 ft. 0 in.	75 ft. 0 in.
Length . .	60 ft. 3 in.	60 ft. 1 in.	60 ft. 1½ in.	60 ft. 4 in.	58 ft. 4 in.
Height . .	17 ft. 0 in.	17 ft. 0 in.	17 ft. 0 in.	16 ft. 9 in.	17 ft. 0 in.
Wing area .	1,450 sq. ft.	1,456 sq. ft.	1,456 sq. ft.	1,563 sq. ft.	1,456 sq. ft.
Tare weight .	—	7,700 lb.	8,600 lb.	8,364 lb.	—
All-up weight .	12,250 lb.	12,000 lb.	13,000 lb.	14,500 lb.	13,780 lb.
Passengers .	12	14	12	14	16
Maximum speed .	115 m.p.h.	104 m.p.h.	103 m.p.h.	114 m.p.h.	100 m.p.h.
Cruising speed .	90 m.p.h.	90 m.p.h.	85 m.p.h.	95 m.p.h.	—
Initial climb .	600 ft./min.	550 ft./min.	—	900 ft./min.	700 ft./min.
Ceiling . .	18,000 ft.	10,600 ft.	13,000 ft.	13,500 ft.	11,000 ft.
Range . . .	500 miles	—	—	400 miles	—

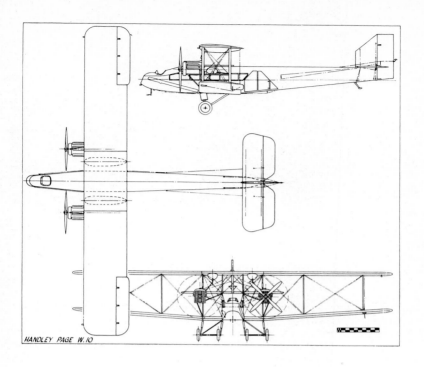

HANDLEY PAGE W.10

'Horatius', second Handley Page H.P.42W, undergoing a pre flight check at Croydon in the 1930s.

Handley Page H.P.42

The H.P.42 was designed specifically for use by Imperial Airways Ltd. on the European and eastern sections of the Empire air routes. A cabin mock-up was exhibited at the Olympia Aero Show of July 1929 and when S/Ldr. A. England and Major J. L. B. H. Cordes took the prototype, G-AAGX, on its maiden flight at Radlett in November 1930, it was seen to be an extremely large biplane in true Handley Page tradition. Although of all-metal construction, with the major part of the fuselage covered with corrugated duralumin plating, all flying surfaces and the rear fuselage were fabric covered. Large automatic slots were fitted to wings braced by Warren girder struts in place of wires, and the biplane tail was fitted with triple fins and rudders. Passenger convenience and comfort had been the designer's watchwords, and the H.P.42 was renowned in its day for setting new standards in furnishing, quietness and cuisine. Ground clearance was such that passengers stepped directly through the cabin door without the aid of steps and the inboard lower mainplanes swept sharply upward to take the main spars over, instead of through, the cabin. The noisy fuselage section adjacent to the engines was occupied by toilets and baggage hold, the passenger cabins being situated fore and aft. Captain and First Officer occupied a glazed compartment high in the nose.

Four geared and moderately supercharged Bristol Jupiter engines were mounted close together to simplify asymmetrical flying in the event of engine failure, and a Bristol gas starter was carried in the port fuselage. A simple device on the throttle quadrant prevented the upper engines being opened up first, thus making it impossible to nose over and emulate the ill-fated Tarrant Tabor. The H.P.42 proceeded majestically and economically along the air routes in the unhurried certainty that its humble 95 m.p.h. could better any surface transport. At the same time it put its passengers completely at ease with its ability to carry them in Pullman comfort and, in an emergency, to land slowly in a confined space. Its appearance brought much ribald criticism, but its unparalleled record of service, safety and revenue earning eventually compelled respect and finally affection.

Including the prototype, total production consisted of four aircraft of each of two versions. Those based at Cairo for the Cairo–Karachi and Cairo–Cape Town sections of the India and South Africa routes were known as the H.P.42E or Eastern model. Initially six, and later 12, passengers were carried in the forward cabin and 12 in the rear, 500 cu. ft. of space being available amidships for the carriage of luggage and mail. The four Croydon-based H.P.42W or Western models were externally identical, but carried 18 passengers forward and 20 in the rear, baggage space being reduced to 250 cu. ft. In post-war years when these aircraft were but a memory, the designation H.P.45 was applied to the Eastern model, but this was not reflected in their constructor's numbers, and was not used during their flying lives. The prototype was completed to H.P.42E standard, named 'Hannibal' and made its first public appearance at a garden party given at Hanworth on June 6, 1931, for members of both Houses of Parliament. Three days later it made the first of a series of proving flights to Paris, carrying its first fare-paying passenger on the 11th. These flights continued until August 8, when a piece of flying metal damaged three airscrews, resulting in a masterly forced landing by Capt. F. Dismore in a field at Tudeley, near Tonbridge. The tail was torn off by telephone wires, but repairs were quickly effected at Croydon. It afterwards left for Cairo to join 'Hadrian', which had made a brief appearance at the Household Brigade Flying Club meeting at Heston on July 22, 1931, before proceeding eastwards. 'Hanno', widely publicised as the first H.P.42E, was in fact the fourth and left Croydon on November 9 piloted by Capt. E. S. Alcock and H. G. Brackley to inaugurate the Empire Air Route to South Africa. While under the command of Capt. H. J. Horsey at Galilee on November 17, 1932, 'Hannibal' suffered damage in a gale. Repairs took six months, after which it gave eight years of unbroken service. 'Horsa' left the factory in September 1931 together with 'Heracles', first of the H.P.42Ws. The remaining three, appearing at Croydon in rapid succession, thereafter became familiar and regular features of the Kent and Sussex skies for many years. 'Heracles' was flown to Hanworth by Capt. W. Rogers on June 19, 1932, to give flights at the garden party of the Royal Aeronautical Society. When leaving, the port wheel sank through a drainage culvert under the aerodrome surface, and for some weeks Middlesex also boasted the silhouette of an H.P.42. Thus, like its Eastern brother, the first Western model became hors de combat right at the beginning of a long and meritorious career. Five years later, on July 23, 1937, 'Heracles' completed its millionth mile on the Paris, Cologne and Zürich routes and by September 11, 1938, seventh anniversary of its first scheduled flight, it had flown $1\frac{1}{4}$ million miles and carried 95,000 passengers.

Utilisation figures for the other H.P.42Ws were equally startling, figures which their Eastern brethren equalled in their own sphere but with different load analyses. 'Helena' was the aircraft chosen to fly to Paris on January 20, 1932, with the first through air mail to Cape Town, 'Hengist' performing a similar function with the first through Australian air mail on

December 8, 1934. Soon afterwards 'Hengist' went east after conversion to H.P.42E, only to be burned out in a hangar fire at Karachi in May 1937. In that year 'Hanno' returned home and was converted to H.P.42W to replace 'Hengist' on European services.

All continued in service until, on September 1, 1939, with war imminent, the Croydon-based machines were evacuated to Whitchurch. Operating from Whitchurch and Exeter, they were mainly used for ferrying war supplies to France. On November 7, 1939 'Horatius' arrived from the Continent to find Exeter enveloped by a storm, forced landed down wind on the golf links at Tiverton, Devon, collided with trees and was written off. It was the beginning of the end of a fleet whose names had been household words for a decade. Three surviving H.P.42Es were flown home, but 'Hannibal' was lost in the Indian Ocean between Jask and Charbah on March 1, 1940. 'Hanno' and 'Heracles' became partially airborne at the end of their picketing ropes during a gale at Whitchurch on March 19, 1940, and were blown together and wrecked. A similar fate overtook 'Hadrian' at Doncaster in 1942 after it had been impressed, together with 'Horsa', for R.A.F. use. The last survivor, 'Helena', was dismantled by the Royal Navy at Donibristle in 1941, and the metal-clad portion of the fuselage, mounted on a wooden cradle, became the Squadron office.

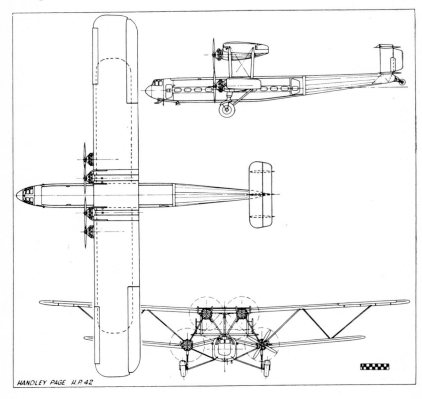

HANDLEY PAGE H.P.42

Manufacturers: Handley Page Ltd., Cricklewood, London, N.W.2, and Radlett
    Aerodrome, Herts.

Power Plants: (H.P.42W) Four 550 h.p. Bristol Jupiter XFBM.
          (H.P.42E) Four 550 h.p. Bristol Jupiter XIF.

Dimensions: Span, 130 ft. 0 in. Length, 89 ft. 9 in. Height, 27 ft. 0 in.

Weights: All-up weight (H.P.42W), 29,500 lb. (H.P.42E), 28,000 lb.

Performance: (H.P.42W) Maximum speed, 127 m.p.h. Cruising speed, 100 m.p.h.
          Initial climb, 670 ft./min.
          (H.P.42E) Maximum speed, 120 m.p.h. Cruising speed, 100 m.p.h.
          Initial climb, 790 ft./min.

G-AIWK, second Halifax C. Mk. 8 to bear the name 'Port of Sydney'.

Handley Page Halifax and Halton

The all-metal Halifax bomber of World War 2 first became a civilian aircraft in February 1946 with the arrival at Radlett of NR169, an H.P.61 Halifax 3 which Handley Page Ltd. converted into a 15-passenger aircraft to the order of A.T.A. Flight-Captain G. N. Wikner, of pre-war Wicko fame. Named 'Waltzing Matilda' and with civil markings G-AGXA emblazoned in white on night camouflage, the Halifax left Hurn on May 26 en route to Australia. Piloted by the owner and carrying two crew and 13 other Australian repatriates, the aircraft touched down at Mascot, Sydney on June 20 in a flying time of 71 hours. After exhibition in aid of R.A.F. charities it was disposed of to Air Carriers Pty., but made only one commercial flight, to Singapore with a load of dogs in June 1947, afterwards limping back to Sydney with an unserviceable port outer engine. It never flew again and suffered dismemberment by local vandals.

As soon as the new H.P.70 Halifax C. Mk. 8 transports erected at Radlett in 1945, came up for disposal, Dr. Graham Humby acquired six and founded London Aero and Motor Services Ltd. They were ferried from High Ercoll to Elstree and converted for freighting duties, for which their large panniers made them eminently suitable. In its blue colour scheme with white markings, the first civil Halifax 8, G-AHZJ, formerly PP247, became the first British civil aeroplane to land at Barcelona after the war. One aircraft, G-AHZM, fully civilianised, suffered undercarriage collapse when taxying out for its first civil test flight on September 16, 1946, and was cannibalised to become a welcome source of spares, but the other five did a brisk trade with fruit from Italy and the South of France. Positioning flights were made to London Airport for each trip, and to eliminate dead flying the firm moved to Stansted on December 14, 1946. Ten more Halifax 8s, G-AIWI–'WR and 'WT, were acquired, 'WO and 'WP being cannibalised during the conversion of the others, which, with the originals, were named after their ports of call. By July 1947 the fleet was importing 500 tons of fruit a month. The expansion of business into full-scale tramping was also attempted with the departure of G-AIWT 'Port of Sydney', Capt. Thiele in command, from Stansted on April 23,

1947. He flew the Halifax to New Zealand via Iceland and the U.S.A., the long haul of 2,500 miles from San Francisco to Honolulu being completed in 11½ hours. Several charters were secured between New Zealand and Australia, the aircraft returning to Stansted on June 5 carrying 7 tons of dripping. As a result, L.A.M.S. (Australia) Ltd. was formed and flights were made between Sydney and the Philippines with turkeys, and to the United Kingdom. L.A.M.S. (Africa) Ltd. began operations with G-AIWR 'Port of Durban', reregistered at the Cape as ZS-BUL for the pilgrim traffic between Istanbul, Nairobi and Jeddah, where on November 25, 1947, its undercarriage was damaged on arrival. The Halifax then flew south to Port Sudan, where it was written off in a crash landing. In spite of this very considerable activity, the company wound up in 1948. G-AIWK, named 'Port of Sydney' in place of 'WT, finding itself marooned at Mascot, was picketed alongside 'Waltzing Matilda' until it suffered a similar fate.

In 1946–48 a demand also developed for the rapid transport of ship's crews and spares, the delivery of machinery to the Overseas Food Corporation in East Africa and for the pilgrim traffic in the Near East. Civil Halifaxes played a prominent part in these charters, notably the fleet of the Lancashire Aircraft Corporation based at Squires Gate and of smaller concerns, such as Skyflight, Alpha Airways, Payloads, Bond Air Services, British American Air Services, Chartair, Air Freight, World Air Freight, Eagle Aviation, Westminster Airways and Petair. A shortage of spares was overcome when 25 H.P.61 Halifax B. Mk. 6s were allotted civil marks and ferried to Bovingdon to be broken up by the Lancashire Aircraft Corporation. This fate also overcame G-ALOM, ferried from Hawarden to Southend by Aviation Traders Ltd. Stansted, Bovingdon, Thame, Southend and Blackbushe became the principal Halifax bases in the south, while in 1947 Gatwick saw the departure of G-AGPC, 'TK, G-AHKK, 'VT, 'WL, G-AJBK and 'XD, to the French operator Aero Cargo. Payloads Ltd. exported G-AJNV, G-AKBP and 'CT to Switzerland, but there is no evidence of their arrival or use. Three others, G-AJNU, 'NX and 'NY were converted at Stansted in 1948 and flown out to Pakistan Airways as AP-ACH, 'BZ and 'CG. The one-time 'NX, Capt. Pearson in command, carrying 27 drums of cable, ran out of fuel on its delivery flight and was

G. N. Wikner's Halifax 3 'Waltzing Matilda' being readied for the Australia flight, May 1946. (*Photo courtesy of 'The Aeroplane'.*)

77

'Falkirk', first of the Halton conversions for B.O.A.C. (*B.O.A.C. Photo.*)

wrecked on the inhospitable coast near Basra on May 10, 1948. Three days later, F-BCJX, the former G-AGTK, inward from Lyons, blocked the Hemel Hempstead road after overshooting at Bovingdon. These were but two of the 14 major accidents to converted Halifaxes. The destruction of G-AIZO of Bond Air Services Ltd. at Berkhampsted on May 23, 1948, caused by the cargo of apricots shifting in the air, was believed to be the first such case on record. G-AJPJ of British American Air Services Ltd. met a different fate. An unauthorised ferry pilot flew it away from White Waltham on July 20, 1948, to an undisclosed destination, although unconfirmed reports suggested that it eventually limped into Lydda on two engines and crash landed, thus just failing to become an Israeli bomber.

The Halifax was also used for airline duties at a time when British Overseas Airways Corporation was faced with fleet shortages caused by the non-delivery of the Avro Tudors. Twelve Halifax C. Mk. 8s were reworked at Radlett by Handley Page Ltd. into transports for 10 passengers, with 8,000 lb. of baggage, freight and mail in the pannier. A large entrance door was fitted in the starboard side of the rear fuselage and square windows provided in the cabin. While retaining the designation H.P.70, a new type name Halton 1 was allotted, the prototype G-AHDU 'Falkirk' being christened by Lady Winster at Radlett on July 18, 1946. The sole Halton 2, G-AGZP, was originally a V.I.P. Halifax operated on behalf of the Maharajah Gaekwar of Baroda by British American Air Services Ltd., which after transporting the owner from India in April 1946, was converted to special standards at Radlett. Following a period in South Africa as ZS-BTA with Alpha Airways, it finished its career in the service of Lancashire Aircraft Corporation. The 12 B.O.A.C. aircraft flew for a year or so on the desert routes from London to Accra until replaced by Canadair C-4s. All 12 then lined up at London Airport until G-AHDR 'Foreland' was sold to the Louis Breguet concern in France and the rest left for Southend on delivery to Aviation Traders Ltd. to join the firm's 22 H.P.71 Halifax A. Mk. 9 paratroop transports granted civil status for ferrying from Hawarden prior to servicing for the Egyptian Air Force. An embargo on arms to Egypt early in 1950 resulted in only half a dozen, G-ALOP, 'OR and 'VJ-'VM leaving for Cairo, the last mentioned being the former RT938, 6,176th and last Halifax built. In

78

Egypt it carried the serial 1161 in Arabic, the others becoming 1155, 1157, 1159, 1160 and 1162 respectively.

In 1948 the initial post-war boom in air freighting collapsed, and the future of the civil Halifaxes was again in jeopardy. They were, however, pressed into use on the Berlin Air Lift, together with the Haltons and G-ALON and 'OS, the only two Halifax 9s converted for civil use. During the period from June 24, 1948, to the last Halifax flight on August 15, 1949, they operated a continuous round-the-clock service into Gatow from their bases at Schleswigsland and Wunsdorf. The fleet consisted of 41 Halifaxes operated by the Lancashire Aircraft Corporation (13), Bond Air Services Ltd. (12), Westminster Airways Ltd. (4), Eagle Aviation Ltd. (4), British American Air Services Ltd. (3), World Air Freight Ltd. (3) and Skyflight Ltd. (2). The phenomenal total of 4,653 freight sorties was flown with an additional 3,509 by Westminster Airways, the Lancashire Aircraft Corporation and British American Air Services, whose

G-ALOS, formerly RT937, was one of two Halifax A.Mk.9 aircraft fully civilianised by Aviation Traders Ltd. It flew 161 sorties for Bond Air Services Ltd. on the Berlin Air Lift.

Halifaxes were converted for the bulk carriage of diesel fuel. Loads averaged 6½ tons, and operations were carried out under extreme difficulties. With few spares available, even minor accidents often resulted in aircraft being scrapped. Thus nine Halifaxes were lost during the operation, many on the ground at Schleswigsland and Tegel, and one, World Air Freight's G-AKGZ, at Gatow on October 8, 1948.

The end of the Berlin Air Lift marked the end of the Halifax as a civil aeroplane. The majority returned to Squires Gate, Woolsington, Southend and Bovingdon, where they were reduced to produce, melted down on site and taken away as ingots. A few survived for a while, including G-AITC, one of two originally civilianised for the College of Aeronautics. This crash landed at Brindisi on January 20, 1950, while in service with World Air Freight Ltd. and carrying a cargo of cloth from Milan to Teheran. Later in the year, one of the surviving Lancashire Halifaxes G-AKEC 'Air Voyager' was sportingly entered for the *Daily Express* Air Race and on September 20 Capt. A. N. Marshall flew it low round the

79

South Coast from Hurn to Herne Bay to come 24th at an average speed of 267 m.p.h., surely the Halifax's only race!

SPECIFICATION

Manufacturers: Handley Page Ltd., Cricklewood, London, N.W.2 and Radlett Aerodrome, Herts.
Power Plants: (Halifax 3 and 9) Four 1,615 h.p. Bristol Hercules 16.
   (Halifax 6 and 8) Four 1,675 h.p. Bristol Hercules 100.
   (Halton 1 and 2) Four 1,675 h.p. Bristol Hercules 100.

	Halifax 3	Halifax 6	Halifax 8	Halifax 9
Span	103 ft. 8 in.	103 ft. 8 in.	103 ft. 8 in.	103 ft. 8 in.
Length	70 ft. 1 in.	73 ft. 7 in.	73 ft. 7 in.	73 ft. 7 in.
Height	21 ft. 7 in.	21 ft. 7 in.	22 ft. 8 in.	21 ft. 7 in.
Wing area	1,275 sq. ft.	1,275 sq. ft.	1,275 sq. ft.	1,275 sq. ft.
Tare weight	—	38,900 lb.	37,750 lb.	37,830 lb.
All-up weight	65,000 lb.	65,000 lb.	68,000 lb.	65,000 lb.
Maximum speed	—	320 m.p.h.	320 m.p.h.	270 m.p.h.
Cruising speed	—	195 m.p.h.	260 m.p.h.	—
Initial climb	—	950 ft./min.	740 ft./min.	700 ft./min.
Ceiling	—	24,000 ft.	21,000 ft.	21,000 ft.
Range	—	2,350 miles	2,530 miles	2,050 miles

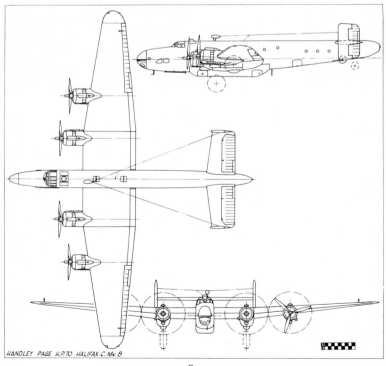

HANDLEY PAGE H.P.70 HALIFAX C.Mk.8

The Handley Page H.P.81 Hermes 4 'Hero' (*B.O.A.C. Photo.*)

Handley Page Hermes

The H.P.68 Hermes 1 four-engined transport was designed during World War 2 for use on future peace-time air routes. A specification issued in 1944 disclosed that seven crew and either 34 first class or 50 tourist class passengers would be accommodated in a pressurised fuselage. The Hermes was thus the first British pressurised passenger aircraft. The prototype, G-AGSS, of all metal construction powered by four Bristol Hercules engines, was built at Cricklewood during 1944–45, and in common with all Handley Page aircraft since the H.P.42, its component parts were taken by road to Radlett Aerodrome for final erection. On Sunday December 3, 1945, the aircraft took off on its first flight piloted by F/Lt. J. R. Talbot, the firm's chief test pilot, but proved unmanageable, probably because of elevator overbalance, stalled and dived upside down into the ground. The pilot and flight observer E. A. Wright lost their lives and the prototype was destroyed by fire.

In spite of this set-back, work proceeded on a military counterpart, the Hastings, the first of which flew successfully during the year. A second civil prototype, the H.P.74 Hermes 2 G-AGUB, was then constructed and made a successful maiden flight in the hands of the company's chief test pilot S/Ldr. H. G. Hazelden at Radlett on September 2, 1947, in time to participate in the S.B.A.C. Show held there a week later. It was a stretched version of the H.P.68 with a 13 ft. extension to the front fuselage and seating 50 passengers in pressurised comfort. Built primarily for development flying, 'UB had a long and useful life which paved the way for the tricycle-undercarriage version, the H.P.81 Hermes 4, 25 of which had been ordered by the Ministry of Supply on behalf of B.O.A.C. in April 1947. Construction of the first, G-AKFP, went ahead rapidly, S/Ldr. Hazelden making the first test flight at Radlett on September 5, 1948. Such was his confidence in the new machine that before landing he flew past at an Elstree air display, and once more a new Hermes was able to put in the qualifying hours before the S.B.A.C. Show. It was publicised as a medium-long-range type for 63 passengers and seven crew, the total payload being 7 tons and the ultimate range 3,500 miles. Its Hercules 763 power plants drove four-bladed de Havilland fully feathering, reversible-pitch airscrews and were installed in quick-access cowlings, notable for their clean aerodynamic form and beauty of line. Two such power units were installed in the outer nacelles of the Hermes 2 prototype, delivered by air to the B.O.A.C. Development Flight at Hurn on May 9, 1949 for a 250 hour programme of test flying under simulated airline conditions. Its work done, the Hermes 2 returned to Radlett, where it languished until fitted with modified windows, a solar compass and camera in 1953 for geophysical research by the Ministry of Supply and is still on the active list in R.A.F. colours.

The Ministry of Supply also ordered two H.P.82 Hermes 5 development aircraft G-ALEU and 'EV, the first of which made its initial flight on August 23, 1949. Both Hermes 5s, exhibited at the 1949, 1950 and '51 S.B.A.C. Shows, were powered by Bristol Theseus turbines and in their day were the world's largest prop jet aircraft. The engines, lighter than the Hercules, were installed farther forward, with the bifurcated jet orifices on each side of the nacelles and passing under the wing. Both were subjected to intensive research flying, during which 'EU, flown by a Handley Page pilot W. Burton, ended its career in a wheels-up landing short of the Chilbolton runway in April 1951 due to engine trouble. The second Mk. 5 'EV, fully furnished to airline standards was flown the 215 miles from London Airport to Orly by D. Bloomfield on June 5, 1951, in the remarkable time of 43 minutes at an average speed of 300 m.p.h. After demonstration to the French Authorities it returned to end its career unspectacularly under the breaker's hammer at Farnborough in 1953.

The B.O.A.C. Hermes 4s were delivered in rapid succession throughout 1950, an achievement made possible by B.O.A.C.'s acceptance of a slight weight penalty resulting partly from the use of Hastings jigs and partly from the tricycle undercarriage. The main oleo attachments for this were moved from the front to the rear spar, which for speed of production was strengthened by modification rather than by redesign. B.O.A.C. accepted the first aircraft on February 22, 1950, the fleet being based initially at Hurn for crew training. After route proving trials in the June, the Hermes fleet took over the West Africa route to Kano, Lagos and Accra and later replaced the Short Solents on the route to South Africa. The Hermes thus became the first British aircraft of post-war construction to enter B.O.A.C. service. In regular airline use they carried five crew and 40 passengers and perpetuated and extended the famous range of mytho-

The Handley Page H.P.68 Hermes 1 at Radlett in December 1945.

G-ALEU, first prototype Handley Page H.P.82 Hermes 5, at Farnborough, September 1949. (*Topical Press.*)

logical names once carried by their illustrious forebears the H.P.42s. Their career was short, and on being replaced by Canadair C-4s in 1952, G-ALDJ was fatigue checked at 3,500 hours flying time. This resulted in a programme of main spar modification, after which they were cocooned at London Airport, but one did not return to suffer this humiliation. G-ALDN 'Horus', victim of a navigational error on the night of May 25–26, 1952, forced landed 11 hours out from Tripoli and lies under the Sahara sand in French West Africa. Several were unexpectedly recommissioned, however, when the Comets were grounded. Fitted with 56 seats, the Hermes 4s began weekly tourist services between London, Dar es Salaam and Nairobi on July 18, 1954.

The second phase in the career of the Hermes 4 began in 1952, when four were sold to Airwork Ltd. for trooping to Kenya and the Egyptian Canal Zone. The Hercules 763 engine, running on special 115 octane fuel, depended on prearranged supplies not always available in the remote areas served by charter operations. It was therefore necessary to modify the engines to burn standard 100 octane fuel, with a change in Hercules nomenclature to 773 and in aircraft designation to Hermes 4A. The first so modified, G-ALDB, went to Entebbe for tropical trials piloted by S/Ldr. Hazelden and the Airwork chief test pilot, Capt. C. D. Stenner. Fitted with 68 strengthened, rearward-facing seats and painted in military markings, the Airwork Hermes 4As plied regularly between Blackbushe and Fayid. The trooping system was later extended, and additional Hermes 4s were acquired by Airwork Ltd. for this purpose. All but one of the remainder were sold to Skyways Ltd. and Britavia Ltd., operating from Bovingdon (later Stansted) and Blackbushe respectively. In 1954 Airwork Ltd. were successful in tendering for the Far East trooping contract to Singapore, for the carriage of 7,000 passengers each way per annum. Several aircraft were lost in this near-military operation, including G-ALDW, blown up by a saboteur's bomb on the ground at Nicosia, Cyprus, in 1956. In that year two of the Skyways aircraft, G-ALDT and 'DX, were detached to Middle East Airlines in Beirut, Lebanon, as OD-ADB and 'ADC, but returned to Stansted after a few months when the pilgrim traffic subsided.

In 1957 fuel supplies were such that reversion to Hermes 4 standard took place on nearly all aircraft. The 17 survivors continued in full employment until 1959 when Hermes 4s were transferred to a new London–

Tunis service, opened by G-ALDO on June 2 and the Silver City Airways 'Silver Arrow' service between Manston and Le Touquet inaugurated by G-ALDP on June 15. At the end of the year G-ALDE and 'DL were converted to 78 seaters and transferred to Bahamas Airways for the Nassau–Miami route.

SPECIFICATION

Manufacturers: Handley Page Ltd., Cricklewood, London, N.W.2 and Radlett Aerodrome, Herts.

Power Plants: (Hermes 1)   Four 1,650 h.p. Bristol Hercules 101.
           (Hermes 2)   Four 1,675 h.p. Bristol Hercules 121.
           (Hermes 4)   Four 2,100 h.p. Bristol Hercules 763.
           (Hermes 4A) Four 2,125 h.p. Bristol Hercules 773.
           (Hermes 5)   Four 2,490 h.p. Bristol Theseus 502.

	Hermes 1	Hermes 2	Hermes 4	Hermes 5
Span	113 ft. 0 in.	113 ft. 0 in.	113 ft. 0 in.	113 ft. 0 in.
Length	81 ft. 6 in.	96 ft. 10 in.	96 ft. 10 in.	96 ft. 10 in.
Height	21 ft. 0 in.	22 ft. 6 in.	29 ft. 11 in.	29 ft. 11 in.
Wing area	1,408 sq. ft.	1,408 sq. ft.	1,408 sq. ft.	1,408 sq. ft.
Tare weight	37,642 lb.	41,689 lb.	55,350 lb.	50,900 lb.
All-up weight	70,000 lb.	80,000 lb.	86,000 lb.	85,000 lb.
Maximum speed	340 m.p.h.	337 m.p.h.	350 m.p.h.	351 m.p.h.
Cruising speed	210 m.p.h.	289 m.p.h.	276 m.p.h.	343 m.p.h.
Initial climb	1,010 ft./min.	750 ft./min.	1,030 ft./min.	2,010 ft./min.
Ceiling	—	23,600 ft.	24,500 ft.	28,600 ft.
Range	2,000 miles	2,000 miles	2,000 miles	2,500 miles

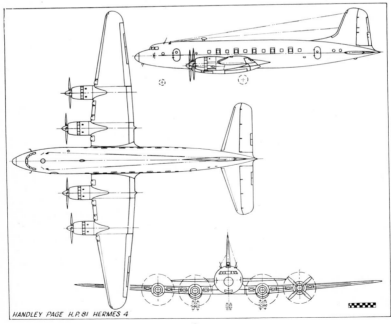

HANDLEY PAGE H.P. 81 HERMES 4

'Millersdale' a Marathon 1A in airline service with Derby Aviation Ltd.

Handley Page (Reading) H.P.R.1 Marathon

The Marathon originated in 1944 when Fred and George Miles and J. H. Lowden of Miles Aircraft Ltd. produced an imaginative design conforming to the Brabazon 5a and 18/44 specifications, three prototypes of which were ordered. Piloted by the Miles chief test pilot K. H. F. 'Ken' Waller, the Marathon, first Miles aeroplane to have four engines, all metal construction and a retractable nose wheel undercarriage, made an uneventful maiden flight under B conditions as U-10 on May 19, 1946, only 14 months after construction began. It was a high-wing, cantilever monoplane with a capacious monocoque fuselage capable of seating two crew and 20 passengers, the fuselage being set low to the ground for ease of entry. The design incorporated Miles pneumatically operated retractable, auxiliary, high-lift flaps and on the power of four supercharged Gipsy Queen 71 engines was the only aircraft of its class to comply with stringent P.I.C.A.O. requirements and could maintain its climb even if two engines failed. Boscombe Down trials were interrupted to permit exhibition at the Radlett S.B.A.C. Show in the September, and fully furnished as G-AGPD, the Marathon was again exhibited in 1947.

During 1946 it became evident that tooling could be planned only for a minimum of 100 Marathons, but total orders amounted to only 25 for the Ministry of Supply and a further 25 for British European Airways Corporation. The latter were to be Mamba powered and designated Miles M.69 Marathon 2. The second Marathon, G-AILH, first flown on February 27, 1947, had two fins and rudders instead of the standard three, and was unfurnished for the purpose of testing the thermal de-icing and cabin heating provided by the Daniel petrol-burning heater, the air intake for which protruded from the top of the rear fuselage. Only the two prototypes had been built before financial difficulties overtook Miles Aircraft Ltd. and work on the Marathon practically ceased. A second blow fell in May 1948, when G-AGPD was totally destroyed in a crash soon after take off from Boscombe Down, with the loss of test pilot Brian Bastable and his flight test observer. Negotiations finally resulted in Handley Page Ltd. taking over Marathon production at Woodley, and for this purpose the name of the firm's historic subsidiary, Handley Page Air Transport Ltd., was changed to Handley Page (Reading) Ltd. on July 5, 1948. The Marathon design was then broken down into seven major assemblies and production began at once. Forty aircraft were built during the next three years with the amended designation Handley Page (Reading) H.P.R.1 Marathon 1, and the Mamba powered Marathon 2 G-AHXU was completed. This became the third British propeller turbine transport to fly when it took off with Handley Page test pilot Hugh Kendall at the controls on July 23, 1949. After exhibition at Farnborough in 1949 and 1950, 'XU was flown by the same pilot into seventh place in the *Daily Express* race from Hurn to Herne Bay on September 16, 1950 at 280·5 m.p.h. It was then transferred to the Ministry of Supply as VX231 and fitted with D.H. reversible-pitch airscrews, the first fitted to turbine engines, in time for demonstrations of backward taxying at the 1951 S.B.A.C. Show. The first production Marathon 1, G-ALUB, left Woodley on January 14, 1950, also piloted by

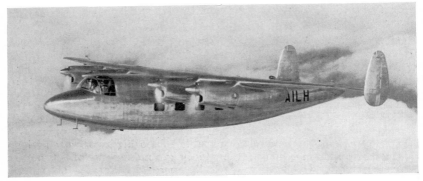

The second prototype Marathon in its original form without the central fin.

Hugh Kendall, accompanied by A. F. 'Bush' Bandidt, on a 40,000 miles sales tour to New Zealand. Demonstrations were staged en route and in Australia and New Guinea, the aircraft returning to Woodley in the May. A year later it was delivered at Northolt for B.E.A.C. acceptance tests, but as had already been foreseen, neither the Marathon 1 nor 2 would be a really suitable Rapide replacement on Scottish services. Thus only seven names were allotted in the proposed Clansman Class, and the order was reduced to seven Marathon 1s. Consequently some 20 undelivered machines were lined up at Woodley and Blackbushe that summer, many of which were later flown to Stansted for storage. G-ALUB reappeared at London Airport in September 1951 in full B.E.A.C. livery with the name 'Rob Roy', but in February 1952 the Corporation finally abandoned the Marathon and the Ministry of Supply diverted 30 aircraft for modification to Marathon T.Mk.11 advanced navigation trainers for the R.A.F. G-AILH, now fitted with the third fin, went to Hullavington as a communications aircraft but was sold to Dan Air Services Ltd. at Lasham when the T.Mk.11s were put up for disposal in 1957. Several others were acquired by the Air Navigation and Trading Co. Ltd. and F. G. Miles Ltd., and flown to Squires Gate and Shoreham for overhaul in 1958–59.

The Mamba powered Marathon 2. (*Photo courtesy of 'The Aeroplane'.*)

The twelfth production Marathon G-AMEO was loaned to West African Airways Corporation in March 1951 as VR-NAI for evaluation over the Nigeria–Gold Coast–Sierra Leone–Gambia network. As a result six Marathons were delivered to the Corporation for regular airline service at the end of 1952, but the Gipsy Queen 70-3 motors were replaced by Gipsy Queen 70-4s, changing the designation to Marathon 1A. When replaced by Herons in 1954, all the Marathons returned for storage at Cranfield or Lasham to await sale. The evaluation aircraft G-AMEO was already at Dusseldorf in service with the German Civil Aviation Board on radio calibration work and another, VR-NAO, went to Jordan as VK-501, a V.I.P. transport for King Hussein. It later returned and tried unsuccessfully to reach the U.S.A. via the northern route after conversion into a juke-box showroom by the Balfour Marine Engineering Co. Ltd. at Southend. Two were handed over to the R.A.E. at Farnborough in March 1955 and were converted to Marathon 1C for special duties. Two others now fly in Derby Aviation livery on scheduled services between Burnaston, the Channel Islands, Isle of Man, Renfrew and elsewhere.

The long-distance tour of 1950 resulted, two years later, in the sale of the last three production Mk.1A aircraft G-AMIA–'IC to Union of Burma Airways at Rangoon. They were employed for several years on services to Akyab, Calcutta, Singapore and Bangkok. An order for two was also received in 1954 from Far East Air Lines in Japan. Thus two aircraft G-AMHY and 'HZ, earmarked for T.Mk.11 conversion, went east instead.

The Mamba Marathon, re-engined with Alvis Leonides Major two-row radials in 1955, was not only a test bed but was fitted with nacelles designed for the projected H.P.R.3 Herald. In this form, redesignated the H.P.R.5, it was based at Baginton with Alvis Motors Ltd. until, in 1958, it moved to Armstrong Siddeley Motors Ltd. for the installation of their new P.181 engines.

Manufacturers: Handley Page (Reading) Ltd., Woodley Aerodrome, Reading, Berks.

Power Plants: (Miles M.60)   Four 330 h.p. de Havilland Gipsy Queen 71.
           (Miles M.69)   Two 1,010 e.h.p. Armstrong Siddeley Mamba 502.
           (Marathon 1)   Four 340 h.p. de Havilland Gipsy Queen 70-3.
           (Marathon 1A) Four 340 h.p. de Havilland Gipsy Queen 70-4.
           (H.P.R.5)   Two 870 h.p. Alvis Leonides Major 701/1.

Dimensions: Span, 65 ft. 0 in. Length, 52 ft. 1½ in. Height, 14 ft. 1 in. Wing area, 498 sq. ft.

	M.60	M.69	Marathon 1
Tare weight . .	11,200 lb.	10,850 lb.	11,688 lb.
All-up weight .	16,240 lb.	18,000 lb.	18,250 lb.
Maximum speed .	230 m.p.h.	290 m.p.h.	232·5 m.p.h.
Cruising speed .	210 m.p.h.	260 m.p.h.	201 m.p.h.
Initial climb .	682 ft./min.	2,100 ft./min.	595 ft./min.
Ceiling . . .	22,000 ft.	35,000 ft.	18,000 ft.
Range . . .	960 miles	900 miles	935 miles

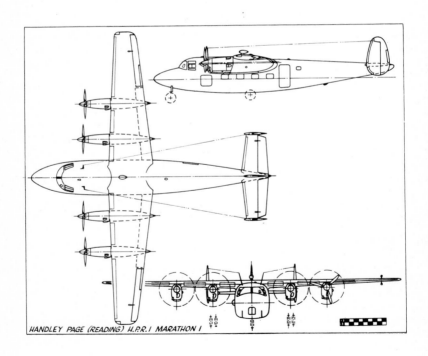

HANDLEY PAGE (READING) H.P.R.1 MARATHON 1

The sole remaining Tomtit retains the standard uncowled engine but has a Spitfire windscreen. (*Photo: Hawker Aircraft Ltd.*)

Hawker Tomtit

In the late 1920s the Air Ministry forsook wooden construction and issued a specification for an all-metal Mongoose powered trainer. Hawker's interpretation of this specification was the Tomtit, a fabric-covered, two seat biplane with Handley Page automatic slots, Frise ailerons on the lower wing only and cockpits behind the centre section for ease of para-chute escape. It was fully aerobatic and a delight to fly. At least 36 were built between 1929 and 1931, mostly for the R.A.F. but four went to the R.N.Z.A.F. and five were registered by the makers as civil aeroplanes. The first two, fitted with Mongoose IIIA radials, were G-AALL and G-ABAX, flown in the 1930 King's Cup Race by S/Ldr. D. S. Don and the Hon. F. E. Guest respectively. The latter came 12th, to record the first of many Tomtit racing failures. A third machine G-AASI appeared in September 1930 fitted experimentally with a Cirrus Hermes I in-line engine and despite its low power put up good aerobatic performances at Brooklands, piloted by P. E. G. Sayer and others.

The original pair were sold to the Hon. F. E. Guest, after which 'LL was fitted with a Mongoose IIIC, standard engine of the R.A.F. machines. After coming 8th piloted by F/O. E. C. T. Edwards in the *Morning Post* Race at Heston on May 21, 1932, it competed for the King's Cup against G-AASI. The latter now boasted a Mongoose IIIC in place of the Hermes, but the pilots, F. E. Guest and H. Wilcox, were unlucky and retired. Last of the civil Tomtits, G-ABII and 'OD, almost certainly the last two built, were registered in 1931. In May 1933 'SI, 'AX and 'OD were sold to Wolseley Motors Ltd. and went to Castle Bromwich as engine test beds, and for that year's King's Cup Race, 'SI and 'AX fitted with geared Wolseley A.R.9 Mk.Ia radials and 'OD with a direct drive A.R.9 Mk.IIa, were flown by Brookland's strongest team, P. W. S. Bulman, P. E. G. Sayer and G. E. Lowdell. Although they averaged 137 m.p.h., the handicapper was not to be beaten, and they faired no better in the following year. In the Hanworth–Isle of Man Race on May 30, 1936, however, Charles Hughesdon came 2nd in G-AASI at 107 m.p.h. Various trial engine installations were made at Castle Bromwich in ensuing years, including that of a Wolseley Aries in 1935. In 1938 'OD, with a Wolseley Aquarius, became personal mount of Hawker test pilot W. Humble, its A.R.9 powered stable mates spending the last year of peace with the Tollerton Aero Club. The Tomtit G-ABII served inconspicuouly as the maker's communications aircraft for 12 years, going camouflaged to Gloster Aircraft Ltd. for the same purpose in 1943. It reappeared at Fairoaks after the war, but owner E. Williams damaged it beyond repair at Cowes in 1948.

Messrs. Bulman, Sayer and Lowdell flying the Wolseley engined Tomtits prior to the 1933 King's Cup Race. Note the ungeared engine of G-ABOD. (*'Flight' Photo.*)

Tomtit G-AASI in 1930 with Cirrus Hermes engine.

Tomtit G-ABOD with the experimental Wolseley Aquarius engine. (*Photo: The H. G. Hawker Engineering Co. Ltd.*)

A second chapter in the history of the type opened in 1935, when the R.A.F. disposed of its obsolete Tomtits by public tender. Nine were civilianised by L. J. Anderson, Hanworth; C. B. Field, Kingswood Knoll; the Leicestershire Aero Club, Braunstone and Southern Aircraft (Gatwick) Ltd. First to appear, G-AEES, carried out aerobatics and pleasure flying with Campbell Black's British Empire Air Displays in 1936–37, eventually going to private ownership at Maylands. G-AEXC saw a year's service at Broxbourne with the Herts and Essex Aero Club and a fleet of four, G-AFIB, 'KB, 'TA and 'VV, operated at the Leicester Club. H. D. Rankin flew his private G-AFFL from Southend, where it was wantonly smashed up at the outbreak of war. C. Plumridge's G-AEVO, on the other hand, survived at Redhill until 1947, when it was burned in an adjacent field.

Six Hawker Tomtits were unique in war-time because G-ABII, G-AFIB, 'KB, 'TA, 'VV and G-AGEF all flew continuously on communications duties as camouflaged civil aeroplanes and somehow resisted impressment. G-AFIB and its successors, 'TA and G-AGEF, were mainly used as personal mounts of Alex Henshaw, test pilot of Spitfires built by the Castle Bromwich Aeroplane Factory.

Following the post-war loss of G-ABII, the only Tomtit now surviving is G-AFTA, fitted with a Spitfire windscreen and a streamlined head-rest, legacy of its wartime Henshaw ownership. After spending 1948 at Chalgrove with R. C. S. Allen, 'TA became the property of Hawker's chief test pilot Neville Duke, thereby becoming well known for its air-racing and aerobatic prowess. Today it is maintained in immaculate condition as a flying museum piece by Hawker Aircraft Ltd. and appears annually at any air display where biplane nostalgia is appreciated.

Manufacturers: H. G. Hawker Engineering Co. Ltd., Canbury Park Road, King-
    ston-on-Thames and Brooklands Aerodrome, Byfleet, Surrey.
Power Plants: One 155 h.p. Armstrong Siddeley Mongoose IIIA.
             One 150 h.p. Armstrong Siddeley Mongoose IIIC.
             One 105 h.p. A.D.C. Cirrus Hermes I.
             One 185 h.p. Wolseley A.R.9 Mk. Ia or IIa.
             One 170 h.p. Wolseley Aquarius.
             One 225 h.p. Wolseley Aries.
Dimensions: Span, 28 ft. 6 in. Length, 23 ft. 8 in. Height, 8 ft. 8 in. Wing area,
    238 sq. ft.
*Weights: Tare weight, 1,100 lb. All-up weight, 2,100 lb.
*Performance: Maximum speed, 124 m.p.h. Cruise, 105 m.p.h. Initial climb,
    1,000 ft./min. Ceiling, 19,500 ft. Range, 350 miles.

* With Mongoose IIIC engine.

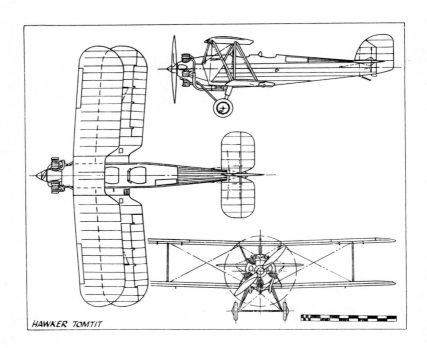

HAWKER TOMTIT

G-AEHJ, last of the three Gipsy VI series I engined Phoenix monoplanes. (*Photo courtesy of 'The Aeroplane'.*)

Heston Type 1 Phoenix

The Heston Type 1 Phoenix five seat commercial or private owner aircraft was, as the name implies, the first product of the Heston Aircraft Co. Ltd. formed in 1934 to take over the assets of Comper Aircraft Ltd. Designed by Mr. George Cornwall, it was of wooden construction, the plywood-covered fuselage consisting of a large rectangular-section cabin terminated by an elliptical section semi-monocoque rear portion. All flying surfaces, including the unflapped mainplane, were of orthodox design, fabric covered with plywood leading edges. Its most revolutionary feature was the Dowty hydraulically operated inward-retracting undercarriage, the first fitted to a British high-wing monoplane. The wheels retracted into a thickened lower stub wing which swept gracefully upward to maintain the line of the rigid N-type wing-bracing struts.

The prototype, G-ADAD, made its first flight at Heston on August 18, 1935 piloted by E. G. Hordern and proved to be 7 m.p.h. faster than the designed top speed. With five occupants, 100 lb. of luggage and fuel for 500 miles, it cruised at 125 m.p.h. on the 200 h.p. of one Gipsy VI. It was particularly notable, not only for the generous leg room and quietness in the cabin but also because no important modifications were recommended after official Martlesham trials. In October 1935 it gained a C. of A. and an effective silver and green colour scheme for demonstration purposes. The second Phoenix VH-AJM was flown to Australia by C. J. Melrose for use on his proposed Melbourne–Adelaide service, but he lost his life when it was struck by lightning near Melton, Victoria, on July 5, 1936. The prototype was sold to a Greek air taxi firm, and a second demonstrator, the blue and silver G-AEHJ, appeared at the Heathrow Garden Party of the Royal Aeronautical Society on May 10, 1936 and the Hatfield S.B.A.C. Show two months later. The fourth Phoenix, G-AEMT, resplendent in silver and red, was the first of three improved models fitted with the Gipsy VI Series II engine driving a de Havilland variable-pitch airscrew which imparted a slightly improved performance. The second

93

improved Phoenix, the yellow G-AESV, was delivered to Standard Telephones and Cables Ltd. at Hatfield in March 1937 as a flying laboratory
for the demonstration and development of their aircraft radio installations.
This particular Phoenix was exhibited at the Heathrow R.Ae.S. Garden
Party on May 9, 1937, but the type did not find a ready market, and only
one other, G-AEYX, was built and sold to joint private owners C. Ran-
drup and S. T. Worth at Heston in May 1939. The two earlier machines
'HJ and 'MT, unsold, but with a two-year record of flying on hire, were
also disposed of in 1939, the first to British American Air Services Ltd. of
Heston and the other to the Luton Flying Club. Both did a considerable
amount of charter flying just prior to the war until 'HJ was damaged beyond repair in an accident. The three survivors, all with Series II motors,
were impressed in 1940 for communications work in the Industry. The
former Standard Telephones machine was allocated to Scottish Aviation
Ltd. during 1942–43, and unlike its two brethren, survived to become a
civil aeroplane once more in 1946. It was used for joyriding at Bembridge
and elsewhere during 1951, finally passing into private ownership with
Mr. A. R. Pilgrim at Elstree. In April 1952 the veteran Phoenix crashed
on a French mountain and the type became extinct.

SPECIFICATION

Manufacturers: The Heston Aircraft Co. Ltd., Heston Airport, Hounslow, Middle-
sex.
Power Plant: One 200 h.p. de Havilland Gipsy VI Series I.
　　　　　　One 205 h.p. de Havilland Gipsy VI Series II.
Dimensions: Span, 40 ft. 4 in. Length, 30 ft. 2 in. Height, 8 ft. 7 in. Wing area,
260 sq. ft.

	Gipsy VI Series I	Gipsy VI Series II
Tare weight . . .	2,000 lb.	2,150 lb.
All-up weight . .	3,300 lb.	3,300 lb.
Maximum speed .	145 m.p.h.	150 m.p.h.
Cruising speed . .	135 m.p.h.	135 m.p.h.
Initial climb . . .	650 ft./min.	850 ft./min.
Ceiling . . .	14,000 ft.	20,000 ft.
Range	500 miles	500 miles

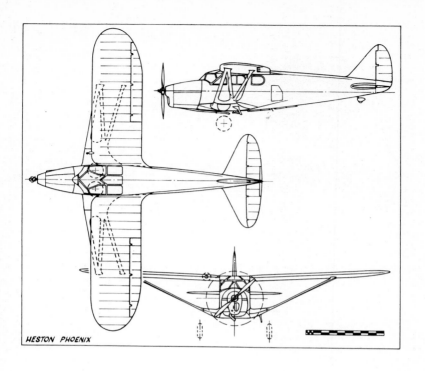

HESTON PHOENIX

One of the fleet of Hillson Pragas used by the Northern School of Aviation at Barton in 1937. (*Photo courtesy of J. G. Ellison.*)

Hillson Praga

Designed by M. Slechta and built at Karlin, a suburb of Prague, Czecho-slovakia, the Praga E.114 light aeroplane first flew in 1934. On August 15, 1935, the second prototype, OK-PGB, landed at Heston, where test pilot Kostalek gave demonstrations. These resulted in the woodworking firm of F. Hills and Sons Ltd. acquiring a licence to build the type in their Trafford Park, Manchester, works. Of all-wood construction with ply-wood covering throughout, the diminutive Praga cantilever monoplane offered cabin comfort for two passengers side by side. Entry was effected by folding back the leading edge of the centre wing (to which was attached the cabin top) and lowering the side windscreens. The engine, also Czech, was a Praga B two cylinder, horizontally opposed, 36 h.p. unit.

In January 1936 a production Praga E.114 OK-PGC was imported from Czechoslovakia by Messrs. Comper and Walker as a pre-produc-tion specimen. Doped a vivid yellow over all, with British markings G-ADXL, it was loaned to C. W. A. Scott's Flying Display at the be-ginning of the 1936 season, but on May 6 left Lympne en route to South Africa piloted by H. L. Brook. He reached the Cape in 16 days 4½ hours, bettering the 23 day trip made by David Llewellyn in Aeronca C-3 G-AEAC three months earlier. In spite of considerable optimism, South African markets did not materialise for these ultra lights, although 'XL was sold locally. After World War 2 it was converted into a glider, and in 1953 was still in existence at Youngsfield Aerodrome, Cape Town.

Production of the British model, known as the Hillson Praga, began at Manchester in 1936, the Praga B engine being built under licence by Jowett Cars Ltd. The first completed aircraft was shipped to Australia and the second, G-AEEU, became the firm's demonstrator. Piloted by R. F. Hall, it won the Manx Air Derby on June 1, 1936, covering three laps of the island at an average speed of 89.5 m.p.h. Aviation on 36 h.p. had little appeal for the British private flier, and the Praga experienced the same sales resistance suffered by its contemporary, the Aeronca 100. Approximately 30 were built, 10 of which were disposed of to the Northern Aviation School and Club Ltd., formed at Barton in 1937 to operate the Pragas for instructional purposes. Five others were used by Straight controlled flying clubs at Ipswich, Ramsgate and Weston-super-Mare, whence all fled when war became imminent. First to go into service, the silver and green G-AEUP arrived at Ipswich on September 1, 1937, but trouble was experienced with the Praga motors, and all five were fitted with 40 h.p. Aeronca J.A.P. J-99 Mk.1A two cylinder engines during 1938. In the following year, in the Straight blue and red colour scheme, they were flown intensively by the Civil Air Guard. Only three Pragas were initially sold elsewhere; G-AELK to Messrs. Jagger, Waugh and Kenworthy, a Barton private ownership group; 'PK to Midland Aircraft Repair Ltd. for use by the North Staffordshire Aero Club at Meir, Stoke-on-Trent; and 'EV to R. J. Pattinson at Sherburn-in-Elmet. En route from Barton to Yeadon in June 1937, 'LK was forced down at Chorley by bad weather and wrecked by striking a wall in the ensuing take off. The syndicate then successfully operated G-AEOL until the outbreak of war.

The little Pragas were not suitable for R.A.F. impressment and were stored until space could no longer be spared and then scrapped. Five managed to survive, 'EU and 'UT at Hooton, 'UP at Perth, 'OL at Barton and 'EV at Doncaster. Two of these, 'UP and 'UT, were overhauled to fly again with Praga B motors replacing the original Aeronca J.A.P.s but were both destroyed in crashes far from home. First to go, G-AEUP was burned out in the Turkish mountains while being flown to the Near East by F/Lt. F. Bosworth in July 1946. The other, serviced at Hooton by the cannibalisation of 'EU, was stored until acquired by Lt. Cdr. G. A. J. Goodhart R.N. and flown to Portsmouth in 1950. It was subsequently owned by V. H. Hallam at Abingdon and finally by Mr. and Mrs. C. M. Roberts at Croydon in 1956. Its end came during an Italian tour in 1957, a forced landing while en route from Peretola to Naples resulting in a destructive collision with trees. The fourth survivor 'EV was acquired by R. Fowler of Hatfield Motor Wreckers near Doncaster in 1945, and for 10 years kept company with the famous Blackburn Dart skeleton until burned at Yeadon in 1955. G-AEOL, overhauled by Astral Aviation Ltd. at Greatham, Co. Durham, in 1947, was nor re-erected and did not fly again.

SPECIFICATION

Manufacturers: F. Hills and Sons Ltd., Trafford Park, Manchester.
Power Plants: One 36 h.p. Praga B.
              One 40 h.p. Aeronca J.A.P. J-99 Mk.1A.
Dimensions: Span, 36 ft. 0 in. Length, 21 ft. 6 in. Height, 5 ft. 6 in. Wing area, 152 sq. ft.
Weights: Tare weight, 584 lb. All-up weight, 1,080 lb.
Performance: Maximum speed, 93·3 m.p.h. Cruising speed, 79·6 m.p.h. Initial climb, 350 ft./min. Range, 280 miles.

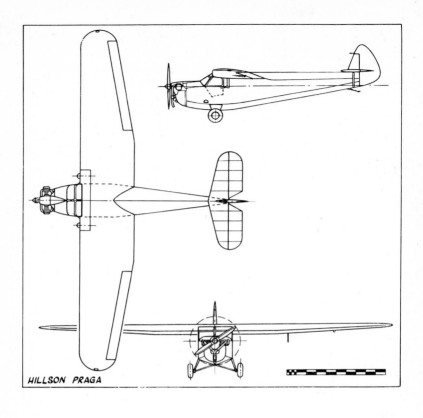

HILLSON PRAGA

'Jason', the Junkers Ju 52/3m freighter outside the British Airways hangar at Heston in 1937.

Junkers Ju 52/3m

The Junkers Ju 52/3m was an all metal, cantilever, low-wing transport first produced at Dessau, Germany in 1932. Fuselage construction followed usual practice, with duralumin frames round four metal longerons, while the wing structure consisted of eight duralumin tubes braced by short struts. The extreme simplicity of the design and the immense strength imparted by the corrugated metal skin, became legendary. Large flaps ran behind and below the trailing edge of the mainplane to form the famous 'double wing' renowned for its low stalling speed. Power was supplied, as the designation indicated, by three B.M.W. licence-built Pratt and Whitney Hornets. The pronounced offsetting of the wing engines was a prominent characteristic of the type. In the years before World War 2, the United Kingdom was unique as one of the few countries not employing the Ju 52/3m. This state of affairs ended in January 1937 when British Airways Ltd. opened a freight service between Heston, Croydon and Hanover with two Ju 52/3m machines named 'Juno' and 'Jupiter' acquired from A.B. Aerotransport in Sweden. In the following August a third aircraft 'Jason', a pure freighter with blanked-off windows was purchased new from Junkers. All three machines were later based at Gatwick, and maintained night mail and freight services to Hanover and Stockholm up to the outbreak of war. From October 1939 they flew a weekly service from Perth to Stavanger, Oslo, Stockholm and Helsinki, but this ended on April 9, 1940, when Norway was invaded and the Germans captured 'Jason' on the ground at Oslo. 'Juno' was at Stockholm but successfully eluded the enemy and rejoined 'Jupiter' at Gatwick. Here they were overhauled and fitted with Pratt and Whitney Wasp engines for which spares were more readily obtainable. After being flown to Speke with a protective escort of fighters they were dismantled and shipped to Lagos as deck cargo. On arrival in November 1940, 'Jupiter' went into service with B.O.A.C. on the trans-African air route between Takoradi and Khartoum. 'Juno' then suffered cannibalisation to service its sister aircraft because the ship carrying the Junkers spares had been torpedoed in the Irish Sea. In September 1941 both were taken over by SABENA in the

Belgian Congo. The fourth Junkers Ju 52/3m of British registry was fitted with Bristol Pegasus VI engines and originated with the Polish airline L.O.T. With other units of the fleet, it escaped the German invasion and on September 12, 1939 flew to Bucharest, where it was acquired by Imperial Airways Ltd. as G-AGAE. In the confusion of the period, the work of repainting with British markings was slow and difficult, and on April 24, 1940, the Air Ministry advised its abandonment.

During the war 2,804 Junkers Ju 52/3m military transports were built for the Luftwaffe. Vast numbers were captured at the end of hostilities, twelve of which, model Ju 52/3m.g8e aircraft, were allocated to British European Airways Corporation for use on internal routes. The first, G-AHBP, of 1939 vintage, was granted a restricted C. of A. for test and freight duties, but was used mainly at Elmdon and Renfrew for crew training. The remaining aircraft were converted by Short Bros. and Harland Ltd. at Belfast at a cost of £125,000. The first Ju 52/3m service, from Croydon to Nutts Corner via Speke, was flown on November 18, 1946, after which they also operated to Nutts Corner non-stop and on the Scottish services from Renfrew and Prestwick to the Orkneys, Shetlands, Inverness and Nutts Corner. One aircraft, G-AHOK, was dismantled for spares following a landing accident at Renfrew early in its career but the rest, referred to as the Jupiter Class in memory of 'Jupiter' the veteran of the African services, continued in use until replaced by Dakotas at the end of 1947. Their ownership was then transferred to the M.C.A. and the aircraft were picketed at Ringway until scrapped by the British Aluminium Co. Ltd. at Warrington in 1948. The initial machine, G-AHBP, was stored at Elmdon until it suffered a similar fate at the hands of Minworth Metals Ltd. at Castle Bromwich in July 1948.

SPECIFICATION

Manufacturers: Junkers Flugzeug und Motorenwerke A.G., Dessau, Germany.
Power Plants: (Ju 52/3m)   Three 770 h.p. Bayerische Motoren Werke 132H.
    Three 600 h.p. Pratt and Whitney Wasp R-1340-S3H1-G.
    Three 775 h.p. Bristol Pegasus VI.
        (Ju 52/3m.g8e) Three 770 h.p. Bayerische Motoren Werke 132Z-3.
Dimensions: Span, 95 ft. 10 in. Length, 62 ft. 0 in. Height, 14 ft. 10 in. Wing area, 1,190 sq. ft.
Weights: Tare weight, 14,325 lb. All-up weight, 23,150 lb.
Performance: Maximum speed, 189 m.p.h. Cruising speed, 160 m.p.h. Initial climb, 750 ft./min. Ceiling, 19,000 ft. Range, 546 miles.

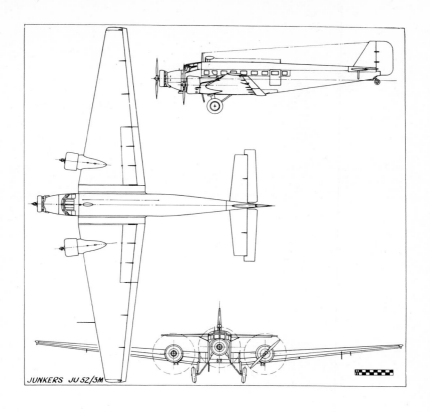

JUNKERS JU 52/3M

Low flying by the Gipsy II powered Klemm L27-IX G-ABOR at Heston in 1935.
(Photo courtesy of 'The Aeroplane'.)

Klemm L25, L26, L27 and L32

The Klemm L25 two seat, low-wing monoplane was the most popular German light aeroplane of the 1920s, and by 1928 production in the Böblingen factory had reached 18–20 a month. In the same year an L25 made a successful landing on the Jungfrau, another completed a world cruise and a third won the premier award at the French light aeroplane trials at Orly. Although of orthodox wooden construction, the varnished natural plywood covering to fuselage and wing leading edges was unusual in those days and imparted the robust qualities essential to private owner-ship. The remainder of the wing and all tail surfaces were fabric covered. For ease of storage the outer wing panels were detachable and provided with special fittings for securing them flat against the fuselage sides.

In May 1929 S. T. Lea Ltd. became sole concessionaries for Klemm aeroplanes in the United Kingdom and a demonstration L25, G-AAFV, was imported and based at Croydon. Registered to Major E. F. Stephen, managing director of the firm, the aircraft was fitted with a 30 h.p. Daimler twin cylinder, horizontally opposed engine. On such low power its performance was not impressive, and at the Olympia Aero Show in the following July the firm's exhibit was powered by a French-built 40 h.p. Salmson A.D.9 nine cylinder radial. This engine gave the aircraft a much improved performance and was the first of many alternative power plants. So varied were they that Herr Klemm devised a system of designations in which the lettered suffix denoted airframe variants and the type of engine was indicated by a hyphenated Roman numeral. The Salmson radial was allotted the numeral I and the aircraft exhibited at Olympia was thus a Klemm L25-I. First of these sold in the United Kingdom was G-AAFU, formerly D-1565, acquired by Col. A. J. Richardson, D.S.O., of the Norfolk and Norwich Aero Club, Mousehold. He was the doyen of the pre-war light aeroplane movement, and on June 27, 1929, at the age of 67, flew 'FU straight across the North Sea to the Rotterdam light plane meeting. The veteran's annual North Sea crossings are now legendary, and iron rations and drinking water for a week were always carried in the front cockpit in case an offshore wind compelled a Klemm style landing on the Dogger Bank. Seven similar machines were sold to British owners, but the C. of A. was not renewed on the Daimler engined model. After a final appearance on the roof of a Kingston-on-Thames cinema to publicise an aviation film in March 1931, it went to the breaker's yard.

The slow and docile Klemms were familiar features of club aerodromes for many years. R. G. J. Nash flew G-AAHL at Brooklands during 1931, but in the following year it was sold to Lord Apsley and wrecked in a collision with a windsock at Whitchurch. A. D. S. Barr's G-AATD, based at Lympne, became well known along the south coast, and in 1938 Roper Brown of Southend acquired the famous 'FU as a replacement for his Avro Baby (see Volume 1, page 85). Three of the original British registered Klemm L25-Is, now thirty years old, are still in existence. One G-AAHW, for so many years the beloved mount of G. R. Lush at Pebsham, Hastings, is now owned by R. H. Grant of Dumfries. The second, G-AAUP, purchased in March 1930 by Major J. C. Hargreaves for private flying at Heston, passed into the hands of Dr. E. V. Beaumont at Mousehold. The third, G-AAXK, suffered five changes of ownership, eventually spending 1938–39 at Leamington, where it was owned and flown by J. Wynn. Credit for the survival of 'UP and 'XK is due to R. H. Grant, who stored them in Dumfries during World War 2. Today 'UP is still intact in storage but 'XK, after several years with J. R. McConnell at Newtownards, County Down, was flown back over the Irish Sea by H. Munro in October 1958 and is now owned by C. C. R. Vick at Biggin Hill.

The small tailplane and unbalanced rectangular rudder of the L25, large enough for normal sedate Klemm style flying, were eventually considered inadequate. It was impossible, for instance, for a pilot to hold the machine in a side slip, consequently the L25a-I appeared with a rounded and horn balanced rudder of greater area. At the same time the tailplane was raised to the top longerons and moved forward to avoid

Roper Brown's veteran Klemm L25-I at the Heathrow Garden Party of the Royal Aeronautical Society in 1938. It was formerly the mount of Col. A. J. Richardson of North Sea fame.

The blue and silver Klemm L25a-I G-AAZH, showing the modified tail surfaces.
(*'Flight' Photo.*)

blanketing the rudder. First to arrive in the United Kingdom was
G-AAZH, which, during its career had six owners, including the Duke
of Richmond and Gordon in 1935. It was the only Klemm impressed
for R.A.F. service during the war. Probably the best known L25a-I was
G-ABCY, which spent much of its life at Castle Bromwich in the hands of
several prominent private owners including A. B. Gibbons, J. V. Rushton,
J. B. Hall and L. W. Hamp. The penultimate British variant of the L25
was the L25b-XI G-ABTE built in 1932 to the order of A. B. Gibbons and
fitted with a Pobjoy R geared radial driving a large two-bladed airscrew.
The change of airframe nomenclature resulted from the fitting of brakes
which, if released with the engine at full throttle, resulted in a take-off run
of the order of 15 yards. An improved model, G-ABZO, for Sir John
Carden, was designated the L25c-XI. With the Pobjoy engine the Klemm
had truly sensational take-off, landing and handling characteristics which
resulted in its manufacture at Hanworth as the B.K. and B.A. Swallow.
(See Volume 1, pages 133–140.)

When the import of Klemm monoplanes came to an end in 1934 the
total flown under British registry had reached 27, the last 14 of which were
remarkable for their detail differences rather than their record of achievement. Basically they were of three major types: the L26, a slightly larger
and heavier version of the L25, the L27 three seater with enlarged front
cockpit and the L32 three seat cabin aircraft. First to appear was R. Denman's Siemens engined L26-II G-AAVS, delivered at Heston in March
1930. Other L26s were fitted with British engines, notably Lord Willoughby de Broke's G-ABBU and Capt. D. I. M. Kennard's G-ABCI,
which had Cirrus IIIs and the designation L26a-III. Another, G-ABRP,
flown at Heston by D. Kinloch was Gipsy III powered and known as an
L26a-X.

For pleasure flights, taxi and aerial photography the three seat L27
series had wide appeal. The white and black Cirrus III powered L27a-
III G-AAWW of British Air Transport Ltd. was a familiar inhabitant of
Croydon until it crashed there in 1933 after taking off with the ailerons
disconnected. An even better known aircraft of this type was G-ABJX, at
first privately owned by A. G. Murray at Lea Airport, Sandown, in 1931,

A. B. Gibbons at Heston with Klemm L32 CH360/G-ACLH in 1933. (*'Flight' Photo.*)

but used by Portsmouth, Southsea and Isle of Wight Aviation Ltd. for the next five years as a joyriding machine at Portsmouth, Ryde and elsewhere. It escaped war-time impressment to become a camouflaged civil communications aircraft, at first with Airwork Ltd. and in 1944 with Vosper Ltd. at Portsmouth. Its career ended in 1945 in a film debut at the National Studios at Elstree, after which it was sold as scrap to C. J. Packer and lapsed into dereliction at Burton, Wilts. G-ABOR was fitted

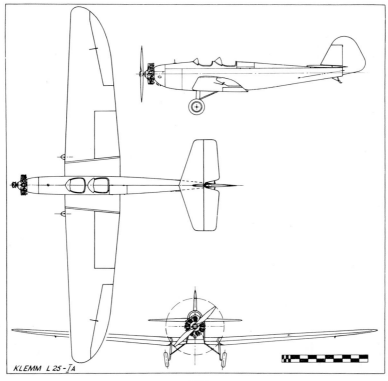

KLEMM L 25 - IA

with the upright Gipsy II engine and flew at Heston as the L27a-IX, first with Airwork Ltd. and in 1936 privately with R. W. Gropler, who eventually sold it in Australia. One other unique specimen also existed, the Hermes IIB powered L27a-VIII G-ABOP, which saw service with British Air Transport Ltd. and Aerofilms Ltd. until sold to Lord Apsley at Whitchurch in May 1935.

Although only two Klemm L32 three seat cabin monoplanes were British operated, each had a unique career. The first started life with an Argus As 8 inverted V type engine in Swiss ownership as CH-360 and flew in the 'Rundflug', or German sponsored International Touring Competition, in August 1932, piloted with distinction by Robert Fretz. In the following year, the well-known Klemm pilot A. B. Gibbons fitted a Gipsy III and brought it to Heston in British colours as G-ACLH with amended designation L32-X. In July 1936 the aircraft was sold in Ireland together with Sir John Carden's Pobjoy powered L25c-XI. The second L32, and final British registered Klemm, powered by the Argus As 8, was originally the demonstrator D-2299. Imported by Aircraft Exchange and Mart Ltd. of Hanworth in September 1934, it was sold to N. R. Littlejohn, an Australian serving in the R.A.F. who kept it at Eastleigh until shipped to Australia in 1937.

SPECIFICATION

Manufacturers: Leichtflugzeugbau Klemm G.m.b.H., Böblingen, Würtemberg, Germany.

Power Plants:	(L25)	One 30 h.p. Daimler.
	(L25-I)	One 40 h.p. Salmson A.D.9.
	(L25a-I)	One 40 h.p. Salmson A.D.9.
	(L25b-VII)	One 70 h.p. Hirth HM60.
	(L25b-XI)	One 75 h.p. Pobjoy R.
	(L25c-XI)	One 75 h.p. Pobjoy R.
	(L26a-II)	One 80 h.p. Siemens & Halske SH13.
	(L26a-III)	One 95 h.p. A.D.C. Cirrus III.
	(L26a-X)	One 120 h.p. de Havilland Gipsy III.
	(L27a-III)	One 95 h.p. A.D.C. Cirrus III.
	(L27a-VIII)	One 105 h.p. Cirrus Hermes IIB.
	(L27a-IX)	One 120 h.p. de Havilland Gipsy II.
	(L32-V)	One 135 h.p. Argus As 8.
	(L32-X)	One 120 h.p. de Havilland Gipsy III.

	L25	L26	L32
Span . . .	42 ft. 7½ in.	42 ft. 7½ in.	39 ft. 4 in.
Length . . .	24 ft. 7 in.	24 ft. 7½ in.	23 ft. 7 in.
Height . . .	7 ft. 10 in.	6 ft. 11 in.	6 ft. 9 in.
Wing area . .	215 sq. ft.	215 sq. ft.	183 sq. ft.
Tare weight . .	627 lb.	882 lb.	1,320 lb.
All-up weight .	1,364 lb.	1,544 lb.	2,090 lb.
Maximum speed .	87 m.p.h.	109 m.p.h.	127·3 m.p.h.
Cruising speed .	65 m.p.h.	—	111·7 m.p.h.
Initial climb . .	500 ft./min.	820 ft./min.	900 ft./min.
Ceiling . . .	21,300 ft.	19,680 ft.	16,400 ft.
Range . . .	600 miles	—	466 miles

G-AEPN, flagship of the British Airways fleet of seven Lockheed Electras. (*Photo: British Airways Ltd.*)

Lockheed Model 10A Electra

In 1936 British Airways Ltd., then extending its routes to Scandinavia, found the de Havilland D.H.86A passenger aircraft, cruising at 140 m.p.h., too slow to make the trip to Stockholm in daylight. The British aircraft industry, fully occupied with the production of military aeroplanes under the R.A.F. expansion scheme, had no replacement type to offer. There was no alternative therefore but to import a suitable foreign aircraft, choice eventually falling on the fast, American designed, Lockheed 10A Electra.

This 10 passenger aircraft had earned a high reputation for speed and economy on the U.S.A. domestic airlines and in Latin America, Canada and Poland. It was a low-wing monoplane of all metal construction, Alclad covered throughout, powered by two 450 h.p. Wasp Junior radials driving two bladed, variable-pitch airscrews. Electrically operated trailing edge flaps and retractable undercarriage were also fitted. Two pilots were accommodated in the nose, which also housed a luggage locker of 35 cu. ft. capacity, with a similar one and a lavatory aft. Four Electras, G-AEPN to 'PR, were shipped to British Airways Ltd. and went into service in March 1937 followed by a fifth, G-AESY, which arrived in the following June. In natural metal finish, with lettering and company titles in black, and piloted by Capts. E. B. Fielden, V. E. Flowerday, C. N. Pelly, S. W. A. Scott and others, they inaugurated the Viking Mail Service. Leaving Croydon at 9.0 a.m., calls were made at Hamburg, Copenhagen and Malmo, Stockholm being reached at 6 p.m. A high-frequency, 90 minute service was also inaugurated between Croydon and Le Bourget. With six return trips scheduled per aircraft per day during the summer season, they revolutionised inter-capital travel. Thus, the Electra G-AEPP made a suitable and interesting exhibit at the garden party of the Royal Aeronautical Society at Heathrow on May 9, 1937. This particular aircraft was wrecked later in the year when making a night landing at Croydon in a blizzard. Its replacement G-AFCS, acquired second-hand from Northwest Airlines in the U.S.A., appeared in February 1938 but was nearly lost soon afterwards when returning from Paris with full load. One motor cut over the Channel, but the pilot made a masterly forced landing on the beach at Pevensey. G-AFEB, seventh and last of the British Airways Electras, went into service in March 1938. In the following June the company moved its London terminal from Croydon to Heston, the Electras continuing to operate on the Stockholm and Paris services with commendable regularity until G-AESY crashed into the sea in the Straits of Storstroem, near Copenhagen. Although salvaged, it was corroded beyond repair and scrapped.

At the outbreak of war the five surviving Electras were hurriedly camouflaged and decorated with fin flashes and lettering underlined in red, white and blue. In this guise they were used extensively on the National Air Communications emergency airlift between Heston, Shoreham and Le Bourget, but after C. of A. overhaul at Whitchurch at the end of 1939, G-AEPN, 'PO and G-AFEB were impressed for R.A.F. communications duties. Based at Hendon, all took part in the evacuation from Dunkirk, where 'PN was abandoned. Rediscovered in time, it was later flown via the northern route to the manufacturers at Burbank, California. Here it was fitted with overload fuel tanks and converted into a very-long-range photo reconnaissance aircraft, later seeing service over Narvik, in the Western Desert and as a glider tug in Sicily. After its return to Hendon in June 1945 it was lost ignominiously in a crash at Leamington.

In April 1940 the two remaining Electras G-AEPN and G-AFCS were taken over by the newly created British Overseas Airways Corporation and transferred to Almaza, Cairo. There they received the names 'Leith' and 'Lea' respectively and were used for two years on routes to West Africa, Kenya and locally in the Near East.

From 1935 the Polish airline Polske Linje Lotnicze (L.O.T.) had operated Electras on services to Hungary, Greece and Rumania and by 1937 owned 10 of these aircraft. After the German invasion of Poland on September 1, 1939, five of them managed to arrive at Bucharest together with six of the company's other types. Negotiations were then opened for their sale to Imperial Airways Ltd., the Electras were allotted registrations G-AGAF to 'AJ and their Polish Cs. of A. were validated for delivery flights to Almaza. In the semi-chaos reigning in Bucharest, it was found impossible to paint them in British colours or to service them for the flight, and they were seized when the Germans later marched into Rumania.

SPECIFICATION

Manufacturers: Lockheed Aircraft Corporation, Burbank, California, U.S.A.
Power Plants: Two 450 h.p. Pratt and Whitney Wasp Junior R-985-SB2.
Dimensions: Span, 55 ft. 0 in. Length, 38 ft. 7 in. Height, 13 ft. 9 in. Wing area, 458·5 sq. ft.
Weights: Tare weight, 6,325 lb. All-up weight, 10,500 lb.
Performance: Maximum speed, 210 m.p.h. Cruising speed, 185 m.p.h. Initial climb, 1,140 ft./min. Ceiling, 21,150 ft. Range, 810 miles.

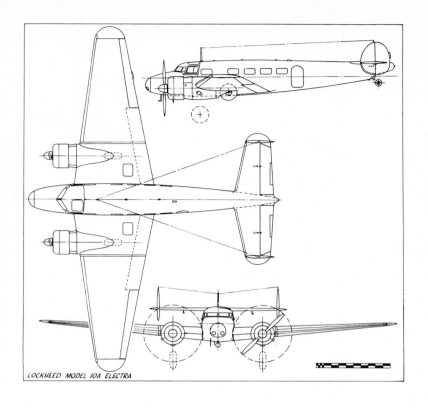

LOCKHEED MODEL 10A ELECTRA

G-AFGN, first Lockheed 14 to become a British civil aeroplane. (*Photo: British Airways Ltd.*)

Lockheed Model 14 and Model 414 Hudson

Introduced in 1937, the Lockheed 14, or so called Super Electra, was a larger and more powerful version of, and a replacement for, the Lockheed 10A Electra. Basic layout and constructional details were identical but accommodation was provided for a maximum of 14 passengers and luggage. The aircraft was consequently larger and the fuselage more rotund, while the installation of Fowler retractable flaps was an innovation which ensured a small field performance despite its relatively high wing loading and cruising speed. Over a hundred had been produced at Burbank by 1940, and many others were built afterwards. Like its predecessor, the Lockheed 14 saw airline service in all parts of the world and four, G-AFGN to 'GR, were shipped to England for British Airways Ltd. They were brought ashore at Southampton Docks and erected at Eastleigh prior to delivery by air to Heston, the first arriving there on September 3, 1938, piloted by Capt. E. G. L. Robinson. A variety of alternative power plants could be installed, the British Airways aircraft, designated Lockheed 14-WF62, being fitted with Wright Cyclone GR-1820-F62s, the first engines with two stage superchargers driving constant-speed, fully feathering airscrews to be used commercially in Britain. During its first month of service, fame came to the flagship G-AFGN as the aircraft used by the late Mr. Neville Chamberlain for his now historic Hitler appeasement flights to Munich and Godesburg.

The Lockheed 14s were acquired primarily for use on a westward extension of the company's routes which were intended ultimately to serve South America. Proving flights, planned in stages, began on October 7, 1938, when two Lockheed 14s were flown from Heston to Cintra Airport, Lisbon by Capts. E. G. L. Robinson and V. E. Flowerday. The second stage of this survey took place at the end of December when the latter reached Lisbon non-stop in 4 hours 59 minutes at an average speed of 208 m.p.h., continuing to Bathurst, Gambia, reached on the 31st. His fellow survey pilot Capt. Robinson had unfortunately been killed a month previously when G-AFGO was burned out in a crash on the rocky Somerset coast at Walton during a test flight. Two additional Lockheed 14-WF62s, G-AFKD and 'KE joined the fleet in November 1938 and a final pair G-AFMO and 'MR in February 1939. The combined fleet of Electra and Lockheed 14 transports enabled British Airways Ltd. to duplicate its Paris and Brussels services and to offer exceptionally fast schedules to Frankfurt (2½ hours), Hamburg (3 hours), Berlin (3¾ hours), Copenhagen (4¾ hours), Budapest (6¼ hours), Warsaw (6½ hours) and Stockholm (7 hours). The flagship 'GN was lost in a crash in France in August 1939 and 'MO made a crash landing at Heston early in 1940. A replacement aircraft for 'GN, a Lockheed 14-WF62 PH-ASL 'Lepelaar' ('Spoonbill'), was purchased second-hand from K.L.M. Royal Dutch Air Lines and became G-AFYU. It was equally unlucky, crashing into the sea off Malta in the following December with the loss of five lives. The five Lockheed 14s absorbed by British Overseas Airways Corporation when it formed on April 1, 1940, were allotted L Class names in common with their two smaller brethren, the Electras. G-AFKD, now fully camouflaged and named 'Loch Invar', lasted but three weeks in B.O.A.C. service, before flying into a mountainside above Loch Lomond and killing the crew and 13 passengers. The remainder were used thereafter solely on maintaining the difficult war-time communications between Britain and Egypt, the first service, flown on June 15, 1940, being routed via Oran, Fort Lamy and Khartoum to Cairo. In the same month G-AFKE 'Lothair' also flew over this route and G-AFGR, 'Lafayette' made a west-bound flight via Kano in Nigeria and Lisbon. On June 28 a ban was placed on flying over French West Africa which cut off the British Isles from the Empire Routes. The Lockheed 14s then remained in Africa, where they spent the rest of their useful lives on the trans-Sahara route from Lagos to Cairo and on local services in the Near East and to Nairobi.

The operational policy of the Polish airline L.O.T. closely followed that of British Airways Ltd. and 10 Lockheed 14-H aircraft, powered as the designation indicated, by Pratt and Whitney Hornet engines, were used to supplement the Electras. Four of these had reached Bucharest after the German invasion of Poland on September 1, 1939, and had been allotted British registrations G-AFZZ, G-AGAA, 'AB and 'AC in readiness for sale to Imperial Airways Ltd. and evacuation to Almaza, Cairo. Without Imperial Airways' knowledge or approval, several of the aircraft were flown on local services by pilots of the Rumanian airline L.A.R.E.S. On July 24, 1940, at the end of one such unauthorised flight from Caracal, SP-BPK/G-AGAA stalled on the approach to Bucharest Airport, crashed through a wooden house and was destroyed. As described in the chapter on the Electra, the scheme was defeated by the German occupation of Rumania. Three other Lockheed 14-H aircraft, SP-LMK, 'BPM and 'BNF, fortunately operating elsewhere in Europe, succeeded in reaching Perth, where they fuelled and proceeded to the Imperial Airways wartime base at Whitchurch, Bristol. Retaining their Polish marks, SP-BNF and 'BPM flew to France in February 1940 and joined the British Airways Lockheeds on the emergency supplies airlift. The third machine remained behind and passed into B.O.A.C. ownership as G-AGAV with its original name 'Lublin'. SP-BNF returned in June 1940 to become G-AGBG, keeping the name 'Lowicz'. At the C. of A. overhaul at Croydon in March 1944, 'Lublin' was found to be seriously corroded, and thereafter remained derelict until the Polish Government permitted its reduction to produce in February 1946. In the same year 'Lowicz' was handed back to L.O.T. at White Waltham but was not repatriated and went instead to Eastleigh to spend a year on long-distance charter operations with Southampton Air Services Ltd. The veteran was then disposed of to Universal Flying Services Ltd. and was later taken over by its parent concern, North Sea Air Transport Ltd. A colourful career came to an end in 1951 when the former 'Lowicz' was sold in Sweden to Airtaca A.B., only to be burned out in a serious crash at Bromma Airport, Stockholm, soon afterwards.

An acute pre-war shortage of R.A.F. general reconnaissance types resulted in a substantial order being placed for a military version of the Lockheed 14 known as the Lockheed 414 Hudson 1. These were armed, operated with a crew of five and were fitted with a more powerful mark of Wright Cyclone engine. The first of the 200 ordered arrived at Liverpool Docks in February 1939 and one, N7364, was allotted to a special R.A.F. Flight at Heston in March 1940. It then became a civil aeroplane G-AGAR under the nominal ownership of Sidney Cotton's company, the Aeronautical Research and Sales Corporation Ltd. Its exact function remained a mystery until 1958 when Constance Babington-Smith unfolded its story. March 30, 1940, found G-AGAR at Habbaniya, Iraq, from whence, devoid of all markings, it photographed Russia's oilfields at Baku. Six days later the Black Sea port of Batum received similar treatment, and in 10 days 'AR was back at Heston with the prints. In June 1940 the Dodecanese were photographed, and it later covered Italian movements in Libya, finally meeting destruction when shot up on the ground at Le Luc Aerodrome near Var in the South of France a year later.

Five other Hudsons were detached from R.A.F. batches and allocated to B.O.A.C. One of these was AM707, a Lockheed 414–13 Hudson 5 delivered to B.O.A.C. on May 9, 1941, and registered as G-AGCE. Test flights revealed unfortunate flying characteristics, and rejection and relegation to No. 10 M.U. followed. The remaining four civil Hudsons G-AGDC, 'DF, 'DK and 'DO designated Lockheed 414–56 Hudson 3, saw useful service, first on the nightly diplomatic and ball-bearing service from Leuchars to Stockholm and from August 1942 on the equally dangerous night service between Gibraltar and Malta. With one exception all returned to the R.A.F., the last to go being G-AGDC and 'DK, which were flown from Croydon to No. 49 M.U. Faygate on August 23, 1945, and scrapped in the following year.

The final Lockheed 14 of British registry was of Canadian origin and 1938 vintage. Originally a Lockheed 14-H2 of Trans Canada Air Lines, it was ferried to Prestwick in 1947 and converted by Scottish Aviation Ltd. to Lockheed 14-08 standard with Twin Wasp motors as G-AKPD. Originally intended for use by Kearsley Airways Ltd., it became instead the executive aircraft of R. A. Brand & Co. Ltd., paper manufacturers. Piloted by Capt. K. Thornton Hall, the aircraft left Croydon on October 29, 1948, en route to Australia, and a few hours later was posted missing. Five years afterwards, on March 22, 1954, during the deep-sea search off Elba for the remains of a crashed Comet, fishermen's nets brought the barnacle encrusted fuselage to the surface.

Manufacturers: Lockheed Aircraft Corporation, Burbank, California, U.S.A.
Power Plants: (Lockheed 14-WF62) Two 760 h.p. Wright Cyclone GR-1820-F62.
    (Lockheed 14-H)   Two 750 h.p. Pratt and Whitney Hornet
                R-1690-S1E2-G.
    (Lockheed 14-08)   Two 1,200 h.p. Pratt and Whitney Twin
                Wasp R-1830-S1C3-G.
    (Lockheed 414-56)   Two 1,200 h.p. Wright Cyclone GR-1820-
                G205A.
Dimensions: Span, 65 ft. 6 in. Length, 44 ft. 4 in. Height, 11 ft. 10½ in. Wing area,
    551 sq. ft.

	Lockheed 14-WF62	Lockheed 14H	Lockheed 414-56
Tare weight . .	10,300 lb.	10,700 lb.	12,536 lb.
All-up weight .	17,500 lb.	17,500 lb.	18,400 lb.
Maximum speed .	249 m.p.h.	227 m.p.h.	253 m.p.h.
Cruising speed .	231 m.p.h.	201 m.p.h.	224 m.p.h.
Initial climb . .	1,230 ft./min.	1,200 ft./min.	2,215 ft./min.
Ceiling . . .	24,200 ft.	23,000 ft.	—
Range . . .	2,125 miles	2,060 miles	2,160 miles

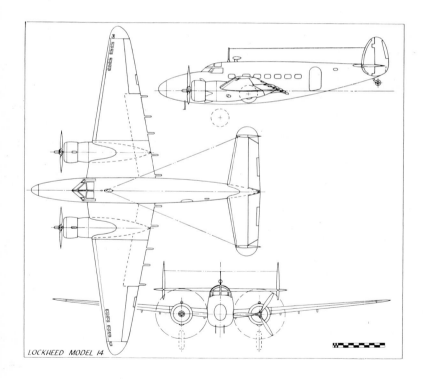

LOCKHEED MODEL 14

Lockheed 18-08 Lodestar G-AGDD 'Loch Losna' in B.O.A.C. wartime colours, flying near Leuchars in 1942. (*Air Ministry Photo.*)

Lockheed Model 18 Lodestar

In 1939 the fourth production Lockheed 14, then in service in the U.S.A. with Northwest Airlines, returned to the Lockheed factory to become the prototype of a larger and faster model known as the Lockheed 18 Lodestar. The fuselage was lengthened to accommodate three crew and 14 passengers, and a new mainplane was fitted incorporating compound taper to the trailing edge. The aircraft made its first flight as a Lodestar on February 2, 1940, and although retaining the original type of Hornet motors, proved capable of carrying a greater load, farther and faster than it had done as a Lockheed 14. Two other Lockheed 14s were similarly converted, and the first production Lodestar was delivered to R. W. Norton on March 13, 1940. Fifty-five production aircraft supplied during 1940 to business houses and scheduled operators in the U.S.A., Latin America, France and South Africa, were the forerunners of 625 built before production ceased in 1943.

Between March and July 1941, nine model 18-07 Lodestars with Hornet engines, ordered by British Overseas Airways Corporation, were delivered by sea to Cape Town. In camouflage as G-AGBO–'BX and bearing L Class names, they joined the Lockheed 14s and de Havilland Flamingoes on the trans-African route, but their numbers proved inadequate to deal with accumulations of east-bound priority loads in West Africa and west-bound ferry pilots in Cairo. Urgent requests for additional Lodestars were met by the R.A.F., which diverted 14 model 18-08s, erstwhile United States civil aircraft which had been impressed by the U.S.A.A.F. prior to being supplied under Lend-Lease. They were converted for B.O.A.C. at Burbank and then shipped to Cape Town for assembly. In peace they had flown with luxury furnishings in the service of Catalina Air Transport, United Air Lines, Walter P. Inman, Harold S. Vanderbilt, R. W. North, the Continental and Superior Oil Companies, the Republic Steel Corporation and the Vaucluse Aviation Company. In war their interiors were stripped, even of the sound proofing, to accommodate 18 passengers on bench-type seats. The Lodestar eventually ousted all other types from the African and Near East services of B.O.A.C., the new arrivals being named after African lakes and carrying the British markings G-AGCL–'CZ. They included 'CT, the first production aircraft, and 'CW, the second of the original Lockheed 14 conversions. Those destined to be 'CL and 'CS were diverted to the Free French and the R.A.F. respectively and did not enter B.O.A.C. service. Two others acquired from Dixie Airlines in the U.S.A. by the Norwegian Purchasing Commission arrived at Leuchars, Fife, in July 1941 to join the Hudsons on the diplomatic flights to Sweden. Manned by Norwegian crews but nominally the property of B.O.A.C., these aircraft, G-AGDD and 'DE, were named 'Loch Losna' and 'Loch Lesja' respectively. In the following year, Hudson losses were made good by 'EI and 'EJ, 'Loch Loen' and 'Loch Lange' and seven others, G-AGIH–'IK, and G-AGLG–'LI, supplied under Lend-Lease. Nightly they ran the cruel gauntlet of the German fighter and anti-aircraft defences in the Skaggerak, until inevitably, two were ditched and lost at sea.

During the siege of Malta the fast and capacious Lodestars proved invaluable in the role of blockade runners, positioning daily at the refuelling point at Gambut in the Western Desert to await nightfall, but 'Lake Rudolf' was lost when the port tyre burst during take off from Malta on May 13, 1942. The replacement, an R.A.F. aircraft HK851, was G-AGEH 'Lake Baringo', a Cyclone engined former U.S.A.A.F. C-60, equivalent to the civil Lockheed 18-56 Lodestar. A number of aircraft of this mark were already in service with the R.A.F., which in September 1943 handed over five to B.O.A.C. as G-AGIG, 'IL–'IM and 'JH, and received in exchange the two surviving Lockheed 14s G-AFKE and 'MR and the Lodestars G-AGBO, 'BP, 'CT, 'CW and 'CX, all of which were in poor condition. The first of the new batch, 'IG 'Lake Karoun', was originally built for the Brazilian Government as a V.I.P. transport for President Vargas with the serial 09 but was impressed by the U.S.A.A.F. before delivery. In the next few years the majority of earlier B.O.A.C. Lodestars were fitted with Cyclone engines and raised to model 18-56 standard.

When the enemy was finally defeated in Africa, the trans-African service was reduced to a skeleton, a number of Lodestars were based at Cairo and, shorn of their camouflage, were fitted with airline seats to maintain services to Turkey, Iraq, Persia, Greece, Transjordan and Kenya. By the end of 1947, however, the majority had been handed back to the R.A.F. at No. 107 M.U., Kasfareet, and by 1953 had all been flown back to the U.S.A. The total B.O.A.C. Lodestar fleet shrank to G-AGBR–'BV and 'BX, six surviving aircraft of the batch purchased outright in 1941. They flew on the Corporation's East African routes until replaced by four engined equipment in 1948, whereupon six were sold to the East African Airways Corporation for £30,000. 'Lowestoft', the sixth, was the only Cairo based Lodestar ever to enter the United Kingdom in British marks, an event celebrated by a minor collision with a hangar on arrival at London Airport at the end of 1947. It was then flown to Australia by its new owner H. W. G. Penny, and after several years of long-distance freighting in Australian marks, is now engaged in crop spraying in New Zealand with Fieldair Ltd.

The prototype Lodestar, converted from a Lockheed 14 in 1939, was disposed of to British West Indian Airways and spent the war years in Trinidad. In 1947 British Aviation Services Ltd. ferried it to Blackbushe, where, as G-AJAW, it became one of the first aircraft operated by Silver City Airways Ltd. In August 1951 it was sold to Aero-Nord of Stockholm, but was never collected from Ciampino Airport, Rome, and was later resold to an American who also failed to collect. Its days therefore ended in corrosion, and in 1958 it was still to be seen at the pickets, an historic but abandoned aircraft. The entire Lodestar fleet of East African Airways Corporation was disposed of in the U.S.A. during 1951 and ferried from Nairobi to New York via the United Kingdom. One, originally B.O.A.C.'s 'Lake Edward', had been sold to the Indamer Corporation but crashed and burned on arrival in New Jersey on January 28, 1952. Nothing remained but the rear fuselage, later enterprisingly grafted on to the front portion of a Hudson by Rauch Aviation. The intention to enter the aircraft, now N367 and renamed Hudstar, in the England–New Zealand Air Race of October 1953, unfortunately came to nought.

In Europe today, only four examples remain of these militant British transports, all acquired in 1953–54 by Dagens Nyheter A.B. of Bromma Airport, Stockholm, for the daily distribution of newspapers to remote areas of Sweden. Two are former B.O.A.C. African air-route machines, 'Lake George' and 'Lake Victoria' still flying as SE-BUF and 'BUU. The others are survivors of the Skaggerak, put up for civilian disposal by the Norwegian Air Force in 1951 and now registered SE-BZE and 'BZK.

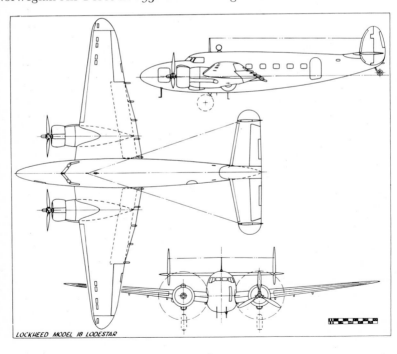

LOCKHEED MODEL 18 LODESTAR

SPECIFICATION

Manufacturers: Lockheed Aircraft Corporation, Burbank, California, U.S.A.
Power Plants: (Model 18-07) Two 875 h.p. Pratt and Whitney Hornet R-1690-
S1E3-G.
(Model 18-08) Two 1,200 h.p. Pratt and Whitney Twin Wasp
R-1830-S1C3-G.
(Model 18-56) Two 1,200 h.p. Wright Cyclone GR-1820-G202A.
Dimensions: Span, 65 ft. 6 in. Length, 49 ft. 10 in. Height, 11 ft. 10½ in. Wing
area, 551 sq. ft.
Weights: Tare weight, 11,790 lb. All-up weight, 17,500 lb.
Performance: Maximum speed 272 m.p.h. Cruising speed, 248 m.p.h. Initial
climb, 1,950 ft./min. Ceiling, 27,000 ft. Range, 1,890 miles.

* Model 18-56.

The British Overseas Airways Corporation Lockheed 049 Constellation 'Baltimore'.
(*B.O.A.C. Photo.*)

Lockheed Model 49 Constellation

A specification for the Lockheed Model 49 was drawn up before the war as a result of consultations between the manufacturers and Transcontinental and Western Airlines. Detail design began in June 1939, and a production line was established at Burbank, California. United States entry into the war resulted in the aircraft being completed to military standards as the C-69, and the prototype made its first flight on January 9, 1943. It was a large, four engined, cantilever low-wing, all-metal monoplane with three fins and rudders and a stressed skin, monocoque fuselage of circular section with slightly up-and-down swept extremities for aerodynamic cleanliness. The two spar mainplane was covered with a flush riveted metal skin and incorporated Fowler flaps. Control surfaces were hydraulically boosted but fitted with emergency manual over-ride and the cabin pressurisation maintained 8,000 ft. at heights over 20,000 ft.

Twenty Lockheed C-69 transports had been delivered to the U.S.A.A.F. before the military contract was cancelled at the end of the war, subsequent airframes being completed to civil standards as the Model 49 Constellation. Accommodation was provided for seven crew and 43 passengers and freight holds were situated fore and aft with a total capacity of 434 cu. ft.

Government permission for British Overseas Airways Corporation to purchase five Constellations in 1946, at a time of acute dollar shortage, provoked considerable criticism. The Tudor having failed, the need for equipment with which to compete with American carriers on the trans-Atlantic route was urgent, and selection of the Constellation, the only available aircraft with sufficient range, was unavoidable. Five of the C-69 aircraft from the tail end of the military contract were overhauled and equipped to B.O.A.C.'s special requirements by Lockheed Aircraft Services Inc. at New York and delivered to the Corporation's maintenance base at Dorval. The first three, 'Bristol II', 'Berwick II' and 'Bangor II', perpetuated the names of the Boeing 314A flying-boats they were to replace over the Atlantic. The fourth, 'Balmoral', Capt. W. S. May, made the first of 10 proving flights on June 16, 1946, reaching London Airport non-stop from New York in 11 hours 24 minutes at an average speed of 310 m.p.h. Serious Constellation accidents in the U.S.A. had been attributed to induction fires in the Duplex Cyclone engines, cabin supercharger drive failures and electrical short-circuits. Pending the result of the enquiry, all Constellations, those of B.O.A.C. included, were temporarily flown unheated and unpressurised until eventually grounded by the U.S. Civil Aeronautics Board. Electrical modifications and the conversion of engines for direct fuel injection proved a lasting cure, and the Constellations gave no further trouble.

Manned by seasoned B.O.A.C. Atlantic Liberator and Boeing captains, the service opened on July 13, 1946, via Shannon and Gander to New York. The first west- and east-bound flights were under the command of Capts. J. T. Percy and O. P. Jones respectively and on February 26, 1947, 'Balmoral', Capt. K. N. Buxton, completed the millionth B.O.A.C. trans-Atlantic mile. 'Baltimore', last of the five, opened the first commercial route to Canada with a flight to Dorval via Prestwick and Gander on April 15, 1947, and was thereafter used almost exclusively on this once-weekly service and on April 4, 1948, made the Corporation's 1,000th Atlantic crossing. A sixth Constellation 'Bedford' was then acquired, arriving from New York with passengers on April 29. By the following September daily utilisation had reached an average of 7·93 hours per aircraft.

Development of the Constellation proceeded via the Model 649 with a more powerful mark of Duplex Cyclone driving Hamilton hydromatic, three bladed, reversible-pitch airscrews, an improved performance, more luxurious furnishings and an increased maximum gross weight of 94,000 lb. The Model 749 which followed, was a long-range version fitted with additional fuel tanks in each outer wing. Although the payload remained the same as for the Model 649, the gross weight rose to 105,000 lb. The designation Model 649 or 749 was equivalent to Model 49 Mk. 6 or Mk. 7, and the original version then became the Model 049 for uniformity. Five Model 749s were purchased with Irish Government approval for trans-Atlantic operation by Aerlinte Eirann. The first three left Burbank with Irish ferry crews on September 16, 1947, but pending the completion of arrangements for a Dublin–New York service, they inaugurated a 'Silver Shamrock' Constellation service to London and Rome. In February 1948, however, Irish plans to operate over the Atlantic were abandoned.

Leisurely Solent schedules to Australia, already outmoded by fast QANTAS and Air-India International services with Model 749 Constellations, were due to cease in January 1949. B.O.A.C. therefore seized the opportunity of acquiring the five Aerlinte aircraft for sterling at a cost of £315,000 each. With its green Irish livery and saintly name replaced by B.O.A.C. blue and gold, 'Banbury' left London under the command of Capt. G. R. Buxton on December 1, 1948, on the Corporation's first Constellation service to Australia. In the following May the B.O.A.C. and QANTAS joint fleet of nine Model 749s was pooled to provide 7–8 return flights per fortnight. The contemporary record for the journey stood at 56 hours 26 minutes set up by a B.O.A.C. 'Connie' which arrived at Sydney on April 13, 1949.

In October 1950 the B.O.A.C. mid-Atlantic Constellation service, operating via the Azores to Bermuda, the Bahamas and Jamaica, was extended across the Andes to Santiago, Chile. The inaugural trip was made by 'Bristol', which like its fellows 'Berwick' and 'Bangor', had then lost the suffix 'II'. The lucrative New York–Bermuda service re-opened with Constellations on May 1, 1951.

'Baltimore', which overshot at Filton during a training flight on January 8, 1951, and suffered major damage in a collision with a petrol store, was disposed of in the U.S.A. and left Avonmouth Docks as deck cargo. After reconstruction by Lockheed Aircraft Service Inc. at New York, using major components from 43-10314, a crashed Lockheed C-69, it went into service on the Los Angeles–Hawaii service of California–Hawaiian Airlines. October 1953 saw it again at London Airport, this time in the colours of Israel's airline El Al. B.O.A.C. did not replace 'Baltimore' until March 1953, when two elderly Model 049s, veterans of eight year's service, first with American Overseas Airlines and from 1950 with Pan American Airways, were added to the fleet as 'Boston' and 'Barnstaple'. Fresh from three months reconstruction at Burbank as Model 049Es, they carried 65 tourist-class passengers at a maximum gross weight, initially of 96,000 lb. and later 98,000 lb. With the Corporation's original Constellations, also modified to Model 049E, they were employed on the 'Mayflower' high-density tourist services to New York, Montreal, Bermuda and Trinidad.

Modifications to the Model 749 introduced in 1949 for the strengthening of centre-section spars and the fitting of heavy-duty undercarriage legs and tyres, had permitted an increase in gross weight to 107,000 lb. with a change of designation to Model 749A. With the exception of 'Belfast', destroyed by fire, with the loss of 33 lives, in a landing accident at Singapore on March 13, 1954, these modifications were made to all the former Irish aircraft. The grounding of the Comet fleet in 1954 caused grave fleet shortages which led to the standardisation of the Model 749A, the purchase of 12 additional aircraft and the formation of a separate Constellation fleet managed by Capt. I. R. Stephens. The Model 049Es were then traded to Capital Airlines in the U.S.A. in part exchange for seven of its Model 749As. When the last 049E left on delivery from London Airport on June 24, 1955, the type had flown 113,207 hours in nine years of B.O.A.C. service.

In their new style B.O.A.C. livery, completely overhauled and boasting brand new Cs. of A., it was difficult to visualise the years of service already standing to the credit of the newly acquired Model 749As. The ex Capital stock had formed the original K.L.M. fleet eight years earlier, one came from Trans World Airlines, four were originally QANTAS aircraft and two had belonged to Air-India. B.O.A.C. tourist and other services were thereafter maintained without incident on the Eastern, Australian and African routes by the fleet of 16 Model 749As until gradually replaced by Britannia 102s in 1957–58. The Constellations then began to filter back to their native land, 'Bala', first to go, leaving London Airport on April 25, 1957, on delivery to Pacific Northern Airlines in Seattle. Others are now frequent visitors to Britain in the colours of Capitol and Transocean Airlines. The last B.O.A.C. scheduled Constellation service was flown by 'Bournemouth' on October 7, 1958 and by June 1959 only four Model 749As remained on the British register—G-ALAK, 'AL, G-ANUP and 'UR, fitted by B.O.A.C. with large double doors for operation by Skyways Ltd. on the Singapore freight service.

SPECIFICATION

Manufacturers: Lockheed Aircraft Corporation, Burbank, California, U.S.A.
Power Plants: (Model 049 and 049E) Four 2,200 h.p. Wright Duplex Cyclone R-3350-C18-BA1.
(Model 749 and 749A) Four 2,500 h.p. Wright Duplex Cyclone R-3350-C18-BD1.
Dimensions: Span, 123 ft. 0 in. Length, 95 ft. 1 in. Height, 23 ft. 8 in. Wing area, 1,650 sq. ft.

	Model 049	Model 749	Model 749A
Tare weight . .	54,600 lb.	58,890 lb.	60,141 lb.
All-up weight .	90,000 lb.	105,000 lb.	107,000 lb.
Maximum speed .	340 m.p.h.	350 m.p.h.	347 m.p.h.
Cruising speed .	308 m.p.h.	328 m.p.h.	298 m.p.h.
Initial climb . .	1,500 ft./min.	—	1,620 ft./min.
Ceiling . . .	24,600 ft.	25,000 ft.	27,300 ft.
Range . . .	3,200 miles	3,000 miles	3,000 miles

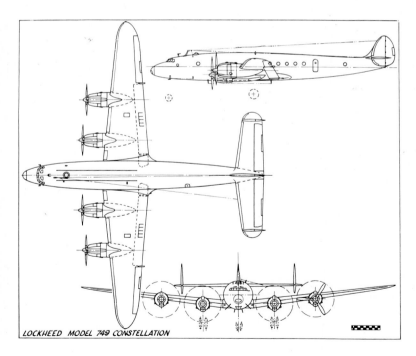

LOCKHEED MODEL 749 CONSTELLATION

F. P. Raynham taking off from Croydon in the single seat Viper engined Martinsyde F.6 G-EBDK at the start of the 1922 King's Cup Race. (*'Flight' Photo.*)

The Martinsydes

Immediately after the First World War, Martinsyde Ltd. produced several civil types, most of which derived from the F.4 single seat fighter, a fabric covered, wooden biplane designed by G. H. Handasyde, with wire braced, box girder fuselage and two spar, single bay wings. Some 280 were constructed, of which only about 50 were delivered to the R.A.F., the remainder, brand new, being stored at the firm's Brooklands works. Their unusually deep and capacious fuselages and relatively high cruising speed made them eminently suitable for civil adaptation as a means of keeping Martinsyde Ltd. in business during peace-time. Piloted by R. H. Nisbet, K-152, the first demilitarised F.4, powered by a 275 h.p. Rolls-Royce Falcon III, gained second place in the Aerial Derby at Hendon on June 21, 1919, at an average speed of 124·61 m.p.h. It was followed by four standard F.4 fighters G-EANM, 'UX, 'YK and 'YP, which received temporary civil status for overseas demonstration. The first left Brooklands piloted by F. P. Raynham on October 6, 1919, performed in Madrid, and on arrival at Lisbon on November 11 was named 'Vasco da Gama' to become the first British aircraft ever to fly in Portugal and the first of a number of F.4s supplied to its air force.

Although incorporating many F.4 components, the Falcon powered Martinsyde Type A Mk. I, long-range two seater, was a two bay biplane considerably larger than its predecessor, built in 1919 to compete for the Australian Government's £10,000 prize for the first England–Australia flight. It fared no better than the Transatlantic Martinsyde Raymor, an essentially similar machine of an earlier era. Capt. C. E. Howell and his navigator Cpl. G. H. Fraser left Hounslow on December 12, 1919, but after making good time, were drowned when forced down in the sea off Corfu five days later. Three other Type A Mk. I machines were built as long-range mailplanes, two of which were exported unregistered in 1920.

A second version, seating four passengers in side-by-side pairs in a glazed cabin ahead of the pilot, was designated Type A Mk. II. No market existed at home, and only the first was of British registry, but four others were exported without marks. One, used for seal spotting in Newfoundland by F. S. Cotton, also took part in the 1921 gold rush at Stag Bay, Labrador. Another went to the Irish Army Air Corps, which gave it the name 'The Big Fellow'.

Construction also proceeded on a racing machine, resembling a scaled-down F.4 and known as the Semiquaver. Flown by F. P. Raynham, it set up a British record of 161·43 m.p.h. over a measured kilometre during Martlesham trials on March 21, 1920, and was later exhibited at the

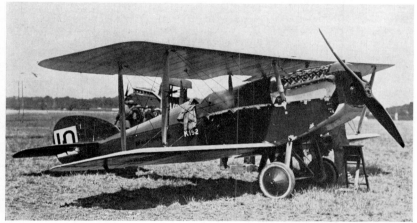

K-152, the Falcon engined Martinsyde F.4 at Hendon on Aerial Derby day 1919. (*'Flight' Photo.*)

A standard F.4 fighter in civil guise at Croydon, just before leaving for Warsaw, January 29, 1921. (*Photo: The Aircraft Disposal Co. Ltd.*)

The ill fated Martinsyde Type A Mk. I leaving Hounslow for Australia, December 12, 1919. ('*Flight*' *Photo.*)

G-EATY, sole example of a Martinsyde Type A Mk. II to bear British civil marks. (*Photo: Martinsyde Ltd.*)

Olympia Aero Show. In the hands of F. T. Courtney it won the Aerial Derby at Hendon on July 28, 1920, at 153·45 m.p.h., but turned over on landing at the end of the race. Short-span wings were then fitted and F. P. Raynham towed it from Brooklands to Etampes behind a car for participation in the Gordon Bennett Race of September 28. In the following year the experimental Alula wing was fitted (see Volume 1, page 405). Although the Semiquaver was the last new type built by Martinsyde Ltd., several F.4 variants were erected and flown. First came the F.4A, a tourer with cockpit for a second occupant ahead of the pilot. Only three were produced, the first, G-EAPP, carrying S/Ldr. T. O'B. Hubbard into 8th place in the 1920 Aerial Derby. The Martinsyde pilot R. H. Nisbet was 6th in G-EAPI, first of two F.6s which were identical to the F.4A except for the heavily staggered centre-section struts. These were vertical in front elevation, whereas those of the F.4 and F.4A were splayed out. The undercarriage was also raked forward and strengthened on the F.6.

G-EAPI, first of the Martinsyde F.6 two seaters. (*Photo: Martinsyde Ltd.*)

Despite the sale of many F.4s to foreign air forces, by 1921 Martinsyde Ltd. found itself in difficulties, a victim of the post-war slump. Its last aeroplane was a low powered F.6, built for F. P. Raynham and fitted with a 200 h.p. Wolseley Viper for more economical private use. First flown at Brooklands on September 29, 1921, the machine later became G-EBDK and was converted into a single seater for racing purposes, coming second in the King's Cup Race of September 8–9, 1922, and competing in the 1924 race piloted by J. King. Its subsequent owners, all well known, were L. C. G. M. Le Champion of Brooklands 1924–25, Leslie Hamilton of Croydon 1925–26 and Major J. C. Savage, Hendon 1927. This famous aircraft was dismantled in Dudley Watt's shed at Brooklands in April 1930, its remains lingering there for several years.

The final chapter in F.4 history opened in 1921, when Martinsyde Ltd. went into liquidation. All surviving airframes were then acquired by the

The Semiquaver fitted with 20 ft. 2 in. wings for the 1920 Aerial Derby.

The Jaguar engined Martinsyde A.D.C.I. (*'Flight' Photo.*)

H. H. Perry leaving Hendon in the Nimbus Martinsyde G-EBOJ at the start of the King's Cup Race, July 9, 1926. (*'Flight' Photo.*)

Amherst Villiers' Martinsyde A.V.I 'Blue Print' at Brooklands in 1931.

Handley Page controlled Aircraft Disposal Co. Ltd. and went by road to Croydon to join the surplus R.A.F. F.4s already held by the company. Four of the latter had lately become civil aircraft in the usual racing and demonstration roles, G-EAXB and 'TD being flown by Major E. L. Foote and R. H. Stocken in the 1921 and 1922 Aerial Derbys respectively. By 1927 a considerable proportion of the F.4 stock had been sold to foreign air forces, 41 going abroad with civil Cs. of A. and two more, G-EBDM and 'FA, in civil marks. To G-EBMI, one of the last to be made airworthy, fell the honour of becoming the only privately owned F.4, property of E. D. A. Bigg at Woodley in March 1930. It crashed a few months later due to failure of the tailplane spar, with the loss of instructor S. W. 'Pat' Giddy.

In 1924 John Kenworthy modernised the F.4 for the Aircraft Disposal Co. Ltd., redesigning the front fuselage to carry a 395 h.p. Armstrong Siddeley Jaguar radial and thereby putting the top speed up to 160 m.p.h. The prototype, G-EBKL, designated Martinsyde A.D.C.I., was first flown at Croydon by the company's test pilot H. H. Perry on October 11, 1924, and competed in the 1925 and 1926 King's Cup Races piloted by W. H. Longton and S/Ldr. H. W. G. Jones respectively. Just as all Martinsydes were affectionately known as 'Tinsydes', 'KL was inevitably dubbed the 'Disposalsyde', forerunner of eight sold to the Latvian Air Force in June 1926. A further redesign with 300 h.p. A.D.C Nimbus appeared in 1926 as the Nimbus Martinsyde and G-EBOJ and 'OL, the only machines of the type, were flown in the 1926 King's Cup Race by H. H. Perry and F. T. Courtney respectively. In the following year, 'OJ, fitted with cylinder head and undercarriage fairings, was re-styled Boreas and won the High Powered Handicap at Hucknall on August 1, 1927, at 141·2 m.p.h. piloted by S/Ldr. H. W. G. Jones. When the Aircraft Disposal Co. Ltd. ceased operations in 1930, all three A.D.C. prototypes were dismantled and burned.

The very last civil Martinsyde was G-ABKH, a two seater known as the Martinsyde A.V.1, erected at Croydon in 1931 by A.D.C. Aircraft Ltd., successors to the disposal company. Externally identical to an F.4A, it embodied many airframe and engine modifications devised by the owner, engine designer C. Amherst Villiers, whose initials it bore. Resplendent in two vivid shades of blue, it was kept at Brooklands until sold to C. B. Field in October 1932. Following an accident at Bekesbourne in February 1933, it lay derelict at the owner's private aerodrome, Kingswood Knoll, Surrey, until scrapped in 1935.

Manufacturers: Martinsyde Ltd., Maybury Hill, Woking, and Brooklands Aerodrome, Byfleet, Surrey; The Aircraft Disposal Co. Ltd., Regent House, Kingsway, W.C.2, and Croydon Aerodrome, Surrey.

Power Plants: (Martinsyde F.4)   One 275 h.p. Rolls-Royce Falcon III.
One 300 h.p. Hispano-Suiza.

(Martinsyde F.4A and A.V.1) One 300 h.p. Hispano-Suiza.

(Martinsyde F.6)   One 300 h.p. Hispano-Suiza.
One 200 h.p. Wolseley Viper.

(Martinsyde Type A Mk. I) One 275 h.p. Rolls-Royce Falcon III.

(Martinsyde Type A Mk. II) One 300 h.p. Hispano-Suiza.

(Semiquaver)   One 300 h.p. Hispano-Suiza.

(Martinsyde A.D.C.I)   One 395 h.p. derated Armstrong Siddeley Jaguar III.

(Nimbus Martinsyde)   One 300 h.p. A.D.C. Nimbus.

	F.4 and F4A	F.6	Type A Mk. I and Mk. II
Span . . .	32 ft. 9⅜ in.	31 ft. 11¼ in.	43 ft. 4 in.
Length . .	25 ft. 5⅝ in.	24 ft. 6 in.	29 ft. 1¼ in.
Height . . .	9 ft. 6 in.	9 ft. 1¼ in.	10 ft. 6 in.
Wing area . .	328·5 sq. ft.	320 sq. ft.	512 sq. ft.
Tare weight . .	1,811 lb.	—	1,800 lb.
All-up weight .	2,300 lb.	2,300 lb.	4,600 lb.
Maximum speed .	145 m.p.h.	—	125 m.p.h.*
Cruising speed .	—	—	100 m.p.h.
Initial climb . .	1,600 ft./min.	—	650 ft./min.
Ceiling . . .	24,000 ft.	—	16,000 ft.
Duration . .	3 hours	3 hours	5 hours

	Semiquaver	A.D.C.I.	Nimbus
Span . . .	20 ft. 2 in.	32 ft. 9⅜ in.	32 ft. 9⅜ in.
Length . . .	19 ft. 3 in.	25 ft. 0 in.	26 ft. 10 in.
Height . . .	—	9 ft. 6 in.	9 ft. 6 in.
Wing area . .	—	320 sq. ft.	320 sq. ft.
Tare weight . .	—	1,865 lb.	2,014 lb.
All-up weight .	2,025 lb.	2,650 lb.	2,665 lb.
Maximum speed .	165 m.p.h.	163 m.p.h.	150 m.p.h.
Cruising speed .	—	—	131 m.p.h.
Initial climb . .	—	2,250 ft./min.	1,350 ft./min.
Ceiling . . .	—	27,000 ft.	23,500 ft.
Duration . .	2·5 hours	3 hours	2·5 hours

* Mk. II 115 m.p.h.

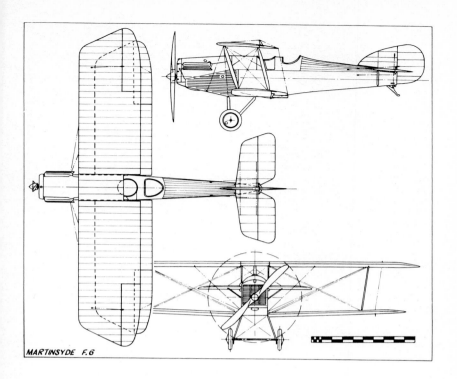

MARTINSYDE F.6

C. L. Storey seated in his Scott Squirrel powered Pou. (*Photo courtesy of R. H. Spence.*)

Mignet H.M.14 Pou du Ciel

In 1933 the French inventor M. Mignet succeeded in flying an aircraft of his own design and construction, afterwards describing it in a best seller entitled 'Le Sport de l'Air'. Aptly named Pou du Ciel, or Sky Louse, it comprised a plywood fuselage carrying rudder, engine, wheels and the lower and smaller of two upswept tandem wings. The upper mainplane was pivoted about the front spar and tilted for longitudinal control. There were no ailerons, turns being made on the rudder, operated by sideways movement of the control column and Mignet claimed that any-one who could make a packing-case could build a Pou and then teach himself to fly it.

The first British Pou du Ciel, G-ADMH, promptly dubbed Flying Flea, was built at Heston by S. V. Appleby and flown for the first time on July 14, 1935, powered by a Carden–Ford unit. Others followed rapidly. G-ADME with Aubier et Dunne engine was built for the Air League by Air Commodore J. A. Chamier, publisher of an English translation of Mignet's book; Cyril Brook coaxed his Scott Squirrel engined G-ADPP into the air at Sherburn-in-Elmet and National Aviation Day Displays Ltd. bought two French built Fleas which cavorted with Cobham's Circus as G-ADSC and 'SD. On July 25 S. V. Appleby turned 'MH over on its back at Heston, giving the well-known sailplane designer L. E. Baynes an opportunity of analysing and remedying defects in the design. He rebuilt the main wing with stouter spars and 5 ft. greater span, the pivot point being moved forward relative to the chord. The front fuselage was also redesigned, totally enclosing engine and radiator. Rae Griffin, also dis-trustful, commissioned Dart Aircraft Ltd. to build his G-ADSE 'Winnie the Pou' from approved materials. It was a true museum piece with the Bristol Cherub III once fitted to the Avro Avis and later to the Supermarine Sparrow, and the wheels and axle from the defunct Gadfly G-AAEY.

Amateur-built models emerged all over the country to be exhibited in motor showrooms, marvelled at in church halls and to make their pathetic hops and occasional circuits from adjacent fields. Overnight they created new problems in certification and insurance, so that the Permit to Fly was created in their honour, No. 1 being issued to Appleby's 'MH on July 24, 1935. By April 1936, some 81 Fleas were complete or under construction, many by groups such as the Glasgow Tramways Flying Club, which built G-AEFP. Fleas were nation wide, ranging from E. M. Lamb's G-ADWX at Canonbridge, Ross-shire, to H. J. Dunning's G-AEEF at Shoreham and from Ray Bullock's G-AEDM at Fraddon, Cornwall, to E. H. Chamber's G-ADXF at Ramsgate. Attempts were also made to build the Flea commercially. F. Hills and Sons Ltd. experimented with G-ADOU at Barton, disliked it and built no more. E. G. Perman and Co. Ltd. constructed 11, G-ADOV, 'PU–'PY, 'ZG, 'ZW and G-AECK–'CM, in mews off Grays Inn Road, London, and fitted a variety of engines, including the Scott Squirrel and the firm's own Perman–Ford conversion. One, G-ADPW, Anzani engined, flew with Campbell Black's Circus piloted by the owner R. G. Doig. S. V. Appleby established Puttnam Aircraft Co. Ltd., which constructed a number of Fleas embodying L. E. Bayne's modifications but only one, G-AEEC, flew at Heston. In the Southend area, C. L. Storey built the Squirrel engined G-ADXS 'Fleeing Fly' and a syndicate produced the gold-painted G-AEDN with A.B.C. Scorpion. The latter had a particularly lively performance, ably demonstrated at the Aero 8 Club Flying Flea Rally held in a field at nearby Ashingdon on April 6, 1936. S. V. Appleby attended in 'EC, flown

G-AEDF, built at Willesden by Arthur Rose, was fitted with a wide-track undercarriage and Anzani engine.

The Austin Seven engine in G-AEEI drove the airscrew through a chain reduction gear. The machine was built by Coopers Garage (Surbiton) Ltd.

from Heston, and F. W. Broughton flew 'MH, fresh from its cross-Channel flight. The others present were C. E. Mercer's Squirrel powered G-AEFV built at West Malling, C. M. Cooper's Surbiton built and Austin Seven engined G-AEEI and the Aero 8 Club's Douglas engined Pou variant 'FW.

At the height of the Flea hysteria came the predicted disaster. On April 20 R. H. Paterson was killed instantly when, soon after take off from Renfrew in G-ADVL, a nose-down attitude gradually developed into a high-speed dive into the ground. Nine more Fleas were built during the next few weeks, but on May 5 F/Lt. Cowell was killed in G-AEEW in exactly similar circumstances at Penshurst, Kent. A fortnight later, on May 21, S/Ldr. C. R. Davidson met the same fate at Digby in the Squirrel engined G-AEBS he had built himself, but blind enthusiasm chose to overlook these grim happenings. E. D. Abbott Ltd. built three examples, G-AEGD, 'JC and 'JD of a strut-braced, push-rod-controlled model designed by L. E. Baynes. Known as Cantilever Poux, they were flown at Heston alongside several privately owned Fleas. 'JC and 'JD competed in the world's only Flea race at Ramsgate on August 3, in which four French and four British machines dashed four times to Manston and back. Edouard Bret won the trophy, but S. V. Appleby made fastest time at 59·5 m.p.h. in his 'veteran' 'MH. The highlight of the meeting was designer Mignet's fighter-like performance in the new H.M.18 cabin Pou fitted with a small elevator in the trailing edge of the rear wing and powered by a Menguin flat twin. It was sold to Appleby in the following month and flew back to France as G-AENV for exhibition at the Paris Aero Show.

Matters came to a head on September 20, when James Goodall was killed at Dyce in his home-built G-ADXY. On the Air League's initiative G-AEFV was tested in the wind tunnel at Farnborough, where the results of French experiments were confirmed. At angles of incidence in excess of − 15 degrees and with the stick hard back, there was insufficient pitching moment to raise the nose. Inevitably the Flea was banned, after 118 had been built or projected, 83 of which had received permits to fly, the last issued on May 1, 1939, to G-AFUL built at Derby by T. H. Fouldes. A few still survive as curios, notably G-AEHM, built at Bristol by H. J. Dolman in April 1936, which is stored at Crayford, Kent, with other Science Museum aircraft; G-AEJX 'The Angus Flea', now at Perth Aerodrome, was built at Brechin by Small and Hardie in June 1936; G-AEKR hangs in Claybourne's Garage near Doncaster Airport, scene of its last flight on June 23, 1937; and G-ADXS is currently exhibited in Storey's motor showroom, Alexandra Street, Southend.

The Puttnam Pou closely resembled the original Appleby machine in its revised form.
(*Photo: Puttnam Aircraft Ltd.*)

The first cantilever Pou, showing the revised bracing and control system.
(*'Flight' Photo.*)

133

The Aero 8 Club's 'high speed' Pou G-AEFW, boasted a streamlined fuselage, normal cockpit, divided undercarriage and Douglas Sprite engine. It crashed south of Gravesend during an attempted flight to France by Claud Oscroft in the summer of 1936.

The H.M.18 cabin Pou, later registered G-AENV. (*'Flight' Photo.*)

Manufacturers: F. Hills and Sons Ltd., Trafford Park, Manchester; E. G. Perman and Co. Ltd., 24 Brownlow Mews, Guildford Street, Grays Inn Road, W.C.1; Puttnam Aircraft Co. Ltd., Victory Works, 407–9 Hornsey Road, London, N.19; E. D. Abbott Ltd., Wrecclesham, Farnham, Surrey; also built in large numbers by home constructors.

Power Plants	Example		
One 35 h.p. A.B.C. Scorpion	G-ADZS	R. R. Little	Bekesbourne
One 35 h.p. Anzani	G-AEEY	R. Butler	Lympne
One 22 h.p. Aubier et Dunne	G-ADME	J. A. Chamier	Hendon
One 847 c.c. Austin Seven	G-AEEI	C. M. Cooper	Surbiton
One 32 h.p. Bristol Cherub III	G-ADSE	R. Griffin	Dunstable
One 30 h.p. Carden-Ford	G-AEIP	C. Oscroft	Ashingdon
One 23 h.p. Douglas Sprite	G-AEFW	Aero 8 Club	Ashingdon
One 38 h.p. Menguin	G-AENV	S. V. Appleby	Heston
One 30 h.p. Perman-Ford	G-AECM	J. E. Foster	Ashingdon
One 25 h.p. Poinsard	G-ADSC	N.A.D. Ltd.	Ford
One 36 h.p. Praga B	G-AEAD	E. W. Kendrew	Leeming
One 25 h.p. Scott Squirrel	G-ADWR	A. U. Tomkins	Brooklands

	H.M.14	Abbott Pou *	Cantilever Pou *	H.M.18 †
Span . .	17 ft. 0 in.	22 ft. 0 in.	22 ft. 0 in.	17 ft. 0 in.
Length . .	11 ft. 10 in.	13 ft. 0 in.	12 ft. 3½ in.	—
Height . .	5 ft. 6 in.	5 ft. 6 in.	5 ft. 6 in.	—
Wing area . .	—	140 sq. ft.	137 sq. ft.	—
Tare weight .	—	350 lb.	327 lb.	250 lb.
All-up weight .	—	550 lb.	550 lb.	—
Maximum speed .	—	70 m.p.h.	—	100 m.p.h.
Cruising speed .	—	60 m.p.h.	—	—
Initial climb .	—	300 ft./min.	—	1,200 ft./min.
Range . .	—	200 miles	—	—

* Carden-Ford.   † Menguin.

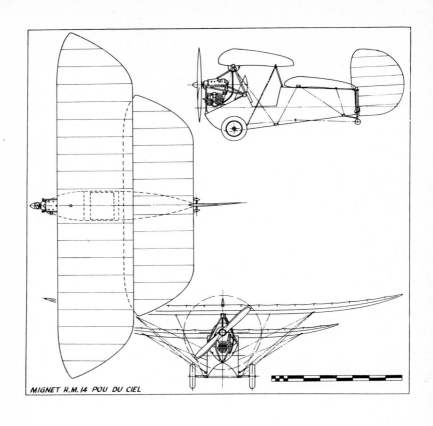

MIGNET H.M. 14 POU DU CIEL

G-ACGH, first of all the Miles Hawks.

Miles M.2 Hawk

The Hawk two seat, low-wing, cantilever monoplane was designed in 1933 by F. G. Miles, and although a structurally orthodox light aeroplane with plywood covered two spar wing and box-built fuselage, excited comment in the heyday of the biplane because its cantilever wing was also designed to fold. Powered by a 95 h.p. A.D.C. Cirrus IIIA, the prototype, G-ACGH, was built at Woodley, Reading, in the workshops of Phillips and Powis Ltd. Piloted by its designer, 'GH made its first flight on the evening of March 29, 1933, and proved so viceless that 53 pilots, mainly inexperienced, flew it within a week.

Without the rigging problems of the biplane and at the attractive price of £395 made possible by the acquisition of new Cirrus engines from a liquidated company in Canada, the Hawk sold without difficulty. In fifteen months, 47 had been supplied to British owners alone. The first production Hawk G-ACHJ was built for Wing Cdr. H. M. Probyn in time for the King's Cup Race of July 8, 1933. Unlike the prototype, which had an undercarriage built from Avian components, 'HJ's was taller and embodied Dowty struts with low pressure wheels. It was flown as a single seater, but forced landed at East Harling with tappet trouble and returned to its base at Farnborough. A fortnight later, the same aircraft and pilot won the Cinque Ports Wakefield Cup Race at an average speed of 115·5 m.p.h., the second production Hawk G-ACHK, belonging to Germ Lubricants Ltd., also competing.

First of four Hawk variants, the Hawk M.2A, a Gipsy III powered cabin version, was built for S. B. Cliff to fly in the Egyptian Oases Rally of January 1934. It was the only one of its kind, and after a couple of years taxi work was destroyed in a hangar fire at Brooklands in 1936. Also built to special order, the solitary M.2B VT-AES was a long-range single seater with Fox Moth sliding hood and Hermes IV inverted engine for Man Mohan Singh's attempt on the England–Cape record in January 1934. This aircraft was cleared for a maximum take-off weight of 2,200 lb. and when fully loaded, carried more than its own weight of fuel. Forced down by an oil leak in darkness at Carcomb (Vaucluse), south of Paris, early on

January 2, 1934, the Hawk was badly damaged and the attempt was abandoned. The one example of the M.2C, a standard Hawk with Gipsy III engine, appeared at about the same time, but left Woodley almost immediately in French markings. In 1934, with travelling air displays at the height of their popularity, Miles produced several three seat Hawks, two of which, G-ACPC and 'PD, went on tour with British Hospitals Air Pageants Ltd. A third lasted only a month in private ownership, and two others, G-ACSC and 'VR, were used for joyriding at Skegness. They were superficially similar to the standard Hawk but had an enlarged rear cockpit for two passengers. The same outer wing panels were used, but the centre section was increased in span by 2 ft. and the undercarriage radius rods were repositioned immediately behind the compression struts.

Several Hawks were sold overseas, a single seater G-ACKX to the Sourabaya Aero Club as PK-SAL; G-ACTO was exhibited at the Geneva International Aero Show as CH-380 in May 1934; G-ACMX was flown to Dublin by F. R. Hill to become EI-ABQ; while 'NX was acquired by Emerson Flying Services, also of Dublin, as EI-AAX. The last mentioned returned in 1935 and, after a succession of owners, crashed at Malmesbury on April 12, 1935, through striking a tree on the approach to a field. After reconstruction and sale to the North Staffordshire Aero Club at Meir, Stoke-on-Trent, it joined the Colonial type Hawk G-ACTN. Like that supplied to Sourabaya, this was strengthened internally, was provided with additional cowling louvres and equipment at an increased tare weight of 1,035 lb. During a snowstorm at Meir on December 15, 1935, 'TN was also involved in a fatal collision with a tree and coincidentally a violent snowstorm also accounted for the destruction of G-ACSD with its owner at Royston, Herts, on April 4, 1935.

As an instructional machine the Hawk was used by the Kent Flying Club, whose yellow G-ACHZ, G-ADBK and 'GI were based at Bekesbourne, by the Ipswich Aero Club with G-ACZD and by the Phillips and Powis School of Flying at Woodley. One Hawk G-ACOP employed by the latter carried the initials of Mr. C. O. Powis. Another, G-ADVR, was a

A standard M.2 Hawk with patent silencing exhaust, optional alternative to a long exhaust pipe on the port side.

The M.2A Hawk was fitted with a cabin for two passengers in tandem. (*'Flight' Photo.*)

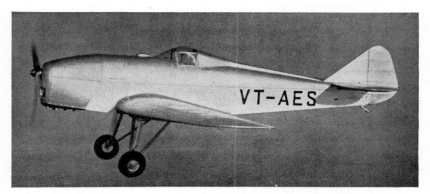

Man Mohan Singh's Hermes powered M.2B Hawk, formerly G-ACKW.

The prototype M.2D Hawk three seater. (*'Flight' Photo.*)

frustrated Rumanian export which had languished at Woodley as YR-ITR before assuming British nationality. The Hawk G-ACTO eventually returned from Switzerland to be operated in turn by the Herts and Essex Aero Club, Ely Aero Club, Cambridgeshire Flying Services and in 1939 by the Kent Flying Club. The last British owned Hawk, G-ADGR, flown at Woodley in 1935 by the Reading Aero Club, carried the initials 'GR in memory of Gerald Royle, killed at Scarborough shortly before. Later sold to the Insurance Flying Club and later still to Julian Rowntree, its career ended on July 18, 1937, in a fatal landing crash at Brussels when returning from Frankfurt. Accidents, mainly serious, had accounted for many of the Hawks, so that by 1939 the only others in existence were G-ACHL of Southern Aircraft (Gatwick) Ltd., 'IZ of W. S. Martin at Tollerton, E. W. Brockhouse's 'MM keeping company at Meir with the rebuilt 'NX, Viscount Clive's G-ACRT at Hanworth, G. G. M. Alington's 'TI and K. W. Hole's 'VO at Hatfield and S. B. Wilmot's 'YA at Hooton. The third production Hawk 'HL was sold to Messrs. P. Steinberg and A. Schrechterman at Tel Aviv early in the war, and two others, G-ACNX and G-ADGI were impressed into the R.A.F. as DG578 and AW150 respectively. The sole example extant today is 'RT, semi-derelict at Kidlington since 1946.

SPECIFICATION

Manufacturers: Phillips and Powis Ltd., Woodley Aerodrome, Reading, Berks.
Power Plants: (M.2) One 95 h.p. A.D.C. Cirrus IIIA.
        (M.2A) One 120 h.p. de Havilland Gipsy III.
        (M.2B) One 120 h.p. A.D.C. Cirrus Hermes IV.
        (M.2C) One 120 h.p. de Havilland Gipsy III.
        (M.2D) One 95 h.p. A.D.C. Cirrus IIIA.
Dimensions: Span, 33 ft. 0 in. (M.2D), 35 ft. 0 in. Length, 24 ft. 0 in. Height, 6 ft. 8 in. Wing area, 169 sq. ft.

	M.2	M.2A	M.2B	M.2D
Tare weight .	1,014 lb.	—	—	1,045 lb.
All-up weight .	1,800 lb.	1,800 lb.	2,200 lb.	1,800 lb.
Maximum speed .	115 m.p.h.	140 m.p.h.	160 m.p.h.	114 m.p.h.
Cruising speed .	100 m.p.h.	125 m.p.h.	140 m.p.h.	98 m.p.h.
Initial climb .	860 ft./min.	—	—	860 ft./min.
Ceiling .	16,000 ft.	—	—	18,000 ft.
Range . .	450 miles	1,000 miles	2,000 miles	450 miles

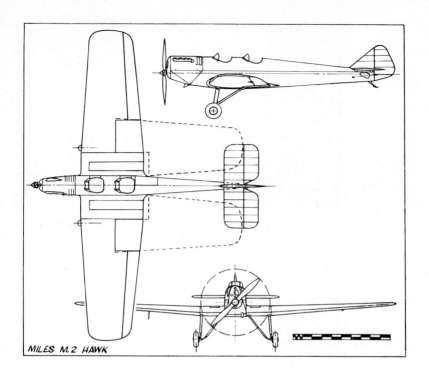

MILES M.2 HAWK

F. G. Miles flying the Hawk Major M.2P G-ADLO near Woodley, July 1935.
(*'Flight' Photo.*)

Miles Hawk Major and Speed Six

The popularity of the M.2 Hawk and the approaching end of limited supplies of Cirrus IIIA engines, compelled the design of a successor which appeared in time to be proved, in traditional style, over the 1934 King's Cup course. Like the M.2C Hawk, it was Gipsy III powered but with metal, instead of wooden engine mounting, and a cantilever, trousered undercarriage. The prototype, G-ACTD, designated the Miles M.2F Hawk Major, temporarily a single seater and flown by Tommy Rose, began the long line of pre-war Miles racing honours by finishing second at an average speed of 147·78 m.p.h. A special single seat variant powered by a 200 h.p. Gipsy Six was entered and flown by Sir Charles Rose, who forced landed at Northolt with ignition trouble. The extra weight of the engine replaced that of a passenger, so that standard characteristics were retained, but with a considerable increase in top speed. This model, only one of which was built, was known as the M.2E Gipsy Six Hawk.

Production Hawk Majors were fitted with Gipsy Major engines and sold in quantity, mainly to private owners. They found their way all over the world, the most famous of them all being ZK-ADJ, otherwise G-ACXU, flown by S/Ldr. M. MacGregor and H. Walker, in the 1934 MacRobertson Race from Mildenhall to Melbourne. This Hawk Major not only averaged 105 m.p.h. to finish 5th in the handicap section but also continued to New Zealand by sea to join the Manawatu Aero Club. Two others, G-ACWV and G-ADGA, were fitted with Savage smoke producing gear by the British Instrument Co. Ltd. at Hendon and became a familiar sight in British skies during their skywriting sorties.

The designation M.2G was given to G-ACYB, a three seat cabin version of the Hawk Major built for the Club George Chazez in Switzerland, where it became well known as HB-OAS. In November 1934 a trailing edge flap was added to the standard aircraft to create the M.2H. This model, with its steepened glide and slow landing, largely replaced the

M.2F on the Woodley production line. By the time the flag fell at the start of the King's Cup Race of September 7, 1935, 56 Hawk Majors had been delivered to British owners. Seven of these, including the cleaned-up M.2H machines G-ADGE, 'LA, 'LB and 'MW, were flown in the race by A.H. Cook, Mrs. Elise Battye, O. Cathcart Jones and A. C. W. Norman. Although the M.2F and M.2H were the versions built in quantity, their important contribution to amateur sporting flying was largely overshadowed by that of the variants. The Hawk Major de Luxe G-ADLN, flown into 2nd place at 157·49 m.p.h. by H. R. A. Edwards, was known as the M.2R, while the designation M.2T was applied to the two long-range, single seat, Cirrus Major powered entries. The first, G-ADNJ, piloted by Alex Henshaw, was ditched with engine trouble 6 miles off Malin Head during the race, and the wreck was later brought ashore at Ardrossan. F. D. Bradbrooke flying the other M.2T, G-ADNK, almost suffered a similar fate, but just reached the coast to forced land near Blackpool. The Gipsy Six Hawk G-ACTE, fitted with sliding hood, rechristened Hawk Speed Six and flown by its new owner W. Humble, was placed 13th at 177·79 m.p.h. The two other Hawk Speed Six aircraft unsuccessfully competing with it were the M.2L G-ADGP of Luis Fontes and the M.2U G-ADOD flown by his sister Miss Ruth Fontes. Both these machines had flaps, wide-track undercarriages and increased dihedral, but differed slightly in cockpit canopy detail and in the fact that a Gipsy Six R high-compression engine was fitted to 'OD. The three Speed Sixes met for the last time in the 1936 Race, in which Tommy Rose averaged 160·5 m.p.h. in 'OD to come 2nd. Later in the year (the then) F/Lt. A. E. Clouston flew it in the Schlesinger Race to Johannesburg. Leaving Portsmouth at 06.34 hours on September 29, 1936, he reached Khartoum at 01.45 hours the next day, but engine trouble and a series of forced landings ended the race and the career of 'OD in a crash at Gwelo, 130 miles S.W. of Salisbury, Southern Rhodesia. An equally spectacular write-off also occurred a few months earlier when, on June 8, the airscrew fractured and the engine fell out of Major R. H. Thornton's M.2H G-ADIG while flying from Budapest to Hamburg. Fortunately the ensuing spin was flat enough to do little damage to the occupants. Another standard M.2H, G-ADEN, purchased by Señor Jose Rabello, was flown to Portugal by the owner and the Reading instructor J. F. Lawn and later saw service in the Spanish Civil War.

J. E. D. Houlder's three seat Hawk Major M.2M at Heathrow in July 1935.

F/O A. E. Clouston running up the Hawk Speed Six M.2U prior to the Portsmouth–Johannesburg Race, September 1936. (*Photo courtesy of 'The Aeroplane'*.)

Hawk Major variants ran consecutively from M.2E to M.2U, with the exception of I, K and N, three more of the range which saw the light of day in British civil marks being J. E. D. Houlder's M.2M G-ADCV, which seated two passengers under a glazed canopy behind the pilot's open cockpit; secondly, the Cardiff Aeroplane Club's G-ADDK and the Airwork Flying School's G-ADLO, which were of the dual-control M.2P type with wider cockpits and 1 ft. greater span; and lastly, G-ADLH, the long-range Gipsy Major powered M.2S built in 1935 for J. H. Van of Broxbourne. Two years later this was bought for an Atlantic flight by an inexperienced Indian pilot G. P. Nair with monies subscribed by his compatriots in Britain. After permission to take off over the North Atlantic had been refused, he decided on a world tour, but was killed near Rouen on October 28, 1937, two hours after leaving Croydon, through stalling on the approach to a field.

A little known conversion without special designation was made by the installation of a Menasco Pirate C.4 engine in the M.2R G-ADLN, which in 1938–39 was operated by the Reading Aero Club along with M.2Hs G-AEGP and 'NS. These were impressed in 1941 as DG664, DG851 and DG848 respectively, a fate which overtook the North Staffs Aero Club G-ACXT (DG577), the Cotswold Aero Club G-ADIT (X5125), the Portsmouth Aero Club G-ADMW (DG590) and the Cardiff Aeroplane Club's G-ADDK (BD180). The total of 10 impressed Hawk Majors was completed by O. F. H. Atkey's de luxe G-AEGE (HL538), F. W. Griffith's G-ACWY (NF748) and Dr. Miles Bickerton's G-ACYO (NF752). Only four survived the war: G-ACYO, restored to the Reading Aero Club in 1947 and winner of the 1954 Air League Challenge Cup at 138 m.p.h., piloted by Miss Freydis Leaf; G-ACYX, serviced at Heston and flown at Broxbourne before sale to France as F-BCEX in 1946; the three seat G-ADCV, denuded of its canopy, flown from Poona to Hamble between November 17 and December 14, 1947, by Lt.-Col. G. H. Wotton, but destroyed at Croydon when a wall collapsed on February 4, 1950; and G-ADMW, currently flown by J. P. Gunner at Eastleigh. The remains of four others were also rediscovered; the prototype 'TD, involved in a fatal crash at Doncaster Airport on August 31, 1936, was used as a target for

R. R. Paine's post-war modifications to the Hawk Speed Six M.2L include a large bubble canopy.

Lincoln bombers at York in 1951; G-ADAB and 'BT were derelict at Walsall and Blackbushe respectively, and G-AEGE is still used as an instructional airframe by the College of Aeronautical Engineering at Redhill.

A major contribution to post-war sporting flying has been made by R. R. Paine's Hawk Speed Six, G-ADGP, modified almost to M.2U standard, fitted with a Gipsy Six 1F and an enormous bubble hood. Each year since 1949 the veteran has fought its private duel with the surviving Mew Gull in the National and other air races, and has a habit of making fastest time, and today holds the 100 km. closed-circuit record in Class C.16 at 192·83 m.p.h.

SPECIFICATION

Manufacturers: Phillips and Powis Aircraft Ltd., Woodley Aerodrome, Reading, Berks.

Power Plant:
(M.2E)	One 200 h.p. de Havilland Gipsy Six.
(M.2F, H, M, P, R)	One 130 h.p. de Havilland Gipsy Major.
(M.2L)	One 200 h.p. de Havilland Gipsy Six 1F.
(M.2S)	One 150 h.p. Blackburn Cirrus Major.
(M.2U)	One 200 h.p. de Havilland Gipsy Six R.

	M.2E, L, U	M.2F, H, M	M.2P, R
Span . . .	33 ft. 0 in.	33 ft. 0 in.	34 ft. 0 in.
Length . . .	24 ft. 0 in.	24 ft. 0 in.	24 ft. 0 in.
Height . . .	6 ft. 8 in.	6 ft. 8 in.	6 ft. 8 in.
Wing area . .	169 sq. ft.	169 sq. ft.	174 sq. ft.
Tare weight . .	1,355 lb.	1,150 lb.	—
All-up weight .	1,900 lb.	1,800 lb.	1,900 lb.
Maximum speed .	185 m.p.h.	150 m.p.h.	150 m.p.h.
Cruising speed .	160 m.p.h.	135 m.p.h.	135 m.p.h.
Initial climb . .	1,450 ft./min.	1,000 ft./min.	—
Ceiling . . .	—	20,000 ft.	—
Range . . .	—	560 miles	—

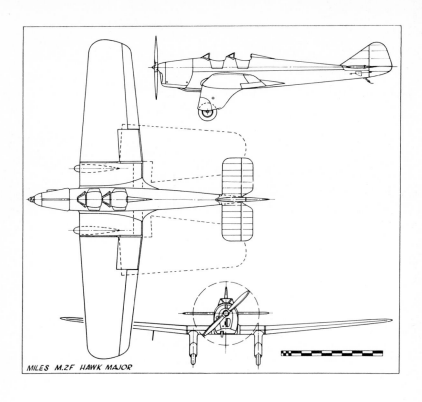

MILES M.2F HAWK MAJOR

Miles M.3A Falcon Major G-ADER of Maddox Airways Ltd. flying near Brooklands, April 1935, showing the production type cabin roof. (*'Flight' Photo.*)

Miles M.3 Falcon

Structurally similar to, and retaining the handling qualities of the Hawk Major, the Falcon was built on more generous lines to accommodate two passengers side by side behind the pilot in a glazed cabin. The split trailing-edge flaps were retained and the dihedral increased from $3\frac{1}{2}$ to 5 degrees to improve stability and lessen pilot fatigue on long flights. The prototype U-3/G-ACTM, designated the M.3, was completed in time for H. L. Brook to fly it, with a passenger, in the MacRobertson Race of October 1934. The engine was the veteran Gipsy Major salvaged from Mr. Brook's ex Mollison Puss Moth 'Heart's Content' (see Volume 1, page 321). Ill luck delayed the Falcon, however, and nearly 27 days were taken to reach Darwin. Flying solo and with extra tanks to give a 2,000 mile range, Brook left Darwin again on March 23, 1935, and reached Lympne in the record time of 7 days 19 hours 15 minutes. During one magnificent stage, the 1,700 miles from Jodhpur to Basra was covered non-stop.

The fuselage of the first production aircraft G-ADBF, first flown at Woodley in January 1935, was not only wider to give comfortable seating for four persons but had a modified cabin top and the now familiar forward-sloping windscreen, estimated to add 4 m.p.h. to the top speed. Designated the M.3A, 'BF went in the following June to Tripoli, temporarily becoming I-ZENA to win the Raduno Sahariano piloted by Signor Parodi. Returning to Woodley in the following year, it was sold in Switzerland but after only a brief stay, went north to Macmerry, where, in 1939, the owner was N. A. Blandford. Nine other M.3A Falcons were delivered to British order during 1935, including G-ADER to Maddox Airways Ltd., Brooklands; G-ADHH to D. W. Gumbley of Heston and last heard of in Lydda in 1940; G-ADFH to E. D. Spratt of Air Service Training Ltd., Hamble, and G-ADIU to the Leicestershire Aero Club, Ratcliffe. G-ADHC was supplied via Galbraith Pembroke and Co. Ltd. to Italy as a second I-ZENA when 'BF returned home.

Like its predecessor, the Falcon was stressed to take engines of higher power, and a Gipsy Six engined M.3B Falcon Six G-ADLC was built in time for the King's Cup Race of September 7, 1935. With Tommy Rose at the controls, the Falcon Six won handsomely at 176·28 m.p.h. and with Hawk Majors 2nd and 3rd, brought the Miles team utter victory. Also competing was the M.3C Falcon Six G-ADLS flown by S. Harris and L. Lipton, who averaged 166·88 m.p.h. to come 5th. Whereas the M.3B was a three seater with the pilot placed centrally, the M.3C held four, with full dual control in the front two seats. It was the only British example, and a year later went to Abbotsinch to remain in the possession of A. D. Farquhar until the war claimed it. At dawn on February 6, 1936, Tommy Rose left Lympne in the King's Cup winner 'LC and succeeded in reducing the Cape record to 3 days 17 hours 37 minutes, leaving again on March 3, to reach Croydon in 6 days 7 hours.

The prototype M.3 Falcon showing the original cabin glazing. (*'Flight' Photo.*)

The last four British registered specimens of the M.3A, retrospectively named the Falcon Major, were delivered in 1936. All were used by Phillips and Powis Ltd. at Woodley for club and taxi work, including G-AEFB flown in the 1936 King's Cup Race by F/Lt. A. E. Clouston. Another, G-AENG, flew in the 1937 race, but Wing Cdrs. E. G. Hilton and P. Sherren lost their lives when the former was thrown out by violent turbulence at the Scarborough Castle turn. Before Falcon production ceased in 1936, eight more Gipsy Six models were built to British order, including G-AEKK based at Castle Bromwich by the Dunlop Rubber Co. Ltd.; G-ADTD and 'ZL, communications aircraft of Vickers and Faireys respectively and E. G. H. Forsyth's G-AEDL. Two others, G-AFAY and 'BF, acquired by Airwork Ltd. from the Austrian and German owners Leopold Block-Baver and Karl Roechling in part exchange for newer aircraft, were operated respectively by Brian Allen Aviation Ltd., Croydon and Birkett Air Services Ltd., Heston. Piloted by C. G. M. Alington and carrying two passengers, 'AY flew to Kenya and back early in 1939.

Henri Deterding's G-AEAG and A. N. T. Rankin's G-AECC embodied a number of detail strengthenings permitting an increase in all-up weight to 2,650 lb. with a change in designation to M.3D. Another version, the

M.3E G-AFCP, also appeared, together with Gipsy Six engined R4071, delivered to the R.A.E. in 1937 for experimental use and eventually civilianised for export to Belgium as G-AGZX by Southern Aircraft (Gatwick) Ltd. in 1946.

Falcon Major G-ADLI and Falcon Sixes G-ADTD and G-AFAY contrived to remain civil communications aircraft throughout the war, but eight others were impressed by the Air Ministry. Only six survived in 1946, one of which, G-AFAY, beyond restoration, was scrapped at Heston. Those that flew again included two Falcon Majors; G-ADFH based at White Waltham and raced for a few seasons until scrapped at Croydon in 1956; and G-ADLI kept at Panshanger by J. W. Haggas until wrecked when taking off from Elstree in 1952. The other three, Gipsy Six powered, comprised M.3B G-AFBF restored to Southampton Air Services in 1946 but sold in the following year to Cunliffe Owen Aircraft Ltd.; G-ADTD, modified to M.3D standard and winner of the 1956 S.B.A.C. Challenge Trophy at 169 m.p.h. piloted by Geoffrey Marler; and finally, G-AECC, raced for nearly a decade by James Rush of Woolsington and winner of the 1950 Norton Griffiths Trophy at 165·5 m.p.h. In 1957 Crop Culture (Aerial) Ltd. acquired it for communication work, in the course of which it was lost at sea between Bembridge and Exeter on May 8, 1959.

SPECIFICATION

Manufacturers: Phillips and Powis Ltd., Woodley Aerodrome, Reading, Berks.
Power Plants: (M.3 and 3A)   One 120 h.p. de Havilland Gipsy Major.
                     (M.3B, 3C and 3D) One 200 h.p. de Havilland Gipsy Six.
Dimensions: Span, 35 ft. 0 in. Length, 25 ft. 0 in. Height, 6 ft. 6 in. Wing area, 174·3 sq. ft.

	M.3	M.3A	M.3B
Tare weight .	1,270 lb.	1,300 lb.	1,550 lb.
All-up weight .	2,000 lb.	2,200 lb.	2,350 lb.
Maximum speed .	148 m.p.h.	145 m.p.h.	180 m.p.h.
Cruising speed .	130 m.p.h.	125 m.p.h.	160 m.p.h.
Initial climb . .	—	750 ft./min.	1,000 ft./min.
Ceiling . . .	—	15,000 ft.	—
Range . . .	—	615 miles	560 miles

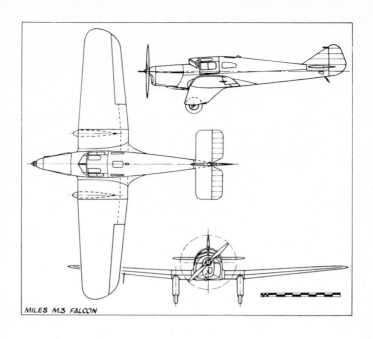

MILES M.3 FALCON

The prototype Miles M.5 Sparrowhawk flying near Woodley in 1935. (*Photo courtesy of 'The Aeroplane'.*)

Miles M.5 Sparrowhawk

The prototype Sparrowhawk G-ADNL was built from standard Hawk components as a mount for F. G. Miles in the King's Cup Race of September 7, 1935, and was, of course, a single seater. A standard fuselage was shortened by 12 in. and the top decking lowered as much as possible, the pilot sitting practically on the floor with his legs over the front spar. The centre section was cut to fuselage width and the wings were attached directly to it, reducing the span by 5 ft. The undercarriage track was widened, and a special Gipsy Major high compression engine was fed from a long range tank. By covering the 953 mile course round Britain at an average speed of 163·64 m.p.h. the Sparrowhawk won the speed prize but came 11th in the final. A constant but unspectacular performer, it came 9th at 165·74 m.p.h. piloted by P. H. Maxwell in 1936 and 7th at 172·5 m.p.h. in the hands of Wing Cdr. F. W. Stent in 1937. Four other Sparrowhawks built in 1936 with specially designed (as opposed to modified Hawk Major) fuselages were designated M.5A. The first, G-ADWW, was J. H. G. McArthur's mount for the King's Cup, and the second, G-AELT, Victor Smith's in the Schlesinger Race to Johannesburg which started at Portsmouth on September 29, 1936. These promising entries shared a common fate, McArthur's was disqualified and Smith's retired at Cairo with oil trouble. Both were then sold abroad, 'WW in the U.S.A., where it still survives in airworthy condition, and 'LT in South Africa. The next Sparrowhawk, G-AFGA, built to the order of L. E. R. Bellairs, was not certificated until raced for the 1938 King's Cup by W. Humble, but was no more successful than the others, coming 7th at 169·4 m.p.h.

The final Sparrowhawk had a more useful, if less spectacular career. Although built in June 1936, it was stored at Woodley until a wartime requirement by Miles Aircraft Ltd. for an experimental aircraft resulted in its assembly and first flight in February 1940. It is believed to have been used under B conditions as U-0223, for high lift flap research. In December of the following year the aircraft reverted to standard and became a camouflaged civil aeroplane G-AGDL for communication duties between the firm's Woodley and South Marston factories. At first fitted with a standard Gipsy Major 1, it later acquired a high compression Gipsy Major 2 (not to be confused with the Gipsy Major series 2, which was intended for variable pitch airscrews). On June 1, 1946, in new cream and red dope, it gave an aerobatic display, piloted by K. H. F. Waller, at the Woodley Garden Party of the Royal Aeronautical Society, and two years later was destroyed in a take off crash at Tollerton while in service with the Nottingham Flying Club.

In 1938 the prototype Sparrowhawk 'NL had passed into the possession of Miss Joan Parsons, and after the war reappeared at Elmdon as the personal aircraft of test pilot C. G. M. Alington. During the early post-war years it was frequently a competitor in major air races and, like its predecessors, constantly averaged 165–170 m.p.h. and although winner of the 1950 race round the Isle of Wight, did not achieve real success.

In December 1950 the aircraft returned to F. G. Miles at Redhill to be remodelled as a jet-powered racing mount for Mr. Fred Dunkerley. An entirely new front fuselage and tail unit were built, and after the firm's move to Shoreham in 1952 modifications were carried out on the wing to house a Turboméca Palas gas turbine in each root end. The aircraft was redesignated the Miles M.77 Sparrowjet and made its first flight at Shoreham piloted by G. H. Miles on December 14, 1953. Although initially dogged by ill luck, the aircraft won the S.B.A.C. Challenge Cup at Yeadon on May 21, 1956, at an average speed of 197·5 m.p.h. Ambition was finally satisfied at Baginton on July 13, 1957, when, after 20 years and a major reconstruction, G-ADNL was brought to victory in the King's Cup Race by Fred Dunkerley at the incredible average speed of 228 m.p.h.

Fred Dunkerley taking off in the Sparrowjet at Shoreham.
(*'Flight' Photo.*)

Manufacturers: Phillips and Powis Aircraft Ltd., Woodley Aerodrome, Reading, Berks.

Power Plants: (Sparrowhawk)   One 147 h.p. de Havilland Gipsy Major h.c.
                                 One 130 h.p. de Havilland Gipsy Major 1.
                                 One 145 h.p. de Havilland Gipsy Major 2.
        (Sparrowjet)   Two 330 lb. s.t. Turboméca Palas.

	Sparrowhawk	Sparrowjet
Span	28 ft. 0 in.	28 ft. 6 in.
Length . . .	23 ft. 6 in.	30 ft. 9½ in.
Height . . .	5 ft. 7 in.	7 ft. 2 in.
Wing area . . .	138 sq. ft.	156 sq. ft.
Tare weight . . .	1,080 lb.	1,578 lb.
All-up weight . .	1,750 lb.	2,400 lb.
Maximum speed . .	180 m.p.h.*	220 m.p.h.
Cruising speed . .	155 m.p.h.*	—
Initial climb . . .	—	2,100 ft./min.
Range	415 miles	270·5 miles

* With Gipsy Major high compression engine.

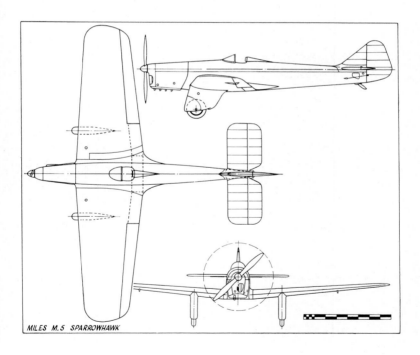

MILES M.5 SPARROWHAWK

153

Miles M.11A Whitney Straight G-AERV was flown pre-war and post-war by the late H. W. H. Moore. (*'Flight' Photo.*)

Miles M.11A Whitney Straight

In 1935 Whitney Straight, then operating a chain of flying clubs in Southern England, laid his conception of a general-purpose light aeroplane before F. G. Miles. The result, first flown in the spring of 1936, afterwards made public debuts at the Heathrow Garden Party of the Royal Aeronautical Society on May 10 and the Hatfield S.B.A.C. Show on June 28. It was a spruce and plywood, low-wing, cantilever monoplane seating two occupants side by side in cabin comfort and provided with generous luggage space in the rear. Designated the Miles M.11 and inevitably bearing the type name Whitney Straight, the prototype G-AECT was reminiscent of a scaled down Falcon, power being supplied by a Gipsy Major. By virtue of its two position, vacuum operated, trailing edge flaps, it could be pulled steeply off the ground at 50 m.p.h. and was fitted with a very robust undercarriage so that if desired it could be landed heavily at low speeds.

Early in the following year production Whitney Straights were already emerging at Woodley but were designated M.11A due to their revised undercarriage detail and one-piece, seamless windscreen in place of the built-up unit of the prototype. The green and silver first production aircraft G-AENH was publicly demonstrated by F. G. Miles with two others at Heston on January 22, 1937. These were Airwork Ltd.'s demonstrator G-AERS and the sole example of the M.11B variant G-AERC. The latter had been acquired by Amherst and Mrs. Maya Villiers as the Heston based test bed for their Villiers Maya I engine. A year earlier this four cylinder inverted unit had flown in the B.A. Eagle G-ADJS, but an increase in compression ratio had now raised the output to 135 h.p.

Before the Second World War halted private flying, 31 additional Whitney Straights, representing the major portion of total production, had been sold on the home market. Immaculately kept by keen private owners

The Miles M.11 G-AECT showing the prototype undercarriage and windscreen.
(*'Flight' Photo.*)

and aircraft firms, they were remarkable for docility rather than spectacular achievement, and included M. H. W. Moore's G-AERV; Hawker's 'UJ; the Rolls-Royce 'UZ; the Earl of Ronaldshay's 'WA; J. A. H. Parke's 'VM, kept at a private field at Hambledon near Godalming; and G-AFCC flown for many years at Magellanes, Chile, by T. Saunders. Capt. A. V. Harvey flew 'VH into 4th place in the 1937 King's Cup Race, but the 63-year-old Brig. Gen. A. C. Lewin did better, coming 2nd in 'ZO at an average speed of 144·5 m.p.h. Less than a month later, on October 9, 1937, 'ZO ran out of fuel while heading south over the Sudan en route to Kenya and was wrecked in a forced landing in the Nile swamp, south of Malakal. The combined efforts of the Imperial Airways flying-boat 'Cassiopeia', No. 47 Squadron R.A.F. and the natives, were necessary to extricate the Brigadier and his wife. G-AERS, on the other hand, had a distinguished overseas career with Army officer R. King Clarke, who flew it back and forth to Ismailia, Egypt, in 1937–38 and later based it at Semakh, Palestine, before flying it to Singapore and back.

Instructional usage was confined to 'RC, fitted with a Gipsy Major in May 1938 for the Ipswich Aero Club; 'VH, sold to the Reading Aero Club in the same month; 'XJ, with Air Service Training Ltd. at Hamble, and G-AFBV, which was shared by the Ipswich and Thanet Aero Clubs until it collided fatally with a windsock.

A fourth and final variant, the M.11C G-AEYI, also appeared, fitted with a Gipsy Major series II driving a variable-pitch airscrew. First flown in May 1937, its take off and climb were quite remarkable, but the aircraft crashed at Harefield, Berks, on June 28, 1938, killing Phillips and Powis test pilot Wing Cdr. F. W. Stent.

Believed to be the last Whitney Straight built, G-AFGK was sold in April 1938 to Miss Rosemary Rees (later of A.T.A.). It served as a civil communications aircraft with Airwork Ltd. throughout the war, and is flown today by the Aldenham Private Flying Group at Elstree. Only the Hawker and Rolls-Royce 'hacks' also enjoyed civil lives during war-time. Even the Phillips and Powis machine U-0227, otherwise G-AFZY, was taken over by the R.A.F., along with 20 others. Nine of these reappeared in 1946; 'RV returned to its pre-war owner, 'UX was flown to Kenya by Wing Cdr. H. M. Probyn, 'VG went to Air Service Training Ltd. to carry on where 'XJ left off and two others were shipped to New Zealand. One aircraft, DR617, fittingly acquired by the Straight Corporation at Weston-super-Mare as G-AITM in 1946, remained unconverted. Loss of pre-war identity and documentation sent it to the scrap heap in 1948. Thus in addition to 'GK, only three remain, 'RV kept at Kidlington by Messrs. Hainge and Nixey, 'UJ now flown at Elstree by C. L. J. Reed and 'WA owned by S. J. Burt at Fairoaks.

SPECIFICATION

Manufacturers: Phillips and Powis Aircraft Ltd., Woodley Aerodrome, Berks.
Power Plants: (M.11 and M.11A) One 130 h.p. Gipsy Major I.
         (M.11B)   One 135 h.p. Villiers Maya I.
         (M.11C)   One 145 h.p. de Havilland Gipsy Major II.
Dimensions: Span, 35 ft. 8 in. Length, 25 ft. 0 in. Height, 6 ft. 6 in. Wing area, 178 sq. ft.
Weights: (M.11A) Tare weight, 1,250 lb. All-up weight, 2,000 lb.
Performance: (M.11A) Maximum speed, 145 m.p.h. Cruising speed, 130 m.p.h. Initial climb, 850 ft./min. Ceiling, 18,500 ft. Range, 570 miles.
        (M.11B) Maximum speed, 155 m.p.h. Cruising speed, 136 m.p.h. Initial climb, 1,050 ft./min.

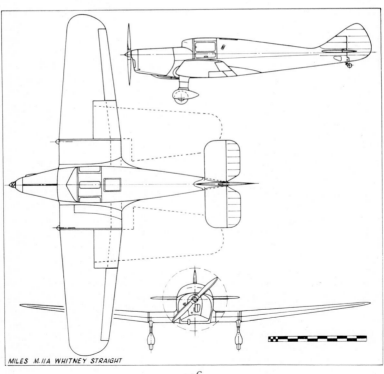

MILES M.11A WHITNEY STRAIGHT

G-AEEL, the last Miles M.2X Hawk Trainer delivered to No. 8 E.R.F.T.S. (*Photo: Phillips and Powis Aircraft Ltd.*)

Miles Hawk Trainers

An improved version of the Hawk Major was built in 1935 to supplement the Tiger Moths then in use at Woodley with No. 8 Elementary and Reserve Flying Training School. They were fitted with dual control, full blind flying equipment, vacuum operated flaps and Gipsy Major engines and were known as Hawk Trainers under the designation M.2W. Only four, G-ADVF and 'WT–'WV, were delivered, nine others built in 1936 having horn-balanced rudders of greater area which amended the type to M.2X. Two others, G-ADZD and G-AEAY, outwardly identical, were registered as M.2Y. Two of the batch, G-ADZC and G-AEAX, were released to the Reading Aero Club in May 1939 and G-ADWT later became the mount of test pilot C. G. M. Alington at Castle Bromwich. With the exception of 'WT and three which met with accidents, all continued in use until impressed en bloc in March 1941. Ten Hawk Trainers were allotted temporary British civil status as G-AEHP to 'HZ for delivery by air to the Rumanian Air Force during 1936, and in the following year the ultimate development of the Hawk Major appeared as the Miles M.14, produced to Air Ministry specification. At a time when the expansion of the R.A.F. into its monoplane era was in full swing, the Miles M.14 was named the Magister and ordered in quantity to teach the new monoplane techniques. Structurally identical to its predecessors, the M.14 had slightly less span, a wide track, spatted undercarriage, anti-spinning strakes and the type of rudder then being fitted to the Monarch. A few were built for civil purposes, with the type name Hawk Trainer Mk. III, the first two flying on test under British marks before despatch to New Zealand in February 1937. The next, G-AEZP, registered as the M.14B Hawk Trainer Mk. II, went to Brough as a test bed for the Blackburn Cirrus Major 2 engine. It was flown by E. C. T. Edwards in the 1937 King's Cup Race but retired at Macmerry. In the following year J. M. Barwick started first in his red Hawk Trainer Mk. III G-AEZR, but finished last at an average speed of 130·5 m.p.h. Three others, G-AEZS, G-AFBS and

'DB, joined the Woodley E.R.F.T.S., and four more, G-AFET–'EW, were allotted to the Straight Corporation's flying clubs at Ipswich, Ramsgate, Exeter and Plymouth respectively. This, the only bona fide civil order, received low priority due to the intensity of military production (1,203 Magisters were built). Consequently the aircraft were delivered by air in primary dope with chalked registrations. During 1938, taller rudders of greater area were fitted to assist recovery from the spin, and the Hawk Trainer Mk. III thereafter assumed the designation M.14A. Except for the Thanet Aero Club's G-AFEU, lost at sea off Cliftonville with two crew in July 1938, all the M.14s were eventually fitted with the new rudder. Pre-war civil deliveries ended with the addition of M.14Bs G-AFTR, 'TS and M.14As G-AFWY, 'XA and 'XB to the Woodley school in 1939, four later aircraft being engulfed by R.A.F. demands. Impressment was inevitable, although, for a time, many flew as civil aircraft in full R.A.F. training camouflage.

One only of the original Hawk Trainers, G-ADWT, survived the war but with an M.2X type rudder. Flown by the Reading Aero Club in 1947, it is owned today by L. D. Blyth of Panshanger. When the Magisters were

One of the original Miles M.14 Hawk Trainer Mk. III aircraft showing the increase in depth of the rear fuselage and change of rudder shape. (*Photo courtesy of C. A. Nepean Bishop.*)

The Miles M.14A Hawk Trainer Mk. III in its final form with enlarged rudder.

Hawk Trainer Coupé G-AKRW at Rochester in 1951. Entry was via a hinged roof.

declared obsolete and came up for civilian disposal, two more pre-war aircraft appeared, G-AFBS to fly with the Airways Aero Association and the Denham Flying Club for a further 12 years and 'XA, overhauled at Croydon but scrapped in 1956. The first Magister of purely military origin civilianised as a Hawk Trainer Mk. III was P6380, certificated on November 19, 1945, as G-AGVW. Following an inauspicious start when 'VW collided with an Auster and fell into the sea off Copenhagen on April 21, 1946, the Hawk Trainer Mk. III settled down to a distinguished post-war career as a club and sporting aircraft. The chief exponents were the Darlington and District, Wiltshire, Rochester, Redhill, Weston, Loch Leven, Scottish, Derby, Elstree, Denham, Fairey and Airways flying clubs and schools.

One of a batch of Magisters acquired by the Herts and Essex Aero Club (1946) Ltd. for civil conversion in 1947, proved to be the Cirrus Major 3 engined prototype L6913. Although fully overhauled and in the club's smart silver and green colours as G-AKNA, it failed to obtain a C. of A. because no such variant had existed pre-war. No designation existed to cover it, and in 1956, it was reduced to spares at Speke. The export market and the ravages of old age inevitably thinned the ranks, and whereas for over a decade every flying function was ensured of a strong contingent of Hawk Trainer Mk. 3s (the 3 was now Arabic), today only 26 remain.

For racing purposes several interesting local modifications, including the fairing in of front or rear seats, took place. The 1950 King's Cup Race, in which eight Hawk Trainer Mk. 3s competed, was won at Wolverhampton by E. Day in a cabin version G-AKRV 'Judith Anne' at 138·5 m.p.h. This modification, later carried out on the Rochester Flying Club's G-AKRW and the Redhill Club's G-AJRT, originated during the war when 'RV, then a Magister T9876, was converted at an R.A.F. station for officer transport. G-AIDF, flown by W. J. Twitchell in the Hurn to Herne Bay Race of September 20, 1950, had both cockpits covered, the pilot's head projecting into a Perspex D.F. loop fairing screwed to the rear cover. His mean speed was 147 m.p.h. One example, G-ALGK, was modified for ground radar co-operation by Short Bros. and Harland Ltd. at Rochester and commissioned in March 1949. The pilot sat in the front seat under a sliding hood, while the completely covered rear cockpit housed

Ekco CE217/12 V.H.F. radio. Its East Anglian patrols came to an end in the water off Burnham-on-Crouch on January 21, 1951.

SPECIFICATION

Manufacturers: Phillips and Powis Aircraft Ltd., Woodley Aerodrome, Reading, Berks.

Power Plants: (M.2W, X and Y) One 130 h.p. de Havilland Gipsy Major.
(M.14) One 130 h.p. de Havilland Gipsy Major I.
(M.14A) One 130 h.p. de Havilland Gipsy Major I.
One 155 h.p. Blackburn Cirrus Major 3.
(M.14B) One 135 h.p. Blackburn Cirrus Major 2.

	M.2W, X, Y	M.14, M.14A
Span	34 ft. 0 in.	33 ft. 10 in.
Length . . .	24 ft. 0 in.	24 ft. 7½ in.
Height . . .	6 ft. 8 in.	6 ft. 8 in.
Wing area . . .	176 sq. ft.	172 sq. ft.
Tare weight . . .	1,210 lb.	1,286 lb.
All-up weight . .	1,720 lb.	1,900 lb.
Maximum speed .	150 m.p.h.	132 m.p.h.
Cruising speed . .	135 m.p.h.	123 m.p.h.
Initial climb . . .	1,300 ft./min.	850 ft./min.
Ceiling . . .	18,000 ft.	18,000 ft.
Range	400 miles	380 miles

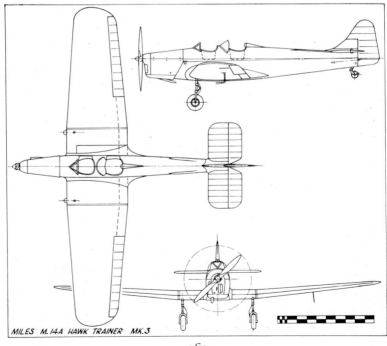

MILES M.14A HAWK TRAINER MK.3

The prototype Monarch flying near Woodley in 1937 piloted by the late H. W. C. Skinner. (*Photo: Miles Aircraft Ltd.*)

Miles M.17 Monarch

Phillips and Powis productive effort in 1937 was almost entirely centred on the Magister contract, and little thought could be spared for the civil market. Only one more private owner type was therefore built at Woodley before the war, an enlarged three seat version of the Whitney Straight known as the Monarch. It was the first Miles aeroplane for which the designer's younger brother G. H. Miles was entirely responsible, and the prototype G-AFCR flew for the first time on February 21, 1938, piloted by H. W. C. Skinner. The fuselage was deeper and roomier than that of its predecessor, the third occupant sitting centrally in part of the luggage space. He was also provided with a window in the starboard but not the port side. Standard Magister outer wing panels were used and a novel interconnected throttle and flap lever provided an appreciable measure of automatic glide control.

Eleven aircraft, including the prototype, were constructed during 1938–39, six to British order. G-AFGL and 'TX were based at Heston by Airwork Ltd. and W. H. Whitbread respectively before being sold abroad in 1939; 'JU was acquired by Sir V. A. G. Warrender; 'JZ went to Blackpool with E. O. Liebert; 'LW to Rolls-Royce Ltd., Hucknall and 'RZ to Lord Malcolm Douglas Hamilton. The fate of this select company paralleled that of the Whitney Straights. The Rolls-Royce machine remained in camouflaged civilian use throughout the war, and the remainder were impressed in February 1940.

In August 1938 a Belgian private pilot M. Camille Gutt had traded his Whitney Straight OO-UMK to Airwork Ltd. in part exchange for a Monarch. The older machine became G-AFJJ, while the new assumed its predecessor's markings. When the Low Countries were overrun in May 1940 the Monarch escaped and returned to Woodley where it was promptly put to good use by Phillips and Powis Aircraft Ltd., first under

B registry as U-0226 and later as G-AGFW. Although returned to M. Gutt's possession in 1944, he was not permitted to fly it in civilian markings, so it went to Hendon to join the Belgian section of the Metropolitan Communications Squadron, eventually returning to Brussels at the end of the year.

E. O. Liebert's G-AFJZ, which had been sold to G. E. Wallace in July 1939, was the only Monarch which failed to return from war service. The others all reappeared in 1946 when the prototype was overhauled for Air Schools Ltd., Burnaston, and 'JU for Lt.-Cdr. H. R. A. Kidston. Rolls-Royce Ltd. were still using the faithful 'LW, but when 'RZ came up for civilian disposal its pre-war identity was overlooked so that it became G-AIDE instead. After overhaul at Christchurch it was flown by B. G. Heron for several years, but at some time in its career the aircraft had acquired a window in the port as well as the starboard side and was the only Monarch so fitted. The well-known sporting pilot W. P. Bowles bought it in 1956 and was successful in winning the Goodyear Trophy at Baginton in July 13, 1957, at an average speed of 131·5 m.p.h. later coming 3rd in the King's Cup Race. In 1958 he again tuned the Monarch successfully, winning the Norton Griffiths Trophy at Baginton on July 12 at 136·16 m.p.h., afterwards coming 2nd in the Osram Cup Race.

With the exception of the prototype, lost in a forced landing in gathering darkness near Venice while touring in its 20th year, all the Monarchs are still airworthy, their careers long and often undistinguished. G-AFJU, veteran of eight post-war owners, has seen industrial service with the Furzehill Laboratories Ltd., Elstree, and S. Smith and Sons (England) Ltd. at Staverton. It also sampled 'circuits and bumps' with the Cotswold Aero Club in 1955. The Rolls-Royce 'hack' 'LW finally left their employ in 1958 and is now in use by the Blackpool and Fylde Aero Club Ltd. at Squires Gate.

SPECIFICATION

Manufacturers: Phillips and Powis Aircraft Ltd., Woodley Aerodrome, Reading, Berks.
Power Plant: One 130 h.p. de Havilland Gipsy Major I.
Dimensions: Span, 35 ft. 7 in. Length, 25 ft. 11¾ in. Height, 8 ft. 9¼ in. Wing area, 180 sq. ft.
Weights: Tare weight, 1,390 lb. All-up weight, 2,200 lb.
Performance: Maximum speed, 145 m.p.h. Cruising speed, 130 m.p.h. Initial climb, 850 ft./min. Ceiling, 17,400 ft. Range, 600 miles.

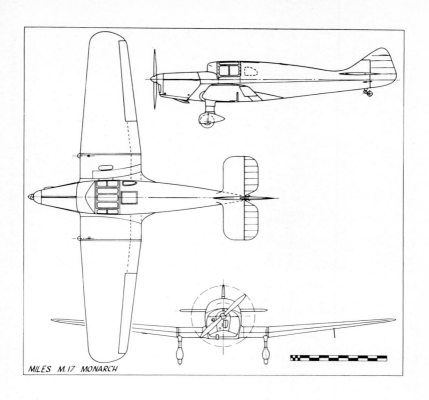

MILES M.17 MONARCH

A standard Miles M.38 Messenger 2A showing the characteristic rear window, auxiliary flap and triple rudders. (*Charles E Brown photograph.*)

Miles M.38 Messenger

Built during the Second World War for light liaison duties, the four seat Messenger handsomely fulfilled an Army specification for a robust aircraft with exceptional slow speed characteristics needing only casual maintenance from unskilled labour. The prototype U-0223, converted from the prototype Miles M.28 Mercury, first flew at Woodley on September 12, 1942. The fuselage, built up from longerons, stringers and U frames, was covered with a plastic-bonded plywood skin, through which passed the twin box spars of the one-piece, plywood covered mainplane. Miles non-retractable auxiliary aerofoil flaps were fitted behind and below the trailing edge, three fins and rudders were fitted to ensure maximum control right down to the stall, and an elementary form of single strut undercarriage was devised to withstand deliberate heavy landings.

Messenger I aircraft with Gipsy Major 1D engines were built in small numbers for the R.A.F., but their potentialities as private aircraft were obvious. After the war production continued to civil standards, and in 1946 an ex Messenger I, G-AHFP, was the first Miles demonstrator, later becoming a joyriding and taxi aircraft with Airwork Ltd. at Gatwick and Croydon. The civil Messenger 2A, identified by the oval instead of square rear window, was powered by a Cirrus Major 3, the test bed for which, a three seat Messenger 2B G-AGPX, was supplied to Blackburn Aircraft Ltd. in June 1945. One three seat Messenger 2C, G-AGUW, with Gipsy Major 1D and oval rear window, was built for export to South Africa and left Woodley on March 8, 1946, piloted by Alex Henshaw.

Late in the war a second prototype Messenger, known as the M.48, had been built with fully retractable flaps and flown under B conditions as

U-0247. This aircraft was registered to Miles Aircraft Ltd. in June 1945 as G-AGOY with the revised designation M.38 Messenger 3. On its return, in 1948, from two years with Aerotaxi A.G. in Zürich, it became well known in private flying circles and still survives in Eire. Production 2As were built at Newtownards, finished aircraft being flown unpainted to Woodley for final doping and sale. When construction ceased in January 1948, 58 had been sold on the British market, the first of which, G-AHZS, was acquired by Air Kruise (Kent) Ltd. A later series of variants also appeared. A Messenger 4 with Gipsy Major 10, built for the Regent of Iraq, left for Baghdad on May 5, 1946, with the British marks G-AHGE. After its loss in an accident, a successor, Messenger 2B G-AHXR, served in Iraq as YI-HRH, returning in 1948 to become British owned. A second Messenger 4, G-AIRY, built to special order later in 1946, was used for several years by the British Aviation Insurance Co. Ltd. and G-AILI, personal aircraft of G. H. Miles, was temporarily fitted and flown in July 1947 with a Praga E flat six engine. Best known of all

The Miles M.48/M.38 Messenger 3 was fitted with retractable flaps, and unlike other marks, had dual control.

Messenger 2A G-AILI with Praga E engine in 1947.

The Bombardier engined Messenger 5 at Shoreham, a few hours before it was written off.

Messengers, however, was Mk. 4 G-AKKG, originally built to Swiss order, which from 1948 to 1957 was flown on Shell business by Mr. Vivian Varcoe and hardly ever missed an aviation meeting.

When the R.A.F. Messenger I with Gipsy Major 1D engine was declared redundant in 1948, almost the entire military production batch was offered for civilian disposal in relatively new condition. Carrying the new designation Messenger 4A, 18 became private, racing and executive aircraft of distinction, as shown in Appendix D. Messenger I RH420, handed over to Blackburn and General Aircraft Ltd. as a test bed for their Bombardier 702 motor, was flown for a considerable time as the Messenger 5 G-2-1. Its first public appearance, as G-ALAC, in the *Daily Express* South Coast Air Race at Shoreham on September 22, 1951, was also its last, test pilot P. G. Lawrence making a forced landing near Faversham in which 'AC was damaged beyond repair.

For over a decade assorted Messengers have found great favour for touring purposes. While thus engaged on June 28, 1947, G-AJEY, subject of the heading photograph, lost its engine near Bait, S.E. France. Boulton Paul chief test pilot R. Lindsay Neale thereupon brought off his historic forced landing by crowding his passengers forward over the dashboard. Although many have been raced, honours have been few. Blackburn test pilot Harold Wood won the 1954 King's Cup in Messenger 2A G-AKBO at 133 m.p.h. and A. J. Spiller the 1952 Siddeley Trophy in G-AKIN at 129 m.p.h. W. P. Bowles, for whom the last Messenger 2A G-AJYZ was erected from stock components by Handley Page (Reading) Ltd. in 1950–51, won the Norton Griffiths Trophy consecutively at Woolsington in 1952 and Southend in 1953.

Manufacturers: Phillips and Powis Aircraft Ltd., Woodley Aerodrome, Reading, Berks. Name changed to Miles Aircraft Ltd. in October 1943, production by Miles Aircraft (N.I.) Ltd., Ards Airport, Newtownards, Co. Down, N.I.

Power Plants: (Messenger 2A, 2B, 3) One 155 h.p. Blackburn Cirrus Major 3.

(Messenger 2C and 4A) One 145 h.p. de Havilland Gipsy Major 1D.

(Messenger 4 and 4B) One 145 h.p. de Havilland Gipsy Major 10.

(Messenger 5) One 180 h.p. Blackburn Bombardier 702.

Dimensions: Span, 36 ft. 2 in. Length, 24 ft. 0 in. Height, 7 ft. 6 in. Wing area, 191 sq. ft.

	Messenger 2A, 2B, 3	Messenger 2C, 4, 4A
Tare weight . .	1,450 lb.	1,360 lb.
All-up weight .	2,400 lb.	2,400 lb.
Maximum speed .	135 m.p.h.	115 m.p.h.
Cruising speed .	124 m.p.h.	100 m.p.h.
Initial climb . .	950 ft./min.	1,100 ft./min.
Ceiling . . .	16,000 ft.	17,000 ft.
Range . . .	460 miles	460 miles

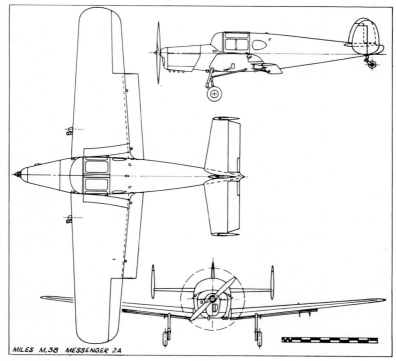

MILES M.38 MESSENGER 2A

Ken Waller flying the Aerovan 1 at Woodley in November 1945.

Miles M.57 Aerovan

Designed by G. H. Miles in 1944 for the short haul transport of bulky loads, the Aerovan contrived to add beauty of line to its unorthodox utilitarian airframe. The short but capacious fuselage of 530 cu. ft. capacity was of plastic bonded wooden construction with the rear portion hinged to form a door large enough for the entry of a small car. Miles auxiliary aerofoil flaps were fitted to the one-piece cantilever wooden mainplane and the triple tail unit was supported on a metal boom. On the power of two Cirrus Major 3 engines the Aerovan would carry a ton of freight or eight passengers for 450 miles at 110–115 m.p.h. The prototype Aerovan 1 was first flown as U-0248 at Woodley by Tommy Rose on January 26, 1945, thereafter appearing at all the early post-war displays as G-AGOZ. In October 1945 it flew to Switzerland with 5,000 ball point pens, and in the following April toured Denmark piloted by Hugh Kendall. In 1947 it flew with a scale mock up of a Mamba nacelle outboard of the starboard engine in readiness for the Miles M.69 Marathon 2. A second prototype of lower structural weight, the Aerovan 2 G-AGWO, which first flew in March 1946 piloted by K. H. F. Waller, was fitted to carry 10 passengers. The front fuselage was extended 18 in., five round instead of four rectangular windows were provided in each side and the outboard rudders were no longer horn balanced. A season of demonstration ended in November 1946 when 'WO went to Newtownards, base of its purchaser Lord Londonderry.

Seven production Aerovan 3s, built during 1946, were outwardly identical to the Aerovan 2 except for a heavy duty door lock under the rear fuselage. Five were employed by Air Contractors Ltd. of Blackbushe for the cross-Channel mixed freight traffic, and a sixth, G-AIIG, for passenger charter by Skytravel Ltd. of Speke. When replaced by Dakotas in 1949 the four survivors went to Beirut, Lebanon, in service with the Arab Contracting and Trading Co. Ltd. They ranged all over the Near East, calling at the landing grounds of the Iraq Petroleum Transport Co. Ltd. in the Syrian Desert, and at Kuwait, Bahrein, Qatar and all along the Trucial coast of Oman. One, G-AHXH, brought up to Aerovan 4 standard, returned to the United Kingdom in 1956.

Main production centred round the Aerovan 4, identified by its four circular windows. Thirty-nine examples were built before the market was satisfied at the end of 1947. All but four were of British registry, two, G-AIDJ and G-AKHG, joining the Aerovan 3s in Beirut. Air Contractors Ltd. acquired G-AIKV and 'SI, the first of which made sensational headlines when washed out to sea after a successful forced landing on the coast near Cherbourg on January 12, 1947. Four were ferried to Aerotechnica S.A. in Madrid as G-AILB–'LE and subsequently did a great deal of flying in Spain as EC-ACP, 'ABA, 'ABB and 'ACQ respectively. Others were acquired for charter work or joyriding by Air Transport (Charter) (C.I.) Ltd., Jersey; Lockwood Flying Services Ltd., Speeton; British Nederland Air Services Ltd.; East Anglian Flying Services Ltd., Southend; North Sea Air Transport Ltd., Brough (later handed over to Universal Flying Services Ltd., Fairoaks); and Kenning Aviation Ltd., Burnaston. G-AJZR, operated for a few months by Skyfreight Ltd., was sold to Turkish State Airlines in January 1949 and became, appropriately, TC-VAN. Several wore elaborate livery and were named. Patrick Aviation Ltd. of Elmdon operated G-AJKP 'County of Stafford' and G-AJOF 'County of Derby', Culliford Airlines Ltd. of Squires Gate had G-AJZG 'Comatas' and Sivewright Airways Ltd., Ringway, G-AJOI 'Oldhamia'. The largest fleet, that of Ulster Aviation Ltd. of Newtownards, comprising G-AJKJ, 'KU, 'OB, 'TD and G-AKHD, was employed in 1947–49 on the Isle of Man tourist traffic and a freight run to Woodley with Ards built Messenger and Gemini assemblies.

The last centre of Aerovan activity was the Channel Islands, whither

An Aerovan 3 of Air Contractors Ltd.

The prototype Aerovan with Mamba nacelle mock-up. (*Photo: Miles Aircraft Ltd.*)

The Lycoming engined Aerovan 6, showing the enlarged tail surfaces.

G-AILF, 'SF, G-AJKP and 'OF gravitated in second-hand condition in 1950–52. They then spent their time with minor operators on charter and joyriding among the Islands and to Dinard. G-AJOF had previously achieved distinction by competing in the *Daily Express* Hurn to Herne Bay Race of September 16, 1950, but owner/pilot E. C. Cathels forced landed at Eastbourne. Two others, 'SF and 'KP, later returned to the fold at Shoreham to commence aerial photography in the colours of Meridian Air Maps Ltd. but crashed fatally at Ringway and Oldbury respectively in 1957. The components of two others, for which registrations G-AMYA and 'YC were reserved by Mrs. O. J. Marmol in 1952, were stored at Elstree for some years.

Early in Aerovan production, Gipsy Major 10 engines were fitted into G-AISJ, thus creating the sole Aerovan 5, later destroyed at Woodley during trials. In 1948 the Aerovan 6 appeared with Lycoming O-435-A motors and the enlarged tail surfaces from the dismantled Miles M.68

The Miles H.D.M.105 G-AHDM flying near the cliffs of Dover. (*'Flight' Photo.*)

prototype. Named 'Northern Exporter', it saw limited service carrying lobsters between Kirkwall and the mainland for Air Cargo Distributors Ltd., afterwards appearing at many air displays piloted by Ian Forbes. The final and most important variant appeared a year later, when G-AJOF emerged from the Miles works rebuilt with Aerovan 6 tail surfaces and a high aspect ratio metal wing designed by Hurel-Dubois of Villacoublay, France. In this form it was renamed the Miles H.D.M.105, flying for the first time on March 30, 1957, as G-35-3 until the very appropriate markings G-AHDM were transferred from a dead Halifax. After serving as a test bed for larger projects it was damaged beyond repair when landing at Shoreham in June 1958.

SPECIFICATION

Manufacturers: Miles Aircraft Ltd., Woodley Aerodrome, Reading, Berks.
Power Plants: (Aerovan 1, 2, 3, 4) Two 155 h.p. Blackburn Cirrus Major 3.
           (Aerovan 5) Two 145 h.p. de Havilland Gipsy Major 10.
           (Aerovan 6) Two 195 h.p. Lycoming O-435-A.
           (H.D.M.105) Two 155 h.p. Blackburn Cirrus Major 3.

	Aerovan 1	Aerovan 2, 3, 4	H.D.M.105
Span . . .	50 ft. 0 in.	50 ft. 0 in.	75 ft. 4 in.
Length . . .	36 ft. 0 in.	36 ft. 0 in.	34 ft. 4 in.
Height . . .	13 ft. 6 in.	13 ft. 6 in.	13 ft. 11 in.
Wing area . .	390 sq. ft.	390 sq. ft.	388 sq. ft.
Tare weight . .	3,410 lb.	3,000 lb.	3,219 lb.
All-up weight .	5,900 lb.	5,800 lb.	6,170 lb.
Maximum speed .	130 m.p.h.	127 m.p.h.	133 m.p.h.
Cruising speed .	110 m.p.h.	112 m.p.h.	116 m.p.h.
Initial climb . .	—	620 ft./min.	650 ft./min.
Ceiling . . .	—	13,250 ft.	18,350 ft.
Range . . .	450 miles	400 miles	—

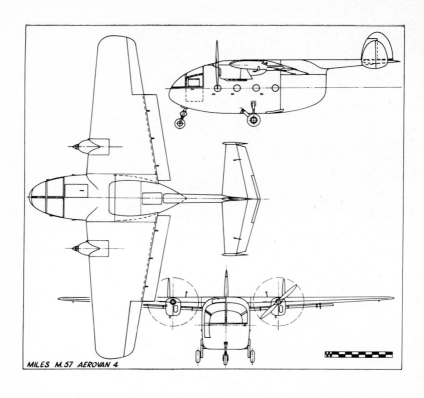

MILES M.57 AEROVAN 4

Group Capt. Bandidt in Gemini 1A G-AILK just before leaving for Australia in 1946.
(*Photo: Miles Aircraft Ltd.*)

Miles M.65 Gemini

The Gemini brought twin engined reliability to the Falcon–Mercury–Messenger family and was the last aeroplane built in quantity at Woodley by Miles Aircraft Ltd. Plastic bonded plywood construction, with cantilever wing and auxiliary aerofoil flaps, was retained, the one-piece, moulded windscreen completing the family likeness. The cream and red Gemini 1 prototype G-AGUS, powered by Cirrus Minor 2 engines, first flown at Woodley by G. H. Miles on October 26, 1945, was demonstrated a few days later to United Nations delegates at Radlett. Although designed with a cantilever undercarriage retracting backward into the engine nacelles, first flight trials were advanced by fitting a temporary fixed undercarriage. During 1946 'US toured Europe and performed at every major British air show, and later flew with the mock-up of a third, central engine.

Large-scale production began at once, G-AIDO, the first demonstration machine with retractable undercarriage, being certificated on August 30, 1946, under the designation Gemini 1A. Five others followed quickly, G-AIHM for Lord Londonderry at Newtownards, G-AIDG International Airways Ltd. at Croydon, G-AIHI exhibited at the November 1946 Paris Salon, G-AHKL for G. W. Harben of Elstree and G-AILK, which left immediately for Australia piloted by Gp. Capt. A. F. 'Bush' Bandidt. His arrival at Truscott, N.T., on January 7, 1947, marked the completion of the first post-war solo flight from the United Kingdom. An unsuccessful attempt to secure a Canadian market was made by shipping G-AJKS on a Canadian aircraft carrier and flying it off on arrival. The aircraft returned to the United Kingdom after demonstration and was sold to Edward Day. Approximately 150 Geminis were built within a year, although the last 10 or so remained unsold and were not immediately assembled. Inevitably the overseas market took toll of these desirable

four seaters, two-thirds of the British registered examples eventually join-
ing those exported direct. In the 12 years during which Geminis have
been permanent features of British civil aerodromes, they have enjoyed
outstanding executive, instructional, commercial and private careers.
Examples of the first were G-AFLT of 'Flight', G-AKGE of the Goodyear
Tyre and Rubber Co. Ltd. and G-AJWC still currently owned by Derek
Crouch (Contractors) Ltd. The prototype, G-AGUS, acquired by Walter
Instruments Ltd. of Redhill in October 1949, was re-engined with
Continental C-125-2 flat six engines as the Gemini 2. Two years service in
this condition ended in July 1952, when it was sold in Sweden as SE-BUY.
Three, G-AKFW, 'HA and 'HS, were used in the Near East, by J. Howard
and Co. Ltd. working on oilfield installations and G-AKEG in the
Lebanon by the Arab Contracting and Trading Co. Ltd. Another,
G-AKZK, was used by the Missionary Aviation Fellowship until it
crashed in the Belgian Congo on July 10, 1948.

The Herts and Essex Aero Club have employed a Gemini for many
years, their current G-AIHM being successor to G-AJEX and G-AKHB.
At Roborough G-AKHW 'City of Plymouth' is the veteran of a decade in
club and taxi service and still wears the dark blue livery of British Overseas
Airways Corporation, the original owners. The Ministry of Civil Aviation
employed two Gemini 1As G-AKDD and G-AIRS for licence testing and
radio calibration from 1947 to 1950, after which 'DD went to Aviation
Traders Ltd. to maintain communications between Southend and Stansted and to play a leading part as a taxi aircraft in the mass movement of
Prentices in 1956–57. 'RS also went to Southend to join the Municipal
Flying School, while G-AJTL was used for the same purpose at Elstree for
several years. The Gemini's commercial activities have been confined
mainly to seaside pleasure flying at Squires Gate, Sandown, Plymouth and
elsewhere, although a number have been used on minor charter operations. As a private aircraft the Gemini, with its high gloss finish and luxury
accommodation, has been the pride and joy of many private owners, for
both air racing and touring. Prince Bira, the racing motorist, owned
G-AJWH 'City of Bangkok' for many years, keeping it at Ramsgate when
not on Continental trips. Major air races since 1948 have always attracted

The Continental engined Gemini 2, with the revised front windscreen fitted in 1952.

174

Gemini 3B G-AJTG with flaps retracted.

Gemini owners to the starting-line, but success has come only to Fred Dunkerley and J.N. 'Nat' Somers. The former's highly polished dark blue G-AKKB, wearing the Lancashire Aero Club's red rose on the fin, became famous as the winner of the Siddeley Trophy in 1949 and 1950, the Kemsley Trophy 1950 and the Air League Challenge Cup 1957. His speeds have continually approached 160 m.p.h., a great performance for a standard aircraft. The Somers Gemini, a version with Gipsy Major 1C engines, known as the Gemini 3, was devised in 1949 at a time when well-known types were no longer beating the handicappers. After flight tests as U-23 and later as G-21-2, it became G-AKDC to win the 1949 King's Cup handsomely at 164·25 m.p.h. Gipsy Major 10s were then fitted, changing the designation to Gemini 3C, and it went on to win the 1953 Siddeley, the 1954 Kemsley and the 1955 Goodyear Trophies. Although it has long since been sold in Kenya, it left in its wake a number of similar variants. First of these was G-ALCS, built as a Gemini 3A for J. M. Houlder of the Elstree Flying Club but later fitted with Gipsy Major 10 Mk. 2 engines to become a Gemini 3C. Two other Geminis of this mark are also in existence, E. Crabtree's G-AKEG and M. B. Rose's G-AKGE, both formerly standard 1As. Several private owners availed themselves of the opportunity to improve their mounts, and today several Gemini 3As are flying, including 'Flight's' G-AKHC, and G-AKEK belonging to T. D. Keegan Ltd., Southend.

The last eight Geminis are of particular interest, all having been constructed from components left over from the main Woodley production. Two erected in 1950 by Handley Page (Reading) Ltd., Gemini 3C G-ALZG and Gemini 1A G-AMEJ, are today owned by Percy Blamire of Baginton and B.K.S. Engineering Ltd. at Southend. Another, G-AMBH, was erected at Redhill by F. G. Miles Ltd. The rest were Gemini 3As, completed to special order by Wolverhampton Aviation Ltd. in 1951. Aerodynamic refinement was confined to the sole Gemini 1B G-AJTG built with retractable flaps for the Hon. Max Aitken in 1950. A succession of owners ended with Edward Day, for whom it was re-equipped with

Gipsy Major 10 Mk. 1–3 engines on the eve of the 1951 King's Cup Race and redesignated Gemini 3B. One Gemini 4 ambulance, G-AKKE, obtained a C. of A. on January 14, 1948, and Gemini 1A G-AKHU, sold in Australia in 1948, has been fitted with Lycoming engines by W. E. James at Bankstown, Sydney, and flies under his initials as VH-WEJ.

At the Fifty Years of Flying Exhibition at Hendon in July 1951, F. G. Miles exhibited the ultimate Gemini development, the M.75 Aries, first flown at Redhill in the previous February. The structure was strengthened to meet the improved performance imparted by two Cirrus Major 3 engines, and redesigned tail surfaces were fitted to increase directional stability during single engine flying. The prototype, G-35-1, later demonstrated as G-AMDJ, was sold to the Hon. M. A. R. Cayzer and then shipped to Australia. It attracted but one order, from Pasolds Ltd., who use G-AOGA for business trips in Europe. Three former Geminis were also raised by modification as near Aries standard as possible, two with Gipsy Major 10 Mk. 2 engines as Gemini 7s for Shell-Mex and B.P. Ltd. and one with Cirrus Major 3s as a Gemini 8 for L. R. Snook of Portsmouth. The Shell machines G-AKHZ and G-AMGF flown respectively by Vivian Varcoe and Gp. Capt. Douglas Bader, are well known everywhere and are distinguishable from the Gemini 8 G-AKFX by their shorter engine nacelles.

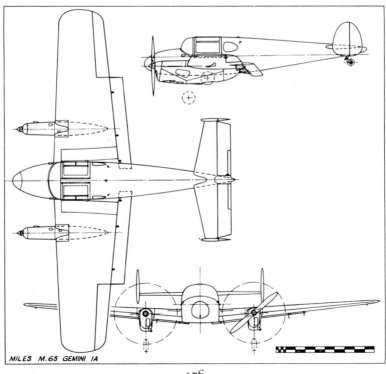

MILES M.65 GEMINI IA

The Miles M.75 Aries operated by Pasolds Ltd.

SPECIFICATION

Manufacturers: Miles Aircraft Ltd., Woodley Aerodrome, Reading, Berks. A number later assembled by Handley Page (Reading) Ltd., Woodley Aerodrome; Wolverhampton Aviation Ltd., Wolverhampton Airport and F. G. Miles Ltd., Redhill Aerodrome.

Power Plants: (Gemini 1, 1A, 1B, 4) Two 100 h.p. Blackburn Cirrus Minor 2.
(Gemini 1A Special) Two 130 h.p. Lycoming O-290-3/1.
(Gemini 2) Two 125 h.p. Continental C-125-2.
(Gemini 3) Two 145 h.p. de Havilland Gipsy Major 1C.
(Gemini 3A) Two 145 h.p. de Havilland Gipsy Major 10 Mk. 1.
(Gemini 3B) Two 145 h.p. de Havilland Gipsy Major 10 Mk. 1–3.
(Gemini 3C, 7) Two 145 h.p. de Havilland Gipsy Major 10 Mk. 2.
(Gemini 8) Two 155 h.p. Blackburn Cirrus Major 3.
(Aries) Two 155 h.p. Blackburn Cirrus Major 3.

Dimensions: Span, 36 ft. 2 in. Length, 22 ft. 3 in. Height, 7 ft. 6 in. Wing area, 191 sq. ft.

	Gemini 1	Gemini 1A	Aries
Tare weight . .	1,896 lb.	1,910 lb.	2,350 lb.
All-up weight .	3,000 lb.	3,000 lb.	3,475 lb.
Maximum speed .	140 m.p.h.	145 m.p.h.	172 m.p.h.
Cruising speed .	125 m.p.h.	135 m.p.h.	150 m.p.h.
Initial climb . .	550 ft./min.	650 ft./min.	1,300 ft./min.
Ceiling . . .	13,500 ft.	13,500 ft.	20,000 ft.
Range . . .	820 miles	820 miles	675 miles

The prototype two seat Hendy 3308 Heck, showing the retractable undercarriage.
(*Photo courtesy of W. K. Kilsby.*)

Parnall Heck

The Heck originated as the Hendy 3308, designed by Basil B. Henderson to the requirements of Whitney Straight, who specified fast cruising coupled with unusually low landing speed. The prototype, built at Yeovil by the Westland Aircraft Works, was a tandem, two seat, low-wing, cabin monoplane, built of spruce with plywood covering throughout. An aerodynamically clean airframe, a Gipsy Six engine and a manually operated, outward retracting undercarriage, ensured a high cruising speed, the second design requirement being met by using camber changing flaps in conjunction with Handley Page leading edge slots. The Heck first flew in July 1934 in red primary dope under the Westland Class B marking P. Unfortunately damage resulting from a collision with a cow in a forced landing en route to Martlesham prevented the completion of airworthiness trials in time for the King's Cup Race. Although in 1934 its speed range, 170–44·8 m.p.h., was a sensation and handsomefully filled the customer's wishes, the aircraft was never used by Whitney Straight.

Parnall Aircraft Ltd. was formed in May 1935 by the amalgamation of George Parnall and Company, the Hendy Aircraft Company and the armament engineering firm of Nash and Thompson Ltd. When, therefore, the prototype went to Hanworth for public demonstration in black and gold as G-ACTC, it had already been restyled the Parnall Heck. Aircraft Exchange and Mart Ltd. prepared to handle sales, and their pilot F/Lt. R. Duncanson demonstrated the Heck at the Hendon S.B.A.C. Show on July 1, 1935. A wheels-up landing at Hanworth in the following month again prevented a King's Cup appearance, but on October 8 it left Hanworth to attack the Cape record piloted by David Llewellyn and Mrs. Jill Wyndham. Forced landings and minor damage en route ruined the attempt, and Cape Town was not reached until the 29th, but on the return journey they beat the previous best time, landing at Lympne on November 11, 6 days 8 hours 27 minutes after leaving Cape Town. On July 10, 1936, 'TC contrived at last to fly in the King's Cup Race piloted

G-AEGH, first production Parnall Heck 2C, showing the revised cabin and fixed under-carriage. (*Photo courtesy of 'The Aeroplane'.*)

The Parnall 382. (*'Flight' Photo.*)

by J. D. Kirwan, but the port undercarriage collapsed when taxying at Whitchurch. It reappeared after repair with the undercarriage permanently locked down and enclosed in trouser type fairings.

A small production line of six Heck 2C aircraft was then laid down by Parnall Aircraft Ltd. at Yate, Gloucestershire. These were three seaters with cabin door, reduced glazing and fixed spatted undercarriages. Five were registered G-AEGH to 'GL, the first of which was decorated in the light and dark blue of Aircraft Exchange and Mart Ltd. and delivered to Hanworth for demonstration in September 1936. None were sold, and with the R.A.F. expansion gathering momentum, 'GH, 'GI and 'GJ were painted dark grey to become communications machines which flew a total of 1,000 miles daily to the squadrons in connection with Parnall's armament interests. A brief respite was granted on July 2, 1938, to allow test pilots H. S. Broad and J. A. C. Warren, in 'GH and 'GI, to compete for the King's Cup. Although their lap speeds averaged 159 m.p.h., they were placed 14th and 10th respectively.

179

Through a clerical error, the letters G-AEGK were not used and the fourth aircraft joined the communications team in 1939 as G-AEMR. When war came, they were camouflaged to continue their normal usage as civil aeroplanes.

The fifth and sixth aircraft, one of which was to have been G-AEGL, were used for the trial installation of the 225 h.p. Wolseley Aries radial and for armament experiments. One, in R.A.F. colours as K8853, with further cabin revision and fitted with a Gipsy VI series II driving a variable-pitch airscrew, was the development vehicle for the gun sight installation in the Hurricane and Spitfire. With war imminent, a two seat, open-cockpit, dual control trainer version known as the Parnall 382, or Heck 3, appeared in February 1939. Using the power plant, tail unit, under-carriage and outer wing panels of its predecessor, the Parnall 382 was the first primary trainer to be fitted with interconnected slots and flaps, and could be flown at 43 m.p.h. No military contract was secured, and only the prototype, G-AFKF, flown under B conditions as J-1, was built. Later in its career the rear cockpit was fitted with a coupé top.

In the course of time 'GJ was cannibalised, but 1942 saw 'GH impressed into the R.A.F. The other two completed their war service with the British Parachute Co. Ltd., at Cardiff, where 'MR was scrapped in 1948. October 1946 found 'GI back at Hanworth to be overhauled and fitted with a Gipsy Queen 3 for Lt.-Cdr. J. G. Crammond, afterwards going to a new home base at Rochester. It was the owner's intention to compete annually against the remaining fast vintage aircraft and at Elmdon on July 29, 1949, came 13th in the King's Cup Race at an average speed of 145·5 m.p.h. In the following June, at Wolverhampton, 'GI reproduced its 1938 form to finish 7th at 159 m.p.h., but after the race its rear end was demolished by the civil Spitfire G-AISU, which struck it when landing. Attempts at reconstruction with spares from 'MR failed and the aircraft was broken up in 1953.

SPECIFICATION

Manufacturers: (Prototype)   Westland Aircraft Works, Yeovil, Somerset.
(Production) Parnall Aircraft Ltd., Yate Aerodrome, Gloucester-shire.

Power Plants: One 200 h.p. de Havilland Gipsy Six.
One 200 h.p. de Havilland Gipsy Queen 3.

	Prototype	Heck 2C	Parnall 382
Span . . .	31 ft. 6 in.	31 ft. 6 in.	33 ft. 6 in.
Length . . .	26 ft. 1½ in.	26 ft. 1½ in.	28 ft. 8 in.
Height . . .	8 ft. 6 in.	8 ft. 6 in.	7 ft. 9 in.
Wing area . .	105·2 sq. ft.	105·2 sq. ft.	155 sq. ft.
Tare weight . .	1,811 lb.	1,750 lb.	1,655 lb.
All-up weight .	2,600 lb.	2,700 lb.	2,450 lb.
Maximum speed .	170 m.p.h.	185 m.p.h.	155 m.p.h.
Cruising speed .	155 m.p.h.	160 m.p.h.	135 m.p.h.
Initial climb . .	—	1,100 ft./min.	—
Ceiling . . .	—	16,700 ft.	—
Range . . .	600 miles	605 miles	—

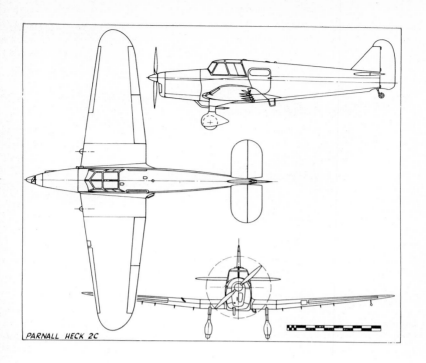

PARNALL HECK 2C

The prototype Gull with unbalanced rudder during early trials. (*Photo: Percival Aircraft Ltd.*)

Percival P.1 Gull Four and P.3 Gull Six

After the Hendy 302 (see Appendix A) had made its successful impact on the aviation fraternity in 1930, Basil B. Henderson left Edgar W. Percival and was replaced by R. H. Bound who designed the three seat Percival Gull, successor to the 302. It followed the same formula, and was an all-wood, low-wing cabin monoplane entered via a hinged roof and folding side. The Henderson patent cantilever mainplane was retained, made to fold about the rear spar and provided with a small flap type air brake under the centre section. The prototype, G-ABUR, powered by a Cirrus Hermes IV, was built at Yate by George Parnall and Company and flown round Britain by E. W. Percival in the King's Cup Race of July 8–9, 1932, at an average speed of 142·73 m.p.h. In the following year, re-engined with a Napier Javelin III, it had a top speed superior to many contemporary fighters, becoming well known at civil aerodromes until written off in Northern Rhodesia during Man Mohan Singh's 1935 Cape record attempt.

The first production batch of 24 Gulls was built at Yate in 1933 under sub-contract to the Percival Aircraft Co. Ltd., newly formed by E. W. Percival and Lt.-Cdr. E. W. B. Leake. Although variously powered, a decade was to pass before a designation system was devised for them. By virtue of its four cylinder Hermes IV, the prototype posthumously became the Percival P.1 Gull Four Mk. I, while production aircraft with improved windscreens and cabin glazing became known as the P.1A Gull Four Mk. II. The first of these, G-ABUV, was Surrey Flying Services Ltd.'s fast charter and photographic machine in 1933–35, and the second, G-ACFY, was used for communications by A. V. Roe and Co. Ltd. Private owners, such as Sir Phillip Sassoon and W. Lindsay Everard, favoured the Javelin engine, so that their respective G-ACGR and 'AL 'Leicestershire Fox'

Jean Batten's Gull Six showing the single strut undercarriage fitted to production aircraft. (*Photo: Hunting Percival Aircraft Ltd.*)

were the first of several of the P.1B Gull Four Mk. IIA type. The British Air Navigation Co. Ltd. of Heston bought 'AL and a Gipsy Major powered P.1C Gull Four Mk. IIB G-ACHM, later in 1933. These were used principally on fast newspaper work, on which the company's chief pilot A. J. 'Bill' Styran and manager I. C. MacGilchrist were engaged when killed in 'AL, returning in bad weather from the scene of the R.101 disaster.

Gull Fours satisfied a lively market and were sold as far afield as Brazil and Japan, and on December 10, 1933, Sir Charles Kingsford Smith arrived at Darwin, Australia in G-ACJV 'Miss Southern Cross' after a record-breaking flight from Heston in 7 days 4 hours 44 minutes. Two others, G-ACIS and 'LG, originally supplied to Air Service Training Ltd. and the Hon. Loel Guinness respectively, were sold to Indian National Airways in 1935 for the Karachi–Lahore mail run. Air Vice Marshal A. E. Borton's private G-ACGP was the only Gull Four flying in Britain at the outbreak of war and, escaping impressment, reappeared at Thame in 1946 but did not fly again.

In 1934 the Percival Aircraft Co. Ltd. established its own works at Gravesend, and A. A. Bage joined the firm as chief designer. The Parnall-built Gull G-ACUL was then modified for Lt. P. Randolph with single strut undercarriage, revised cabin top and side entrance doors to become a P.1D Gull Four Mk. III. Three unsold Gulls, G-ACHA, 'PA and 'XY, similarly modified and fitted with Gipsy Six engines, were in later years allotted the type number P.3. Twenty-two Gulls were built at Gravesend before the company moved to Luton in 1936, including two P.1Ds, one of which went to Heston as G-ADGK for Mrs. E. M. Highfield. Another, G-ADOE, was the sole P.1E, acquired by the North Sea Aerial and General Transport Co. Ltd. as a test bed for the Cirrus Major engine Mks. 1 and 2 and raced by C. S. Napier.

Several notable flights were made in 1935 in Gull Sixes, which, with overload cabin tank and a 2,000 mile range, was an ideal mount for long-distance pilots of that great record-breaking age. E. W. Percival's dash from Gravesend to Oran and back in a day, using G-ADEP, was followed by Jean Batten's Britannia Trophy winning flight to Brazil in G-ADPR, including a 13 hour 15 minute crossing of the South Atlantic. On October 5, 1936, she again took off from Lympne, this time reaching Darwin in the record time of 5 days 21 hours 3 minutes and lowering the time for the Tasman crossing to reach her native Auckland, New Zealand, in the fastest-ever time from England of 11 days 45 minutes. The last British registered Gull Six, G-ADZO, was that used by Amy Mollison between May 4 and 12, 1936, for her out-and-home record to the Cape in 7 days 22 hours 45 minutes and by H. L. Brook in May 1937 for his fastest unofficial flight from the Cape to Heston in 4 days 18 minutes.

During the Italo-Abyssinian War of 1935 the fast Gulls of Brian Allen Aviation Ltd. were obvious mounts for enterprising newspapermen. C. F. French and Brian Allen were away many months with G-ACHM and G-ADPA, but the Gipsy Six prototype was lost in a crash en route at Avignon. The Gull Six was also used executively and privately, G-ACUP by Miss Diana Williams and later S. K. Davies of Cardiff; G-ADFA by Charles Gardner to win the 1935 Siddeley Trophy at 170·08 m.p.h.; G-ADKX by the Shell Company of Egypt and later by Lt.-Col. Blandford-Hewson at Almaza; and G-ADSG, first by the Duchess of Bedford and later by R. C. Preston. The Maharajah of Patiala received G-ACYS

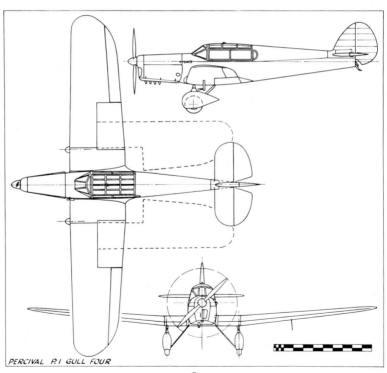

PERCIVAL P.I GULL FOUR

184

in 1935, in which year G-ADEU went to the R.A.E. for extended evaluation leading to an order for the Vega Gull.

Jean Batten's 'Jean' was impressed during the war years, returning to the Hunting Percival fold at Luton after the Kemble sale of December 1945, to be preserved for all time. Blackburn and Vickers retained G-ADOE and 'FA as camouflaged civil 'hacks', but only the former survived. After a Gipsy Major was fitted by Air Couriers Ltd. at Heston in 1946, 'OE was sold to a Jersey private owner but crashed in the Channel a year later.

SPECIFICATION

Manufacturers: George Parnall and Company, Yate Aerodrome, Gloucestershire and the Percival Aircraft Co. Ltd., Gravesend Airport, Kent.

Power Plants: Gull Four.

(P.1 Mk. I)	One 130 h.p. Cirrus Hermes IV.
(P.1A Mk. II)	One 130 h.p. Cirrus Hermes IV.
(P.1B Mk. IIA)	One 160 h.p. Napier Javelin III.
(P.1C Mk. IIB)	One 130 h.p. de Havilland Gipsy Major.
(P.1E Mk. III)	One 135 h.p. Blackburn Cirrus Major I or II.

Gull Six.

(P.3)	One 200 h.p. de Havilland Gipsy Six.

Dimensions: Span, 36 ft. 2 in. Length, 24 ft. 9 in. Height, 7 ft. 4½ in. Wing area, 169 sq. ft.

	Hermes IV	Javelin III	Gipsy Major and Cirrus Major I	Gipsy Six
Tare weight .	1,170 lb.	1,170 lb.	1,290 lb.	1,500 lb.
All-up weight .	2,050 lb.	2,250 lb.	2,300 lb.	2,450 lb.
Maximum speed.	145 m.p.h.	160 m.p.h.	155 m.p.h.	178 m.p.h.
Cruising speed .	125 m.p.h.	140 m.p.h.	133 m.p.h.	160 m.p.h.
Initial climb .	850 ft./min.	—	—	—
Ceiling . .	16,000 ft.	—	18,000 ft.	20,000 ft.
Range . .	700 miles	700 miles	745 miles	640 miles

Edgar Percival flying the short span Mew Gull IIA G-AFAA.

Percival P.2 and P.6 Mew Gull

The remarkable career of the Gull, built for touring but already famous as racer and record breaker, made it easy for Edgar Percival to visualise the success which might come to a pure racing version. Thus inspired, he and R. H. Bound designed and built the Mew Gull single seater in a few months in the Gravesend works, first flights taking place in March 1934. It was an incredibly small low-wing monoplane with spatted, strutted undercarriage and powered by a Javelin 1A. A single strut undercarriage and Gipsy Six engine were fitted for its one public appearance, at Hatfield for the King's Cup Race of July 13, 1934. Failing to beat the handicappers, even though lapping at 191 m.p.h., it returned to Gravesend and was broken up. When Percival designations were regularised after the Second World War, this prototype became the Percival P.2 Mew Gull Mk. I. Its successor the Percival P.6 Mew Gull Mk. II, designed by A. A. Bage, was an entirely different aeroplane, also registered G-ACND, which had a longer fuselage, redesigned undercarriage and tail surfaces, trailing edge flaps and a Gipsy Six engine. After its first public appearance at the Hendon S.B.A.C. Show on July 1, 1935, it was rapidly and temporarily re-engined with a French 180 h.p. Regnier, of less than 8 litres capacity to qualify for entry in the Coupe Armand Esders. Over a 1,046 mile course from Deauville to Cannes and back, the Comte de Chateaubrun, Percival agent in France, averaged 188 m.p.h. to win the premier award. With Gipsy Six replaced, it returned home to come 6th at 208·9 m.p.h. in the King's Cup Race, 3rd at 198·5 m.p.h. in the Folkestone Trophy Race and to score its first success by winning the Heston–Cardiff Race at 218 m.p.h.

The next Mew Gull, G-AEKL, flown by E. W. Percival in the 1936 King's Cup and Folkestone Trophy Races, came 4th and 7th respectively. It was then sold to Air Publicity Ltd. at Heston and modified with additional fuselage tanks, Gipsy Six series II engine and variable pitch airscrew as a mount for Tom Campbell Black in the Schlesinger Race to Johannesberg. On September 19, 1936, 'KL went to Speke to be named

'Miss Liverpool'. There its illustrious pilot was mortally injured by the airscrew of a Hawker Hart with which it collided on the ground. Two exactly similar Mew Gulls which took off from Portsmouth 10 days later to race to Johannesberg were ZS-AHM 'The Golden City' and ZS-AHO 'Baragwanath' built for the veteran South African pilots Major A. M. Miller and Capt. S. S. Halse. The latter's aircraft, temporarily G-AEMO prior to the race, made a meteoric dash southward, but earth jammed the spats and the machine was wrecked when it went over on its back in a forced landing near Salisbury, Southern Rhodesia. Miller ran out of fuel, made a dead stick landing almost within sight of the first control at Belgrade, flew in on low-grade spirit, retired and returned to England.

In 1937 the sixth and last Mew Gull, G-AFAA, with reduced span and Gipsy Six series II, was built for E. W. Percival and retrospectively designated the P.6A Mew Gull Mk. IIA. The tragic G-AEKL was also rebuilt for Charles Gardner, while Alex Henshaw acquired Capt. Miller's aircraft, now fitted with a standard Gipsy Six and boasting the British label G-AEXF. During the season, Gardner won the Newcastle Race at 221 m.p.h. and Henshaw the Folkestone Trophy at 210 m.p.h. Later all three Mew Gulls faced the King's Cup starter, Gardner winning handsomely at 233·7 m.p.h., with Percival making fastest time to reach 3rd place at 238·7 m.p.h. In the following year 'KL was raced by Giles Guthrie and 'XF went to Gravesend, where Essex Aero Ltd. fitted a Gipsy Six R engine and a French Ratier variable pitch airscrew from the D.H.88 Comet G-ACSS. The two Mew Gulls fought a duel in the Isle of Man Races and met Percival's 'AA at the King's Cup. 'XF now had a de Havilland variable pitch airscrew on a short extension shaft, with resultant changes in nose and spinner shape. The cowling was also flattened and the aircraft given a more wicked look, Essex Aero Ltd. having remodelled the whole decking above the longerons to lower the canopy 4 in. and seat the pilot on the floor. It won the 1938 King's Cup at the phenomenal speed of 236·25 m.p.h., with Guthrie 2nd and Percival 6th.

'XF then retired to Gravesend to be groomed for Alex Henshaw's

The first Mew Gull, G-ACND, with Napier Javelin engine. (*Fox Photos.*)

Alex Henshaw's G-AEXF fitted with Gipsy Six R and de Havilland airscrew, lowered cabin and cut away spats for the 1938 King's Cup Race. (*Photo courtesy of 'The Aeroplane'.*)

Mew Gull G-AEXF as it is today, with raised cockpit enclosure.

fantastic out-and-home Cape record. Fitted with Gipsy Six series II, radio and long-range tanks and cleared for a take off weight of 2,350 lb., it left Gravesend on February 5, 1939, and arrived back 4 days 10 hours 16 minutes later. In the following July it was sold in France and survived war-time storage north of Lyons until re-discovered by H. E. Scrope 11 years later. With no previous Mew Gull experience and with the engine misfiring, he flew non-stop from Bron to Blackbushe on July 2, 1950. After overhaul at White Waltham it was entered for the abortive 1951 King's Cup Race, but following a landing accident at Shoreham in the August, was rebuilt by D. E. Bianchi with raised and enlarged cockpit canopy. J. N. Somers bought and raced it for the Kemsley Trophy at Southend in June 1953, and in the following year the canopy was raised still more by Adie Aviation Ltd. at Croydon. In the hands of P. S. Clifford, flying on behalf of the owner Fred Dunkerley, the veteran Mew Gull has performed annually at Baginton, winning the King's and S.B.A.C.

Cups on August 20, 1955, at 213·5 m.p.h., the Norton Griffiths Trophy on July 14, 1957, at 200·75 m.p.h. and the Air League Challenge Trophy on July 12, 1958, at 202·66 m.p.h.

SPECIFICATION

Manufacturers: Percival Aircraft Ltd., Gravesend Airport, Kent, moved to Luton
    Airport, Beds., 1936.
Power Plants: (Mew Gull I)   One 165 h.p. Napier Javelin IA.
                        One 200 h.p. de Havilland Gipsy Six.
        (Mew Gull II)   One 200 h.p. de Havilland Gipsy Six.
                        One 180 h.p. Regnier.
                        One 205 h.p. de Havilland Gipsy Six series II.
                        One 230 h.p. de Havilland Gipsy Six R.
      (Mew Gull IIA) One 205 h.p. de Havilland Gipsy Six series II.

	Mew Gull I Javelin	Mew Gull I Gipsy Six	Mew Gull II Gipsy Six	Mew Gull II Gipsy Six series II	Mew Gull IIA
Span	24 ft. 0 in.	24 ft. 0 in.	24 ft. 0 in.	24 ft. 0 in.	22 ft. 9 in.
Length	18 ft. 3 in.	18 ft. 3 in.	20 ft. 3 in.	20 ft. 3 in.	20 ft. 3 in.
Height	6 ft. 10 in.	6 ft. 10 in.	6 ft. 10 in.	6 ft. 10 in.	6 ft. 10 in.
Wing area	78 sq. ft.	78 sq. ft.	78 sq. ft.	78 sq. ft.	75 sq. ft.
Tare weight	996 lb.	1,040 lb.	1,080 lb.	1,150 lb.	1,150 lb.
All-up weight	1,460 lb.	1,545 lb.	1,800 lb.	2,125 lb.	2,125 lb.
Maximum speed	195 m.p.h.	204 m.p.h.	225 m.p.h.	230 m.p.h.	235 m.p.h.
Cruising speed	175 m.p.h.	180 m.p.h.	190 m.p.h.	205 m.p.h.	232 m.p.h.
Initial climb	—	1,400 ft./min.	1,400 ft./min.	1,700 ft./min.	1,800 ft./min.
Ceiling	—	—	—	21,000 ft.	21,000 ft.
Range	550 miles	500 miles	575 miles	800 miles	875 miles

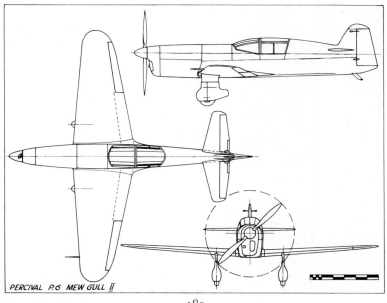

PERCIVAL P.6 MEW GULL II

The prototype Vega Gull G-AEAB on an early flight with the final registration letter incorrectly painted as D. (*Photo: Percival Aircraft Ltd.*)

Percival P.10 Vega Gull

The Vega Gull, designed by A. A. Bage, was a direct development of the Gull Six using the same form of wooden construction but the fuselage was lengthened by 9 in. and widened to 44 in. to allow side-by-side seating for two pairs. Dual control was fitted in the front seats, split trailing edge flaps were incorporated in folding wings and the Vega Gull possessed a high all-round performance which made it famous as a fast touring or charter aircraft. The prototype, G-AEAB, initially mispainted as G-AEAD, was built at Gravesend and first flown by E. W. Percival in December 1935.

Four Vega Gulls, comprising the prototype, G-AEKD, Sir Connop Guthrie's 'KE and W. Lindsay Everard's G-AELE 'Leicestershire Fox IV', flown respectively by Misri Chand, P. Randolph, Charles Gardner and P. Q. Reiss, fought a private duel with the Miles team in the King's Cup Race of July 10–11, 1936. Fitted with long-range cabin and centre section tanks for the 1,224 mile eliminating race, Gardner's was the winner at an average speed of 164·47 m.p.h. After the race, 'KE and the prototype, similarly tanked, were fitted with Gipsy Six series II engines driving variable pitch airscrews for entry in the Schlesinger Race to Johannesberg. Flown by C. W. A. Scott and the owner's son Giles Guthrie, 'KE was the only finisher, landing at Rand Airport on October 1, 1936, 52 hours 56 minutes 48·2 seconds out from Portsmouth. Amid the glare of resultant publicity, the Percival works transferred to larger premises at Luton, where a Vega Gull production line prospered until the 89th and final aircraft took off on July 27, 1939.

In later years Vega Gulls with Gipsy Six and Gipsy Six series II engines were designated Percival P.10 and P.10A Vega Gull Mk. I. Late production models, fitted with the rounded windscreen of the Proctor I, became known as the P.10B Vega Gull Mk. II. First of two Mk. I machines modified in this manner for export was G-AEEM, originally delivered to Sir Charles Rose, sold in Sweden as SE-AHR in May 1939, only to be shot down by a German fighter two years later. The other was Lt.-Col. Hamilton Gault's G-AEIF sold in France as F-AQMZ in April 1938. Of the 44 Vega Gulls delivered to the home market, the following were used commercially: G-AEJJ Commercial Air Hire Ltd., Heston, 'LW the Anglo American Oil Co. Ltd., Heston; 'RL Air Service Training Ltd., Hamble; 'TF the de Havilland Aircraft Co. Ltd.; 'WS European Air Communications Ltd., Gatwick; 'XV Air Commerce Ltd., Heston; G-AFAV Air Hire Ltd., Castle Bromwich; 'IE Smiths Aircraft Instruments Ltd., Hatfield. Prominent private owners were the Marquess of Douglas and Clydesdale G-AELF; Sir George Lewis 'LS; G. W. Harben 'MB; P. G. Aldrich-Blake

Percival P.10B Vega Gull 2 G-AEXV in the colours of British and Continental Airways, 1947, showing the rounded windscreen.

'PS; W. H. Whitbread 'TE; D. Schreiber 'ZJ; G. M. Tonge 'ZK; F. J. C. Butler 'ZL; R. E. Gardner G-AFBW and 'IT; Alex Henshaw owned 'EA, the machine in which he made a survey flight down the west coast of Africa in the spring of 1938.

Fitted with much of the equipment from the undelivered and solitary two seat, open-cockpit Percival P.8 Gull Six, built for the Maharajah of Jodhpur in 1935, Vega Gull G-AFBR went to Bombay for demonstration. It returned to crash at Luton on June 1, 1938, with the loss of its pilot Sir Alastair McRobert and two passengers. Prior to the Second World War the Vega Gull was a persistent air race performer, but the start of the Isle of Man Race at Hanworth on May 19, 1937, cost S. W. Sparkes his life when G-AERH went through a house in an attempt to catch Patrick Randolph's 'KD.

A Service version of the machine, retrospectively designated the P.10C Vega Gull Mk. III, was supplied to the Air Ministry in 1938–39. Two of these, L7272 and P5992, were allotted civil status in June 1939 as G-AFWG and 'VI respectively as personal aircraft of the Air Attachés in Buenos Aires and Lisbon. A Mk. II Vega Gull, G-AFBO, commissioned in August 1937 for the use of the Attaché in Berlin, was seized by the Germans at the outbreak of war, together with Mrs. H. M. Russell-Cooke's G-AFIM, stranded in France. By March 1940, 19 British owned Vega Gulls had been impressed for communications work as shown in Appendix D. Their ranks were sadly thinned, many served overseas, including W. L. Runciman's G-AEXU at Aboukir in 1943, and only six survived the war. They were G-AEXV, flown at Southend by British and Continental Airways Ltd. in 1947; G-AFAU, the identity of which had been lost, employed on taxi work from Croydon by St. Christopher Travelways Ltd. as G-AIIT in 1946; 'BC, personal aircraft of Lady Sherbourn, ex-A.T.A., in which Gp. Capt. C. M. M. Grece was killed at Eastleigh on July 12, 1954; 'EA, sold abroad in 1952 after war service with Gloster Aircraft Ltd. and post-war ownership by Dr. D. F. Little; and finally 'EH, a charter aircraft with the Lancashire Aircraft Corporation Ltd. from 1946 to 1953.

Today but two remain, Vega Gull Mk. II, G-AEYC, resurrected at Kidlington in 1946 and currently owned by G. P. Layton, and an ex Air Ministry Vega Gull Mk. III, G-AHET. Now based at Fairwood Common by E. N. Husbands, it was once P5989, delivered to No. 24 Squadron at Hendon on April 5, 1939. After the war it was civilianised for the first time at Gravesend by Essex Aero Ltd.

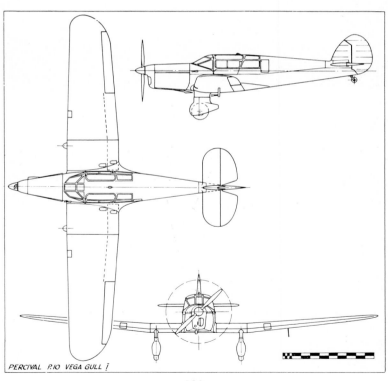

PERCIVAL P.10 VEGA GULL I

Manufacturers: Percival Aircraft Ltd., Gravesend Airport, Kent, moved to Luton
   Airport, Beds., 1936.

Power Plants: (P.10)   One 200 h.p. de Havilland Gipsy Six.
         (P.10B)   One 200 h.p. de Havilland Gipsy Six.
                          One 205 h.p. de Havilland Gipsy Six series II.
         (P.10A and P.10C) One 205 h.p. de Havilland Gipsy Six series II.

Dimensions: Span, 39 ft. 6 in. Length, 25 ft. 6 in. Height, 7 ft. 4 in. Wing area,
   184 sq. ft.

	Gipsy Six	Gipsy Six series II
Tare weight . . .	1,575 lb.	1,740 lb.
All-up weight . .	2,750 lb.	3,250 lb.
Maximum speed . .	170 m.p.h.	174 m.p.h.
Cruising speed . .	160 m.p.h.	150 m.p.h.
Initial climb . . .	—	1,020 ft./min.
Ceiling . . .	18,000 ft.	17,000 ft.
Range	620 miles	660 miles

E. W. Percival flying the turquoise and silver prototype Q.6 near Luton in 1937.
(*Photo courtesy of 'The Aeroplane'.*)

Percival P.16 Q.6

Designed by A. A. Bage in 1937 to carry two crew and four passengers, the Q.6 marked the entry of Percival Aircraft Ltd. into the twin engined market. The fuselage was basically a plywood box faired with fabric over external frames and stringers, and the cantilever wing consisted of two wooden box spars with spruce ribs and plywood skin. Percival split trailing edge flaps were fitted, all control surfaces were fabric covered and the nacelles, integrated with the trousered undercarriage, housed Gipsy Six series II engines driving de Havilland variable pitch airscrews. The prototype, G-AEYE, later allotted the type number P.16, was first flown at Luton by E. W. Percival on September 14, 1937, the construction of 26 production aircraft commencing in the following year. These were retrospectively designated P.16A, nine being sold initially for executive use and scheduled services at home.

Sir Phillip Sassoon took delivery of G-AFFD, the grey and silver first production aircraft, at Lympne on March 2, 1938. During the next 12 months G-AFFE went to H. B. Legge and Sons Ltd. at Warlingham; 'HG to Lord Londonderry, Newtownards; 'IW to Vickers Aviation Ltd. at Brooklands; 'GX to Intava; 'KG to L. A. Hordern, Hatfield; and 'KC to Almaza, Cairo, for Lt.-Col. E. T. Peel. A retractable undercarriage was an optional extra, only four aircraft being so fitted, eventually to be allotted the designation P.16D. First of these, VH-ABL, built to the order of the famous Australian pilot and navigator Capt. P. G. Taylor, was involved in an accident during undercarriage trials at Martlesham in June 1938. The second, G-AFIX, delivered to W. A. H. B. Burnside at Croydon on December 12, 1938, carried the red and blue livery of Western Airways Ltd. on the Castle Bromwich–Whitchurch–Weston–Cardiff

Western Airways' Q.6 G-AFIX flying with undercarriage retracted, 1939.

route during the summer of 1939. A third, G-AFMV, became the personal aircraft of Viscount Forbes in March 1939 and the fourth was shipped to Australia.

In June 1939 Western Airways Ltd. added to its fleet G-AFVC, which had been delivered under French marks a year earlier to Baron L. de Armella. Soon afterwards Vickers-Armstrongs Ltd. acquired the retractable prototype, repaired and fitted with a fixed undercarriage before taking up residence at Eastleigh as G-AFMT. With one exception the civil Q.6s all served in the R.A.F. during World War 2, the prototype inaugurating the process on March 6, 1940, when it flew away from Luton as X9328. Three days later, P5640, last of seven P.16E Petrels built under Air Ministry contract, was delivered to No. 36 M.U. Sealand for R.A.F. communications duties. Impressment came to an end in May 1940, when G-AFVC, flown since the previous September in all yellow colour scheme with small black markings on the rear fuselage, departed from Weston to become AX860. The Vickers 'hack' 'IW retained its civil status throughout hostilities and although transferred to J. Brockhouse and Co. Ltd. at Minworth in 1943 and damaged in an accident in Corsica in 1945, it survived to become Lt.-Cdr. R. E. Bibby's private aeroplane in 1946.

The return of peace witnessed the reappearance of four other Percival Q.6s, including the prototype, restored by Southern Aircraft (Gatwick) Ltd. and named 'Southernaire'; G-AFFD operated by the Yorkshire Aeroplane Club at Sherburn-in-Elmet until sold in April 1952 to Walter Instruments Ltd., Redhill; and 'IX demobilised with a fixed undercarriage. The last was mainly used by Fremantle Overseas Radio Ltd., but ended its career in 1949 as a taxi and joyriding aircraft with Starways Ltd. at Speke. Not unexpectedly, three R.A.F. Petrels also survived to be converted for civilian use by Whitney Straight Ltd. at Weston-super-Mare in 1946. One, formerly P5637 of the Woodley Communications Flight, originally delivered on August 18, 1939, went to Denham as G-AHOM and carried out several long-distance charters to Italy and North Africa piloted by A. R. Lewis of Airways Individual Reservations Ltd. Following a crash landing at Jury's Gap, Dungeness, when flying from Le Bourget to Lympne in bad visibility on Christmas Eve 1946, it returned to Weston for reconstruction. It then went on to enjoy a useful life with the Yellow Air Taxi Co. (Midlands) Ltd. at Elmdon in 1947, with Ductility Steels Ltd., Wolverhampton, with the name 'Ductility' in 1948, with W. J.

Twitchell at Luton in 1950, and with its originator E. W. Percival during the E.P.9 production in 1956.

After the war the last production Petrel, P5640, originally delivered to No. 11 Group Station Flight at Northolt on June 2, 1939, was civilianised as G-AHTA for the London and Oxford Steel Co. Ltd. The same firm acquired G-AHTB, formerly P5634, but both aircraft were comparatively short lived. G-AHTA, sold to the Brussels taxi firm COGEA in November 1946, was damaged beyond repair in 1954, while 'TB went into executive use at Southend with S. E. Norman, only to meet a similar fate at Almaza. After more than 20 years, three aircraft of the type still exist, but only the prototype, flown privately at Cambridge by J. B. Peak, has a current C. of A.

SPECIFICATION

Manufacturers: Percival Aircraft Ltd., Luton Airport, Luton, Beds.
Power Plants: Two 205 h.p. de Havilland Gipsy Six series II.
Dimensions: Span, 46 ft. 8 in. Length, 32 ft. 3 in. Height, 9 ft. 9 in. Wing area, 278 sq. ft.
Weights: Tare weight (Prototype), 3,100 lb. (Production), 3,500 lb.
  All-up weight (Prototype), 5,250 lb. (Production), 5,500 lb.
Performance: Maximum speed, 195 m.p.h. Cruise, 175 m.p.h.* Initial climb, 1,150 ft./min. Ceiling, 21,000 ft. Range, 750 miles.

* 183 m.p.h. with undercarriage retracted.

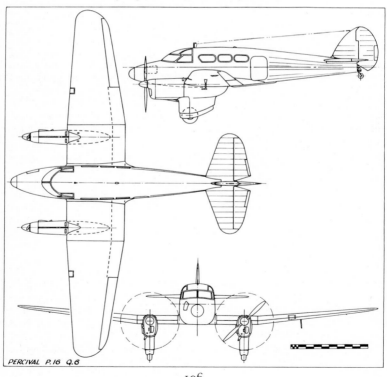

PERCIVAL P.16 Q.6

Proctor 3 G-AKWV, formerly HM350, was first used by the Cinque Ports Flying Club at Lympne. (*Photo: Skyfotos Ltd.*)

Percival P.28, P.30 and P.34 Proctor
1, 2 and 3

The Percival P.28 Proctor I three seat communications aircraft was a strengthened version of the Vega Gull Mk. III built to Air Ministry specification. The prototype, P5998, first flown at Luton on October 8, 1939, was followed by 246 production aircraft, 25 of which were built under sub-contract at Manchester by F. Hills and Sons Ltd. Further deliveries totalled 196 externally identical P.30 Proctor II and 436 P.34 Proctor III radio trainers, nearly all of which were built at Manchester. In October 1944 the Proctor III DX198 was earmarked as G-AGLC, replacement for the Air Attaché's Vega Gull G-AFWG in Buenos Aires. The scheme fell through, and the same Proctor was used until recently as G-ALUJ by J. M. S. Procter at Yeadon. The first active civil Proctor was a Mk. III LZ599 used, initially in camouflage, by the Ministry of Civil Aviation as G-AGLJ for licence testing from 1944 to 1950. Concurrently HM460 was in similar employ at Almaza as G-AGOG, and HM397 became G-AGTH 'Star Pixie', first and smallest aircraft of British South American Airways. Another Proctor 3 (Arabic mark numbers replaced Roman in 1948) served the Air Attachés in Berne and Prague. This was LZ734, civil as G-AGWB from 1946 to 1951 and now restored as the based radio test vehicle of Avionics Ltd., Biggin Hill.

After the war some 225 surplus Proctors 1, 2 and 3 were denuded of military equipment for private ownership, charter work and training, all three marks thereby becoming identical and their intended civil designations P.28B, P.30B and P.34A were never used. The first conversion was carried out on Proctor 1 P6197 at Weston-super-Mare in March 1946, and

197

as G-AGWV the machine made a few runs on the Western Airways service to Cardiff prior to six years in private ownership. The Cardiff–Whitchurch route was later operated by Cambrian Air Services' Proctor 1s G-AHEU 'Montgomery' and 'EV 'Denbigh'. Many post-war charter firms commenced operations with Proctors, notably Air Taxis (Croydon) Ltd. with G-AGYA and 'YB; Olley Air Services Ltd., G-AIIL; Reid and Sigrist Ltd., Desford, G-AIIW and 'KK; Portsmouth Aviation Ltd., G-AHTC; Scottish Aviation Ltd., G-AHMP and 'MT; Lancashire Aircraft Corporation Ltd., G-AIHD and the ex A.T.A. pilot Rosemary Rees with G-AILP. In later years Morton Air Services Ltd., Croydon, used G-AKWF and G-AHFW operated in Beirut, Lebanon, with the Arab Contracting and Trading Co. Ltd.

Radio and navigation trainers G-AHTV and 'KZN carried the black and silver of Air Service Training Ltd., Hamble, from 1946 to 1952, while G-AGZL, 'ZM and G-AHLW had varying careers with the Herts and Essex Aero Club, G-AIEX being concurrently in service with the Yorkshire Aeroplane Club. Smith's Aircraft Instruments Ltd. maintained G-AHFK for many years for test and executive purposes, and G-AILN was the first of several 'Windmill Girls' operated by the theatre company. G-AHMP, a Scottish Airways air taxi in 1946 and John Grierson's 'Rouge et Noir' in 1948, currently flies on communications for the de Havilland Engine Co. Ltd., Leavesden, a function carried out for several years at Brough for Blackburn Aircraft Ltd. by G-AHVG.

A large number of civil Proctors were sold overseas. Many of these were ferried in the early post-war years by Colonials returning home, as in the case of W/O J. Dyer, R.A.A.F., who left Hanworth for Australia in G-AHTN on July 20, 1946, a few days before F/Lt. J. Dalton in G-AHMG 'Dominion Lass' and F/Lt. F. Ogden in G-AHFX 'Yorkshire Lass'. In the following November G-AIEI 'Baby Baroda', piloted by F. James, was the first to reach the Cape. LZ804, first flown on December 2, 1943, and the last Proctor 3 constructed, was also one of the last delivered by air to Australia, leaving Croydon as G-ANGC in December 1957.

As a private aircraft the early Proctors chiefly found favour with sporting pilots such as A. S. K. 'Buster' Paine, whose red G-AHNA 'Nannie Ann', probably best known of all Proctors, won the Kemsley Trophy at Southend on June 20, 1953, at 149 m.p.h. and the Air League Challenge Trophy at Baginton on July 21, 1956, at 153·5 m.p.h. Other memorable Proctor successes included N. W. Chorlton's victory in G-AHUZ 'Nicodemus' in the Hurn to Herne Bay Race of September 16, 1950; the dead heat for the Osram Cup at Baginton on July 21, 1956, between T. G. Knox in G-AMBS and A. Barker in G-ANWY; and S/Ldr. W. I. Lashbrooke's win in G-AIHD in the Air League Challenge Trophy Race at Yeadon on July 22, 1950. T. G. Knox carried off the same trophy in G-ALCK on August 20, 1955, and P. G. Lawrence the Kemsley Trophy in G-AHVG at Woolsington on July 11, 1952. The veteran R. H. McIntosh, constant performer in G-AHGA, flew G-AOEJ into second place at 152 m.p.h. in the 1958 King's Cup Race.

Modifications to the type were few. G-AHAB, Farnborough based mount of C. E. Berens for 13 years, underwent prototype four seat conversion. This found no general favour, although G-AIIR was similarly modified for British and Continental Airways Ltd. at Southend in 1947.

Other modifications were confined to the long, silencing exhaust on G-AHAB and the enlarged rear cabin windows on H. W. J. Bethell's G-AMAL, wrecked in bad weather in a collision with a hillside near Peebles on October 1, 1950. In 1959 only 33 Proctors 1, 2 and 3 were in current British use, these including G-AHBS of the Fakenham Flying Group, G-AIED flown for many years on Shell business by J. C. C. Taylor, G-AJLS owned by Air Vice Marshal D. C. T. Bennett, the Wiltshire School of Flying's G-AKWP and 'ZN and No. 604 Sqn. Flying Group's G-ALOK.

SPECIFICATION

Manufacturers: Percival Aircraft Ltd., Luton Airport, Beds., sub-contracted by F. Hills and Sons Ltd., Trafford Park, Manchester.
Power Plant: One 210 h.p. de Havilland Gipsy Queen 2.
Dimensions: Span, 39 ft. 6 in. Length, 25 ft. 10 in. Height, 7 ft. 3 in. Wing area, 197 sq. ft.
Weights: Tare weight, 1,875 lb. All-up weight, 3,250 lb.
Performance: Maximum speed, 165 m.p.h. Cruising speed, 150 m.p.h. Initial climb, 1,020 ft./min. Ceiling, 17,000 ft. Range, 660 miles.

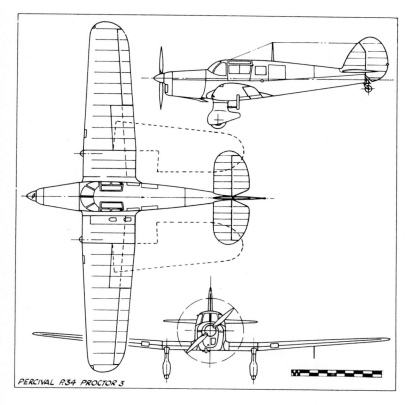

PERCIVAL P.34 PROCTOR 3

The turquoise and silver Proctor 5 G-AGTC, first English demonstrator.

Percival P.31 and P.44 Proctor 4 and 5

In 1943 the Proctor was entirely redesigned and strengthened by A. A. Bage, chief designer of Percival Aircraft Ltd. The fuselage was widened, lengthened and deepened to accommodate two side-by-side pairs, the windscreen and cabin windows enlarged and the tailplane raised to improve recovery from the spin. First known as the Preceptor, it was almost immediately renamed Proctor IV (later Proctor 4). Eight pre-production aircraft constructed at Luton and 250 others built at Manchester as radio trainers were among the first British wooden aeroplanes to employ plastic bonded construction.

In June 1945 a Proctor 4 RM161 was released to the Ministry of Civil Aviation as G-AGPA and after conversion at Luton went to Gatwick on radio calibration duties. A few others were declared surplus to R.A.F. requirements in 1947, a batch of 16, G-AJMH–'MX, being civilianised at Tollerton and Croydon by Field Aircraft Services Ltd., who exhibited 'MP at that year's Radlett S.B.A.C. Show. 'MH became well known at Redhill in the hands of private owner E. Williams, 'MW and 'MX operated the Rochester Air Charter Service of Short Bros. Ltd. and several were sold abroad. 'MU, named 'Thursday's Child', was fitted with extra tanks for a world flight by Mrs. R. Morrow-Tait with M. Townsend navigating. Leaving Croydon in August 1948, it flew via India, Japan and a 1,730 mile North Pacific crossing, only to be damaged beyond repair in a forced landing on the Alaskan Highway on November 21. Six others civilianised at Squires Gate as G-AKLB–'LD and 'YI–'YK, went into charter service at Yeadon in the red and green of Lancashire Aircraft Corporation Ltd. One of the few British examples of structural failure in the air occurred on August 19, 1949, when 'LC was destroyed at Shipley, Yorks. Two others, G-AKWL and 'LEO, served the flying schools at Southend and Thruxton for a number of years.

Early in 1955 the R.A.F. declared obsolete all its remaining Proctor 4s, approximately 60 being acquired by civilian firms. Few saw any real service, although G-ANGM flew with East Anglian Flying Services Ltd. at Ipswich; 'XR on communications with Folland Aircraft Ltd., Hamble; 'YP with the Wiltshire School of Flying; 'YV as the camera ship of Film Aviation Services Ltd. and G-AOAR 'The Instrument Rater' in current use by the Airways Aero Club. The rest were flown mainly under temporary civil marks to Panshanger, White Waltham and elsewhere to be scrapped after the removal of valuable engines and instruments. These included the second prototype LA589, ferried to Exeter by C. E. Harper and Co. Ltd. as G-ANXI.

When the Proctor 4 contract was terminated by the end of hostilities in 1945, three new aircraft RM193, 196 and 197 went to Luton to become prototypes of a purely civil version, the Proctor 5. Registered G-AGSW–'SY as demonstrators, the first and third went by sea to Canada and Australia respectively. The other, together with 'SZ, was handed over to the associate company Hunting Air Travel Ltd. and on January 1, 1946, the inaugural day of post-war civil flying, made an initial return charter flight from Luton to Croydon piloted by former Imperial Airways pilot W. Rogers. Series production of 150 Proctor 5s then began at Luton, 89 of which were of British registry. After 14 years, one of the first, G-AGTC, is still flying for Hunting Aircraft Ltd. G-AHTA, fitted with long-range tanks, made a delivery flight to Brazil piloted by J. A. Mollison, who left St. Mawgan, Cornwall, on January 28, 1946. The flying time of $37\frac{1}{2}$ hours for the 4,640 mile flight included a 15 hour crossing of the South Atlantic.

The Proctor 5, fastest of post-war four seaters, was used executively by the Dunlop Rubber Co. Ltd. with G-AHBA, Helliwells Ltd. 'GT, Shell 'WU, Intava 'ZY, and D. Napier and Son Ltd. 'WV. It saw charter service with Island Air Services Ltd., Marshalls Flying School Ltd., Butlins Ltd., Kenning Aviation Ltd., Atlas Aviation Ltd., Kearsley Airways Ltd., Blue Line Airways Ltd., Skytravel Ltd., International Airways Ltd., Somerton Airways Ltd. and Northern Air Charter Ltd. The last, operating at Woolsington for a short time in 1946, employed two Proctor 5s, G-AGTD and G-AHTK, specially fitted with rounded rear windows. Outstanding examples of personal Proctor 5s were G-AHGL currently

One of two Proctor 5s built with rounded rear windows for Northern Air Charter in 1946.

The recess for the sliding window distinguished the Proctor 4, shown here, from the Proctor 5. G-AJMX was an air taxi operated by Short Bros. Ltd. at Rochester in 1947.

owned and flown for 13 years by E. S. Davis; G-AIET, now the sole Mk. 5A with Gipsy Queen 30-2 engine, currently J. J. Duke's Eastleigh based 'Fourflusher' but previously one of the 'Windmill Girl' series; and G-AHGN, commissioned by the M.C.A. in 1946 for the Civil Air Attaché in Washington and now flown in the Bahamas under American marks as N558E. Many long-distance flights were made, including those of N. S. Norway to Australia in G-AKIW 1949 and A. J. Bradshaw to New Zealand in G-AHWW 'Kiwi Wanderer' 1951.

In true Vega Gull tradition, the 92nd–95th production aircraft were delivered to the R.A.F. in September 1946 for Air Attaché duties in Rome and other European capitals as VN895–8. VN896 did not survive, but in September 1953 the others came up for disposal and were civilianised at Croydon, Squires Gate and Eastleigh respectively as G-ANAT, 'MD and 'GG.

SPECIFICATION

Manufacturers: (Proctor 4) Percival Aircraft Ltd., Luton Airport, Beds., sub-contracted by F. Hills and Sons Ltd., Trafford Park, Manchester.

(Proctor 5) Percival Aircraft Ltd., Luton Airport, Beds.

Power Plants: (Proctor 4 and 5) One 210 h.p. de Havilland Gipsy Queen 2.

(Proctor 5A) One 250 h.p. de Havilland Gipsy Queen 30-2.

Dimensions: Span, 39 ft. 6 in. Length, 28 ft. 2 in. Height, 7 ft. 3 in. Wing area, 202 sq. ft.

Weights: Tare weight, 2,340 lb. All-up weight, 3,500 lb.

Performance: Maximum speed, 157 m.p.h. Cruising speed, 135 m.p.h. Initial climb, 700 ft./min. Ceiling, 14,000 ft. Range, 500 miles.

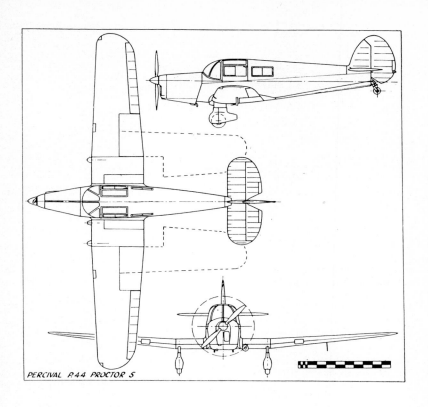

PERCIVAL P.44 PROCTOR 5

203

The prototype seven seat Prentice conversion G-APJE flying near Southend, August 1959. (*'The Aeroplane' Photo.*)

Percival P.40 Prentice 1

Thirty pre-production and 323 production Prentices were delivered to the R.A.F. in 1948, superseding the Tiger Moth as the basic trainer and introducing variable pitch airscrew, flap and radio techniques into ab initio instruction. Originally intended to carry an instructor and two pupils, they were employed in practice as side-by-side two seaters and were of all metal construction powered by one Gipsy Queen 32 motor. Cut-away elevators and turned-up wing tips were modifications made when prototype trials revealed inadequate rudder control and some lateral instability. The Prentices came from two production lines, one in the parent factory at Luton and one at Brough, where they were built under sub-contract by Blackburn and General Aircraft Ltd.

In November 1947 two pre-production machines, VR209 and VR210, were allotted civil markings G-AKLF and 'LG for overseas demonstration flights which resulted in production orders from the Argentine, Lebanese and Indian Air Forces.

Ousted from R.A.F. service by the Hunting Percival Provost, the Prentice was finally struck off charge in 1955, 248 being sold to Aviation Traders Ltd. early in the following year. Between April and July 1956, 33 pilots ferried 92 Prentices to Southend from R.A.F. maintenance units at Cosford, High Ercall and Shawbury and another 58 to Stansted. All carried roughly daubed civil markings, and in the following October–November, 26 more were delivered at Stansted and four at Southend, where five more landed on May 31, 1957. Thirty others arrived at Stansted that summer, half of which, stranded at M.U.s with unserviceable power plants, were ferried by means of four slave engines. The R.A.F. Signallers' School at Swanton Morley, last employer of the R.A.F. Prentice, then added its fleet of 22 aircraft to Aviation Traders' stock. Even the six airframes used for ground instruction at St. Athan were acquired, and in September 1958 a solitary pre-production Prentice VR189, surviving at R.A.E. Bedford, was located, bought and registered G-APPL to bring the company's grand total to 252. The aircraft were then prepared for long-term storage, withdrawals being made from the vast dumps at

Stansted and Southend as required. One other Prentice, VS652, registered to Vendair Ltd. in November 1957 and flown to Croydon for conversion as G-APIF, was the only aircraft not acquired by Aviation Traders Ltd. Civilianisation was abandoned, and in July 1958 the machine was scrapped on the dump of Minworth Metals Ltd., Castle Bromwich, along with VR209 and VR210, civil demonstrators of a decade earlier.

Stripped of military equipment, the relatively new Prentices were ripe for development as five seaters in the private, executive and charter roles. Modifications to engine and airframe necessary to satisfy civil requirements proved long and tedious, and two aircraft, G-AOKT and 'WT, selected as test vehicles were needed to carry out intensive flight trials at Southend, which lasted from June to November 1956. The results were incorporated in the 'prototype' G-AOPL, rolled out in the following March, granted a full C. of A. on September 9, 1957, and despatched on a sales tour of West, East and South Africa by the Balfour (Marine) Engineering Co. Ltd. a year later. Next 'off', G-AONS, with seven hour tankage and named 'Koomela', left Southend on March 5, 1958, piloted by D. J. Hill, who with wife as passenger, reached Melbourne on April 29. Others converted at Southend during 1958–59 included G-APIU, fitted with two stage amber instrument flying screens and decorated in the distinctive blue and yellow of the Surrey Flying Club; a similar machine G-APIT for the Airwork Flying School, Perth; a single seater G-APIY fitted with a steel banner and glider towing yoke under the rudder; the four seat G-AOPO fitted for towing and delivered from Southend to a Belgian operator, on September 9, 1958; G-AOLP, 'PL and G-APPL, delivered to private owners; 'KF and 'LU for Maitland Air Charters Ltd., Biggin Hill; 'MK for T. D. Keegan at Lulsgate; 'NB for No. 600 Sqn. Flying Group, Biggin Hill; and the test vehicle 'WT, fitted with long-range tanks for Trans Mediterranean Airways, Beirut, Lebanon. Recent developments include G-APJE with bench type front seat for three abreast, increasing the short range seating capacity to seven, and also the trial installation of the Gipsy Queen 70 engine.

Overseas demonstrator G-AKLG at Redhill in 1948, inscribed 'Percival Prentice' in Greek and Arabic.

Manufacturers: Percival Aircraft Ltd., Luton Airport, Beds, sub-contracted by
Blackburn and General Aircraft Ltd., Brough, E. Yorks.

Power Plant: One 250 h.p. de Havilland Gipsy Queen 30–2.
One 340 h.p. de Havilland Gipsy Queen 70.

Dimensions: Span, 46 ft. 0 in. Length, 31 ft. 6½ in. Height, 10 ft. 0 in. Wing area,
305 sq. ft.

Weights: Tare weight, 3,232 lb. All-up weight, 4,350 lb.

Performance: Maximum speed, 143 m.p.h. Cruising speed, 126 m.p.h. Initial
climb, 650 ft./min. Ceiling, 10,500 ft. Range, 350 miles.

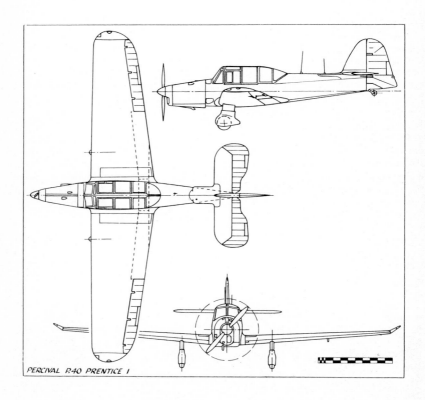

PERCIVAL P.40 PRENTICE I

The first production Prince after conversion to Mk. 2 with sloping windscreen.
(*Photo: Percival Aircraft Ltd.*)

Percival P.50 Prince

After the war Percival Aircraft Ltd. produced the five seat P.48 Merganser, which was of all-metal, stressed-skin construction with fabric-covered control surfaces and built primarily for passenger convenience. Chief designer A. A. Bage therefore chose the high-wing layout to give the best possible view and built an exceptionally roomy fuselage mounted on a retractable tricycle undercarriage to give a low, level floor for ease of entry. The fuselage was completed in November 1946 and immediately despatched by train ferry to the Paris Aero Show. Non-availability of the production Gipsy Queen 51 or suitable alternatives had already doomed the Merganser to extinction, but two such engines were loaned from the Ministry of Supply development order. With these, the first flight took place at Luton on May 9, 1947, the aircraft carrying the Class B marking X-2 in place of its allotted G-AHMH. Extensive flight trials culminated in its appearance at the Radlett S.B.A.C. Show in the following September and in data which speeded the production of a larger type, the P.50 Prince.

This medium range transport, fitted with Alvis Leonides nine cylinder radials, inaugurated an era of fruitful co-operation between Percivals and Alvis Ltd. in which engine development made possible the full exploitation of the basic airframe. The prototype Prince, G-23-1, later G-ALCM, flown for the first time at Luton on May 13, 1948, by Wing Cdr. H. P. Powell, shared the robust single engined performance of its predecessor and the addition of a small dorsal fin was the only major modification found necessary. Outwardly resembling the Merganser, its heavy-duty, fork-mounted mainwheels and fluted, metal-clad control surfaces were the only visible concessions to the increased weight and speed.

An initial batch of 10 Princes, laid down during prototype trials, benefited from further wind tunnel tests at Toulouse in September 1948. In the following March Capt. R. W. Hornall took off from Luton in the first production Prince 1, G-ALFZ, on a 25,000 mile proving flight to the Cape, carrying out tropical trials at Khartoum, Nairobi and Accra en route. The next machine, G-ALJA, made a demonstration tour to Bombay via the Near East, flying continuously to simulated airline schedules. G-ALRY, a survey version built for Percival's associate company, Hunting Aerosurveys Ltd., and designated P.54, was exhibited at the Farnborough S.B.A.C. Show in September 1949. Operated by a crew of three, it had an observer's station in a lengthened nose as well as vertical and oblique camera hatches. Piloted by J. H. Saffery, it left via Bovingdon on February 2, 1950, on the 3,200 mile positioning flight to Sharjah on the Persian Gulf for a four month oil prospecting contract, first of several carried out in Persia, Turkey, Siam and Kuwait. From May 1956 to January 1959 it was seconded to the firm's East African branch at Nairobi.

The sloping front windscreen, an aesthetic and aerodynamic refinement incorporated in the survey version, was also fitted to the Prince 1s 'FZ and 'JA in April 1950. This and main spar modifications permitting an increase in all-up weight to 11,000 lb., created the Prince 2. A contract for four 10-passenger Prince 2s for Transportes Aereos Norte do Brasil

The Merganser in Class B markings, showing the single front and double rear doors.

Percival P.54 Prince 4D G-AMOT, formerly operated by Hunting Aerosurveys Ltd., showing the survey nose. (*Photo: Hunting Percival Aircraft Ltd.*)

The President 1 prototype. (*Photo: Hunting Percival Aircraft Ltd.*)

resulted in the passage of 'FZ through Prestwick on August 7, 1950. Carrying a 100 gallon overload fuel tank in the cabin, the delivery flight was made via Keflavik, Bluie West One, Goose Bay, Dorval, Miami and Jamaica, a route already flown by the Shell Company's Prince 2s G-ALWG and 'WH. Fitted as six seat executive and eight seat convertible freighter respectively, these had arrived at Maracaibo, Venezuela, on April 18, 1950, having covered the 6,500 miles from Luton in 14 days. The much travelled 'JA, also convertible, left Luton on May 30, 1950, piloted by Gp. Capt. Douglas Bader to further Shell's interests in Borneo.

Development of the Leonides engine resulting in the 550 h.p. series 502/4 driving de Havilland constant speed, feathering and reversing airscrews made possible the presentation of the much improved Prince 3 G-AMMB at the 1952 S.B.A.C. Show. Operating at higher economical cruising speed at an all-up weight of 11,500 lb., the demonstrator was equipped for six seat executive use and later sold to the South African Iron and Steel Industrial Corporation. Of the five ordered by the Shell Refining and Marketing Co. Ltd., G-AMKK and 'LX went to Borneo, G-AMLW and 'LY to Venezuela, 'LZ being based in Britain. A special executive model, G-AMPR, designated Prince 3E, was delivered to the

Standard Motor Co. Ltd. at Baginton, but the appearance of series 502/5 engines then created the Prince 3B. Three of these, G-AMLW–'LY, were equipped with radar nose, astrodome and the necessary equipment for calibrating airfield radio, radar and navigational aids by the M.T.C.A. Flight at Stansted. Progressive engine development resulted in their upgrading to Prince 4B in November 1956 and to Prince 6B in July 1958.

Although a number of Prince 3s were sold overseas, only one, a long-nosed survey model, G-AMNT, designated Prince 3A, was ferried in British marks. Later, in Thai Air Force colours, it carried out survey work for the Mapping Organisation of the Ministry of Defence. Another survey machine, G-AMOT, specially equipped with airborne magnetometer equipment for use in Canada by Hunting Aerosurveys Ltd., was designated Prince 3D. On its return in the following year it was upgraded to Prince 4D and transferred to the uranium survey in Kenya, where it was destroyed in a wheels-up landing in the jungle in 1958. Similar work was carried on in Australia by the one-time Shell Prince 3, 'LW, which returned from Venezuela for modification to Prince 4 before being flown from Elstree to Mascot by R. Keeling in December 1954 and handed over to Hunting Adastra Geophysics Ltd. It flew with appropriate and phonetic Australian marks until its return to Luton in February 1959.

Large military contracts for the wide span P.66 Pembroke ended Prince production in 1953 but led to a demand for second-hand specimens. G-ALWH was flown home from South America and sold to the Sperry

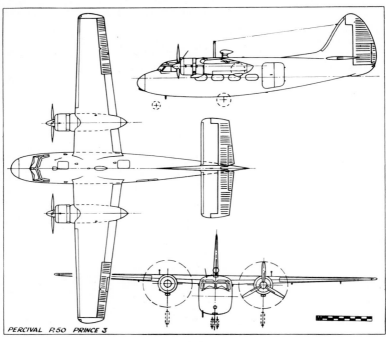

PERCIVAL P.50 PRINCE 3

Gyroscope Co. Ltd. as a test and demonstration vehicle. G-AMLY followed suit for executive use by Martin-Baker Aircraft Ltd. in 1955, but after upgrading to Prince 4 passed through Bahrein on September 3, 1958, en route to the British Malayan Petroleum Co. Ltd. in Borneo. Fitted with series 503/4 engines, the executive Prince 3E G-AMPR became the sole Prince 4E, prior to sale to the Tanganyika Government who named it 'Prince Hal' in February 1956.

The ultimate development of the type, G-AOJG, initially the Prince 5 but later known as the President 1, first flew at Luton on August 26, 1956, differing from the Pembroke only in the shape of the nacelles, modified at the rear to improve single engined handling. It was shown at the 1956 S.B.A.C. Show as an executive six seater and left Luton on April 29, 1957, for a European sales tour resulting in a frustrated order for three Presidents for a Spanish airline. The first example of the President 2, G-APMO, built for the M.T.C.A. Flight, was exhibited at the 1958 S.B.A.C. Show, but the second was actually the third Spaniard EC-APC, reworked for demonstration abroad as G-APVJ. One military Pembroke, formerly in service with the Empire Test Pilots' School, was delivered to the Air Navigation and Trading Co. Ltd. at Squires Gate on June 29, 1958, for civil conversion as G-APNL.

SPECIFICATION

Manufacturers: Percival Aircraft Ltd., Luton Airport, Beds., name changed to Hunting Percival Aircraft Ltd. April 26, 1954, further changed to Hunting Aircraft Ltd., December 5, 1957.

Power Plants:
(Merganser)	Two 296 h.p. de Havilland Gipsy Queen 51.
(Prince 1 and 2)	Two 520 h.p. Alvis Leonides 501/4.
(P.54)	Two 520 h.p. Alvis Leonides 501/4.
(Prince 3, 3A, 3E)	Two 550 h.p. Alvis Leonides 502/4.
(Prince 3B and 3D)	Two 560 h.p. Alvis Leonides 502/5.
(Prince 4 and 4E)	Two 550 h.p. Alvis Leonides 503/4.
(Prince 4B and 4D)	Two 550 h.p. Alvis Leonides 503/5.
(Prince 6B)	Two 540 h.p. Alvis Leonides 504/5A.
(President 1)	Two 520 h.p. Alvis Leonides 503/5A.
	Two 540 h.p. Alvis Leonides 504/5A.
(President 2)	Two 560 h.p. Alvis Leonides 514/5A.
(Pembroke)	Two 550 h.p. Alvis Leonides 127.

	Merganser	Prince 1 and 2	P.54	Prince 3, 4, 6	President 1, 2 and Pembroke
Span	47 ft. 9 in.	56 ft. 0 in.	56 ft. 0 in.	56 ft. 0 in.	64 ft. 6 in.
Length	40 ft. 8 in.	42 ft. 10 in.	45 ft. 3½ in.	42 ft. 10 in.†	46 ft. 4 in.
Height	13 ft. 9 in.	16 ft. 1 in.	16 ft. 1 in.	16 ft. 1 in.	16 ft. 0 in.
Wing area	319 sq. ft.	365 sq. ft.	365 sq. ft.	365 sq. ft.	400 sq. ft.
Tare weight	5,300 lb.	7,364 lb.	7,607 lb.	8,038 lb.	9,136 lb.
All-up weight	7,300 lb.	10,659 lb.*	11,000 lb.	11,000 lb.‡	13,500 lb.
Maximum speed	193 m.p.h.	216 m.p.h.	202 m.p.h.	229 m.p.h.	212 m.p.h.
Cruising speed	160 m.p.h.	179 m.p.h.	168 m.p.h.	197 m.p.h.	164 m.p.h.
Initial climb	1,010 ft./min.	1,110 ft./min.	1,100 ft./min.	1,650 ft./min.	1,500 ft./min.
Ceiling	24,000 ft.	23,500 ft.	23,000 ft.	23,400 ft.	22,000 ft.
Range	800 miles	940 miles	1,300 miles	894 miles	1,075 miles

* Prince 2 A.U.W. 11,000 lb. † Prince 3A length 45 ft. 3½ in. ‡ Improved braking on Prince 4 and 6, permitting A.U.W. of 11,500 lb. and 11,800 lb. respectively.

P. G. Masefield flying the Cub L-4H G-AIYX, experimentally fitted with the 55 h.p. Coventry Victor Flying Neptune engine in 1955. (*Photo courtesy of 'The Aeroplane'.*)

Piper Cub

The Cub strut-braced, high-wing, cabin monoplane, produced in 1935 by the Taylor Aircraft Company in the U.S.A., was a simple, robust and fool-proof light aeroplane designed for mass production. A mainplane with spruce spars and duralumin ribs was bolted directly to the top of a fabric-covered, welded steel tube fuselage seating two occupants in tandem. Power was supplied by a 40 h.p. Continental flat four, and the Cub would cruise for 4 hours at 75 m.p.h. on 10 gallons of fuel. It was cheap, could be flown in and out of small fields, would land at 30 m.p.h. and found such favour among inexperienced pilots that 761 were sold by the end of 1936.

A. J. Walter, then of the Tollerton Aero Club, and now of Gatwick, sole British concessionaire for over 20 years, imported a demonstrator, G-AEIK, first of five British owned Taylor Cub J-2 aircraft. Flown by P. J. Field-Richards, it averaged 76·75 m.p.h. to reach third place in the Folkestone Trophy Race at Lympne on August 1, 1936. A second Cub, G-AESK, arrived in the following year for Miss E. B. Walter of Croydon and won the Thanet Air Trophy at Ramsgate on August 21, 1937, at 71·5 m.p.h. piloted by P. B. Elwell. Two others, 'XY and 'XZ, later joined by 'IK, were the first aircraft of the newly formed County Flying Club at Rearsby. The Taylor Aircraft Company was reorganised in 1937 as the Piper Aircraft Corporation under the direction of W. T. Piper. The company's former president and chief engineer C. G. Taylor then left to form the Taylor–Young Airplane Company. Thereafter the aircraft were re-named Piper Cubs, the last British J-2, G-AFFH, being delivered to R. E. Gardner at Hamsey Green in August 1938 and flown round the coast on floats later in the year.

Introduced in 1938, the Cub J-3 featured a horn balanced rudder, better upholstery and improved instrumentation, but whereas the hinged starboard side panels of the J-2 were detachable for open cockpit flying, those of the newer type were not. G-AFFJ, first of four J-3s imported by A. J. Walter, experimentally fitted with a single bladed airscrew and demonstrated by P. B. Elwell at the Royal Aeronautical Society's Heathrow Garden Party on May 8, 1938, was later sold to the County Flying Club. Then followed 'IO, also with single bladed airscrew, and 'IY flown from the fields of Workshop Farm, Withybrook, Coventry, by H. Perkins. Finally came 'IZ fitted with a 50 h.p. Continental, designated J-3C-50 and kept at Hanworth by K. B. Hobbs.

The side-by-side, two seat Cub Coupé G-AFPP arrived at Hanworth in February 1939, first of 24 imported to enjoy one brief pre-war summer. With the exception of 'PP, which was a J-4 with 50 h.p. Continental and the Ipswich Aero Club's 'TC, a J-4B with Franklin engine, all were J-4As with the 65 h.p. Continental. They brought a sharp reduction in the cost of instructional flying, for which purpose the Wiltshire School of Flying, High Post, used 'PP, 'SY, 'SZ and 'WR; the Ipswich Aero Club 'TB, 'TC,

First Cub ever imported into Britain, G-AEIK was built by the Taylor Aircraft Company and boasted long exhaust pipes.

Cub J-3 G-AFIO at Hanworth in 1938, with single bladed airscrew.

213

Cub Coupé J-4A G-AFSZ at Shoreham on Goodyear Trophy day, August 28, 1954.

Cub L-4H G-AJBE at Elstree in April 1947, showing the extended rear windows of the military type. This aircraft donated its markings to a Halifax, became G-AKNC in April 1948, later flew under American ownership and crashed in Finland as OH-CPC on January 15, 1952.

'VF, 'VG and 'VM; the Midland Aero Club (Rearsby) Ltd. 'TE; the Inverness Aero Club 'WA and 'WB; the Plymouth and District Aero Club 'WS, 'WU, 'WV and 'WW; and C.T.F. Aviation Ltd., Watchfield, 'XS and 'XT. The farm-based J-3 'IY was sold to the West Suffolk Aero Club and replaced by Cub Coupé 'TD. One other, 'VL, also entered private ownership with E. G. A. Bramall in a field at Blandford, Dorset.

Soon after the outbreak of war the majority of the Cub Coupés were impressed for R.A.F. communications, but the earlier models were considered unsuitable. In 1946 the Cub J-2s G-AFFH, G-AEXY and 'XZ emerged from storage along with J-3s 'FJ and 'IZ, only to be faced with import restrictions on American spares. With the exception of 'XZ, still extant but unairworthy at Farnborough Grange, they flew privately with numerous owners until this situation forced their sale abroad, the little

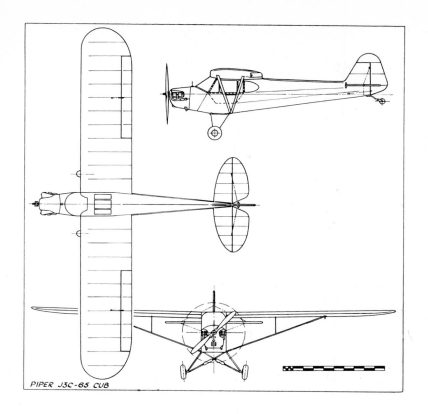

PIPER J3C-65 CUB

J-2s leaving Croydon on March 21, 1953, for the long delivery flight to Spain. The spares problem also proved the undoing of six Cub Coupés which survived the war, although 'PP flew at Cambridge with one owner, W. Smyth, for 10 years until sold in Germany in 1956. The others included 'TC (converted to J-4A), 'WS and 'XS overhauled by Western Airways Ltd. in 1946. Today only G-AFSZ remains, flying in true Cub fashion from E. R. Barker's private strip at Cranleigh, Surrey.

The final phase in the Cub's history as a British civil aeroplane came in 1946-49 when 13 war-surplus U.S.A.F. Piper L-4H Grasshopper light liaison monoplanes were civilianised. Differing from the pre-war Cub J-3 by their mark of engine and extra rear window area, they were loosely and incorrectly described as Cubs J3C-65. The largest batch, comprising eight aircraft G-AISP, 'SV–SX, 'YU, 'YV, 'YX and G-AJDS, was overhauled at Hanworth in 1947, four each for W. S. Shackleton Ltd. and V.I.P. Services Ltd. They went into service with the Wolverhampton Flying School Ltd.; W. A. Herbert, Workington; G. Bickley, Wolverhampton; the Community Flying Club, Woodley; and the Denham Aero Club. One, G-AISW, was flown by C. J. Packer, owner of several vintage aircraft relics, from a field behind his garage at Burton, Wiltshire. He was drowned in the North Sea, east of the Goodwins, on February 16, 1948, while flying 'SW home from Le Touquet. G-AIYX, used by the B.K.S. Flying Group at Southend during the 1954 season, was modified by the company in 1955 as a vehicle for the 50 hour flight test programme of the 55 h.p. Coventry Victor Flying Neptune flat four engine. Another, G-AJDS, counted the Blackpool and Fylde Aero Club among its many owners, and G-AIYV returned to American ownership in July 1958 to fly with the U.S.A.F. sponsored Mildenhall Aero Club. Four newly built Cubs with several post-war modifications, correctly designated J3C-65, were imported by A. J. Walter in 1947 for resale abroad. After erection and test flying at Redhill they were despatched to Eire, Portugal and Spain, where dollar expenditure was unrestricted. Several other ex-U.S.A.F. L-4H machines saw considerable service. G-AIIH, civilianised at Sywell for A. C. Cox in 1947, is currently flown by W. T. Knapton from College Farm, Heyford, Oxford. Airborne Taxi Services' one-time be-spatted and Elstree based G-AKAA, now flies at Stansted with the Sky-ways Flying Group. H. Tinsley's G-ALGH and E. N. Heywood's G-ALMA, kept at Elstree and Broxbourne respectively in the early 'fifties were eventually sold abroad together with the final British Cubs. These were both former American Embassy Flying Club aircraft, the first, G-ALVR, overhauled by A. J. Walter at Gatwick in 1950, spent many years at Balado with G. Whyte. The second, G-ANXP, converted by Hants and Sussex Aviation Ltd. at Portsmouth in five days, left for Germany via Ferryfield on October 14, 1955.

SPECIFICATION

Manufacturers: Taylor Aircraft Company, Lockhaven, Pennsylvania, U.S.A., name
    changed to Piper Aircraft Corporation in 1937.
Power Plants: (J-2)   One 40 h.p. Continental A-40-4.
                   One 50 h.p. Continental A-50-5.
      (J-3)   One 50 h.p. Continental A-50-5 or A-50-7.
                   One 65 h.p. Continental A-65-1.
      (J-4)   One 50 h.p. Continental A-50-3.
      (J-4A) One 65 h.p. Continental A-65-1 or A-65-3.
      (J-4B) One 60 h.p. Franklin 4AC-171.
      (L-4H) One 65 h.p. Continental A-65-8S.
      (J-3C) One 65 h.p. Continental A-65-F8.

	Cub J-2	Cub J-4A	Cub J3C-65
Span . . .	35 ft. 2½ in.	36 ft. 2 in.	35 ft. 2½ in.
Length . . .	22 ft. 5 in.	22 ft. 6 in.	22 ft. 4½ in.
Height . . .	6 ft. 8 in.	6 ft. 8 in.	6 ft. 8 in.
Wing area . .	178·5 sq. ft.	183·75 sq. ft.	178·5 sq. ft.
Tare weight . .	563 lb.	710 lb.	730 lb.
All-up weight .	970 lb.	1,200 lb.	1,220 lb.
Maximum speed .	87 m.p.h.	93 m.p.h.	100 m.p.h.
Cruising speed .	74 m.p.h.	83 m.p.h.	87 m.p.h.
Initial climb . .	450 ft./min.	650 ft./min.	514 ft./min.
Ceiling . . .	12,000 ft.	12,000 ft.	14,000 ft.
Range . . .	210 miles	340 miles	300 miles

G-ABDO, first of the Genet engined Redwing II aircraft. (*'Flight' Photo.*)

Robinson Redwing

The Redwing side-by-side two seater appeared in May 1930 at the height of the popular enthusiasm for light aeroplanes. Designed by John Kenworthy and built in a workshop near Croydon by the Robinson Aircraft Co. Ltd., newly founded by Capt. P. G. Robinson, the prototype G-AAUO was powered by a 75 h.p. A.B.C. Hornet flat four engine. Its plywood-covered fuselage was supported on a wide-track, split-axle undercarriage, the shock legs of which were attached to the top longerons. As the name suggested, the Redwing's folding mainplanes were doped red overall and were of generous proportions to give easy flying and slow landing characteristics. In the light of early trials, the Genet IIA five cylinder radial was chosen as a more suitable engine and powered the Redwing II prototype G-ABDO which first flew in October 1930. The firm was then financially reorganised as Redwing Aircraft Ltd. and larger premises were obtained in one of the former A.D.C. hangars at Croydon Aerodrome, enabling work to begin on a small batch of production aircraft.

Both prototypes were sold, Redwing I to the Scarborough Aeroplane Club and Redwing II to the newly formed L.G.O.C. Flying Club at Broxbourne, where F/Lt. N. M. S. Russell, test pilot to the manufacturers, became the busmen's first instructor. By the end of 1931, eight more Redwings had been constructed, two of which, G-ABLA and 'MF, went to High Post for use by the Wiltshire School of Flying Ltd. Another, 'MJ, spent two months at Scarborough, thereafter counting comedian Will Hay, Miss Delphine Reynolds of Gatwick and Miss Rosalind Norman among its several owners. The Croydon premises were vacated in March 1932 and the works transferred to Blue Barns Aerodrome, Colchester, where Redwings G-ABMU, 'MV and 'NP could be serviced for the Colchester branch of the Eastern Counties Aeroplane Club Ltd., Ipswich.

The official opening of Blue Barns on March 10 was quickly followed by a similar ceremony at Gatwick on July 1, when the firm also took over the Surrey Aero Club and added Redwings G-ABMJ and 'OK to its fleet, eight Redwings being lined up on the aerodrome for the occasion. The firm had again been reconstituted and now numbered designer John Kenworthy and the Junkers concessionaire H. R. Trost among its directors.

Only two more aircraft were built, however, both Redwing IIIs, using the same fuselage, empennage and engine installation but with reduced wing area for improved cross country performance. Better streamlining of the undercarriage also contributed to its higher cruising speed. The first Redwing III, G-ABRL, was delivered at Gatwick from the Colchester factory on May 11, 1933, but the second, 'RM, reverted to Mk. II standard before sale to the Eastern Counties Aeroplane Club. The Colchester branch having closed down, 'RM went to Ipswich to join the surviving Redwing II 'NP, both continuing in service until 1934. Frequent breakages where the main undercarriage legs met the top longerons, coupled with shortage of spares, resulted in cannibalisation and the eventual emergence of 'RM, re-erected with most of the major assemblies of 'NP. It remained on the club's strength until wrecked in a forced landing at Frinton in the autumn of 1935.

In Mk. III form, G-ABRL was not found particularly successful and gained no C. of A. until it reverted to Mk. II with standard wings in 1934. Leaving Croydon for Cape Town on January 4, 1935, piloted by Mrs. Keith Miller, 'RL crossed the Sahara, to reach Gao on the 24th. A few days later it made a forced landing 10 miles from Kotonu, Dahomey, and was wrecked through striking a tree in swerving to avoid natives.

Today the only surviving Redwing is G-ABNX, last Redwing II to be built and originally sold to C. P. Hunter at Rhos Ucha, North Wales, 1933–35. After service with S. Reid at Macmerry, it was acquired by C. W. Morrison and reappeared in dismantled condition at Elstree in

The Hornet engined prototype Redwing I. (*'Flight' Photo.*)

The Redwing III sesquiplane. (*'Flight' Photo.*)

1945. After delivery by road to the College of Aeronautical Engineering at Redhill on April 16, 1951, it was superficially reconditioned for the Fifty Years of Flying Exhibition at Hendon in the following July. After several years at Panshanger awaiting overhaul and the reconditioning of its Genet engine, it was put into storage at Heath End, near Farnham, Surrey, until acquired by John Pothecary and E. H. Gould and taken to Christchurch on December 18, 1959 for reconstruction.

SPECIFICATION

Manufacturers: The Robinson Aircraft Co. Ltd., Stafford Road, Wallington, Surrey. Name changed to Redwing Aircraft Ltd. April 1931, works moved to Blue Barns Aerodrome, Colchester, March 10, 1932. Registered office moved to Gatwick Airport, Horley, Surrey, July 1, 1932.

Power Plants: (Redwing I) One 75 h.p. A.B.C. Hornet.
(Redwing II and III) One 80 h.p. Armstrong Siddeley Genet IIA.

	Redwing I	Redwing II	Redwing III
Span . . .	30 ft. 6 in.	30 ft. 6 in.	24 ft. 0 in.
Length . . .	22 ft. 3 in.	22 ft. 8 in.	22 ft. 8 in.
Height . . .	8 ft. 7 in.	8 ft. 7 in.	—
Wing area . .	250 sq. ft.	250 sq. ft.	154 sq. ft.
Tare weight . .	860 lb.	870 lb.	850 lb.
All-up weight .	1,325 lb.	1,450 lb.*	1,500 lb.
Maximum speed .	92 m.p.h.	95 m.p.h.	—
Cruising speed .	84 m.p.h.	85 m.p.h.	90 m.p.h.
Initial climb . .	650 ft./min.	800 ft./min.	—
Range . . .	—	275 miles	550 miles

* Increased to 1,500 lb. in 1938.

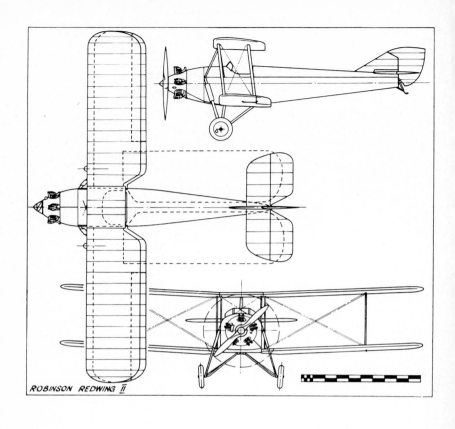

ROBINSON REDWING II

220

G-ACDP, an Air Service Training Cutty Sark with Genet Major engines, taking off from Southampton Water. (*Photo courtesy of W. K. Kilsby.*)

Saro A.17 Cutty Sark

In 1928 Sir Alliott Verdon Roe joined forces with Mr. John Lord and acquired a controlling interest in S. E. Saunders Ltd., flying-boat builders of Cowes, Isle of Wight. The firm was then reconstituted as Saunders-Roe Ltd., its first product being the twin engined, four seat, Cutty Sark cabin flying-boat. The Avro-Fokker, watertight, plywood-covered, cantilever wing was bolted directly to the gunwales of the corrosion-resisting Alclad hull. Two 105 h.p. A.D.C. Hermes I engines were mounted on pylons, well clear of the spray, with generous outboard floats just below, beaching being carried out by passing a wheeled axle through a sleeve built into the hull. The prototype, G-AAIP, made its first flight at Cowes on July 4, 1929, piloted by F/O Chilton and left the water in 6 seconds. After its public presentation at the Olympia Aero Show, the same pilot flew the Cutty Sark to La Baule Seaplane Rally on September 14, 1929, carrying the Director of Civil Aviation, Sir Sefton Brancker. A wide-track, retractable, amphibian undercarriage was then fitted and the machine sold to Norman Holden, for whom it was flown by E. Hordern. Shortly after, it was acquired by Messrs. Kirston and Mace for a service between Woolston, Southampton and Jersey. Later the performance was considerably improved by the installation of closely cowled 120 h.p. Gipsy II engines and between March 26 and April 23, 1931, the manufacturers' chief test pilot S. D. Scott carried out a 3,000 mile sales tour to Dubrovnik, Belgrade and Budapest and also to the Stockholm Exhibition in the June. Early in 1932 Messrs. Kirston and Mace formed British Amphibious Air Lines Ltd. and acquired a second Cutty Sark, G-ABBC, formerly the Heston-based private aircraft of Mr. Francis Francis. Both amphibians were based at Squires Gate and operated via Liverpool to the Isle of Man, landing in Douglas Harbour or at Ronaldsway according to the weather.

Twelve Cutty Sarks were constructed, eight of British registry. G-AAVX, originally built as a flying-boat for the Hon. A. E. Guinness and launched in May 1930, spent several years under tropical conditions on club and taxi work as an amphibian with the Royal Singapore Flying Club, until the plywood wing became so warped that the aircraft was

221

scrapped in 1935. The ninth aircraft, allotted British marks G-ABVF for test flying at Cowes, was a pure flying-boat to the order of a Japanese pilot Yoshihara for a flight from San Francisco to Japan. Long-range tanks and blind-flying equipment were fitted and 'VF, powered by a 240 h.p. Lynx radial, was unique as the only single engined Cutty Sark.

The remaining aircraft were powered by 140 h.p. Genet Major seven-cylinder radials. Two were shipped to Hong Kong, one for instructional use by the Far East Flying School as VR-HAY and the other for sale in China. Another, G-ADAF, was exported to the island of San Domingo in the West Indies by R. H. Kulka Ltd. The remaining two, G-ACDP and 'DR, delivered to Air Service Training Ltd., Hamble, were the best known of all Cutty Sarks, familiar sights in the Solent from 1933 to 1938 on their

The prototype Cutty Sark in its ultimate form with amphibian undercarriage and Gipsy II engines. (*'Flight' Photo.*)

The long range single engined Cutty Sark G-ABVF, built to Japanese order. (*Photo: Saunders-Roe Ltd.*)

instructional, navigational and seamanship sorties. In 1937 they were joined by the machine which had lain at Hong Kong after the sale to China had fallen through five years previously. This became G-AETI and, in common with 'DP and G-ABBC of British Air Lines, was broken up during the war.

SPECIFICATION

Manufacturers: Saunders-Roe Ltd., East Cowes, Isle of Wight.
Power Plants: Two 105 h.p. A.D.C. Cirrus Hermes I.
          Two 120 h.p. de Havilland Gipsy II.
          Two 130 h.p. de Havilland Gipsy III.
          Two 140 h.p. Armstrong Siddeley Genet Major I.
          One 240 h.p. Armstrong Siddeley Lynx IVC.
Dimensions: Span, 45 ft. 0 in. Length, 34 ft. 4 in. Height, 11 ft. 2 in. Wing area, 320 sq. ft.

	As flying-boat	As amphibian	
	Hermes I	Gipsy II	Genet Major
Tare weight . .	2,375 lb.	2,670 lb.	2,725 lb.
All-up weight .	3,500 lb.	3,850 lb.	3,900 lb.
Maximum speed .	105 m.p.h.	103 m.p.h.	107 m.p.h.
Cruising speed .	85 m.p.h.	85 m.p.h.	90 m.p.h.
Initial climb . .	600 ft./min.	550 ft./min.	500 ft./min.
Ceiling . . .	9,500 ft.	9,000 ft.	9,000 ft.
Range . . .	340 miles	300 miles	315 miles

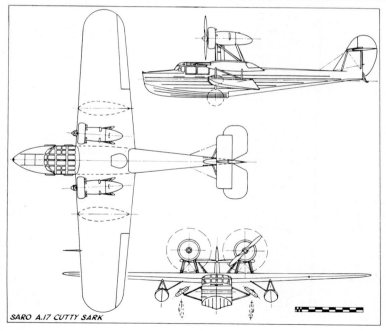

SARO A.17 CUTTY SARK

The prototype Pioneer flying slowly with slots and flaps extended. (*'Flight' Photo.*)

Scottish Aviation Prestwick Pioneer

First aircraft produced by Scottish Aviation Ltd., the Prestwick Pioneer was designed by Robert McIntyre to meet an Air Ministry requirement for a communications aircraft capable of operating into, and out of, confined spaces. It was a strut-braced, high-wing cabin monoplane of all-metal, stressed-skin construction powered by a 240 h.p. Gipsy Queen 32. Full span, controllable leading edge slats and Fowler type trailing edge flaps of generous area imparted sensational take off, landing and slow flying characteristics. Adequate trimming and control at forward speeds of the order of 30 m.p.h. were achieved by the use of an electrically operated, variable incidence tailplane and an unusually large rudder and elevator. The pilot sat centrally with maximum view, three passengers and luggage being accommodated behind.

VL515, the first prototype, made its debut at the Radlett S.B.A.C. Show in September 1947, but when no military contract was awarded, development continued for civil purposes. Trials proceeded throughout 1948 in the hands of test pilots N. J. Capper and R. C. W. Ellison, the aircraft, re-engined with a Gipsy Queen 34, flying under B conditions as G-31-1. It was exhibited as such at the 1948 S.B.A.C. Show, even though already registered G-AKBF. A decision to increase the passenger seats to four and improve the performance called for the installation of a more powerful engine. A number of power plants were considered, including the Pratt and Whitney Wasp R-1340, several of which were available following the dismantling of the company's Fokker F.22 G-AFZP. Final choice fell on the Alvis Leonides nine cylinder radial, the reworked prototype making its first flight as the Pioneer 2 in June 1950. Steep take off and short landing demonstrations by N. J. Capper at the 1950, 1951 and 1952 S.B.A.C. Shows drew attention, not only to its improved military potential and civil applications in the light transport, ambulance or agricultural roles but also to its docility. With the port half of the elevator torn away in a steep take off at the 1952 Show, the Pioneer continued its circuit to make an uneventful landing. The issue of an unrestricted C. of A. in May 1952, followed by helicopter style landings on 100 yard strips on the Hebridean islands of Mull and Iona, rounded off the development of Scotland's first commercial design and Britain's first STOL* transport.

The adoption of the Pioneer for casualty evacuation in the Malayan jungles by the R.A.F. necessitated a production line at Prestwick, and by the end of 1958 56 aircraft had been completed, including several for the Ceylon and Malayan Air Forces. During this period six aircraft were employed by the manufacturers as temporary civil demonstrators. The third R.A.F. aircraft became G-ANAZ for a few days in September 1953, purely for ferrying to, and exhibition at, the Farnborough S.B.A.C. Show. The fifth aircraft appeared in the following year as G-ANRG and afterwards masqueraded as an R.A.F. aircraft XH469 for participation in Exercise Battle Royal and the Battle of Britain display at Hendon. In the following June 'RG was despatched to the Far East, but during demonstration flights at Rangoon by A. F. Coker on July 23, 1955, was seriously damaged and shipped home for repair. A new demonstrator G-AODZ then completed the Far East sales tour and continues in the company's service to the present day. It was leased to Film Aviation Services Ltd. early in 1958 and went on location in French Equatorial Africa, piloted by K. Sissons, during the filming of 'Roots of Heaven', but returned to Prestwick for overhaul before leaving on a sales tour of Israel on August 24, 1958. European sales tours had been undertaken with G-AOGF and 'GK in 1956. In the same year G-AOUE went to the U.S.A. for evaluation by the American Authorities but nosed over when taking off on loose sand from Fort Bragg, North Carolina on November 6, returning as U.S.A.F. air freight to Prestwick, where it was deemed irrepairable and scrapped.

To avoid confusion with the Twin Pioneer, production of which was increasing, the civil Prestwick Pioneer 2 was redesignated Pioneer 1 in March 1957. Demonstrators G-AOFG and 'GK were eventually sold and left Prestwick together on March 2, 1958, at the commencement of their delivery flight to the Iranian Customs Authority and are now engaged on anti-smuggling patrols. Two others, test flown during the following summer under civil marks as G-APNW and 'NX, were crated and despatched to the Royal Ceylon Air Force.

* STOL—Short Take Off and Landing.

Manufacturers: Scottish Aviation Ltd., Prestwick Airport, Ayrshire, Scotland.
Power Plants: (Pioneer 1) One 240 h.p. de Havilland Gipsy Queen 32.
　　　　　　　　　　　One 250 h.p. de Havilland Gipsy Queen 34.
　　　　　(Pioneer 2*) One 520 h.p. Alvis Leonides 501/3.
　　　　　　　　　　　One 520 h.p. Alvis Leonides 501/4.
　　　　　　　　　　　One 560 h.p. Alvis Leonides 502/4.
　　　　　　　　　　　One 560 h.p. Alvis Leonides 502/7.
Dimensions: Span, 49 ft. 9 in. Length, 34 ft. 9 in. Height, 10 ft. 2½ in. Wing area,
　　390 sq. ft.

	Pioneer 1	Pioneer 2 *
Tare weight . . .	3,215 lb.	3,900 lb.
All-up weight . .	4,250 lb.	5,800 lb.
Maximum speed . .	126 m.p.h.	162 m.p.h.
Cruising speed . .	114 m.p.h.	121 m.p.h.
Initial climb . . .	900 ft./min.	880 ft./min.
Ceiling . . .	14,500 ft.	23,000 ft.
Range	500 miles	420 miles

* Redesignated Pioneer 1 in March 1957.

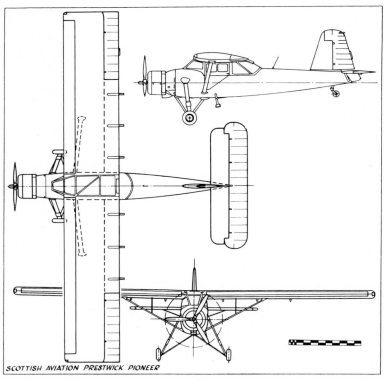

SCOTTISH AVIATION PRESTWICK PIONEER

Twin Pioneer G-APLW flying over the Scottish mountains. (*Photo : Scottish Aviation Ltd.*)

Scottish Aviation Twin Pioneer

The prototype Twin Pioneer G-ANTP, first flown at Prestwick on June 25, 1955, was a twin Leonides powered STOL transport of rugged aspect, carrying 16 passengers and two crew. It incorporated many of the well-proven features of its single engined predecessor, used identical outer wing panels, the same type of all-metal, stressed-skin construction, leading edge slats and Fowler flaps. A long travel undercarriage and generous triple tail surfaces guaranteed viceless behaviour when landing slowly in confined spaces. Flight trials proved its outstanding short run take off and landing ability, and the aircraft was presented at the 1955 Farnborough S.B.A.C. Show by Capt. Roy Smith. Three pre-production Twin Pioneers, G-AOEN, 'EO and 'EP, built and flown during 1956, embodied two important modifications. Leading edge slats inboard of the engines were found unnecessary and deleted. Ailerons which originally extended to the wing tips were clipped and full-chord tip fairings fitted. G-AOEN and 'EO made their appearance at the 1956 S.B.A.C. Show painted respectively in the colour schemes of Swissair and the K.L.M. subsidiary de Kroonduif.

Convinced that the Twin Pioneer had a high sales potential, Scottish Aviation Ltd. laid plans for the production of 200 aircraft and instituted a world-wide sales campaign. In January 1957 'EO was despatched to St. Moritz for a three month evaluation on Swissair's mountain ski traffic; 'EP, captained by Roy Smith, left for demonstrations in the Far East and Australia, while 'EN crossed the Atlantic by the Northern route for a tour of Central and South America. Both 'EP and 'EN carried spares for six months, in which time they covered 46,000 miles in 500 flying hours and 'EN crossed the Andes three times. It also gave full-load demonstrations at La Paz (13,404 ft.) and spent two years in Central America and the Caribbean, during which its annual C. of A. overhauls took place in Mexico. A fourth aircraft, G-AOER, was sold to Rio Tinto Fiance and Exploration Ltd., but remained in the factory until 1959 for the installation of airborne magnetometer equipment in special wing tip containers.

Trials were carried out with the prototype at Aden and Asmara to confirm the calculated performance under tropical conditions, and in June 1957 'EO excited considerable comment by flying a passenger service from Issy heliport to the Paris Aero Show at Le Bourget in competition with two Vertol helicopters. It left Prestwick for a South African sales sortie in the following December and was demonstrated en route to the oil companies at Tripoli, Libya. Here it suffered fatigue failure of a structural member in the port wing and crashed with the loss of the firm's managing director D. F. McIntyre, Capt. R. Smith and the engineer officer. Modifications having already been incorporated in subsequent aircraft, the production programme was not seriously affected, and by the end of 1958 over 70 Twin Pioneers had been delivered or were on order, 15 of which were of British registry.

One of these, G-APLW, the 32nd aircraft, became the firm's demonstrator in succession to 'EO and spent June 1958 visiting the Near East, the Sudan and Italy, King Hussein of Jordan and the Sudanese Prime Minister being among those who flew in it. With one exception, the remaining British aircraft received civil status for delivery to distant operational bases, G-APHX and 'HY to the Kuwait Oil Company in October 1957, and during 1958 G-APIR and 'PH left for Umm Said in the Qatar Peninsula to transport freight and personnel to new drilling sites of the Iraq Petroleum Co. Ltd. G-APLM and 'LN went to Nigeria for similar transport duties in connection with the oil prospecting contract of Fison-Airwork Ltd. G-APJT 'Lang Rajawali' (King Eagle) left Prestwick on March 31, 1958, to make the long flight to Singapore, where it became the first aircraft of the newly formed Malayan Air Force. One other export, G-APMT, flew to Iran in July of the same year, where it carried out many mercy flights for the Red Lion and Sun Organisation to areas affected by the earthquake.

The chief variant to date has been G-APPW, appropriately marked, fitted with Pratt and Whitney R-1340 motors for A.R.B. and C.A.A. certification in readiness for the delivery of five similarly powered Twin Pioneers to Philippine Airlines. Piloted by Tom Hope, 'PW was flown for the first time on August 31, 1958. When long stroke Leonides 531 radials became available and were fitted to the prototype G-ANTP for certification trials, Twin Pioneer series numbers were reorganised as shown in the table below and the Series 3, with its enhanced performance, became the 1959 model. The first production model G-AOEN which at last returned to Prestwick from Central America piloted by Beverley Snook on May 1, 1959, was modified to Series 3 standard, leaving again on July 21 for an African sales tour. This ended in a forced landing on an island in the Zambesi, near Luabo, Mozambique on December 12. Two other Twin Pioneer 3s went overseas in October 1959, 'RS to Fison-Airwork Ltd. and 'UM to the Iraq Petroleum Transport Co. Ltd.

SPECIFICATION

Manufacturers: Scottish Aviation Ltd., Prestwick Airport, Ayrshire.
Power Plants: (Prototype) Two 540 h.p. Alvis Leonides 503/8.
        (Series 1)   Two 560 h.p. Alvis Leonides 514/8.
                      Two 560 h.p. Alvis Leonides 514/8A.
        (Series 2)   Two 600 h.p. Pratt and Whitney Wasp
                                    R-1340-S1H1-G.
        (Series 3)   Two 640 h.p. Alvis Leonides 531.
Dimensions: Span, 76 ft. 6 in. Length, 45 ft. 3 in. Height, 12 ft. 3 in. Wing area, 670 sq. ft.

	Twin Pioneer		
	Series 1	Series 2	Series 3
Tare weight . .	9,969 lb.	10,900 lb.	10,200 lb.
All-up weight .	14,000 lb.	14,000 lb.	14,600 lb.
Maximum speed .	186·5 m.p.h.	186·5 m.p.h.	186·5 m.p.h.
Cruising speed .	117·5 m.p.h.	122 m.p.h.	131·25 m.p.h.
Initial climb . .	750 ft./min.	600 ft./min.	880 ft./min.
Ceiling .	17,000 ft.	15,800 ft.	18,000 ft.
Range . .	670 miles	670 miles	700 miles

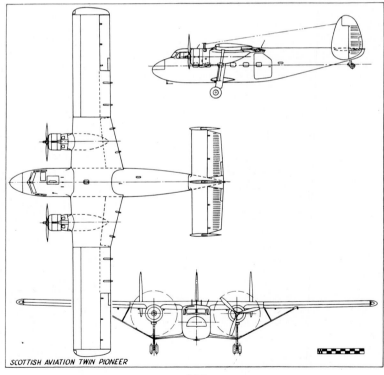

SCOTTISH AVIATION TWIN PIONEER

E. E. Stammers taking off in Mrs. Elliott-Lynn's S.E.5A at the start of the Bournemouth Killjoy Trophy Race, April 18, 1927. (*'Flight' Photo.*)

S.E.5A

Designed in 1916 at the Royal Aircraft Factory, Farnborough by H. P.
Folland, the S.E.5A was probably the greatest single seat fighter of the
First World War. It was built in the traditional manner of the period, with
spruce primary structure braced with piano wire and fabric covered. A
number of engines were fitted, but a large proportion of the main production was powered by the 200 h.p. Wolseley Viper, cooled by a car-type
radiator in the nose. Vast quantities of surplus S.E.5A airframes, spares
and engines were taken over by the Aircraft Disposal Co. Ltd. at Croydon
in 1920 and reconditioned for sale to foreign air forces. One of the original
design requirements was that the aircraft should be inherently stable and
capable of being flown by inexperienced pilots. This feature commended
the S.E.5A to the disposals company as a possible private or sporting aircraft, and in May 1920 the S.E.5A F9022 was stripped of armament,
registered G-EATE and offered for civil use at £700. Eight more,
G-EAXQ–'XX, were then erected, six of which were loaned to the Royal
Aero Club for the one and only Oxford *v.* Cambridge Air Race, won by
Cambridge at Hendon on July 16, 1921.

The first privately owned specimen was G-EAZT fitted with a 90 h.p.
R.A.F. IA aircooled engine for the late Dr. E. D. Whitehead Reid of
Canterbury, who flew from Bekesbourne to land in convenient fields
when visiting outlying patients. Underpowered to a degree, it proved very
slow, and its short life ended when it stood on its nose and destroyed the
front fuselage early in 1923. Its replacement, G-EBCA, secured in time for
participation in the Grosvenor Trophy Race at Lympne on June 23, 1923,
had a venerable 80 h.p. Renault engine imparting a top speed of some 65
m.p.h. In civil form the S.E.5A will be associated forever with Major
J. C. Savage and skywriting, his first aircraft G-EATE being used by

Cyril Turner for the first public demonstration of black smoke writing on May 30, 1922. Smoke producing chemicals of secret formula were carried in a specially installed tank in the fuselage and could be fed at will, by means of a cock, into the hot exhaust gases. The smoke was led through a special pipe under the fuselage and the starboard elevator fabric was partly removed to prevent charring. This system was soon superseded by white smoke led through lengthened exhause pipes to a Y junction at the sternpost. Such pilots as Turner, L. R. Tait-Cox, M. M. L. Bramson and Sidney St. Barbe are legendary as perfectionists in the art of mirror writing in smoke, an art learned at Hendon by riding the letter shapes in reverse on a bicycle. The advertising value of a word in the sky, often visible over a 50 mile radius, was so immense that to satisfy the demand, which included *Daily Mail*, Players, Ronuk, Persil and Buick contracts, batches G-EBFF–'FI, 'GJ–'GM and 'IA–'IF were converted at Hendon. Two were shipped to America, where they wrote 'Hello, New York' over the city and then carried out a million dollar contract with the American Tobacco Company. They operated as the Skywriting Corporation of America whose fleet eventually numbered 11, five of which were later Americanised with underslung radiators and steamlined, spin polished cowlings. In this form they continued to write 'Lucky Strike' until the end of 1924, when they passed into local ownership and were allotted new constructor's and licence numbers 1–5 and NC2677-81 respectively.

The Hendon based S.E.5As ranged far and wide over the British Isles and in almost every European country, one trio, G-EBQA–'QC, spending much of its time in Germany. By 1929 the heyday of smoke writing was over and the fleet of tired S.E.5As then dispersed, five to Gesellschaft für Himmelschrift und Wolkenprojektion m.b.H. at Düsseldorf and others to demolition at Anderson's yard in Hounslow. The one survivor, G-EBVB, gave itinerant aerobatic displays until 1938. With the exception of his first machine, Major Savage used only aircraft which had been obtained in new condition from Vickers, Austin and Wolseley, three of the many S.E.5A sub-contractors. Ten other S.E.5As sold by the Aircraft Disposal Co. Ltd. had seen R.A.F. service before entering private ownership, and included Dudley Watt's G-EBOG, Mrs. S. C. Elliott Lynn's

Rear view of the original civil S.E.5A G-EATE with prototype skywriting modifications, including underslung smoke stack and cut away elevator fabric. (*Photo: Aerofilms Ltd.*)

The Savage Skywriting Company's S.E.5A 'The Sweep' at Gothenberg during M. L. Bramson's demonstrations in 1923. The rudder was cut away to make way for the exhaust junction. (*Photo courtesy of Leonard Bridgman.*)

Short exhaust pipes were retained on S.E.5As reworked for skywriting in the U.S.A. The identity mark G-EBGL is faintly visible on the under fin. (*Photo: Real Photographs Company.*)

'PA, A. H. Wheeler's 'QM, K. Hunter's 'QK, 1929 Schneider Trophy winner H. R. D. Waghorn's 'PD and G-EBQQ in which Lt. Gwynne Maddocks spun in and was killed at Brooklands on November 9, 1928. Nearly all appeared at the various race meetings held in 1926–27, F/O A. F. Scroggs winning the Sherburn Private Owners Handicap in 'QK on October 1, 1927, at 113 m.p.h. and Mrs. S. C. Elliott Lynn the Wattle Handicap at the same meeting at 116 m.p.h.

Dudley Watt flew 'OG to victory in the Hotels Handicap at Bournemouth on April 18, 1927, at 114.2 m.p.h. and afterwards rebuilt it as a high performance machine, designated the D.W.1, powered by a 300 h.p. Hispano-Suiza enclosed in a streamlined cowling and cooled by under-slung radiators. The rear fuselage decking was also redesigned and built up to form a streamlined headrest. Work on the D.W.1 was carried out in a shed at Brooklands near the Henderson School of Flying hangars in which two non-standard S.E.5As with aircooled engines driving four bladed airscrews were erected in 1927. First of these, G-EBTK, belonged to L. R. Oldmeadows and was powered by a 90 h.p. R.A.F. IA. In July 1930 'TK was acquired by Kent Aircraft Services and went to Kingsdown, Kent, and lay dismantled until sold to C. B. Field at Kingswood Knoll, Surrey, in August 1932, but never flew again. The other, 'TO, built for comedian Will Hay, was fitted with a 120 h.p. Airdisco motor and flew from Sherburn-in-Elmet until January 1929, when it was purchased by W. L. Handley and moved south to Castle Bromwich.

Today three S.E.5As of the former Savage Skywriting Co. Ltd. are the only survivors. G-EBIA was reconstructed for the Shuttleworth Trust by the Farnborough apprentices and staff 1957–59 and flew again on

Dr. E. D. Whitehead Reid seated in his Renault engined S.E.5A before the start of the 1923 Grosvenor Trophy Race at Lympne. (*'Flight' Photo.*)

Dudley Watt, wearing his famous black and yellow check helmet, seated in the D.W.1 at Whitchurch, 1930. (*Photo courtesy of W. K. Kilsby.*)

The R.A.F.IA engined S.E.5A built at Brooklands for L. R. Oldmeadows in 1927.

Walley Handley's S.E.5A G-EBTO, with 120 h.p. Airdisco aircooled engine.

August 4, 1959 in military colours with suitable but incorrect serial D7000, piloted by Air Commodore A. H. Wheeler. The engine is a 200 h.p. Hispano-Suiza retrieved from the Science Museum store. G-EBIB, last flown in 1914–18 camouflage at the 1937 Hendon R.A.F. Display by F/Lt. R. C. Jonas, now hangs from the roof of the South Kensington Science Museum and the third, 'IC, is now housed at London Airport. Stripped of the long exhaust pipes at 39 M.U. Colerne in 1950 and bearing R.A.F. markings and a spurious serial number B4563, it is to be preserved for all time by the Royal Aeronautical Society.

Manufacturers: (1) The Royal Aircraft Factory, Farnborough, Hants. (2) The Austin Motor Co. (1914) Ltd., Northfield, Birmingham. (3) The Air Navigation and Engineering Co. Ltd., Addlestone, Surrey. (4) Martinsyde Ltd., Brooklands, Byfleet, Surrey. (5) Vickers Ltd., Crayford and Weybridge. (6) Wolseley Motors Ltd., Adderley Park, Birmingham. (*The numbers in parentheses form the key to manufacturers in Appendix D.*)

Power Plants: One 200 h.p. Wolseley Viper.
One 300 h.p. Hispano-Suiza.
One 120 h.p. Airdisco.
One 90 h.p. R.A.F.IA.
One 80 h.p. Renault.

Dimensions: Span, 26 ft. 7½ in. Length, 20 ft. 11 in. Height, 9 ft. 6 in. Wing area, 244 sq. ft.

Weights: (Viper) Tare weight, 1,322 lb. All-up weight, 2,052 lb.
(R.A.F.IA) Tare weight, 1,630 lb. All-up weight, 2,050 lb.
(Renault) Tare weight, 1,241 lb. All-up weight, 1,829 lb.

*Performance: Maximum speed, 137 m.p.h. Cruising speed, 100 m.p.h. Initial climb, 1,175 ft./min. Ceiling, 19,500 ft. Range, 250 miles.

* With Wolseley Viper engine.

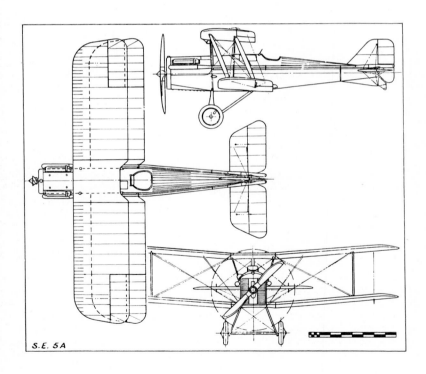

S.E. 5A

The prototype Calcutta flying with the emergency aerial masts in position on the upper mainplane. (*'Flight' Photo.*)

Short S.8 Calcutta and S.17 Kent

The Calcutta was historically important as the first flying-boat with stressed-skin metal hull to go into commercial service, being designed in 1927 by Arthur Gouge for the Mediterranean section of the Imperial Airways route to India, in the light of experience gained with the Singapore I and the metal hulled F.5 of 1923. With the exception of certain stainless steel fittings and the fabric covering of flying and control surfaces, the entire structure was of duralumin. Three Jupiter radials gave multi-engined safety and the fuel tanks were located in the upper mainplane to enable smoking to be permitted in the cabin. Comfortable accommodation was provided for 15 passengers, a steward served hot or cold meals from a buffet, and supplementary freight and mail was carried in the rear of the hull.

G-EBVG, first of two aircraft ordered, was first flown by chief test pilot J. Lankester Parker on February 21, 1928, from the Medway outside Short's works at Rochester. After air and seaworthiness tests at the M.A.E.E., Felixstowe, and acceptance tests by the Imperial Airways superintendent H. G. Brackley, 'VG was flown to London, landing on the Thames at Westminster on August 1, 1928. A three day visit enabled Members of Parliament to inspect an aircraft destined to forge important links in Empire communications. Proving and crew training flights were made to Guernsey on August 5, Jersey on the 21st, and to Cherbourg on the 27th. The second Calcutta, 'VH, delivered from Rochester to Southampton on September 12, 1928, left two days later on a tour to Stranraer and Liverpool, carrying the Imperial Airways chairman, Sir Eric Geddes. After operating a daily service between Liverpool and Belfast for one week, it joined 'VG in a number of scheduled runs to Jersey over the route formerly operated with Supermarine Sea Eagles.

On April 16, 1929, 'VG left for Genoa to inaugurate the Mediterranean service. Passengers for India flew from Croydon to Basle by A. W. Argosy, thence by sleeping car express to Genoa, continuing by Short Calcutta to

Alexandria via Rome, Naples, Corfu, Athens, Suda Bay and Tobruk. The final stage to Karachi was flown by D.H.66 Hercules, the whole service operating to a seven day schedule. A third Calcutta, G-AADN 'City of Rome', was commissioned in March 1929, the originals being allotted the names 'City of Alexandria' and 'City of Athens' respectively, but in the following October 'DN was forced down off Spezia in a gale and foundered with all hands, including the pilot, Capt. Birt. Two other boats, 'SJ and 'TZ, were already under construction, the latter receiving the name 'City of Salonika' following the transference of the flying-boat terminal to that port as a result of political unrest in Italy. Brave attempts to fly Argosies to Salonika were defeated by weather and terrain, but eventually the Calcuttas returned to their Italian terminal at Genoa, after a short period at Brindisi. In 1931 the schedule was cut to six days by re-routing via Athens, Haifa and the Sea of Galilee to Baghdad.

Imperial Airways Ltd. then placed an order for three Kent flying-boats, which were enlarged four engined developments of the Calcutta. Their lower mainplanes were approximately equal in span to the upper mainplanes of their predecessors, the crew was housed in an enclosed cockpit, and 16 passengers enjoyed Pullman comfort in four rows of seats with folding tables. They were considered the most comfortable transports of their age, with room for walking about and a galley for preparing hot meals in the air. The prototype, G-ABFA 'Scipio', made its first flight from the Medway piloted by J. Lankester Parker on February 24, 1931, and it was Short's proud boast that scarcely a single modification was found necessary. After routine trials, 'Scipio' was ferried to the Mediterranean on May 5, 1931, followed 10 days later by 'FB 'Sylvanus'. The third Kent, 'FC 'Satyrus', delivered on May 26, gained wide publicity by carrying H.R.H. The Prince of Wales on a tour of the Solent area.

As forecast by the name 'City of Khartoum' allotted to Calcutta 'SJ, the difficult Khartoum–Kisumu section of the route to South Africa, opened in January 1932, was operated by Calcuttas released from the Mediterranean by Kents. Their enforced open-air life, often in the tropics, had

Calcutta G-EBVG fitted with three Armstrong Siddeley Tiger radials, Hamble 1936.

237

The Short Kent 'Scipio' at Rochester in February 1931. The enormous Calcutta and Kent rudders were actuated by a large servo. (*'Flight' Photo*.)

literally no effect on their rugged structures, and by mid-1932 Calcuttas had completed 308,000 miles over the Mediterranean and 186,000 miles along the Upper Nile. By August 1932 the three Kents had flown 98,270, 90,565 and 77,484 miles respectively on the Brindisi–Alexandria run without a single mechanical breakdown. The combined fleet of seven flying-boats gave uninterrupted service until brought low by a series of tragedies three years later. 'Sylvanus' was set on fire at her moorings at Brindisi by an Italian in November 1935, and a month later Calcutta 'SJ ran out of fuel and made a sudden forced landing from 500 ft. in darkness, and foundered just outside the harbour breakwater at Alexandria. Capt. V. G. Wilson escaped from the open cockpit, but 12 passengers were killed. Eight months later 'Scipio' crashed on alighting at Mirabella, Crete, in exceptionally bad weather, but Capt. A. S. Wilcockson, crew, and all but two passengers escaped.

In September 1935, after more than seven years in the Mediterranean, Calcuttas 'VG and 'TZ were flown to Rochester for conversion to trainers in readiness for the commissioning of the Empire Boats. Flying 'TZ, long renamed 'City of Swanage', H. G. Brackley made a number of experimental landings on reservoirs, lakes and rivers in France on the way home, reaching Southampton Water on October 1, 1935.

The prototype 'VG was re-engined with Tiger radials and spent the last year of its flying life with Air Pilots Training Ltd. at Hamble, joining its sister ship 'TZ and a Short S.8/8 Rangoon G-AEIM. The last was externally similar to a Calcutta but equipped with an enclosed cockpit and aft gun positions. First flown in August 1930 as S1433, it had been the first of six Rangoons built for R.A.F. use at Basra on the Persian Gulf. Flown out by R. L. Ragg (now Air Vice Marshal, Rtd.), in February 1931, it returned to Rochester for trainer conversion alongside its civil relatives four years later.

Manufacturers: Short Bros. (Rochester and Bedford) Ltd., Seaplane Works, Rochester, Kent.

Power Plants: (Calcutta) Three 540 h.p. Bristol Jupiter XIF.
Three 840 h.p. Armstrong Siddeley Tiger VI.
(Rangoon) Three 540 h.p. Bristol Jupiter XIF.
(Kent) Four 555 h.p. Bristol Jupiter XFBM.

	S.8 Calcutta	S.8/8 Rangoon	S.17 Kent
Span . . .	93 ft. 0 in.	93 ft. 0 in.	113 ft. 0 in.
Length . . .	66 ft. 9 in.	66 ft. 9½ in.	78 ft. 5 in.
Height . . .	23 ft. 9 in.	23 ft. 9 in.	28 ft. 0 in.
Wing area . .	1,825 sq. ft.	1,828 sq. ft.	2,640 sq. ft.
Tare weight . .	13,845 lb.	14,000 lb.	20,460 lb.
All-up weight .	22,500 lb.	22,500 lb.	32,000 lb.
Maximum speed .	118 m.p.h.	115 m.p.h.	137 m.p.h.
Cruising speed .	97 m.p.h.	92 m.p.h.	105 m.p.h.
Initial climb . .	750 ft./min.	550 ft./min.	840 ft./min.
Ceiling . . .	13,500 ft.	12,000 ft.	17,500 ft.
Range . . .	650 miles	650 miles	450 miles

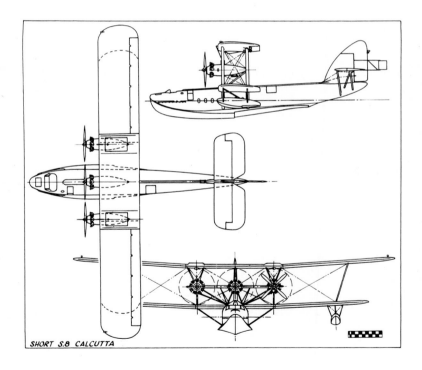

SHORT S.8 CALCUTTA

Scion 2 G-ADDN at Southend in 1935.

Short S.16 Scion

In pre-war days the name Short was synonymous with marine aircraft, so that the Scion twin engined cantilever monoplane was a break with tradition. Designed by Arthur Gouge for feeder-line work, it comprised a welded steel fuselage and single-spar, fabric-covered metal wing, pilot and five passengers being carried on the power of two uncowled 75 h.p. Pobjoy R radials. The prototype, G-ACJI, first flown at Gravesend by test pilot J. Lankester Parker in September 1933, had a flat top to the rear fuselage, but during the following month a large curved decking was added and became standard. Completion of the first production aircraft, G-ACUV, powered by closely cowled 90 h.p. Pobjoy Niagara Is, was rushed through in time for the same pilot to demonstrate its remarkable quietness at the Hendon S.B.A.C Show of July 1, 1934. Three others, G-ACUW–'UY, completed in the seaplane works later in 1934, included 'UX equipped with twin floats for export to Port Moresby, Papua. Its long and active life came to an end as a landplane with Marshall Airways, giving pleasure flights at Sydney in 1954.

Well-planned flight trials with the early Scions, including 1,082 scheduled flights by the prototype from Rochester to Southend between June and September 1934, led to a 1935 model known as the Scion 2. The nacelles were raised to bring the thrust line level with the leading edge of the wing, a sixth passenger seat was added and considerable improvements were made to cockpit and cabin glazing. The first Scion 2, G-ACUZ, sold to Nottingham Airport Ltd. via Airwork Ltd., was followed by a batch of 10 constructed in the company's new works at Rochester Airport. During 1935–36 an hourly service between Southend and Rochester was operated jointly by Shorts with Scion 1 'UY and Southend Flying Services Ltd. with Scion 2 'DN. G-ADDO was based at Shoreham by Olley Air Service Ltd. for pleasure flights and occasional jockey transport, and 'DS was sold to Adelaide Airways in South Australia. In the

North, 'DP served West of Scotland Airways Ltd. on a route from Renfrew to the Island of Mull, the first Scion 1, 'UV, operated in the Orkneys with Aberdeen Airways Ltd. and the prototype, 'JI, settled down at Yeadon with Yorkshire Airways Ltd., after a season's joyriding with C. W. A. Scott's Air Display in the hands of L. J. Rimmer. The last of the batch of Scion 2s, G-ADDV and 'DX, were operated respectively by Ramsgate and Plymouth Airports Ltd., giving pleasure flights to thousands of holiday-makers in their day. In 1938 'DV went to Ipswich and ran a daily service to Clacton and the Scottish 'DP went to Squires Gate for joyriding with Williams and Company.

The sole long distance flight by a Scion began at Croydon on January 21, 1936, when C. E. Gardner left for India in the Pobjoy company's machine 'DT. Before its return on March 13, 15,932 miles were covered, including 1,500 miles at full throttle to come 6th in the Viceroy's Cup Race at Delhi on February 14. The aircraft then went on tour with Campbell Black's Air Display. Gouge trailing edge flaps designed for the new Short Empire Boats were air tested in 1935 on the Scion 2 G-ADDR fitted with a tapered wooden wing and flown under B conditions as M-3. Preoccupation with the Empire Boat contract finally resulted in Scion production

The prototype Scion in its original condition without rear decking. (*Photo: Short Bros. Ltd.*)

Scion 1 floatplane G-ACUX of Papuan Concessions Ltd. moored in the Medway, February 1935. (*'Flight' Photo.*)

The experimental Scion 2 G-ADDR with tapered wing, Gouge flaps and Class B marking M-3, November 1935. (*Imperial War Museum Photo MH.3348.*)

being handed over to the Pobjoy company, which built the last six aircraft. These were near identical with the Short-built machines, but carried the amended type number S.16/1. Two were exported to Palestine Airways Ltd., but the others were of British registry, the first, G-AEIL, going to Khormaksar, Aden, for service with Arabian Airways Ltd. Here it joined the company's first Scion, G-AEOY, which had been built from the crashed remains of that exported to Adelaide Airways two years previously. The second Pobjoy Scion, G-AEJN, entered private ownership at Gatwick, initially with C. G. M. Alington and in 1939 with D. E. Spratt. The final Scion, G-AEZF, went to Freetown, Sierra Leone, to operate on floats with Elders Colonial Airways Ltd. Returning by sea, it became a civil communications aircraft with No. 24 E.F.T.S. at Barton-in-the-Clay, Beds., in November 1941, continuing in the same employ until demobilised at Sealand in 1945. After a brief period of post-war activity at Exeter and elsewhere, 'ZF lapsed into unserviceability at Croydon and was eventually dismantled at Redhill and taken to Southend by road on June 2, 1959.

From April 1935 a daily passenger and mail service was operated between Barnstaple and Lundy Island by Lundy and Atlantic Coast Air Lines Ltd. with Scion 1 G-ACUW. Four years later it was joined by Pobjoy Scion G-AETT and the service continued until the latter crashed in February 1940. The survivor, in common with the majority of Scions, was then impressed for R.A.F. war service. A number were overhauled at Gatwick during the war, and 'JN eventually became an instructional airframe at Kemble, but thereafter all but 'ZF faded into obscurity.

Manufacturers: Short Bros. (Rochester and Bedford) Ltd., Seaplane Works, Rochester, and Rochester Airport, Kent; Pobjoy Airmotors and Aircraft Ltd., Rochester Airport, Kent.

Power Plants: (Prototype) Two 75 h.p. Pobjoy R.
  (Scion 1)　　Two 85 h.p. Pobjoy Niagara I or II.
  (Scion 2)　　Two 90 h.p. Pobjoy Niagara III.

Dimensions: Span, 42 ft. 0 in. Length, 31 ft. 6 in. Height, 10 ft. 4½ in. Wing area, 255·3 sq. ft.

	Prototype	Scion 1	Scion 2
Tare weight .	1,700 lb.	1,710 lb.	1,770 lb.
All-up weight	3,000 lb.	3,050 lb.	3,200 lb.
Maximum speed	117 m.p.h.	125 m.p.h.	128 m.p.h.*
Cruising speed	90 m.p.h.	102 m.p.h.	116 m.p.h.
Initial climb .	600 ft./min.	600 ft./min.	625 ft./min.
Ceiling .	11,500 ft.	13,000 ft.	13,000 ft.
Range .	360 miles	380 miles	390 miles

* Floatplane 117 m.p.h.

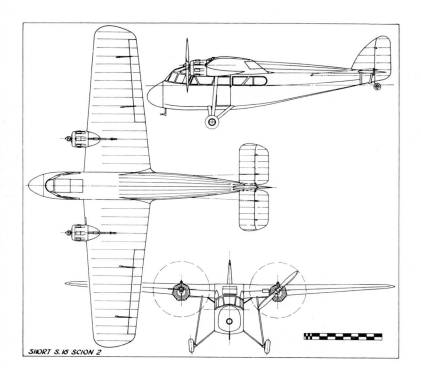

SHORT S.16 SCION 2

Short S.30 'Champion' taking off from Durban. (*Imperial War Museum Photo CH.* *14759.*)

Short S.23 Empire Flying Boat

A British Government decision made in 1935, to carry all mail without surcharge by air within the Empire, called for a fleet of fast aircraft capable of handling vastly increased loads. Short's team, led by A. Gouge, was designing an all-metal flying-boat with monocoque hull of considerable beauty of line, mounting a metal-clad, tapered, cantilever wing carrying four Bristol Pegasus XC radials driving three bladed de Havilland variable pitch airscrews. Electrically operated Gouge retractable trailing edge flaps were incorporated to improve take off and to reduce the landing speed by some 12 m.p.h. The $3\frac{1}{2}$ ton payload included $1\frac{1}{2}$ tons of mail and 24 day passengers, with alternative 16 sleeping berth layout, while on long flights passengers were able to stroll into a promenade lounge. Traditional pilots' cockpits disappeared in favour of a spacious crew cabin for captain, first officer, navigator and flight clerk, and a steward's pantry was situated amidships.

It was a remarkable design, far ahead of its day, and Imperial Airways Ltd. took the unprecedented step of ordering 28 straight from the drawing-board. This far sighted decision was fully vindicated on July 4, 1936, when test pilot J. Lankester Parker took the prototype, 'Canopus', C Class flagship, on a trouble-free maiden flight at Rochester. Empire Boats were, without question, the most famous and successful of all pre-war civil transports, due to Short's carefully planned tank, wind tunnel and practical flying tests. Scale-model Gouge trailing edge flaps had been flight tested on a Scion, while the handling qualities had been reproduced in advance with the four motor Scion Senior, aerodynamically a half-scale Empire Boat.

'Canopus' was ferried to Genoa by H. G. Brackley on October 22, 1936, and went into service over the Mediterranean on the 31st, the rest of the fleet following at an average rate of two per month. From February 4, 1937, regular services on the Empire routes began at Hythe, the last of the old overland schedules terminating at Croydon on March 4. In conjunction with QANTAS Empire Airways, the Empire Boats flew right through to Sydney and from June 28, 1937, superseded the miscellaneous aircraft operating in Africa when 'Centaurus', Capt. F. L. Bailey, opened a through service to Durban. The fourth boat, 'Cavalier', was shipped to Bermuda and there assembled for the service to New York which opened on May 25, 1937. By 1938 Empire Boats were flying seven services a week to Egypt, four to India, three to East Africa and two each to South Africa, Malaya, Hong Kong and Australia. Increases in mail reduced the passengers carried to 17, an extra half ton of mail occupying the forward cabin.

Government plans for a Transatlantic mail service led to the completion of the second boat 'Caledonia' with long range tanks and strengthened for operation at an all-up weight of 45,000 lb. Capts. W. N. Cumming and A. S. Wilcockson took it from Hythe to Alexandria on December 18, 1936, and flew back to Marseilles, a distance of 1,700 miles, non-stop in $11\frac{1}{4}$ hours. Experimental long distance trials continued with 2,300 mile non-stop flights on February 17 and March 4, 1937, between Hythe and Alexandria and back, a distance 400 miles greater than from Ireland to Newfoundland. The first ocean crossing without payload was made from Foynes to Botwood by Capt. A. S. Wilcockson on the night of July 5–6, 1937, arriving at New York three days later. A second long range boat, 'Cambria', made similar survey flights on July 29 and August 27, 'Caledonia' completing the series with crossings on August 15 and September 13.

Three additional Empire Boats, initially of British registry, G-AFBJ–'BL, were delivered to QANTAS Empire Airways at the beginning of 1938. They joined three others, G-AEUG–'UI, which, after initial transfer to QANTAS in August 1937, returned temporarily to Imperial Airways Ltd. in January 1938 before finally settling down under Australian ownership six months later. The close ties between the joint operators was further emphasised in September 1939 when two Australian boats 'Corio' and 'Coorong' reverted to British marks in exchange for 'Centaurus' and 'Calypso'. The Australian deliveries brought the final total of S.23 boats to 31, but in the first two years of operation the ranks were sadly depleted by the loss of 'Capricornus', 'Courtier', 'Cygnus', 'Calpurnia', 'Capella', 'Challenger', 'Cavalier' and 'Centurion' in major fatal crashes. Shortest lived of all Empire Boats, 'Capricornus', Capt. Paterson, crashed in the Beaujolais Mountains in France on March 24, 1937, soon after leaving Hythe on its maiden flight.

Eight S.30 boats powered by Bristol Perseus XIIC sleeve valve radials and strengthened for operation at an all-up weight of 48,000 lb. were delivered in 1938–39. The first four, intended for Transatlantic services, were fitted for flight refuelling and cleared for flight, and later take off, at a maximum weight of 53,000 lb. 'Connemara', lost in a refuelling fire at Hythe a few weeks after delivery, was replaced by 'Cathay' in the following year. The S.30s 'Cabot' and 'Caribou' inaugurated the North Atlantic mail route on August 8, 1939, completing eight round trips before war intervened, additional fuel being taken on from Harrow tankers over Foynes and Botwood (see page 482). Together with Capts. Gordon Store, S. G. Long and crews, they were impressed in October 1939 and worked with No. 119 Squadron from Invergordon and Islay on early A.S.V. radar trials. Both were attacked and sunk by German aircraft at Bodo, Norway,

245

in May 1940 while disembarking an R.A.F. radar unit. Their replacements were the S.23 boats 'Clio' and 'Cordelia', which, equipped with four dorsal radar masts, tail and dorsal gun turrets at Belfast, were redesignated S.23M and spent 1941 patrolling between Loch Indail and Iceland.

Three S.30 boats, laid down as 'Captain Cook', 'Canterbury' and 'Cumberland', were sold before completion to Tasman Empire Airways Ltd. Two, renamed 'Awarua' and 'Aotearoa', operated on the Auckland–Sydney route for $7\frac{1}{2}$ years with over 90% regularity, the first service being flown by Capt. J. W. Burgess in 'Aotearoa' on April 30, 1940. The third boat 'Australia', eventually retained by Imperial Airways, was seriously damaged on take off from Basra on August 9, 1939, returned to England, was renamed 'Clare' and fitted with long range tanks. 'Clyde', originally built to replace the ill-fated 'Cavalier' on the New York–Bermuda route, then joined 'Clare', six return crossings of the Atlantic with passengers being made in 1940. Italy's entry into the war closed the Mediterranean and the majority of boats, including 'Corsair', were transferred to Durban. This boat had been forced down by fuel shortage and bad weather on a small river at Faraje in the Belgian Congo in March 1939. Holed by a rock, it required an epic of engineering skill to repair it and dam the river, before Capt. J. C. Kelly Rogers brought it out of the jungle on January 6, 1940. The fleet also included 'Clifton' and 'Cleopatra', the last Empire Boats to be built. Carrying the type number S.33, they were hybrids with Pegasus XC engines and hulls strengthened for a maximum take off weight of 53,000 lb.

From this new base, the Horseshoe Route was operated through East Africa, India and Malaya to Australia. Promenade decks and luxury equipment were removed, seating was increased to 29 and the maximum take off weight of the S.23s increased to 32,500 lb. 'Champion', 'Clare' and 'Cathay' remained at Poole, and during 1941 worked the Poole–Foynes shuttle, to West Africa and between October 1941 and March 1942 on the hazardous Gibraltar–Malta–Cairo lifeline. The fleet of Empire Boats was irrevocably split by the Japanese occupation of Malaya in 1942, and the story of those marooned in Antipodean waters, told in graphic detail in E. Bennett Bremner's 'Frontline Airline', is one of supreme sacrifice by man and machine under appalling conditions. Ten of these noble craft, including three loaned to the R.A.A.F., fell victim to Japanese attack. Nearer home, 'Cambria' and 'Coorong' evacuated 469 British troops from Crete to Alexandria in 1941.

Thirteen S.23, S.30 and S.33 boats survived the war, having been fitted, for spares economy, with 1,010 h.p. Pegasus 22 radials similar to those fitted to the Corporation's newer Sunderlands. Their useful lives were, however, drawing to a close. 'Castor', stripped of camouflage, flew the last Karachi–Cairo Horseshoe Service on January 15, 1947, and the Hythe–Durban route closed down at the end of the year. As Cs. of A. expired, the veterans were broken up on Southampton Water, one of the first to go being the mighty 'Canopus' herself. At the end of 1947 the same fate overtook her sister craft in the Antipodes. 'Aotearoa' made its 442nd and final Tasman crossing on October 29 and retired in Auckland as a coffee bar, and 'Coriolanus' was broken up at Rose Bay, Sydney, after her last scheduled flight on the Fiji–Sydney route of QANTAS on

December 23. In 11 years of service the Empire Boats flew a grand total of 37,779,242 miles, over two million of which were flown by 'Canopus'.

SPECIFICATION

Manufacturers: Short Bros. (Rochester and Bedford) Ltd., Seaplane Works, Rochester, Kent.

Power Plants: (S.23) Four 920 h.p. Bristol Pegasus XC.
Four 1,010 h.p. Bristol Pegasus XXII.
(S.30) Four 890 h.p. Bristol Perseus XII.
(S.33) Four 920 h.p. Bristol Pegasus XC.
Four 1,010 h.p. Bristol Pegasus XXII.

Dimensions: Span, 114 ft. 0 in. Length, 88 ft. 0 in. Height, 31 ft. 9¾ in. Wing area, 1,500 sq. ft.

Weights: (S.23) Tare weight, 23,500 lb. All-up weight, 40,500 lb.*
(S.30) Tare weight, 27,180 lb. All-up weight, 48,000 lb.†
(S.33) Tare weight, 27,180 lb. All-up weight, 53,000 lb.

Performance: Maximum speed, 200 m.p.h. Cruising speed, 165 m.p.h. Initial climb, 950 ft./min. Ceiling, 20,000 ft. Range (S.23 and S.33), 760 miles; (S.30), 1,300 miles; ('Caledonia' and 'Cambria'), 3,300 miles; ('Cavalier'), 1,500 miles; ('Cabot' and 'Caribou'), 2,500 miles.

    * Later 43,500 lb.
    † 'Cabot' and 'Caribou' 53,000 lb. airborne.

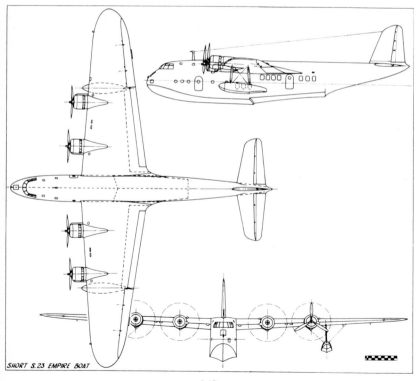

SHORT S.23 EMPIRE BOAT

A Sunderland 3, later 'Hamilton', in wartime civil colours, at moorings, Lagos 1943.
(*B.O.A.C. Photo.*)

Short S.25 Sunderland 3 and Sandringham

R.A.F. Sunderland 3 flying-boats powered by four Pegasus XVIII motors, carrying priority passengers and mail on joint B.O.A.C. and Transport Command routes in 1942, were stripped of all armament and fitted with bench-type seats. Gun turrets were replaced by bulbous fairings, the nose fairing being retractable for mooring purposes. From January 1943 they gradually assumed civil markings and went into B.O.A.C. service between Poole and West Africa, and late in the following year a 5,039-mile proving flight, carrying seven passengers and freight, was made to Karachi in 28 hours flying time. It marked the beginning of B.O.A.C. research into the aircraft's flying attitude and power output which eventually halved England–India flight times. After VE Day the Sunderlands were stripped of camouflage, engines were upgraded to Pegasus 38 (later 48), and the interiors modified for the carriage of 24 day or 16 night passengers and 6,500 lb. of mail. They were then known as the Hythe Class, 18 being converted by B.O.A.C. at Hythe and four by Shorts at Belfast in readiness for the reopening of the Empire routes. The Singapore service was reintroduced on January 31, 1946, and on February 22, 'Hythe' arrived at Sydney in the record time of 54 hours and continued to Auckland with V.I.P. passengers. A Poole–Calcutta Sunderland service was withdrawn on May 12, 1946, and replaced by the first post-war through service to Sydney. Inaugural east- and west-bound flights were made by B.O.A.C. and QANTAS crews in 'Hudson' and 'Henley' respectively, operating to a $5\frac{1}{2}$-day schedule. A memorable year of Sunderland achievement included the reopening of the Dragon route from Poole to Hong Kong by 'Hamilton' on August 24.

Simple conversion of military airframes was not sufficient to fully exploit the Sunderland's commercial potential, and in 1945 'Himalaya' returned to Rochester for extensive remodelling by Shorts. It emerged as the Sandringham 1 with S.26 type nose and tail and the whole interior

248

reconstructed with two decks, dining-saloon, cocktail bar and accommodation for 24 day or 16 night passengers. Initially flown in Transport Command markings as OQZF/ML788, its public debut before returning to B.O.A.C. was made as G-AGKX at the Victory Air Pageant, Eastleigh, on June 22, 1946, and at Farnborough a week later. It was the only Sandringham 1, but a considerable number of similar conversions were made to Twin Wasp engined Sunderland 5s by Short Bros. and Harland Ltd. at Belfast 1945–48.

'Argentina', 'Uruguay' and 'Paraguay', designated Short S.25/V Sandringham 2, built to the order of the Argentine operator Dodero, carried 45 day passengers with cocktail bar on the upper deck. They were ferried under British marks by B.O.A.C. crews, 'Argentina', Capt. Dudley Travers, reaching Buenos Aires on November 25, 1945, after covering the 7,330 miles from Poole in 45 hours 47 minutes flying time. Two similar boats, 'Brazil' and 'Ingleterra', also flown out, were Sandringham 3s with dining-saloon and galley on the upper deck and 21 passenger seats on the lower. G-AGWW and 'WX, delivered by air early in 1946 to the Uruguayan airline CAUSA and the Argentine ALFA respectively, were Sunderland 3s with Sandringham interiors, but were without special designation.

B.O.A.C. took delivery of nine Twin Wasp powered Sandringham 5s during 1947. These were known as the Plymouth Class and carried 22 day or 16 night passengers. The second aircraft, G-AHYZ 'Perth', damaged beyond repair during conversion at Belfast, was replaced by G-AJMZ with the same name. By the end of 1947 the Sandringham 5s were relieving the more elderly Sunderlands on routes from Poole to Sydney, Bahrein and Hong Kong, and on the Singapore–Hong Kong shuttle. On April 1, 1948, an enlarged and more convenient flying-boat terminal was opened at Berth 50, Southampton Water, at a time when luxurious flying-boat travel was at the height of its popularity. Three final Sandringhams, Mk. 7s equipped to carry 30 passengers and known as the Bermuda Class, were then added to the B.O.A.C. fleet.

In 1949 the Sunderlands were replaced by Constellations after covering 10 million miles and carrying 31,000 passengers on the Australia route

'Helmsdale', final B.O.A.C. Sunderland 3, was a freighter which retained the wartime bomb doors and had only two additional windows.

Sandringham 2 'Uruguay'. (*Photo: Short and Harland Ltd.*)

alone. In the same year Sandringhams were superseded on Far East routes by Canadair C-4s, after flying nearly six million miles in the Corporation's employ. Three Sunderlands, 'Hampshire', 'Hazlemere' and 'Halstead', sold to Aquila Airways Ltd., were thereafter maintained at Hamble, but continued to use Berth 50 when making 6, 118 and 141 sorties respectively to the Havel Lake, during the Berlin Air Lift, June 26, 1948, to October 6, 1949. Seven more ex B.O.A.C. Sunderlands and the Sandringham I were then acquired, some for scheduled services to Madeira and the Canary Islands and others for reduction to spares. An ex R.A.F. Sunderland 5 PP162, ferried to Hamble in 1953, was destroyed in a storm before conversion to G-ANAK, so that, paradoxically, the last Sunderland to remain in service was 'Hadfield', the first ever civilianised. Three former B.O.A.C. Sandringham 3s went to the Pacific in QANTAS service, and two Sandringham 7s joined their sister ships in Uruguay. The third, 'St. George', was overhauled at Cowes by Saunders-Roe Ltd. for Capt. Sir Gordon P. G. ('Bill') Taylor, who took delivery on October 14, 1954, afterwards flying home to Australia to inaugurate a series of South Sea flying-boat cruises.

B.O.A.C. Sandringham 5 'Portmarnock'.

Manufacturers: Short Bros. (Rochester and Bedford) Ltd., Seaplane Works, Rochester, Kent and Windermere, Cumberland; Short Bros. and Harland Ltd., Queen's Island, Belfast, N.I.; Blackburn Aircraft Ltd., Dumbarton, Dunbartonshire.

Power Plants: (Sunderland 3) Four 1,030 Bristol Pegasus XVIII, 38 or 48.
(Sandringham 1) Four 1,030 h.p. Bristol Pegasus 38.
(Sandringham 2) Four 1,200 h.p. Pratt and Whitney Twin Wasp R-1830-92.
(Sandringham 3) Four 1,200 h.p. Pratt and Whitney Twin Wasp R-1830-92B
(Sandringham 5 and 7) Four 1,200 h.p. Pratt and Whitney Twin Wasp R-1830-90D.

	Sunderland 3	Sandringham 1	Sandringham 2 and 3	Sandringham 5 and 7
Span	112 ft. 9½ in.	112 ft. 9½ in.	112 ft. 9½ in.	112 ft. 9½ in.
Length	88 ft. 6¾ in.	85 ft. 4¼ in.	86 ft. 3 in.	86 ft. 3 in.
Height	22 ft. 10½ in.	22 ft. 10½ in.	22 ft. 10½ in.	22 ft. 10½ in.
Wing area	1,687 sq. ft.	1,687 sq. ft.	1,687 sq. ft.	1,687 sq. ft.
Tare weight	35,862 lb.	34,150 lb.	41,370 lb.	39,498 lb.
All-up weight	50,000 lb.	56,000 lb.	56,000 lb.	60,000 lb.
Maximum speed	178 m.p.h.	216 m.p.h.	238 m.p.h.	206 m.p.h.
Cruising speed	165 m.p.h.	184 m.p.h.	221 m.p.h.	176 m.p.h.
Initial climb	720 ft./min.	557 ft./min.	1,000 ft./min.	840 ft./min.
Ceiling	16,000 ft.	16,150 ft.	21,300 ft.	17,900 ft.
Range	2,350 miles	2,550 miles	2,410 miles	2,440 miles

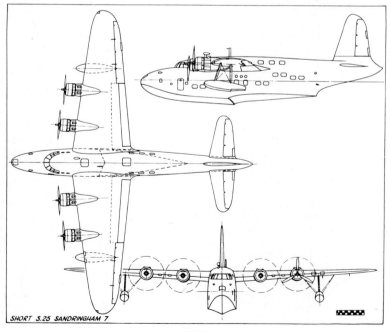

SHORT S.25 SANDRINGHAM 7

251

'Golden Hind' taking off on its maiden flight, piloted by J. Lankester Parker, June 1939. (*'Flight' Photo.*)

Short S.26

'Golden Hind', launched in June 1939, was the first of three Short S.26 G Class flying-boats ordered by Imperial Airways Ltd. for non-stop mail services across the Atlantic. The second and third boats, laid down as 'Grenville' and 'Grenadier', were completed as 'Golden Fleece' and 'Golden Horn'. Although developed from, and superficially resembling an Empire Boat, the S.26 was considerably larger and embodied the four-crew control cabin and modified rear step of the Sunderland I. Power was supplied by four Bristol Hercules IV sleeve valve engines driving three bladed de Havilland constant speed airscrews, and normal tankage gave a cruising range of over 3,000 miles.

When war brought Transatlantic aspirations to an end, the three S.26 boats and their crews were commandeered for long range reconnaissance duties with No. 119 Squadron, based first at Invergordon and later in Islay and West Africa. Military modifications, carried out at Rochester, included tail and dorsal Boulton and Paul gun-turret installations, internal depth-charge housing and full camouflage. 'Golden Fleece' was lost off Finisterre in August 1941 when two motors failed together, the surviving crew being picked up by an enemy submarine, so that only two S.26s returned to civil life under B.O.A.C. ownership when the squadron disbanded at Pembroke Dock at the end of the year. They were then reconditioned and fitted for the carriage of 40 passengers, receiving civil certificates of airworthiness for the first time. Tail cones removed during military conversion had been lost, and both boats retained the rear gun-turret housing. Based at Poole, they reinforced the service operating through Lisbon, Bathurst, Accra and Freetown to Lagos, the long range S.26 being particularly suited to the 13-hour Lisbon–Bathurst stage. Only priority passengers and diplomatic mail were carried, but on the final north-bound stage Lisbon–Foynes, loads of European refugees were evacuated.

During a test flight after an engine change at Lisbon on January 9, 1943, 'Golden Horn' suffered an engine fire, crashing into the Tagus with the loss of 13 occupants, including Capt. J. H. Lock, pioneer Hillman, Imperial Airways and Railways Air Services pilot. 'Golden Hind' was then relegated to the Poole–Foynes shuttle until it emerged from a third conversion at Hythe in 1944, equipped to full airline standard for 38 passengers and seven crew. Capt. Mollard then flew it to Durban for operation between Mombasa, Madagascar, Seychelles and Ceylon. After the war it was fitted with Hercules XIV motors at Belfast and ended its airline days on the occasional Poole–Athens–Cairo service inaugurated in January 1946. On retirement at the end of 1947, the aircraft was ferried

'Golden Horn' being launched at Lisbon after wing-tip float repairs, January 1943.
Note the disused rear gun turret.

to Rochester and passed first into the hands of F. J. Cork of Gillingham, Kent, and later to Buchan Marine Services Ltd. 'Golden Hind' remained at her moorings outside the former seaplane works for five years, maintained in serviceable condition with a watchman aboard. Plans to use her on tourist flights abroad came to nought, and in October 1953 the old aircraft was sold to F. C. Bettison and towed away for overhaul at Hamble. The tow ended in the Swale at Harty Ferry, where 'Golden Hind', last of the pre-war flying-boats, was sunk in a gale in May 1954.

SPECIFICATION

Manufacturers: Short Bros. (Rochester and Bedford) Ltd., Seaplane Works, Rochester, Kent.
Power Plants: Four 1,380 h.p. Bristol Hercules IV.
        Four 1,380 h.p. Bristol Hercules XIV.
Dimensions: Span, 134 ft. 4 in. Length, 101 ft. 4 in. Height, 37 ft. 7 in. Wing area, 2,160 sq. ft.
Weights: Tare weight, 37,700 lb. All-up weight, 73,500 lb.
Performance: Maximum speed, 209 m.p.h. Cruising speed, 180 m.p.h. Range, 3,200 miles.

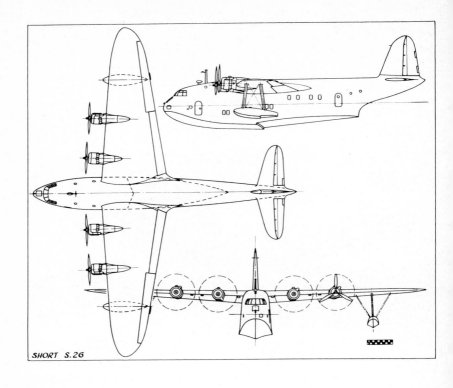

SHORT S.26

Solent 2 'Southampton' of British Overseas Airways Corporation, showing the original type of wing-tip floats. (*Charles E. Brown Photograph.*)

Short S.45 Solent 2, 3 and 4

A larger and longer version of the Sunderland, 1 ft. wider in the beam, with a planing bottom of increased area to permit a greater take-off weight, was flown in 1945 as the Seaford 1, and NJ201, one of a small batch built for the R.A.F., was loaned to B.O.A.C. for civil evaluation as G-AGWU in 1946. As a result, an order was placed for 12 similar aircraft, powered by Hercules 637 engines, for operation with seven crew and up to 30 passengers on two decks, with full promenade, cocktail bar and dining-saloon facilities. Construction was undertaken at Rochester, where the prototype, G-AHIL 'Salisbury', designated Solent 2, was launched on November 11, 1946. The twelfth, G-AHIY 'Southsea', launched on April 8, 1948, was the last aircraft ever built at Rochester.

During its $2\frac{1}{2}$-year accident-free B.O.A.C. service, the Solent 2 became famous for the luxury travel it introduced after replacing the Yorks on the South Africa route. 'Southampton', christened by the Mayoress of that city on April 14, 1948, made a proving flight which terminated at Vaaldam, the lake near Johannesburg, on May 1, and three days later the first Solent passenger service left Southampton. The route lay via Marseilles, Augusta in Sicily, Cairo, Port Bell on Lake Victoria and Victoria Falls, three services a week operating to a $4\frac{1}{2}$-day schedule. Teething trouble with the wing-tip floats necessitated the withdrawal of the Solent fleet on July 22, and the boats remained out of service until October 17, during which time the floats were strengthened and re-installed on a V strut mounting 7 ft. outboard and 18 in. forward of their original position.

The Solent fleet was on lease from the M.C.A. and not owned outright

Solent 2 'Solway' flying low at the 1949 Farnborough S.B.A.C. Show to show the revised strutting of wing-tip floats.

by B.O.A.C., and in 1948 arrangements were made whereby six new Seaford 1s, under construction at Belfast, should be completed as Solents for the Corporation. Equipped for 39 passengers and designated Solent 3, they were externally identified by two extra rectangular windows in the upper rear part of the hull. The first Solent 3, G-AKNO, landed on the Thames at Limehouse Reach, London, on May 5, 1949, to receive the name 'City of London' from the Lord Mayor at Tower Pier five days later. Together with later Solent 3s, 'NO then served to reinforce the earlier boats on the South Africa run. From May 15 they were also routed to Lake Naivasha, Kenya, replacing Yorks on the Nairobi service and cutting the journey from 48 to 27½ hours. Ten days later they also relieved Sandringhams on the Karachi service, but with the departure of 'Somerset' to South Africa from Berth 50 on November 10, 1950, all B.O.A.C. flying-boat operations ceased. A number were sold, and the rest were dispersed to storage at Belfast, Felixstowe and Hamworthy. 'Somerset' and 'City of Cardiff', two of three flown to Australia for the Pacific services of Trans-Oceanic Airlines, were sold again, arriving at Oakland, California, in June 1956 as N9945F and '46F respectively. They acquired South Pacific Airlines livery and were joined by N9947F, formerly G-AKNT, which arrived from Belfast via Australia and Honolulu. Solent 3 'City of Belfast' was sold to Tasman Empire Airways Ltd. and flew out via San Francisco and Honolulu, leaving Loch Erne, Northern Ireland, on August 22, 1951, and making the 2,055-mile crossing to Gander en route. 'City of Liverpool' was loaned to the Marine Aircraft Experimental Establishment during the major part of 1951 for stability investigations at overload weights up to 84,000 lb. Take off and landing tests were conducted at Felixstowe, Gibraltar and Tangiers Bay in military marks as WM759.

T.E.A.L. already operated four Solent 4s, custom built to carry 44 passengers on the 1,350-mile ocean crossing from Auckland to Sydney. They included 'Aotearoa II' named by H.M. The Queen (then Princess

Elizabeth) at Belfast in June 1949 and used for certification trials before leaving for New Zealand on November 26, 1949. Superseded by Douglas DC-6Bs in 1954, 'Aotearoa II', and a sister ship 'Awateri', flew back to Hamble for use on Aquila Airways routes to Montreux, Santa Margherita, Madeira and the Canary Islands. The last Solent 3, G-AKNU, in use by the company since December 1951, was joined in April 1954 by the most remarkable of all Solents. Originally the turretted evaluation Seaford 1 G-AGWU, it was later fitted with Solent nose and tail as a trainer but retained its original serial NJ201, and flew from Hythe to Felixstowe on November 7, 1950, when the B.O.A.C. fleet disbanded. Aquila Airways Ltd. brought it back to Hamble in 1953 for conversion to Solent 3 standards as G-ANAJ. One other Seaford 1, NJ200, registered to R. L. Whyham as G-ALIJ in February 1949, was not collected from the R.A.F.

All British commercial flying-boat activity ceased on September 30, 1958, when Aquila Airways Ltd. withdrew its Madeira service. The three surviving Solents G-AHIN, G-ANYI and G-AOBL were then taken over by Aerovias Aquila, to resume their flights to Madeira under Portuguese registry. The scheme fell through and all three now lie beached in the Tagus estuary at Lisbon.

The Aquila Airways Solent 'Sydney', a Mk. 3 identifiable by the extra windows at the rear of the upper deck. (*Photo courtesy of W. K. Kilsby.*)

Manufacturers: Short Bros. (Rochester and Bedford) Ltd., Seaplane Works, Rochester, Kent; Short Bros. and Harland Ltd., Queens Island, Belfast, N.I.

Power Plants: (Seaford 1)   Four 1,800 h.p. Bristol Hercules 130.
(Solent 2 and 3) Four 1,690 h.p. Bristol Hercules 637.
(Solent 4)   Four 2,040 h.p. Bristol Hercules 733.

Dimensions: Span, 112 ft. 9½ in. Length, 87 ft. 8 in. Height, 34 ft. 3¼ in. Wing area, 1,687 sq. ft.

	Seaford 1	Solent 2	Solent 3	Solent 4
Tare weight .	45,000 lb.	47,760 lb.	48,210 lb.	49,145 lb.
All-up weight .	75,000 lb.	78,000 lb.	78,600 lb.	81,000 lb.
Maximum speed .	242 m.p.h.	273 m.p.h.	267 m.p.h.	282 m.p.h.
Cruising speed .	207 m.p.h.	244 m.p.h.	236 m.p.h.	251 m.p.h.
Initial climb .	875 ft./min.	925 ft./min.	830 ft./min.	925 ft./min.
Ceiling . .	13,000 ft.	17,000 ft.	15,500 ft.	17,100 ft.
Range . .	2,800 miles	1,800 miles	2,190 miles	3,000 miles

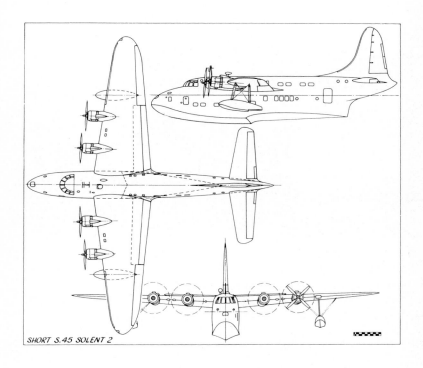

SHORT S.45 SOLENT 2

Sealand G-AKLO photographed en route to the 1950 S.B.A.C. Show. (*Photo: Short Bros. and Harland Ltd.*)

Short S.A.6 Sealand

Allotted the S.B.A.C. designation S.A.6, the all-metal Sealand, designed in 1947 by C. T. P. Lipscomb, was Britain's only post-war civil amphibian and carried up to seven passengers with two crew on the power of two Gipsy Queen 70 motors. The hull was of the normal single step type, fitted with a pneumatically retractable undercarriage for land operations. G-AIVX, the prototype, made its maiden flight from the waters of Belfast Harbour, piloted by H. L. Piper on January 22, 1948, and a production batch of 14, later increased to 24, was laid down. They were intended primarily for export during the financially difficult post-war period, but it was four years before the 24th and final Sealand left Belfast. The first production machine, G-AKLM, averaged 169 m.p.h. in the Elmdon King's Cup Race of August 1, 1949, and later left on a sales tour of Scandinavia, but was burned out with the loss of F/Lt. D. G. McCall and crew when it hit a mountainside in fog at the southern tip of Norway in the October. The fourth aircraft, G-AKLP, first of three ordered by British West Indian Airways for inter-island services, was exhibited as VP-TBA 'R.M.A. St. Vincent' at the 1949 Farnborough S.B.A.C. Show. During the completion of tropical trials in the West Indies, Short's chief test pilot, T. W. Brook-Smith, found that the Sealands were expected to operate from unsuitable areas of open sea at St. Vincent and Dominica and re-commended the shelving of the scheme. 'St. Vincent' therefore reverted to the manufacturers, was renamed 'Festival of Britain' and left Trinidad on January 6, 1951, under British marks for a 50,000-mile sales tour of South and North America, which included a double crossing of the Andes. The second and third West Indian aircraft were then disposed of to Yugoslovenski Aero Transport for services along the Dalmatian coast and passed through Short's establishment at Rochester en route to Zagreb in September 1951. During 1950–52 the European demonstrator G-AKLO ranged far and wide, from the Canary Islands in the south to

Scandinavia in the north, resulting in the purchase by Vestlandske Luft-fartselskap, Bergen, of 'LN and 'LU for scheduled services without under-carriages along the difficult coastline to Trondheim. G-AKLO was also chartered to NATO and used by Sir Patrick Brind for an extensive tour of his naval command, returning to Rochester in January 1952. It then set out on one last tour, covering 55,000 miles over Northern Europe, reaching the Arctic Circle from a base at Fornebu, Oslo. G-AKLN, shown at the 1951 Farnborough S.B.A.C. Show, was important as the first Sealand with strengthened hull, wing fences and 2 ft. 6 in. greater wing span. Shell then acquired the European and American demonstrators 'LO and 'LP, which, after long periods in storage at Rochester and Croydon respectively, departed for Balik Papaan for amphibious service over remote jungle areas in Borneo. Another, 'LW, sold to an Egyptian Pasha, left via Croydon on February 23, 1952, as SU-AHY.

The disposal of 'LT to the Christian and Missionary Alliance in January 1951 was a triumph of salesmanship. This, the first post-war British aero-plane sold to an American buyer, was shipped to Djakarta for operation by the veteran bush pilot evangelist Mason, from a base at Tandjoengselor, Indonesia. Like those in Borneo, it reduced a month's trek to a matter of minutes, but ended its year's career in a jungle water-course after a forced landing with a split fuel tank. Three others went to Dacca, East Bengal. The first, 'LV 'Pegasus', left Blackbushe on May 7, 1952, on delivery to Ralli Bros. Ltd. for operation along their riverside jute stations as AP-AFM, while the others flew for the local Transport Commission.

Only the first 12 of the total production of 24 Sealands were initially of British registry, the last two being first of 10 special aircraft built for the Indian Navy in 1952. They were equipped with dual control, tankage for 6 hours endurance and, for higher continuous cruising power, Gipsy Queen 70-4 engines driving constant speed feathering and reversing air-screws. The first, INS-101, left Rochester on January 13, 1953, piloted by C. R. Dash of Short's Ferry Flight, en route to Cochin.

The only Sealand currently registered in the United Kingdom is 'Pegasus', which arrived at Tilbury Docks from Pakistan in October 1957 consigned to Shorts at Rochester, but application for renewal of C. of A. has not yet been made.

Manufacturers: Short Bros. and Harland Ltd., Queen's Island, Belfast, N.I.
Power Plants: (Prototype) Two 345 h.p. de Havilland Gipsy Queen 70-2.
(Production) Two 340 h.p. de Havilland Gipsy Queen 70-3.
(Indian) Two 340 h.p. de Havilland Gipsy Queen 70-4.

	Prototype and Early Production	Late Production
Span	59 ft. 0 in.	61 ft. 6 in.
Length . . .	42 ft. 2 in.	42 ft. 2 in.
Height . . .	15 ft. 0 in.	15 ft. 0 in.
Wing area . . .	353 sq. ft.	358·6 sq. ft.
Tare weight . . .	7,397 lb.	7,065 lb.
All-up weight . .	9,100 lb.	9,100 lb.
Maximum speed .	189 m.p.h.	185 m.p.h.
Cruising speed . .	175 m.p.h.	169 m.p.h.
Initial climb . . .	880 ft./min.	780 ft./min.
Ceiling . . .	20,600 ft.	21,000 ft.
Range	660 miles	525 miles

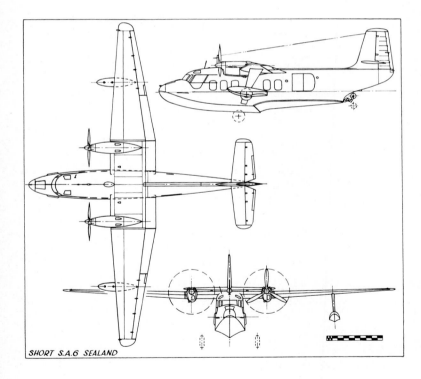

SHORT S.A.6 SEALAND

T. Neville Stack demonstrating the prototype Simmonds Spartan G-EBYU at Croydon in 1928. (*'Flight' Photo.*)

Simmonds Spartan

Dissatisfied with the high manufacturing and maintenance costs of contemporary light aeroplanes, the former Supermarine designer O. E. Simmonds built a wooden two seat biplane in 1928 which sought economy through interchangeability. All four wings and ailerons were identical and had a symmetrical aerofoil section to enable one spare wing to fit in any of the four positions. The rudder was also interchangeable with the half elevator, the fin was identical with the outer third of the tailplane, each half of the undercarriage would fit on either the port or starboard side and all main bracing wires were of the same length and size. Spares needed to cover even serious damage were therefore few. The aircraft was otherwise structurally orthodox, with plywood fuselage and fabric-covered wooden wings.

Known as the Simmonds Spartan and powered by a Cirrus III, the prototype, G-EBYU, was rushed through in time for the King's Cup Race of July 20–21, 1928. Repairs following a landing accident during early test flights left no time for adequate tuning, and F/Lt. S. N. Webster averaged only 73·06 m.p.h. to come 18th. Later in the year the Spartan was loaned to the short-lived Isle of Purbeck Flying Club, the chief instructor of which, F/O H. W. R. Banting, flew the machine from Croydon to the Berlin Aero Show on October 24, 1928, in the remarkable non-stop time of 7 hours 10 minutes. Lt.-Col. L. A. Strange was carried as passenger, and the return trip was made on the 27th in 5 hours 55 minutes.

Production then began at Weston, Southampton, final erection and test flying taking place at Hamble, but prejudice against the alleged spinning tendencies of the symmetrical wing section killed the Simmonds Spartan in 15 months. In that short time 48 were built, the majority for the

Dominions, but 23 were of British registry, including G-AAMA–'ML, a fleet of 12 ordered by National Flying Services Ltd. for instructional use at Hanworth. Unlike those of the prototype, the main undercarriage legs were not raked forward on production aircraft, four of which, G-AAFP, 'GN, 'GY and 'MC, were flown without success in the King's Cup Race of July 5–6, 1929, piloted by R. W. Jackson, C. S. Staniland, T. B. Bruce and F/O G. E. F. Boyes respectively.

Four engine variants were produced, G-AAGO temporarily fitted with a Gipsy II as H. T. Andrew's mount in the King's Cup Race, July 5, 1930; G-AAHA supplied to C. Coombes of Shanklin had the Hermes II, as did the first and last N.F.S. machines, the rest being Hermes I powered. Finally, G-ABNU, built at Brooklands in 1931 as an exercise by students of the College of Aeronautical Engineering, was fitted with a Gipsy I.

First of three airframe variants, G-AAMH was experimentally fitted with wings of 4 ft. greater span, with a consequent improvement in take-off and climb. Another, 'MG, was evaluated at the M.A.E.E. Felixstowe on twin metal floats and fitted with an enlarged rudder of the type fitted to O. E. Simmond's later design, the Spartan Arrow. Several aircraft were also built to seat two passengers in tandem in a double cockpit ahead of the pilot, but were otherwise similar to the two seater and used all the same interchangeable assemblies. The three sold on the home market were G-AAGV (Cirrus III) and 'HV (Hermes I), which went to Cramlington for joyriding with Pleasure Flying Services Ltd., and 'JB flown by F/O H. R. L. Wood in the 1930 King's Cup Race. 'GV crashed in September 1930, but was painstakingly rebuilt by Cramlington Aircraft Ltd. to reappear in June 1932 as G-ABXO. After a long joyriding career along the South Coast it went in 1938 to Cambridge, owned by H. G. Hubbard, and was one of several derelict aircraft burned at Gatwick in 1948 after storage there during the war. Its sister machine 'HV passed through several ownerships, including that of an air-minded cleric, who used it as an open-air pulpit along the East Coast in 1935, and the London and

The 20th production Simmonds Spartan, showing the revised undercarriage.

Provincial Aviation Co. Ltd. at Croydon. Today it is the only surviving Simmonds Spartan relic and is stored at Denham after long years in Herefordshire and Hampshire barns.

When National Flying Services Ltd. standardised the Moth at the end of 1930, its remaining Spartans were retired. G-AAMD was then modified at Hanworth and fitted with a Gipsy I and seven hour tankage for Lt. Finch White, who left Hanworth on January 29, 1931, in an abortive attempt to reach India, crashing at Tunis a few days later. G-AAMB was flown for a time by Alexander Duckham and Co. Ltd. to publicise the firm's oils and then went to High Post with the Wiltshire School of Flying Ltd.

G-AAHV, third and last of the British registered Simmonds Spartan three seaters.

G-AAGY was the only other used for this purpose, spending 1929 and 1930 in the ownership of B. S. Thynne and F/O J. F. X. McKenna, before going to the Phillips and Powis School of Flying at Woodley in 1933 and to the short-lived Eastern Flying Club at Warley, Essex, in 1938.

Fame rarely came to the Simmonds Spartan, but the former N.F.S. machine G-AAMI was equipped with skis and sold to Wilhelm Omsted at Oslo in April 1930. It made many Arctic flights, covering more than 45,000 miles over the mountain ranges of Northern Norway. In the racing field the Spartan's chief success occurred during the King's Cup Race of July 25, 1931, when F/Lt. F. G. Gibbons came second in the single-seat Hermes II engined G-AAHA at 109·1 m.p.h.

Manufacturers: Simmonds Aircraft Ltd., Weston, Southampton, and Hamble
   Aerodrome, Hants.
Power Plants: One 95 h.p. A.D.C. Cirrus III.
           One 100 h.p. de Havilland Gipsy I.
           One 120 h.p. de Havilland Gipsy II.
           One 100 h.p. A.D.C. Hermes I.
           One 105 h.p. A.D.C. Hermes II.
Dimensions: Span, 28 ft. 7 in. Length, 23 ft. 11 in. Height, 9 ft. 3 in. Wing area,
   240 sq. ft.
Weights: (Two seater) Tare weight, 940 lb. All-up weight, 1,680 lb.
            (Three seater) Tare weight, 1,050 lb. All-up weight, 1,750 lb.
Performance: (Two seater) Maximum speed, 100 m.p.h. Cruising speed,
                         85 m.p.h. Initial climb, 600 ft./min. Range,
                         320 miles.
            (Three seater) Maximum speed, 107 m.p.h. Cruising speed,
                         95 m.p.h. Initial climb, 500 ft./min. Ceiling,
                         16,000 ft. Range, 300 miles.

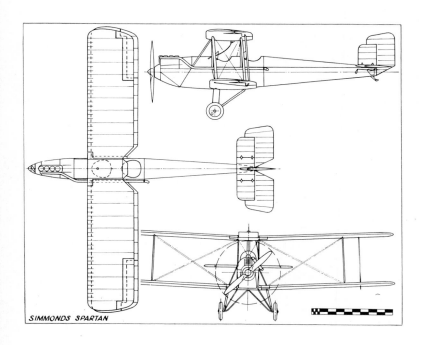

SIMMONDS SPARTAN

Harry Hawker flying the prototype cabin Gnu K-101, second British civil registered aeroplane, at Hendon, May 29, 1919. (*'Flight' Photo.*)

Sopwith Gnu

Introduced in May 1919, the Sopwith Gnu three seat tourer was one of the first cabin aircraft designed for civil use. It was an orthodox two bay biplane of fabric-covered wooden construction, seating the pilot in an open cockpit under the centre section, one panel of which was left open for improved vision. Two passengers sat side by side in the rear cockpit under a hinged and glazed cabin roof.

Fresh from his famous mid-Atlantic rescue, Harry Hawker flew his wife from Brooklands to Hendon in the Bentley B.R.2 powered prototype Gnu, K-101, on May 29, 1919, to attend the reception given to the crews of the successful American Transatlantic flying-boats NC-1, 2 and 4. The honour of making the first passenger flight in the Gnu, piloted by the idol of the aviation world, fell to a Miss Daisy King of Leeds, who paid 60 guineas in an auction conducted by Mr. Grahame-White. Excluding the prototype, total Gnu production amounted to 12 aircraft, the first of which, K-136, fitted, like most subsequent aircraft, with a 110 h.p. Le Rhône rotary, flew to Hendon in formation with the prototype. The third machine, K-140, was the first of several open models, and when Gnu production ceased six months later, three had been shipped to the Larkin-Sopwith Aviation Co. Ltd. in Australia. Four remained unsold, one of which was exhibited without markings at the Olympia Aero Show of July 1920 and another, G-EAMG, the last Gnu delivered, was eventually flown with a B.R.2.

Only the first and fourth production Gnus had lengthy careers in the United Kingdom. These were the cabin model G-EADB and the open cockpit 'GP. The latter became the property of Lt.-Col. F. K. McClean and won the Grosvenor Trophy at Lympne on June 23, 1923, piloted by F/Lt. W. H. Longton. The 404 mile course round Southern England was completed at an average speed of 87·6 m.p.h., the Filton–Croydon leg being covered in 62 minutes. The other Gnu, 'DP, was owned and flown during 1923–24 by E. A. D. Eldridge, but in June 1925 was sold to J. R. King, who entered it for the Lympne Races on August 1–3, 1925. The Gnu's performance was not outstanding, and 'DB came fourth at 86·95 m.p.h. in the 100 mile International Handicap, and fifth at 84·86 m.p.h. in the 50 mile Private Owners' Handicap.

Both Gnus were then purchased by the Southern Counties Aviation Company of Shoreham and spent the remainder of the 1925 season giving pleasure flights from fields along the South Coast. In the following year they were taken over by G. M. Lloyd, a professional stunt man, who extended their activities to embrace the East Coast and to include exhibition flying to attract would-be passengers. It was their undoing, the first to go being 'DB, which stalled on the approach to a field at Horley, Surrey, on March 2, 1926, injuring the pilot, L. R. Goodman. Two months later 'GP spun into a cemetery at King's Lynn, killing the pilot A. O. Bigg-Wither after the engine failed at the conclusion of a wing walking exhibition by G. M. Lloyd.

W. H. Longton taxying in at Lympne after winning the 1923 Grosvenor Trophy in the open cockpit Gnu G-EAGP. (*'Flight' Photo.*)

SPECIFICATION

Manufacturers: The Sopwith Aviation Co. Ltd., Canbury Park Road, Kingston-on-Thames, Surrey. Name changed to The Sopwith Aviation and Engineering Co. Ltd., June 1919.
Power Plants: One 200 h.p. Bentley B.R.2.
         One 110 h.p. Le Rhône.
Dimensions: Span, 38 ft. 1 in. Length, 25 ft. 10 in. Height, 9 ft. 10 in.
Weights: All-up weight, 3,350 lb.
Performance: Maximum speed, 93 m.p.h. Initial climb, 645 ft./min. Range, 300 miles.

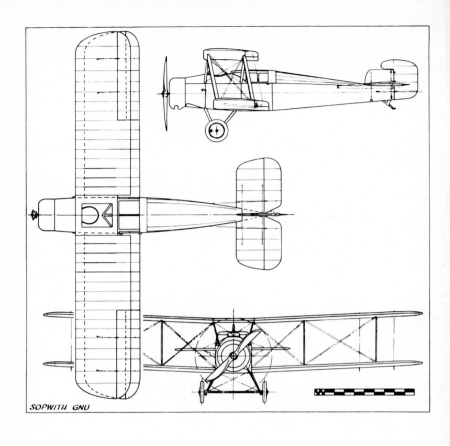

SOPWITH GNU

268

The prototype Martlet with Hornet engine. (*'Flight' Photo.*)

Southern Martlet

The prototype Martlet, G-AAII, first flown in August 1929, was an Avro Baby (see Volume 1, page 84), modernised at Shoreham by a team consisting of F. G. Miles, G. H. Miles, D. L. Brown and H. Hull. Its identity is uncertain, but was, no doubt, a new and unsold airframe from Avro's Hamble works. Existing mainplanes and fuselage were married to an entirely new tail unit, and a new oleo and coil spring undercarriage was designed for it by the Hendy Aircraft Company. New controls and an aircooled A.B.C. Hornet flat four were also fitted and the result was an incredibly manoeuvrable aircraft, suitable for amateur aerobatics. The Martlet made its first public appearance at the opening of Hanworth on August 30, 1929, but was re-engined with a Genet II radial soon afterwards.

Five dissimilar production aircraft were built at Shoreham during 1930–31, G-AAVD with Genet II for W. R. Westhead, 'YX with Genet Major and untapered ailerons for L. E. R. Bellairs, 'YZ with Gipsy II for the Rt. Hon. F. E. Guest, G-ABBN with Genet II for the Marquess of Douglas and Clydesdale and G-ABIF with Genet II and untapered ailerons for Mrs. Freeman-Thomas. Although obvious racing mounts, their King's Cup record was disappointing. Miss Winifred Spooner flew 'YZ into 14th place in the 1930 event at a round-Britain speed of 125·5 m.p.h., but F. G. Miles, in 'VD retired at Hanworth. That redoubtable pair M. L. Bramson and H. H. Leech were no luckier in 1931. Flying 'BN and 'IF, they retired at Shoreham and Sherburn-in-Elmet respectively, while in the following year, F/O E. C. T. Edwards, then the owner of 'YZ, damaged it in a forced landing near Runcorn. In 1933 T. C. Sanders retired in 'IF in traditional fashion, and for the 1934 race, 'YZ was fitted with a Gipsy I, bringing Edwards into 6th place at 119·77 m.p.h., but Martlets were never again flown in the classic event.

G-ABBN was acquired by National Aviation Day Displays Ltd. in 1932, and for one season toured the country giving aerobatic and aerodrome racing performances. The prototype, veteran of six ownerships, spent 1935 at Hanworth in the possession of A. H. Tweddle and was then sold in Eire. In common with the other Martlets, 'VD had several owners, ending its flying days at Redhill in 1939 with H. Whittaker after a period at Walsall with H. M. Goodwin. The Gipsy model, 'YZ, spent 1935–37 in a red colour

G-AAYZ, the Gipsy II Martlet at Brooklands prior to the start of the King's Cup Race, July 8, 1932. (*'Flight' Photo.*)

The last production Martlet G-ABIF combined the Genet II with untapered ailerons. (*Photo: Miles Aircraft Ltd.*)

The Metal Martlet, G-ABJW, showing the incorrect lettering.

scheme with Marius Maxwell at Croydon, while 'IF toured with C. W. A. Scott's Air Display 1936–37, flown by pilots of Air Travel Ltd. When war came, its final owner, G. D. Tucker of Hatfield, gave it to the A.T.C.

Unique among Martlets by virtue of its Genet Major engine, G-AAYX was at first the all-red personal mount of F. G. Miles and went with him to Reading, passing into the ownership of Phillips and Powis Aircraft Ltd. in August 1934. Its presence among the new Reading-built Miles machines then gave rise to the oft used, but wholly inaccurate, designation Miles Martlet. After spending 1937–38 at West Malling with G. K. Lawrence and W. K. Vinson, it was taken to Witney by M. N. Mavrogordato. One of the first pre-war aircraft to reappear after VJ Day, it flew again at Woodley on June 17, 1947, after overhaul by Miles Aircraft Ltd. for Butlins Ltd., who acquired it for the aerobatic entertainment of holiday-makers at Broomhall, Pwllheli. In 1949 it was sold to the Ultra Light Association, but finally returned to its birthplace and progressive dereliction. Today, as the only survivor of an important breed, it is in the hands of the Shuttleworth Trust at Old Warden.

The last Martlet left the Shoreham works in 1931, but was followed by a new version, the Metal Martlet. This had a fuselage of plate-jointed steel tubing covered by detachable wood and fabric fairings and split axle undercarriage with low pressure wheels and differential brakes. Powered by a Hermes I, it had unstaggered folding wings and little in common with the true Martlet. Registered G-ABJW, it flew at Shoreham during the 1931 season, mispainted first as G-AAII and later as G-AAJW, and then went to the scrap heap. A second machine, G-ABMM, ordered by W. R. Westhead, was not completed.

Manufacturers: Southern Aircraft Ltd., Shoreham Aerodrome, Sussex.

Power Plants: (Martlet)   One 85 h.p. A.B.C. Hornet
                         One 80 h.p. Armstrong Siddeley Genet II.
                         One 100 h.p. Armstrong Siddeley Genet Major.
                         One 100 h.p. de Havilland Gipsy I.
                         One 120 h.p. de Havilland Gipsy II.
          (Metal Martlet) One 105 h.p. A.D.C. Hermes I.

Dimensions: (Martlet)   Span, 25 ft. 0 in. Length, 20 ft. 3 in. Height, 7 ft. 7 in. Wing area, 180 sq. ft.
         (Metal Martlet) Span, 23 ft. 6 in. Length, 20 ft. 6 in. Height, 8 ft. 0 in. Wing area, 156 sq. ft.

	Martlet			Metal Martlet
	Hornet	Genet II	Gipsy II	
Tare weight .	630 lb.	705 lb.	—	—
All-up weight .	1,040 lb.	1,030 lb.	1,105 lb.	—
Maximum speed.	112 m.p.h.	112·5 m.p.h.	130 m.p.h.	130 m.p.h.
Cruising speed .	—	95·5 m.p.h.	95 m.p.h.	115 m.p.h.
Initial climb .	1,100 ft./min.	1,100 ft./min.	1,700 ft./min.	1,400 ft./min.
Ceiling .	—	—	—	20,000 ft.
Range .	—	280 miles	—	400 miles

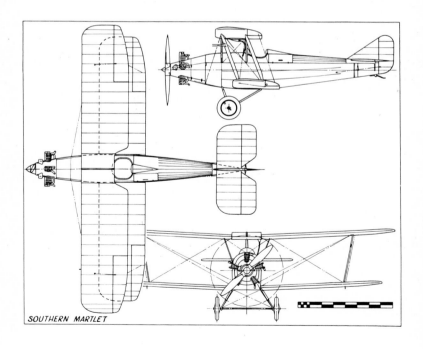

SOUTHERN MARTLET

A late production Arrow with ailerons on lower wings only.

Spartan Arrow

Simmonds Aircraft Ltd. was reconstituted early in 1930 and renamed Spartan Aircraft Ltd., members of the board including Mr. O. E. Simmonds, Lt.-Col. L. A. Strange and Capt. H. H. Balfour. Realising that sales resistance to the Simmonds Spartan was probably due to an unwarranted distrust of the symmetrical aerofoil section, a new two seater, the Spartan Arrow, was built. Although a non-symmetrical wing section was employed, much of the original interchangeability was ingeniously retained by a system of detachable wing tips and trailing edge sections which enabled a wing to be fitted on either side and the aileron at either end. The two halves of the undercarriage were still interchangeable, but the vertical tail surfaces were of entirely new outline. The Arrow was otherwise structurally orthodox, with spruce and plywood fuselage and wooden, fabric-covered, folding wings, but the cockpits, entered via large doors, were more roomy than on contemporary light aircraft.

Use of the Clark Y, high lift, aerofoil section and an increase of 2 ft. in the span, imparted a rate of climb much superior to that of its predecessor. Two prototypes, G-AAWY and 'WZ, flew with Gipsy I engines in May 1930, but 'WZ and G-ABBE, first of the 12 production Arrows, were fitted with Gipsy IIs for the King's Cup Race of July 5, 1930. Results were disappointing, the aircraft finishing 54th and 58th, piloted by W. A. Andrews and Capt. N. H. Balfour at average speeds of 100·5 and 94·3 m.p.h. respectively. The Andrews/'WZ combination put up a fine performance, however, in the International Round Europe Touring Competition a month later. First deliveries, in December 1930, were G-ABGW to B. S. Thynne, Hamble, and 'HR, the only Arrow fitted with a Cirrus III, to the Household Brigade Flying Club, Heston. G-ABKL went to the Bristol and Wessex Aeroplane Club, Whitchurch, in April 1931. A single seater, 'HD, with Gipsy II, was delivered to the Australian pilot

G. P. Fairbairn at Hanworth on January 25, 1931, for an attempt on the Australia record, but the flight ended ignominiously at Nice on February 20, one day after leaving Hanworth. The remaining distance was covered by sea, the Arrow subsequently seeing considerable service before crashing at Essendon on June 11, 1935.

Capt. Balfour's 'BE went to the M.A.E.E., Felixstowe, at the end of 1930 for floatplane trials, which were followed by an order from the Hon. A. E. Guinness for G-ABMK, a Hermes powered Arrow on floats. This was first flown at Cowes under B conditions as S-1 in June 1931, but the owner's interest in larger marine aircraft led to its sale as a landplane to George Duller at Woodley in February 1933.

Although no Arrow ever again raced for the King's Cup, F/Lt. G. H. Stainforth flew the 9th production aircraft, G-ABOB, in the *Morning Post* Race at Heston on May 21, 1932, but averaged a humble 79·2 m.p.h. to come 13th, an unhappy position reached in the same machine by Lt.-Col. L. A. Strange in the Heston–Cramlington Race of August 16, 1933. It went on to enjoy a successful career in private and club ownership, ended with the Exeter and Thanet Aero Clubs in 1938–39, but was more note-worthy as the last Arrow fitted with ailerons on all four wings. The re-maining six Arrows had them only on the lower mainplanes, and in-cluded a special aircraft, G-ABST, with non-standard rudder, built as a flying test bed for the new Napier E.97 six cylinder, aircooled engine, later known as the Javelin. Relays of pilots put in hundreds of hours of test flying with this Arrow at Heston in 1932–33. During the same period the second prototype, 'WZ, was in similar employ at Croydon by Cirrus Aero Engines Ltd., fitted with their Hermes II and flown by J. V. Holman.

Production of the Arrow ended in 1933 with the delivery of G-ACHE, 'HF and 'HG, the second of which was the centre of a fatal drama at Brooklands on September 13, 1933, when its first owner, Lady Clayton

The Gipsy powered Arrow floatplane G-ABBE at Felixstowe, December 1930. (*Crown Copyright Reserved.*)

G-ABST, the Napier Javelin III flying test bed. (*'Flight' Photo.*)

East Clayton, fell out on take off and was killed. Later it went to Lympne to be flown by the Marquess of Kildare in 1935 and by T. A. S. Webb in the following year, coming 4th in the Wakefield Trophy Race. Bought by the Romford Flying Club in March 1939, its end came in the fire at May-lands on February 2, 1940. Its career was rivalled only by the fifth pro-duction Arrow, G-ABWR, which, between 1932 and its sale in Denmark in August 1938, was owned successively by R. V. L'Estrange Malone, Heston; H. V. K. Atkinson and Flying Hire Ltd. at Chilworth; Rollason Aircraft Services Ltd., Croydon, and W. J. Gunther, Gravesend.

At the outbreak of war the first prototype, re-engined with a Hermes II, was in use by the Isle of Wight Flying Club at Sandown, where it was eventually dismantled and the parts used to build a primary glider. The second Arrow, 'WZ, was at Ford with the Yapton Aero Club and 'KL, owned by E. D. Ward, was destroyed in the Hooton fire of July 11, 1940. One other, the Hermes II model G-ABWP, bought by R. O. Shuttleworth in December 1936, reappeared at the Fifty Years of Flying Exhibition at Hendon in July 1951 after years in storage at Old Warden. Two years later it began a post-war career with a brand new C. of A. with W. G. Lilleystone's group at Croydon, passing in April 1955 into the hands of the Spartan Group with which it still flies at Denham.

Manufacturers: Spartan Aircraft Ltd., Weston, Southampton, moved to East
Cowes, Isle of Wight, February 20, 1931.

Power Plants: One 100 h.p. de Havilland Gipsy I.
One 120 h.p. de Havilland Gipsy II.
One 95 h.p. A.D.C. Cirrus III.
One 105 h.p. Cirrus Hermes II.
One 160 h.p. Napier Javelin III.

Dimensions: Span, 30 ft. 7 in. Length, 25 ft. 0 in. Height, 9 ft. 6 in. Wing area,
251 sq. ft.

Weights:　　(Standard) Tare weight, 965 lb. All-up weight, 1,750 lb.*
(Javelin)　Tare weight, 1,207 lb. All-up weight, 1,730 lb.

Performance: Maximum speed, 106 m.p.h. Cruising speed, 92 m.p.h. Initial climb,
830 ft./min. Range, 432 miles.

* Late production 1,850 lb.

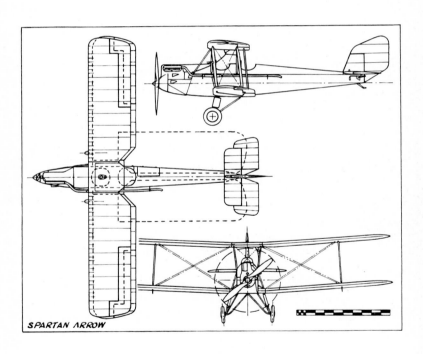

SPARTAN ARROW

The Hermes II powered Spartan Three Seater I G-ABRA of the Spartan Air Circus 1932.

Spartan Three Seater I and II

When Spartan Aircraft Ltd. took over the former Simmonds Aircraft Co. Ltd., the symmetrical wing section was abandoned in favour of the Clark Y. Two and three seat successors to the original Simmonds Spartan were then produced and designated Spartan Arrow and Spartan Three Seater respectively. The latter was structurally similar to the Arrow, with plywood fuselage and wooden wings, but retained the characteristic rudder of the original Simmonds Spartan. Commencing with Sandown and Shanklin Flying Services' red G-ABAZ 'Island Queen', 19 Three Seaters were built at Cowes 1930–32, all of British registry except the 11th, which was to Australian order. Upright engines were fitted, five having Gipsy IIs and the rest Hermes IIs.

Although few in number, Spartan Three Seaters became one of the mainstays of the pleasure flight trade in the 1930s. In 1939 'AZ was still circuiting Sandown Bay, while the second and third aircraft, 'ET and 'KJ, were similarly employed along the East Coast by Lawn Parks (Skegness) Ltd. British Air Transport's black and white G-ABTU worthily upheld the Avro tradition at Croydon, Addiscombe and Redhill, 'JS toured with C. D. Barnard's Circus in 1931, 'WU spent 1933 doing 10s. flights round Southend Pier, Rollason's 'WV toured with National Aviation Day Displays and 'LJ spent its life on the same errand, first with Portsmouth, Southsea and Isle of Wight Aviation Ltd. and later at Ford with the Yapton Aero Club. Hayling Island's Three Seater was 'YH, destroyed there in 1935 in a fatal crash when attempting a publicity loop at low altitude. Spartan joyriding activities also extended to Africa, where G-ABPZ, 'RA and 'RB of Skywork Ltd., piloted by Oscar Garden, E. D. Ayre and others, toured 64 towns in 1932. 'RA then returned home to spend a season at Allhallows, Kent, piloted by John Stark, 'PZ staying at the Cape while Oscar Garden took 'RB into the Sudan and Egypt with Tanganyikan marks during 1933.

Trading as Air Trips Ltd., those immortal ladies Pauline Gower and Dorothy Spicer made 'KK the best remembered of the Spartan Three Seaters. Named 'Helen of Troy', it ranged between Shoreham, Blackpool and Haldon with the Crimson Fleet in 1932, visited 185 towns with British Hospital's Air Pageants in 1933 and spent 1934–35 at Hunstanton and with Jubilee Air Displays. The end came in 1936 with Campbell Black's Air Circus, in a take off collision at Westwood, Coventry. Several flying clubs augmented their incomes with Spartan joyriding, including Peterborough with 'KT and Romford with 'WO in 1939, but few were privately owned. J. Miskelly kept the cabin Three Seater 'WX at Dumfries for a few months in 1933 and Neville Browning had 'YG at Abridge in 1935. 'LJ, kept at Tangmere by A. C. Douglas in 1939, was acquired by C. J. Rice in 1942 and conveyed on a trailer to Leicester, where it was given to the A.T.C. Only one Three Seater essayed a racing career, 'TT, winner of a local race at Skegness on May 14, 1932, piloted by Capt. Gordon Store of Imperial Airways. Exactly a week later it flew into a tree during the *Morning Post* Race, killing F/Lt. F. G. Gibbons.

Two years at the most gruelling form of aerial work had shown the need for better pilot view and less difficult entry for passengers. In the Three Seater II, the prototype of which, G-ABTR, was introduced by Lt.-Col. L. A. Strange at Henlys' Rally, Heston on June 4, 1932, both requirements were brilliantly met by cockpit reversal and the use of the Hermes IIB inverted engine. The earlier model then became known as the Three Seater I, but neither should be identified with the original three seat Simmonds Spartan, which was an entirely different aeroplane. 'TR then embarked on a racing programme for publicity purposes, winning the Skegness Race at 100·25 m.p.h. on July 31, coming 4th in the Heston–Cramlington Race on August 6 and winning the Thanet Air Race at Ramsgate at 96·5 m.p.h. on September 17.

Only six production models were built, all Hermes IV powered. The first, 'YN, privately owned by E. G. Croskin at Hedon, Hull in 1935, eventually went to Ireland and was still flying in Tipperary in 1950. Aerofilms

G-ABWX, only Three Seater I to be fitted with an enclosed passenger cockpit. (*Photo: Aerofilms Ltd.*)

Prototype Spartan Three Seater II G-ABTR (Hermes IIB) and the first production machine G-ABYN (Hermes IV) at the special Spartan demonstration, Heston, August 30, 1932. (*'Flight' Photo.*)

Sole example of a cabin Three Seater II, G-ABTR flew with Spartan Air Lines during the 1933 season. (*'Flight' Photo.*)

Ltd. used 'ZH as a photographic aircraft, but it also toured with the circuses, as did the Cornwall Aviation Company's G-ACAF, and 'AD successor to the Gower/Spicer 'KK. The last Spartan of all, 'EF, privately owned at Christchurch by H. Pritchett 1935–37, ended its days with Malling Aviation Ltd. Only one, 'ZI, exchanged a hard-working for an eventful career, going to Iraq Airwork Ltd. as YI-AAB in January 1933 and returning to Hendon two years later for the use of officers of No. 601 Squadron. It was burned out on the roof of the station buildings at Farnborough in August 1936 after an haphazard take off.

No Spartan Three Seater exists today, the last, 'TR, operated by United Airways Ltd. and British Airways Ltd. 1934–36 and later employed joyriding with F. G. Barnard at Hayling Island, was burned as a derelict in 1947 after wartime storage at Gatwick.

SPECIFICATION

Manufacturers: Spartan Aircraft Ltd., Weston, Southampton, moved to East Cowes, Isle of Wight, February 20, 1931.

Power Plants: (Three Seater I)   One 120 h.p. de Havilland Gipsy II.
                                   One 115 h.p. Cirrus Hermes II.
                (Three Seater II) One 115 h.p. Cirrus Hermes IIB.
                                   One 120 h.p. Cirrus Hermes IV.

Dimensions: Span, 28 ft. 10 in. Length, 26 ft. 3 in. Height, 9 ft. 8 in. Wing area, 240 sq. ft.

Weights: Tare weight (Mk. I), 1,030 lb. (Mk. II), 1,150 lb. All-up weight (Mk. I), 1,680 lb. (Mk. II), 1,850 lb.

Performance: (Three Seater I)   Maximum speed, 103 m.p.h. Cruising speed, 90 m.p.h. Initial climb, 600 ft./min. Ceiling, 15,000 ft. Range, 300 miles.
               (Three Seater II) Maximum speed, 107 m.p.h. Cruising speed, 95 m.p.h. Initial climb, 750 ft./min. Range, 260 miles.

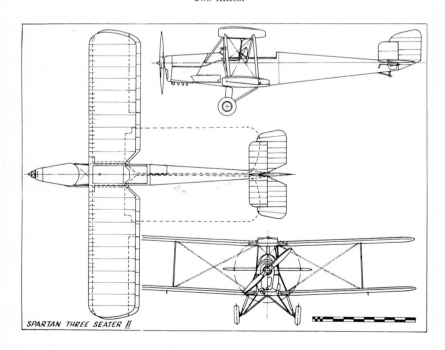

SPARTAN THREE SEATER II

Cruiser II G-ACVT at Croydon in 1934 showing the revised windscreen and cabin windows incorporated in the four final aircraft.

Spartan Cruiser

No better example of joint effort can be envisaged than the hard-worked Spartan Cruiser of the 1930s. It stemmed from the Saunders-Roe A.24 Mailplane G-ABLI, built in 1931 to the designs of E. W. Percival. The only one of its kind, this low-wing monoplane was typically Percival, with plywood fuselage and wooden wing, but was powered by three Gipsy III engines, and seated a single pilot ahead of a small mail compartment. Close ties between the Saunders-Roe and Spartan concerns, both of East Cowes, resulted in development being transferred to Spartan and the designation changed to Spartan Mailplane. In 1932 the single fin and rudder was replaced by a twin unit, and after further rudder modification the aircraft was flown to India by T. Neville Stack. Named 'Blackpool', it left Stanley Park Aerodrome with civic blessings on June 15, 1932, reaching Drigh Road, Karachi, in an elapsed time of 5 days 23 hours 50 minutes. After demonstration before the Director of Civil Aviation, it returned home, making a forced landing in Greece with an oil leak en route.

Although the pure mail carrier had no future, the design held promise for passenger work, team effort at East Cowes being rewarded by successful trials of the Spartan Cruiser I, G-ABTY, by Lt.-Col. L. A. Strange in May 1932. As indicated by the constructor's number 24M, E. W. Percival's low-wing trimotor layout had been retained, but an all-metal fuselage had been built to accommodate six passengers and two crew. The structural features of the stressed-skin hull and plywood-covered wing of the Cutty Sark, had been adapted for the Cruiser, which also used cabin glazing reminiscent of the Saro Segrave Meteor. The new machine was demonstrated at the first Hendon S.B.A.C. Show of June 27, 1932, and alongside its predecessor, the Mailplane, at the Spartan demonstration at Heston on August 30. Piloted by Lt.-Col. L. A. Strange, it conveyed H.R.H. the Prince of Wales from Sunningdale to Croydon on September 22, carried the Lord Mayor of London from Heston to Maylands to open the Essex Air Display on the 24th and left on October 14 for a European sales tour. On its return to Heston on the 25th, 3,593 miles had been covered at an average speed of 113 m.p.h. Demonstrations made to the Jugoslav airline Aeroput at Belgrade on October 19 eventually led to an order for four aircraft.

The first Cruiser II, flown in February 1933, was ordered by Iraq Airwork Ltd. for an experimental air route between Baghdad and Mosul, and although initially registered G-ACBM, was flown out in Airwork white and green as YI-AAA by T. Neville Stack. It was powered by three Hermes IVs and entered by a cabin door instead of via folding side and roof panels, while the pilot's windscreen was V-shaped for improved vision. During the next two years, eleven more Cruiser IIs were built, five of which, fruits of the overseas sales tours, were sold abroad. Two were flown to Belgrade on delivery to the Jugoslav airline Aeroput and two to the Bata Shoe Company at Zlin, Czechoslovakia. In May–June 1934 the first of these, G-ACNO/OK-ATQ 'Cape of Good Hope', carried out a successful 21,900 mile business trip of Europe, the Near East, Egypt, Sudan and South Africa. The 5th Cruiser was shipped to the Maharajah of Patiala in November 1933. The majority were Gipsy Major powered but G-ACOU had Walter Major 4s and the Indian was fitted with Hermes IVs.

An operating company known as Spartan Air Lines Ltd., formed to open an internal air route between Heston and Cowes, began operations on April 1, 1933, with the Cruiser I and two new Cruiser IIs, G-ACDW and 'DX. The firm's chief pilot, P. W. Lynch Blosse, flew 'DW, specially named 'Faithful City', to Australia and back at the end of the season, on charter to Capt. W. P. Crawford Green and Lord Apsley. Leaving on

The Saro A.24 Mailplane. (*Photo: Saunders-Roe Ltd.*)

Cruiser I showing the early type of cabin glazing. (*Photo: Saunders-Roe Ltd.*)

Cruiser III G-ADEM, last of all the Cruisers. (*Photo courtesy of J. G. Ellison.*)

October 9, 1933, Sydney was reached on the 30th, and the machine eventually arrived home to make a precautionary landing on St. Osyth beach, Essex. The Southern Railway then acquired a controlling interest in Spartan Air Lines and the London terminus was transferred to Croydon on May 1, 1934. Two new Cruiser IIs, 'SM and 'VT, were then commissioned together with 'BM, back from Iraq to replace 'DW, which had left Heston as SU-ABL on delivery to Misr Airwork Ltd., at Almaza, Cairo, in April. They were joined in the following year by the final Cruiser II, 'ZM, built to replace the Cruiser I, sold to the Hon. Mrs. Victor Bruce in February 1935. It was then employed on charter work by Channel Air Lines, mainly on the early morning newspaper run to Le Bourget, until it forced landed in the Channel and was lost a few months later. The penultimate Cruiser II, 'YL, built for United Airways Ltd., operated the company's service between Heston, Stanley Park and Ronaldsway throughout 1935.

Cruiser production finally ended in May 1935 with the delivery to Spartan Air Lines of the third Spartan Cruiser III, of similar design to the Mk. II but with aerodynamically refined fuselage, modified windscreen, empennage and trousered undercarriage. Passenger accommodation was increased to eight and the prototype, G-ACYK, made its public debut at the Heathrow Garden Party of the Royal Aeronautical Society on May 5, 1935.

The year 1936 saw the absorption of Spartan Air Lines by British Airways Ltd., and the transference of the surviving Cruisers to a new base at Eastleigh, from which they worked over the Isle of Wight, Heston, Blackpool, Isle of Man network. The Cruiser IIIs carried Railway Air Services Ltd.'s livery during the season, but 'EM was burned out at Stanley Park in the November and Capt. O'Connell and a passenger killed through flying into a hangar when taking off in fog. The four surviving Cruisers were then taken over by Northern and Scottish Airways Ltd., Renfrew, continuing in service to the Highlands and Islands until the outbreak of war. From June 1938 they did so under Scottish Airways ownership, three being impressed by the R.A.F. in April 1940.

Manufacturers: Spartan Aircraft Ltd., East Cowes, Isle of Wight, Hants.

Power Plants: (Mailplane)   Three 120 h.p. de Havilland Gipsy III.
       (Cruiser I)   Three 120 h.p. de Havilland Gipsy III.
      (Cruiser II)   Three 130 h.p. de Havilland Gipsy Major.
                     Three 130 h.p. Cirrus Hermes IV.
                     Three 130 h.p. Walter Major 4.
     (Cruiser III) Three 130 h.p. de Havilland Gipsy Major.

	Mailplane	Cruiser I	Cruiser II	Cruiser III
Span . .	56 ft. 0 in.	54 ft. 0 in.	54 ft. 0 in.	54 ft. 0 in.
Length . .	41 ft. 6 in.	39 ft. 2 in.	39 ft. 2 in.	41 ft. 0 in.
Height . .	9 ft. 0 in.	10 ft. 0 in.	10 ft. 0 in.	9 ft. 6 in.
Wing area . .	470 sq. ft.	436 sq. ft.	436 sq. ft.	436 sq. ft.
Tare weight .	4,425 lb.	3,400 lb.	3,650 lb.	4,010 lb.
All-up weight .	5,645 lb.	5,500 lb.	6,200 lb.	6,200 lb.
Maximum speed .	122 m.p.h.	135 m.p.h.	133 m.p.h.	135 m.p.h.
Cruising speed .	105 m.p.h.	110 m.p.h.	115 m.p.h.	118 m.p.h.
Initial climb .	500 ft./min.	600 ft./min.	630 ft./min.	600 ft./min.
Ceiling . .	—	13,000 ft.	15,000 ft.	15,000 ft.
Range . .	400 miles	660 miles	310 miles	550 miles

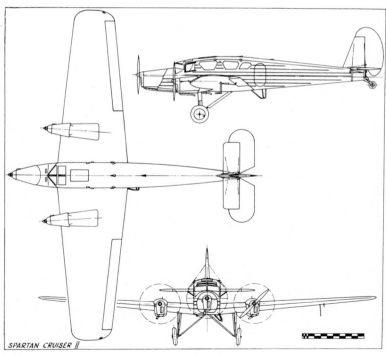

SPARTAN CRUISER II

G-EAED/N1529, the first civil Channel, leaving Southampton on the inaugural flight to Le Havre, August 1919. (*Photo: The Supermarine Aviation Works Ltd.*)

Supermarine Channel

The A.D. two-seat patrol flying-boat of 1916 bore the initials of the Air Department of the Admiralty, for which it was designed jointly by Lt. Linton Hope, Harold Bolas, Harold Yendall and Clifford W. Tinson. Such a team could not fail to produce an outstanding aircraft, the flexible wooden monocoque hull of which unconcernedly absorbed every type of punishment in rough seas and high wind. Power was supplied by either a 150 h.p. or 200 h.p. Hispano-Suiza engine driving a four bladed pusher airscrew, and the wings folded forward. Construction took place at the Woolston, Southampton, works of Pemberton Billing Ltd., and at the Armistice 27 had been built, nine of which were undelivered. A number were repurchased from the Air Ministry by the Supermarine Aviation Works Ltd., successors to the Pemberton Billing concern, and converted for civil use. The more economical 160 h.p. Beardmore engine was fitted and the forward part of the hull modified to seat two passengers in tandem in the main cockpit, with a third in the bows and the pilot behind.

An initial batch of 10 rebuilt A.D. boats, redesignated Supermarine Channels, were registered to the manufacturers as G-EAED–'EM on June 11, 1919. Three, 'ED, 'EE and 'EK, still bearing their former R.A.F. serials, at once began pleasure flights along the South Coast, becoming, on July 23, 1919, the first commercial flying-boats to receive British certificates of airworthiness. Brisk business was done at Bournemouth Pier, so that the chief pilot Cdr. B. D. Hobbs, organised the daily positioning flight from Woolston into a regular service. During Cowes Week, a Channel was stationed in the Medina for the entertainment of members of the Royal Yacht Squadron and on August 7 was chartered for a flight round H.M.S. *Renown* as it left Portsmouth with H.R.H. the Prince of

Wales aboard. Later in the month 'ED received a civic send off at the inauguration of the world's first international flying-boat service to Le Havre. A local service to Cowes also began, the Channels taxying from the Woolston works to embark passengers at Royal Pier, but 'EE overturned and sank during a pleasure flight at Bournemouth on August 15 and the company ceased commercial operations at the end of the season.

In 1920 three Channels, originally earmarked as G-EAEH, 'EI and 'EL, were despatched to Norway in crates for use by Norske Luftreideri on a mail and passenger service between Stavanger and Bergen. From difficult anchorages, over difficult terrain and often in marginal weather, they operated with 94·4% regularity until the company ceased operations in December 1920. A fourth Channel, believed to have been G-EAEM, was fitted with dual control and supplied to the Royal Norwegian Navy base at Horten.

G-EAEF, 'EG and 'EJ, last of the initial batch of Channels, were shipped to Bermuda in April 1920, and spent the following winter in highly successful pleasure flying operations with the Bermuda and Western Atlantic Aviation Co. Ltd. One of several novel charters involved overtaking and landing alongside a United States bound steamship and transferring actress Pearl White. Shortage of spares ended their careers within a few months, but 'EG was shipped to Trinidad in March 1921 to join two Channel Mk. II flying-boats. Powered by the 240 h.p. Siddeley Puma engine, these had strutted wing tip floats and watertight camera doors let into the hull bottoms. Flown by C. E. Ward and F. Bailey of the Bermuda and Western Atlantic Aviation Co. Ltd., they carried out an oil prospecting expedition in the Orinoco Delta, Venezuela, under the direction of Major Cochran Patrick. Although neither carried markings, one was registered G-EAWC and later one of them was detached for the aerial survey of Georgetown, British Guiana, but sank in the River Essequibo after a collision with driftwood.

Launching Channel G-EAEJ of the Bermuda and Western Atlantic Aviation Co. Ltd.

Channel Mk. II G-EAWP, taking off at Fiji, July 1921. In addition to the Puma engine, the Channel Mk. II was fitted with strutted wing-tip floats. (*Photo: The Supermarine Aviation Works Ltd.*)

In July 1921 another unmarked Channel Mk. II, actually G-EAWP, was engaged in flights between the main islands of the Fiji group, later completing a photographic survey of the coastline of Viti Levu. Six similar machines also received certificates of airworthiness in 1920–21 for export without markings, including four for the Imperial Japanese Navy, one for the Royal Norwegian Navy and one each for commercial use in Cuba and New Zealand.

SPECIFICATION

Manufacturers: The Supermarine Aviation Works Ltd., Woolston, Southampton, Hants.
Power Plants: (Channel Mk. I) One 160 h.p. Beardmore.
              (Channel Mk. II) One 240 h.p. Siddeley Puma.
Dimensions: Span, 50 ft. 4 in. Length, 30 ft. 7 in. Height, 13 ft. 1 in. Wing area, 479 sq. ft.
*Weights: All-up weight 3,400 lb.
*Performance: Maximum speed 100 m.p.h. Ceiling 10,000 ft. Duration 5 hours.

* Channel Mk. I.

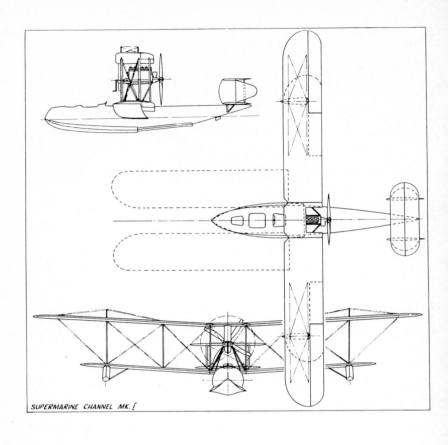

SUPERMARINE CHANNEL MK. I

The Romford Flying Club's Taylorcraft Plus C, flying at Maylands, August 1939.
(*Photo courtesy of 'The Aeroplane'*.)

Taylorcraft Plus C and D

Taylorcraft Aeroplanes (England) Ltd. was formed in November 1938 to build the Taylorcraft side-by-side, two-seat, high-wing monoplane under licence from the Taylor Young Airplane Corporation in the U.S.A. Following contemporary American practice, the Taylorcraft Model A was fabric covered with welded steel tube fuselage and a wing of mixed construction braced by steel struts. Six examples, powered by the 40 h.p. Continental flat four engine had already been imported, the first of which, G-AFDN, was exhibited as a 'Taylor Young' at the Heathrow Garden Party of the Royal Aeronautical Society on May 8, 1938. After a season with C. N. Prentice at Ipswich, it joined a similar machine, 'KN, at the West Suffolk Aero Club, Bury St. Edmunds. The other four comprised 'HF of Cambridgeshire Flying Services Ltd., Ely; 'JO with Reid and Sigrist Ltd., Desford; 'JP at Meir with the South Staffs Aero Club, and 'JW with the County Flying Club, Rearsby, Leicester. A seventh, 'KO, a Model B with 50 h.p. Continental, was also based at Rearsby for publicity and test purposes by the new British licensee, who had opened a factory at Thurmaston, three miles away.

To differentiate them from the American machines the British versions were designated Taylorcraft C, later changed to Taylorcraft Plus C. The prototype, G-AFNW, completed at Thurmaston in April 1939, was taken to Rearsby for erection and flight, over a road traversed by all aircraft built by the firm during the next seven years. Powered by a 55 h.p.

Lycoming and fitted with dual control for use by the County Flying Club, 'NW was the forerunner of 22 production aircraft delivered in the summer of 1939 to private owners, the Coventry, Derby, Grimsby, Luton, Maidstone, Romford and West Suffolk clubs and the Wiltshire School of Flying.

The 11th airframe, built with 90 h.p. Cirrus Minor 1 in June 1939, was delivered to the R.A.F. as T9120 under the designation Auster I. Two months later the 25th aircraft, G-AFWN, also flew with this type of engine to become prototype of the civil Taylorcraft Plus D. Eight production aircraft appeared too late for bona fide civil use, four being impressed in 1940 for communications work in France and A.O.P. duties with No. 651 Squadron, a fate which befell the majority of Plus C machines. They were then re-engined by the R.A.F. with Cirrus Minor 1s

Taylorcraft Plus D G-AHUG, formerly an Auster I LB282, currently operated by the Reading Aero Club at Woodley, but previously in executive use by Feltrex Ltd. and Polythene Ltd.

and redesignated Taylorcraft Plus C.2. In 1947 this modification was also carried out on G-AFUA, which somehow managed to escape impressment. The prototype Plus D, G-AFWN, remained stored in a crashed condition until rebuilt as the prototype Autocrat in 1945 (See Volume 1, page 55).

Air Ministry trials of the Auster I led to a contract for 100 similar aircraft in 1941, final development work being undertaken at Larkhill by No. 651 Squadron with the last two civil machines G-AGBF and 'DB in August 1940 and September 1941 respectively. After a short Service life, the Auster Is, many in new condition, were stored at M.U.s until disposed of by public tender in 1945–46, when 58 became civil as Taylorcraft Plus Ds. Seven pre-war civil machines also survived, four of which had lost their previous identities and received post-war registrations. The prototype Auster I T9120 also reappeared to fly at Thruxton with the Wiltshire School of Flying as G-AHAF until wrecked by a sister machine G-AHUG, which landed on top of it on May 29, 1948. At Rearsby, three former R.A.F. aircraft G-AHCR, 'GX and 'HC were temporarily fitted with 55 h.p. Lycoming engines in 1947, approximating to Plus Cs until the Cirrus Minors were re-installed in 1948.

In 13 years of post-war flying, Taylorcraft Plus C.2 and D aircraft have done yeoman service as private aircraft, they have taken the hard knocks of instructional flying and they have served with the Boston, Bristol and Wessex, Cambridge, Channel Islands, Cotswold, Croydon, Denham, Edinburgh, Fairoaks, Hereford, Lancashire, Liverpool, Luton, Midland, Newcastle, Northampton, Penguin, Reading, Rochester, Staverton, West London, Wycombe and Yorkshire Flying Clubs. Seldom in the sporting headlines, the type made history at Woolsington on July 12, 1952, when Cyril Gregory flew a brilliant race in G-AHGZ, cunningly tuned, to win the King's Cup at an average speed of 113·5 m.p.h.

Advancing age, accidents and sales in Finland, Southern Rhodesia, Germany, Eire and Switzerland have taken toll, and in 1959 but 22 remain, including Plus C.2s G-AFTN and 'HLJ belonging to H. Plain, Exeter and the Fairoaks Aero Club respectively. Delivered to the West Suffolk Aero Club in May 1939 as G-AFTZ, the latter aircraft saw service at Luton before impressment and 12 post-war years at Chilbolton on Vickers-Armstrongs communications work. Two American built Taylorcraft Model As, G-AFJO and 'JP, spent the war in storage, to fly again in 1946 with P. S. Clifford, Walsall, and T. C. Sparrow, Christchurch, respectively. For six years mainstay of the Rotol Flying Club at Staverton, 'JO crashed in 1952, a year before the other passed away at Woodbridge, Suffolk, under group ownership with the Flying Tiger Cubs.

SPECIFICATION

Manufacturers: (Taylorcraft A) Taylor Young Airplane Corporation, Alliance, Ohio, U.S.A.

(Taylorcraft Plus C and D) Taylorcraft Aeroplanes (England) Ltd., Britannia Works, Thurmaston and Rearsby Aerodrome, Leicester.

Power Plants: (Taylorcraft A) One 40 h.p. Continental A-40-4.
One 40 h.p. Continental A-40-5.
One 50 h.p. Continental A-50.

(Taylorcraft Plus C) One 55 h.p. Lycoming O-145-A2.
(Taylorcraft Plus C.2 and D) One 90 h.p. Blackburn Cirrus Minor 1.

Dimensions: Span, 36 ft. 0 in. Length, 22 ft. 10 in. Height, 8 ft. 0 in. Wing area, 167 sq. ft.

	Model A	Model C	Model C.2	Model D
Tare weight .	586 lb.	720 lb.	833 lb.	890 lb.
All-up weight .	1,050 lb.	1,200 lb.	1,300 lb.	1,450 lb.
Maximum speed.	91 m.p.h.	110 m.p.h.	125 m.p.h.	120 m.p.h.
Cruising speed .	80 m.p.h.	90 m.p.h.	107 m.p.h.	102 m.p.h.
Initial climb .	390 ft./min.	550 ft./min.	1,000 ft./min.	1,000 ft./min.
Ceiling . .	14,000 ft.	—	—	—
Range . .	230 miles	275 miles	325 miles	325 miles

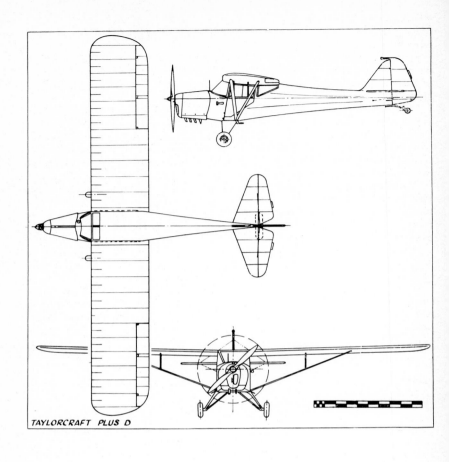

TAYLORCRAFT PLUS D

G-AESU, second Douglas powered Tipsy S.2 built by Aero Engines Ltd., Bristol.
(*Photo: The Fairey Aviation Co. Ltd.*)

Tipsy S.2

Unlike many pre-war ultra lights, the Tipsy S.2 was of orthodox appearance and had something of the clean, sturdy lines of the Spitfire. The name derived from that of the designer, E. O. Tips of Avions Fairey S.A., the Gosselies, Belgium, subsidiary of the Fairey Aviation Co., Ltd., in whose works the prototype, appropriately registered OO-TIP and designated Tipsy S.1, was built in 1935. It was mainly of wood, with plywood fuselage, fin and tailplane, the cantilever mainplane and all control surfaces being fabric covered. A Douglas Sprite two cylinder engine was carried on a tubular steel mounting and the wide track undercarriage ensured ease of taxying. At the Belgian light aeroplane trials in June 1935 the S.1 covered 63 miles per hour per gallon, and in May 1936 was flown to England for demonstration at Fairey's aerodrome, Heathrow, by M. Eyskens, chief test pilot of Avions Fairey. Thereafter it became a familiar sight at all the British aviation meetings, piloted by C. S. Staniland and others until scrapped at West Malling in 1938.

Interest was such that arrangements were made for the S.2 production version to be built, not only at Gosselies, but also under licence at Kingswood, Bristol, by Aero Engines Ltd., manufacturers of the Douglas engine. OO-ASA, the eighth Belgian built S.2, was delivered to Bristol as a specimen in October 1936, becoming British as G-AENF when sold to E. H. Chambers at Aylesbury in the following January. In August 1937 it was acquired by Neville Browning, flew in civil camouflage during the war and was eventually burned. Nine British S.2s were built during 1937, some of which were test flown at Whitchurch before despatch to Hanworth, where a sales organisation, the Tipsy Aircraft Co. Ltd., had been set up. The first, G-AEOB, in common with OO-TIP was fitted with an early model engine started by pulling a cord round a bobbin, but subsequent aircraft had improved engines with impulse starters and dual ignition, permitting a more streamlined top cowling. The reason for the failure of the lively little S.2 will remain for ever one of aviation's mysteries. None survived the year in which they were built, only two received Authorisations to Fly and only a few arrived at Hanworth. The third, 'WJ, was exhibited at the Heathrow Garden Party of the Royal Aeronautical Society on May 9, 1937, but crashed at Broadstairs a month later. E. D. Ward took the fourth, 'XK, to Hooton, but it only lasted three months, and with the arrival of 'YG at the opening of Ramsgate Airport on July 3, 1937, the career of the British built S.2 was at an end.

Meanwhile, production in Belgium had reached 20, and on March 5, 1938, the 16th machine, OO-ASJ, powered by a 32 h.p. Sarolea Epervier, landed at Croydon on delivery to Brian Allen Aviation Ltd. As G-AFFN, it was shown at the Royal Aeronautical Society's Garden Party at Heathrow on May 8, 1938, remaining in storage at Heston throughout the war to pass into the hands of G. A. Chamberlain at Blackbushe in February 1951. A final Tipsy, the 9th Belgian, OO-ASB, imported in June 1939, was used privately by R. C. S. Allen as G-AFVH, but later reverted to the Fairey Aviation Co. Ltd. It reappeared with a new Authorisation to Fly at White Waltham in December 1946 and made a last appearance there on January 18, 1947, at the Informal Light Aeroplane Committee's meeting, afterwards returning to Belgium for preservation as OO-TIP, the registration properly belonging to its prototype.

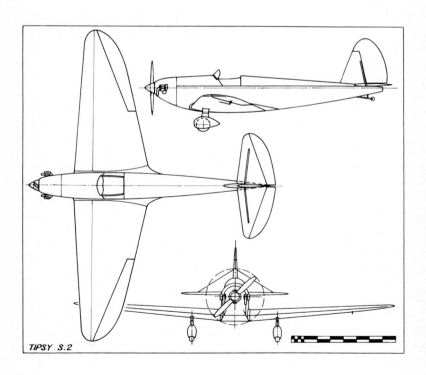

TIPSY S.2

The Air Ministry Competition Vimy Commercial at Martlesham in August 1920.
(*Photo courtesy of G. Clephane.*)

Vickers F.B.27A Vimy IV and F.B.28 Vimy Commercial

Although it saw no war service, the Vickers F.B.27A Vimy IV twin-engined bomber of 1918 was the fastest weight lifter of its age. Designed by the late R. K. Pierson, the Vimy IV was a three bay, fabric covered biplane of mixed construction, powered by two 360 h.p. Rolls-Royce Eagle VIIIs. Built in quantity for the R.A.F., it found employment in many Service roles, and four became civil aeroplanes of distinction. The first of these, the famous Atlantic flight Vimy of 1919, was not theoretically a civil aeroplane at all, as it was in Newfoundland being prepared for its historic crossing a month or so before civil flying was officially permitted. Piloted by John Alcock, and navigated by Lt. Arthur Whitten Brown, the Vimy took off from Munday's Pond, St. John's, Newfoundland, on June 14, 1919, with 865 gallons of petrol and 50 gallons of oil, at an all-up weight of 13,300 lb. Fifteen hours and 57 minutes later the aircraft touched down 1,890 miles away at Clifden, Ireland, bogged and broken at the end of the world's first Transatlantic flight.

The first Vimy IV registered as a civil aeroplane was allotted the markings G-EAAR on May 1, 1919, one day after the official commencement of non-military flying. These markings were never carried, and during its short career, a flight from Brooklands to Amsterdam in August 1919 for exhibition on the Vickers stand at the First Air Traffic Exhibition, the machine wore its constructor's number C-105. Active flying by the Vickers contingent was carried out with K-107, the Vickers F.B.27B Vimy Commercial prototype. First flown at Joyce Green on April 13, 1919, allegedly by Capt. Alcock, this aircraft used standard Vimy wing structure and empennage mated to a rotund, oval section, plywood, monocoque front fuselage seating 10 passengers. Entry was via a narrow opening, closed by a roller blind, in the port side of the front fuselage, adjacent to the open cockpit in which two pilots sat side by side.

First flown on September 20, 1919, the next civil Vimy IV, G-EAOL, was equipped as a three seat bomber and left Brooklands in the following month for demonstration to the Spanish Government. Although it disappeared into obscurity at Madrid, its sister ship, G-EAOU, fourth and last of the species, achieved immortality as winner of the Australian Government's £10,000 prize for the first flight from England to Australia. Piloted by Capts. Ross and Keith Smith and carrying Sgts. W. H. Shiers and J. M. Bennett as engineers, 'OU left Hounslow on November 12, 1919, and landed 11,340 miles away at Fanny Bay, Darwin, on

Sir John Alcock of Atlantic flight fame, with Sir Ross and Keith Smith's 1919 Australia Flight Vimy IV. (*Shell Photo.*)

December 10, 27 days 21 hours later. The route via Lyons, Rome, Cairo, Damascus, Basra, Karachi, Calcutta, Bangkok, Singapore and Java was covered in 135 flying hours at an average speed of 75 m.p.h., an incredible feat, for which both pilots were knighted. After Sir Ross Smith's death in the Viking IV accident at Brooklands in 1922 (see page 452), the Vimy was stored for 35 years, the last few of which were spent at Canberra. In 1957 a decision was made to place it on permanent exhibition in a concrete-and-glass mausoleum at Adelaide, South Australia, the long journey south being made on two R.A.A.F. trailer vehicles. Unfortunately the mainplanes, airscrews and cowlings were damaged by fire at Keith, 160 miles east of Adelaide, while in transit on November 3, 1957. After lengthy repairs the veteran was finally placed on show two years later.

Inspired by the Australian Government's example, the *Daily Mail* put up a £10,000 prize for a flight from Cairo to the Cape. Three aircraft competed, the Handley Page 0/400 G-EAMC (see page 61), a South African Vimy IV G-UABA 'Silver Queen' manned by Lt.-Col. P. Van Ryneveld and F/Lt. C. J. Quintin Brand, who were the ultimate winners, and the Vimy Commercial prototype. After Martlesham trials this prototype had returned to Brooklands for modification, emerging in 1920 with the circular portholes replaced by round-cornered rectangular windows and an additional door, with built-in steps, in the rear fuselage. Carrying the permanent markings G-EAAV, it left Brooklands under the sponsorship of *The Times* on January 24, 1920, piloted by Capts. S. Cockerell and F. C. G. Broome, but crashed at Tabora, Tanganyika, on February 27.

Following the award of a contract for Vimy Commercials by the Chinese Government, large-scale production of the F.B.28, without the front door, began at Brooklands. The British air transport pioneers S. Instone and Co. Ltd. took delivery of G-EASI, named 'City of London' for its inaugural flight from Croydon to Brussels with jockeys on May 9, 1920. This aeroplane was undoubtedly the best known of all pre-war passenger aircraft, flying continually, almost relentlessly, on the Paris, Brussels and

K-107, the F.B.27B prototype at Hendon in July 1919, showing the circular windows.
(*Photo: Central Press Ltd.*)

Cologne routes piloted by F. L. Barnard, G. J. Powell and others. On October 3, 1922, it became the first civil aircraft to make a scheduled flight to Cologne, reached via Brussels in 3 hours 25 minutes.

As early as July 1921 it had completed 360 hours flying and had carried 10,600 passengers, many on pleasure flights, and when handed over to Imperial Airways Ltd. on April 1, 1924, had flown 107,950 miles. Finally scrapped in 1926, the cabin was acquired by the inimitable K.L.M. representative Spry Leverton and ended its days as a summer-house in Waterer Rise, Wallington.

There were only two other Vimy Commercials of British registry, one of which, G-EAUY, almost certainly became the Vernon I prototype J6864. The other, 'UL, runner up, piloted by Capts. Cockerell and Broome, in the Air Ministry's Heavy Commercial Aeroplane Competition at Martlesham in August 1920, was afterwards sold to the French Government.

Manufacturers: Vickers Ltd., Vickers House, Broadway, Westminster, S.W.1, Brooklands Aerodrome, Surrey and Joyce Green Aerodrome, Kent.

Power Plants: Two 360 h.p. Rolls-Royce Eagle VIII.

Dimensions: Span, 67 ft. 2 in. Height, 15 ft. 3 in. Wing area, 1,330 sq. ft. Length (Vimy IV), 43 ft. 6½ in. (Commercial), 42 ft. 8 in.

Weights: (Vimy IV)   Tare weight, 7,101 lb. All-up weight, 12,500 lb.

           (Commercial) Tare weight, 7,790 lb. All-up weight, 12,500 lb.

Performance: (Vimy IV)   Maximum speed, 103 m.p.h. Initial climb, 300 ft./min. Ceiling, 10,500 ft.

           (Commercial) Maximum speed, 103 m.p.h. Cruising speed, 84 m.p.h. Initial climb, 375 ft./min. Ceiling, 10,500 ft. Range, 450 miles.

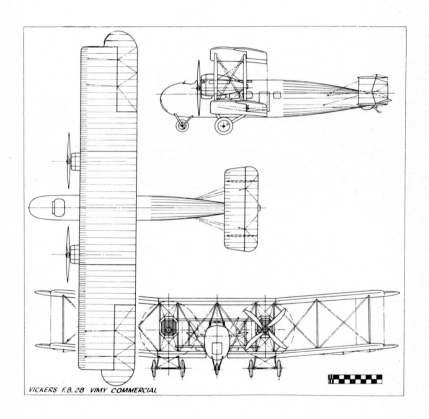

VICKERS F.B.28 VIMY COMMERCIAL

The prototype Vulcan before the addition of the small central fin. (*Photo: Vickers Ltd.*)

Vickers Type 61 Vulcan

Designed by R. K. Pierson and first flown at Brooklands by chief test pilot S. Cockerell in May 1922, the Vulcan was an attempt to build a commercial aeroplane which would pay its way without Government subsidy, performance being rated second to low initial cost and cheapness of operation. It was a compact, single bay biplane of great rotundity, every inch a descendant of the Vimy Commercial. Pilot, eight passengers and baggage were carried into the air on the mere 360 h.p. of one Rolls-Royce Eagle VIII, an engine renowned for reliability and obtainable in new condition at a fraction of original cost from the Aircraft Disposal Co. Ltd. The entire mainplane gap was occupied by an oval section, plywood front fuselage, with the stout wooden box girder of the rear fuselage faired to the same generous proportions and supporting a small, typically Vickers, biplane tail unit. The single pilot sat in front of the upper mainplane with a magnificent view, the nose falling away sharply to the car type radiator in the nose.

Early trials revealed some directional instability and the necessity for a central auxiliary fin, and also a reluctance to take off at the designed maximum weight. Nevertheless, the construction of eight more Vulcans began at Brooklands, two of which, G-EBDH and 'EA, were sold with the prototype 'BL to Instone Air Line Ltd. Delivery in the company's dark-blue livery took place in August 1922 at Croydon, where their obese appearance, small tails, squat undercarriages and snub noses promptly earned them the permanent soubriquet of 'Flying Pigs'. The three Vulcans were chiefly employed on the Brussels route, 'BL 'City of Antwerp' alone receiving a name. A fourth Vulcan, 'EK, was completed to Air Ministry order as the Type 63 freighter without windows and subjected to exhaustive Martlesham trials. The next, 'EM, was acquired by Douglas Vickers, M.P., for entry in the first King's Cup Race. Piloted by Capt. S. Cockerell and carrying several passengers, it started from Croydon on September 8, 1922, arriving back in 7th place on the following day, having covered the 810 mile course to Renfrew and back in 9 hours 24 minutes flying time.

Later in 1922 two Vulcans, G-EBES and 'ET, were registered to Queensland and Northern Territories Aerial Services Ltd. and 'ET was

The Air Council's windowless Type 63 Vulcan freighter G-EBEK. (*Photo courtesy of the Royal Aeronautical Society.*)

Lion powered Type 74 Vulcans were identified by two exhaust stacks on the starboard side. (*Photo: Vickers Ltd.*)

shipped to Melbourne to be evaluated for the Charleville–Cloncurry service. With midsummer temperatures standing at 110 degrees in the shade, tests on 'ET at Longreach in March 1923 proved the Vulcan's performance entirely inadequate and it was shipped back to England. The aircraft's lack of power reserve was further underlined by the loss of Instone's 'DH in a crash at Oxted, Surrey, after which 'EA was relegated to the scrap heap. Surprisingly the prototype was then overhauled for renewal of C. of A., re-issued on May 31, 1923, for an increased all-up weight of 6,750 lb. After one proving flight on August 4, 1923, over Instone Air Lines' newly extended route to Prague, via Cologne, piloted by F. L. Barnard and carrying five passengers, it followed its stable mate into oblivion.

Experience with 'BL led to the installation of the more powerful Napier Lion engine in the last two Vulcans 'FC and 'LB, both of which operated at the increased maximum weight as Type 74. G-EBFC, first flown on March 3, 1923, was Douglas Vickers' entry in the 1923 King's Cup Race, but retired on the first leg. In December 1924 it was delivered to the newly formed Imperial Airways Ltd., which also acquired 'LB in the following May. Additional power enabled these Vulcans to be employed on Continental scheduled services, their work being publicised at the 1925 Empire Exhibition, Wembley, by the presence of the Air Council's freighter 'EK, described as an Imperial Airways machine, even though it was not.

In the following year 'FC was withdrawn from service, dismantled and burned, leaving only the Eagle engined 'EM and the Lion powered 'LB, airworthy. They were thereafter relegated to charter work, the first, leased to Leslie Hamilton by the manufacturers to succeed his Viking IV G-EBED, was lost at sea off the Italian coast in May 1926. The second, 'LB, completed more flying hours than any other Vulcan, remaining in commission until July 1928, when it crashed and burned in Purley with the loss of several Imperial Airways employees, soon after taking off on a test flight.

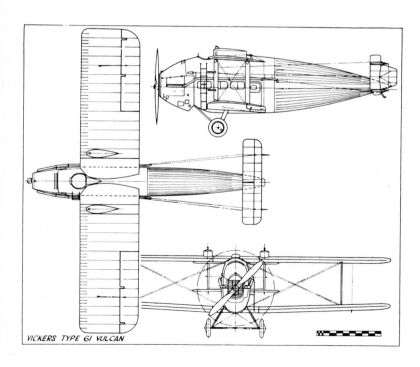

VICKERS TYPE 61 VULCAN

Manufacturers: Vickers Ltd., Vickers House, Broadway, Westminster, London, S.W.1 and Brooklands Aerodrome, Surrey.

Power Plants: One 360 h.p. Rolls-Royce Eagle VIII.
One 450 h.p. Napier Lion.

Dimensions: Span, 49 ft. 0 in. Length, 37 ft. 6 in. Height, 14 ft. 3 in. Wing area, 840 sq. ft.

Weights: (Eagle) Tare weight, 3,775 lb. All-up weight, 6,150 lb.
(Lion) All-up weight, 6,750 lb.

*Performance: Maximum speed, 105 m.p.h. Cruising speed, 90 m.p.h. Initial climb, 450 ft./min. Range, 360 miles.

* With Eagle VIII engine.

G-AHPC, in Hunting service as Type 639, showing the seven cabin windows of the short nose Viking 1.

Vickers Viking

For over 12 years the Vickers Commercial 1, or V.C.1 Viking, has been one of the mainstays of British aviation, first with British European Airways Corporation, and in recent years with independent operators. It was the first post-war British transport aeroplane to enter airline work, the first ever to be built in quantity and the last to be designed by R. K. Pierson. Assessing in advance the possible peacetime requirement for a medium–short haul passenger aircraft, the Ministry of Supply and Aircraft Production ordered three prototype 'Wellington Transport Aircraft' in 1944, R.A.F. serials TT194, 197 and 181 being allotted. For speed and cheapness of production the greatest possible use was made of Wellington bomber assemblies, including the fabric-covered geodetic outer wing panels and nacelle/undercarriage units. The entirely new, large-capacity, stressed-skin, metal fuselage, seating 21 passengers, perpetuated the familiar rotundity of every Vickers transport since the Vimy Commercial of 1919. A crew of four was carried consisting of two pilots, radio officer and stewardess.

When the first prototype, designated Type 491, made its maiden flight in the hands of J. 'Mutt' Summers at Wisley on June 22, 1945, it did so as a civil aeroplane G-AGOK, all three R.A.F. serials having been transferred to aircraft built by other firms. Continuing existing practice, each new Viking prototype or custom-built production variant was allotted a distinguishing type number. Thus the second prototype, G-AGOL, was Type 495 by virtue of increased fin area and the third, G-AGOM, became Type 496. Development proceeded apace, and by December 1945 the three aircraft had completed 100, 50 and 10 hours respectively. Nineteen Type 498 aircraft were then ordered for the European services of B.O.A.C. (later reorganised as B.E.A.C.), the first aircraft, G-AGON, flying on March 23, 1946. Together with subsequent Vikings 'RM and 'RN and all three prototypes, 'ON was later taken over by the R.A.F. for trials which

'Sir Bertram Ramsey', an eight windowed long nose Viking 1B in the Admiral Class livery of British European Airways Corporation, 1952. (*B.E.A.C. Photo.*)

led to orders for military counterparts, the Viking. C.Mk.2 and Valetta C.Mk.1. Three aircraft were earmarked for crew training at Northolt, and five were modified internally as Type 657 for service in Trinidad with British West Indian Airways, leaving only 11 to earn revenue for B.E.A.C. and to receive V Class names (see Appendix D). Following a proving flight Northolt–Stavanger–Oslo by Capt. J. W. James in 'Vagrant' on August 20, 1946, 'Valerie' inaugurated the first regular Viking service over the same route on September 1.

A second batch of Vikings included 13 Type 614 for B.E.A.C., commencing with 'Vanguard', delivered in October 1946. In response to the operator's wishes they were fitted with mainplanes of stressed skin, instead of geodetic construction, with the designation Viking 1, the earlier model becoming the Viking 1A. As before, certain B.E.A.C. aircraft were released to associate companies, three to B.W.I.A., one to Central African Airways and one to South Africa. Twelve Type 621 Viking C.Mk.2 freighters were also built for the Ministry of Supply, two of which were used by the Civil Air Test Section, Boscombe Down, for a number of years in alternate military and civil roles as VL226/G-AIJE and VL227/G-AIKN.

The 20th airframe, completed as VT-AZA for Indian National Airways and first flown on August 6, 1946, was the first 'long nose' Viking 1B with a 28-in. extension to the front fuselage permitting the carriage of three more passengers over stage lengths of up to 600 miles. A preliminary batch of eight Vikings 1B Type 610, G-AHPK-'PS, was delivered to B.E.A.C. early in 1947, followed by G-AIHA, a Type 616 flown out to Central African Airways. Large-scale production followed for the Argentine, Southern Rhodesia, Denmark and Eire. Additionally 68 (later reduced to 39) were ordered for B.E.A.C., three of which were released to Iraqi Airways and one to Central African Airways. The manufacturers also commissioned a demonstrator G-AJJN, Type 636, which left Hurn on April 13, 1947, piloted by S/Ldr. P. Robarts, for a sales tour to New Zealand, covering 40,000 miles and returning on June 15. It was sold to

B.E.A.C. and named 'Vulcan' in 1950. By the end of 1947 Vikings had ousted the well-worn Dakota from all major European services and were working between Northolt and Paris, Amsterdam, Brussels, Geneva, Lisbon, Gibraltar, Berlin, Prague, Oslo, Aberdeen and Belfast.

Viking production terminated at the end of 1947, when 113 long-nosed aircraft had been delivered in addition to the original 48 short-nosed type. Final deliveries included eight Type 635 to South African Airways.

The unobtrusively efficient Viking seldom made headline news, but did so tragically when 'Vimy' was lost with 10 passengers and crew on April 5, 1948, its starboard wing cut off in collision with a Soviet Yak fighter when approaching to land at Gatow, Berlin. Two years later, on the night of April 13, 1950, 'Vigilant', Capt. J. Harvey, suffered an internal explosion which almost severed the tail unit. The immense strength of the Viking, coupled with superb airmanship, brought the 31 occupants safely back to Northolt. The aircraft was then rebuilt by Airwork Ltd. at Gatwick, reappearing in January 1951 in a new colour scheme, which, in modified form, was adopted as the Corporation's new Admiral Class livery, prelude to a complete new naming process (see Appendix D). Operating at an increased all-up weight of 36,712 lb. and carrying 36 instead of 27 passengers, Admiral Class Vikings entered service on October 1, 1952, and made possible the first cheap fare of £9 15s. return between London and Paris. All eight South African Airways Viking 1Bs were eventually purchased to augment the already considerable B.E.A.C. fleet, four in time for the 1951 season as G-AMGG–'GJ and four a year later as G-AMNJ, 'NR, 'NS and 'NX. The fleet continued in service until replaced by Viscounts in 1954, and in eight years of service flew 65 million miles in 414,000 hours, carried 2,748,000 passengers and earned £35 million revenue.

As a charter aircraft the Viking began its career in 1948 with Hunting Air Transport Ltd., which acquired nine redundant B.E.A.C. Viking 1A and 1 aircraft G-AGRP, 'RV, 'RW, G-AHOY, 'PB–'PD, 'PI and 'PJ. Geodetic wings were eventually scrapped and all became Viking 1s, joined in 1951 by G-AMNK, a former Egyptian Airlines Viking 1B

The Nene Viking G-AJPH showing the modified undercarriage with small twin wheels.

The Varsity 1, ultimate Viking variant, used by Kelvin and Hughes Ltd. (*Photo: The College of Aeronautics.*)

SU-AFM, reclaimed from a desert crash after an epic feat of reconstruction by an engineering team from Field Aircraft Services Ltd. The other main users, both of Blackbushe, were Airwork Ltd., which has owned 13 Vikings, and Eagle Aviation Ltd., which in 1953 took over the majority of B.E.A.C. Viking 1Bs as they were replaced by Viscounts. Both firms flew regular trooping services to the Canal Zone in 1954, the Vikings conforming to international agreement by flying in R.A.F. colours. A considerable number were sold in West Germany when flying was again permitted in 1956, and now form the backbone of German charter operations. British owned fleets today number 16 Viking 1, 3 Viking 1A and 27 Viking 1B, which are in use as 32 seaters on high-density tourist traffic with Overseas Aviation (C.I.) Ltd., Eagle Aviation Ltd., Hunting-Clan Airservices Ltd., Airwork Ltd., African Air Safaris Ltd., Orion Airways Ltd., Continental Air Services Ltd., East Anglian Flying Services Ltd., Falcon Airways Ltd. and Tradair Ltd.

Non-standard aircraft also played an important part in the Viking story. The 107th airframe, completed to Ministry of Supply order with two Rolls-Royce Nene turbojets, metal-clad elevators and heavier main and tail plane skinning, became the first British pure jet transport. First flown at Wisley by J. Summers on April 6, 1948, as the Type 618 G-AJPH/VX856, the 24 passenger Nene Viking set up a new fashion in intercapital speed by flying from London Airport to Villacoublay, Paris, in 34 minutes 7 seconds on July 25, 1948, 39th anniversary of Bleriot's first cross-Channel flight. It was eventually sold to Eagle Aviation Ltd. and converted into a Viking 1B freighter with $5\frac{1}{2}$ ft. square door and named 'Lord Dundonald' by P. G. Masefield at Northolt on September 24, 1954. Both Ministry of Supply Type 621 Vikings C.2 G-AIJE and 'KN also returned, the former to Independent Air Travel Ltd., in whose service it crashed at Southall, Middlesex, on September 2, 1958, and the latter to fly with Continental Air Services Ltd. in the Netherlands.

Five former R.A.F. Viking C.Mk.2s are also in current civil use as the Viking 2, G-APAT 'Lord Hood' with Eagle Aviation Ltd., three former Queen's Flight Type 623 machines delivered to Tradair Ltd. at Southend as G-APOO–'OR on August 12, 1958 and VL229, once the Napier Naiad test bed, delivered from Ringway to the same owners on October 10, 1959. Three ex R.A.F. Type 607 Valetta C.Mk.1s, differing from the Viking 1B externally mainly by their lack of tail cone, have also gained civil status, G-APKR converted at Biggin Hill for the Decca Navigator Co. Ltd. and G-APII and 'IJ awaiting sale by Eagle Aviation Ltd. One example of the wide-span, long-fuselage, tricycle undercarriage R.A.F. trainer variant, the Type 668 Varsity T.Mk.1, is also in current research use at Cranfield as G-APAZ by Kelvin and Hughes Ltd.

SPECIFICATION

Manufacturers: Vickers-Armstrongs Ltd., Broadway, Westminster, London, S.W.1; Brooklands and Wisley Aerodromes, Surrey.

Power Plants: (Prototypes Type 401, 495, 496) Two 1,675 h.p. Bristol Hercules 130.

(Viking 1A Type 498)   Two 1,690 h.p. Bristol Hercules 630.

(Viking 1, 1B and C.2 Types 610, 614, 616, 621, 623) Two 1,690 h.p. Bristol Hercules 634.

(Nene Viking Type 618)   Two 5,000 lb. s.t. Rolls-Royce Nene 1.

(Valetta C.Mk.1 Type 607)   Two 1,975 h.p. Bristol Hercules 710.

(Varsity T.Mk.1 Type 668)   Two 1,950 h.p. Bristol Hercules 764.

	Viking 1 and 1A	Viking 1B	Nene Viking	Valetta C.Mk.1	Varsity T.Mk.1
Span . . .	89 ft. 3 in.	89 ft. 3 in.	89 ft. 3 in.	89 ft. 3 in.	95 ft. 7 in.
Length . .	65 ft. 2 in.	65 ft. 2 in.	65 ft. 2 in.	62 ft. 11 in.	67 ft. 6 in.
Height . .	19 ft. 6 in.	19 ft. 6 in.	19 ft. 6 in.	19 ft. 6 in.	23 ft. 11 in.
Wing area .	882 sq. ft.	882 sq. ft.	882 sq. ft.	882 sq. ft.	974 sq. ft.
Tare weight .	22,910 lb.	23,250 lb.	21,050 lb.	24,854 lb.	27,040 lb.
All-up weight	34,000 lb.	34,000 lb.	34,000 lb.	36,500 lb.	37,500 lb.
Maximum speed .	252 m.p.h.	263 m.p.h.	457 m.p.h.	294 m.p.h.	288 m.p.h.
Cruising speed .	210 m.p.h.	210 m.p.h.	393 m.p.h.	172 m.p.h.	239 m.p.h.
Initial climb . .	1,390 ft./min.	1,275 ft./min.	3,500 ft./min.	1,200 ft./min.	1,400 ft./min.
Ceiling . .	22,000 ft.	23,750 ft.	44,000 ft.	22,200 ft.	27,000 ft.
Maximum range .	1,875 miles	1,700 miles	312 miles	1,410 miles	2,648 miles

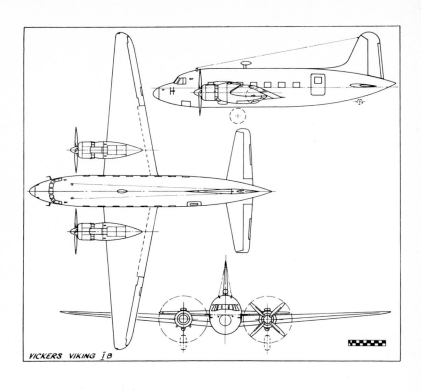

VICKERS VIKING I B

The British European Airways Corporation Viscount 802 G-AOJC 'R.M.A. Robert O'Hara Burke'. (*B.E.A.C. Photo.*)

Vickers Viscount

In April 1945 the Vickers design team led by R. K. Pierson began to consider an unpressurised Viking development with four turbine engines. Following the publication a month later of the Brabazon IIB specification, a pressurised double-bubble fuselage was substituted, which in the December gave place to a circular-section fuselage with the now familiar Viscount oval windows. These and subsidiary projects were all referred to as the Vickers Type 453 V.C.2, but following R. K. Pierson's appointment as chief engineer in September 1945, design responsibility fell to his successor G. R. (now Sir George) Edwards. Two Armstrong Siddeley Mamba powered prototypes, known as the V.609 Viceroy, to carry 32 passengers, were ordered by the Ministry of Supply on March 9, 1946, with Vickers to finance a third. It was later decided to complete the Ministry's prototypes G-AHRF and 'RG with four Rolls-Royce Darts as V.630 and Vickers' third aircraft G-AJZW with four Napier Naiads as V.640. Construction then went ahead at Foxwarren, but in 1947 the partition of India resulted in a change of name to Viscount. When the first aircraft, G-AHRF, assembled at Wisley, made its maiden flight on July 16, 1948, piloted by J. Summers and G. R. Bryce, it was not merely the world's first turbo-prop transport, a natural flier and an almost trouble-free prototype but also a truly sensational advance over contemporary piston-engined aircraft.

The prospect of a developed Dart, the R.Da.3 (Mk. 505) giving 50% more power, made it possible to design a stretched 40 seat version, more exactly fulfilling British European Airways Corporation requirements. Construction of a prototype, known as the V.700 with fuselage lengthened by 6 ft. 8 in. and the inner span increased by 5 ft. was then undertaken, the second V.630 being diverted to military research flying as the V.663.

313

Powered by two Rolls-Royce Tay turbojets, the latter made its first flight in R.A.F. marks as VX217 at Wisley on March 15, 1950, and after demonstration at the Farnborough S.B.A.C. Show in the following September, was used in the development of powered controls for the Valiant bomber. It was later flown experimentally by Boulton Paul Ltd. at Seighford as test bed for their electronic control system. The first V.630 G-AHRF flew as VX211 during trials, which culminated in the issue of a restricted C. of A. on August 19, 1949, and eventually to full passenger carrying clearance for a month's scheduled operations with B.E.A.C. commencing on July 29, 1950. This historic aircraft remained in continual use until written off at Khartoum on August 27, 1952, after completing 931 hours 50 minutes of experimental flying.

Components intended for the abandoned third prototype were used in the construction of the V.700 prototype G-AMAV, the fuselage of which was built at South Marston and the wings at Itchen. Assembly took place at Brooklands, and after the first flight on April 19, 1950, 20 (later increased to 27), slightly modified 53 seat V.701 production aircraft were ordered by B.E.A.C. The prototype V.700 was shown at the S.B.A.C. Show a month later, completing 250 hours of test flying before leaving on October 5, 1951, for tropical trials at Khartoum, captained by S. N. Sloan. The same pilot took it to India, Pakistan and the Near East for demonstration in the June and July, Capt. A. S. Johnson made the first B.E.A.C. proving flight in it to Rome, Athens and Cyprus on August 21, and George Lowdell showed its paces in West Germany a month later. Six weeks winterisation trials in Canada were completed when G. R. Bryce returned to Wisley via the northern route on April 5, 1953. Meanwhile the first V.701, G-ALWE, flown on August 20, 1952, in time for exhibition at the S.B.A.C. Show, had been named at Wisley by Lady Douglas on February 11, 1953, as flagship of the new Discovery Class. Rapid de-

The first prototype Viscount 630 G-AHRF in B.E.A.C. styling, July 1950. (*Photo: Vickers-Armstrongs Ltd.*)

VX217/G-AHRG, the Tay Viscount 663. (*Photo courtesy of Charles W. Cain.*)

liveries then permitted route proving trials on all the Corporation's services in Europe, Scandinavia and the United Kingdom, culminating with the Viscount's introduction into regular scheduled operations on April 17, 1953.

In B.E.A.C. styling, numbered 23, and bearing the Discovery Class name 'Endeavour', the prototype, 'AV, was flown by a B.E.A.C. crew headed by Chief Flight Capt. W. Baillie, in the England–New Zealand Air Race. Leaving London Airport on October 8, 1953, the 11,795 miles to Harewood Airport, Christchurch, New Zealand, were covered in an elapsed time of 40 hours 45 minutes at an official average speed of 290 m.p.h. Orders then materialised from all over the world, so that Vickers instituted a system of type numbers to cover individual customer requirements. Viscounts in the V.700 series used by other British operators, however, included only Airwork Ltd.'s V.736s G-AODG and 'DH used for long-distance charter and the West African Colonial Coach Service; Kuwait Airways' former Capital Airlines V.745s G-APNF and 'NG and former British West Indian Airways V.702s G-APOW and 'PX; and Hunting-Clan Air Transport Ltd.'s V.732s G-ANRR and 'RS.

The still more powerful Dart R.Da.6 (Mk. 510) of 1954 encouraged a 3 ft. 10 in. extension to the fuselage and an aft movement of the rear pressure bulkhead to permit an increase in seating to 65. A B.E.A.C. order for 14 improved Viscounts (later increased to 24), designated V.802, was placed on April 14, 1954. All V.700 series construction was then concentrated at Weybridge and a V.800 series production line set up at Hurn. In January 1956 B.E.A.C. placed an additional order for 59 seat mixed-class aircraft powered by the improved Dart R.Da.7 (Mk. 520) and known as the V.806. The first of these, G-AOYF 'Michael Faraday', was used by the makers for certification trials but made a crash landing at Johannesberg on October 20, 1957, and never saw B.E.A.C. service. Designated V.806A, it first flew on August 9, 1957, with Dart R.Da.7/1 (Mk. 525), an even more powerful engine destined for the V.810 series aircraft then under construction. Due to their higher design weight and speed, these are the first Viscounts to embody major structural strengthening and modification, and are externally recognisable by the simplified aerodynamic balance of the rudder. The first V.810 G-AOYV, which first flew on December 23, 1957, became the maker's test vehicle and was assisted throughout the certification trials by the V.700 prototype G-AMAV, re-engined with Dart R.Da.7 for the purpose. Although the majority of the new type are being delivered in the United States, two V.831s, G-APND and 'NE, have been acquired by Airwork Ltd., to join the five other British owned Viscount V.800s. These comprise V.805s G-APDW and 'DX delivered to Eagle Aviation at Blackbushe in December 1957, for operation in Bermuda, and V.804s G-AOXU, 'XV and G-APKG employed for long distance charter and tourist services by Transair Ltd., Gatwick.

Thirty-four per cent of European transport aircraft are now Viscounts, 62 of which are operated by B.E.A.C. on internal and external services, the earlier V.701s now modified to 63 passenger layout with two additional windows and fitted with airstairs. By December 31, 1958, an average all-the-year-round daily utilisation of $6\frac{3}{4}$ hours per day per aircraft had been achieved with the V.701s and $5\frac{3}{4}$ hours with the V.802s and V.806s. In 1959, reworked V.701s were flown on new internal German services and also from Gatwick to Cologne, Jersey and Dinard and V.802/806s on a new London–Klagenfurt route. A proving flight to Moscow via Copenhagen on April 21, 1959 by G-AOYI 'Sir Humphry Davy' under the command of Capt. G. G. McLannahan, heralded a permanent twice weekly V.806 mixed class service to the Soviet capital, inaugurated on May 14 by G-AOYS 'George Stephenson'.

SPECIFICATION

Manufacturers: Vickers-Armstrongs (Aircraft) Ltd., Vickers House, Westminster, S.W.1; Brooklands Aerodrome, Byfleet, Surrey; Hurn Airport, near Bournemouth, Hants.

Viscount Type	630	663	700	701
Engines . . .	Dart R.Da.1	Tay R.Ta.1	Dart R.Da.3	Dart R.Da.3
Mark . . .	502	—	505	506
Power . . .	1,380 e.h.p.	6,250 lb.s.t.	1,540 e.h.p.	1,540 e.h.p.
Span . . .	88 ft. 11 in.	88 ft. 11 in.	93 ft. 8½ in.	93 ft. 8½ in.
Length . . .	74 ft. 6 in.	74 ft. 6 in.	81 ft. 2 in.	81 ft. 2 in.
Wing area . .	885 sq. ft.	885 sq. ft.	963 sq. ft.	963 sq. ft.
Passengers . .	32	—	47	47
Tare weight .	29,060 lb.	—	32,000 lb.	35,522 lb.
All-up weight .	40,400 lb.	—	50,000 lb.	60,000 lb.
Economical cruising .	276 m.p.h.	—	316 m.p.h.	316 m.p.h.
Maximum range .	1,380 miles	—	950 miles	1,450 miles

Viscount Type	802	806	810
Engines . . .	Dart R.Da.6	Dart R.Da.7	Dart R.Da.7/1
Mark . . .	510	520	525
Power . . .	1,742 e.h.p.	1,890 e.h.p.	1,990 e.h.p.
Span . . .	93 ft. 8½ in.	93 ft. 8½ in.	93 ft. 8½ in.
Length . . .	85 ft. 8 in.	85 ft. 8 in.	85 ft. 8 in.
Wing area . .	963 sq. ft.	963 sq. ft.	963 sq. ft.
Passengers . .	53–65	59	52–75
Tare weight .	40,430 lb.	40,980 lb.	41,276 lb.
All-up weight .	63,000 lb.	64,500 lb.	67,500 lb.
Economical cruising .	320 m.p.h.	320 m.p.h.	360 m.p.h.
Maximum range .	1,490 miles	—	1,380 miles

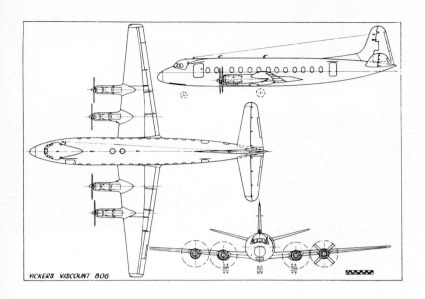

VICKERS VISCOUNT 806

The prototype Falcon powered Limousine I. (*Photo: The Westland Aircraft Works.*)

Westland Limousine

Designed by Arthur Davenport, the Limousine I was the Westland Aircraft Works' first commercial aeroplane and one of the earliest attempts to introduce saloon-car comfort into flying. It was a two bay biplane of conventional fabric-covered, wooden construction powered by one well-proven and economical 275 h.p. Rolls-Royce Falcon III, complete with Bristol Fighter type radiator. Situated amidships, the cabin was a ply-wood-covered structure for three passengers and pilot, the latter in the port rear seat, 30 in. higher than the passengers, with his head through a hole in the roof, open cockpit fashion. The prototype, K-126, first flown at Yeovil by chief test pilot Capt. A. S. Keep in July 1919, made a considerable number of publicity flights in 1919–20, including that during which Westland director R. J. Norton's secretary typed letters to his dictation in flight.

October 1919 saw the completion of the Limousine II, G-EAJL, also with a 275 h.p. Rolls-Royce Falcon but externally identified by the rectangular radiator and increased fin and rudder area. After demonstration at the air meeting held at Winton racecourse by the Bournemouth Aviation Company on May 1, 1920, the prototype, now registered G-EAFO, joined 'JL at Croydon, on loan to Air Post of Banks Ltd. They spent the next few months on an experimental service to Paris, 'JL making the fastest crossing of September 1920 in a time of 1 hour 52 minutes. This firm, whose chief pilot was F. T. Courtney, was short lived and the Limousines returned to Yeovil, where'FO became the manufacturer's communications aircraft. It gave useful service until struck and demolished by a Fairey Fawn on the ground at Netheravon in September 1925, while on a business visit, piloted by Major L. P. Openshaw.

A third Limousine, also Mk. II, had flown in April 1920, as test bed for the new 400 h.p. Cosmos Jupiter but later reverted to standard. It was followed by a small batch of four, two of which, 'RE and 'RF, flown in October 1920, were leased to Instone Air Ltd., flying regularly on the Paris and Brussels routes until purchased outright in June 1922. Limousine 'RE, which was fitted with a 300 h.p. Hispano-Suiza, set up a new London–Brussels time of 2 hours 8 minutes later in the year.

Publication of the rules for the 1920 Air Ministry Commercial Aeroplane Competition resulted in the construction of the Lion powered Limousine III, a much larger, three bay biplane for pilot and five passengers. It was fitted with wheel brakes and a nose wheel to permit their maximum use in the short landing test. Fuel tanks were fitted under the lower mainplanes to reduce fire risk and to allow smoking in the cabin, a

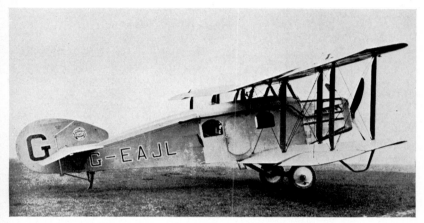

Limousine II G-EAJL with 275 h.p. Rolls-Royce Falcon and enlarged vertical tail surfaces. (*Photo: The Westland Aircraft Works.*)

The Jupiter powered Limousine II. The pilot's head can be seen projecting above the fuselage. (*Photo: Westland Aircraft Works.*)

G-EARV, first of the two Limousine IIIs and winner of the Air Ministry prize, 1920.
(*Photo courtesy of the Royal Aeronautical Society.*)

feature also incorporated in the Instone Air Line Limousine IIs. Piloted at Martlesham by A. S. Keep, it just beat the Sopwith Antelope to win £7,500, first prize in the small commercial aeroplane section. An interesting sidelight was the presence of maker's serial W.A.C.7 on the rear fuselage in contradiction of the aircraft's documents, which quoted W.A.C.8. It is therefore probable that construction of the true W.A.C.7, the final Limousine II, G-EARH, was not completed. Although inherently stable and in advance of the time—Capt. Keep was able to leave the controls and join his passengers in the cabin—the market for commercial aeroplanes was non-existent due to the post-war slump, and only one other Limousine III, G-EAWF, was built. Supplied to the Air Council in April 1921, it joined the small fleet of miscellaneous transports on loan to approved firms under the Government's subsidy scheme. It thus became the Instone Air Line reserve aircraft, joining its smaller brethren 'RE and 'RF at Croydon until all three were pensioned off in 1923.

Competition winner 'RV pioneered air transport in Newfoundland with F. S. Cotton's Aerial Survey Company, to which it was sold for seal and fishery spotting in January 1921. Successful, if difficult, operation on wheels and skis was followed by participation in the gold rush to Stag Bay, Labrador, flown by T. K. Breakell. In July 1922 the Limousine IIs 'JL and 'MV were overhauled for C. of A. renewal and then also shipped to Newfoundland, followed by 'RG in the November.

Manufacturers: The Westland Aircraft Works, Yeovil, Somerset.
Power Plants: (Limousine I and II) One 275 Rolls-Royce Falcon III.
          (Limousine II)   One 300 h.p. Hispano-Suiza.
                                 One 410 h.p. Cosmos Jupiter III.
         (Limousine III)   One 450 h.p. Napier Lion.

	Limousine I	Limousine II	Limousine III
Span . . .	38 ft. 2 in.	37 ft. 9 in.	54 ft. 0 in.
Length . . .	27 ft. 9 in.	27 ft. 9 in.	33 ft. 6 in.
Height . . .	10 ft. 9 in.	10 ft. 9 in.	12 ft. 6 in.
Wing area .	440 sq. ft.	440 sq. ft.	726 sq. ft.
Tare weight . .	2,183 lb.	2,010 lb.	3,823 lb.
All-up weight .	3,383 lb.	3,800 lb.	5,850 lb.
Maximum speed .	100 m.p.h.	100 m.p.h.	118 m.p.h.
Cruising speed .	85 m.p.h.	90 m.p.h.	90 m.p.h.
Initial climb . .	600 ft./min.	650 ft./min.	—
Ceiling . . .	17,000 ft.	17,000 ft.	12,300 ft.
Range . . .	290 miles	400 miles	520 miles

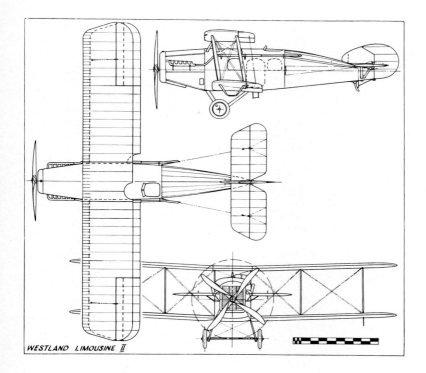

WESTLAND LIMOUSINE II

The late Carill S. Napier landing his Gipsy I powered Widgeon III. (*Photo courtesy of* '*The Aeroplane*'.)

Westland Widgeon

Built for the 1924 Lympne Trials, the two seat Widgeon was a parasol monoplane with fabric-covered, spruce girder fuselage powered by a 35 h.p. Blackburne Thrush. The unusual folding wing tapered sharply in chord and thickness to give the pilot an exceptional range of vision. The maiden flight took place at Yeovil on September 22, 1924, but during a qualifying circuit of the Lympne course on the 27th, the Widgeon encountered a down current and sideslipped into the ground. Capt. Winstanley was uninjured, and the damaged aircraft, obviously underpowered, was rebuilt as the Widgeon II with 60 h.p. Armstrong Siddeley Genet I and less rudder area. Competitive trials against the Woodpigeon led to the eclipse of the biplane and to the introduction of the Widgeon III, a redesign for ease of production. With a plywood fuselage and rigidly braced constant chord wing, the Widgeon III was not only robust and free of rigging problems but also faster than contemporary light biplanes. The Cirrus II powered prototype, G-EBPW, first flown by chief test pilot L. P. Openshaw in April 1927, was piloted by S/Ldr. T. H. England in the Bournemouth Easter Races in competition with the Widgeon II. During Whitsun racing over the same course, 'PW collided in the air with Blackburn Bluebird G-EBKD, both aircraft being burned out with the loss of pilots L. P. Openshaw and W. H. Longton. Dr. E. D. Whitehead Reid bought Widgeon II G-EBJT in January 1928, flying from Bekesbourne until he was killed through striking trees in a dusk forced landing at East Sutton Park, near Detling, Kent, in October 1930.

Pressure of work on the Wapiti contract brought production to an end in 1929 after some 30 Widgeons had been constructed, 17 of which were of British registry, sold in two well-defined batches in 1927 and 1929. Westland managing director R. A. Bruce's G-EBRL, second in the 1927

King's Cup Race at 102·8 m.p.h. piloted by W. J. McDonough, was experimentally fitted, but not flown, with an 80 h.p. A.B.C. Hornet in 1928. It was also flown at Cowes on Saunders-Roe floats with 95 h.p. Cirrus III in 1929. Two others had roving tendencies. Winner of the 1928 Grosvenor Trophy, S/Ldr. H. M. Probyn's 'RQ was unique in having an alternative centre section giving 11 instead of 4 in. of sweep back, to compensate for the lower installed weight of a 75 h.p. Genet II. During the winter of 1928–29, owner and wife made a 4,200 mile tour to Naples, Catania, Tunis, Algiers, Seville, Madrid and Biarritz in a flying time of 60 hours 50 minutes. Cirrus Widgeon G-EBRO, Gipsy Widgeon G-AADE flown respectively by J. G. Ormston and C. S. Napier, and 'RQ, all competed without success in the King's Cup Race of July 1930, averaging 98 m.p.h.

The Widgeon I with three cylinder Thrush radial before the Lympne Trials, September 1924. (*Photo: Westland Aircraft Works.*)

The Widgeon II, showing Genet engine and revised rudder. (*'Flight' Photo.*)

323

Widgeon III G-EBRL with 80 h.p. A.B.C. Hornet flat four aircooled engine.

Widgeon III G-EBRO with the temporary cabin fitted in 1928.

Sq. Ldr. H. M. Probyn's unique Genet II powered Widgeon III G-EBRQ.

G-EBRN, Cirrus II engined single seater with 50 gallon fuel tank in the front cockpit, left Lympne for Australia on April 23, 1928, piloted by Wing Cdr. E. R. Manning. After considerable bad luck the flight was abandoned at Baghdad and 'RN was shipped home and sold to H. R. Law for a similar attempt. Again damaged, this time at Athens on January 18, 1930, it returned to become the longest-lived British owned Widgeon, flown privately by F/Lt. (now Air Commodore) A. H. Wheeler from November 1933 until the outbreak of war. After C. of A. renewal at Balado in February 1948, however, it was burned at Stranraer by an owner who could no longer house it.

The remaining aircraft of the first batch, G-EBRM, built for R. G. Cazalet, was the first of several Widgeon IIIA aircraft with metal fuselage and divided undercarriage. With the original Cirrus III replaced by a 105 h.p. Hermes I, 'RM made fastest time in the Grosvenor Trophy Race at Cramlington on October 5, 1929.

The second, or 1929 batch, comprised C. S. Napier's Gipsy I powered Widgeon III G-AADE and five Widgeon IIIAs. These included Miss C. R. Leathart's Cramlington based G-AAJF, Westland's Cirrus III powered demonstrator G-AAFN, the Anglo-American Oil Co. Ltd.'s Gipsy I engined G-AAFD 'Miss Ethyl', and G-AALB taken to Canada by W. J. McDonough.

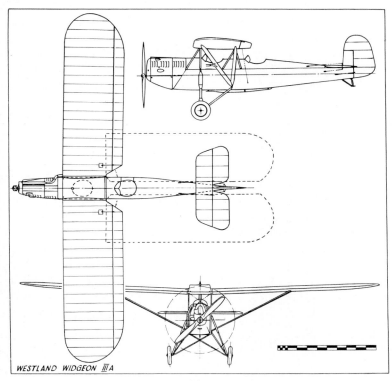

WESTLAND WIDGEON IIIA

Westland Aircraft Ltd.'s famous communications Widgeon G-AAGH, Hermes II engine, showing the divided undercarriage of the Mk. IIIA and the wartime civil markings.

Last of all the Widgeons, G-AAGH, fitted with a Hermes I, was the manufacturer's communications aircraft for over 19 years, flown throughout the war in military colours with civil marks. In the hands of H. J. Penrose it gave memorable post-war displays until burned out at Merryfield in July 1948 after striking a hangar during an attempted pilotless take off.

SPECIFICATION

Manufacturers: The Westland Aircraft Works, Yeovil, Somerset.
Power Plants: (Widgeon I)   One 35 h.p. Blackburne Thrush.
        (Widgeon II)   One 60 h.p. Armstrong Siddeley Genet I.
        (Widgeon III)   One 85 h.p. A.D.C. Cirrus II.
                    One 90 h.p. A.D.C. Cirrus III.
                    One 75 h.p. Armstrong Siddeley Genet II.
                    One 85 h.p. A.B.C. Hornet.
                    One 100 h.p. de Havilland Gipsy I.
        (Widgeon IIIA) One 90 h.p. A.D.C. Cirrus III.
                    One 100 h.p. de Havilland Gipsy I.
                    One 105 h.p. Cirrus Hermes I.
                    One 120 h.p. Cirrus Hermes II.

	Widgeon I	Widgeon II	Widgeon III	Widgeon IIIA
Span . .	30 ft. 8 in.	30 ft. 8 in.	36 ft. 4½ in.	36 ft. 4½ in.
Length . .	21 ft. 0 in.	21 ft. 0 in.	23 ft. 5¼ in.	23 ft. 5¼ in.
Height . .	7 ft. 3 in.	7 ft. 3 in.	8 ft. 5 in.	8 ft. 5 in.
Wing area . .	145 sq. ft.	145 sq. ft.	200 sq. ft.	200 sq. ft.
Tare weight .	475 lb.	—	852 lb.*	935 lb.
All-up weight .	815 lb.	1,150 lb.	1,400 lb.*	1,650 lb.
Maximum speed .	72 m.p.h.	110 m.p.h.	100 m.p.h.	104 m.p.h.
Cruising speed .	—	—	85 m.p.h.	86 m.p.h.
Initial climb .	300 ft./min.	—	560 ft./min.	640 ft./min.
Ceiling . .	—	—	14,000 ft.	15,000 ft.
Range . .	—	—	—	315 miles

* 775 lb. and 1,323 lb. respectively with Genet II.

G-ACIJ, the V.I.P. Wessex supplied to the Egyptian Air Force in 1934. Late production machines had metal clad front fuselages. (*Photo: Westland Aircraft Works.*)

Westland IV and Wessex

The Westland IV, designed in 1928, was a small, high-wing, taxi or feeder-line aircraft built of wood, fabric covered and fitted with standard Wapiti rudder. Risk of forced landings was lessened by fitting three 95 h.p. Cirrus III engines, the outboard units mounted on the undercarriage outriggers. Pilot, mechanic and four passengers were carried, with a generous baggage compartment behind the cabin. The prototype, G-EBXK, was first flown at Yeovil by chief test pilot L. C. Paget on February 22, 1929, and a second was completed for exhibition at the Olympia Aero Show in the July. The new machine, G-AAGW, boasted a rear fuselage of metal construction and three closely cowled 105 h.p. Hermes I engines. After the show it went into service with the private hire department of Imperial Airways Ltd. at Croydon, and construction of another, G-AAJI, ordered by Wilson Airways Ltd., Nairobi, was begun. After extensive trials, the use of in-line engines was discontinued, and when the Wilson Airways order fell through, 'JI was completed as the prototype Wessex, G-ABAJ/P-1, with three 105 h.p. Armstrong Siddeley Genet Major radials. The outboard nacelles were not only of better streamline form, but were, for the first time, strutted to the mainplane. First flights were made in May 1930, after which the Wessex became the first of four used on the Continental services of the Belgian air line SABENA. The original Westland IV, also re-engined and strutted, continued as the manufacturer's demonstration and communications aircraft until 1935.

Early in 1931 the Armstrong Siddeley company introduced the Genet Major IA, a 140 h.p. engine with seven instead of five cylinders. When fitted to the Wessex, it imparted a considerable improvement in performance and the demonstrator G-ABEG was chartered for a survey of the South Yorkshire canals in 1931. It was also used by H.R.H. the Prince of Wales for the opening of Roborough Aerodrome on July 15, 1931, and for a trip to the French Riviera. On Saturday 24, 1932, it also carried the Lord Mayor's guests to the Essex Air Display at Maylands. Both 'EG and another 'high performance' Wessex G-ACHI were acquired by Imperial Airways Ltd. in 1933, joining their original Westland IV 'GW, which had been modified to the same standard. Chartered by the Great Western Railway, 'GW operated a pioneer internal air route from Cardiff to Plymouth via Haldon from April 12–May 20, 1933, then extended to Castle Bromwich until the service ceased on September 30. In the following year 'EG went to Baghdad on charter to the Iraq Petroleum Transport Co. Ltd., and spent 1935 in service with Rhodesian and Nyasaland Airways, finally coming to grief in a forced landing at Chirindu, Northern Rhodesia. Its sister aircraft were then relegated to radio and navigation training with Air Pilots Training Ltd., Hamble, until 1940. Only two more Wessex aircraft were built, the first of which, G-ABVB, was a special machine with square dural tubes replacing wood in the wings, for use on the Portsmouth–Ryde and Shoreham–Portsmouth high density ferry services of Portsmouth, Southsea and Isle of Wight Aviation Ltd. Eight passengers were accommodated by a reduction in baggage space, while the cockpit was raised, undercarriage strengthened and rudder area increased. G-ACIJ, the final Wessex, a standard aircraft, left Heston in March 1934 on delivery to the Egyptian Air Force.

The Cirrus III powered Westland IV prototype landing at Croydon. (*'Flight' Photo.*)

G-AAGW in its original form with Hermes engines. (*Photo: Westland Aircraft Works.*)

The special Wessex built for Portsmouth, Southsea and Isle of Wight Aviation Ltd. in 1932.

Three survivors of the SABENA Wessex fleet returned in March 1935 for use as G-ABAJ, G-ADEW and 'FZ by Cobham Air Routes Ltd. on a Portsmouth–Christchurch–Guernsey service which opened on May 6, 1935. Two months later the starboard engine of G-ADEW failed half an hour out from Guernsey and the machine sank after a forced landing at sea off the Needles. The route then closed and 'AJ became a Ryde ferry, while 'FZ and the veteran 'XK joined National Aviation Day Displays Ltd. for pleasure flying. Early in 1936 'AJ and 'FZ were taken over by the Trafalgar Advertising Co. Ltd. and were based at Croydon, carrying out nightly publicity sorties with battery-operated neon advertising under the wings.

SPECIFICATION

Manufacturers: The Westland Aircraft Works, Yeovil, Somerset.
Power Plants: (Westland IV) Three 95 h.p. A.D.C. Cirrus III.
                             Three 105 h.p. Cirrus Hermes I.
         (Wessex) Three 105 h.p. Armstrong Siddeley Genet Major.
                             Three 140 h.p. Armstrong Siddeley Genet Major 1A.
Dimensions: Span, 57 ft. 6 in. Length, 38 ft. 0 in. Height, 9 ft. 6 in. Wing area, 490 sq. ft.

		Wessex		
	Westland IV	Genet Major	Genet Major IA	G-ABVB
Tare weight .	3,150 lb.	3,810 lb.	3,891 lb.	3,930 lb.
All-up weight .	5,500 lb.*	5,750 lb.	6,300 lb.	6,300 lb.
Maximum speed .	108 m.p.h.	118 m.p.h.	122 m.p.h.	122 m.p.h.
Cruising speed .	100 m.p.h.	100 m.p.h.	100 m.p.h.	108 m.p.h.
Initial climb .	520 ft./min.	600 ft./min.	680 ft./min.	610 ft./min.
Ceiling . .	14,000 ft.	12,300 ft.	14,900 ft.	13,700 ft.
Range . .	525 miles	520 miles	420 miles	340 miles

* Prototype 4,900 lb.

329

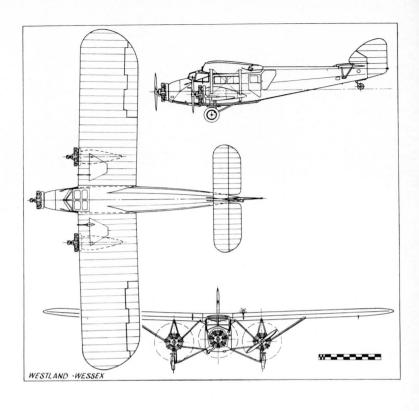

WESTLAND · WESSEX

G-AMRE, a standard S-51 Mk. 1A built at Yeovil in 1952. (*Photo: Westland Aircraft Ltd.*)

Westland Sikorsky S-51

At the end of 1946 Westland Aircraft Ltd. concluded an agreement with the United Aircraft Corporation in the United States for the production of the all-metal four seat Sikorsky S-51 helicopter in England. Six American built specimens were imported in 1947; the first, G-AJHW, for evaluation and demonstration; one each for agricultural use by Pest Control Ltd. and military trials by the Ministry of Supply, and three for use by British European Airways Corporation. Development flying began under Wing Cdr. R. A. C. Brie at Yeovil, but later moved to Westwood, Peterborough, base for the Corporation's experimental helicopter service to the major Norfolk towns in 1948. It was also the scene of the first night helicopter service when G-AKCU took off for Norwich on February 21, 1949. This aircraft was short lived, coming to grief in the following May while carrying sand and cement on Britain's first industrial airlift, to the Croesor Dam in the Welsh mountains. It was replaced by demonstrator 'HW, and on June 1, 1950, the B.E.A.C. unit inaugurated the world's first scheduled helicopter service, between Speke and Cardiff. G-AJHW and 'OV assisted in flood relief in Holland in February 1953 and spent several years on crop-spraying work with Autair Ltd. at home and in Germany before sale to Wheeler Airlines Ltd. at Montreal in June 1957.

The first British built S-51, G-AKTW, was completed and flown at Yeovil in time for the 1948 Farnborough S.B.A.C. Show. Three early production machines, G-ALEG, 'IL and 'MC, powered, like the prototype, by the 550 h.p. Alvis Leonides 521 and designated S-51 Mk. 1A, were supplied to the Ministry of Supply for trials which resulted in large orders

The prototype Widgeon flying with pilot and four passengers. (*Photo: Westland Aircraft Ltd.*)

for a naval and R.A.F. version known as the Dragonfly. By 1959 over 140 had been produced, but the majority of the 27 British civil examples were sold to foreign governments, including three to Italy, three to Thailand and four to Japan. Two supplied to the Egyptian Air Force in November 1949 and three to the Belgian Congo Government in 1951–52 were fitted with the Wasp Junior engine under the designation S-51 Mk.1B.

Few S-51 helicopters have been used on normal British civil duties. Pest Control Ltd. operated G-ALEG and 'EI fitted with spray bars on extensive agricultural work, until the latter crashed in Switzerland and returned to Yeovil to become a rotor test bed. The *Evening Standard* acquired G-ANAL for publicity purposes early in 1953, using it for photographic and advertising sorties, equipped with large signboards. Today it is maintained at White Waltham as G-ANZL, personal aircraft of Mr. Richard Fairey. The largest S-51 fleet, comprising G-AKTW, G-ALIK, G-AMRE, G-ANLV, 'LW and G-AOAJ, was operated by the Westland Helicopter Training School at Yeovil. Two of its aircraft, G-AMRE and G-ANLV were noteworthy, the first having spent 1953 in the Antarctic as a whale spotter under Norwegian marks while the other, in service with Silver City Airways in July 1954, was the first helicopter to operate on a cross-Channel route.

Early in 1955 G-ALIK was withdrawn from the school to be flown experimentally with the rotor head of its larger brother the S-55, in preparation for conversion to full five seater. This involved the fitment of an entirely new Westland-designed light-weight front fuselage with stepped windscreen. The first flight in revised form as the S-51 Series 2 Widgeon was made on August 23, 1955, piloted by R. Bradley, followed by 10 hours flying in two days to qualify for exhibition at the S.B.A.C. Show. The veteran 'TW, which also flew as a Widgeon on January 3, 1956, went to South Africa on an extended sales tour in 1957. It was followed by 'LW, converted in 1958 to operate a local service to the Brussels Exhibition in SABENA colours. Four other Widgeons have since received British civil status. The first pair, G-APBK and 'BL, were equipped with loud hailers and delivered to the Hong Kong Police Force for crowd control duties in September 1957. Two others, G-AOZD and 'ZE, supplied to Bristow

Helicopters Ltd., operate with the oil drilling expedition at Doha on the Persian Gulf, together with the original Widgeons 'TW and 'IK, re-registered G-APPR and 'PS and flown out in a K.L.M. Douglas DC-6A on December 7, 1958.

Manufacturers: (Sikorsky S-51) United Aircraft Corporation, Bridge-port, Connecticut, U.S.A.

(Westland S-51) Westland Aircraft Ltd., Yeovil, Somer-set.

Power Plants: (Sikorsky S-51) One 450 h.p. Pratt and Whitney Wasp Junior R-985-B4.

(Westland S-51 Mk. 1A) One 540 h.p. Alvis Leonides 521/1.

(Westland S-51 Mk. 1B) One 450 h.p. Pratt and Whitney Wasp Junior R-985-B4.

(Widgeon) One 520 h.p. Alvis Leonides 521/2.

Dimensions: Rotor diameter (S-51), 49 ft. 0 in. (Widgeon), 49 ft. 2 in. Height, 12 ft. 11 in. Length (S-51), 57 ft. 6½ in. (Widgeon), 57 ft. 8 in.

		Sikorsky S-51	Westland S-51 Mk. 1A	Widgeon
Tare weight .	.	3,805 lb.	4,397 lb.	4,322 lb.
All-up weight	.	5,500 lb.	5,700 lb.	5,900 lb.
Cruising speed	.	85 m.p.h.	80 m.p.h.	88 m.p.h.
Initial climb .	.	1,000 ft./min.	680 ft./min.	1,190 ft./min.
Ceiling .	.	13,500 ft.	14,000 ft.	10,500 ft.
Range .	.	260 miles	300 miles	310 miles

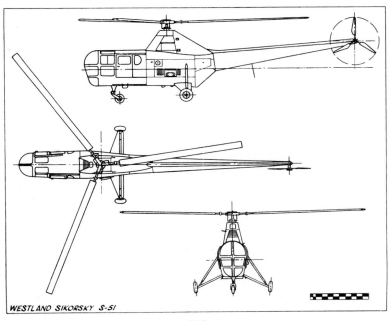

WESTLAND SIKORSKY S-51

333

The British European Airways Corporation's S-55 Series I 'Sir Ector'.   (*B.E.A.C. Photo.*)

Westland Sikorsky S-55

In November 1950 Westland Aircraft Ltd. announced its intention to manufacture the all-metal, eight seat, Sikorsky S-55 helicopter under licence and an American built specimen G-AMHK was imported for inspection and trials. This aircraft took on many roles in its two year career in Britain, taking part in R.A.F. and Royal Navy exercises until finally sold to a Norwegian whaling firm in September 1953. The first Yeovil built machine G-AMJT flew in November 1952, but was taken over by the Royal Navy in March 1953 for minesweeping and other trials which resulted in large orders for a military version known as the Whirlwind. A similar function was carried out by the second civil S-55 G-AMYN, delivered to the French Navy in April 1954. By 1959 almost 300 had been built, 26 of British registry, the first of which, G-ANFH 'Sir Ector' and 'UK 'Sir Kay', were sold to British European Airways Corporation for an experimental passenger service inaugurated on July 25, 1955, between the London South Bank and London Airport. For this purpose they were equipped with silencers and also twin floats in case of forced landings when following the Thames. The 1956 programme, inaugurated on July 1, consisted of a daily service between Birmingham, Nottingham and Leicester which made a loss and was discontinued, the S-55s thereafter engaging on charter work, and in 1958 on the more profitable potato-spraying contracts in East Anglia. A third S-55, G-AOCF, originally acquired for Civil Defence exercises and flown under Home Office contract, is now based with the Corporation's remaining S-55 'FH at Gatwick, where on May 17, 1958, Capt. J. Reid used it as a flying crane for installing the rotary light on the 85-ft. airport beacon.

Four Westland S-55s were also sold to the South Georgia Co. Ltd. for whale spotting in the Antarctic, the first two, G-ANJT and 'JV, joining the whaling factory ship *Southern Venturer* in the Tyne on October 24, 1954, the others, 'JS and 'JU, landing on *Southern Harvester* on the 31st. Each year they came back for C. of A. overhaul, first to Henstridge and, from 1957, to Staverton, returning to their ships each October. The hazards of their calling are emphasised by the loss at sea of 'JS in 1955, 'JU in 1956 and 'JT in 1958, and their replacement by the former B.E.A.C. 'Sir Kay' and a new aircraft G-AOHE. Two aircraft, G-ANZN and 'ZO, were crated for shipment to Bahamas Airways Ltd. in July 1955 and two more, acquired by the Shell Company, arrived at Doha on September 28, 1955, for oil prospecting work on the Persian Gulf. Four others, 'DO, 'DP, 'YB and 'ZK, are currently in use by Fison-Airwork Ltd. for the same purpose, the first two in Nigeria and the others in Kenya.

Initially flown on June 16, 1955, and subsequently exhibited at the S.B.A.C. and Paris Aero Shows, a Westland demonstration S-55, G-AOCZ, was re-engined with an Alvis Leonides Major engine in place of the customary Pratt and Whitney Wasp. It was also modified with down-tilted tail boom and horizontal instead of anhedral stabilisers, under the designation S-55 Series 2, first of six such machines civil registered to date. During the winter of 1957, 'CZ demonstrated landings and take offs in the Austrian Alps at an altitude of 11,600 ft. with seven people on board. Two similar aircraft, 'YY and 'YZ, were crated in July 1957 and despatched to Wheeler Airlines Ltd. at Montreal, while the current demonstrator G-APDY made its maiden flight at Yeovil on August 25, 1957.

The S-55 Series 2 prototype showing the tilted boom, modified tail and revised cabin windows. (*Photo: Westland Aircraft Ltd.*)

SPECIFICATION

Manufacturers: (Sikorsky S-55)   United Aircraft Corporation, Bridge-port, Connecticut, U.S.A.

(Westland S-55)   Westland Aircraft Ltd., Yeovil, Somerset.

Power Plants: (Sikorsky S-55 and Westland S-55 Series 1)
One 600 h.p. Pratt and Whitney Wasp R-1340-40.

(Westland S-55 Series 2) One 850 h.p. Alvis Leonides Major 755/1.

Dimensions: Rotor diameter, 53 ft. 0 in. Length, 41 ft. 8½ in. Height, 15 ft. 4½ in.

Weights: (Series 1) Tare weight, 5,010 lb. All-up weight, 7,500 lb.

(Series 2) Tare weight, 5,262 lb. All-up weight, 7,800 lb.

Performance: (Series 1) Cruising speed, 87 m.p.h. Initial climb, 750 ft./min. Ceiling, 7,000 ft. Range, 282 miles.

(Series 2) Cruising speed, 87 m.p.h. Initial climb, 910 ft./min. Ceiling, 13,300 ft. Range, 354 miles.

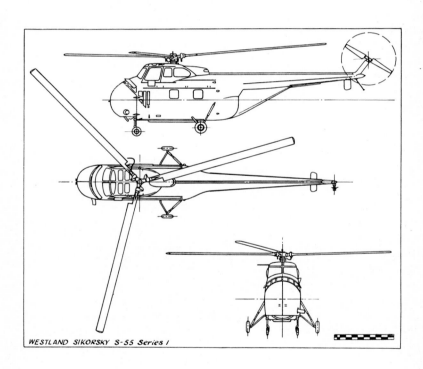

WESTLAND SIKORSKY S-55 Series 1

APPENDIX A

Miscellaneous Civil Aircraft

This section includes all bona-fide civil aircraft which existed only in prototype form or in small numbers. The text should be read in conjunction with the following notes:

1. The date of issue of Certificate of Airworthiness is given for each individual aircraft and its omission is equivalent to a direct statement that none was issued.

2. The number of aircraft built has been stated in three ways, examples being given hereunder—

    a. (One) aircraft only—indicates no other built.

    b. (One) civil aircraft only—indicates that other aircraft of the same type were built for military use.

    c. (One) British aircraft only—indicates that other civil or military aircraft of the same type were exported. If an aeroplane of foreign origin, (one) only was imported.

ENGLISH ELECTRIC WREN

Single seat ultra light powered by one 398 c.c. A.B.C., designed by W. O. Manning and built at Lytham St. Annes 1923 by the English Electric Co. Ltd. One civil aircraft only, c/n 4, flown in the 1923 Lympne Trials with competition number 3 by S/Ldr. M. E. A. Wright. Registered for civil flying 9.4.26 as G-EBNV by Alan Smith at Sherburn-in-Elmet. Withdrawn from use 1929, stored in Bradford and later Dumfries. Cannibalised at Warton, Lancs. 1957 to service another Wren, number 4, c/n 3, currently airworthy with the Shuttleworth Trust, Old Warden. Span, 37 ft. 0 in. Length, 24 ft. 3 in. Tare wt., 232 lb. A.U.W., 420 lb. Max speed, 50 m.p.h. Range, 75 miles.

ERCOUPE 415-CD

Two seater with interconnected rudders and ailerons, powered by one 75 h.p. Continental C-75-12F, built by the Engineering and Research Corporation at Riversdale, U.S.A. One British aircraft only, G-AKFC, c/n 4784, built 1947 as NC7465H, imported from Belgium as OO-ERU by Ministry of Supply, C. of A. issued 29.8.47. Evaluated at Boscombe Down 1947–52 as VX147, restored to Aviation Traders Ltd., Southend 2.52; flown by Blackpool & Fylde Aero Club 1955; C. W. Morley, Southend 1956; current owner S. V. Parkin, Jersey. Span, 30 ft. 0 in. Length, 20 ft. 9 in. Tare wt., 750 lb. A.U.W., 1,260 lb. Max. speed, 127 m.p.h. Cruise, 110 m.p.h.

338

(*Photo: Fairey Aviation Co. Ltd.*)

FAIREY GYRODYNE

Four seat helicopter powered by one 505 h.p. Alvis Leonides LE.22.HM, built at Hayes, Mx. 1947. Two prototype aircraft only: G-AIKP, c/n F.B.1, exhibited Radlett S.B.A.C. Show 9.47, first flown at Heston by B. H. Arkell 7.12.47, broke International helicopter 3 Km closed-circuit record at 124·3 m.p.h., White Waltham 28.6.48, crashed at Ufton near Reading 17.4.49, chief test pilot F. H. Dixon killed; G-AJJP, c/n F.B.2, exhibited at Farnborough S.B.A.C. Show 9.48, converted to Jet Gyrodyne XD759 in 1954. Rotor diameter, 52 ft. 0 in. Tare wt., 3,270 lb. A.U.W., 4,500 lb. Max. speed, 124 m.p.h. Cruise, 100 m.p.h.

(*Photo: Fairey Aviation Co. Ltd.*)

FAIREY PRIMER

Trainer developed from the Tipsy M, built at Hamble 1948. Two prototype aircraft only, G-ALBL, c/n F.8455, one 145 h.p. de Havilland Gipsy Major 10, C. of A. issued 22.10.48, test flown as G-6-4, later flown without rear decking, dismantled 1949; G-ALEW, c/n F.8456, one 155 h.p. Blackburn Cirrus Major 3, evaluated against the Chipmunk at Boscombe Down 11.48 as G-6-5, dismantled 1951. Span, 32 ft. 10 in. Length, 27 ft. 6 in. Tare wt., 1,572 lb. A.U.W., 1,960 lb. Max. speed (Cirrus Major 3), 141 m.p.h. Cruise, 125 m.p.h.

(P. R. Keating Photo)

FIAT G.212

Twenty-six seat transport powered by three 1,215 h.p. Pratt and Whitney Twin Wasp R-1830-92, built by Aeronautica D'Italia S.A. (Fiat) at Turin 1948. One British aircraft only, G-ANOE, c/n 10, formerly F-BCUX, originally I-ENEA, C. of A. issued 31.5.54, owner H. E. Shaikh Du'ag Salman al-Subah, operating Arabian Desert Airlines. Unserviceable at Kuwait since C. of A. expiry 12.1.56. Span, 96 ft. 4 in. Length, 75 ft. 7 in. Tare wt., 24,640 lb. A.U.W., 39,600 lb. Max. speed, 236 m.p.h. Cruise, 199 m.p.h.

(M. J. G. Gradidge Photo)

FIRTH HELICOPTER

Two seat twin rotor helicopter powered by two 145 h.p. de Havilland Gipsy Major 10, designed by Messrs. Heenan, Winn and Steele to American Landgraf principles and built at Thame by Firth Helicopters Ltd. 1954, using the magnesium alloy monocoque fuselage of the second prototype Planet Satellite. One aircraft only, G-ALXP, c/n FH-01/4, construction not completed, airframe presented to the museum of the College of Aeronautics, Cranfield, in 1955. Cruise, 125 m.p.h. Range, 250 miles.

('*The Aeroplane*' *Photo*)

FLEET F.7C-2

Two seater powered by one 135 h.p. Armstrong Siddeley Genet Major, built 1937 by Fleet Aircraft Ltd. at Fort Erie, Ontario, Canada. One British civil aircraft only, G-AEJY, c/n 69, imported by Amalgamated Aircraft Builders Ltd., first flown at Gatwick 14.7.38, C. of A. issued 26.7.38. Sold to A. G. A. Fisher, Croydon; to Aero Industries Ltd., Heston 1939; C. R. Dunn, Langley 1943; C. W. Blankley 1946. Damaged landing at Kidlington 14.4.46, stored until transferred to Ringway 5.58, scrapped at Altrincham 7.59. Span, 28 ft. 0 in. Length, 21 ft. 8 in. Tare wt., 1,100 lb. A.U.W., 1,750 lb. Max. speed, 113 m.p.h. Cruise, 98 m.p.h.

('*The Aeroplane*' *Photo*)

FOCKE WULF Fw200B CONDOR

Transport for 22 passengers powered by four 880 h.p. B.M.W. Hornet 132-G/1, built at Bremen, Germany 1938. One British civil aircraft only, G-AGAY, c/n 2894, formerly Danish Air Lines OY-DAM 'Dania', Danish C. of A. issued 21.7.38. Seized at Shoreham 5.40, flown to Whitchurch with a prize crew, allotted B.O.A.C. name 'Wolf', impressed by the R.A.F. 1.41 as DX177, damaged beyond repair at White Waltham 12.7.41. Span, 108 ft. 0 in. Length 78 ft. 0 in. Tare wt., 24,860 lb. A.U.W., 32,600 lb. Max. speed, 267 m.p.h. Cruise, 258 m.p.h.

341

(*'The Aeroplane' Photo*)

GARLAND-BIANCHI LINNET

French designed Piel CP-301 Emeraude low-wing, side-by-side two seater, modified to meet British airworthiness requirements, fitted with one 90 h.p. Continental C.90/14F and built at Maidenhead by the Garland Aircraft Co. Three aircraft to date: G-APNS, c/n 001, first flown by S/Ldr. Neville Duke at Fairoaks 1.9.58, C. of A. issued 8.10.58; G-APRH, c/n 002, registered 12.58; G-APVO, c/n 003, Croydon Aero Club, registered 8.59. Span, 26 ft. 4 in. Length, 20 ft. 9 in. Tare wt., 802 lb. A.U.W., 1,400 lb. Max. speed, 130 m.p.h. Cruise, 115 m.p.h.

GENERAL AIRCRAFT MONOSPAR ST-18 CROYDON

Transport for 10 passengers, powered by two 450 h.p. Pratt and Whitney Wasp Junior SB-9, built at Hanworth 1935. One aircraft only, G-AECB, c/n 501, first flown as T-22, C. of A. issued 16.6.36. Sold to Major C. R. Anson 2.7.36, left Croydon for Australia 30.7.36 piloted by H. Wood. Abandoned on return journey on Seringapatam Reef, 175 miles off N.W. coast of Australia 7.10.36. Failed to make landfall across Timor Sea due to compass error. Span, 59 ft. 6 in. Length, 43 ft. 3 in. Tare wt., 7,974 lb., A.U.W., 11,500 lb. Max. speed, 203 m.p.h. Cruise, 190 m.p.h.

(Photo: General Aircraft Ltd.)

GENERAL AIRCRAFT G.A.L.45 OWLET

All-metal, two seat trainer with tricycle undercarriage developed from the G.A.L.42 Cygnet. One aircraft only, G-AGBK, c/n 134, powered by one 150 h.p. Blackburn Cirrus Major 1, built Hanworth 1940, first flown 5.9.40, C. of A. issued 10.1.41. Impressed 8.7.41 as DP240 for training Douglas Boston pilots at No. 51 O.T.U. Damaged beyond repair in heavy landing at White Waltham. Span, 32 ft. 5 in. Length, 24 ft. 7 in. Tare wt., 1,563 lb. A.U.W., 2,300 lb. Max. speed, 125 m.p.h. Cruise, 110 m.p.h.

GLOBE GC-1B SWIFT

Two seater built at Dallas, Texas, U.S.A., by the Texas Engineering and Manufacturing Co. Inc. Three British aircraft only: G-AHUU, c/n 1003, 125 h.p. Continental C-125-1, imported by Helliwells Ltd., Walsall, for demonstration 6.46, C. of A. issued 26.2.47, sold in Norway 5.54 as LN-BDE; G-AHWG, c/n 1, to have been built by Helliwells Ltd., not proceeded with; G-AHWH, c/n 1243, 125 h.p. Continental C-125-2, C. of A. issued 19.3.47, owned by C. G. Wheatley, Clifton. Span, 29 ft. 4 in. Length, 20 ft. 10¾ in. Tare wt., 1,139 lb. A.U.W., 1,710 lb. Max. speed, 150 m.p.h. Cruise, 140 m.p.h.

('*Flight*' *Photo*)

GLOSTER MARS I BAMEL

Single seat racer powered by one 450 h.p. Napier Lion II, designed by H. P. Folland as a development of the Nieuport Nighthawk and built by the Gloucestershire Aircraft Co. Ltd. for the 1921 Aerial Derby. One aircraft only, G-EAXZ, won the race at 163·34 m.p.h. Then fitted with twin Lamblin radiators (illustrated), but retired in Coupe Deutsch Race at Etampes 1.10.21 with loose wing fabric. British speed record raised to 196·4 m.p.h. at Martlesham 19.12.21. Fastest time in 1922 Aerial Derby at 177·85 m.p.h. Pilot J. H. James. Span, 23 ft. 0 in. Length, 22 ft. 0 in. Tare wt., 1,890 lb. A.U.W., 2,500 lb. Max. speed, 196 m.p.h.

(*Photo via C. W. Cain*)

GLOSTER MARS I BAMEL (1922)

The Bamel rebuilt for the Coupe Deutsche Race, Etampes 30.9.22, with single Lamblin radiator, square cut tail surfaces of S.E.5 outline, stream-lined wheels and reduced wing area. Retired when J. H. James lost his maps, but later raised the British speed record to 212·2 m.p.h. Span, 20 ft. 0 in. Length, 22 ft. 0 in. A.U.W., 2,700 lb. Max. speed, 212 m.p.h.

(*Leonard Bridgman Photo*)

GLOSTER I

Bamel modified in 1923 to have fuel tanks inside the top wing and a strutted centre section. Won the 1923 Aerial Derby at Croydon at 192·4 m.p.h. piloted by Larry Carter. To the R.A.F. 12.12.23 as J7234, converted into a training seaplane for the 1925 and 1927 Schneider Trophy contests. Scrapped 1927. Span, 21 ft. 0 in. Length, 20 ft. 0 in. A.U.W., 2,650 lb. Max speed, 220 m.p.h.

(*Gloster Photo*)

GLOSTER II

Racing seaplane developed from the Bamel, built at Sunningend, Cheltenham, to Air Ministry order and powered by one 585 h.p. Napier Lion. One civil aircraft only, G-EBJZ, c/n Gloster II, racing number 1. Registered for participation in the 1924 Schneider Trophy Race in the U.S.A. Flown by Hubert Broad in Felixstowe trials, undercarriage collapsed after landing 19.9.24, aircraft sank and was written off. 1924 contest then postponed till 1925. Span, 20 ft. 0 in.

(*Photo via H. G. Martin*)

GLOSTER III

Successor to Gloster II, fitted with twin floats and powered by one special 680 h.p. Napier Lion VII, built at Sunningend for the Schneider Trophy Race at Baltimore, U.S.A. 26.10.25. Two Air Ministry aircraft N194 and N195 only, the former registered G-EBLJ 3.6.25, C. of A. issued 4.10.25,

(*Gloster Photo*)

GLOSTER GANNET (Carden)

Single seat ultra light with folding wings, built for the 1923 *Daily Mail* Light Aeroplane Competitions at Lympne. One aircraft only, G-EBHU, c/n 1, first flown 23.11.23, powered by one 750 c.c. Carden two stroke. Retired with engine trouble. Span, 18 ft. 0 in. Length, 16 ft. 0 in. Tare wt., 248 lb. A.U.W., 417 lb. Max speed, 72 m.p.h.

(*Gloster Photo*)

GLOSTER GANNET (Tomtit)

G-EBHU re-engined 1924 with 698 c.c. Blackburne Tomtit. Exhibited at Olympia, London during the Aero Show of July 1929. Span, 18 ft. 0 in. Length, 16 ft. 6 in. Tare wt., 292 lb. A.U.W., 460 lb. Max speed, 72 m.p.h. Cruise, 64 m.p.h.

---

continued from page 346.

as principal contender, racing number 5. Piloted by Hubert Broad, gained second place at 199·169 m.p.h. Reverted to R.A.F. use and converted to Gloster IIIA trainer for 1927 contest. Span, 20 ft. 0 in. Length, 26 ft. 10 in. A.U.W., 2,650 lb. Max speed, 220 m.p.h.

('*Flight*' Photo)

GLOSTER A.S.31 SURVEY

Developed from the D.H.67 design, the A.S.31 was the first Gloster twin engined aircraft. Carrying two pilots and camera operator it was used by the Aircraft Operating Co. Ltd. for the survey of Northern Rhodesia. One civil aircraft only, G-AADO, no c/n, powered by two 525 h.p. Bristol Jupiter XI, first flown 6.29, C. of A. issued 30.1.30. Left Heston 20.3.30 and delivered by air to Cape Town by A. S. and Mrs. Butler. Sold abroad 5.33. Span, 61 ft. 6 in. Length, 48 ft. 6 in. Tare wt., 5,615 lb. A.U.W., 8,750 lb. Max. speed, 131 m.p.h. Cruise, 110 m.p.h.

('*Flight*' Photo)

GNOSSPELIUS GULL

Single seat ultra light with wooden monocoque fuselage, powered by one 698 c.c. Blackburne Tomtit with twin chain driven pusher airscrews, designed by Major O. T. Gnosspelius for the 1923 Lympne Trials and built at Rochester by Short Bros. Ltd. Two aircraft only: G-EBGN, c/n 1, rudder projecting above fin, first flown by J. Lankester Parker 26.5.23; c/n 2, unregistered, equal fin and rudder, flown at Lympne as No. 19, crashed at Cramlington, S. A. Packman killed 18.6.26. Span, 36 ft. 4 in. Length, 19 ft. 6 in. Tare wt., 360 lb. A.U.W., 570 lb. Max. speed, 70 m.p.h. Cruise, 45 m.p.h.

('*The Aeroplane*' Photo)

GORDON DOVE

Single seat ultra light powered by one 750 c.c. Douglas Sprite, designed by S. C. Buszard and built at Maylands Aerodrome, Romford by Premier Aircraft Constructions Ltd., 1937. Three aircraft only: G-AETU, c/n S.C.B. III, first flown 3.3.37, A. to F. issued 4.3.37, Romford Flying Club, burned in hangar fire Maylands 6.2.40; G-AEZA, c/n S.B.IV, A. to F. issued 1.7.37, Earl of Cardigan, Marlborough, scrapped 5.39; G-AEZB, c/n 3, A. to F. issued 24.9.37, J. K. Flower, damaged beyond repair Tilbury 9.9.37, G-AFAC–'AG not built. Span, 27 ft. 3 in. Length, 18 ft. 3 in. Tare wt., 382 lb. A.U.W., 600 lb. Max. speed, 95 m.p.h. Cruise, 81 m.p.h.

GRAHAME-WHITE G.W.E.6 BANTAM

Single seat sporting biplane powered by one 80 h.p. Le Rhône rotary, designed by M. Boudot and built by The Grahame-White Aviation Co. Ltd. at Hendon 1919. Two aircraft only: K-150/G-EAFK, c/n G.W.E.6; K-153/G-EAFL, c/n G.W.E.6A; both raced in 1919 Aerial Derby and at Hendon. K-150 crashed into hangar at Hendon 6.7.19, 'FL stored until reconditioned by Gnat Aero Co., Shoreham in 1926. Span, 20 ft. 0 in. Length, 16 ft. 6 in. Tare wt., 640 lb. A.U.W., 995 lb. Max. speed, 100 m.p.h.

(*Grahame-White Photo*)

GRAHAME-WHITE G.W.E.7

Luxury transport with folding wings designed by M. Boudot to seat four passengers in the cabin in the nose and the pilot in a glazed compartment between the centre section struts. One aircraft only, G-EALR, c/n G.W.E.7, powered by two 320 h.p. Rolls-Royce Eagle V, built at Hendon by The Grahame-White Aviation Co. Ltd. 8.19, damaged beyond repair in forced landing in 1919, burned 1920. Span, 60 ft. 0 in. Length 39 ft. 0 in. Tare wt., 5,785 lb. A.U.W., 7,947 lb. Max. speed, 116 m.p.h. Cruise, 104 m.p.h.

(*Photo: D. Napier and Son Ltd.*)

GRAHAME-WHITE G.W.E.9 GANYMEDE

The twin fuselage three engined G.W.E.4 Ganymede bomber of 1918, converted for civil use by The Grahame-White Aviation Co. Ltd., at Hendon 1919. One aircraft only, G-EAMW, c/n G.W.E.9, powered by two 450 h.p. Napier Lion, formerly C3481, registered to the manufacturers 12.9.19, burned 9.20. Two pilots in an open cockpit sat ahead of about 12 passengers in a glazed central nacelle. Span, 89 ft. 3 in. Length, 49 ft. 9 in.

GRANGER ARCHAEOPTERYX

Single seater with pterodactyl wing but retaining normal rudder. Designed with the assistance of C. H. Latimer-Needham and built at Attenborough, Notts, 1926–30 by R. F. T. and R. J. T. Granger. One aircraft only, G-ABXL, c/n 3A, powered by one 32 h.p. Bristol Cherub I. First flown at Hucknall 10.30, flown without markings until registered 3.6.32. Regularly flown at Tollerton, longest flight was to R.A.F. Flying Club Display, Hatfield, 15.6.35. Span, 27 ft. 6 in. Length, 15 ft. 0 in. Max. speed, 95 m.p.h. Cruise, 75 m.p.h.

(R. W. Brown Photo)

GRUMMAN G.21A GOOSE

All-metal amphibian for two crew and six passengers, powered by two 450 h.p. Pratt and Whitney Wasp Junior R-985-SB2, in production 1937 by the Grumman Aircraft Engineering Corp'n. at Bethpage, Long Island, N.Y., U.S.A. Two British civil aircraft only: G-AFCH, c/n 1009, registered to Lord Beaverbrook 26.10.37, sold in the Dutch East Indies 7.38; G-AFKJ, c/n 1049, C. of A. issued 4.1.39, same owner, impressed 18.2.41. Span, 49 ft. 0 in. Length, 38 ft. 4 in. Tare wt., 5,425 lb. A.U.W., 8,500 lb. Max. speed, 205 m.p.h. Cruise, 191 m.p.h.

351

('*The Aeroplane*' Photo)

HAFNER A.R.III Mk.2 GYROPLANE

Single seat, experimental, vertical lift autogiro with variable incidence rotor blades, designed by Raoul Hafner and built by the A.R.III Construction Co. in the Martin-Baker Aircraft Company's factory, Denham, 1936. One aircraft only, G-ADMV, c/n A.R.III, (A.R. signifying 'Auto Rotation'), one 90 h.p. Pobjoy Niagara, registered to T. V. Welsh, Heston 26.7.35. First flown 6.2.37 and later tested at Farnborough by A. E. Clouston. Leased to R.A.E. for research, scrapped during war. Rotor diameter, 32 ft. 10 in. Length, 17 ft. 10 in. Tare wt., 640 lb. A.U.W., 900 lb. Max. speed, 120 m.p.h. Cruise, 110 m.p.h.

('*Flight*' Photo)

HALTON H.A.C.I MAYFLY

Two seater powered by one 32 h.p. Bristol Cherub III, designed by C. H. Latimer-Needham and built by the Halton Aero Club 1926–27. One aircraft only, G-EBOO, c/n 1, first flown by F/Lt. C. F. Le Poer Trench 31.1.27. Converted to single seater, C. of A. issued 13.5.27, won the President's, Selfridge and Leeming Cups, £150 in prize money and competed in the King's Cup Race. Completed 2,700 miles in 40 flying hours as a biplane. Span, 28 ft. 6 in. Length, 22 ft. 0 in. Tare wt., 480 lb. A.U.W., 920 lb. Max. speed, 83·5 m.p.h. Cruise, 75 m.p.h.

HALTON H.A.C.II MINUS

The Mayfly single seater converted to parasol monoplane, second in the Blackpool Open Handicap Race 7.7.28 at 87·75 m.p.h., won the Wakefield Trophy, Hamble, piloted by F/Lt. C. F. Le Poer Trench. Flown by same pilot in 1928 King's Cup Race, retired at Leeds with broken magneto drive. Entered by C. H. Latimer-Needham and flown by F/Lt. G. R. Ashton in 1929 King's Cup Race, retired at Newcastle. Dismantled at Halton 1930. Tare wt., 450 lb. A.U.W., 720 lb. Max. speed, 95 m.p.h. Cruise, 85 m.p.h.

HANDLEY PAGE H.P.32 HAMLET (Lucifer)

Transport for six passengers, fitted with full span slots and slotted flaps, powered by three 120 h.p. Bristol Lucifer IV three cylinder radials, built to Air Ministry order at Cricklewood 1926. One aircraft only, G-EBNS, c/n 1, first flown 10.26. Span, 52 ft. 0 in. Length, 34 ft. 10 in. Tare wt., 3,105 lb. A.U.W., 5,000 lb. Max. speed, 118 m.p.h. Cruise, 100 m.p.h.

HANDLEY PAGE H.P.32 HAMLET (Lynx)

G-EBNS fitted with curved fin and re-engined with two 220 h.p. Armstrong Siddeley Lynx due to the excessive vibration of the Lucifer installation. Flown at the Hendon R.A.F. Display 2.7.27. Scrapped 1929. A.U.W., 5,000 lb. Max. speed, 114 m.p.h.

HANDLEY PAGE H.P.39 GUGNUNC

Two seat biplane fitted with Handley Page full span slots and flaps, powered by one 155 h.p. Armstrong Siddeley Mongoose II, built at Cricklewood 1929 for the Guggenheim air safety competition in the U.S.A. One aircraft only, G-AACN, no c/n, runner up in competition; flown in 1930 Hendon R.A.F. Display by F/O H. H. Leech, transferred to the R.A.E. 12.30 as K1908, currently in the Science Museum store, Knockholt, Kent. Span, 40 ft. 0 in. Length, 26 ft. 9 in. Tare wt., 1,362 lb. A.U.W., 2,150 lb. Max. speed, 112·5 m.p.h. Min. speed, 33·5 m.p.h.

HANDLEY PAGE (READING) H.P.R.3 HERALD

Medium-haul pressurised transport for two crew and a maximum of 44 passengers, powered by four 870 h.p. Alvis Leonides Major 701/1, built at Woodley 1955. Two aircraft only: G-AODE, c/n 147, first flown at Radlett 25.8.55, C. of A. issued 20.7.56, flown at 1955 Farnborough S.B.A.C. Show in Queensland Airlines colours; G-AODF, c/n 148, C. of A. issued 27.8.56, flown at 1956 Farnborough S.B.A.C. Show. Span, 94 ft. 9½ in. Length, 71 ft. 11 in. Tare wt., 21,136 lb. A.U.W., 33,500 lb. Cruise, 199 m.p.h. Range, 1,452 miles with 6,929 lb. payload.

HANDLEY PAGE (READING) H.P.R.7 DART HERALD

Two H.P.R.3 Herald prototypes remodelled with two 2,105 e.h.p. Rolls-Royce Dart 527 turboprops. G-AODE, c/n 147, first flown at Woodley 11.3.58, C. of A. issued 22.4.58, forced landed in flames at Milford, near Godalming, Surrey, 30.8.58 by S/Ldr. H. G. Hazelden; G-AODF, c/n 148, first flown at Woodley 17.12.58, C. of A. issued 31.12.58. Production batch, G-APWA–'WJ laid down 1959. G-APWA, C. of A. issued 25.11.59, first of three for B.E.A.C. evaluation. Tare wt., 22,808 lb. A.U.W. 39,000 lb. Cruise, 275 m.p.h. Max range, 1,450 miles.

HANTS. AND SUSSEX HERALD

Single seat ultra light with tricycle undercarriage, powered by one 40 h.p. Aeronca-J.A.P. J-99, built at Portsmouth 1949 by Hants. and Sussex Aviation Ltd. One aircraft only, G-ALYA, c/n HS/AC/001, few ground hops only at Portsmouth 1953, dismantled 1954. Span, 29 ft. 0 in. Length, 21 ft. 6 in. Tare wt., 580 lb. A.U.W., 800 lb. Max. speed, 92 m.p.h. Cruise, 82 m.p.h.

('*Flight*' *Photo*)

HAWKER CYGNET (Scorpion)

Two seater powered by one 30 h.p. A.B.C. Scorpion, designed by W. G. Carter and Sydney Camm and built at Kingston for the 1924 Lympne Trials. One aircraft only, G-EBJH, c/n 1, flown as No. 15 by F. P. Raynham. Presented to the R.A.E. Aero Club 26.1.26, fitted with 32 h.p. Bristol Cherub III, C. of A. issued 21.8.26. Second in 1926 Trials piloted by F/Lt. J. S. Chick. Crashed at Lympne 8.27 when taking off for nonstop flight to Bucharest piloted by F/Lt. R. L. Ragg. Span, 28 ft. 0 in. Length, 20 ft. 3 in. Tare wt. (Scorpion), 373 lb. A.U.W., 780 lb.

(*Rolls-Royce Photo*)

HEINKEL He70

Transport for two crew and four passengers fitted with retractable under-carriage, built at Warnemünde 1935. One British aircraft only, G-ADZF, c/n 1692, built to the order of Rolls-Royce Ltd. for Kestrel engine development. C. of A. issued 6.4.36, based at Hucknall, demonstrated at the Heathrow Garden Party of the Royal Aeronautical Society 10.5.36, broken up 1944. Span, 48 ft. 6½ in. Length, 37 ft. 9 in. Tare wt., 5,291 lb. A.U.W., 7,700 lb.

(*'Flight' Photo*)

HELMY AEROGYPT I

Four seater powered by three 22 h.p. Douglas Sprites, designed and built at Heston by S. Helmy, an Egyptian, 1938. One aircraft only, G-AFFG, c/n 3, incorporating hinged roof acting as landing flap, first flown at Heston 2.39. Later flown as Aerogypt II with hinged roof removed. Last flown 26.9.40 as Aerogypt III with end plate fins. Span, 26 ft. 4 in. Length, 19 ft. 0 in.

HELMY AEROGYPT IV

G-AFFG modified to Aerogypt IV at White Waltham 1943 with two 65 h.p. Continental A-65 and tricycle undercarriage by the newly formed Aerogypt High Speed Development Co. Ltd., C. of A. issued 29.10.46. Dropped by salvage crane and damaged beyond repair following a landing accident at Northolt 26.11.46 when outward bound for Egypt. Tare wt., 1,150 lb. A.U.W., 2,400 lb. Max. speed, 160 m.p.h. Cruise, 145 m.p.h.

HENDERSON H.S.F.I. (Cabin version)

Twin boom, cabin six seat, pusher monoplane, powered by one 240 h.p. Siddeley Puma, designed by J. Bewsher and built at Brooklands 1928 by the Henderson School of Flying Ltd. One aircraft only, G-EBVF, c/n H.S.F.I., not flown with the canopy fitted. Span 51 ft. 0 in. Length, 38 ft. 0 in. Tare wt., 2,000 lb. A.U.W. 3,200 lb. Max. speed 105 m.p.h.

HENDERSON H.S.F.I. (Open version)

The original Henderson H.S.F.I. G-EBVF modified later in 1928 with open cockpit and uncowled 240 h.p. Siddeley Puma engine and flown by Col. G. L. P. Henderson at Brooklands, some 30 passengers being carried on the first day. Its promising joyriding career was prevented by the death of Col. Henderson (see page 369) and the aircraft was broken up. Span, 51 ft. 0 in. Length, 38 ft. 0 in. A Martlesham report dated 5.30 gives tare wt., 3,300 lb. and A.U.W. 4,112 lb.

HENDERSON-GLENNY H.S.F.II GADFLY I

Single seat ultra light powered by one 35 h.p. A.B.C. Scorpion II, designed by K. N. Pearson and built 1929 by Glenny and Henderson Ltd. at York Road, Byfleet, Surrey. One aircraft only, G-AAEY, c/n 1, first flown at Brooklands 4.29. World's height record for aircraft under 200 Kg tare weight, Brooklands 17.5.29 piloted by G. L. P. Henderson. Span, 25 ft. 10 in. Length, 17 ft. 10 in. Tare wt., 455 lb. A.U.W., 750 lb. Max. speed, 91 m.p.h. Cruise, 72 m.p.h.

(*J. McNulty Photo*)

HENDERSON-GLENNY H.S.F.II GADFLY II

Gadfly I fitted with rotary ailerons invented by K. N. Pearson. Two aircraft only, G-AAEY modified for exhibition at Olympia 7.29, C. of A. issued 16.9.29, sold to Oscar Greig, Brooklands, 9.29; C. F. Parker, Wolverhampton, 5.31; E. Bradley, Wolverhampton, 2.33; scrapped 6.34: G-AARJ, c/n 2, built 8.29, C. of A. issued 31.10.29 owner A. A. Anderson, the constructor's chief engineer. Sold in Canada 6.30 as CF-AMG, crashed at Salt, Ontario, 7.30. Specification as for Gadfly I.

(*'The Aeroplane' Photo*)

HENDERSON-GLENNY H.S.F.II GADFLY III

Gadfly II fitted with 40 h.p. Salmson A.D.9 radial. One aircraft only, G-AARK, c/n 1, built 7.29, owner G. L. P. Henderson, demonstrated at Heston 20.7.29. Withdrawn from use 1930, in storage at Brooklands until 6.33. Dimensions as for Gadfly I.

(*'The Aeroplane' Photo*)

HENDY 281 HOBO (Scorpion)

Single seat ultra light powered by one 35 h.p. A.B.C. Scorpion, designed by Basil B. Henderson and built by the Hendy Aircraft Company at Shoreham 1929. One aircraft only, G-AAIG, c/n 1, first flown by E. W. Percival 10.29, based at Shoreham until 1934. Span, 32 ft. 0 in. Length, 19 ft. 6 in. A.U.W., 650 lb. Max. speed, 100 m.p.h.

(*'Flight' Photo*)

HENDY 281 HOBO (Cataract)

G-AAIG rebuilt at Shoreham 1934 with 90 h.p. Pobjoy Cataract, mass balanced ailerons and modified undercarriage to the order of Lord Patrick Crichton-Stuart for racing purposes. C. of A. issued 9.7.34, owner won Hatfield–Cardiff race 6.10.34 at 125·4 m.p.h. Raced with varying success until 1939. Dimensions as for original.

HENDY 302

Two seat cabin monoplane powered by one 105 h.p. Cirrus Hermes I, designed by Basil B. Henderson and built at Yate 1929 by George Parnall and Company. One aircraft only, G-AAVT, c/n 1, C. of A. issued 27.6.30. Averaged 121·51 m.p.h. in the 1930 King's Cup Race and 145 m.p.h. in the 1931 Heston–Newcastle Race, owner/pilot E. W. Percival. Sold as test bed to Cirrus Hermes Engineering Co. Ltd. 7.31 and to C. S. Napier 4.33. Span, 35 ft. 0 in. Length, 22 ft. 10 in. Tare wt., 1,045 lb. A.U.W., 1,900 lb. Max. speed, 132 m.p.h. Cruise, 112 m.p.h.

('*Flight*' *Photo*)

HENDY 302A

G-AAVT rebuilt at Croydon 1934 for C. S. Napier by the Cirrus Hermes Engineering Co. Ltd. Fitted with 130 h.p. Cirrus Hermes IV inverted engine, revised cabin top and spatted undercarriage. Averaged 133·5 m.p.h. in the 1934 King's Cup Race, pilot C. S. Napier. Used as test bed for the 150 h.p. Cirrus Major II engine, retired at Edinburgh in 1936 King's Cup Race. Scrapped 1936. Dimensions as Hendy 302, A.U.W., 1,900 lb. Max. speed, 136 m.p.h.

(*Photo: D. Napier and Son Ltd.*)

HESTON TYPE 5 RACER

Wooden single seater designed by A. E. Hagg and G. Cornwall for an attempt on the world's air speed record, powered by one 2,300 h.p. derated Napier Sabre. Two aircraft only, financed by Lord Nuffield, built by the Heston Aircraft Co. Ltd. 1939–40 and registered to D. Napier and Son Ltd. G-AFOK, c/n 1, made one flight at Heston 12.6.40 piloted by S/Ldr. G. L. G. Richmond. Damaged beyond repair in forced landing with over-heated engine and inadequate elevator control after five minutes flight. G-AFOL, c/n 2, construction not completed. Span, 32 ft. o$\frac{1}{2}$ in. Length, 24 ft. 7$\frac{1}{4}$ in. A.U.W., 7,200 lb. Duration, 18 minutes. Estimated max. speed, 480 m.p.h.

HILLER 360

Three seater designed by Stanley Hiller, Jnr., built by United Helicopters Inc. at Palo Alto, California, U.S.A. Ten British civil Series UH-12A powered by the 178 h.p. Franklin 6V4-178-B33, used for crop spraying by Fison-Airwork Ltd. in the United Kingdom, the Near East and Jamaica. Ten Series UH-12B powered by the 200 h.p. Franklin 6V4-200-C33, formerly used by Air Service Training Ltd., Hamble, and currently by crop spraying operators; thirteen Series UH-12C, similarly powered and operated. Details in Appendix D. Rotor diameter, 35 ft. 0 in. Length, 26 ft. 6 in. Tare wt., 1,628 lb. A.U.W. (UH-12A), 2,400 lb.; (UH-12B and C) 2,500 lb. Max. speed, 84 m.p.h. Cruise, 76 m.p.h.

HILLSON HELVELLYN

Two seat, mid-wing training monoplane powered by one 90 h.p. Blackburn Cirrus Minor 1, designed by Norman Sykes and built by F. Hills and Sons Ltd. at Manchester 1939. One aircraft only, G-AFKT, c/n HA.200, A. to F. issued 30.4.40, flown early in the war on the firm's communications duties, mainly between Barton and Ipswich. Dismantled 11.42. Span, 33 ft. 0 in. Length, 22 ft. 0 in. Tare wt., 900 lb. A.U.W., 1,500 lb. Cruise, 110 m.p.h.

('*Flight*' *Photo*)

HINKLER IBIS

Two seat, wooden monoplane powered by two 40 h.p. Salmson A.D.9, designed and built at Hamble 1929–31 by H. J. Hinkler with the assistance of R. H. Bound. The wing was designed by Basil B. Henderson and built at Shoreham by Hendy Aircraft Ltd. One aircraft only, G-AAIS, c/n 1, flown at Hamble without markings late in 1931, thereafter stored in Hinkler's garden at Sholing, Southampton. Rediscovered, semi-derelict 2.53, acquired by H. C. G. Stisted and exhibited at the Hatfield Garden Party of the R.Ae.S. 14.6.53, scrapped at Lee-on-Solent 1959.

HIRTENBERG H.S.9A

Two seater powered by one 120 h.p. de Havilland Gipsy Major, built by the Hirtenberger Patronen Zündhutchen und Metallwarenfabrik A.G. at Hirtenberg, Austria. One British aircraft only, c/n 001, built for J. H. Davies 7.37 as OE-DJH. Flew to England as D-EDJH 7.39, registered G-AGAK, C. of A. issued 22.11.39. Stored at Filton until overhauled at Gatwick 10.46. Flown privately by J. H. Davis, sold to D. D. Budworth at Boxted and named 'Zamiel' 9.50, to A. J. Stocks 8.54, J. E. Coxon 11.55 and C. H. Cosmelli, Denham, 4.56. Crashed at Butser Hill, Petersfield, Hants, 15.2.58. Span, 36 ft. 0 in. Length, 26 ft. 5 in. Tare wt., 1,254 lb. A.U.W., 2,090 lb. Max. speed, 118 m.p.h. Cruise, 102 m.p.h.

('*Flight*' *Photo*)

HORDERN-RICHMOND AUTOPLANE

Three seat, low-wing monoplane of wooden construction, powered by two 40 h.p. Continental A-40. Built at Heston 1936 by the Heston Aircraft Co. Ltd. to the joint specification of their test pilot E. G. Hordern and the Duke of Richmond and Gordon. Rudder control from wheel on control column. One aircraft only, G-AEOG, c/n 1, A. to F. issued 16.10.36, owned by the Duke of Richmond and Gordon and after 14.4.38 by Hordern-Richmond Aircraft Ltd. at Denham. Scrapped during the war. Span, 43 ft. 4 in. Length, 24 ft. 6 in. Tare wt., 1,125 lb. A.U.W., 1,750 lb. Max. speed, 100 m.p.h. Cruise, 85 m.p.h.

JODEL D.117

Side-by-side, two seat, cabin monoplane of wooden construction, powered by one 90 h.p. Continental C90-14F designed by MM. Joly and Dele-montez and built in quantity by the Société Aeronautique Normande at Bernay, France. One British aircraft only, G-APOZ, c/n 846, built 1958, C. of A. issued 1.10.58, ferried from Bernay to Croydon by Norman Jones 4.10.58. Demonstration aircraft of Rollason Aircraft and Engines Ltd., British concessionaires. Span, 27 ft. 0 in. Length, 20 ft. 2½ in. Tare wt., 808 lb. A.U.W., 1,357 lb. Max. speed, 130 m.p.h. Cruise, 120 m.p.h.

(Photo courtesy of the Royal Aeronautical Society)

JUNKERS F.13fe

Low-wing monoplane of all-metal construction for two crew in open cockpit and four cabin passengers, powered by one 385 h.p. Junkers L.5, in production from 1919 by the Junkers Flugzeug und Motorenwerke A.G. at Dessau, Germany. One British aircraft only, G-EBZV, c/n 2024, C. of A. issued 13.7.28, owner Rt. Hon. F. E. Guest of Hanworth, sold 5.30 to L. Beardmore, Hanworth, fitted with 450 h.p. Bristol Jupiter VI engine 1930. Sold to Lord Sempill 5.32. Sold in Sweden 4.37 as SE-AFW. Span, 58 ft. 3 in. Length, 31 ft. 6 in. Tare wt., 3,330 lb. A.U.W., 5,960 lb. Max. speed, 123 m.p.h. Cruise, 106 m.p.h.

(Photo courtesy of the Royal Aeronautical Society)

JUNKERS F.13

1929 model with enclosed cockpit, revised windows and locker. Four British aircraft only: G-AAGU, no known c/n, C. of A. issued 30.5.29, Trost Bros. Ltd. of Croydon, to Walcot Air Lines 5.30, to South African Airways 12.32 as ZS-AEN; G-AAZK, c/n 2052, C. of A. issued 4.6.30, Walcot Air Lines, structural failure in the air, Meopham, Kent, 21.7.30, G. L. P. Henderson and five passengers killed; G-ABDC, c/n 2074, C. of A. issued 23.8.30, Personal Flying Services Ltd., Heston, to Brooklands Airways Ltd. 4.33, sold in Sweden 12.34 as SE-AEC; G-ABDD, c/n 2005, C. of A. issued 22.7.30, Trost Bros. Ltd. Sold abroad 8.30. Span, 58 ft. 3 in. Length, 31 ft. 6 in.

('*Flight*' Photo)

JUNKERS A.50 JUNIOR

Two seat monoplane of all metal construction powered by one 80 h.p. Armstrong Siddeley Genet II, in production at Dessau, Germany from 1929. Two British aircraft only: G-AATH, c/n 3512, formerly D-2155, C. of A. issued 26.3.30, owner H. R. Trost, sold abroad 6.31; G-AAXB, c/n 3523, C. of A. issued 22.5.30 owner J. Parkes, crashed 6.31. Span, 32 ft. 10 in. Length, 23 ft. 6 in. Tare wt., 770 lb. A.U.W., 1,330 lb. Max. speed, 109 m.p.h. Cruise, 87 m.p.h.

KAY GYROPLANE TYPE 33/1

Single seat autogiro with collective pitch control, powered by one 75 h.p. Pobjoy R, designed by David Kay and built by Oddie, Bradbury and Cull Ltd. at Eastleigh 1934–35. One aircraft only, G-ACVA, c/n 1002, registered to Kay Gyroplanes Ltd., last flown at Perth 16.8.47, currently stored there. A second aircraft G-ACVB, c/n 1003, not completed. An earlier model, type 32/1, flown at Leuchars in 1932, was not registered as a civil aircraft. Rotor diameter, 22 ft. 0 in. Length, 17 ft. 11 in. Tare wt., 664 lb. A.U.W., 920 lb.

('The Aeroplane' Photo)

KRONFELD MONOPLANE

Single seat parasol monoplane powered by one 30 h.p. Carden-Ford driving a pusher airscrew, designed as a Drone replacement by Robert Kronfeld and built at Hanworth 1937. One aircraft only, G-AESG, c/n 33, A. to F. issued 7.5.37, first public appearance at the Heathrow Garden Party of the Royal Aeronautical Society 9.5.37. Scrapped during the war. Span, 39 ft. 8 in. Length, 21 ft. 2 in. Tare wt., 390 lb. A.U.W., 640 lb. Max. speed, 73 m.p.h. Cruise, 65 m.p.h.

KZ-VII LARK

Four seat, high-wing monoplane powered by one 125 h.p. Continental C-125-2, in production at Copenhagen by Skandinavisk Aero Industri A.S. from 1946. Two British aircraft only, imported by R. K. Dundas Ltd.: G-AJHM, c/n 148, formerly OY-AAN, C. of A. issued 21.7.47, sold to G. J. Dawson and later to the Guernsey Salvage Co. Ltd., sold in France 7.49 as F-BFXA: G-AJZV, c/n 151, C. of A. issued 10.9.47, crashed 4 miles N.W. of Manston, Kent 20.12.47. Span, 31 ft. 6 in. Length, 21 ft. 6 in. Tare wt., 1,022 lb. A.U.W., 1,911 lb. Max. speed, 125 m.p.h. Cruise, 115 m.p.h.

371

L. AND P. BIPLANE

Two seater powered by one 50 h.p. Gnôme, designed by A. A. Fletcher, built at Hendon 1916 by the London and Provincial Aviation Company as Type No. 4 for their own flying school. After the Armistice, five were registered for use at Stag Lane, Edgware: K-117/G-EABQ, c/n E121; K-118/G-EABR, c/n E120; K-119/G-EABS, c/n D147, all registered 20.5.19, broken up 8.19 when A.I.D. approval was refused. K-138/G-EADT, c/n E122, registered 11.6.19, crashed 10.20. Improved version G-EAQW, 100 h.p. Anzani (illustrated), no c/n, used during the war for parachuting experiments, registered to R. A. Whitehead 6.2.20, later sold to J. Coe and scrapped. Span, 37 ft. 0 in. Length, 25 ft. 0 in. Duration 3 hours.

LOCKHEED MODEL 5 VEGA

Transport for six passengers, powered by one Pratt and Whitney Wasp SC1, built at Los Angeles by Lockheed Aircraft Inc. 1929. One British aircraft only, G-ABFE, c/n 155, formerly NC372E, re-registered G-ABGK using initials of owner Glen Kidston, C. of A. issued 3.1.31. Left Netheravon 31.3.31 and lowered the Cape record to 6 days 9 hours, piloted by O. Cathcart Jones and owner. Sold to H. C. Miller 8.34, named 'Puck', flown in MacRobertson Race by D. C. T. Bennett, crash landed at Aleppo 21.10.34. Shipped to Australia, rebuilt 1936 as VH-UVK. Span, 41 ft. 0 in. Length, 27 ft. 6 in. Tare wt., 2,725 lb. A.U.W., 4,750 lb. Max. speed, 195 m.p.h. Cruise, 170 m.p.h.

(*Lockheed Photo*)

LOCKHEED MODEL 8D ALTAIR

Two seat, long distance monoplane of wooden monocoque construction fitted with retractable undercarriage, powered by one 550 h.p. Pratt and Whitney Wasp S1D1. One British aircraft only, c/n 152, built at Los Angeles, U.S.A. 1934 for Sir Charles Kingsford Smith by Lockheed Aircraft Inc., test flown as X118W 'Anzac' and shipped to Australia 27.6.34. Became VH-USB 'Lady Southern Cross', made first eastbound trans-Pacific flight, Brisbane–San Francisco 20.10.34–4.11.34. Shipped to U.K., taken ashore by barge at Allhallows, Kent, and flown to Croydon 8.10.35, registered G-ADUS, C. of A. issued 18.10.35, for attempt on England–Australia record. Left Croydon 23.10.35 with J. T. Pethyridge navigating, but icing damage over Greece compelled its return. Left 6.11.35, lost in Bay of Bengal 8.11.35. Wreckage found 20 years later suggested that the Altair had struck the summit of a mountainous island in bad visibility. Span, 42 ft. 9½ in. Length, 27 ft. 10 in. Tare wt., 3,297 lb. A.U.W., 5,800 lb. Max. speed, 230 m.p.h. Cruise, 205 m.p.h.

LOCKHEED MODEL 12A

All-metal transport for 2 pilots and 6 passengers powered by two 450 h.p. Pratt and Whitney Wasp Junior R-985-SB2, built at Burbank, California, from 1936. Thirteen British civil aircraft listed in Appendix D. *Prewar:* G-AEMZ and 'OI, executive transports for Lord Beaverbrook and Viscount Furness respectively; G-AFCO, 'KR, 'PF and 'XP imported

Continued overleaf

LOWE H.L.(M).9 MARLBURIAN

Side-by-side, two seat braced monoplane powered by one 60 h.p. Gnôme rotary, designed and built at Heaton, Newcastle-upon-Tyne, 1921 by F. Harold Lowe, trading as the Northern Aerial Transport Company. One aircraft only, G-EBEX, c/n H.L.(M).9, registered to the designer 7.10.22, crashed 25.11.22. Span, 28 ft. 6 in. Length, 17 ft. 0 in. Tare wt. 450 lb Max. speed, 100 m.p.h. Cruise, 85 m.p.h.

Lockheed Model 12A—continued.

for resale by the Aeronautical Research and Sales Corporation; G-AFTL used by F. S. Cotton to photograph Wilhelmshaven 16.9.39, destroyed by land mine at Heston 19.9.40. *Wartime:* G-AGDT for communications work with Cunliffe-Owen Aircraft Ltd. *Postwar* with R-985-AN3 motors: G-AGVZ, 'WM, 'WN, impressed U.S. transports demobilised after R.A.F. service; G-AGTL 'Caprice' used for eleven years on radio aid development by F. S. Cotton, currently owned by K. McAlpine, Luton; G-AHLH, currently based at Toussus-le-Noble, France, by the Earl of Granard. Span, 49 ft. 6 in. Length, 36 ft. 4 in. Tare wt., 6,040 lb. A.U.W., 9,200 lb. Max. speed, 225 m.p.h.. Cruise, 212 m.p.h.

('*Flight*' Photo)

LUTON BUZZARD I

Open cockpit, single seat ultra light of wooden construction, powered by one 35 h.p. Anzani inverted twin, designed by C. H. Latimer-Needham and built by Luton Aircraft Ltd. at Barton-in-the-Clay, Beds. One aircraft only, G-ADYX, c/n L.A.B./1, first flown 1936, fitted with split flaps and all-flying tailplane. Crashed at Christchurch 16.11.36, pilot R. L. Porteous. Span, 40 ft. 0 in. Length, 20 ft. 0 in. Tare wt., 600 lb. A.U.W., 800 lb. Max. speed, 85 m.p.h. Cruise, 75 m.p.h.

('*The Aeroplane*' Photo)

LUTON BUZZARD II

The original Buzzard G-ADYX, rebuilt with short-span wings, enclosed cockpit, orthodox tailplane, revised cowlings and undercarriage 1937, A. to F. issued 8.8.36. Damaged beyond repair in baulked landing during demonstration by Robert Kronfeld at the Heathrow Garden Party of the Royal Aeronautical Society 8.5.38. Destroyed in hangar fire Gerrards Cross 1943. Span, 35 ft. 6 in. Length, 21 ft. 6 in. Tare wt., 400 lb. A.U.W., 600 lb. Max. speed, 95 m.p.h. Cruise, 81 m.p.h.

('*The Aeroplane*' Photo)

LUTON MINOR

Single seat ultra light of wooden construction powered by one 35 h.p.
Anzani, designed by C. H. Latimer-Needham and built 1936 by Luton
Aircraft Ltd. at Barton-in-the-Clay, Beds, using fuselage and other com-
ponents of the experimental Luton L.A.2 tandem wing aircraft. One air-
craft only, G-AEPD, c/n L.A.2, A. to F. issued 3.3.37, sold 5.39 to A. J.
Cook, Anstruther, Fife, still extant in Dumbarton. Span, 25 ft. 0 in.
Length, 20 ft. 0 in. Tare wt., 380 lb. A.U.W., 600 lb. Max. speed,
85 m.p.h. Cruise, 75 m.p.h.

LUTON MINOR (Modified)

Basic airframe modified for home construction and better ground handling, with undercarriage incorporating rubber shock absorbers, parallel
wing bracing struts and single, in place of double, front centre section
strut. Five aircraft only: G-AFIR, c/n J.S.S.2, 35 h.p. Anzani, A. to F.
issued 14.8.38, built by J. S. Squires at Rearsby; G-AFRC, c/n J.E.C.1,
35 h.p. Anzani, A. to F. issued 8.3.39, built by J. E. Carine at Douglas,
and based at Hall Caine Airport, Isle of Man, crashed at Jurby 2.9.39.
Specification as for works model.

(C. H. Latimer-Needham Photo)

LUTON MINOR (Scorpion)

The modified airframe fitted with one 40 h.p. A.B.C. Scorpion. Three aircraft only: G-AFBP, c/n L.A.4, built by Luton Aircraft Ltd. at Gerrards Cross 1937, destroyed there in hangar fire 1943; G-AFUG, c/n W.S.H.1, one 40 h.p. A.B.C. Scorpion, built by W. S. Henry at Newtownards, County Down, 1939; G-AHMO, built by R. S. Finch at Darwen, Lancs, 1946 and fitted with the Scorpion engine from 'UG. Specification as for works model.

LUTON MINOR (Aeronca J.A.P. J-99)

The modified airframe fitted with one 40 h.p. Aeronca J.A.P. J-99 Four aircraft to date: G-AFIR, rebuilt 1950 at Pinner, Middlesex, by A. W. J. G. Ord-Hume, crashed at Oxhey, Herts., 1.5.51, rebuilt, A. to F. reissued 20.7.56, currently owned by F. J. Parker, White Waltham; G-AGEP, built by L. R. Miller at Seaton, Devon 1942, currently owned by C. M. Roberts, Luton: G-ALUZ reserved for D. E. Felce; G-AMUW construction commenced by W. Petrie, Orkney 1952, G-APVI, J. T. Hayes, construction begun at Lincoln, 1959. Span, 25 ft. 0 in. Length, 21 ft. 6 in. Tare wt., 340 lb. A.U.W., 620 lb. Max. speed, 85 m.p.h. Cruise, 75 m.p.h.

(Photo: Cambridge Daily News)

LUTON MINOR (Cherub)

The modified type fitted with one 32 h.p. Bristol Cherub III. One aircraft only, G-AMAW 'Sunbury', built at Oakington 1949–50 by F/Lt. J. R. Coates, first flown at Waterbeach, A. to F. issued 3.10.50. Currently based at Luton. Specification as for Aeronca J.A.P. version.

LUTON MAJOR

Two seat light aircraft powered by one 62 h.p. Walter Mikron II, designed by C. H. Latimer-Needham and built by Luton Aircraft Ltd. at Gerrards Cross 1939. Three aircraft to date: G-AFMU, c/n L.A.5/1, A. to F. issued 4.3.39, first flown by S/Ldr. E. L. Mole 12.3.39, exhibited at the Heathrow Garden Party of the R.Ae.S. 14.5.39, destroyed in hangar fire, Gerrards Cross 1943. G-APUG, c/n PAL.1203, and 'UN, c/n PFA/120, now under construction by L. D. Blyth, Sawbridgeworth and W. G. Cooper, Weybridge, from drawings revised by Phoenix Aircraft Ltd., 1958. Span, 35 ft. 2 in. Length, 23 ft. 9 in. Tare wt., 600 lb. A.U.W., 1,030 lb. Max. speed, 105 m.p.h. Cruise, 90 m.p.h.

378

MARENDAZ Mk.III

Four seater with retractable undercarriage, powered by one 200 h.p. de Havilland Gipsy VI, designed by D. M. K. Marendaz and built by International Aircraft and Engineering Ltd. Two aircraft only: an unregistered prototype, c/n 1, built at Cordwallis Works, Maidenhead, was lost when the factory was destroyed by fire 6.37; G-AFGG, c/n 2, built at Barton-in-the-Clay, Beds, was exhibited in unfinished state at the Heathrow Garden Party of the Royal Aeronautical Society 8.5.38. The machine remained uncompleted and was destroyed in 1940.

('*The Aeroplane*' *Photo*)

MARENDAZ TRAINER

Two seat instructional aircraft powered by one 90 h.p. Blackburn Cirrus Minor I, designed by D. M. K. Marendaz and built by Marendaz Aircraft Ltd. at Barton-in-the-Clay, Beds, 1939. One aircraft only, G-AFZX, c/n A.B.T.1, first flown 12.39, given to the Halton Squadron of the Air Training Corps, 1940. Span, 34 ft. 0 in. Length, 22 ft. 4 in. Tare wt., 960 lb. A.U.W., 1,500 lb. Max. speed, 124 m.p.h. Cruise, 95 m.p.h.

MARTIN MONOPLANE

Single seater using some D.H.53 components, designed by C. H. Latimer-Needham and built for F/O Martin Hopkinson by Luton Aircraft Ltd. 1937. One aircraft only, G-AEYY, c/n 1, fitted with one 32 h.p. Bristol Cherub III, first flown at Denham 10.37, A. to F. issued 4.11.37. Max. speed, 80 m.p.h.

MARTIN-BAKER M.B.1

Two seat, all-metal, experimental aircraft powered by one 160 h.p. Napier Javelin IIIA, designed by James Martin and built by the Martin-Baker Aircraft Co. Ltd. at Denham, Bucks, 1934, to demonstrate the Martin system of lattice girder construction. One aircraft only, G-ADCS, c/n M.B.1, first flown by V. H. Baker 3.35, destroyed by fire 3.38. Span, 37 ft. 0 in. Length, 28 ft. 10½ in.

MESSERSCHMITT Bf108 TAIFUN

Four seat luxury tourer of all-metal, stressed-skin construction, fitted with retractable undercarriage. In production by the Bayerische Flugzeugwerke A.G. at Augsburg, Germany, from 1938. Four British civil aircraft only: G-AFRN, c/n 2039, one 270 h.p. Argus AS10-E, imported by A.F.N. Ltd., Heston, C. of A. issued 26.6.39, impressed 5.41 as DK280. G-AFZO, c/n 1660, 270 h.p. Argus AS10-C3, formerly a German Embassy aircraft D-IDBT, seized 9.39, handed over to A.F.N. Ltd., impressed 9.41 as ES955 but incorrectly painted as ES995. A second Embassy aircraft D-IJHW also seized and directly impressed as AW167. AW167 and 'ES995' demobilised at Heston 26.9.46 under A.F.N. Ltd. ownership to masquerade as G-AFZO and 'RN respectively until sold in Switzerland 4.50 as HB-ESM and 'SL; G-AGUZ, c/n Nord 1000 No. 15, ex Luftwaffe, owner T. N. L. B. Guinness, unconverted at Gatwick 1946; G-AKZY, c/n 3059, Air Couriers Ltd., sold abroad unconverted 1.50. Span, 34 ft. 5 in. Length, 27 ft. 2 in. Tare wt., 1,887 lb. A.U.W., 3,087 lb. Max. speed, 196 m.p.h. Cruise, 187 m.p.h.

MILES M.1 SATYR

Single seat wooden aerobatic biplane powered by one 75 h.p. Pobjoy R, designed by F. G. Miles and built by George Parnall and Company at Yate, Glos., 1932. One aircraft only, G-ABVG, c/n 1 (later J.7), first flown 8.32, C. of A. issued 1.2.33. Sold to the Hon. Mrs. Victor Bruce's firm Luxury Air Tours Ltd. 5.33, painted in red and white squares and flown by J. B. Pugh at the displays of British Hospitals Air Pageants Ltd. until crashed 9.36. Span, 21 ft. 0 in. Length, 17 ft. 8 in. Tare wt., 594 lb. A.U.W., 900 lb. Max. speed, 122 m.p.h.

MILES M.4A MERLIN

Fast taxi aircraft for pilot and four passengers, powered by one 200 h.p. de Havilland Gipsy Six, built at Woodley by Phillips and Powis Aircraft Ltd. 1935. One British aircraft only, G-ADFE, c/n 151, prototype, built for Birkett Air Services Ltd., Heston, first flown as U-8, C. of A. issued 15.5.35. Used on charter to the Abyssinian War 1935–36 and throughout Europe until 1939. All trace of it was lost during the war. Span, 37 ft. 0 in. Length, 25 ft. 10 in. Tare wt., 1,700 lb. A.U.W., 3,000 lb. Max. speed, 155 m.p.h. Cruise, 140 m.p.h.

MILES M.7 NIGHTHAWK

Four seat instrument trainer powered by one 200 h.p. de Havilland Gipsy Six, built at Woodley from 1935. Four British civil aircraft only: G-ADXA, c/n 263, prototype, first flown as U-5, C. of A. issued 7.12.35, crashed during spinning trials at Woodley 22.1.36, Wing Cdr. F. W. Stent escaped by parachute; G-AEBP, c/n 282, C. of A. issued 19.3.36, withdrawn 5.37; G-AEHN and 'HO, c/n 283–4, Cs. of A. issued 14.8.36, left on delivery to the Rumanian Air Force 15.8.36. Span, 35 ft. 0 in. Length, 25 ft. 0 in. Tare wt., 1,650 lb. A.U.W., 2,400 lb. Max. speed, 175 m.p.h. Cruise, 155 m.p.h.

MILES M.7A NIGHTHAWK

Four seater erected in 1944 using a Nighthawk fuselage, the wings of the second Mohawk, revised glazing, rudder trim tab and one 205 h.p. de Havilland Gipsy Six series II driving a variable pitch airscrew. One aircraft only, c/n 286, flown by Miles Aircraft Ltd. as U-0225 and later as G-AGWT, C. of A. issued 15.3.46. Taxi work by Raceways Ltd., Woodley, 1946–47; raced by Tommy Rose and owners E. Williams, R. Crewdson and Gp. Capt. C. M. M. Grece 1947–54; sold in Kenya 6.54 as VP-KMM. Dimensions as for M.7, A.U.W., 2,650 lb. Max. speed, 170 m.p.h. Cruise, 150 m.p.h.

MILES M.8 PEREGRINE

The first Miles twin engined aircraft. Transport with retractable under-
carriage, carrying two crew and six passengers, powered by two 205 h.p.
Gipsy Six II, built at Woodley 1936. One civil aircraft only, G-AEDE,
c/n 300, first flown as U-9 by C. O. Powis 8.36. Entered for the Schlesinger
Race to Johannesburg by F/Lt. H. R. A. Edwards and S/Ldr. B. S.
Thynne but was not ready in time. Dismantled 12.37. Span, 46 ft. 0 in.
Length, 32 ft. 0 in. Tare wt., 3,000 lb. A.U.W., 5,200 lb. Max. speed,
188 m.p.h. Cruise, 164 m.p.h.

MILES M.12 MOHAWK

Two seater powered by one 250 h.p. Menasco Buccaneer B6-S, built at
Woodley 1936 to the specification of Col. Charles Lindbergh. Two air-
craft only, G-AEKW, c/n 298, C. of A. issued 28.1.37, used by Lindbergh
and wife for European inter-Capital travel 1937. Impressed 11.41 as
HM503, restored 5.46 by Southern Aircraft (Gatwick) Ltd., flown in 1947
Folkestone Trophy Race by Wing Cdr. Earle. Sold to E. G. F. Lyder
1947; to B. P. Pini, Broxbourne 7.48 and converted to open cockpits.
Sold in Spain 2.50; G-AEKX, c/n 301, built but not erected. Span,
35 ft. 0 in. Length, 25 ft. 6 in. Tare wt., 1,605 lb. A.U.W., 2,620 lb.
Max. speed, 190 m.p.h. Cruise, 170 m.p.h.

MILES M.13 HOBBY

Single seat research monoplane with retractable undercarriage, powered by one 145 h.p. de Havilland Gipsy Major 2 driving a variable pitch airscrew. One aircraft only, G-AFAW, c/n 1.Y, completed at Woodley and flown by F. G. Miles as U-2 a day or so before the King's Cup Race of September 11, 1937. Retraction difficulties prevented it from competing, although a public appearance was made at Hatfield on that day. Sold to the R.A.E. for full-scale wind tunnel research 5.38. Span, 21 ft. 5 in. Length, 22 ft. 8 in. Tare wt., 1,140 lb. A.U.W., 1,527 lb. Max. speed, 200+ m.p.h.

MILES M.18 Mk.1

Two seat trainer powered by one 130 h.p. de Havilland Gipsy Major 1, designed by W. Capley. One aircraft only, G-AFRO, c/n 1075, first flown at Woodley by F. G. Miles 4.12.38 as U-2. Converted to single seater in 1941 with tricycle undercarriage and fin and rudder moved forward 22 in. Flown as U-0222. Reverted to tail wheel undercarriage, flew with span reduced to 22 ft. and in 1946-47 with 110 h.p. Jameson FF engine. Scrapped 12.47. Span, 31 ft. 0 in. Length, 24 ft. 10 in. Tare wt., 1,180 lb. A.U.W., 1,800 lb. Max. speed, 140 m.p.h.

MILES M.18 Mk.2

Second prototype M.18 with fin and rudder moved forward 22 in., powered by one 150 h.p. Blackburn Cirrus Major III. One aircraft only, c/n 4426, first flown at Woodley 11.39 as U-8 and on Air Ministry acceptance trials as U-0224. Miles communications aircraft as HM545 until civilianised post-war as G-AHKY, C. of A. issued 29.8.46. Sold to F/Lt. H. B. Iles 3.48, won 1956 Goodyear Trophy at 130 m.p.h., 1957 Osram Cup at 136 m.p.h. Span, 31 ft. 0 in. Length, 24 ft. 10 in. Tare wt., 1,306 lb. A.U.W., 1,925 lb. Max. speed, 130 m.p.h. Cruise, 120 m.p.h.

MILES M.18 Mk.3

Third prototype M.18 fitted with enclosed cockpits and powered by one 150 h.p. Blackburn Cirrus Major III. One aircraft only, c/n 4432, first flown at Woodley 10.42 as U-0238. Used for communications, becoming U-3 in 1945 and civil as G-AHOA in 1946, C. of A. issued 3.4.48. Owned by Mrs. E. M. Porteous, Burnaston 1948, sold to T. W. Hayhow, crashed at Littondale, Yorks, 25.5.50. Specification as for M.18 Mk. 2.

MILES M.28 MERCURY 2

Three seater with knuckled retractable undercarriage, designed by G. H. Miles, built at Woodley 1942. One aircraft only, U-0237 later HM583, initially powered by one 145 h.p. de Havilland Gipsy Major IIA and later one 140 h.p. Blackburn Cirrus Major II. Civilianised 1947 as G-AJVX and fitted with 150 h.p. Blackburn Cirrus Major III for the Hulland Gravel Co. Ltd., Burnaston, C. of A. issued 11.12.47. Sold to J. E. Nicholson, Croft, flown to Australia in 64 days as VH-BBK by F. Burt, arrived Perth, W.A., 17.1.51. Span, 30 ft. 8 in. Length, 24 ft. 0 in. Tare wt., 1,400 lb. A.U.W., 2,500 lb. Max. speed, 155 m.p.h. Cruise, 135 m.p.h.

(Air Ministry Photo)

MILES M.28 MERCURY 3

Three seat, triple control trainer with thinner centre section allowing retracted wheels to protrude, powered by one 150 h.p. Blackburn Cirrus Major III. One aircraft only, c/n 4684, built 1943, initially flown as U-0242 and later PW937. Registration G-AISH reserved 12.46, scrapped 2.48. Span, 30 ft. 8 in. Length, 24 ft. 0 in. Tare wt., 1,480 lb. A.U.W., 2,500 lb. Max. speed, 155 m.p.h. Cruise, 135 m.p.h.

MILES M.28 MERCURY 4

Four seat tourer powered by one 145 h.p. de Havilland Gipsy Major IIA driving a constant speed airscrew. One aircraft only, c/n 4685, built at Woodley 1944, first flown as U-0243, registered to Miles Aircraft Ltd. 11.45 as G-AGVX, C. of A. issued 26.4.46. Sold to Aerotaxi A.G. Zürich 4.47 as HB-EED, restored to H. W. H. Moore 3.48, five subsequent owners. Sold in Australia 1.53 as VH-AKH, later VH-AKC. Span, 30 ft. 8 in. Length, 24 ft. 0 in. Tare wt., 1,425 lb. A.U.W., 2,400 lb. Max. speed, 157 m.p.h. Cruise, 139 m.p.h.

MILES M.28 MERCURY 5

Four seater powered by one 150 h.p. Blackburn Cirrus Major III, fitted with revised undercarriage and the square rear window. One aircraft only, G-AJFE, c/n 6697, built at Woodley 1947, C. of A. issued 28.10.47, sold to K. Hole, White Waltham, and later J. F. Schumaker, Geneva. Re-registered in Switzerland 6.51 as HB-EEF. Restored to A. T. C. Carey, Denham, 12.54, damaged beyond repair in forced landing at West Hyde, Bucks, 13.3.55. Span, 30 ft. 8 in. Length, 24 ft. 0 in. Tare wt., 1,460 lb. A.U.W., 2,500 lb. Max. speed, 157 m.p.h. Cruise, 139 m.p.h.

MILES M.28 MERCURY 6

Four seater powered by one 150 h.p. Blackburn Cirrus Major III, fitted with the oval rear window of the Messenger 2A. One aircraft only, G-AHAA, c/n 6268, built at Woodley 1946, C. of A. issued 3.5.46, personal aircraft of chairman of B.E.A.C., used by the Airways Aero Association 1947, sold 3.48 to K. E. Millard & Co. Ltd., Wolverhampton. Sold in Germany 9.56 by Adie Aviation Ltd. as D-EHAB. Specification as for Mercury 5.

MILES M.68

Aerovan derivative carrying one crew and 1,600 lb. of freight, unofficially known as the Boxcar and powered by four 90 h.p. Blackburn Cirrus Minor II. One aircraft only, G-AJJM, c/n 6696, built at Woodley 1947, fitted with detachable and roadable central freight hold. Flown with and without hold at the Radlett S.B.A.C. Show 9.47. Scrapped 1948. Span, 50 ft. 0 in. Length, 36 ft. 0 in. Max. speed, 140 m.p.h. Cruise, 130 m.p.h.

MILES M.71 MERCHANTMAN

The largest Aerovan development, of all-metal construction, powered by four 250 h.p. de Havilland Gipsy Queen 30 and carrying two crew and 20 passengers or 5,000 lb. of freight. One aircraft only, G-AILJ, c/n 6695, built at Woodley 1947 and flown under B conditions as U-21. Demonstrated at the Radlett S.B.A.C. Show 9.47. Scrapped 1948. Span, 66 ft. 6 in. Length, 42 ft. 9 in. A.U.W., 13,000 lb. Max. speed, 163 m.p.h. Cruise, 157 m.p.h.

MILES M.100 STUDENT

Two seat, side-by-side, private-venture trainer powered by one 880 lb. s.t. Blackburn Turboméca Marboré 2A turbojet, designed by G. H. Miles and built at Shoreham 1956–57. One aircraft to date: G-APLK, c/n 100/1008, first flown by the designer 14.5.57 and exhibited at the Farnborough S.B.A.C. Show 9.57 under B conditions as G-35-4. C. of A. issued 20.6.58, for Continental tour 7.58. Used in London–Paris Race 7.59. Span, 29 ft. 2 in. Length, 31 ft. 6 in. Tare wt., 2,400 lb. A.U.W., 3,900 lb. Max. speed, 298 m.p.h. Cruise, 262 m.p.h.

Continued from page 391.

5W40, imported by J. E. Carberry for the International Light Plane Tour of Europe 20.7.30–7.8.30, C. of A. issued 8.7.30. Fitted with Townend Ring, averaged 141·8 m.p.h. in 1931 Heston–Cramlington Race, sold to Air Taxis Ltd. 3.32, sold in Germany to Leo Lammertz 7.33. Span, 32 ft. 0 in. Length, 20 ft. 5 in. Tare wt., 888 lb. A.U.W., 1,519 lb. Max. speed, 98 m.p.h. Cruise, 85 m.p.h.

MONOCOUPE 60

Tandem, two seat, cabin monoplane powered by one 60 h.p. Velie radial, built 1928 by Mono Aircraft Inc. at Moline, Illinois, U.S.A. One British aircraft only, G-AADG, c/n 194, imported 12.28 by H. G. Hamer, sold to R. W. H. Knight, Hereford, 2.31, re-engined with 80 h.p. Armstrong Siddeley Genet II, C. of A. issued 14.7.31, flown to Guernsey and back 25–27.3.32. Last owner A. O. Humble-Smith, Maylands, 1939. Stored during war, broken up at Gatwick 1947. Span, 30 ft. 0 in. Length, 19 ft. 9 in. Tare wt., 700 lb. A.U.W., 1,175 lb. Max. speed, 92 m.p.h.

('New York Times' Photo)

MONOCOUPE 90

Side-by-side, two seat, cabin monoplane powered by one 125 h.p. Warner Scarab, built 1930 by Mono Aircraft Inc. at Moline, Illinois, U.S.A. One British aircraft only, G-ABBR, initially mispainted as G-ABAR, c/n

391

('*The Aeroplane*' *Photo*)

MOONEY M20A

Four seat tourer with metal monocoque fuselage, wooden wing and retractable undercarriage, powered by one 180 h.p. Lycoming O-360-A1A, built by Mooney Aircraft Inc. at Kerrville, Texas, U.S.A. 1959. One British aircraft to date, G-APVV, c/n 1474, previously N8164E, freighted to London in Constellation N6501C 17.7.59, erected at Croydon, delivered to D. M. B. Carnegie, Luton and C. of A. issued 30.7.59. Span, 35 ft. 0 in. Length, 23 ft. 2 in. Tare wt., 1,415 lb. A.U.W., 2,450 lb. Max. speed, 190 m.p.h. Cruise, 180 m.p.h.

('*The Aeroplane*' *Photo*)

MORANE-SAULNIER M.S.760 PARIS

All metal four seater powered by two 880 lb. s.t. Turboméca Marboré IIC, built by Aéroplanes Morane-Saulnier at Puteaux, Seine, France 1958. One British aircraft to date, G-APRU, c/n 8, delivered to the College of Aeronautics at Cranfield 10.12.58 as F-WJAC. Later flown as G-26-2 and equipped as a high performance flying classroom. Flown in the London–Paris Race 7.59. Span, 33 ft. 3 in. Length, 33 ft. Tare wt., 4,280 lb. A.U.W. 7,725 lb. Max. speed, 405 m.p.h. Cruise, 350 m.p.h.

MOSS M.A.1 (Cabin)

Two seat monoplane of wooden construction powered by one 95 h.p. Pobjoy Niagara III, designed and built by Moss Bros. Aircraft Ltd. at Chorley, Lancs., 1937. One aircraft only, G-AEST, c/n 1, C. of A. issued 6.9.37. Converted to open cockpits 1938. Span, 34 ft. 0 in. Length, 23 ft. 3 in. Tare wt., 950 lb. A.U.W., 1,400 lb. Max. speed, 130 m.p.h. Cruise, 120 m.p.h.

MOSS M.A.1 (Open)

The original M.A.1 rebuilt with open cockpits 1938, stored during the war, rear seat faired in 1949, flown by W. H. Moss in the 1949 and 1950 King's Cup Races, crashed during the latter at Newport, near Wolverhampton, and pilot killed 17.6.50. Reservations G-AFHA and 'JV for two additional aircraft were not taken up. Specification as for cabin model.

MOSS M.A.2 (Open)

Two seat trainer similar to M.A.1, powered by one 90 h.p. Blackburn
Cirrus Minor I, built at Chorley 1939. One aircraft only, G-AFMS,
shown at R.Ae.S. Garden Party, Heathrow, 14.5.39. Converted to cabin
model 1940. Span, 34 ft. 0 in. Length, 23 ft. 3 in. Tare wt., 950 lb.
A.U.W., 1,400 lb. Max. speed, 125 m.p.h. Cruise, 110 m.p.h.

MOSS M.A.2 (Cabin)

The original M.A.2 rebuilt with cabin top, C. of A. issued 18.10.40.
Shipped to Canada as CF-BUB, became the first light aircraft to cross the
Rockies, 1941. Returned 1947, flown in 1949 King's Cup Race by W. H.
Moss, in 1950 by G. F. Bullen, sold to T. W. Hayhow 3.53, to the Fair-
wood Flying Group 9.53, crashed 10 miles south of Builth Wells 7.7.58.
Specification as for open model except: Tare wt., 800 lb. Max. speed,
120 m.p.h. Cruise, 105 m.p.h.

NEWBURY A.P.4 EON

Four seater powered by one 100 h.p. Blackburn Cirrus Minor II, designed by Aviation and Engineering Projects Ltd. and built 1947 by Elliotts of Newbury Ltd. One aircraft only, G-AKBC, c/n EON/1, first flown at Welford by P. Stanbury 8.8.47, C. of A. issued 8.9.47. Fitted 7.48 with 145 h.p. de Havilland Gipsy Major 10 and lengthened nose-wheel leg, and redesignated EON 2. Destroyed in pilotless take-off at Lympne 14.4.50. Span, 37 ft. 0 in. Length, 25 ft. 0 in. (EON 1) A.U.W., 1,950 lb. Max. speed, 112 m.p.h. Cruise, 100 m.p.h. (EON 2) A.U.W., 2,340 lb. Max. speed, 136 m.p.h. Cruise, 115 m.p.h.

(M. J. G. Gradidge Photo)

N.H.I. H-3 KOLIBRIE SERIES I

Two seat, two bladed helicopter powered by two 49·5 lb. s.t. TJ-5 tip mounted ramjets, built by N. V. Nederlandse Helicopter Industrie at Rotterdam 1958. Two British aircraft to date: G-APRZ, c/n 3009, formerly PH-ACD, delivered to European Helicopters Ltd. at Ipswich for agricultural use 11.58, C. of A. issued 6.4.59; PH-NIW, c/n 3011, was to have been G-APVB, same owners, crashed at St. Andrews, Fife 4.6.59. Rotor diameter, 33 ft. 0 in. Length, 13 ft. 10½ in. Tare wt., 530 lb. A.U.W., 1,430 lb. Max. speed, 62 m.p.h. Operating speed 15–50 m.p.h.

('*Flight*' Photo)

NIEUPORT NIGHTHAWK

Two seater designed by H. P. Folland, powered by one 320 h.p. A.B.C.
Dragonfly I and built from Nighthawk single seat fighter components by
the Nieuport and General Aircraft Co. Ltd. at Cricklewood 1919. One
British civil aircraft only, K-151, c/n L.C.1 No. 1, flown in the Aerial
Derby, Hendon, 21.6.19 by L. R. Tait-Cox, forced landed at West
Thurrock. Became G-EAEQ, C. of A. issued 7.7.19, made first newspaper
flight in India, from Bombay to Poona 2.20. Sold in India 9.20. Span,
28 ft. 0 in. Length, 18 ft. 0 in. Tare wt., 1,500 lb. A.U.W., 2,180 lb.
Max. speed, 138 m.p.h.

('*Flight*' Photo)

NIEUPORT NIEUHAWK

Single seat wooden racing and demonstration aircraft powered by one
320 h.p. A.B.C. Dragonfly I, designed by H. P. Folland and built at
Cricklewood 1919 by the Nieuport and General Aircraft Co. Ltd. One

NIEUPORT GOSHAWK

Single seat racing biplane powered by one 320 h.p. A.B.C. Dragonfly Ia, designed by H. P. Folland and built at Cricklewood 1920. One aircraft only, G-EASK, c/n L.S.3 No. 1, set up British speed record of 166·5 m.p.h. in Class C4B piloted by L. R. Tait-Cox at Martlesham 17.6.20. Forced down at Brooklands in the Aerial Derby 24.7.20, same pilot. Flown to Etampes by J. H. James for the Gordon Bennett Race 26–27.9.20. H. G. Hawker suffered haemorrhage in the air and was killed when the machine crashed at Hendon 12.7.21. Span, 20 ft. 6 in. Max. speed, 167 m.p.h.

Continued from page 396.

aircraft only, G-EAJY, c/n L.C.1 No. 2, first flown 3.9.19, fourth at 132·67 m.p.h. in the Aerial Derby, Hendon, 24.7.20 piloted by J. H. James. Forced landed after completing one lap of the Aerial Derby 16.7.21 at 142·6 m.p.h. piloted by F/Lt. J. Noakes. Sold 1921 to C. P. B. Ogilvie, Willesden. Span, 26 ft. 0 in. Length, 18 ft. 6 in. A.U.W., 2,120 lb. Max. speed, 151 m.p.h.

NORTHROP DELTA 1C

Transport for eight passengers, powered by one 700 h.p. Pratt and
Whitney Hornet SD, built at Los Angeles by the Northrop Corporation
1934. Third production aircraft, c/n 7, sold to A. B. Aerotransport,
Stockholm, as SE-ADI. Non-starter in the Australia Race 10.34.
Acquired by Mrs. Beryl Markham as G-AEXR for long distance flight
5.37. Not delivered. Went to Iraq as YI-OSF. Span, 47 ft. 9 in.
Length, 33 ft. 1 in. Tare wt., 4,200 lb. A.U.W., 7,350 lb. Max. speed,
221 m.p.h. Cruise, 201 m.p.h.

NORTHROP 2L GAMMA COMMERCIAL

Two seater of all-metal, monocoque construction, built at Santa Monica,
California, 1937. One British aircraft only, G-AFBT, c/n 347, imported by
the Bristol Aeroplane Co. Ltd. 9.37 and flown at Filton as test bed during
the early flight trials of the 1,400 h.p. Bristol Hercules, 14 cylinder, two row
radial. Dismantled at Filton during the war. Span, 47 ft. 8 in. Length,
31 ft. 8⅝ in. A.U.W., 8,315 lb. Max. speed, 270 m.p.h. Cruise, 230 m.p.h.

(*P. T. Capon Photo*)

PARNALL PIXIE I AND II

Single seater of wooden construction designed by Harold Bolas and built at Coliseum Works, Bristol, by George Parnall and Company for the 1923 Lympne Trials. One aircraft only, with two sets of interchangeable mainplanes and engines. As Pixie I with 29 ft. wings and 500 c.c. Douglas for the consumption test, first flown at Filton 13.9.23. As Pixie II with 18 ft. wings and 736 c.c. Douglas, first flown 4.10.23. Averaged 76·1 m.p.h. to win the £500 speed prize at Lympne 11.10.23. Won the Wakefield Prize at 81 m.p.h., Hendon 27.10.23. Piloted throughout by Capt. N. Macmillan. Reconditioned as Pixie II with 696 c.c. Blackburne Tomtit, flown at the Hendon R.A.F. Display 28.6.24 as J7323. Flown by F. T. Courtney in the Grosvenor Trophy Race at Lympne 4.10.24, registered G-EBKM 2.12.24. Fitted with large rudder and flown in the Lympne Races 8.25 by F. T. Courtney. Stored until sold to F. J. Cleare, Maylands 17.4.36, A. to F. issued 7.8.37, sold to Ray Bullock, Fraddon, Cornwall, 1.39, crashed 4.39. Span, 18 ft. 0 in. Length, 18 ft. 0 in. Tare wt., 280 lb. A.U.W., 450 lb. Max. speed, 81 m.p.h.

(*Photo courtesy of the Royal Aeronautical Society*)

PARNALL PIXIE IIIA

Two seater with detachable upper mainplane, designed by Harold Bolas for the 1924 Lympne Trials. Two aircraft only: G-EBJG, 32 h.p. Bristol Cherub III, first flown at Yate 5.9.24, flown as No. 18 by F/Lt. R. A. de Haga Haig; G-EBKK, 35 h.p. Blackburne Thrush, flown as No. 19 by Wing Cdr. W. F. Sholto Douglas, both retired with engine trouble. G-EBKK fitted with 1,100 c.c. Anzani (illustrated) in 1925. Span, 32 ft. 5 in. Length, 21 ft. 2 in. Tare wt., 540 lb. A.U.W., 891 lb.

399

PARNALL PIXIE III

The two Pixie IIIA biplanes permanently converted to monoplanes with 32 h.p. Bristol Cherub III engines 1926. G-EBJG, C. of A. issued 4.9.26, sold to C. B. Thompson, Rugby, 3.33, to S. L. Dodwell, Hinckley, 4.35, stored at Hanworth 1936, at Kirklinton by R. G. Carr during the war, at Carlisle by D. I. Taylor 1957, and currently derelict at Reigate; G-EBKK, re-engined with Cherub III, flown as No. 14 into 4th place in the 1926 Lympne Trials by F. T. Courtney, sold to the Bristol and Wessex Aeroplane Club 2.30, crashed 9.30. Span, 32 ft. 5 in. Length, 21 ft. 2 in. Tare wt., 522 lb. A.U.W., 925 lb.

PARNALL IMP

Two seat cantilever biplane with fuselage of plywood-covered, stressed-skin construction, powered by one 80 h.p. Armstrong Siddeley Genet II, designed by Harold Bolas, first flown at Yate 1927. One aircraft only, G-EBTE, C. of A. issued 4.5.28, 8th in the 1928 King's Cup Race at 109·93 m.p.h. piloted by F/Lt. D. W. Bonham Carter. Later used for flight trials of the 65 h.p. Pobjoy P prototype radial. Sold to F/O A. T. Orchard, Worthy Down, 8.33, scrapped 12.33. Span, 25 ft. 6 in. Length, 21 ft. 2 in. Tare wt., 850 lb. A.U.W., 1,320 lb.

PARNALL ELF I

Two seat biplane with plywood-covered fuselage and Warren girder-braced, fabric-covered, folding wings, powered by one 105 h.p. A.D.C. Hermes I, designed by Harold Bolas and built at Yate 1928–29. One aircraft only, G-AAFH, c/n 1, exhibited without markings at the Olympia Aero Show 7.29, C. of A. issued 25.6.30, sold to Lord Apsley 12.32, damaged beyond repair in a forced landing at Herongate, Rickmansworth, Herts 20.3.34. Span, 31 ft. $3\frac{1}{2}$ in. Length, 22 ft. $10\frac{1}{2}$ in. Tare wt., 1,020 lb. A.U.W., 1,700 lb. Max. speed, 116 m.p.h. Cruise, 103 m.p.h.

(*W. K. Kilsby Photo*)

PARNALL ELF II

Similar aircraft to Elf I but with horn balanced rudder and one 120 h.p. A.D.C. Hermes II. Two aircraft only: G-AAIN, c/n 2 (later J.6), C. of A. issued 15.6.32, sold to Lord Apsley 11.34, stored during the war, restored by W. J. Nobbs at Fairoaks 1950, now preserved by the Shuttleworth Trust at Old Warden Park, Biggleswade; G-AAIO, c/n 3 (later J.5), C. of A. issued 2.9.31, sold to R. Hall of the Cotswold Aero Club 11.33, crashed and burned due to fuel pump failure, killing owner and son 13.1.34. Specification as for Elf I.

PERMAN PARASOL

Single seat ultra light, powered by one 30 h.p. Perman-Ford, designed and built by E. G. Perman and Co. Ltd. at Brownlow Mews, Guildford St., Grays Inn Road, W.C.1, and first flown at Gravesend 5.36. One aircraft only, G-ADZX, c/n E.G.P.56, using marks originally reserved for one of the company's Poux du Ciel. Sold to Airworthiness Ltd., Gravesend, 13.10.36, and believed burned at fire fighting display 7.37. Span, 25 ft. 6 in. Length, 15 ft. 6 in. A.U.W., 600 lb. Max. speed, 80 m.p.h.

PIAGGIO P.136-L

Five seat amphibian built by Societa per Azioni Piaggio at Finale Ligure, Italy. Two British aircraft only, both imported by Lamberts Trust Ltd.: G-AOFN, c/n 195, model P.136-L1, two 260 h.p. Lycoming GO-435-C2B, C. of A. issued 4.8.55, later based at Monte Carlo by Onassis, sold in Italy 9.58; G·APNY 'Christine', c/n 242, model P.136-L2, two 320 h.p. Lycoming GSO-480-B1C6, C. of A. issued 14.8.58, sold in Switzerland 8.59 as HB-LAV. Span, 44 ft. 4$\frac{5}{8}$ in. Length, 35 ft. 5$\frac{1}{4}$ in. Tare wt., 4,460 lb. (L1) A.U.W., 6,000 lb. Max. speed, 173 m.p.h. Cruise, 153 m.p.h. (L2) A.U.W., 6,615 lb. Max. speed, 182 m.p.h. Cruise, 167 m.p.h.

PIAGGIO P.166

All metal six/eight seat executive transport powered by two 340 h.p. Lycoming GSO-480-B1C6 driving pusher airscrews, built by Societa per Azioni Piaggio at Finale Ligure, Italy, 1959. Two British aircraft to date: G-APSJ, c/n 354, delivered to the aviation division of Sir Robert McAlpine and Sons, Luton, 19.4.59, C. of A. issued 30.5.59; G-APVE, c/n 355, C. of A. issued 4.8.59, currently based at Speke by the Earl of Derby. Span, 46 ft. 9 in. Length, 38 ft. 0¼ in. Tare wt., 5,004 lb. A.U.W., 8,115 lb. Max. speed, 226 m.p.h. Cruise, 208 m.p.h.

PICKERING-PEARSON KP.2

Single seat, experimental pusher of wooden construction powered by one 40 h.p. Aeronca E.117 designed by K. N. Pearson and built at Hanworth 1933 by G. L. Pickering. No rudder was fitted, directional and lateral control being effected by the Pearson rotary ailerons. One aircraft only, G-ACMR, c/n 2, completed 10.33, scrapped 1935.

PIPER PA-12 SUPERCRUISER

Three seater powered by one 104 h.p. Lycoming O-235-C, in production by the Piper Aircraft Corporation at Lockhaven, Penn., U.S.A., from 1945. Three British aircraft only: G-AJGY, c/n 12-1118, C. of A. issued 16.5.47, erected at Hanworth, sold to C. G. Reid-Walker 10.47, won the Goodyear Trophy 28.5.49 at 115 m.p.h., sold in France 1.53 as F-BGQY; G-AKDM, c/n 12-3966, C. of A. issued 23.9.47, erected at Redhill, sold to E. C. S. Harper, Gatwick, 9.48, sold in South Africa 1.51; G-AKJC, c/n 12-3994, C. of A. issued 3.10.47, sold abroad 23.10.47. Span, 35 ft. 5½ in. Length, 22 ft. 10 in. Tare wt., 960 lb. A.U.W., 1,750 lb. Max. speed, 115 m.p.h. Cruise, 105 m.p.h.

PIPER PA-18A SUPER CUB

Two seater powered by one 150 h.p. Lycoming O-320, currently in production by the Piper Aircraft Corporation. Seven British aircraft to date, currently in use by crop spraying firms at home and abroad. Full details in Appendix D. Span, 35 ft. 2½ in. Length, 22 ft. 6 in. Tare wt., 1,126 lb. A.U.W., 2,070 lb. Max. speed, 128 m.p.h. Cruise, 113 m.p.h.

PIPER PA-22 TRI-PACER

Four seat, cabin monoplane of fabric-covered, metal construction, powered by one 125 h.p. Lycoming O-290-D2, currently in large-scale production by the Piper Aircraft Corporation. Seven British aircraft to date, used for private and executive purposes at home and abroad. Full details in Appendix D. Span, 29 ft. 4 in. Length, 20 ft. 4¾ in. Tare wt., 1,005 lb. A.U.W., 1,950 lb. Max. speed, 137 m.p.h. Cruise, 132 m.p.h.

PIPER PA-23 APACHE

Four seat, cabin monoplane powered by two 150 h.p. Lycoming O-320, currently in large-scale production by the Piper Aircraft Corporation. Four British aircraft to date: G-APCL, c/n 23-1159, C. of A. issued 18.9.57, J. N. Somers Ltd., Panshangar; G-APLJ, c/n 23-1366, C. of A. issued 16.6.58, K. McAlpine, Luton; G-APMY, c/n 23-1258, C. of A. issued 19.6.58, United Steel Companies Ltd., Yeadon; G-APVK, c/n 23-1719, McVitie and Price Ltd., Turnhouse. Span, 37 ft. 0 in. Length, 27 ft. 1¼ in. Tare wt., 2,200 lb. A.U.W., 3,800 lb. Max speed, 180 m.p.h. Cruise, 162 m.p.h.

PIPER PA-24 COMANCHE 250

All metal four seat tourer powered by one 250 h.p. Lycoming O-540-A1A, in production by the Piper Aircraft Corporation at Lockhaven, Penn., U.S.A. from 1958. Six British aircraft to date, G-APUZ, c/n 24-1094, C. of A. issued 7.7.59, L. R. Snook, Portsmouth; G-APXJ, c/n 24-291, ex VR-NDA, C. of A. issued 19.1.60, Mrs. D. I. Senn, Eastleigh; G-APZF–'ZI reserved for Vigors Aviation Ltd., Kidlington. Span, 36 ft. 0 in. Length, 24 ft. 9 in. Tare wt., 1,600 lb. A.U.W., 2,800 lb. Max. speed, 190 m.p.h. Cruise, 171 m.p.h.

PITCAIRN PA-19

Four seat autogiro powered by one 420 h.p. Wright Whirlwind R975-E, built by the Pitcairn Autogiro Company Inc., at Willow Grove, Pennsylvania, U.S.A., 1934–35. Two British aircraft only, both imported by the Hon. A. E. Guinness; G-ADAM, c/n H.89, C. of A. issued 27.12.34, believed crashed at Newtownards 1935; replaced by G-ADBE, c/n H.87, C. of A. issued 11.1.36, based at Eastleigh until 1939, stored during the war, broken up at Kenley 1950. Rotor diameter, 50 ft. 7½ in. Length, 25 ft. 9 in. Tare wt., 2,690 lb. A.U.W., 4,250 lb. Max. speed, 120 m.p.h. Cruise, 100 m.p.h.

(*R. H. Nicholls Photo*)

PLANET SATELLITE

Four seater of magnesium alloy construction, with retractable under-carriage, ventral fin and rudder and one 250 h.p. de Havilland Gipsy Queen 32 amidships driving a pusher airscrew in the tail. Designed by J. N. D. Heenan, built in the Redwing factory, Croydon, erected at Red-hill 1948. One aircraft only, c/n 1, shown at the Farnborough S.B.A.C. Show 9.48, registered G-ALOI 4.49. Initial take off attempts at Black-bushe abandoned and the aircraft never flew. Dismantled at Redhill and melted down 1958. Span, 33 ft. 6 in. Length, 26 ft. 3 in. Tare wt., 1,600 lb. A.U.W., 2,905 lb. Max. speed, 208 m.p.h. Cruise, 191 m.p.h.

(*'Flight' Photo*)

PORTERFIELD 35-70

Tandem two seater with steel tube fuselage and wooden wing, powered by one 70 h.p. Le Blond radial, built 1936 by the Porterfield Aircraft Cor-poration at Kansas City, U.S.A. One British aircraft only, G-AEOK, c/n 246, C. of A. issued 11.12.36, imported by U.K. agents, Surrey Flying Services Ltd. Used for tuition at Croydon 1937–39, stored during the war, broken up at Gatwick 1947. Span, 32 ft. 0 in. Length, 20 ft. 0 in. Tare wt., 813 lb. A.U.W., 1,310 lb. Max. speed, 115 m.p.h. Cruise, 100 m.p.h.

(*Photo: Portsmouth Aviation Ltd.*)

PORTSMOUTH AEROCAR MAJOR

Twin-boom, high-wing monoplane with retractable undercarriage, powered by two 155 h.p. Blackburn Cirrus Major III, seating pilot and five passengers in a pod type fuselage. One aircraft only, G-AGTG, c/n 2, built by Portsmouth Aviation Ltd. at Portsmouth City Airport 1947, first flown by F. L. Luxmoore 18.6.47, exhibited at 1948 and 1949 S.B.A.C. Shows, C. of A. issued 3.9.48. Series production abandoned, scrapped 1950. Span, 42 ft. 0 in. Length, 26 ft. 3 in. Tare wt., 2,600 lb. A.U.W., 3,950 lb. Max. speed, 167 m.p.h. Cruise, 153 m.p.h.

(*'Flight' Photo*)

POTEZ 36

Cabin two seater powered by one 95 h.p. Renault 4Pb, in production by the Société des Avions Henri Potez at Méaulte, Somme, France, from 1929. One British aircraft only, G-ABNB, c/n 2359, imported 6.31 for joyriding with C. D. Barnard's Air Display. Retained French markings F-ALJC until returned to the manufacturers at the end of the season. Span, 33 ft. 3 in. Length, 25 ft. 2 in. Tare wt., 994 lb. A.U.W., 1,676 lb. Max. speed, 93 m.p.h.

R.A.E. ZEPHYR

Single seat, twin-boom ultra light powered by one 500 c.c. Douglas driving a pusher airscrew, designed and built at Farnborough 1922–23 by the Royal Aircraft Establishment Aero Club. One aircraft only, G-EBGW, c/n 1, first flight (illustrated) at Farnborough by F/Lt. P. W. S. Bulman 6.9.23, scrapped 1925. Span, 29 ft. 0 in. A.U.W., 635 lb. Cruise, 45 m.p.h.

R.A.E. HURRICANE (Douglas)

Single seat ultra light powered by one 600 c.c. Douglas with chain driven airscrew, designed by S. Childs and built at Farnborough 1922–23 by the Royal Aircraft Establishment Aero Club. One aircraft only, G-EBHS, c/n 2, flown in the Lympne Trials 10.23 by F/Lt. P. W. S. Bulman but proved underpowered. Span, 23 ft. 0 in. Length, 17 ft. $7\frac{3}{4}$ in. Tare wt., 375 lb. A.U.W., 565 lb. Max. speed, 58·5 m.p.h.

R.A.E. HURRICANE (Cherub)

The original Hurricane G-EBHS, rebuilt with 32 h.p. Bristol Cherub III and strutted undercarriage for the Lympne Races 1–3.8.25, C. of A. issued 2.8.25. Piloted by F/Lt. J. S. Chick, won the International Handicap at 73·41 m.p.h., the Grosvenor Cup at 81·19 m.p.h., the Private Owners' Handicap at 81·55 m.p.h. and carried off £300 in prize money. Scrapped 1926. Span, 23 ft. 0 in. Length, 17 ft. 7¾ in. Max. speed, 85 m.p.h.

R.A.E. SCARAB

Single seater using D.H.53 fuselage, mainplanes and empennage, powered by one 32 h.p. Bristol Cherub III. Built at Farnborough 1930–31 by the Royal Aircraft Establishment Aero Club to the designs of P. G. N. Peters and C. R. Brewer, whose initials gave its alternative designation P. B. Scarab. One aircraft only, G-ABOH, c/n 5, first flown by F/O H. H. Leech 2.32, stored from 1938 until scrapped at Farnborough 1945. Span, 30 ft. 0 in. Length, 21 ft. 0 in. A.U.W., 650 lb. Max. speed, 78 m.p.h.

SARO A.19 CLOUD (Whirlwinds)

Amphibian with metal hull and wooden wing, for two crew and eight passengers, powered by two 300 h.p. Wright Whirlwind J-6, built by Saunders-Roe Ltd., East Cowes, 1930–33. Two aircraft only: G-ABCJ, prototype, c/n A.19/1, C. of A. issued 1.8.30, owner Capt. R. Holt, to Canada 12.31 as CF-ARB, returned to makers for trial engine installations 1.34; G-ABXW 'Cloud of Iona', c/n A.19/4, C. of A. issued 15.7.32, used on the Glasgow–Belfast service of British Flying Boats Ltd., to Guernsey Airways Ltd. 9.34, lost off Jersey with 10 occupants 31.7.36. Span, 64 ft. 0 in. Length, 47 ft. 9 in. Tare wt., 5,500 lb. A.U.W., 8,100 lb. Max. speed, 120 m.p.h. Cruise, 95 m.p.h.

SARO A.19 CLOUD (Lynx)

Special Cloud amphibian built for the Hon. A. E. Guinness 1930, powered by three 215 h.p. Armstrong Siddeley Lynx IVC. One aircraft only, G-ABHG, c/n A.19/2, nominally registered to the owner's pilot O. S. Baker, test flown 12.30 by S/Ldr. L. S. Ash. Re-engined with Wasps before delivery. Specification as for Whirlwind model except: Tare wt., 6,075 lb.

('*The Aeroplane*' Photo)

SARO A.19 CLOUD (Wasps)

The Hon. A. E. Guinness' Cloud G-ABHG, named 'Flying Amo' and re-engined 1931 with two 425 h.p. Pratt and Whitney Wasp C radials (of the type fitted to the owner's Ford 5AT-D), driving three bladed airscrews. Lower landing speed and improved directional control achieved by fitting auxiliary aerofoil and twin fins and rudders. C. of A. issued 31.7.31. Based at Eastleigh until sold to Imperial Airways Ltd. for crew training 1.40, damaged beyond repair at Ibsley 6.41. Sold as scrap, fuselage used as caravan, St. Leonards, Ringwood, Hants, 1952. Specification as Whirlwind model except: Tare wt., 5,687 lb. A.U.W., 10,000 lb.

(*Photo: D. Napier and Son Ltd.*)

SARO A.19 CLOUD (Rapiers)

The prototype Cloud G-ABCJ re-engined 1934 with two 340 h.p. Napier Rapier IV and fitted with small auxiliary aerofoil behind and below the engine nacelles to smooth out the airflow and improve control. Allotted revised c/n A.19/1A. Demonstrated at Hendon S.B.A.C. Shows of 1.7.34 and 1.7.35, loaned to Jersey Airways Ltd. 8.35, withdrawn from use 12.36. Span, 64 ft. 0 in. Length, 49 ft. 9 in. Tare wt., 6,450 lb. A.U.W., 9,700 lb. Max. speed, 121 m.p.h. Cruise, 102 m.p.h.

SARO A.19 CLOUD (Servals)

Cloud amphibian fitted with two 340 h.p. Armstrong Siddeley Serval III. One aircraft only, G-ACGO, c/n A.19/5, first flown 15.7.33, C. of A. issued 23.6.33, manufacturers' demonstrator, flown by test pilot S. D. Scott to Holland, Scandinavia, Latvia, Estonia, Poland, Germany and Belgium, returned to Cowes 10.8.33. Sold in Czechoslovakia 7.34 as OK-BAK. Span, 64 ft. 0 in. Length, 49 ft. 9 in. Tare wt., 6,500 lb. A.U.W., 9,500 lb. Max. speed, 118 m.p.h. Cruise, 95 m.p.h.

(Air Ministry Photo)

SARO A.21 WINDHOVER

Amphibian with metal hull and wooden wing, for two crew and six passengers, powered by three 120 h.p. de Havilland Gipsy II, built by Saunders-Roe Ltd., 1930–31. One British aircraft only, G-ABJP, c/n A.21/2, C. of A. issued 8.7.31, owner Francis Francis, Heston. To Gibraltar Airways 9.31 for the Tangier service. To the Hon. Mrs. Victor Bruce 7.32, named 'City of Portsmouth', wheels removed and tankage increased for flight-refuelled endurance record of 54 hours 13 minutes 9–11.8.32. Sold to Jersey Airways Ltd. as amphibian 5.35. Withdrawn 1938. Span, 54 ft. 4 in. Length, 41 ft. 4 in. Tare wt., 4,200 lb. A.U.W., 5,700 lb. Max. speed, 110 m.p.h. Cruise, 90 m.p.h.

(*Photo: Saunders-Roe Ltd.*)

SARO A.37 SHRIMP

Two seat, flying scale research aircraft of metal construction, powered by
four 95 h.p. Pobjoy Niagara III, designed by H. Knowler and built as part
of a development programme on large flying-boat design by Saunders-Roe
Ltd. at Cowes 1939. One aircraft only, G-AFZS, c/n A.37/1, first flown
1940, handed over to the R.A.F. 5.41. Later became TK580 for flight
testing a scale Short Shetland tail unit. Broken up at Felixstowe 1949.
Span, 50 ft. 0 in. Length, 42 ft. 8¾ in.

(*Photo: Saunders-Roe Ltd.*)

SARO S.R.45 PRINCESS

All-metal, 200-passenger flying-boat powered by ten 3,780 e.h.p. Bristol
Proteus 600, designed by H. Knowler and built by Saunders-Roe Ltd.
1947–52. Three aircraft only, ordered for B.O.A.C. 1946, registered to the
Ministry of Supply 13.10.49: G-ALUN, c/n SR.901, launched 20.8.52,
first flown by Geoffrey Tyson 22.8.52, flown at 1952 and 1953 S.B.A.C.
Shows, cocooned at Cowes 1954; G-ALUO, c/n SR.902, launched in
cocooned state 13.2.53, beached at Calshot next day; G-ALUP, c/n
SR.903, cocooned and beached at Calshot 1953. Span, 219 ft. 6 in.
Length, 148 ft. 0 in. Tare wt., 191,000 lb. A.U.W., 330,000 lb. Cruise,
360 m.p.h. Max. range, 5,270 miles.

(*Photo: Saunders-Roe Ltd.*)

SARO SKEETER

All-metal, two seat helicopter developed from the Cierva W.14 Skeeter 2 (Volume 1, page 451), built at East Cowes and flown at Eastleigh by Saunders-Roe Ltd. Seven civil aircraft to date: G-AMTZ, Mk. 5, c/n SR.907, 180 h.p. Cirrus Bombardier 702, conceived as the Cierva Skeeter 5 G-AMDC, evaluated at Boscombe Down 1954 as XG303, modified to Skeeter 6 with 200 h.p. de Havilland Gipsy Major 201 in 1957, C. of A. issued 21.5.57; G-ANMG, Mk. 6, c/n SR.904, C. of A. issued 8.6.55, to the R.A.F. 11.55 as XK773, G-ANMH, Mk. 6, c/n SR.905, first flown 29.8.54, to the R.A.F. 11.55 as XJ355; G-ANMI, Mk. 6, c/n SR.906, to the R.A.F. as XK964; G-APOI–'OJ, Mk. 8, c/n S2/5081, 5091, 5111. Rotor diameter, 32 ft. 0 in. Length, 31 ft. 1½ in. Tare wt., 1,590 lb. A.U.W., 2,150 lb. Cruise, 99 m.p.h.

(*Photo: Saunders-Roe Ltd.*)

SARO SKEETER (Modified)

Skeeter 6 fitted with Napier NRE.19 liquid fuel rockets at the rotor tips, with fuel tank over the rotor head. Two aircraft only: G-ANMI, first flown with rocket boost 5.8.56, shown at the 1956 S.B.A.C. Show; Mk. 5 G-AMTZ modified to Mk. 6 for the purpose, shown at the 1957 S.B.A.C. Show with stretcher panniers, since removed.

(*Photo: Saunders-Roe Ltd.*)

SARO P.531

Private venture all metal five seat helicopter built by Saunders-Roe Ltd. at East Cowes 1958–59. Four civil prototype aircraft to date. Two Mk. 1 with 300 s.h.p. Blackburn Turboméca Turmo 600; G-APNU, c/n S2/5267, first flown at Eastleigh by K. M. Reed 20.7.58; G-APNV, c/n S2/5268, evaluated by the Royal Navy 1959 as XN332. Two Mk. 2; G-APVL, c/n S2/5311, 650 s.h.p. Blackburn A.129, first flown at Eastleigh 9.8.59; G-APVM, c/n S2/5312, derated 1000 s.h.p. de Havilland Gnome H.1000. Rotor diameter, 32 ft. 6 in. Length, 29 ft. 0 in. Tare wt., 2,092 lb. A.U.W., 3,800 lb. Cruise, 115 m.p.h.

(*C. A. Nepean Bishop Photo*)

S.C.A.L. F.B.30 AVION BASSOU

Two seater of wooden construction powered by one 40 h.p. Menguin driving a pusher airscrew, built by Société de Constructions et d'Aviation Légère, Paris, 1935. One British aircraft only, G-AFCD, c/n 2, formerly F-APDT, imported 6.37 by H. McClelland, A. to F. issued 18.10.37, sold to W. L. Lewis, Hanworth, 5.38. Destroyed in fatal crash, Hanworth, 12.6.38. Span, 30 ft. 4 in. Length, 19 ft. 8 in. Tare wt., 572 lb. A.U.W., 1,100 lb. Max. speed, 106·8 m.p.h. Cruise, 93 m.p.h.

(*W. K. Kilsby Photo*)

SHACKLETON-MURRAY S.M.1

Two seat, wooden, parasol monoplane powered by one 70 h.p. Hirth H.M.60 driving a pusher airscrew, designed by W. S. Shackleton and L. C. Murray and built by Airspeed Ltd. at York 1933. One aircraft only, G-ACBP, Airspeed c/n 8, first flown at Sherburn-in-Elmet 1933, C. of A. issued 28.9.33, based at Hanworth until sold to Lord Apsley, Whitchurch, 1.35. Dismantled 1937. Span, 40 ft. 0 in. Length, 25 ft. 7 in. Tare wt., 840 lb. A.U.W., 1,450 lb. Max. speed, 90·5 m.p.h. Cruise, 75 m.p.h.

(*W. K. Kilsby Photo*)

SHAPLEY KITTIWAKE

Side-by-side two seater with gull wing, designed and built at Torquay by E. S. Shapley 1937–38. Two aircraft only: G-AEZN, c/n E.S.S.1, Mk. 1 open model, 50 h.p. Continental A.50, first flown at Roborough, A. to F. issued 29.6.37, dismantled pre-war; G-AFRP, c/n E.S.S.2, Mk. 2 cabin model, 90 h.p. Pobjoy Niagara III, flown at Roborough 1938, stored, flown at Rochester 4.46, crashed on Dartmoor 12.46. Mk. 2 data in parentheses. Span, 20 ft. 3 in. (32 ft. 0 in.). Length, 20 ft. 3 in. (20 ft. 10 in.). Tare wt., 630 lb. (901 lb.). A.U.W., 1,000 lb. (1,600 lb.). Max. speed, 116 m.p.h. (120 m.p.h.). Cruise, 99 m.p.h. (110 m.p.h.).

SHORT SHRIMP

Commercial seaplane sometimes known as the Short Sporting Type, powered by one 240 h.p. Siddeley Puma, built at Rochester 1919–20. Two front seats in tandem with dual control, two rear seats side by side. Three aircraft only: G-EAPZ, c/n S.540, initially with 160 h.p. Beardmore, sold in Australia 1.21 as G-AUPZ; G-EAUA, c/n S.541, exhibited at Olympia 7.20, damaged in heavy landing, Rochester 21.9.20, rebuilt with 300 h.p. Hispano-Suiza and camber changing flaps; G-EAUB, c/n S.542, completed 10.2.21, first flown 10.12.21, dismantled 1923. Span, 44 ft. 6 in. Length, 36 ft. 9 in. A.U.W., 3,554 lb. Max. speed, 85 m.p.h.

SHORT SILVER STREAK

The first British all-metal aeroplane. A single seater powered by one 240 h.p. Siddeley Puma, with semi-monocoque duralumin fuselage and duralumin-covered wings with steel tubular spars, built by Short Bros. Ltd. at Rochester 1920. One aircraft only, G-EARQ, c/n S.543, exhibited without markings at the Olympia Aero Show 7.20, sold to the Air Ministry for evaluation 1.21. Flown to Farnborough 1.2.21, flight tests 5.21, static tests 6.21, 100 hours of vibration testing 9–11.21. Span, 37 ft. 6 in. Length, 26 ft. 6 in. Tare wt., 1,865 lb. A.U.W., 2,870 lb. Max. speed, 120 m.p.h. Cruise, 90 m.p.h.

(*Short Photo*)

SHORT S.1 COCKLE

Single seat, all-metal flying-boat powered by two 696 c.c. Blackburne
Tomtit driving tractor airscrews through extension shafts, built by Short
Bros. Ltd. at Rochester 1924 for, but not delivered to, Lebbeus Hordern.
One aircraft only, G-EBKA, c/n S.638, first flown 10.24, handed over to
the R.A.F. 7.25 as N193, returned to Rochester and scrapped 8.26. Span,
36 ft. 0 in. Length, 24 ft. 8½ in. A.U.W., 880 lb. Max. speed, 68 m.p.h.

('*Flight*' *Photo*)

SHORT S.4 SATELLITE

Two seater with metal monocoque fuselage, powered by one 32 h.p.
Bristol Cherub III, built at Rochester for the 1924 Lympne Trials. One
aircraft only, G-EBJU, c/n S.644, first flown 16.9.24, competed as No. 8
piloted by J. Lankester Parker, who raced it as a single seater, Lympne
1–3.8.25. Fitted with 40 h.p. A.B.C. Scorpion II by the Seven Aero Club,
C. of A. issued 8.9.26, flown in the 1926 Lympne Trials and Grosvenor
Trophy Race by F/O G. E. F. Boyes. Dismantled 1.28. Span, 34 ft. 0 in.
Length, 23 ft. 9 in. (Cherub III) Tare wt., 640 lb. A.U.W., 1,014 lb.
(Scorpion II) Tare wt., 610 lb. A.U.W., 1,010 lb.

SHORT S.7 MUSSEL I

Two seat seaplane with metal fuselage powered by one 60 h.p. A.D.C. Cirrus I, built at Rochester 1925. One aircraft only, G-EBMJ, c/n S.678, first flown 5.26, converted to landplane 9.26, C. of A. issued 16.9.26, flown by J. Lankester Parker in the 1926 Grosvenor Trophy Race and at the 1927 Bournemouth Easter Meeting. Fitted with floats and enclosed 85 h.p. Cirrus II, raised the world's altitude class record to 13,400 ft. piloted by Lady Heath 10.7.28. Sank in the Medway 24.8.28, rebuilt as landplane, scrapped 1.29 after 120 hours flying. Span, 36 ft. 0 in. Length, 25 ft. 0 in. Tare wt., 907 lb. A.U.W., 1,400 lb. (Cirrus II 1,135 lb. and 1,636 lb.). Max. speed, 82 m.p.h. Cruise, 65 m.p.h.

SHORT S.7 MUSSEL II

Similar floatplane with revised undercarriage strutting, powered by one 90 h.p. A.D.C. Cirrus III, built at Rochester 1929. One aircraft only, G-AAFZ, c/n S.750, exhibited at the Olympia Aero Show 7.29. Fitted with Short amphibian undercarriage and flown 3.30 under B conditions as M-1, scrapped 1933. Span, 37 ft. 3½ in. Length, 24 ft. 11½ in. Tare wt., 1,061 lb. (Amphibian 1,300 lb.) A.U.W., 1,640 lb. Max. speed, 102 m.p.h.

(Air Ministry Photo)

SHORT S.11 VALETTA

Transport for 16 passengers and two crew built to Air Ministry order for comparison with the pure flying-boat, and in its day was the world's largest floatplane. One aircraft only, G-AAJY, c/n S.747, powered by three 525 h.p. Bristol Jupiter XIF, built at Rochester 1929–30, first flown 7.30, C. of A. issued 17.7.31. Left Rochester 22.7.31 piloted by Sir Alan Cobham on an African survey flight to Lakes Albert, Victoria, Edward and Kivu, covering 12,300 miles before returning to Rochester 1.9.31. Span, 107 ft. 0 in. Length, 70 ft. 5 in. Tare wt., 14,535 lb. A.U.W., 23,000 lb. Max. speed, 135 m.p.h. Cruise, 110 m.p.h.

('Flight' Photo)

SHORT S.11 VALETTA (Landplane)

One aircraft only, G-AAJY, fitted with wheeled undercarriage for further evaluation, demonstrated at Croydon by J. Lankester Parker 14.5.32, exhibited at the Hendon R.A.F. Display 25.6.32, subsequently employed by the Air Ministry as a radio test vehicle, scrapped 1.34. Span, 107 ft. 0 in. Length, 69 ft. 8 in. Tare wt., 16,070 lb. A.U.W., 23,000 lb. Max. speed, 137 m.p.h. Cruise, 105 m.p.h.

SHORT L.17

Transport for 39 passengers powered by four 595 h.p. Bristol Jupiter XF.BM, using the superstructure and tail unit of the S.17 Kent, built at Rochester for the Croydon–Paris and Brussels services of Imperial Airways Ltd. 1933–34. Two aircraft only: G-ACJI 'Scylla', c/n S.768, first flown by J. Lankester Parker 4.34, C. of A. issued 1.5.34, later flown experimentally with trim tab replacing servo rudder, wrecked by gale in Scotland 9.9.40; G-ACJK 'Syrinx', c/n S.769, C. of A. issued 8.6.34, re-engined 1935 with four 660 h.p. Bristol Pegasus XC. Carried out flight trials with two Bristol Perseus inboard. Scrapped 1940. Span, 113 ft. 0 in. Length, 83 ft. 10 in. Tare wt., 22,650 lb. A.U.W., 33,500 lb. Max. speed, 137 m.p.h. Cruise, 105 m.p.h.

SHORT-MAYO S.20/S.21 COMPOSITE

Built to test Major R. H. Mayo's theory of extending the range of one aircraft by assisting it into the air on another. *Upper component:* Short S.20 G-ADHJ 'Mercury', c/n S.796, four 340 h.p. Napier Rapier V, launched 25.8.37, first flown 5.9.37, C. of A. issued 2.7.38, later fitted with four 370 h.p. Rapier VI, flown Hythe–Felixstowe 18.6.40 by Capt. D. C. T. Bennett and handed over to a Dutch seaplane reconnaissance unit. Span, 73 ft. 0 in. Length, 51 ft. 0 in. Tare wt., 10,000 lb. A.U.W. (individual flying), 15,500 lb.; (air launched), 20,500 lb. Max. speed, 207 m.p.h. Cruise, 180 m.p.h. *Lower component:* Short S.21 G-ADHK 'Maia', c/n S.797, four 920 h.p. Bristol Pegasus XC, first flown 8.37, C. of A. issued 1.6.38, used as a navigational trainer when not employed in its composite role, destroyed by enemy action on the water, Poole 4.41. Span, 114 ft. 0 in. Length, 84 ft. 10¾ in. Tare wt., 24,000 lb. A.U.W. (individual flying), 38,000 lb. Max. speed, 200 m.p.h. Cruise, 165 m.p.h. *Composite:* First flown at Rochester 4.1.38 with J. Lankester Parker in 'Maia' and H. L. Piper in 'Mercury'. First separation in the air 6.2.38, first commercial separation at Foynes 21.7.38, when 'Mercury', piloted by Capt. D. C. T. Bennett, flew non-stop to Montreal in 20 hours 20 minutes. Returned via Azores, reached from New York in 7 hours 33 minutes. Last recorded separation at Dundee 6.10.38 when Capt. Bennett flew 'Mercury' 6,045 miles non-stop to the mouth of the Orange River, South Africa, to establish a World's long distance record for seaplanes. Dimensions as S.21. Tare wt., 34,000 lb. A.U.W. 47,500 lb. Max speed, 195 m.p.h. Cruise, 167 m.p.h.

(*Short Photo*)

SHORT S.22 SCION SENIOR

Floatplane for nine passengers and pilot, powered by four 90 h.p. Pobjoy Niagara III, built at Rochester 1935–36. Four British civil aircraft only: G-ACZG, c/n S.779, C. of A. issued 11.1.36, to the Irrawaddy Flotilla Co. Ltd., Rangoon, 10.35 as VT-AGU; G-ADIP, c/n S.810, C. of A. issued 19.8.36, to the same owner 6.36 as VT-AHI; G-AENX, c/n S.835, C. of A. issued 11.9.37, used on the Greenock Harbour–Hebrides service of West of Scotland Airways Ltd., to Elders Colonial Airways Ltd., Sierra Leone, 2.38, scrapped during the war; G-AETH, c/n S.836, reservation. Span, 55 ft. 0 in. Length, 42 ft. 0 in. Tare wt., 3,886 lb. A.U.W., 5,750 lb. Max. speed, 134 m.p.h. Cruise, 115 m.p.h.

(*Short Photo*)

SHORT S.22 SCION SENIOR (Landplane)

Landplane version. One civil aircraft only, G-AECU, c/n S.834, C. of A. issued 28.7.36, demonstrator, flown by H. L. Piper in the King's Cup Race 11.9.37, loaned to Jersey Airways Ltd. 1938, sold to the Iraq Petroleum Transport Co. Ltd., Haifa, 12.38, impressed in the Middle East 2.42 as HK868. Dimensions as floatplane. Tare wt., 3,546 lb. A.U.W., 5,750 lb. Max. speed, 140 m.p.h. Cruise, 122 m.p.h.

(Associated Press Photo)

SHORT S.35 SHETLAND 2

All-metal flying-boat for 40 passengers and crew of 11, powered by four 2,500 h.p. Bristol Centaurus 660, built at Rochester 1945–47. One civil aircraft only, G-AGVD, c/n S.1313, second prototype, allotted R.A.F. serial DX171 during construction, launched 15.9.47, first flown 17.9.47, evaluated by Ministry of Supply, broken up at Belfast 1951. Span, 150 ft. 4 in. Length, 105 ft. 0 in. Tare wt., 80,140 lb. A.U.W., 125,000 lb. Cruise, 240 m.p.h. Range, 2,780 miles.

SIKORSKY S.38B

Five seat amphibian powered by two 420 h.p. Pratt and Whitney Wasp, built at Bridgeport, Connecticut, U.S.A., 1930, by the Sikorsky Aircraft Division of the United Aircraft Manufacturing Corporation. One British aircraft only, G-ABYS 'Blue Falcon', c/n 814–19, formerly NC15V, shipped to Southampton for Francis Francis, ferried to Heston 5.6.32, C. of A. issued 4.8.32, flown to Geneva 3.9.32 on delivery to R. H. Parrott, sold in France 5.36 as F-AOUC, crashed at Calabar, Niger Colony 12.8.39. Span, 71 ft. 8 in. Length, 40 ft. 3 in. Tare wt., 6,500 lb. A.U.W., 10,480 lb. Max. speed, 125 m.p.h. Cruise, 110 m.p.h.

SIKORSKY S.39A

Four seat amphibian powered by one 300 h.p. Pratt and Whitney Wasp Junior, built at Bridgeport, Connecticut, U.S.A., 1930 by the Sikorsky Aircraft Division of the United Aircraft Manufacturing Corporation. One British aircraft only, G-ABFN, c/n 908, previously NC806W, C. of A. issued 22.10.30. Imported by W. S. Cottingham for use by Personal Flying Services Ltd., Heston. Sold abroad 7.35. Span, 52 ft. 0 in. Length, 31 ft. 11 in. Tare wt., 2,678 lb. A.U.W., 4,000 lb. Max. speed, 120 m.p.h. Cruise, 100 m.p.h.

SLINGSBY T.29B MOTOR TUTOR

Single seater comprising a Slingsby Tutor primary glider airframe fitted with an undercarriage and one 40 h.p. Aeronca J.A.P. J-99. Two aircraft only, built by Slingsby Sailplanes Ltd. at Kirbymoorside 1948: G-AKEY, c/n W.N.544, first flown 6.48 as AB-1 and later as G-26-1, dismantled at Kirbymoorside 4.53; G-AKJD, c/n W.N.599, A. to F. issued 3.11.50, evaluated by the Southend Municipal Flying School 1951, sold to J. M. Alcock, Waddington, 4.54 and to current owners A. F. Gotch and partners, Lasham, 7.55. Span, 43 ft. 3¾ in. Length, 20 ft. 0 in. Tare wt., 555 lb. A.U.W., 798 lb. Max. speed, 75 m.p.h. Cruise, 65 m.p.h.

(R. A. Cole Photo)

SOMERS-KENDALL SK-1

Two seat wooden jet racer with retractable bicycle undercarriage, powered by one 330 lb. s.t. Turboméca Palas 1 turbojet, designed by Hugh Kendall and built for J. N. Somers by Somers-Kendall Aircraft Ltd. at Woodley 1954–55. One aircraft only, G-AOBG, c/n 1, C. of A. issued 27.3.56. Minor defects prevented participation in 1956 racing events, and the aircraft has been stored at Cranfield since turbine failure in the air 11.7.57. Span, 22 ft. 9½ in. Length, 20 ft. 10½ in. Tare wt., 685 lb. A.U.W., 1,500 lb. Max. speed, 332 m.p.h. Cruise, 285 m.p.h.

SOPWITH DOVE

Two seat version of the Pup, with swept-back wings and 80 h.p. Le Rhône, built at Kingston-on-Thames by the Sopwith Aviation and Engineering Co. Ltd. 1919–20. Ten British civil aircraft shown in Appendix D. Last machine modernised 1925 with horn balanced rudder as G-EBKY, C. of A. issued 12.4.27. Sold to C. H. Lowe-Wylde 9.30, abandoned at West Malling after owner's death 1933, rebuilt as Pup by R. O. Shuttleworth 1937–38. Span 24 ft. 9½ in. Length, 19 ft. 4 in. Tare wt., 1,065 lb. A.U.W., 1,430 lb. Max. speed, 95 m.p.h.

(L. T. Mason Photo)

SOPWITH GRASSHOPPER

Two seat tourer of wooden construction powered by one 100 h.p. Anzani, built at Kingston-on-Thames by the Sopwith Aviation and Engineering Co. Ltd. 1919. One aircraft only, G-EAIN, c/n W/O 2698/1, C. of A. issued 22.3.20. Sold 12.22 to L. C. G. M. Le Champion, 5.23 to E. A. D. Eldridge, 2.25 to John R. Cobb, 8.25 to Dudley Watt, all of Brooklands; 2.28 to Miss C. R. Leathart, Cramlington. C. of A. not renewed on expiry 30.5.29. Span, 33 ft. 1 in. Length, 23 ft. 1 in. A.U.W., 1,670 lb. Max. speed, 90 m.p.h.

(*Bristol Photo*)

SOPWITH SCHNEIDER

Single seat racer of fabric-covered wooden construction with $2\frac{1}{2}$ in. backward stagger, powered by one 450 h.p. Cosmos Jupiter, built at Kingston-on-Thames for the 1919 Schneider Trophy contest. One aircraft only, G-EAKI, c/n W/O 3067, flown in the race by H. G. Hawker over a course between Bournemouth and Swanage 10.9.19. Retired through fog, contest abandoned. Span, 24 ft. 0 in. Length, 21 ft. 6 in. A.U.W., 2,200 lb. Max. speed, 170 m.p.h.

(*'Flight' Photo*)

SOPWITH RAINBOW

Sopwith Schneider with wheeled undercarriage and a 320 h.p. A.B.C. Dragonfly as a mount for H. G. Hawker in the Hendon Aerial Derby 24.7.20. Disqualified for incorrect finish. Rebuilt 1922 with 500 h.p. Bristol Jupiter II by the H. G. Hawker Engineering Co. Ltd., and is the only aircraft to which the transitional nomenclature Sopwith/Hawker may strictly be applied. Second in the 1923 Aerial Derby at Croydon piloted by F/Lt. W. H. Longton at 165 m.p.h. Re-registered to the Hawker Company 18.7.23, crashed 5.10.23. Span, 24 ft. 0 in. Length, 18 ft. 0 in. Max. speed (Dragonfly), 165 m.p.h.; (Jupiter), 175 m.p.h.

433

(*Sopwith Photo*)

SOPWITH WALLABY

Long range open biplane with two seats retracting into the cabin, powered by one 375 h.p. Rolls-Royce Eagle VIII, built at Kingston-on-Thames 1919 to compete for the Australian Government's £10,000 England–Australia Flight prize. One aircraft only, G-EAKS, c/n W/O 3109, left Hounslow 21.10.19 piloted by Capt. G. C. Matthews and Sgt. T. Kay, C. of A. issued 22.10.19, crashed landing on the Island of Bali, Dutch East Indies, 17.4.20. Shipped to Australia, rebuilt as an 8 seater G-AUDU. Span, 46 ft. 6 in. Length, 31 ft. 6 in. Tare wt., 2,780 lb. A.U.W., 5,200 lb. Max. speed, 115 m.p.h. Cruise, 107 m.p.h.

(*Sopwith Photo*)

SOPWITH ANTELOPE

Transport seating two passengers in a cabin behind the pilot's open cockpit, powered by one 200 h.p. Wolseley Viper, built at Kingston-on-Thames 1919. One aircraft only, G-EASS, c/n W/O 3398, modified with four wheel braked undercarriage, C. of A. issued 10.8.20, awarded the second prize of £3,000 in the Air Ministry Small Commercial Aeroplane Competition Martlesham 8.20, piloted by H. G. Hawker. Won the Surrey Open Handicap Race, Croydon 5.6.22, piloted by F. P. Raynham. To the Larkin Aviation Company with Puma engine 4.23 as G-AUSS. Span, 46 ft. 6 in. Length, 31 ft. 0 in. Tare wt., 2,387 lb. A.U.W., 3,450 lb. Max. speed, 110·5 m.p.h. Cruise, 84 m.p.h.

(*Photo: Spartan Aircraft Ltd.*)

SPARTAN CLIPPER

Two seater using outer wings of the Monospar ST-4, powered by one 75 h.p. Pobjoy R, designed by H. E. Broadsmith and built at East Cowes by Spartan Aircraft Ltd. 1932. One aircraft only, c/n 201, first flown 14.12.32 as S-5. After undercarriage, cabin glazing and cowling modifications, registered as G-ACEG, C. of A. issued 29.6.33, averaged 93·39 m.p.h. in the 1933 King's Cup Race piloted by L. A. Strange. Fitted with 90 h.p. Pobjoy Niagara III in 1938, used on the firm's communications, destroyed in an air raid, Cowes, 4.5.42. Span, 34 ft. 0 in. Length, 28 ft. 2 in. Tare wt., 770 lb. A.U.W., 1,300 lb. Max. speed, 110 m.p.h.

SPERRY MESSENGER

Single seater powered by one 60 h.p. Wright L-4 radial, designed by the Engineering Division, U.S. Air Service, McCook Field, Dayton, Ohio, and built by the Lawrence Sperry Aircraft Co. Inc. at Long Island, N.Y., U.S.A., 1923. One British aircraft only, G-EBIJ, c/n 12, brought to England by Lawrence Sperry 1923, registered to the Sperry Gyroscope Co. Ltd. 9.11.23. Forced landed in the English Channel off Rye, Sussex, 13.12.23. Recovered intact by lifeboat, but Sperry was never found. Span, 20 ft. 0 in. Length, 18 ft. 9 in. Tare wt., 581 lb. A.U.W., 820 lb. Max. speed, 95 m.p.h.

('*Flight*' Photo)

STINSON JUNIOR R

Four seater powered by one 215 h.p. Lycoming R-680, built by the Stinson Aircraft Corporation at Wayne, Michigan, U.S.A. 1932. One British aircraft only, G-AFUW, c/n 8510, imported 5.39 by Southern Aircraft (Gatwick) Ltd., C. of A. issued 4.8.39, impressed into the R.A.F. 2.40 as X8522. This machine was originally NC12157 (illustrated), delivered to J. H. White of the Vacuum Oil Company at Heston 7.32, used by the Club d'Aviateurs de Bruxelles as OO-HVS 1933-39. Span, 41 ft. 8 in. Length, 29 ft. 0 in. Max. speed, 125 m.p.h. Cruise, 103 m.p.h.

STINSON JUNIOR S

Four seater powered by one 215 h.p. Lycoming R-680, built at Wayne 1931. Four British aircraft only: G-ABSU, c/n 8066, formerly NC10897, C. of A. issued 23.11.31, Lt.-Col. E. P. Johnston, Heston, sold abroad 7.36 by R. P. G. Denman; G-ABTZ, c/n 8050, formerly NC10879, C. of A. issued 26.2.32, E. James, Hanworth, to Lady A. C. E. Nelson, Hanworth 8.33, last owner C. Permetta, Broxbourne, scrapped 1940; G-ABZY, c/n 8093, C. of A. issued 21.10.32, the Nairn Motor Transport Co. Ltd., Baghdad, sold abroad 1.34. Span, 42 ft. 1 in. Length, 28 ft. 11 in. Tare wt., 2,152 lb. A.U.W., 3,265 lb. Max. speed, 125 m.p.h. Cruise, 105 m.p.h.

STINSON SR-5 RELIANT

Four seater of mixed construction powered by one 215 h.p. Lycoming R-680, built at Wayne, 1934–35. Two British aircraft only: G-ACSV, c/n 8779, formerly NC13824, C. of A. issued 22.5.34, imported for W. Adamson, Sherburn, last owner E. G. Hayes, Heston, impressed 2.40 as X8518; G-ADDG, c/n 9326, C. of A. issued 30.5.35, imported for W. Caldwell, last owner C. E. Horne, Hatfield, impressed 2.40 as X8519. Span, 43 ft. 3 in. Length, 27 ft. 0 in. Tare wt., 2,250 lb. A.U.W., 3,325 lb. Max. speed, 138 m.p.h. Cruise, 120 m.p.h.

STINSON SR-6A RELIANT

Enlarged four seater of mixed construction powered by one 225 h.p. Lycoming R-680-4, built at Wayne, Michigan, 1935. Two British aircraft only: G-ADJK, c/n 9613, C. of A. issued 30.9.35, imported for Halford Constant, Croydon, sold abroad 7.37; G-AEJT, c/n 9646, formerly NC15169, C. of A. issued 5.6.36, imported for Aeropolis Ltd., Heston, delivered to C. W. F. Wood, Dar-es-Salaam, Tanganyika, 1.37, sold abroad 5.37. Span, 43 ft. 3 in. Length, 27 ft. 0 in. Tare wt., 2,270 lb. A.U.W., 3,325 lb. Max. speed, 138 m.p.h. Cruise, 126 m.p.h.

STINSON SR-7B RELIANT

Four seater with compound tapered wing and single bracing struts, powered by one 245 h.p. Lycoming R-680-B6, built at Wayne, Michigan, 1936. One British aircraft only, G-AEFY, c/n 9691, C. of A. issued 20.6.36, imported for L. C. Desoutter, Hanworth, with whom it was in constant use until impressed into the R.A.F. 2.40 as W7979. Span, 41 ft. 10 in. Length, 28 ft. 0 in.

(W. T. Larkins Photo)

STINSON SR-8 RELIANT

Five seat version of the SR-7 Reliant, built at Wayne 1936. Four British aircraft only. Two SR-8B, 245 h.p. Lycoming R-680-B6; G-AEMC, c/n 9758, formerly NC16175, C. of A. issued 11.11.36, personal aircraft of Richard Fairey, Heathrow, crashed 9.39; G-AEOR, c/n 9820, C. of A. issued 22.1.37, Fairey Aviation Co. Ltd. communications, scrapped at Ringway 12.42. Two SR-8D, 320 h.p. Wright Whirlwind R-760-E1; G-AEJI, c/n 9728, C. of A. issued 18.9.36, imported for J. C. Knowles, Hatfield, last owner Brian Allen Aviation Ltd., Croydon, impressed 3.40 as X8520; G-AELU, c/n 9759, C. of A. issued 4.11.36, imported by Brian Allen Aviation Ltd., sold to Aeropolis Ltd., Heston, 5.38, impressed 5.40 as X9596. Span, 41 ft. 10¼ in. Length, 27 ft. 5⅜ in. Cruise, 140 m.p.h.

STINSON SR-9 RELIANT

Improved five seater with rounded front windscreen, powered by one 245 h.p. Lycoming R-680-B6 or R-680-D6 (SR-9B), one 245 h.p. Lycoming R-680-D5 (SR-9C) or one 320 h.p. Wright Whirlwind R-760-E1 (SR-9D), built at Wayne 1937. Six British aircraft as detailed in Appendix D. Span, 41 ft. 10 in. Length, 27 ft. 11 in. Tare wt., 2,530 lb. A.U.W., 3,700 lb. Cruise, 143 m.p.h.

STINSON SR-10 RELIANT

Five seater with panelled windscreen and modified rudder horn balance, powered by one 245 h.p. Lycoming R-680-D6 or R-680-E3 in helmeted cowling (SR-10B and SR-10J), or R-680-D5 in smooth cowling (SR-10C), built at Wayne 1938. Four British aircraft only, see Appendix D: G-AFHB (SR-10B, later SR-10J); G-AFRS, 'VT and G-AGZV (SR-10C). G-AFVT, now SR-10J, has seen 19 years service with the Fairey Aviation Co. Ltd. Span, 41 ft. 10½ in. Length, 27 ft. 7½ in. Tare wt. (SR-10C), 2,525 lb.; (SR-10J), 2,610 lb. A.U.W. (SR-10C), 3,900 lb.; (SR-10J), 4,500 lb. Cruise (SR-10C), 147 m.p.h.; (SR-10J), 151 m.p.h.

STINSON V-77 RELIANT

Navigational trainer powered by one 290 h.p. Lycoming R-680-E3B, built in quantity for the Royal Navy by the Stinson Aircraft Division of Vultee Aircraft Inc., at Wayne, Michigan, U.S.A., 1942. Two British civil aircraft only: G-AIYW, c/n 1410, formerly U.S.A.A.F. 43-44123 and Royal Navy FB682, civilianised by Scottish Aviation Ltd., C. of A. issued 28.4.47, delivered to Noon and Pearce Air Charters Ltd., Nairobi, 10.47 as VP-KEH; G-AJKZ, c/n 1404, reserved for Noon and Pearce 22.3.47, not proceeded with. Span, 41 ft. 10½ in. Length, 29 ft. 4¼ in. Tare wt., 2,810 lb. A.U.W., 4,000 lb. Max. speed, 141 m.p.h. Cruise, 130 m.p.h.

STINSON 105 VOYAGER

Two seater of mixed construction, powered by one 80 h.p. Continental A-80-9, in production pre-war by the Stinson Division of the Aviation Manufacturing Corporation at Wayne, Michigan, U.S.A. One British aircraft only, c/n 7504, built 1940, purchased by the Air Council for experimental use at Farnborough as X1050. Sold to the Clifford Cab Co. Ltd. 1.46, civilianised by Southampton Air Services Ltd. at Eastleigh as G-AGZW 9.46, sold to R. R. Harrington, White Waltham 9.51 and to A. S. Dubey, Croydon 4.53. Sold in Sweden 5.53 as SE-BYI. Span, 34 ft. 0 in. Length, 22 ft. 0 in. Tare wt., 923 lb. A.U.W., 1,580 lb. Max. speed, 115 m.p.h. Cruise, 109 m.p.h.

T.K.2

Wooden two seater powered by one 140 h.p. de Havilland Gipsy Major IC, designed by de Havilland Technical School students and built at Hatfield 1935. One aircraft only, G-ADNO, c/n 1998, completed as a single seater with long range tank in place of passenger, first flown 16.8.35 as E-3, C. of A. issued 29.8.35, 4th in the King's Cup Race 6–7.9.35 at 165·88 m.p.h. piloted by Hubert Broad. Span, 32 ft. 0 in. Length, 22 ft. 2½ in. Tare wt., 1,078 lb. A.U.W., 1,600 lb. Max. speed, 174 m.p.h.

T.K.2 (First Modification)

The original T.K.2 with aerodynamically refined cockpit canopy and lengthened spats. Sixth in the King's Cup Race 11.7.36 at 172·05 m.p.h. piloted by R. J. Waight, won the Heston–Cardiff race at 190 m.p.h. Second in the Heston–Newcastle race 3.7.37, piloted by Geoffrey de Havilland, who won the Heston–Cardiff race 10.7.37 at 161·4 m.p.h. but retired in the King's Cup Race 11.9.37 after averaging 165 m.p.h. Specification as before except: A.U.W., 1,630 lb.

('*The Aeroplane*' *Photo*)

T.K.2 (Second Modification)

G-ADNO modified for the 1938 season with reduced span, improved cabin glazing and 140 h.p. de Havilland Gipsy Major II, test flown as E-5. Piloted by Geoffrey de Havilland, won the 1938 Heston–Cardiff race at 187·5 m.p.h. and the 1939 Heston–Isle of Man at 168·4 m.p.h. Flew on de Havilland's communications as E-0235 during the war, 2nd in 1947 Manx Air Derby at 179 m.p.h. piloted by Bruce Campbell. Final appearance in Folkestone Trophy Race 31.8.47 when W. I. P. Fillingham broke the 100 Km closed circuit class record at 178·33 m.p.h. Scrapped 12.47. Span, 28 ft. 0 in. Length, 22 ft. 5 in. Tare wt., 1,135 lb. A.U.W., 1,650 lb. Max. speed, 182 m.p.h.

('*The Aeroplane*' *Photo*)

T.K.4

Built at Hatfield by de Havilland Technical School students in 1937 as the smallest single seat racer that could be designed around a 140 h.p. de Havilland Gipsy Major II. It was equipped with retractable undercarriage, variable pitch airscrew, slots and flaps. One aircraft only, G-AETK, c/n 2265, first flown 7.37 as E-4, C. of A. issued 1.9.37. Ninth in King's Cup Race 11.9.37 at 230·5 m.p.h. piloted by R. J. Waight, who was killed when the aircraft crashed near Hatfield 1.10.37 while practising for an attempt on the 100 Km class record. Span, 19 ft. 8 in. Length, 15 ft. 6 in. Tare wt., 928 lb. A.U.W., 1,357 lb.

('The Aeroplane' Photo)

T.K.5

Last of the T.K. series, designed and built at Hatfield 1938–39. Single seat canard research aircraft powered by one 140 h.p. de Havilland Gipsy Major IC driving a pusher airscrew. One aircraft only, G-AFTK, c/n 2266, completed late 1939, tested by Geoffrey de Havilland, but refused to leave the ground and was scrapped. Span, 25 ft. 8 in. Length, 18 ft. 3 in. A.U.W., 1,366 lb. Estimated max. speed, 170 m.p.h.

(Vickers Photo)

VICKERS TYPE 54 VIKING I

Four seat cabin amphibian of wooden construction powered by one 375 h.p. Rolls-Royce Eagle VIII, designed by R. K. Pierson and built at Weybridge 1918 by Vickers Ltd. One aircraft only, G-EAOV, registered to the manufacturers 21.10.19, crashed near Rouen 18.12.19, pilot Sir John Alcock of Atlantic flight fame killed. Span, 46 ft. 0 in. Length, 32 ft. 0 in. A.U.W., 4,545 lb. Max. speed, 104 m.p.h. Cruise, 85 m.p.h.

(*'Flight' Photo*)

VICKERS TYPE 59 VIKING II AND III

Four seat open amphibian powered by one 375 h.p. Rolls-Royce Eagle VIII (Viking II) or one 450 h.p. Napier Lion (Viking III). Two British aircraft only: G-EASC Viking II exhibited at Olympia 7.20, 1st prize in the Antwerp Seaplane Trials 8.20, later crashed; G-EAUK Viking III, 1st prize in the Air Ministry Amphibian Competition 9.20 piloted by Capt. S. Cockerell. Sold to the Air Council 19.1.21 as N147. Trial landings on the Thames at Westminster 7.2.21 and 17.3.21, and on the Seine, Paris, 29.4.21, scrapped 1925. Span, 46 ft. o in. Length, 32 ft. o in. Tare wt., 2,740 lb. A.U.W., 4,545 lb. Max. speed, 110 m.p.h. Cruise, 90 m.p.h.

VICKERS TYPE 60 VIKING IV

Six seat amphibian powered by one 450 h.p. Napier Lion. Two British civil aircraft only: G-EBBZ, c/n 15, registered to Sir Ross Smith 14.3.22 for a world flight, crashed on test at Brooklands 13.4.22, Sir Ross and Lt. Bennett, who made the Vimy flight to Australia, killed; G-EBED, c/n 17, C. of A. issued 6.10.22 for demonstration in Madrid, operated on winter sports service between Croydon, St. Moritz and Nice, 21.1.26 to 1.3.26, by Leslie Hamilton, to whom it was sold 7.26. Scrapped 12.29. Span, 50 ft. o in. Length, 35 ft. o in. Tare wt., 3,728 lb. A.U.W., 5,600 lb. Max. speed, 105 m.p.h. Cruise, 90 m.p.h.

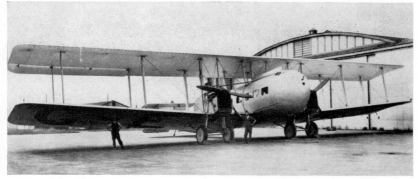

(*Vickers Photo*)

VICKERS TYPE 62 VANGUARD

Transport of wood and fabric construction for 22 passengers and two crew, designed by R. K. Pierson as a development of the Vimy Commercial. One civil aircraft only, G-EBCP, c/n 1, powered by two 450 h.p. Napier Lion, built at Weybridge for the Air Council 1922. Span, 88 ft. 4 in. Length, 53 ft. 10 in. Tare wt., 9,068 lb. A.U.W., 16,400 lb. Max. speed, 109 m.p.h.

VICKERS TYPE 89 VIGET

Single seat wooden ultra light powered by one 500 c.c. Douglas, designed by R. K. Pierson and built at Weybridge for the 1923 Lympne Trials. One aircraft only, G-EBHN, c/n 1, flown in the trials by chief test pilot S. Cockerell. Performed well but earned no prize money. Fitted with 35 h.p. Blackburne Thrush in 1924. Withdrawn from use 1928. Span, 25 ft. 0 in. Length, 17 ft. 3 in. Tare wt., 395 lb. A.U.W. (Douglas), 575 lb.; (Thrush), 625 lb. Max. speed, 58·1 m.p.h.

(*Vickers Photo*)

VICKERS TYPE 95 VULTURE

Three seat amphibian powered by one 450 h.p. Napier Lion, designed by
R. K. Pierson for a round the world flight and built at Weybridge 1923–24.
Two aircraft only: G-EBHO, c/n 2, C. of A. issued 18.2.24, left Calshot
25.3.24 in command of S/Ldr. A. C. S. MacLaren and piloted by F/O J.
Plenderleith, crashed on take off at Akyab 24.5.24; G-EBGO, c/n 1,
C. of A. issued 11.11.23, spare aircraft positioned at Tokyo, shipped back
to Akyab, left 25.6.24, wrecked in forced landing in heavy seas near the
Aleutian Islands 2.8.24. Span, 49 ft. 0 in. Length, 38 ft. 2 in. A.U.W.,
6,000 lb. Max. speed, 104 m.p.h. Cruise, 82 m.p.h.

(*Vickers Photo*)

VICKERS TYPE 98 VAGABOND

Two seat wooden ultra light powered by one 32 h.p. Bristol Cherub III,
designed for the 1924 Lympne Trials and built for Vickers Ltd. by A. V.
Roe and Co. Ltd. at Hamble. One aircraft only, G-EBJF, c/n 1, not flown
until fitted with one 35 h.p. Blackburne Thrush (illustrated) in 1925.
Scrapped 1927. Span, 28 ft. 0 in. Length, 21 ft. 0 in. Tare wt., 527 lb.
A.U.W., 887 lb. Max. speed, 77 m.p.h.

VICKERS TYPE 103 VANGUARD

The original Vanguard G-EBCP fitted in 1925 with two 650 h.p. Rolls-Royce Condor III and improved accommodation for 20 passengers, C. of A. issued 11.3.26. Reconditioned as Type 170 and loaned to Imperial Airways Ltd. for trial under airline conditions on the Croydon–Le Bourget service during the summer of 1928, broke the world's load-carrying record 6.7.28. Crashed and burned near Shepperton, Middlesex, 16.5.29, chief test pilot E. R. C. Scholefield killed. Span, 87 ft. 9 in. Length, 53 ft. 10 in. Tare wt., 12,040 lb. A.U.W., 18,500 lb. Max. speed, 115 m.p.h.

(Vickers Photo)

VICKERS TYPE 133 VENDACE II

Two seat, general purpose aircraft of mixed construction powered by one 300 h.p. A.D.C. Nimbus, built by Vickers Ltd. at Weybridge 1926. One British civil aircraft only, G-EBPX, c/n 1, C. of A. issued 10.1.28, sold to the Aircraft Operating Co. Ltd. 6.28, equipped with cameras and twin float undercarriage for the aerial survey of Rio de Janeiro, shipped on S.S. *Andorra* 6.6.28, withdrawn from use 9.30. Span, 45 ft. 0 in. Length, 31 ft. 4 in. Tare wt., 2,604 lb. A.U.W., 3,270 lb. Max. speed, 119 m.p.h.

VICKERS TYPE 134 VELLORE I

All-metal, two seat freighter powered by one 525 h.p. Bristol Jupiter IX, built to Air Ministry order at Weybridge 1928. One aircraft only, G-EBYX, allocated R.A.F. serial J8906 during construction, shown at Hendon R.A.F. Display 30.6.28. Fitted with one 490 h.p. Armstrong Siddeley Jaguar IV for Australia flight by F/Lt. S. J. Moir and P/O H. C. Owen, C. of A. issued 14.3.29, left Brooklands 18.3.29, crashed at Cape Don, Northern Territory, 26.5.29. Span, 76 ft. 0 in. Length, 51 ft. 6 in. Tare wt., 4,771 lb. A.U.W., 9,500 lb. Max. speed, 110 m.p.h.

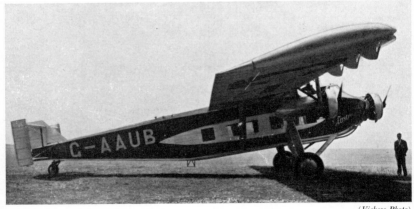

VICKERS TYPE 160 VIASTRA I

All-metal transport for 10 passengers, two crew and 800 lb. of baggage, powered by three 200 h.p. Armstrong Siddeley Lynx V, built at the Supermarine Aircraft Works, Southampton, 1929–30. One experimental aircraft only, G-AAUB, c/n 1, converted to Type 199 in 1931. Span, 70 ft. 0 in. Length, 48 ft. 6 in. A.U.W., 11,850 lb. Max. speed, 130 m.p.h. Cruise, 105 m.p.h.

(*Vickers Photo*)

VICKERS TYPE 172 VELLORE III

Metal transport for two crew and eight passengers developed from Vellore I. Two aircraft only: G-AASW, c/n 1, powered by two 550 h.p. Bristol Jupiter IXF, last aircraft built at Joyce Green. C. of A. issued 27.6.30, averaged 126·8 m.p.h. in the King's Cup Race 5.7.30, flown by F/O J. 'Mutt' Summers. Tested on floats as O-4, scrapped 1934; G-ABKC, c/n 1, completed as mailplane Type 173 with two 525 h.p. Bristol Jupiter XIF, transferred to the R.A.F. 8.31 as K2133. Span, 76 ft. o in. Length, 48 ft. o in. Tare wt., 7,435 lb. A.U.W., 12,000 lb. Max. speed, 138 m.p.h. Cruise, 120 m.p.h.

(*Vickers Photo*)

VICKERS TYPE 199 VIASTRA III

Prototype Viastra G-AAUB converted to twin engined layout 1931 and fitted with two 490 h.p. Armstrong Siddeley Jaguar VIC. Converted to Viastra VIII in 1932. Length, 48 ft. 6 in. A.U.W., 12,350 lb. Cruise, 125 m.p.h.

(*Vickers Photo*)

VICKERS TYPE 203 VIASTRA VI

Single engined variant powered by one 540 h.p. Bristol Jupiter IXF built at Southampton to the order of West Australian Airways Ltd. 1932. One aircraft only, G-ABVM, c/n 1, flown to Brooklands 3.32 under B conditions as N-1. Not delivered to Australia, flown for test purposes as O-6 (illustrated), scrapped 12.32. Tare wt., 6,440 lb. A.U.W., 9,960 lb. Max. speed, 127 m.p.h. Cruise, 103 m.p.h.

(*W. K. Kilsby Photo*)

VICKERS TYPE 212 VELLOX

Fabric-covered freighter of metal construction powered by two 580 h.p. Bristol Pegasus I built at Weybridge 1931. One aircraft only, G-ABKY, c/n 1, first public appearance at the Hendon S.B.A.C. Show 1.1.34, C. of A. issued 30.1.34, sold to Imperial Airways Ltd. for night freighting 5.36. Fitted with the Bristol Perseus engines removed from Short L.17 'Syrinx', burned out in night take off crash at Croydon 10.8.36. Span, 76 ft. 0 in. Length, 48 ft. 0 in. Tare wt., 7,280 lb. A.U.W., 13,500 lb. Max. speed, 160 m.p.h. Cruise, 130 m.p.h.

(*Bristol Photo*)

VICKERS TYPE 220 VIASTRA VIII

Prototype Viastra G-AAUB reconverted to trimotor layout in 1932, with three 450 h.p. Bristol Jupiter VI and equipped for the carriage of 12 passengers and two crew. Scrapped 12.33. Span, 70 ft. 0 in. Length, 48 ft. 6 in. A.U.W., 12,950 lb. Max. speed, 152 m.p.h. Cruise, 130 m.p.h.

(*W. K. Kilsby Photo*)

VICKERS TYPE 259 VIASTRA X

Special version of the proposed Type 242 Viastra IX built at Southampton for the use of H.R.H. the Prince of Wales 1932, with seating for seven passengers and two crew, powered by two 650 h.p. Bristol Pegasus II.L3 in nacelles attached directly to the wing. One aircraft only, G-ACCC, c/n 1, C. of A. issued 16.5.33, stationed at Hendon with the Royal Flight and flown by F/Lt. E. H. Fielden. Based at Croydon under Secretary of State for Air ownership from 5.35 for radio test purposes. Broken up 1937. Span, 70 ft. 0 in. Length, 45 ft. 6 in. Tare wt., 7,880 lb. A.U.W., 12,350 lb. Max. speed, 160 m.p.h. Cruise, 130 m.p.h.

VICKERS TYPE 951 VANGUARD

Transport for four crew and up to 135 passengers, powered by four 5,525 e.h.p. Rolls-Royce Tyne 506 turboprops, built at Weybridge 1958. Prototype, G-AOYW, c/n 703, first flown by G. R. Bryce 20.1.59. Twenty, G-APEA–'EU, c/n 704–723, ordered by B.E.A.C. 5.6.56, twelve of which will be Type 953 with increased payload. See Appendix D. Span, 118 ft. 0 in. Length, 122 ft. 10½ in. Tare wt., 83,500 lb. A.U.W., 141,000 lb. Cruise, 422 m.p.h. Max. range, 3,800 miles.

('*Flight*' *Photo*)

WACO UIC

Fabric-covered, metal four seater powered by one 210 h.p. Continental R-670, built by The Waco Aircraft Company at Troy, Ohio, U.S.A., 1933. One British aircraft only, G-ACGJ, c/n 3749, shipped to Hamble, flown to Heston by H. F. Jenkins 2.6.33 on delivery to Lady Hay Drummond Hay, C. of A. issued 19.6.33. Sold in Australia 8.35 as VH-UAX, crashed at Brisbane 22.5.41. Span, 33 ft. 3 in. Length, 25 ft. 2½ in. Tare wt., 1,755 lb. A.U.W., 2,800 lb. Max. speed, 143·5 m.p.h. Cruise, 120 m.p.h.

('*Flight*' Photo)

WATKINSON DINGBAT

Single seat ultra light of wooden construction powered by one 30 h.p.
Carden Ford, designed by E. T. Watkinson and C. W. Taylor and built at
Teddington, Middlesex, 1938. One aircraft only, G-AFJA, c/n DB.100,
first flown at Heston 6.38 by R. L. Porteous, P. to F. issued 29.7.38, shown
at the R.Ae.S. Garden Party, Heathrow 14.5.39. Restored post-war to
J. A. Allen but not re-erected, dismantled at Croydon 4.53. Rebuilt by
J. H. Pickrell and D. O. Wallis 1959, A. to F. reissued 10.12.59, currently
based at Ipswich. Span, 28 ft. o in. Length, 16 ft. o in. Tare wt., 460 lb.
A.U.W., 700 lb. Max. speed, 90 m.p.h. Cruise, 80 m.p.h.

(*Westland* Photo)

WESTLAND WOODPIGEON I

Wooden two seater built for the 1924 Lympne Trials, powered by one
32 h.p. Bristol Cherub III. Two aircraft only: G-EBIY, c/n W.P.1, and
G-EBJV, c/n W.P.2. The latter first flown by L. P. Openshaw 17.9.24,
piloted in the Trials as No. 5 without success by F/O Gaskell. Second in
the Grosvenor Trophy Race 4.10.24. Re-engined with 30 h.p. A.B.C.
Scorpion (illustrated) for the Seven Aero Club, C. of A. issued 8.9.26,
unsuccessful in the 1926 Lympne Trials. Span, 22 ft. 9 in. Length,
19 ft. 6 in. Tare wt., 439 lb. A.U.W., 779 lb. Max. speed, 72 m.p.h.

WESTLAND WOODPIGEON II

The original Woodpigeons fitted with 60 h.p. Anzani radials and main-planes of greater span in 1927. G-EBIY sold to F/O A. F. Scroggs, Henlow, C. of A. issued 12.5.27, last owner Miss Cicele O'Brien 8.30, currently in Bowers' scrap yard, Ferrybridge, Yorks: G-EBJV, sold to L. Taylor 6.27; to L. J. C. Mitchell, Chard 10.27, to J. E. Crossland McClure, No. 41 (Fighter) Sqn., Netheravon, 2.30. Last C. of A. renewal at Northolt 6.5.32. Span, 27 ft. 0 in. Length, 20 ft. 9 in. Tare wt., 515 lb. A.U.W., 890 lb.

(Westland Photo)

WESTLAND WESTMINSTER

Experimental helicopter powered by two 2,400 e.h.p. Napier Eland 229 gas turbines and using the rotor and control systems of the Sikorsky S.58. Two aircraft to date, G-APLE, c/n W.A.1, prototype of projected 45 seat transport, first flown at Yeovil by W. H. 'Slim' Sear 15.6.58, first demonstrated at Farnborough S.B.A.C. Show 9.58; G-APTX, c/n W.A.2, first flown 4.9.59. Rotor diameter, 72 ft. 0 in. Length, 86 ft. 9 in. Tare wt., 21,245 lb. A.U.W., 33,000 lb. Cruise, 173 m.p.h. Range, 390 miles.

(Photo courtesy of Air Comm. A. H. Wheeler)

WHEELER SLYMPH

Single seater powered by one 696 c.c. Blackburne Tomtit designed and built by F/Lt. (now Air Commodore) A. H. Wheeler at the Aircraft Depot, Hinaidi, Iraq, 1931. One aircraft only, G-ABOI, c/n A.H.W.1, modified and re-engined with one 35 h.p. A.B.C. Scorpion at R.A.F. Henlow 1932. Never flown, currently stored at Old Warden, Beds., with the Shuttleworth collection. Span, 22 ft. 0 in. Length, 14 ft. 9 in. A.U.W., 530 lb.

WILLOUGHBY DELTA F

Wooden experimental two seater with triangular aerofoil section tail booms, powered by two 125 h.p. Menasco Pirate C-4, designed by P. N. Willoughby and built by the Willoughby Delta Company at Witney 1938–39. One aircraft only, G-AFPX 'St. Francis', c/n 1, demonstrated by A. N. Kingwill at the Heathrow Garden Party of the R.Ae.S. 14.5.39, destroyed in crash at Caulcott, near Bicester 10.7.39, pilot H. N. Olley and designer killed. Span, 34 ft. 6 in. Length, 26 ft. 1 in. Tare wt., 1,585 lb. A.U.W., 2,350 lb. Max. speed, 183 m.p.h. Cruise, 165 m.p.h.

YOUNGMAN–BAYNES HIGH LIFT

Experimental two seater using some Proctor components, designed by
L. E. Baynes to incorporate a system of full span, slotted flaps invented by
R. T. Youngman and built by Heston Aircraft Ltd. 1947. One aircraft
only, c/n 1, powered by one 250 h.p. Gipsy Queen 32, first flown at
Heston 5.2.48 as VT789 by R. Munday. Registered to R. T. Youngman
as G-AMBL, 10.5.50, shown at the White Waltham Garden Party of the
R.Ae.S. 6.5.51, presented to the College of Aeronautics, Cranfield, 1954.
Span, 33 ft. 0 in. Length, 29 ft. 0 in. Tare wt., 2,380 lb. A.U.W., 3,500 lb.
Max. speed, 180 m.p.h.

ZLIN 12

Open two seater of wooden construction powered by one 45 h.p. Persy II,
designed and built by Zlinska Letecka A.S. at Zlin, Czechoslovakia, 1938.
Two British aircraft only, imported by Essex Aero Ltd. 1938 and employed on Civil Air Guard training by Southend Flying Services Ltd. until
September 1939: G-AFMW, c/n 1001, formerly OK-LZX; G-AFMX,
c/n 153, formerly a cabin model OK-TBK; Cs. of A. issued 18.1.39,
scrapped at Gravesend during the war. Span, 32 ft. 9½ in. Length, 25 ft.
7 in. Tare wt., 650 lb. A.U.W., 1,102 lb. Max. speed, 93 m.p.h. Cruise,
77 m.p.h.

APPENDIX B

Military Types Used for Civil Purposes

Aircraft listed in this section were either demilitarised in small numbers for normal commercial or private usage or flew under civil markings for demonstration, test or overseas delivery. As it constitutes a breach of international law to fly an aircraft in military marks over foreign soil without permission, British military aircraft being delivered by air often receive temporary civil status.

The notes given in Appendix A concerning Certificates of Airworthiness and the number of aircraft on register apply equally to Appendix B.

F.E.2B

Two seat fighter powered by one 160 h.p. Beardmore, designed by the Royal Aircraft Factory, Farnborough, 1915 and widely sub-contracted. One British civil aircraft only, G-EAHC, formerly D3832, built by Richard Garrett and Sons at Leiston, Suffolk. Registered 14.7.19 to J. Carter Smith, C. of A. issued 8.8.19, sold to the Bournemouth Aviation Co. Ltd. 31.3.20 for instruction and joyriding. Crashed prior to 10.1.23. Span, 47 ft. 9 in. Length, 32 ft. 3 in. Tare wt., 2,061 lb. A.U.W., 3,037 lb. Max. speed, 91·5 m.p.h.

(Imperial War Museum Photo MH. 2945)

FAIREY FREMANTLE

Four seat, long range seaplane powered by one 650 h.p. Rolls-Royce Condor III, designed 1922 for projected round-the-world flight piloted by R. H. McIntosh but construction not completed until 1925. One aircraft only, G-EBLZ, c/n F.420, registered to the Air Council but flown in Service markings as N173. Handed over to the R.A.E. for radio navigation development 1926. Span, 68 ft. 6 in. A.U.W., 12,550 lb. Max. speed, 100 m.p.h. Cruise, 80 m.p.h.

FAIREY FOX I

Two seat day bomber powered by one 450 h.p. Curtiss D-12 (Fairey Felix), built at Hayes, Middlesex, for No. 12 Sqn. R.A.F. in 1926, put up for civilian disposal 1932. Three civil aircraft only, full details in Appendix D: G-ACAS of Luxury Air Tours Ltd., flown by F/Lt. J. B. Pugh with C. W. A. Scott's Circus 1933; G-ACXO and 'XX flown in MacRobertson Race to Australia October 1934, former by R. J. P. Parer (See Volume 1, page 269) and G. E. Hemsworth, latter by J. K. C. Baines and H. D. Gilman. Span, 37 ft. 8½ in. Length, 31 ft. 2 in. Tare wt., 2,600 lb. A.U.W., 4,300 lb. Max. speed, 156·5 m.p.h.

FAIREY FOX II

All-metal development of Fox I powered by one 480 h.p. Rolls-Royce Kestrel IIB. Built Hayes, Middlesex, 1929. One civil aircraft only, G-ABFG, c/n F.1138, formerly the prototype J9834, C. of A. issued 6.10.30. Demonstrated to Belgian Air Force at Evere, Brussels, by C. S. Staniland 1930, converted to demonstration two seat fighter 1931, withdrawn from use 11.32. Span, 38 ft. 0 in. Length, 24 ft. 6 in. Max. speed, 190 m.p.h.

(*Photo: Fairey Aviation Co. Ltd.*)

FAIREY FOX III

Three seat variant of Fox III day bomber, powered by one 525 h.p. Rolls-Royce Kestrel IIMS, built Hayes, Middlesex, 1932. One aircraft only, G-ABYY, c/n F.1842, C. of A. issued 23.6.33. Exhibited at Hendon S.B.A.C. Show 26.6.33, later shipped to Shanghai for demonstration to Chinese military authorities. Span, 38 ft. 0 in. Length, 29 ft. 8 in. A.U.W., 5,000 lb. Max. speed, 185 m.p.h.

(*Photo: Fairey Aviation Co. Ltd.*)

FAIREY FOX III TRAINER

Two seat trainer variant of Fox III with full dual control, powered by one 340 h.p. Armstrong Siddeley Serval, built Hayes, Middlesex, 1933. One British civil aircraft only, G-ACKH, c/n F.1925, later allotted Avions Fairey c/n A.F.3032, C. of A. issued 22.12.33, sold to the Belgian Air Force 3.34. Span, 38 ft. 0 in. Length, 31 ft. 4 in. A.U.W., 4,296 lb. Max. speed 138 m.p.h.

('The Aeroplane' Photo)

FAIREY FIREFLY IIM

Prototype single seat interceptor fighter powered by one 480 h.p. Rolls-Royce Kestrel IIS, built Hayes, Middlesex 1929. One civil aircraft only, G-ABCN, c/n F.1130, first flown at Northolt 5.2.29, registered 9.7.30, C. of A. issued 10.7.30. Flown at Hendon R.A.F. Display 28.6.30 and employed as demonstrator at home and on the continent until the end of 1932. Span, 32 ft. 0 in. Length, 24 ft. 6 in. A.U.W., 3,404 lb. Max. speed, 212 m.p.h.

(P. T. Capon Photo)

FAIREY FIREFLY III

Ship-borne version of Firefly II with increased span, powered by one 480 h.p. Rolls-Royce Kestrel IIS, built Hayes, Middlesex, 1931. One aircraft only, S1592, c/n F.1138, allotted civil markings G-ABFH during manufacture, completed as floatplane trainer for 1931 Schneider Trophy team. Fitted with land undercarriage, demonstrated by C. S. Staniland at major air displays 1932. Span, 33 ft. 6 in. Length, 25 ft. 6 in. A.U.W., 3,500 lb. Max. speed, 214 m.p.h.

(*Photo: Fairey Aviation Co. Ltd.*)

FAIREY FANTÔME

Single seat fighter powered by one 925 h.p. Hispano Suiza 12 Ycrs, built at Hayes, Middlesex, 1935 for the Belgian Government's International Fighter Competition. One civil aircraft only, G-ADIF, c/n F.6, first flown under B conditions 6.35 as F-6. Demonstrated at Hendon S.B.A.C. Show 1.7.35 by C. S. Staniland. Crashed at Evere, Brussels, 17.7.35 during the Competition and test pilot S. H. G. Trower killed. Span, 34 ft. 6 in. Length, 27 ft. 6 in. A.U.W., 4,120 lb. Max. speed, 270 m.p.h. Cruise, 216 m.p.h.

FAIREY SWORDFISH

Three seat torpedo-bomber in production 1935–45. One British civil aircraft only, G-AJVH, formerly LS326, powered by one 750 h.p. Bristol Pegasus 30, built at Brough 1943 by Blackburn Aircraft Ltd. Flown post-war in Service marks for communications and demonstration, exhibited at Fifty Years of Flying Exhibition, Hendon, 7.51, civilianised at Hamble 10.55 as flying museum piece for preservation by the Fairey Aviation Co. Ltd. Flown annually at displays, reverted to military marks 6.59. Span, 45 ft. 6 in. Length, 35 ft. 8 in. Tare wt., 4,700 lb. A.U.W., 7,510 lb. Max. speed, 138 m.p.h. Cruise, 131 m.p.h.

(*Charles E. Brown Photo*)

FAIREY FULMAR 2

Two seat naval fighter built by the Fairey Aviation Co. Ltd. at Heaton Chapel, Stockport. One civil aircraft only, G-AIBE, c/n F.3707, formerly the prototype N1854, first flown at Ringway 4.1.40. Civilianised at Ringway 1946 as communications aircraft powered by one 1,300 h.p. Rolls-Royce Merlin 30F, C. of A. issued 26.2.47. Preserved by makers as flying museum piece, reverted to military marks 6.59. Span, 46 ft. 4½ in. Length, 40 ft. 3 in. A.U.W., 9,672 lb. Max. speed, 280 m.p.h. Cruise, 235 m.p.h.

(*Photo: Fairey Aviation Co. Ltd.*)

FAIREY FIREFLY TRAINER MK. 1

Two seat naval trainer powered by one 1,815 h.p. Rolls-Royce Griffon XII, developed from Firefly 1 two seat fighter. One British civil aircraft only, G-AHYA, formerly MB750, first flown at Heston 7.46 as F-1, demonstrated at Les Mureaux, France, and Valkenborg, Netherlands, 11.46–2.47. Then reverted to the Admiralty as MB750, coming 3rd in Lympne High Speed Handicap 31.8.47 piloted by G/C. R. G. Slade at 290·21 m.p.h. Span, 44 ft. 6 in. Length, 37 ft. 7¼ in. Tare wt., 9,906 lb. A.U.W., 12,300 lb. Max speed, 305 m.p.h.

(*Photo: Fairey Aviation Co. Ltd.*)

FAIREY ULTRA LIGHT HELICOPTER

Two bladed A.O.P. two seater powered by one 252 lb. s.t. Blackburn Turboméca Palouste 505 supplying compressed air to pressure jet rotor tip burners, built at Hayes, Mx. 1955–58. Three prototypes only:

[*continued on p. 511*

('*The Aeroplane*' Photo)

FANE F1/40

Two seat Air Observation Post with fully flapped and slotted wing, developed by Capt. Gerard Fane from the Comper Scamp design, powered by one 80 h.p. Continental A-80 driving a pusher airscrew. Built at Norbury by the Fane Aircraft Co. Ltd. 1941. One aircraft only, c/n F.1, on charge at Heston D.G.R.D. 21–26.3.41 as T1788, registered G-AGDJ 11.9.41, A. to F. issued 17.9.41, scrapped during the war. Span, 37 ft. 0 in. Length, 23 ft. 5 in. A.U.W., 1,500 lb.

(Short Photo)

FELIXSTOWE F.3

Patrol boat designed by John Porte, powered by two 345 h.p. Rolls-Royce Eagle VIII. Two British civil aircraft only: G-EAQT, c/n S.607, ex N4019, built by Short Bros. Ltd. at Rochester 1918, remodelled with cabin for L. Horden 3.20, shipped to Botany Bay, not erected; G-EBDQ, ex N4177, built by the Phoenix Dynamo Co. Ltd., Bradford, 1918, shipped to Montreal by the Aircraft Disposal Co. Ltd. 7.22 for the final, Atlantic, section of Major W. T. Blake's abortive world flight (see page 26), sold in Canada 11.22. Span, 102 ft. 0 in. Length, 49 ft. 2 in. Tare wt., 7,958 lb. A.U.W., 12,235 lb. Max. speed, 91 m.p.h.

(Photo: General Aircraft Ltd.)

GENERAL AIRCRAFT G.A.L.47

Two seat, twin-boom Air Observation Post powered by one 90 h.p. Blackburn Cirrus Minor driving a pusher airscrew, built at Hanworth 1940. One aircraft only, G-AGBL, c/n 135, first flown as T-47 and later as T-0224, civil registration not used. Destroyed 2.4.42. Span, 37 ft. 10 in. Length, 25 ft. 9 in. A.U.W., 1,615 lb. Cruise, 75 m.p.h.

GLOSTER MARS III SPARROWHAWK

Two seat trainer powered by one 230 h.p. Bentley B.R.2 rotary, designed by H. P. Folland and built by the Gloucestershire Aircraft Co. Ltd. at Sunningend 1921. One British aircraft only, G-EAYN, c/n Mars III, C. of A. issued 24.7.22, flown in 1922 Aerial Derby by L. R. Tait-Cox but retired. Converted to Grouse I in 1923. Span, 23 ft. o in. A.U.W., 2,154 lb.

(Gloster Photo)

GLOSTER GROUSE I

Sparrowhawk demonstrator rebuilt 1923 with square-cut vertical tail surfaces and fitted with single bay sesquiplane wings incorporating the Gloster H.L.B. high/medium lift feature. One aircraft only, G-EAYN, c/n 1, converted to Grouse II in 1924. Span, 28 ft. o in. Length, 19 ft. o in. Tare wt., 1,357 lb. A.U.W., 2,120 lb. Max. speed, 118 m.p.h.

GLOSTER GROUSE II

Grouse I prototype re-engined 1924 with 180 h.p. Armstrong Siddeley Lynx II radial as ab initio trainer. One British civil aircraft only, G-EAYN, c/n 2, C. of A. reissued 21.4.25, demonstrator, sold abroad 9.12.25. Span, 27 ft. 10 in. Length, 20 ft. 0 in. A.U.W., 2,120 lb. Max. speed, 118 m.p.h.

GLOSTER GREBE (Jaguar)

Single seat fighter designed by H. P. Folland and built for the R.A.F. by the Gloucestershire Aircraft Co. Ltd. at Sunningend. One civil aircraft only, G-EBHA, no c/n, demonstrator powered by one 385 h.p. Armstrong Siddeley Jaguar IIIA, first flown 6.7.23, C. of A. issued 11.7.23. Scratch machine in 1923 King's Cup Race, piloted by L. L. Carter, retired at Manchester. Span, 29 ft. 4 in. Length, 19 ft. 4 in. A.U.W., 2,570 lb. Max. speed, 152 m.p.h.

GLOSTER GREBE (Jupiter)

G-EBHA rebuilt 1926 with one 425 h.p. Bristol Jupiter IV and Gamecock type undercarriage, rudder and top ailerons, C. of A. renewed 30.3.27. Used to flight test and demonstrate Gloster-Hele-Shaw-Beacham experimental variable pitch airscrew. Scrapped 1930. Dimensions as before. A.U.W., 2,600 lb. Max. speed, 152 m.p.h.

GLOSTER GAMECOCK (Special)

Standard aircraft J8047 rebuilt by Glosters with lengthened fuselage, modified fin and rudder, narrow chord ailerons and wide track under-carriage, delivered to the R.A.E. 28.11.28. Temporarily fitted with one

('*Flight*' *Photo*)

GLOSTER GAMECOCK

Single seat fighter developed from the Grebe and built in quantity at Hucclecote for the R.A.F. Two civil aircraft only: G-EBNT, c/n 95/12877 powered by one 460 h.p. Bristol Jupiter VI, C. of A. issued 26.3.26, demonstrator, withdrawn from use 1927; G-EBOE, no c/n, reserved for experimental private venture installation of 495 h.p. Bristol Orion exhaust-turbo-supercharged engine which was not completed due to unsuccessful bench tests. Registration cancelled 3.28. Span, 29 ft. 7½ in. Length, 19 ft. 10½ in. Tare wt., 1,052 lb. A.U.W. (Jupiter), 2,750 lb.; (Orion), 2,823 lb. Max. speed, 150 m.p.h.

Continued from page 476.

530 h.p. Bristol Jupiter VII and Hele-Shaw variable pitch airscrew 1929–30, disposed of to scrap dealer at Hornchurch 10.4.34, sold to J. W. Tomkins 5.34 and rebuilt for private use with Jupiter VIIFP as G-ADIN at Apethorpe, Northants, C. of A. issued 24.9.35. Flown at Apethorpe and Sywell, withdrawn from use at C. of A. expiry 9.36.

(*Sport and General Photo*)

GLOSTER G.41F METEOR 4

Single seat fighter powered by two 3,500 lb. s.t. Rolls-Royce Derwent 5, in large-scale production at Hucclecote from 1946. One British civil aircraft only, G-AIDC, demonstrator built 1946, finished in scarlet and silver, C. of A. issued 14.4.47, left same day on Continental tour piloted by S/Ldr. D. V. Cotes-Preedy. Established Brussels–Copenhagen record 22.4.47 at 630 m.p.h. Seriously damaged by a Belgian pilot. Major components salvaged and returned to manufacturers. Span, 37 ft. 2 in. Length, 41 ft. 3 in. Tare wt., 10,740 lb. A.U.W., 15,175 lb. Max. speed, 588 m.p.h. Cruise, 375 m.p.h.

(*Gloster Photo*)

GLOSTER G.43 METEOR T.Mk.7

Two seat trainer powered by two 3,500 lb. s.t. Rolls-Royce Derwent 5, built in quantity at Hucclecote. One British civil aircraft only, G-AKPK, prototype, c/n G.5/201, constructed from wings, rear fuselage and tail unit of Meteor 4 G-AIDC, first flown 19.3.48, C. of A. issued 12.4.48, sales tour of Turkey 5.48, flew Lord Mayor's letter from Biggin Hill to Orly 30.9.48 in 27·5 minutes. Sold to Royal Netherlands Air Force 11.48 as I.1. Span, 37 ft. 2 in. Length, 43 ft. 9 in. Tare wt., 10,540 lb. A.U.W., 14,230 lb. Max. speed, 585 m.p.h. Cruise, 555 m.p.h.

(*Gloster Photo*)

GLOSTER METEOR P.V.7–8

Two seat demonstration and photographic aircraft powered by two 3,600 lb. s.t. Rolls-Royce Derwent 8. One aircraft only, G-ANSO, c/n G.5/1525, constructed 1954 by fitting a Mk. 7 two seat cockpit to the demilitarised P.V. ground-attack prototype G-7-1. C. of A. issued 9.7.54, exhibited at the Farnborough S.B.A.C. Show 9.54, finished in larkspur blue and ivory as Hawker-Siddeley Group camera ship. C. of A. not renewed since 26.9.56. Span, 42 ft. 0 in. A.U.W., 18,500 lb.

(*Gloster Photo*)

GLOSTER METEOR Mk.8

Single seat, private venture attack fighter powered by two 3,600 lb. s.t. Rolls-Royce Derwent 8, modified from a production Meteor F. Mk. 8 to carry RATOG, external rockets, ventral cannon and tip tanks. Rectilineal vertical tail surfaces without underkeel. One aircraft only, G-AMCJ, c/n G.5/1210, exhibited at the Farnborough S.B.A.C. Show 9.50, sold to the Danish Air Force 2.51 as '490'. Span, 37 ft. 2 in. Length, 44 ft. 7 in.

(*Gloster Photo*)

GLOSTER GLADIATOR

All-metal, single seat fighter powered by one 840 h.p. Bristol Mercury
VIIIA, 527 built at Hucclecote 1937–40. One civil aircraft only,
G-AMRK, largely composed of the former R.A.F. aircraft L8032, made
airworthy at Eastleigh 1952 by V. H. Bellamy. Flown at air displays until
sold to Gloster Aircraft Ltd. 1956 as museum piece. Now flown for exhibition purposes in R.A.F. colours with incorrect serial K8032. Span,
32 ft. 3 in. Length, 27 ft. 5 in. Tare wt., 3,745 lb. A.U.W., 5,420 lb.
Max. speed, 250 m.p.h. Cruise, 212 m.p.h.

GOSPORT FLYING-BOAT

Felixstowe F.5 four seater powered by two 345 h.p. Rolls-Royce Eagle
VIII. One civil aircraft only, G-EAIK, c/n G6/100, an R.A.F. aircraft
N4634, built at Northam 1919 by the Gosport Aviation Co. Ltd., C. of A.
issued 7.8.19, registered to the makers as a 'Gosport Flying Boat'. Flown
to Amsterdam 8.8.19 by Lt.-Col. R. Hope-Vere for exhibition at the First
Air Traffic Exhibition and demonstration flights from the River Ij.
Returned to Felixstowe 28.8.19, withdrawn from use at C. of A. expiry.
Span, 102 ft. 0 in. Length, 49 ft. 2 in. Tare wt., 7,958 lb. A.U.W.,
12,235 lb. Max. speed, 93 m.p.h.

(*Fox Photo*)

HANDLEY PAGE H.P.33 CLIVE I

Transport for 16 passengers powered by two 550 h.p. Bristol Jupiter IX, built at Cricklewood 1927. One civil aircraft only, c/n H.P.33, first flown 2.28 as the wooden prototype J9126. Registered to the Air Council 13.8.32 as G-ABYX, C. of A. issued 9.9.32. Sold to Sir Alan Cobham 4.33 and named 'Youth of Australia' for joyriding and flight refuelling experiments. Renamed 'Astra', scrapped 1935 after carrying 120,000 passengers. Registration G-ABIP reserved by the Air Council 2.2.31, but not used, for the metal prototype H.P.35 Clive II, J9949, c/n H.P.35/1. Span, 75 ft. o in. Length, 59 ft. 2 in. A.U.W., 14,500 lb. Max. speed, 111 m.p.h.

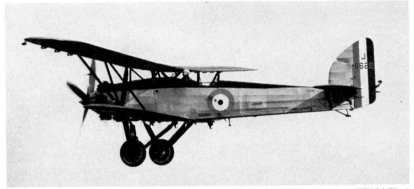

('*Flight*' Photo)

HANDLEY PAGE H.P.34 HARE

Two seat day bomber of metal construction, designed by G. R. Volkert, powered by one 485 h.p. Bristol Jupiter VIII, built at Cricklewood 1928. One aircraft only, J8622, first flown 24.2.28, struck off R.A.F. charge 1932, sold to J. N. Addinsell and registered G-ACEL for proposed long distance flight. Flown to Hanworth 3.33, where it was redoped in a civil colour scheme of blue and silver but was not flown again. Progressively broken up by vandals until the remains were scrapped in 1937. Span, 50 ft. o in. Length, 32 ft. 2 in. Tare wt., 3,050 lb. A.U.W., 5,720 lb. Max. speed, 145 m.p.h. Range, 1,000 miles.

(*J. McNulty Photo*)

HANDLEY PAGE H.P.54 HARROW II

Short range tanker, powered by two 925 h.p. Bristol Pegasus XX. Three R.A.F. aircraft built at Cricklewood 1936–37, loaned to Sir Alan Cobham for refuelling experiments 1939. G-AFRG, prototype Mk.I K6933, C. of A. issued 4.4.39; G-AFRH, ex K7029, C. of A. issued 4.4.39; G-AFRL, ex K7027, C. of A. issued 20.7.39. The first two arrived by sea in Montreal 30.4.39 to refuel the Transatlantic Empire Boats off New-foundland. Impressed by the R.C.A.F. at Rockliffe, Ottawa, where 'RG became '794' and 'RH was cannibalised. G-AFRL refuelled the Empire Boats over Foynes and was destroyed by enemy action at Ford, Sussex, 6.40. Span, 88 ft. 5 in. Length, 82 ft. 2 in. Tare wt., 13,600 lb. A.U.W., 25,240 lb. Max. speed, 200 m.p.h. Cruise, 163 m.p.h.

HANRIOT HD-1

Single seat fighter powered by one 110 h.p. Le Rhône, in production by Hanriot et Cie. at Billancourt, France 1916–18. One British aircraft only, G-AFDX, a Belgian Air Force machine civilianised 1934 as OO-APJ, flown from Brussels to Old Warden, Beds, by R. Shuttleworth and ex-hibited at the R.Ae.S. Garden Party, Heathrow, 8.5.38. Lost a wheel on take off from Brooklands 17.6.39, turned over landing at Old Warden. Wings destroyed by bombing at Brooklands 1940, fuselage currently stored at Old Warden. Span, 28 ft. 6½ in. Length, 19 ft. 1⅞ in. Tare wt., 904 lb. A.U.W., 1,521 lb. Max. speed, 100 m.p.h.

('*Flight*' *Photo*)

HAWKER WOODCOCK MK.II

Single seat fighter of wooden construction powered by one 420 h.p.
Bristol Jupiter IV, designed by W. G. Carter, built at Kingston-on-
Thames, Surrey, 1925–27 by the H. G. Hawker Engineering Co. Ltd.
The fourth production R.A.F. aircraft J7515, prepared for Scandinavian
Tour as G-EBMA. Entered by T. O. M. Sopwith and flown in the King's
Cup Race 3.7.25 by F/Lt. P. W. S. Bulman, crash landed in fog at Luton.
Span, 32 ft. 6 in. Length, 23 ft. 3 in. Tare wt., 2,075 lb. A.U.W., 3,040 lb.
Max. speed, 138 m.p.h.

('*Flight*' *Photo*)

HAWKER HAWFINCH

Single seat fighter of metal construction powered by one 530 h.p. Bristol
Jupiter VIIF, designed by W. G. Carter and built at Kingston-on-Thames,
Surrey, by the H. G. Hawker Engineering Co. Ltd. 1927. One prototype
only, J8776, registered to the manufacturers 27.7.29 as G-AAKH for
experimental flying with increased camber aerofoil sections at Brooklands
and Farnborough. Marks cancelled 10.29. Span, 33 ft. 6 in. Length,
24 ft. 4 in. Max. speed, 171 m.p.h.

(*Photo: Hawker Aircraft Ltd.*)

HAWKER HERON

Single seat fighter powered by one 515 h.p. Bristol Jupiter VI, designed by W. G. Carter and built at Kingston-on-Thames 1926. The first Hawker metal aircraft. One prototype only, J6989, c/n 1B, civilianised as G-EBYC, C. of A. issued 21.5.28, for the King's Cup Race of 20.7.28. Collided with a car at Hendon before the start. Scrapped 1.30. Span, 35 ft. 0 in. Length, 23 ft. 2 in. A.U.W., 2,780 lb. Max. speed, 160 m.p.h.

HAWKER HART II (Kestrel)

Two seat day bomber designed by Sydney Camm, in production from 1931. One demonstrator only, G-ABMR, c/n H.H.1, C. of A. issued 1.8.31, initially with one 525 h.p. Rolls-Royce Kestrel IB. Fitted 1938 with 525 h.p. Kestrel IIS and Osprey rudder for icing experiments and photographic duties. Fitted 1949 with 560 h.p. Kestrel IIIS and redoped blue and gold. Averaged 170 m.p.h. in Kemsley and King's Cup Races 1952 piloted by G. F. Bullen. Repainted 1959 as J9933. Span, 37 ft. 3 in. Length, 29 ft. 4 in. Tare wt., 2,530 lb. A.U.W., 4,635 lb. Max. speed, 184 m.p.h. Cruise, 140 m.p.h.

(Photo: Hawker Aircraft Ltd.)

HAWKER HART (Jupiter)

Hart bomber initially fitted with 480 h.p. Bristol Jupiter VIII, built at Kingston 1931. One British civil aircraft only, G-ABTN, c/n H.H.3; re-engined with 595 h.p. Jupiter XFAM, first flown thus 1.3.32, C. of A. issued 25.6.32; re-engined with 570 h.p. Bristol Pegasus IM.2, first flown 24.11.32. Flown from Heston to the Paris Aero Show 27.11.32 by P. E. G. Sayer, lost at sea off Ostend on the return journey, 30.11.32, pilot rescued. Span, 37 ft. 3 in. Length (Jupiter VIII) 36 ft. 10 in. (Jupiter XFAM) 35 ft. 10 in. (Pegasus) 35 ft. 9½ in. Tare wt., 2,937 lb. A.U.W. (Jupiter VIII) 4,500 lb. (Pegasus) 4,852 lb. Max. speed (Jupiter VIII) 161 m.p.h. (Pegasus) 177 m.p.h.

(Photo: Hawker Aircraft Ltd.)

HAWKER OSPREY

Deck-landing, fighter-reconnaissance version of the Hart. One British civil aircraft only, G-AEBD, c/n S.O.1 (i.e. Spanish Osprey 1), specially fitted with one 595 h.p. Hispano-Suiza 12Nbr for demonstration in Spain, where it was sold 6.36 as EA-KAJ. Span, 37 ft. 3 in. Length, 30 ft. 0 in. A.U.W., 4,780 lb. Max. speed. 164 m.p.h.

485

(Photo: Hawker Aircraft Ltd.)

HAWKER FURY I

Single seat fighter powered by one 525 h.p. Rolls-Royce Kestrel IIs, designed by Sydney Camm and built by the H. G. Hawker Engineering Co. Ltd. at Kingston-on-Thames 1931. One British civil aircraft only, G-ABSE, c/n H.F.4, C. of A. issued 10.5.32. Used as export demonstrator and later for research within the Hawker-Siddeley Group until allocated to Air Service Training Ltd., Hamble, for aerobatics in 1936. Scrapped 1938. Span, 30 ft. 0 in. Length, 26 ft. 8½ in. Tare wt., 2,623 lb. A.U.W., 3,367 lb. Max. speed, 207 m.p.h.

HAWKER FURY F.MK.1

Single seat fighter powered by one 2,500 h.p. Bristol Centaurus 18. First prototype, first flown at Brooklands 2.9.44 as NX798, allotted civil marks G-AKRY 1948 for overseas delivery, C. of A. issued 13.4.48, crashed in Egypt 1949. Third prototype, LA610, first flown at Brooklands 27.11.44 with one Rolls-Royce Griffon 81 engine, converted in 1946 to take one 2,700 h.p. Napier Sabre 7 with leading edge radiators. Civil marks G-AKRZ reserved by Hawker Aircraft Ltd. 29.1.48, scrapped 1949. Span, 38 ft. 4¾ in. Length, 34 ft. 8 in. Tare wt., 9,240 lb. A.U.W., 12,500 lb. Max. speed, 460 m.p.h.

HAWKER HURRICANE Mk. 1

Single seat fighter of fabric-covered, metal construction, fitted with retractable undercarriage, designed by Sidney Camm, in production by Hawker Aircraft Ltd. from 1938. One civil aircraft only, G-AFKX, c/n W/O 5436, formerly L1606 of No. 56 Sqn. powered by one 1,030 h.p. Rolls-Royce Merlin III, first civil flight at Brooklands 24.1.29, C. of A. issued 25.5.39, first flown with metal wings and experimental 1,210 h.p. Merlin RM4S 9.6.40, later fitted with 1,585 h.p. Merlin 45. Span, 40 ft. 0 in. Length, 31 ft. 5 in. Tare wt., 4,670 lb. A.U.W., 6,600 lb. Max. speed, 316 m.p.h.

HAWKER HURRICANE Mk. 2 C

Four-cannon version powered by one 1,280 h.p. Rolls-Royce Merlin 20, in large-scale production from 1940. The 12,780th and final Hurricane, PZ865 'Last of the Many', first flown by Gp. Capt. P. W. S. Bulman at Langley 8.44, stripped of armament as demonstrator and museum piece. First appearance in blue and gold at R.Ae.S. Garden Party, White Waltham, 14.5.50, C. of A. issued 23.5.50. Second in King's Cup Race 17.6.50 at 283 m.p.h. piloted by Gp. Capt. P. Townsend. Currently flying with Merlin 24. Span, 40 ft. 0 in. Length, 32 ft. 0 in. Tare wt., 5,800 lb. A.U.W., 7,600 lb. Max. speed, 339 m.p.h.

(*J. M. G. Gradidge Photo*)

HAWKER HUNTER T.Mk.66A

All metal, two seat fighter trainer powered by one 10,050 lb. s.t. Rolls-Royce Avon 203 turbojet. One civil aircraft to date, G-APUX, c/n H.IF.19, erected at Dunsfold 7.59 using the nose section of Indian Hunter 66 BS369 and fuselage of Belgian Hunter 6 IF.19. Fitted with braking nose wheel. C. of A. issued 4.9.59, demonstrated at the S.B.A.C. Show 9.59 by chief test pilot A. W. Bedford. Span, 33 ft. 7 in. Length, 48 ft. 10½ in. A.U.W., 25,000 lb.

(*J. A. Bagley Photo*)

HUNTING PERCIVAL P.56 PROVOST I

Two seat, side-by-side, all-metal, basic trainer, powered by one 550 h.p. Alvis Leonides 503/6, in production by Hunting Percival Aircraft Ltd. at Luton from 1953. One civil aircraft only, G-AMZM, c/n 20, C. of A. issued 29.6.53, sales tour of Turkey 7.53, demonstrated at Blackbushe 9.53, S.B.A.C. Show 1954, flown by R. G. Wheldon in the Lockheed Aerobatic Contest, Baginton, 20.7.56. Stored at Luton since C. of A. expiry 3.10.57. Span, 35 ft. 2 in. Length, 28 ft. 8 in. Tare wt., 3,350 lb. A.U.W., 4,700 lb. Max. speed, 200 m.p.h. Cruise, 162 m.p.h.

HUNTING PERCIVAL P.84 JET PROVOST 1

Two seat, side-by-side, all-metal, basic trainer using Provost mainplane and empennage, powered by one 1,640 lb. s.t. Armstrong Siddeley Viper 5 Mk.101 turbojet, built by Hunting Percival Aircraft Ltd. at Luton 1954. One civil aircraft only, G-AOBU, c/n 6, C. of A. issued 25.5.55; demonstrated at Blackbushe 9.55; flight trials of Viper 8 at Bitteswell 1956 as G-42-1; in current use by Hunting Aircraft Ltd. Span, 35 ft. 5 in. Length, 31 ft. 11 in. A.U.W., 6,038 lb. Max. speed, 330 m.p.h. Cruise, 303 m.p.h.

HUNTING PERCIVAL P.84 JET PROVOST 2

Developed version with shortened undercarriage legs, improved fuselage lines and dorsal fin. Two civil aircraft only: G-AOHD, c/n 12, 1,750 lb. s.t. Viper 8 Mk.102, C. of A. issued 30.5.56, flown at the ILSY Display, Ypenberg, 10.6.57, to Trinidad by sea for 8,400 miles sales tour of South America piloted by R. N. Rumbelow 5.4.58–2.8.58; G-AOUS, Mk.2B c/n 14, 2,500 lb. s.t. Viper 11, C. of A. issued 25.9.56, demonstrator. Dimensions as Jet Provost 1. A.U.W. (G-AOHD), 6,200 lb.; (G-AOUS), 7,150 lb. Max. speed, 330 m.p.h. Cruise, 282 m.p.h.

MARTIN-BAKER M.B.2

Private-venture, single seat, eight-gun fighter to Specification F.5/34, powered by one 1,000 h.p. Napier Dagger III, designed by James Martin and built at Heston by the Martin-Baker Aircraft Co. Ltd. 1937. One aircraft only, G-AEZD, c/n M.B.2, first flown at Heston under B conditions as M-B-1 by V. H. Baker 1938. Transferred to the R.A.F. 3.39 as P9594. Span, 34 ft. 0 in. Length, 34 ft. 6 in. A.U.W., 5,400 lb. Max. speed, 300+ m.p.h.

MILES M.9 KESTREL TRAINER

Private-venture, two seat advanced trainer of wooden construction, fitted with retractable undercarriage, powered by one 745 h.p. Rolls-Royce Kestrel XVI, designed by F. G. Miles and built by Phillips and Powis Aircraft Ltd. at Woodley 1937. One aircraft only, G-AEOC, c/n 330, registered 6.10.36, first flown 5.37, demonstrated at the Hendon R.A.F. Display 26.6.37, flown on manufacturer's trials under B conditions as U-5 until scrapped 5.38. Span, 39 ft. 0 in. Length, 29 ft. 6 in. Tare wt., 4,159 lb. A.U.W., 5,337 lb. Max. speed, 296 m.p.h. Cruise, 254 m.p.h.

MILES M.16 MENTOR

Three seat training and communications aircraft developed from the Miles Nighthawk and powered by one 200 h.p. de Havilland Gipsy Six series 1. One aircraft only, L4420, c/n 462, sole survivor of 45 Mentors supplied to the R.A.F. 1938–39, civilianised at White Waltham as G-AHKM 1947. Based at Wolverhampton by P. W. Bayliss, sold to J. C. Turnhill 12.48. Competed for 1948 Siddeley Trophy and 1949 King's Cup. Crashed in bad visibility at Clayhidon, Devon, 1.4.50, en route Wolverhampton–Exeter, J. C. Turnhill killed. Span, 34 ft. 9½ in. Length, 26 ft. 1¾ in. Tare wt., 1,978 lb. A.U.W., 2,710 lb. Max. speed, 156 m.p.h.

MILES M.19 MASTER 2

Two seat advanced trainer of all-wood construction powered by one 870 h.p. Bristol Mercury 20, 1,799 built by Phillips and Powis Aircraft Ltd. at Woodley from 1940. Three British civil aircraft only: G-AHOB, c/n 6434, converted at Woodley 5.46 for demonstration flying, scrapped 1950; G-AIZM and 'ZN, formerly EM300 and DM442 respectively, registered to Southern Aircraft (Gatwick) Ltd. 30.12.46, not converted, broken up for spares 1948. Span, 35 ft. 9 in. Length, 29 ft. 6 in. Tare wt., 4,053 lb. A.U.W., 5,673 lb. Max. speed, 243 m.p.h.

MILES M.27 MASTER 3

As Master 2 but powered by one 825 h.p. Pratt and Whitney Twin Wasp
Junior R-1535-SB4G, 602 built by Phillips and Powis Aircraft Ltd. at
Woodley from 1940. One British civil aircraft only, G-AGEK, R.A.F.
serial DL670, registered to the Secretary of State for Air 3.7.42 and ferried
in civil markings to the Irish Air Corps. Span, 35 ft. 9 in. Length,
30 ft. 2 in. Tare wt., 4,204 lb. A.U.W., 5,570 lb. Max. speed, 232 m.p.h.

PARNALL PANTHER

Two seat Fleet reconnaissance biplane of wooden monocoque construction,
powered by one 200 h.p. Bentley B.R.2 rotary, designed 1917 by Harold
Bolas for Parnall and Sons, 150 built by the British and Colonial Aeroplane Co. Ltd. at Filton 1919–21. One civil aircraft only, G-EBCM,
formerly N7530, completed at Filton 23.6.20. First flown at Croydon
13.4.22, after conversion by the Aircraft Disposal Co. Ltd., solely for the
Royal Aero Club race meeting at Croydon 17.4.22, at which it was flown
by A. F. Muir. Span, 29 ft. 6 in. Length, 24 ft. 11 in. Tare wt., 1,328 lb.
A.U.W., 2,369 lb. Max. speed, 108·5 m.p.h.

PARNALL PLOVER

Single seat Fleet fighter powered by one 420 h.p. Bristol Jupiter III, designed by Harold Bolas and built at Coliseum Works, Bristol, by George Parnall and Company 1923–24. One civil aircraft only, G-EBON, formerly N9705, C. of A. issued 7.7.26, flown in the King's Cup Race of 9–10.7.26 by S/Ldr. Sir C. J. Quintin Brand, retired with petrol feed trouble. Crashed 1.29. Span, 29 ft. o in. Length, 23 ft. o in. Tare wt., 2,035 lb. A.U.W., 3,020 lb.

(Photo courtesy of S/Ldr. C. A. Rea)

SHORT 184

Two seater designed by Short Bros. Ltd. in 1915 and widely sub-contracted. Five British civil aircraft only, all with 260 h.p. Sunbeam Maori III, converted to five seaters for one season's seaside pleasure flying: G-EAJT, ex N2986, C. of A. issued 8.8.19 and G-EALC, ex N2998, C. of A. issued 17.6.19, the Eastbourne Aviation Co. Ltd., scrapped 8.20; G-EBBM ex N9096, C. of A. issued 24.8.22 and G-EBBN ex N9118, C. of A. issued 1.6.22, Seaplane and Pleasure Trip Co. Ltd.; G-EBGP ex N2996, Manchester Airways, not converted. Span, 63 ft. 6¼ in. Length, 40 ft. 7½ in. Tare wt., 3,638 lb. A.U.W., 5,287 lb. Max. speed, 82 m.p.h.

('*Flight*' *Photo*)

SHORT S.5 SINGAPORE I

The first large all-metal flying-boat. One aircraft only, N179, c/n S.677, two 650 h.p. Rolls-Royce Condor IIIA, first flown by J. Lankester Parker at Rochester 8.26. Loaned to Sir Alan Cobham by the Air Council 1927 as G-EBUP for a 20,000 mile African Survey Flight, C. of A. issued 7.11.27. Left Rochester 17.11.27, held up at Malta until 21.1.28, first flying-boat to visit the Cape 30.3.28, returned to Rochester 4.6.28. Returned to the R.A.F. 10.28 as N179, exhibited at Olympia 7.29. Later fitted with Rolls-Royce Buzzard engines. Span, 93 ft. 0 in. Length, 65 ft. 6 in. Tare wt., 12,955 lb. A.U.W., 21,000 lb. Max. speed, 128 m.p.h.

SHORT S.29 STIRLING 5

All-metal transport powered by four 1,600 h.p. Bristol Hercules XVI, 160 built at Belfast 1945 by Short and Harland Ltd. One British civil aircraft only, G-AKPC, formerly PK148, illustrated, registered 6.1.48 for ferrying from R.A.F. Polebrook to Airtech Ltd., Thame, for overhaul and delivery to the Belgian operator Trans-Air as OO-XAM. The Belgian marks were not taken up, and the aircraft is believed to have been reduced to produce at Thame late in 1948. Span, 99 ft. 1 in. Length, 90 ft. 6¾ in. Tare wt., 43,500 lb. A.U.W., 70,000 lb. Max. speed, 280 m.p.h. Cruise, 233 m.p.h.

(*P. T. Capon Photo*)

SOPWITH PUP

Single seat fighter powered by one 80 h.p. Le Rhône, designed 1916. Eight civilianised surplus R.A.F. aircraft: G-EAVF and 'VV–'VZ by the Aircraft Disposal Co. Ltd. 1920 ('VX damaged in the 1921 Aerial Derby by D. L. Forestier-Walker); G-EBAZ, first flown 10.8.18, based at Erith, Kent, by H. Sykes 1922; G-EBFJ, first flown 27.12.18, converted by J. T. Norquay 1923. G-EBKY was a rebuilt Sopwith Dove (see page 432), currently owned by the Shuttleworth Trust as N5180. A replica, G-APUP, currently under construction at Dorking by K. C. D. St. Cyrien. Span, 26 ft. 6 in. Length, 19 ft. $3\frac{3}{4}$ in. Tare wt., 787 lb. A.U.W., 1,330 lb. Max. speed, 111·5 m.p.h.

(*Photo courtesy of P. D. Roberts*)

SOPWITH F.1 CAMEL

Single seat fighter designed 1916, widely sub-contracted. Two British civil aircraft only, powered by the 130 h.p. Clerget, built 1918 by Boulton and Paul Ltd.: G-EAWN ex H2700, first flown 12.12.19, owner H. S. Broad, 6th in the Aerial Derby 16.7.21 at 95·61 m.p.h., aerobatics for the Welsh Aviation Company 8.21, dismantled at Stag Lane 1922; G-EBER ex F6302 registered to F/O W. J. McDonough 9.8.22, crashed 4.11.22. Span, 28 ft. 0 in. Length, 18 ft. 9 in. Tare wt., 929 lb. A.U.W., 1,474 lb. Max. speed, 115 m.p.h.

('*Flight*' *Photo*)

SOPWITH R.M.1 SNAPPER

Fabric-covered, wooden, single seat fighter powered by one 360 h.p.
A.B.C. Dragonfly IA, built by the Sopwith Aviation Co. Ltd. at Kingston-
on-Thames 1919. One civil aircraft only, K-149/G-EAFJ, c/n P.W.14,
demilitarised and registered to the manufacturers 19.6.19. Flown to
Hendon by H. G. Hawker for the Aerial Derby 21.6.19, but participation
was forbidden as the Dragonfly engine was still on the Secret List.
Scrapped 8.20. Span, 28 ft. 0 in. Length, 20 ft. 7 in. Tare wt., 1,244 lb.
A.U.W., 2,190 lb. Max. speed, 140 m.p.h.

(*P. T. Capon Photo*)

SOPWITH SCOOTER

Single seat monoplane comprising a Sopwith Camel fuselage fitted with
a wire-braced wing and powered by one 130 h.p. Clerget. One aircraft
only, somewhat resembling the Sopwith Swallow; first flown at Brooklands 6.18, registered K-135/G-EACZ 29.5.19 as an aerobatic mount for
H. G. Hawker, to whom it was sold 4.21. Overhauled for C. Clayton,
Hendon, 5.25, C. of A. issued 1.8.25, exhibition flying by J. Phillips, sold
8.26 to Dudley Watt, by whom it was extensively raced. Sold as scrap
1927. Wing area, 162 sq. ft. Length, 18 ft. 9 in. Tare wt., 890 lb.
A.U.W., 1,420 lb. Max. speed, 115 m.p.h.

('*Flight*' Photo)

SOPWITH 7F.1 SNIPE

Single seat fighter powered by one 230 h.p. Bentley B.R.2, widely sub-contracted from 1918. Four unused R.A.F. aircraft registered 1920 by the Aircraft Disposal Company: G-EATF ex J365, built at Lincoln by Ruston and Hornsby Ltd., demonstrator; G-EAUU ex J459; G-EAUV ex J453; G-EAUW (illustrated) ex J455; built at Norwich by Boulton and Paul Ltd. and flown in the Hendon Aerial Derby 24.7.20 by J. S. T. Fall, W. H. Longton (both forced landed) and W. L. Jordan (5th) respectively. A fifth Snipe G-EBBE ex J461, Norwich built, registered 13.1.22, sold abroad 3.22. Span, 31 ft. 1 in. Length, 19 ft. 10 in. Tare wt., 1,127 lb. A.U.W., 2,075 lb. Max. speed, 121 m.p.h.

STINSON L-5 SENTINEL

Two seat, fabric-covered, metal communications aircraft powered by one 185 h.p. Lycoming O-435-1, built by Vultee Aircraft Inc., Wayne, Michigan, 1942. One British civil aircraft only, G-AKYF, formerly U.S.A.A.F. 42-98552, first flown at Fairoaks 4.48 with R.A.F. colours and unofficial serial LG552, C. of A. issued 29.7.48, owned successively by R. C. Cox, H. C. V. Hext and Southern Aircraft (Gatwick) Ltd. Sold in Kenya 9.49 as VP-KHM. Span, 34 ft. 0 in. Length, 24 ft. 1¾ in. Tare wt., 1,472 lb. A.U.W., 2,045 lb. Max. speed, 120 m.p.h.

SUPERMARINE SEAGULL III

Fleet Air Arm amphibian powered by one 450 h.p. Napier Lion V, built by the Supermarine Aviation Works Ltd., Woolston, 1923. Three aircraft converted to civil six seaters 1928–29: G-EBXH ex N9653, C. of A. issued 16.7.28 to F. Tyllyer and F. H. Winn, t/a Coastal Flying Boat Services, Shoreham, for South Coast joyrides and abortive Dieppe service; G-EBXI ex N9654, same owners, both scrapped 1930; G-AAIZ, ex N9605, Lion IIB, C. of A. issued 10.7.29, Travel and Tour Association Ltd., Brooklands, flown to Jersey 10.29, sold to G. W. Higgs 2.30, burned at Brooklands 12.33. Span, 46 ft. 0 in. Length, 37 ft. 0 in. Tare wt., 3,897 lb. A.U.W., 5,668 lb. Max. speed, 108 m.p.h.

(Photo: Supermarine Aviation Works)

SUPERMARINE SOLENT

Torpedo-carrying derivative of the Southampton powered by three 420 h.p. Armstrong Siddeley Jaguar IVA built for the Danish Navy as the Nanok (Ice Bear) in 1928. One undelivered aircraft only, Danish serial 99, c/n 1244, civilianised as G-AAAB for the Hon. A. E. Guinness and re-designated Solent, C. of A. issued 5.9.28. Numerous flights between Woolston and the Irish ports. Scrapped 1934. Span, 75 ft. 0 in. Length, 50 ft. 2 in. Tare wt., 9,849 lb. A.U.W., 16,300 lb. Max. speed, 111 m.p.h. Cruise, 90 m.p.h.

(*Vickers Photo*)

VICKERS TYPE 71 VIXEN I

Two seat general-purpose biplane powered by one 450 h.p. Napier Lion,
built at Weybridge 1922. One civil aircraft only, G-EBEC, c/n 1, C. of A.
issued 10.9.23. Modified to Type 87 Vixen II in 1924, with modified
decking, cowlings and wing tanks. Further modified to Type 124 in 1928.
Span, 40 ft. 0 in. Length, 29 ft. 0 in. Tare wt., 3,098 lb. A.U.W., 4,720 lb.

(*Imperial War Museum Photo MH. 2948*)

VICKERS TYPE 91 VIXEN III

Two seat marine reconnaissance biplane similar to Vixen II, powered by
one 450 h.p. Napier Lion with modified cowlings, decking and rudder horn
balance. One civil aircraft only, G-EBIP, c/n 1, built at Weybridge 1923,
evaluated by the M.A.E.E. Felixstowe, converted to landplane, registered
to Douglas Vickers 8.24, 5th in the 1924 King's Cup Race, piloted by
S/Ldr. H. J. Payn. Later modified to Type 148. Span, 45 ft. 1 in.
Length, 36 ft. 6 in. Tare wt., 3,900 lb. A.U.W., 5,500 lb. Max. speed,
125 m.p.h.

VICKERS TYPE 113 VESPA I

Fabric-covered, high-altitude Army Co-operation biplane of wooden construction powered by one 515 h.p. Bristol Jupiter VI, built by Vickers Ltd. at Weybridge 1925. One British civil demonstrator only, G-EBLD, c/n 1, C. of A. issued 28.1.26. Flown with gun blisters removed in the King's Cup Race 30.7.27 by S/Ldr. H. J. Payn, averaging 115·5 m.p.h. until damaged in flight by loose Hucks starter claw. Rebuilt as Type 210 in 1930. Span, 50 ft. 0 in. Length, 33 ft. 0 in. Tare wt., 2,468 lb. A.U.W., 4,370 lb. Max. speed, 126 m.p.h.

VICKERS TYPE 123

Single seat fighter of fabric-covered, metal construction powered by one 400 h.p. Hispano-Suiza Type 52, built at Weybridge 1926. One aircraft only, G-EBNQ, c/n 1, first flown 11.9.26, modified to Type 141 in 1928. Span, 34 ft. 0 in. Length, 28 ft. 6 in. Tare wt., 2,278 lb. A.U.W., 3,300 lb. Max. speed, 149 m.p.h.

(*Vickers Photo*)

VICKERS TYPE 124 VIXEN VI

The Vixen II demonstrator G-EBEC modified in 1928 with improved
fuselage lines, modified aileron circuit and horn balances to all controls,
and fitted with one 650 h.p. Rolls-Royce Condor IIIA. Flown by Charles
Russell on experimental mail flights to connect with Transatlantic liners,
commencing Croydon–Baldonnel 21.8.29. Scrapped 1930. Span, 45 ft.
1 in. Length, 34 ft. 6 in. A.U.W., 5,550 lb. Max. speed, 159 m.p.h.

(*Vickers Photo*)

VICKERS TYPE 131 VALIANT

Two seat, general-purpose biplane of fabric-covered, metal construction,
powered by one 515 h.p. Bristol Jupiter VI, built at Weybridge 1927.
One aircraft only, c/n 1, shown as No. 11 in the New Types park at the
Hendon R.A.F. Display 2.7.27. Registered G-EBVM as a civil demonstrator 15.12.27, C. of A. issued 3.1.28, sold abroad 12.28. Span, 45 ft. 7 in.
Length, 34 ft. 0 in. Tare wt., 2,973 lb. A.U.W., 5,550 lb. Max. speed,
125 m.p.h.

(*Air Ministry Photo*)

VICKERS TYPE 132 VILDEBEESTE I

Two seat torpedoplane of fabric-covered, metal construction powered by one 480 h.p. Bristol Jupiter IX, built at Weybridge 1930. One British civil demonstrator only, G-ABGE, c/n 1, C. of A. issued 1.12.30, modified 9.31 to Spanish requirements as Type 216. Span, 49 ft. 0 in. Length, 36 ft. 8 in. Tare wt., 3,990 lb. A.U.W., 7,915 lb. Max. speed, 128 m.p.h.

(*Vickers Photo*)

VICKERS TYPE 141

Vickers Type 123 G-EBNQ modified in 1928 as ship's fighter to A.M. Spec. N.21/26 with one 480 h.p. Rolls-Royce F.XI. Scratch machine in the King's Cup Race, 5–6.7.29 piloted by F/O J. Summers, retired at Castle Bromwich. Later fitted with 480 h.p. Rolls-Royce F.XII supercharged engine, scrapped 1930.

('*Flight*' *Photo*)

VICKERS TYPE 146 VIVID

Two seat, general-purpose biplane powered by one 590 h.p. Napier Lion
XIA, built at Weybridge 1926. One aircraft only, G-EBPY, c/n 1, C. of A.
issued 29.8.28, flown at Woolston on twin floats and to Bucharest as a
landplane by F/Lt. E. R. C. Scholefield 6.9.28. Sold to J. R. Chaplin 3.31,
set up one-day out-and-home records from Heston piloted by T. Neville
Stack and owner, Berlin 12.4.31, Copenhagen 23.5.31, Warsaw 24.6.31.
Damaged landing at Broomfield, Essex 8.32, burned at Brooklands 10.32.
Span, 45 ft. 1 in. Length, 34 ft. 5 in. Tare wt., 3,560 lb. A.U.W., 5,550 lb.
Max. speed, 153 m.p.h. Cruise, 130 m.p.h.

('*Flight*' *Photo*)

VICKERS TYPE 148 VIXEN III

The original Vixen III G-EBIP demilitarised as a high performance two
seater, C. of A. issued 1.2.26, 2nd and 3rd respectively in the 1926 and
1927 King's Cup Races, averaging 141·6 m.p.h., piloted by E. R. C.
Scholefield, scrapped 1929. Span, 45 ft. 1 in. Length, 36 ft. 6 in. Tare
wt., 3,900 lb. A.U.W., 5,500 lb. Max. speed, 125 m.p.h.

(*Bristol Photo*)

VICKERS TYPE 210 VESPA VI

Vespa I G-EBLD converted to two seat fighter prototype with modified undercarriage but retaining the Jupiter VI engine. Re-registered G-ABIL 1.31, C. of A. issued 12.3.31 for demonstration tour of China, ending at Nankin. Loaned to the Bristol Aeroplane Co. Ltd., converted to single seater and fitted with one 550 h.p. Bristol Pegasus 1S3 under the direction of F. S. Barnwell. Pegasus development flights at Filton under B conditions as O-5, culminating in a new world's altitude record of 43,976 ft. piloted by C. F. Uwins 16.9.32. To the R.A.F. 6.33 as K3588. Span, 50 ft. 0 in. Length, 33 ft. 0 in.

·(*Vickers Photo*)

VICKERS TYPE 216 VILDEBEESTE VII

Similar to Type 132 Vildebeeste I but fitted with one 595 h.p. Hispano-Suiza 12Lbr. Two British civil aircraft only: demonstrator G-ABGE flown at Woolston 10.31 with twin float undercarriage, and later with wheeled undercarriage as O-3, C. of A. reissued 22.3.32, sold to Spanish Ministry of Marine, ferried to Seville as EC-W11 by H. W. R. Banting 24–27.3.32; markings G-ABJK, reserved 10.3.31, but not taken up, for a prototype Vildebeeste VII, c/n 1, believed to have been the exhibition airframe Type 217. Span, 49 ft. 0 in. Length, 40 ft. 0 in. Tare wt., 5,100 lb. A.U.W., 7,752 lb. Max. speed, 134·5 m.p.h. Cruise, 106 m.p.h.

(Vickers Photo)

VICKERS TYPE 252 VILDEBEEST XI

Developed aircraft with amended name, fitted with one 660 h.p. Bristol Pegasus IIM3, built in quantity for the R.A.F. at Weybridge 1934 as the Vildebeest II. One civil experimental aircraft only, G-ACYV, c/n 1, scrapped 1938. Span, 49 ft. 0 in. Length, 38 ft. 6 in. Tare wt., 4,229 lb. A.U.W. 8,100 lb. Max speed, 143 m.p.h.

(Air Ministry Photo)

VICKERS TYPE 456 WARWICK I

Long range transport of fabric-covered, geodetic construction, powered by two 1,850 h.p. Pratt and Whitney Double Wasp R-2800-S1A4-G, designed by B. N. Wallis and built at Weybridge 1942. Fourteen British civil aircraft only: G-AGEX–'FK, R.A.F. aircraft BV243–BV256, diverted 11.42 for wartime use by British Overseas Airways Corporation on routes to North Africa and the Mediterranean. All transferred to No. 167 Sqn., Holmesley South 8.43. Span, 96 ft. 8½ in. Length, 70 ft. 9 in. A.U.W., 45,000 lb. Max. speed, 260 m.p.h. Cruise, 180 m.p.h.

VICKERS TYPE 490 WELLINGTON T.Mk.10

Navigation trainer of fabric-covered, geodetic construction powered by two 1,650 h.p. Bristol Hercules 16, designed by B. N. Wallis. One temporary British civil aircraft only, G-ALUH, an R.A.F. aircraft RP468, fitted at Langley 1949 with a tail boom radar device and allotted civil status for test flights to the Norwegian coast. C. of A. issued 22.7.49, called at Ringway 8.9.49, returned to the R.A.F. 10.49 as RP468. Span, 86 ft. 2 in. Length (without boom), 60 ft. 10 in.

(W. K. Kilsby Photo)

VICKERS-SUPERMARINE TYPE 236 WALRUS

Three seat amphibian with fabric-covered mainplanes and metal hull (Supermarine built Mk. I) or wooden hull (Saunders-Roe built Mk. II), designed by R. J. Mitchell and powered by one 775 h.p. Bristol Pegasus VI. Seventeen war surplus aircraft converted, or earmarked for conversion for civil use (see Appendix D). None saw real service except G-AHFL–'FO, three of which spotted for whales aboard the S.S. *Balaena* in the Antarctic 1947. G-AHFN, pilot John Grierson, won the Folkestone Trophy at 121 m.p.h., Lympne 31.8.46. Span, 45 ft. 10 in. Length, 37 ft. 7 in. Tare wt., 4,900 lb. A.U.W., 7,200 lb. Max. speed, 135 m.p.h. Cruise, 95 m.p.h.

WESTLAND WHIRLWIND

All-metal, single seat fighter powered by two 885 h.p. Rolls-Royce Peregrine I, 112 built at Yeovil for the R.A.F. 1940–42. One civil aircraft only, G-AGOI, formerly P7048, civilianised at Yeovil by Westland Aircraft Ltd. 1945–46, C. of A. issued 23.10.46, dismantled 5.47. Span, 45 ft. 0 in. Length, 32 ft. 9 in. Tare wt., 7,840 lb. A.U.W., 10,270 lb. Max. speed, 360 m.p.h.

Fairey Ultra Light Helicopter (continued from page 472)
G-AOUK, c/n F.9426, first flown at White Waltham 8.55, fitted with triple tail 1957, withdrawn from use 1958; G-AOUJ, c/n F.9424, modified version built 1956, shown with 'UJ at the S.B.A.C. Shows 9.56 and 9.57, C. of A. issued 30.9.58; G-APJJ, c/n F.9428, shown at the S.B.A.C. Show 9.58, C. of A. issued 2.10.58, evaluated by the Royal Navy with 'UJ 1958. Rotor diameter, 28 ft. 3½ in. Length, 14 ft. 8 in. A.U.W., 1,650 lb. Cruise, 80 m.p.h. Climb, 950 ft./min.

APPENDIX C

This section gives details of aircraft for which illustrations have not been found despite intensive and painstaking search. It also describes those which were not completed and therefore not photographed and also those at present under construction.

The introductory notes to Appendix A apply equally to this section.

FARMAN S-11 SHORTHORN

Two seat pusher biplane powered by one 80 h.p. Renault, designed 1914 by Henri & Maurice Farman. One British civil aircraft only, G-EAAZ, formerly an R.A.F. trainer B4674, built at Hendon by the Aircraft Manufacturing Co. Ltd., August 1917, registered to Major H. S. Shield 3.5.19. Flown from Old Sarum to Squires Gate by the owner in May 1919. Span, 53 ft. 0 in. Length, 30 ft. 8 in. Tare wt., 1,441 lb. A.U.W., 2,046 lb. Max. speed, 66 m.p.h.

FENTON CHEEL

Two seat light aircraft designed and built 1930–31 by J. B. Fenton of Beggar's Roost, Stanmore, Middlesex. One aircraft only, G-ABHZ, c/n F.Mk.1, construction abandoned.

FOKKER D.VII

Single seat fighter powered by one 160 h.p. Mercedes water cooled engine, built for the German Air Force by Fokker Flugzeugwerke, Schwerin, 1918. One British civil aircraft only, G-EANH, registered to J. Forgan Potts 18.9.19, registration cancelled 9.20. Span, 29 ft. $3\frac{1}{2}$ in. Length, 23 ft. 0 in. Tare wt., 1,540 lb. A.U.W., 1,936 lb. Max. speed, 120 m.p.h.

GRAHAME-WHITE G.W.15

Two seat box kite pusher trainer, normally powered by one 80 h.p. Gnôme or 80 h.p. Le Rhône rotary, built by The Grahame-White Aviation Co. Ltd. at Hendon 1916–17. Three civil aircraft only, K-111 to K-113, later G-EABB–'BD, c/n 401–403, registered to the manufacturers 6.5.19. It is probable that they were rebuilt military stock, intended for use by the Grahame-White flying school, but none of the three appears to have actually flown. One flew at Hendon with racing number 24 in September 1919.

GRUMMAN G.73 MALLARD

Commercial amphibian for 10 passengers and two crew, powered by two 600 h.p. Pratt and Whitney Wasp R-1340-S3H1, built by the Grumman Aircraft Engineering Corp'n. at Bethpage, Long Island, New York, U.S.A. 1949. One British aircraft only, G-ALLJ, c/n J-41, C. of A. issued 6.4.49. Registered to the Shell Refining and Marketing Co. Ltd. for ferrying from Amsterdam to Djakarta. Sold on arrival to N.V. Bataafsche Petroleum Maatschappij as PK-AKE. Burned out during maintenance, Djakarta 27.1.51. Span, 66 ft. 8 in. Length, 48 ft. 4 in. Tare wt., 9,350 lb. A.U.W., 12,750 lb. Max. speed, 215 m.p.h. Cruise, 180 m.p.h.

GUNTON SPECIAL

Single seat ultra-light monoplane powered by one 40 h.p. A.B.C. Scorpion, designed and built by T. F. W. Gunton at Spalding, Lincs, 1939. One aircraft only, G-AFRW, c/n T.F.W.G.1, construction not completed. Sold to R. G. Bracewell at Gorleston 5.45 and converted into the Pivot single seat parasol monoplane G-AGOO, construction of which was also not completed. Scrapped 12.46.

HAWKER HEDGEHOG

Three seat fleet reconnaissance aircraft powered by one 382 h.p. Bristol Jupiter IV, built Kingston-on-Thames 1923–24. One prototype only, N187, intended as civil demonstrator. Registration G-EBJN reserved 16.7.24 by H. G. Hawker Engineering Co. Ltd. but not used.

HILLSON PENNINE

Side-by-side, two seat cabin monoplane powered by one 36 h.p. Praga B, designed 1937 by Norman Sykes and built by F. Hills and Sons Ltd., Trafford Park, Manchester. Fitted with an unorthodox control system consisting solely of normal elevator with spoilers on leading edge of wing. One aircraft only, G-AFBX, c/n H.A.100, registered to the manufacturers 27.10.37, construction abandoned.

HOWITT MONOPLANE

Single seat monoplane designed by R. C. Howitt, built at Shelley Road, Oxford, 1937. One aircraft only, G-AEXS, c/n H32D, construction abandoned.

HUNTING H.107

Short-haul transport for two crew and 48–56 passengers, with swept wing and two 6,810 lb. s.t. Bristol Siddeley Orpheus B.Or.12B turbojets mounted externally at the rear of fuselage. One projected aircraft only, for which the registration G-APOH was reserved 7.58. Span, 80 ft. 0 in. Length, 85 ft. 2 in. Tare wt., 22,770 lb. A.U.W., 44,900 lb. Cruise, 500 m.p.h.

KIRBY KITTEN

An unidentified aircraft, c/n 1, registered to the Speedbird Flying Club Ltd. at Denham 11.1.49 as G-ALGA. The existence of an aircraft using a name so well known in gliding circles has never been publicised. It is assumed to have been the dismantled and engineless, single seat, low-wing monoplane resembling an enlarged Tipsy S.2 which was stored at Denham at the time. Diligent investigation failed to reveal anyone with the slightest connection with this aircraft, and the registration was cancelled in May 1953.

MILES M.25 MARTINET

Two seat target tug using many Master 2 components, powered by one 870 h.p. Bristol Mercury 20 engine, 1,724 built by Phillips and Powis Aircraft Ltd. at Woodley from 1942. Five British civil aircraft only, as shown in Appendix D; G-AJJK, 'JL and 'JO registered to D. E. Masters 27.2.47, crated at Hanworth, shipped to Svensk Flygtjänst A.B. 23.5.47; G-AJZB and 'ZC registered to W. S. Shackleton Ltd. 18.6.47, broken up at Bovingdon 3.48. Span, 39 ft. 0 in. Length, 30 ft. 11 in. Tare wt., 4,600 lb. A.U.W., 6,600 lb. Max. speed, 232 m.p.h. Cruise, 225 m.p.h.

MILES M.37 MARTINET TRAINER

Two seat trainer conversion of the Miles M.25 Martinet powered by one 870 h.p. Bristol Mercury 20. One British civil aircraft only, G-AKOS, second prototype, formerly JN668, registered 22.12.47 to L. A. Andrews, trading as the Gloucester Flying Club, Staverton. Not converted for civil use, becoming derelict in an orchard adjacent to the aerodrome in 1949. Specification as standard Martinet.

NORMAN THOMPSON N.T.2B

Two bay, two seat, biplane flying-boat of wooden construction powered by one 160 h.p. Beardmore driving a pusher airscrew. One British civil aircraft only, G-EAQO, formerly an Admiralty trainer N2290, built 1918 by the Norman Thompson Flight Co. Ltd. at Bognor, Sussex. Believed to have been the aircraft exhibited at Harrods, Knightsbridge, by Handley Page Ltd. 3.19. Registered to Handley Page Ltd. 9.1.20, sold abroad 1.21. Span, 48 ft. 4¾ in. Length, 27 ft. 4½ in.

NORMAN THOMPSON N.T.4A

Three seat coastal and training biplane flying-boat of wooden construction, powered by two 200 h.p. Hispano-Suiza engines driving pusher airscrews. One civil aircraft only, G-EAOY, formerly N2155, built 1917 by the Norman Thompson Flight Co. Ltd. at Bognor, Sussex. Registered to Handley Page Ltd. 29.10.19, believed not civilianised. Span, 78 ft. 7 in. Length, 41 ft. 6 in. Tare wt., 4,572 lb. A.U.W., 6,469 lb. Max. speed, 95 m.p.h.

PARMENTIER WEE MITE

Two seater powered by one 35 h.p. A.B.C. Scorpion, designed and built in Guernsey 1932 by Messrs. Noel and Parmentier. One aircraft only, c/n 1, trial hops from the sands of Vazon Bay 4.33, metal airscrew burst, damaging the front fuselage. Rebuilt with lengthened fuselage, 18 in. of wing sweep back and 40 h.p. Salmson A.D.9 radial. Successfully flown round the island by C. W. Noel for 50 minutes 9.33. Registered G-ACRL 24.4.34, dismantled 3.36. (With Salmson engine.) Span, 31 ft. 0 in. Length, 20 ft. 0 in. Tare wt., 650 lb. A.U.W., 970 lb. Max. speed, 92 m.p.h. Cruise, 75 m.p.h.

PARNALL PETO

Two seat reconnaissance biplane of fabric-covered, stainless steel construction powered by one 135 h.p. Armstrong Siddeley Mongoose or one 120 h.p. Bristol Lucifer IV, fitted with twin metal floats for operation from the submarine *M.2*. Two prototypes N181 and N182 and six production aircraft commencing N255 built by George Parnall and Company at Yate 1929–30. An unidentified Peto was acquired in 1934 for civil use as G-ACOJ by F. C. H. Allen of Selsey, Sussex. Stored at Ford Aerodrome during 1935 but not converted. Span, 28 ft. 5 in. Length, 22 ft. 6½ in. Tare wt., 1,300 lb. A.U.W., 1,950 lb. Max. speed, 113 m.p.h.

PETERBOROUGH GUARDIAN

Side-by-side, two seat, cabin monoplane with tricycle undercarriage, powered by one 90 h.p. Blackburn Cirrus Minor I, designed by J. H. Payne for the Peterborough Aero Club, 1939. One aircraft only, G-AFZT, c/n G.1, completion abandoned due to the outbreak of war, unfinished airframe transferred to Slingsby Sailplanes Ltd., Kirbymoorside. Span, 33 ft. 4 in. Length, 23 ft. 4 in. A.U.W., 1,350 lb. Max. speed, 120 m.p.h. Cruise, 100 m.p.h.

POBJOY PIRATE

Two seat light aeroplane powered by one Pobjoy radial. The prototype, G-ADEY, c/n 101, partially built by Pobjoy Airmotors and Aircraft Ltd. at Rochester Airport, Kent 1935–36 but construction abandoned 5.36. No details were released.

PORTSMOUTH AEROCAR MINOR

Twin boom, high-wing monoplane with retractable undercarriage, powered by two 90 h.p. Blackburn Cirrus Minor 2, seating pilot and four passengers in a pod type fuselage. Prototype G-AGNJ, c/n 1, partially constructed by Portsmouth Aviation Ltd. at Portsmouth City Airport 1946. Completion abandoned 1947. Span, 42 ft. 0 in. Length, 25 ft. 7 in. A.U.W., 3,450 lb. Max. speed, 131 m.p.h. Cruise, 120 m.p.h.

R.A.E. SIROCCO

Single seat, ultra light monoplane powered by one 32 h.p. Bristol Cherub III, designed by the Royal Aircraft Establishment Aero Club, Farnborough, Hants, in 1926. One aircraft only, G-EBNL, c/n 3, registered 26.1.26, as a projected entry for the Grosvenor Trophy Race, Lympne, 18.9.26. Non-starter, completion abandoned.

SALMON TANDEM MONOPLANE

Single seat, ultra light monoplane powered by one $3\frac{1}{2}$ h.p. Bradshaw, designed and built at Farnborough by Percy Salmon. One aircraft only, G-EBHQ, registered to the designer 11.8.23, construction completed 9.23. A.U.W., 445 lb.

SHORT S.32

Projected long range transport for 16 day or 12 night passengers, with alternative high-density layout for 24, powered by four 1,250 h.p. Bristol Hercules, designed by Arthur Gouge for construction at Rochester by Short Bros. (Rochester and Bedford) Ltd. Three prototypes G-AFMK–'MM, c/n S.1022–4, one of which was to have been pressurised for high-altitude operation, registered to the Secretary of State for Air 19.12.38. Construction abandoned due to the manufacturer's preoccupation with Stirling production. (Standard model) Span, 127 ft. 0 in. Length, 89 ft. 0 in. Tare wt., 39,050 lb. A.U.W., 71,000 lb. Max. speed, 275 m.p.h. Cruise, 246 m.p.h. Range, 3,420 miles. (High altitude) Tare wt., 41,310 lb. Max. speed, 331 m.p.h. Cruise, 275 m.p.h. Range, 3,370 miles.

SOPWITH 1½ STRUTTER

Two seat day bomber of fabric-covered, wooden construction, in large-scale production by The Sopwith Aviation Co. Ltd., Canbury Park Road, Kingston-on-Thames, and numerous sub-contractors from 1915. One civil aircraft only, G-EAVB, c/n 3541, converted to three seater and powered by one 130 h.p. Clerget rotary, registered to C. H. Oliver 7.8.20. Span, 33 ft. 6 in. Length, 25 ft. 3 in. Tare wt., 1,305 lb. A.U.W., 2,200 lb. Max. speed, 100 m.p.h.

SOPWITH 5F.1 DOLPHIN

Single seat fighter biplane with backward stagger powered by one 200 h.p. Hispano-Suiza, in large-scale production 1917–18. One civil aircraft only, G-EATC, a surplus R.A.F. machine D5369 built by Hooper and Co. Ltd. Registered to Handley Page Ltd. 7.5.20 for demonstration and overseas ferrying by the Aircraft Disposal Company Ltd. Span, 32 ft. 6 in. Length, 22 ft. 3 in. Tare wt., 1,406 lb. A.U.W., 1,911 lb. Max. speed, 131·5 m.p.h.

SUPERMARINE SOUTHAMPTON II

Five seat reconnaissance flying-boat with metal hull and fabric-covered wooden wings, powered by two 500 h.p. Napier Lion V, in production at the Supermarine Aviation Works, Woolston, Southampton, 1925–28. One British civil aircraft only, G-AASH, c/n 1235, C. of A. issued 12.11.29, an R.A.F. flying-boat loaned to Imperial Airways Ltd. for the carriage of mail between Genoa and Alexandria during the three month gap between the loss of Short Calcutta G-AADN and the delivery of its replacement G-AASJ. The Southampton returned to the R.A.F. at Lee-on-Solent 3.30. Span, 75 ft. 0 in. Length, 51 ft. 1½ in. Tare wt., 9,000 lb. A.U.W., 15,200 lb. Max. speed, 108 m.p.h. Cruise, 83 m.p.h.

VICKERS-SUPERMARINE TYPE 179

All-metal transport monoplane flying-boat for seven crew and 40 day passengers, powered by six Rolls-Royce Buzzard. One aircraft only, G-ABLE, c/n 1316, design commenced 8.29, keel laid 1931, registered to the Air Council 7.4.31, construction abandoned. Span, 165 ft. 0 in.

TAYLOR EXPERIMENTAL

Two seater of fabric-covered metal construction, powered by one 90 h.p. Cirrus Minor I, incorporating many untried features such as lattice girder wing spars and a system of diagonal surface bracing. One aircraft only, G-AEPX, c/n T.E.2, designed and built at Hamsey Green Aerodrome, Surrey, 1936 by Richard Taylor, who was killed when the wings failed on its first flight 7.1.37. Two similar aircraft: G-AEPY, c/n T.E.3, a single seater and G-AEPZ, c/n T.E.4, two seater, were registered 7.12.36 but not built. Registration G-AERA was reserved for a fourth Taylor Experimental.

VICKERS F.B.14

Two seat, single bay, fighter-reconnaissance biplane powered by one 160 h.p. Beardmore, built by Vickers Ltd. and first flown 8.16. Total production 150 aircraft. Two civil machines only: G-EAAS and 'AT, c/n C.103 and C.102, registered to Vickers Ltd. 1.5.19 and 13.5.19 respectively. Registrations cancelled 7.19. It is probable that these aircraft were never converted for civil use. Span, 39 ft. 6 in. Length, 28 ft. 5 in. Tare wt., 1,662 lb. A.U.W., 2,603 lb. Max. speed, 99·5 m.p.h.

VICKERS F.B.19

Single seat, single bay, fighter biplane powered variously by the 100 h.p. Gnôme 110 h.p. Le Rhône and 110 h.p. Clerget rotary engines, built by Vickers Ltd. and first flown 8.19. One civil aircraft only, G-EAAU, c/n C.104, registered to Vickers Ltd. 13.5.19, registration cancelled 7.19, believed not civilianised. Span, 24 ft. 0 in. Length, 18 ft. 2 in. In the absence of information on the precise mark number of this aircraft, no further details can be given.

VICKERS TYPE 196 JOCKEY III

Single seat fighter of metal construction powered by one 530 h.p. Bristol Jupiter VIIF. Registration G-AAWG, reserved by Vickers Ltd. 5.4.33 for projected aircraft, c/n 1, which was never built.

VICKERS TYPE 473 WARWICK V

Coastal reconnaissance version of the Warwick produced in 1944 to carry a crew of six and powered by two 2,520 h.p. Bristol Centaurus VII. One civil aircraft only, G-AGLD, former R.A.F. aircraft PN703, C. of A. issued 17.10.44, loaned to the B.O.A.C. Development Flight at Hurn as a Centaurus VII test bed. Flown to South Africa 10.45, broken up at Wisley 10.46. Span, 96 ft. 8½ in. Length, 70 ft. 6 in. A.U.W., 50,000 lb. Max. speed, 290 m.p.h.

VICKERS-SUPERMARINE TYPE 300 SPITFIRE IB

Single seat fighter of all-metal, monocoque construction, armed with four machine guns and two cannon, powered by one 1,030 h.p. Rolls-Royce Merlin II, designed by R. J. Mitchell, 1,566 built for the R.A.F. 1937–39. Civil marks G-AIST reserved 25.10.46 for one aircraft, AR213, by Gp. Capt. (now Air Commodore) A. H. Wheeler. Currently stored, dismantled and unconverted, at Old Warden, Beds. Span, 36 ft. 10 in. Length, 29 ft. 11 in. A.U.W., 5,820 lb. Max. speed, 355 m.p.h.

WESTLAND WAPITI I

Two seat, general-purpose biplane of fabric-covered, metal construction powered by one 550 h.p. Bristol Jupiter XFA, built by the Westland Aircraft Works Ltd. at Yeovil 1931. One civil aircraft only, G-ABUY, c/n WA.2298c, registered to the manufacturers 9.3.32, transferred to the R.A.F. 12.32. Span, 46 ft. 5 in. Length, 32 ft. 6 in. Tare wt., 3,180 lb. A.U.W., 5,400 lb. Max. speed, 135 m.p.h. Cruise, 110 m.p.h.

WESTLAND WESSEX I

Transport helicopter for two crew, 12 passengers and baggage, powered by one 1,450 s.h.p. Napier Gazelle N.Ga.13 turbine. Based on the Sikorsky S-58 and built by Westland Aircraft Ltd. at Yeovil, Somerset. Registration G-APLF reserved by the manufacturers 2.58 for civil demonstrator, c/n WA.53, not yet constructed. Rotor diameter, 56 ft. 0 in. Length, 65 ft. 9½ in. Tare wt., 8,350 lb. A.U.W., 12,600 lb. Cruise, 127 m.p.h. Range, 630 miles.

WREN GOLDCREST

Single seat, ultra light, low-wing monoplane powered by one 25 h.p. Scott Squirrel designed by R. G. Carr and built by the Wren Aircraft Co. Ltd. at Kirklinton, Carlisle, 1946. One aircraft only, G-AICX, c/n 1, registered to the designer 13.8.46, scrapped 1947. Span, 23 ft. 0 in. Length, 16 ft. 8 in. Tare wt., 370 lb. A.U.W., 580 lb. Max. speed, 98 m.p.h. Cruise, 75 m.p.h.

APPENDIX D

Individual Aircraft Histories

Every single aircraft of every main type and variant is listed herein. In the case of aircraft built in limited numbers, it has been possible to include precise details on individual constructor's number, registration, date of issue of Certificate of Airworthiness and disposal.

Where blocks of allocated registrations are quoted for the more popular aircraft types, the order given is that in which they were constructed, in preference to an alphabetical listing of registration markings.

Constructor's No. and Registration	C. of A. Issued	Remarks

EDGAR PERCIVAL E.P.9

20	G-AOFU	30.10.56	Prototype, operated by Air Ads Ltd., Stapleford
21	G-APCR	9. 9.57	Crashed near Tripoli, Libya, 8.58
23	G-AOZY	14. 2.57	Crashed at Mesmerode near Wunsdorf 6.5.57
24	G-AFCS	26. 7.57	Bahamas Helicopters (U.K.) Ltd., Libya
25	G-APCT	26. 7.57	,, ,, ,,
26	G-APBF	14. 5.57	To Ernst Lund A.G. 11.57 as D-EDUV
27	G-APAD	23. 4.57	Sold in Australia 9.58
28	G-APBR	29. 5.57	To Super Spread Av. Pty. Ltd. 10.57 as VH-SSV
29	G-AOZO*	6. 3.57	British demonstrator
32	G-APFY	17. 9.57	To Super Spread Av. Pty. Ltd. 10.57 as VH-SSW
33	G-APIA	15.10.57	To Skyspread Ltd., Australia 5.58 as VH-FBY
34	G-APIB	11.10.57	To Skyspread Ltd., Australia 5.58 as VH-FBZ
35	G-APLP	31. 3.58	Forced landed, Blackpool beach 15.7.59, submerged by tide
41	G-APWX*	22.10.59	Current demonstration aircraft

* Redesignated Lancashire Prospector Type E.P.9.

FAIRCHILD 24

2718	G-AECO	14. 4.36	Model 24C8-C impressed 10.40 as BK869
3126	G-AEOU	9.11.36	Model 24C8-F impressed 10.40 as BS817
3120	G-AFFK	10. 6.38	Model 24C8-F impressed 7.41 as EF523
2817	G-AFKW	17. 3.39	Model 24C8-E impressed 14.10.40

FAIRCHILD 24W-41A ARGUS 2

Allocation: G-AITG, 'XC, 'XM, 'YO, 'ZE; G-AJAT, 'BF, 'DO, 'DT, 'FY, 'GW, 'LB, 'MY, 'NN, 'OW–'PE, 'PI, 'RZ–'SB, 'SG, 'SH, 'SM–'SY, 'TR, 'VI, 'VM, 'XA; G-AKCJ, 'FN, 'GW, 'IZ–'JB, 'JK–'JM; G-AMAZ

FAIRCHILD 24R ARGUS 3

1130	G-AJDD	nil	F. Bosworth, burned out at Bahrein 18.4.49
960	G-AKPX	nil	R. L. Whyham, sold in Finland 6.50 as OH-FCA
1146	G-AMBA	nil	Gulf Aviation Co. Ltd., withdrawn 1952

FAIREY III to IIIF

F.127	K-103	nil	III, later G-EAAJ, to Norway 5.20 as N-20

F.128	G-EALQ	nil	III, 1919 Schneider Trophy, amphibian in 1920
F.246	G-EADZ	nil	IIIA, 3 seater, Navarro Aviation Co.
F.246	G-EAMY	nil	IIIC, formerly G-EADZ, to Sweden, crashed 8.20
F.302	G-EAPV	nil	IIIC, sold in Sweden 12.20
F.333	G-EARS	nil	IIIC, two seat seaplane demonstrator
F.33(c)*	G-EBDI	nil	IIIC, W. T. Blake, sunk Gulf of Assam 25.8.22
F.576	G-EBKE	17.10.24	IIID, Eagle IX, scrapped in British Guiana 1929
Not given	G-EBPZ	5. 2.27	IIID, Lion, damaged beyond repair 30.4.27
F.1129	G-AABY	27. 7.29	IIIF, Lion, sold in Australia 4.35 as VH-UTT
F.1272	G-AASK	20.12.29	IIIF, Jaguar, withdrawn from use 1934
F.1315	G-AATT	5. 2.30	IIIF, Jaguar, crashed 10.30

* As documented. True c/n painted on aircraft appeared to be F.336.

FAIREY FOX I

(Former R.A.F. serial given in Column 4)

FA.35756*	G-ACAS	23. 3.33		Caught fire in the air, burned out on landing, Littlehampton, 14.7.33
F.856	G-ACXO	17. 9.34	J7950	Sold in New Guinea 1935 as VH-UTR
F.876	G-ACXX	18.10.34	J8424	Crashed and burned out at Apulia, Italy 20.10.34

* As documented. Believed to be fuselage part number.

FOKKER F.III to F.XII

(Former registration given in Column 5)

4938	G-EBPL	nil	F.VIIA	H-NADH	F. E. Guest, crashed 1.27, remains sold to K.L.M.
4982	G-EBPV	nil	F.VIIA/3m	H-NADS	F. E. Guest, sold abroad 3.27
5023	G-EBTQ	24. 8.27	F.VIIA	H-NAEC	'St. Raphael', lost 31.8.27
4953	G-EBTS	2. 9.27	F.VIIA	H-NADK	'Princess Xenia'/'The Spider'
422	G-EBUT	16.11.27	F.XI	NC3199	To Australia 12.35 as VH-UTO
5063	G-EBYI	30. 5.28	F.VIIA/3m	H-NAEK	D. H. Drew, sold abroad 3.30
5087	G-EBZJ	7. 7.28	F.VIIA/3m	H-NAEL	A. P. Holt, sold abroad 10.30
Not given	G-AADZ	8. 2.29	F.VIIB/3m	H-NADP	V. L. B. Ltd., sold abroad 12.30

Constructor's No. and Registration		C. of A. Issued			Remarks

FOKKER F.III to F.XII (contd.)

1558	G-AALC	23. 8.29	F.III	T-DOFF	Delivered Amsterdam–Croydon 7.8.29; crashed Croydon 11.9.29
Not given	G-AARG	12.10.29	F.III	T-DOFC	Delivered Copenhagen–Croydon 17.9.29; scrapped 12.31
5206	G-AATG	10. 2.30	F.VIIC/3m	PH-AGW	W. Z. Ltd., sold abroad 6.35
5284	G-ADZH	23. 3.36	F.XII	PH-AFV	Sold in Spain 8.36
5285	G-ADZI	31. 1.36	F.XII	PH-AFU	,, ,,
5292	G-ADZJ	8. 1.36	F.XII	PH-AIE	,, ,,
5301	G-ADZK	7. 2.36	F.XII	PH-AII	,, ,,
4984	G-AEHE	*nil*	F.VIIA	PH-ADX	Sold 12.36 as PH-EHE
4952	G-AEHF	*nil*	F.VIIA	PH-ADN	Sold abroad 12.36
5291	G-AEOS	3.11.36	F.XII	PH-AID	Scrapped 6.40
5300	G-AEOT	3.11.36	F.XII	PH-AIH	Crashed Gatwick 19.11.36
5043	G-AEPT	13. 1.37	F.VIII	PH-AEF	Withdrawn 5.38
5046	G-AEPU	21. 5.37	F.VIII	PH-AEI	Sold in Sweden 4.39 as SE-AHA

FORD TRIMOTOR

(Original American identity given in Column 5)

4AT-61	G-ABEF	15.10.30	4AT-E	NC9678	To New Guinea 6.35 as VH-UDY, impressed 1942 as A45-2
5AT-68	G-ABFF	15.10.30	5AT-C	NC409H	Re-registered 1.31 as G-ABHF
5AT-68	G-ABHF	15.10.30	5AT-C		To New Guinea 12.34 as VH-UTB
5AT-60	G-ABHO	20.12.30	5AT-C	NC401H	To New Guinea 6.35 as VH-UBI, impressed 1942 as A45-1
5AT-170	G-ACAE	13. 4.33	5AT-D	NC440H	Hon. A. E. Guinness, to R.A.F. 4.40
4AT-68	G-ACAK	8. 4.33	4AT-E	NC8406	Formerly EC-KKA, to New Guinea 12.34 as VH-USX

FOSTER WIKNER WICKO G.M.1

1	G-AENU	19. 9.36	Prototype, converted to F.W.2, scrapped at Plymouth 1952
2	G-AEZZ	8. 9.37	F.W.3 converted to G.M.1, impressed 7.41 as ES943
4	G-AFAZ	19. 9.38	Bristol Club, impressed 5.41 as ES924
5	G-AFJB	1.11.38	Impressed 4.41 as DR613, restored 16.10.45, currently flying

6	G-AFKS	5. 1.39	Impressed 8.42 as HM574, scrapped at Eastleigh 9.46
7	G-AFKU	14. 6.39	Impressed 6.41 as ES947
8	G-AFKK	3. 7.39	Impressed 5.41 as ES913
9	G-AFVK	*nil*	Impressed 10.41 as HM499
11	G-AGPE	4. 4.46	Scrapped at Eastleigh 5.49 after accident

GENERAL AIRCRAFT MONOSPAR ST-3 AND ST-4 Mk. I

(Last owner given in Remarks Column for all Monospar type aircraft)

S.S.1	G-AARP	21. 7.31	ST-3; scrapped at Hanworth 9.32
1	G-ABUZ	27. 7.32	P. Bailey, Croydon; scrapped during the war
2	G-ABVN	19. 8.32	C. Kelman, Heston; scrapped at Sydney, Australia 1954
3	G-ABVO	22.10.32	Sold to Maharajah of Patiala 11.34 as VT-ADT
4	G-ABVP	12. 8.32	Ace Air Services, Speke; impressed 5.40 as X9434
5	G-ABVR	14.11.32	Sold to W. Hocklin, Switzerland 11.32 as CH-347
6	G-ABVS	26. 1.33	Yapton Aero Club, scrapped 1939

GENERAL AIRCRAFT MONOSPAR ST-4 Mk. II

8	G-ACCO	2. 3.33	G. H. Ambler; impressed 31.3.40 as X9376, later DR849
10	G-ACCP	17. 3.33	Lundy and Atlantic Coast Air Lines; scrapped during the war
11	G-ACEW	6. 4.33	Highland Airways Ltd. 'Inverness', crashed 12.37
12	G-ACFR	13. 4.33	Herts and Essex Aero Club, scrapped 1936
15	G-ACHS	12. 5.33	Asiatic Petroleum Co. Ltd., Cairo; sold 4.34
17	G-ACGM	31. 5.33	General Aircraft Ltd., cancelled 10.33
18	G-ACHU	13. 6.33	R. G. Cazalet, converted to ST-6
19	G-ACJF	3. 8.33	G. S. Davison, scrapped at Heston 1945
21	G-ACJE	18. 8.33	International Air Lines Ltd.; to Italy 12.34 as I-AGAR
26	G-ADBY	9. 3.35	General Aircraft Ltd., to S. Africa 8.36 as ZS-AHE
27	G-ADIK	4. 6.35	Commercial Air Hire Ltd., crashed 5.36
28	G-ADJP	29. 6.35	R. K. Dundas Ltd., impressed 3.40 as X9343
29	G-ACKT	25.11.33	Crashed at Thrupp's Farm, Lidlington, 5.12.33
30	G-ADLM	22. 7.35	Fatal crash on take off, Croydon, 16.5.36

GENERAL AIRCRAFT MONOSPAR ST-6

14	G-ACGI	1. 7.33	Southern Airways Ltd., impressed 5.40 as AV979
18	G-ACHU	13. 6.33	Murphy Bros., Wolverhampton, scrapped during war
20	G-ACIC	21. 7.33	Romford Flying Club, burned at Maylands 6.2.40

GENERAL AIRCRAFT MONOSPAR ST-10 AND ST-12

32	G-ACTS	3. 7.34	ST-10, impressed 4.40 as X9453
35	G-ADBN	1. 3.35	Air Dispatch Ltd., impressed 11.8.40 as BD150
39	G-ADDY	8. 4.35	R. J. B. Seaman, sold abroad 12.36
40	G-ADDZ	9. 4.35	Demonstrator, sold abroad 6.37
45	G-ADLL	19. 7.35	G. O. E. Roberts, impressed 27.3.40 as X9341

GENERAL AIRCRAFT MONOSPAR ST-25 JUBILEE

46	G-ADIV	21. 6.35	Prototype; crashed and sank, Wigtown Bay, 11.8.36
47	G-ADMC	23. 7.35	Marshalls Flying School, sold abroad 10.38
49	G-ADMD	4. 7.35	H. R. d'Erlanger; crashed 2.1.37
50	G-ADLT	2. 8.35	Sold in France 5.37 as F-AQAC
51	G-ADNM	9. 8.35	Sold in Netherlands 9.35 as PH-IPM
52	G-ADNN	22. 8.35	Aircraft Exchange & Mart Ltd., sold in Kenya 12.36 as VP-KCB
53	G-ADMZ	17. 9.35	Sir M. Assheton-Smith, to Spain 6.36 as EC-AFF
54	G-ADPI	5. 9.35	Hubert Holliday, Hanworth; to Spanish civil war 8.36
55	G-ADPK	9. 9.35	P.S. and I.O.W., impressed 3.40 as X9348, later DR848
57	G-ADPL	19. 9.35	P.S. and I.O.W., impressed 3.40 as X9369
58	G-ADPM	1.10.35	Burned out in hangar fire at Hooton 11.7.40
59	G-ADTE	1.10.35	Mrs. Ursula Lloyd; crashed 4.37
61	G-ADVG	16.10.35	Aircraft Exchange & Mart Ltd., to Spanish civil war 8.36
62	G-ADVH	25.10.35	F/Lt. G. Shaw, Thornaby; impressed 3.40 as X9365
63	G-ADWH	6.11.35	Sold in France by makers 5.37 as F-AQAD
64	G-ADWI	29.10.35	Sold in France by makers 6.37 as F-AQCL

71	G-AHBK	6. 6.46	Ex K8308; N. L. Hayman, Fairoaks; crashed near Cirencester 2.6.47
72	G-AEDY	12. 3.36	Converted via de Luxe to Universal 1936
73	G-ADYN	4. 2.36	Williams and Co.; impressed 3.40 as X9373
75	G-AEAT	21. 4.36	Aerial Sites Ltd., crashed Brasted, Kent 16.3.38
80	G-AEGX	8. 5.36	Dennis Corrigan; sold abroad 3.37

GENERAL AIRCRAFT MONOSPAR ST-25 UNIVERSAL

72	G-AEDY	12. 3.36	Utility Airways, scrapped at Hooton 1940
77	G-AEVN	15. 3.37	Ambulance; N. Montefiore, cancelled 1.39
78	G-AEWN	28. 4.37	Ambulance; R. B. Pickett, cancelled 12.37
79	G-AESS	19. 5.37	General Aircraft Ltd., cancelled 1943
82	G-AEJB	29. 7.36	A. Besse and Co. (Aden) Ltd., scrapped during war
83	G-AEJV	22. 6.36	W. E. Davies, crashed at Lympne 12.3.38
84	G-AEJW	11. 7.36	Sold in New Zealand 12.36 as ZK-AFF
87	G-AEPG	19.11.36	Sold in France 6.38 as F-AQOM
88	G-AEMN	25. 9.36	General Aircraft Ltd., sold abroad 11.36
89	G-AGDN	29. 9.36	Ex CF-BAH; C. G. M. Alington, scrapped 1.47
93	G-AEGY	15. 5.36	J. W. Adamson; impressed 3.40 as X9377
94	G-AEPA	4.12.36	Blackpool Flying Services Ltd., impressed 3.40 as X9372
95	G-AEYF	8. 6.37	Ambulance demonstrator, sold abroad 3.39
96	G-AFBM	1.10.37	Freighter, sold in Canada by makers 11.37
97	G-AFBN	1.10.37	,, ,, ,,
98	G-AFDE	16.12.37	General Aircraft Ltd., sold abroad 1.38
99	G-AFIP	12. 7.38	General Aircraft Ltd., impressed 3.40 as X9333
100	G-AFIV	31. 3.39	General Aircraft Ltd., impressed 3.40 as X9334
101	G-AFSA	22. 4.39	General Aircraft Ltd., impressed 3.40 as X9331
102	G-AFSB	22. 4.39	General Aircraft Ltd., impressed 3.40 as X9330
103	G-AFWP	5. 8.39	General Aircraft Ltd., impressed 3.40 as X9335

527

GENERAL AIRCRAFT G.A.L.42 CYGNET II

0001	G-AEMA	2. 9.37	Converted C.W. design, scrapped during war
109	G-AFVR	5. 7.39	Impressed as HL539, currently flying
110	G-AGAL	17. 2.41	Impressed as DG566, with No. 24 Sqn. in 1941
112	G-AGAW	28. 9.40	To Werner J. Hein, Brazil 3.41
113	G-AGBA	13. 6.41	Impressed as HM495, melted down at Kirby, Lancs., 16.1.57
114	G-AGAX	7.11.44	Crashed Midhope Common, near Barnsley, 4.4.55
117	G-AGAS	12. 9.40	To T. L. Bridges, Argentina, 8.41 as LV-FAH
118	G-AGAU	24. 9.46	Crashed at Cowes 28.8.49

HANDLEY PAGE 0/400

(Former R.A.F. serial given in Column 4; key to manufacturer at end)

nil	G-EAAE	1. 5.19	D8350	'Vulture', scrapped 8.20	(1)
nil	G-EAAF	1. 5.19	F5414	Converted into H.P.0/7	(1)
nil	G-EAAG	1. 5.19	F5418	'Penguin', crashed 4.20	(1)
nil	G-EAAW	1. 5.19	F5417	Withdrawn at census 10.1.23	(1)
HP-16	G-EAKE	25. 8.19	J2252	Crashed near Stockholm 6.20	(2)
nil	G-EAKF	10.10.19	J2249	Scrapped 10.20	(2)
HP-20	G-EAKG	6. 9.19	J2250	Scrapped 8.20	(2)
HP-21	G-EALX	31.10.19	J2251	Crashed 4.21	(2)
HP-24	G-EALY	17.10.19	J2247	Scrapped 10.20	(2)
HP-23	G-EALZ	23.12.19	J2243	Scrapped 10.20	(2)
HP-26	G-EAMB	23.12.19	D4623	Scrapped 10.20	(2)
HP-27	G-EAMC	28. 1.20	D4624	Crashed in the Sudan 25.2.20	(2)
HP-28	G-EAMD	1.12.19	D4633	Sold to Polish Government 11.20	(2)
HP-33	G-EASO	*nil*	D5444	Lion engines, dismantled 4.21	(3)

HANDLEY PAGE 0/7

nil	G-EAAF	14. 8.19	F5414	Withdrawn at census 10.1.23	(1)
HP-1	K-162	8. 8.19		Later G-EAGN, not taken up	
HP-25	G-EAMA	7.11.19	J2248	Crashed at Golders Green 14.12.20	(2)
HP-7	G-EANV	2.10.19		'Commando', to South Africa 9.20	

HP-11	G-EAPA	9.12.19		Sold abroad 1.21	
HP-12	G-EAPB	23. 4.20		,, ,,	
HP-10	G-EAQZ	18. 2.20		Sold abroad 2.21	

HANDLEY PAGE o/10

HP-34	G-EASX	15.10.20	F308	Sold abroad 4.21	(3)
HP-35	G-EASY	23. 6.20	D4614	,, ,,	(2)
HP-36	G-EASZ	25. 6.20	F310	,, ,,	(3)
HP-37	G-EATG	23. 6.20	D4618	Withdrawn from use 1922	(2)
HP-38	G-EATH	30. 6.20	D4631	Withdrawn from use 9.23	(2)
HP-39	G-EATJ	25. 6.20	F307	Withdrawn from use 1922	(3)
HP-40	G-EATK	15. 7.20	J2262	Jupiter installation, scrapped 11.22	(2)
HP-41	G-EATL	30. 8.20	F312	Withdrawn from use 5.22	(3)
HP-42	G-EATM	30. 7.20	D4609	Withdrawn from use 1.22	(2)
HP-43	G-EATN	13. 7.20	J2261	Withdrawn from use 5.22	(2)

HANDLEY PAGE o/11

*	G-EASL	26. 3.20	C9699	Crashed 4.20	(1)
*	G-EASM	26. 3.20	C9731	Withdrawn from use 4.21	(1)
*	G-EASN	23. 6.20	D4611	Withdrawn from use 4.21	(2)

* Conversion numbers not recorded.

HANDLEY PAGE W8 to W10

W8-1	G-EAPJ	7. 8.20	Prototype, crashed 22.11.23
W8a	G-EAVJ	*nil*	Registered 6.9.20, not built
W8-2	G-EBBG	9. 6.22	'Princess Mary', crashed at Abbeville 15.2.28
W8-3	G-EBBH	10. 6.22	'Prince George', scrapped 2.31
W8-4	G-EBBI	30. 6.22	'Prince Henry', scrapped 10.32
W8-7	G-EBIX	27. 6.24	'City of Washington', crashed Boulogne 30.10.30
W9-1	G-EBLE	20. 1.26	'City of New York', to New Guinea 10.29 as VH-ULK
W10-1	G-EBMM	5. 3.26	'City of Melbourne', crashed at Ashton Clinton 24.9.34
W10-2	G-EBMR	9. 3.26	'City of Pretoria', sold abroad 11.34
W10-3	G-EBMS	9. 3.26	'City of London', crashed in Channel 21.10.26
W10-4	G-EBMT	13. 3.26	'City of Ottawa', crashed in Channel 17.6.29
1	G-ACDO	*nil*	Formerly OO-AHJ, scrapped at Ford 1934

HANDLEY PAGE H.P.42

42/1	G-AAGX	5. 6.31	'Hannibal', lost at sea 1.3.40
42/4	G-AAUC	19. 9.31	'Horsa', delivery to R.A.F. 31.5.40
42/3	G-AAUD	30. 7.31	'Hanno', wrecked at Whitchurch 19.3.40
42/2	G-AAUE	10. 7.31	'Hadrian', impressed 8.40 as AS982

529

HANDLEY PAGE H.P.42 (contd.)

42/5	G-AAXC	31. 8.31	'Heracles', wrecked at Whitchurch 19.3.40
42/6	G-AAXD	13.11.31	'Horatius', wrecked at Tiverton 7.11.39
42/7	G-AAXE	10.12.31	'Hengist', burned out at Karachi 31.5.37
42/8	G-AAXF	31.12.31	'Helena', delivery to R.A.F. 8.6.40

HANDLEY PAGE H.P.61 HALIFAX B.Mk.3

(Former R.A.F. serial given in lieu of constructor's number)

NR169	G-AGXA	16. 5.46	Sold in Australia 7.47 as VH-BDT
NA684	G-AJPG	*nil*	Instructional airframe, scrapped Cranfield 12.48

HANDLEY PAGE H.P.61 HALIFAX B.Mk.6

Allocation: G-AIBG; G-AJBE, 'SZ, 'TX–'UB; G-AKAP, 'AW, 'BI, 'JI, 'JJ, 'LI–'LK, 'NG–'NL, 'UT, 'UU; G-ALCD, 'CY, 'CZ, 'DZ–'EE, 'OM

HANDLEY PAGE H.P.70 HALIFAX C.Mk.8

Allocation: G-AGFC, 'TK; G-AHKK, 'VT, 'WL–'WN, 'YH, 'YI, 'ZJ–'ZO; G-AIAN–'AS, 'HU–'HY, 'ID, 'LO, 'OH, 'OI, 'TC, 'WI–'WR, 'WT, 'ZO; G-AJBK, 'BL, 'CG, 'NT–'NZ, 'PJ, 'PK, 'XD, 'ZY, 'ZZ; G-AKAC, 'AD, 'BA, 'BB, 'BJ, 'BK, 'BP, 'BR, 'CT, 'EC, 'GN–'GP, 'GZ, 'IE, 'JF, 'XT; G-ALBS–'BV, 'BZ, 'CX, 'EF

London Aero and Motor Services Ltd. fleet 1947

G-AHZJ	Port of Marseilles	G-AIWK	Port of Sydney (2)
G-AHZK	Port of Naples	G-AIWM	Merchant Venturer
G-AHZL	Port of Oslo	G-AIWN	Port of Darwin
G-AHZO	Port of London	G-AIWR	Port of Durban
G-AIWJ	Port of Athens	G-AIWT	Port of Sydney (1)

Lancashire Aircraft Corporation Ltd. fleet 1947–1950

G-AHWN	Air Viceroy	G-AJZY	Air Monarch
G-AHYH	Air Merchant II	G-AJZZ	*nil*
G-AIHU	Air Adventurer	G-AKBJ	Air Ambassador
G-AIHV	Air Trader	G-AKBK	Air Enterprise
G-AIHX	Air Merchant	G-AKEC	Air Voyager
G-AIHY	Air Explorer	G-AKXT	Air Rover
G-AILO	Air Courier	G-ALBZ	*nil*
		G-ALCX	Air Regent

HANDLEY PAGE H.P.70 HALTON

(Former Royal Air Force serial given in Column 4)

1398	G-AGZP	20. 3.46	PP336	Series 2, scrapped at Bovingdon 3.53
1308	G-AHDL	18. 9.46	PP224	'Fitzroy', crashed at Gatow 1.4.49

1312	G-AHDM	20. 7.46	PP228	'Falmouth', scrapped at Black-bushe 9.50
1318	G-AHDN	24. 3.47	PP234	'Flamborough', scrapped at Southend 11.50
1320	G-AHDO	13. 8.47	PP236	'Forfar', scrapped at Southend 11.50
1341	G-AHDP	24. 3.47	PP268	'Fleetwood', crashed Schleswig-land 27.3.51
1342	G-AHDR	7. 7.47	PP269	'Foreland', to France 6.48 as F-BECK
1350	G-AHDS	24. 8.46	PP277	'Freemantle', destroyed 27.3.51
1370	G-AHDT	4. 6.47	PP308	'Fife', scrapped in Germany 11.49
1372	G-AHDU	10. 7.46	PP310	'Falkirk', scrapped at Southend 11.50
1376	G-AHDV	19. 8.46	PP314	'Finisterre', wrecked in gale, Squires Gate 17.10.52
1377	G-AHDW	29. 7.46	PP315	'Falaise', scrapped at Southend 11.50
1378	G-AHDX	4. 6.47	PP316	'Folkestone', crashed in Alps 16.4.50

HANDLEY PAGE H.P.71 HALIFAX A.Mk.9
Allocation: G-AKKP, 'KU; G-ALIR, 'ON–'OS, 'SK, 'SL, 'UT–'UV, 'VH–'VM, 'YI–'YN; G-AMBX, 'CB–'CG

HANDLEY PAGE HERMES
(*Temporary trooping serial follows B.O.A.C. name and operator*)

H.P.68/1	G-AGSS	*nil*	Crashed at Kendall's Hall, Radlett 3.12.45
H.P.74/1	G-AGUB	2. 9.48	To Ministry of Supply 10.53 as VX234
H.P.81/1	G-AKFP	14.10.49	'Hamilcar' Airwork XD632 Beyond repair in collision with Dakota, Calcutta 1.9.57
H.P.81/2	G-ALDA	14.10.52	'Hecuba' Airwork WZ838 Currently operated by Falcon Airways
H.P.81/3	G-ALDB	30.11.49	'Hebe' Airwork WZ839 Burned out in crash at Pithiviers, France 23.7.52
H.P.81/4	G-ALDC	14.12.49	'Hermione' Airwork WZ840 Currently operated by Falcon Airways
H.P.81/5	G-ALDD	19.12.49	'Horatius' Skyways
H.P.81/6	G-ALDE	7. 2.50	'Hanno' To Bahamas 1.60 as VP-BBO
H.P.81/7	G-ALDF	27. 2.50	'Hadrian' Airwork WZ841 Lost at sea off Trapani, Sicily 25.8.52
H.P.81/8	G-ALDG	9. 3.50	'Horsa' Britavia
H.P.81/9	G-ALDH	20. 3.50	'Heracles' Skyways
H.P.81/10	G-ALDI	6. 7.50	'Hannibal' Britavia XJ309

Constructor's No. and Registration		C. of A. Issued		Remarks

HANDLEY PAGE HERMES (contd.)

H.P.81/11	G-ALDJ	7. 7.50		'Hengist' Britavia
				Destroyed in night landing Blackbushe 5–6.11.56
H.P.81/12	G-ALDK	12. 7.50		'Helena' Britavia XJ281
				Crash landed Drigh Road Aerodrome, Karachi 5.8.56
H.P.81/13	G-ALDL	21. 2.51		'Hector' To Bahamas 1.60 as VP-BBP
H.P.81/14	G-ALDM	17. 7.50		'Hero' Air Safaris Ltd.
H.P.81/15	G-ALDN	20. 7.50		'Horus', forced landed in Sahara, 150 miles S.E. of Port Etienne, French West Africa 26.5.52
H.P.81/16	G-ALDO	20. 7.50		'Heron', scrapped at Blackbushe 3.59
H.P.81/17	G-ALDP	24. 8.50		'Homer' Britavia XJ269
H.P.81/18	G-ALDR	29. 8.50		'Herodotus' Skyways
H.P.81/19	G-ALDS	6. 9.50		'Hesperides' Skyways
H.P.81/20	G-ALDT	13. 9.50		'Hestia' Skyways
H.P.81/21	G-ALDU	12.10.50		'Halcyone' Britavia XJ280
H.P.81/22	G-ALDV	29. 9.50		'Hera' Skyways
				Burned out in fatal crash, Meesden Green, Herts., 1.4.58
H.P.81/23	G-ALDW	30.10.50		'Helios' Skyways
				Blown up by saboteur, Nicosia, Cyprus, 4.3.56
H.P.81/24	G-ALDX	13.12.50		'Hyperion' Britavia XJ267
				Withdrawn from use 1.60
H.P.81/25	G-ALDY	16. 1.51		'Honor' Skyways
H.P.82/1	G-ALEU	nil		Damaged beyond repair, Chilbolton, 10.4.51
H.P.82/2	G-ALEV	nil		Reduced to produce, Farnborough, 9.53

HANDLEY PAGE (READING) H.P.R.1 MARATHON

(Subsequent identities given in Column 4)

6265	G-AGPD	4. 9.47		Formerly U-10, crashed at Amesbury 28.5.48
6430	G-AILH	28.10.49	VX229	Dismantled and sold 1957
6544	G-AHXU	19. 4.50	VX231	Trial engine installations
101	G-ALUB	13. 1.50	XA249	Formerly B.E.A.C. 'Rob Roy'
102	G-ALVW	28.12.51	XA250	1952 S.B.A.C. exhibit
103	G-ALVX	15. 1.51	XA251	Transferred to R.A.F. 4.52
104	G-ALVY	28. 9.50	XA252	Transferred to R.A.F. 4.52. Restored to Miles 6.59
105	G-ALXR	15. 1.51	XA253	Transferred to R.A.F. 4.52.
106	G-AMAX	28. 9.50	XA254	,, ,,
107	G-AMAY	5.10.50	XA255	,, ,,

108	G-AMDH	13.11.50	XA256	Transferred to R.A.F. 4.52
109	G-AMEK	19. 1.51	XA257	,, ,,
110	G-AMEL	14. 9.51	XA258	Converted 11.51 to Mk. 1A
111	G-AMEM	23. 2.51	XA259	Transferred to R.A.F. 4.52
112	G-AMEO	12. 3.52		VR-NAI in 1951, to Germany 8.55 as D-CFSA
113–115	G-AMEP, 'ER, 'ET	23. 2.51*	XA260–XA262	To the R.A.F. 4.52
116–117	G-AMEU–'EV	30. 4.51*	XA263–XA264	,, ,,
118	G-AMEW	29. 6.51	XA265	Now Derby Aviation Ltd.
119–123	G-AMGN–'GS	29. 6.51*	XA266–XA270	To the R.A.F. 4.52
124	G-AMGT	17. 8.51	XA271	Destroyed in crash at Calne 30.9.54
125	G-AMGU	17. 8.51	XA272	Transferred to R.A.F. 4.52
126	G-AMGV	17. 8.51	XA273	,, ,,
127	G-AMGW	10. 9.51	VR-NAN	Now Derby Aviation Ltd. 'Millersdale'
128	G-AMGX	21. 9.51	VR-NAO	Scrapped at Southend 1959
129	G-AMHR	21. 9.51	VR-NAR	Now Derby Aviation 'Monsaldale'
130	G-AMHS	19.10.51	VR-NAS	To R.A.E. 3.55 as XJ830. Restored to Air Navigation & Trading Co. Ltd. 3.59
131	G-AMHT	30.11.51	XA274	Transferred to R.A.F. 4.52. Restored to F. G. Miles Ltd. 6.59
132	G-AMHU	16.11.51	XA275	Transferred to R.A.F. 4.52
133	G-AMHV	19.10.51	VR-NAT	To R.A.E. 3.55 as XJ831. Restored to Air Navigation & Trading Co. Ltd. 3.59
134	G-AMHW	3.10.51	VR-NAU	
135	G-AMHX	16.11.51	XA276	Transferred to R.A.F. 4.52
136	G-AMHY	16.11.51	(XA277)†	To Japan 7.54 as JA-6009
137	G-AMHZ	19.12.51	(XA278)†	To Japan 1.55 as JA-6010
138	G-AMIA	18. 1.52		Sold in Burma 7.52 as XY-ACX
139	G-AMIB	28. 2.52		Sold in Burma 7.52 as XY-ACY
140	G-AMIC	28. 2.52		Sold in Burma 7.52 as XY-ACZ

* Issue date of first aircraft.   † Allocation only.

HAWKER TOMTIT

(Former R.A.F. serial given in Column 1 where applicable)

9	G-AALL	11. 6.30	Scrapped in 1937
12	G-AASI	30. 9.30	W. Humble, Firbeck; scrapped during war
27	G-ABAX	26. 6.30	Tollerton Aero Club; scrapped during war

Constructor's No. and Registration	C. of A. Issued	Remarks

HAWKER TOMTIT (contd.)

54	G-ABII	31. 1.31	Damaged beyond repair, Cowes, 10.4.48
55	G-ABOD	2. 1.33	Tollerton Aero Club, scrapped during war
K1782	G-AEES	11. 5.36	Destroyed in hangar fire, Maylands, 6.2.40
K1451	G-AEVO	1. 4.37	Scrapped at Redhill 1946–47
J9782	G-AEVP	nil	Not taken up, re-registered G-AFFL
J9781	G-AEXC	5. 4.38	Herts and Essex Aero Club, scrapped during war
J9782	G-AFFL	11. 3.38	H. D. Rankin, broken up at Southend 1940
K1781	G-AFIB	15. 8.38	Vickers 1941, road block Chilbolton 10.43
K1785	G-AFKB	2.11.38	Crashed at Braunstone, Leics, 13.7.39
K1786	G-AFTA	28. 4.39	Currently stored at Old Warden
K1784	G-AFVV	4. 7.39	Alex Henshaw 1941
K1783	G-AGEF	8. 7.42	Scrapped following accident 18.10.43

HESTON TYPE 1 PHOENIX

1/1	G-ADAD	1.10.35	Prototype; to E. Xidis, Athens, 9.36 as SX-AAH
1/3	G-AEHJ	7. 5.36	British American A/S; crashed 1939
1/4	G-AEMT	22. 5.37	Ser. II, Luton Flying Club, impressed 4.40 as X9393
1/5	G-AESV	23. 3.37	Ser. II, impressed as X2891, crashed in France 4.52
1/6	G-AEYX	25. 6.37	Ser. II, Randrup and Worth, impressed 4.40 as X9338

HILLER 360 SERIES UH-12A

166	G-AMDN	3.10.50	Currently owned by Fison-Airwork Ltd.
172	G-AMDO	3.10.50	Crashed in Panama 3.3.58
165	G-AMGY	18. 1.51	Currently owned by Fison-Airwork Ltd.
148	G-AMMY	3.11.51	Formerly N8148H and OO-MAT, crashed at Grantchester, Cambs 20.11.56
170	G-ANOA	22. 2.54	Currently owned by Fison-Airwork Ltd. Formerly F-BEEG
120	G-ANOB	20. 4.54	Currently owned by Fison-Airwork Ltd. Formerly N8120H, HB-XAI, I-ELAM and F-BGGZ
115	G-ANOC	25. 3.54	Formerly F-BFGY, crashed at Gleatham, Lincs, 23.8.55
106	G-ANZM	1. 2.56	Currently owned by Fison-Airwork Ltd. Formerly N8106H and OO-APR. Rebuilt 1.56 with fuselage of LN-FOH, c/n 122

| 337 | G-APKX* | 30. 6.58 | Currently owned by Fison-Airwork Ltd. Formerly N24C and CF-HAP |
| 137 | G-APLA | 24. 4.58 | Formerly F-BFLX, crashed at High Roding, Essex, 28.5.58 |

* Fitted with 200 h.p. Franklin 6V4-200-C33 engine.

HILLER 360 SERIES UH-12B

745	G-AOFK	28. 6.55	Crashed and burned, Hamble, 4.10.55
746	G-AOFL	28. 6.55 ⎫	Air Service Training Ltd., sold to Heli-
748	G-AOFV	14.11.55 ⎭	copter Services Ltd., Luton, 7.59
686	G-APJN	7. 2.58	Currently owned by Fison-Airwork Ltd. Formerly HB-XAH
673	G-APKY	4. 6.58	Currently owned by Fison-Airwork Ltd. Formerly PH-NFL
747	G-APSH	4. 3.59	Currently owned by Fison-Airwork Ltd. Formerly N5313V
555	G-APSL	25.4.59	Currently owned by Fison-Airwork Ltd. Formerly N5300V
674	G-APTM	10. 6.59	Currently owned by Fison-Airwork Ltd. Formerly PI-C364
680	G-APTN	10. 6.59	Currently owned by Fison-Airwork Ltd. Formerly PI-C365
744	G-APUH	29. 5.59	Burned out in the Sahara 19.12.59 Formerly D-HABA

HILLER 360 SERIES UH-12C

785	G-AOFA	18. 9.56	Air Service Training Ltd., sold to Heli- copter Services Ltd., Luton, 7.59
847	G-AOZR	5. 4.57	Currently owned by Fison-Airwork Ltd.
848	G-AOZS	5. 4.57	,, ,,
849	G-APDU	31. 7.57	,, ,,
856	G-APDV	31. 7.57	,, ,,
1041	G-APMP	21. 7.58	,, ,,
1037	G-APMR	6. 6.58	,, ,,
1038	G-APMS	6. 6.58	,, ,,
1039	G-APNI	14. 7.58	Crashed in Panama 4.59
784	G-APNR	3. 7.58	Currently owned by Fison-Airwork Ltd. Formerly F-BHTG
776	G-APOF	31. 7.58	Currently owned by Fison-Airwork Ltd. Formerly F-BBDZ
1040	G-APOT	2. 9.58	Currently owned by Fison-Airwork Ltd.
777	G-APRD	31.12.58	Currently owned by Fison-Airwork Ltd. Formerly N5319V

HILLSON PRAGA

107	G-ADXL	27. 2.36	Formerly OK-PGC, sold in S. Africa 6.36 as ZS-AHL
H.A.2	G-AEEU	13. 4.36	Demonstrator, cannibalised at Hooton 1947
H.A.3	G-AEEV	13. 4.36	Preserved at Hatfield, Yorks.

535

HILLSON PRAGA (contd.)

H.A.12	G-AEPI	21.12.36	Northern Aviation School and Club Ltd., Barton
H.A.13	G-AELK	11. 9.36	Crashed at Abbey Village, near Chorley, 7.6.37
H.A.14	G-AELL	25.10.36	Remained unsold
H.A.15	G-AEOL	9.12.36	R. Jagger and partners, Barton
H.A.16	G-AEOM	18. 1.37	Remained unsold
H.A.20	G-AEON	4.12.36	F. Hills and Sons Ltd., sold abroad 12.36
H.A.23	G-AEPL	4. 2.37	Malayan Motors Ltd., Singapore, sold abroad 1937
H.A.24	G-AEPM	1. 2.37	Malayan Motors Ltd., sold 1937 as VR-SAU
H.A.25	G-AEPJ	11. 2.37	Northern Aviation School and Club Ltd., Barton
H.A.26	G-AEPK	16. 3.37	N. Staffs. Club, sold to Northern Aviation School and Club Ltd. 4.39
H.A.27–31	G-AEUK–'UO	23. 3.37*	Northern Aviation School and Club Ltd., Barton
H.A.32	G-AEUP	31. 7.37	Crashed in Turkey 21.7.46
H.A.33	G-AEUR	12. 8.37	Northern Aviation School and Club Ltd., crashed 22.6.39
H.A.34	G-AEUS	21. 9.37	
H.A.35	G-AEUT	5. 1.38	Crashed at Sinalunga, Siena, Italy 19.6.57
H.A.36	G-AEUU	30.12.37	Ipswich Aero Club Ltd.
H.A.37	G-AEYK	15.12.37	Northern Aviation School and Club Ltd.
H.A.38	G-AEYL	19. 1.38	Thanet and Ipswich Aero Clubs
H.A.39	G-AEYM	19. 1.38	Ipswich Aero Club, crashed Weston-super-Mare, 1.9.39
H.A.40–46	G-AEYN–'YU	nil	Construction not completed

* Date of issue for G-AEUK.

HUNTING PRESIDENT 1 and 2

HPAL/PEM/79	G-AOJG	20.12.56		To the Danish Air Force 7.59 as '697'
PAC/PRES 2/1071	G-APMO	29. 9.58		Current owner Ministry of Aviation
HPAC/PRES 2/114	G-APVJ	4. 9.59		Formerly EC-APC; to the Sudanese Air Force 3.60

JUNKERS Ju 52/3m

(Previous identity given in Column 4)

5440	G-AERU	19. 2.37	SE-AER	'Juno', cannibalised at Lagos 1941
5518	G-AERX	7. 4.37	SE-AES	'Jupiter', to SABENA 9.41 as OO-CAP
5881	G-AFAP	28. 1.38	nil	'Jason', captured by the Germans at Oslo 9.4.40
5588	G-AGAE	7.11.39	SP-AKX	Interned in Rumania 1939

JUNKERS Ju 52/3m.g8e

(Previous R.A.F. serial given in lieu of constructor's number)

VM908	G-AHBP	7.10.46	Scrapped at Castle Bromwich 2.48
VM923	G-AHOC	5.11.46	Scrapped at Warrington 2.48
VN740	G-AHOD	12.12.46	,, ,, ,,
VN723	G-AHOE	11.11.46	,, ,, ,,
VN729	G-AHOF	29.11.46	,, ,, ,,
VM979	G-AHOG	5.11.46	,, ,, ,,
VN746	G-AHOH	14. 3.47	,, ,, ,,
VN744	G-AHOI	8. 2.47	,, ,, ,,
VN756	G-AHOJ	28. 2.47	,, ,, ,,
VN742	G-AHOK	8. 1.47	Damaged beyond repair, Renfrew 26.1.47
VN741	G-AHOL	19.12.46	Scrapped at Warrington 2.48

KLEMM MONOPLANES

(Designation given in Column 4 should be used in conjunction with table on page 106 to show type of engine fitted)

135	G-AAFU	20. 6.29	L25-I	Burned out in hangar, Maylands 6.2.40
136	G-AAFV	8. 5.29	L25	E. F. Stephen, Croydon; scrapped 1931
144	G-AAHL	26. 8.29	L25-I	Lord Apsley, crashed Whitchurch 27.2.32
152	G-AAHW	26. 8.29	L25-I	Currently owned by R. H. Grant, Dumfries
	G-AARO	nil		Registration not taken up
163	G-AATD	4. 1.30	L25-I	F/O F. M. Smith, Eastchurch; sold abroad
145	G-AAUP	5. 3.30	L25-I	Currently stored at Dumfries by R. H. Grant
197	G-AAVS	26. 3.30	L26a-II	Sold abroad by Brian Lewis 1934
181	G-AAWE	7. 4.30	L25-I	C. H. Phillips, Broxbourne, 1933
196	G-AAWW	17. 4.30	L27a-III	British Air Transport Ltd., crashed at Croydon 2.33
182	G-AAXK	16. 6.30	L25-I	Currently owned by C. C. R. Vick, Biggin Hill
180	G-AAZH	14. 7.30	L25a-I	L. A. Willard, Whitley; impressed 10.5.40 as X5009
216	G-ABBT	27.11.30	L25a-I	Formerly D-1776, cancelled 5.36
225	G-ABBU	2. 7.30	L26a-III	H. J. Sykes, High Post, 1936
226	G-ABCI	7. 7.30	L26a-III	Sold in the Netherlands 9.37 as PH-APA

537

Constructor's No. and Registration		C. of A. Issued		Remarks

KLEMM MONOPLANES (contd.)

215	G-ABCY	16. 7.30	L25a-I	F/O C. E. R. Tait, Hanworth, 1938
208	G-ABFS	nil	L26a-II	Formerly D-1833, sold abroad 9.33
247	G-ABJX	27. 3.31	L27a-III	Scrapped at Burton, Wilts, 1946
325	G-ABOJ	21. 7.31	L26a-III	Scrapped at Knowle by D. C. Burgoyne 1945
307	G-ABOP	21. 8.31	L27a-VIII	Lord Apsley, Whitchurch; scrapped 1939
330	G-ABOR	25. 8.31	L27a-IX	Sold in Australia as VH-USZ, crashed 13.3.38
214	G-ABOS	3.10.31	L25a-I	G. L. Young, Gravesend, 1936
358	G-ABRG	12.10.31	L25b-VII	Formerly D-2393, sold abroad 1.33
350	G-ABRP	7.11.31	L26a-X	D. Kinloch, Heston, 1935
360	G-ABTE	25. 1.32	L25b-XI	Wiltshire School of Flying 1936
413	G-ABZO	30. 9.32	L25c-XI	Sold in Ireland 10.36 as EI-ABJ
668	G-ACLH	17.11.33	L32-X	Sold in Ireland 11.36 as EI-ABF
402	G-ACYU	19.11.34	L32-V	Sold in Australia as VH-UVE, burned out 28.6.39

LOCKHEED MODEL 10A ELECTRA

1080	G-AEPN	12. 3.37	Impressed into the R.A.F. 18.12.39 as W9105
1081	G-AEPO	17. 3.37	Impressed into the R.A.F. 1.1.40 as W9106
1082	G-AEPP	17. 3.37	Crashed at Croydon 13.12.37
1083	G-AEPR	17. 3.37	'Leith'; destroyed in accident 1944
1102	G-AESY	15. 6.37	Crashed into sea off Danish coast 15.8.39
1025	G-AFCS	16. 2.38	'Lea', formerly NC14936, crashed at Almaza 19.11.43
1122	G-AFEB	14. 3.38	Impressed into the R.A.F. 18.12.39 as W9104
1087	G-AGAF	7.11.39	Formerly SP-BGG ⎤
1047	G-AGAG	7.11.39	Formerly SP-AYC ⎟ Interned by the
1086	G-AGAH	7.11.39	Formerly SP-BGF ⎬ Rumanian Government 12.39
1085	G-AGAI	7.11.39	Formerly SP-BGE ⎟ ment 12.39
1088	G-AGAJ	7.11.39	Formerly SP-BGH ⎦

LOCKHEED MODEL 12A

(Previous identity given in Column 4)

1203	G-AFTL	11. 6.39	NC16077	Sold to British West Indian Airways 11.42 as VP-TAI
1206	G-AEMZ	3. 4.37	*nil*	Impressed 9.39, to R.A.E. as R8987
1211	G-AGWM	*nil*	LA620	Sold to Roger Hansez 3.47 as OO-AFA
1212	G-AEOI	10. 3.37	*nil*	Impressed as X9316, sold to Shell company in Venezuela 1948
1226	G-AHLH	28. 5.47	NC18130	Currently owned by the Earl of Granard
1238	G-AFCO	18.11.37	*nil*	To Maharajah of Jammu and Kashmir 3.38 as VT-AJS, impressed 11.42 as AX803
1267	G-AFKR	15. 2.39	*nil*	Sold in France 5.39 as F-ARQA
1270	G-AFPF	*nil*	*nil*	Sold in France 5.39 as F-ARPP
1274	G-AFXP	12. 1.40	*nil*	To Maharajah of Jaipur 3.40 as VT-AMB, impressed as HX798
1275	G-AGWN	21. 5.47	LA623	Sold in Australia 2.53 as VH-BHH
1277	G-AGVZ	*nil*	LA621	Sold to U.S. owner 2.47 as NC79820
1285	G-AGDT	13. 9.40	Y-0233	Sold in Sweden 3.51 as SE-BTO
1287	G-AGTL	5.12.46	USN.02947	Currently owned by K. McAlpine, Luton

LOCKHEED MODEL 14-WF62

1467	G-AFGN	15. 9.38	Crashed in France 11.8.39
1468	G-AFGO	15. 9.38	Crashed at Walton, Somerset 22.11.38
1469	G-AFGP	15. 9.38	'Livingstone', crashed at Khartoum 4.8.41
1470	G-AFGR	15. 9.38	'Lafayette', crashed at El Fasher 19.1.41
1484	G-AFKD	22.11.38	'Loch Invar', crashed near Loch Lomond 22.4.40
1485	G-AFKE	30.11.38	'Lothair', transferred to R.A.F. 10.43 as HK982
1490	G-AFMO	18. 3.39	Damaged beyond repair at Heston 15.1.40
1491	G-AFMR	21. 3.39	'Leander', broken up at R.A.F. Kabrit 11.43, serial HK984 allotted but not used
1444	G-AFYU	19. 8.39	Formerly PH-ASL, lost at sea near Malta 21.12.39

LOCKHEED MODEL 14-H

1493	G-AFZZ	7.11.39	Formerly SP-BPL, crashed at Bucharest 24.7.40
1492	G-AGAA	7.11.39	Formerly SP-BPK, interned in Rumania 1939
1420	G-AGAB	7.11.39	Formerly SP-BNE, interned in Rumania 1939
1423	G-AGAC	7.11.39	Formerly SP-BNH, interned in Rumania 1939
1425	G-AGAV	15. 3.38	Formerly SP-LMK, broken up at Croydon 2.46
1421	G-AGBG	13.10.38	Formerly SP-BNF, sold in Sweden 3.51 as SE-BTN
1429	G-AKPD*	27. 7.48	Formerly CF-TCD, lost at sea off Elba 29.10.48

* Converted to Lockheed Model 14-08.

LOCKHEED MODEL 414 HUDSON

(Previous R.A.F. serial given in Column 4 where applicable)

1761	G-AGAR	3. 5.40	N7364	Destroyed by enemy, Le Luc Southern France, 29.5.41
2789	G-AGCE	6. 6.41	AM707	Transferred to the R.A.F. 8.41
2585	G-AGDC	8. 7.41	V9061	'Loch Lomond', to R.A.F. 8.45 as VJ416
3772	G-AGDF	29. 9.41		'Loch Leven', crashed off Swedish coast near Skredewick 23.6.42
3757	G-AGDK	28. 1.42		'Loch Lyon', to R.A.F. 8.45 as VJ421
Not given	G-AGDO	*nil*	AE581	'Loch Loyal', handed back to R.A.F. 4.42

LOCKHEED MODEL 18-07 LODESTAR

1954	G-AJAW	17. 2.47	Formerly Lockheed 14H NC17385, c/n 1404; became Lodestar NX17835 and VP-TAE. Sold as SE-BTL 10.51
2018	G-AGBO	3. 1.41	'Lanark', to R.A.F. 10.43 as HK973
2024	G-AGBP	3. 1.41	'Leicester', to R.A.F. 10.43 as HK980
2070	G-AGBR*	3. 2.41	'Lewes', later 'Lake George', to E.A.A.C. 4.48 as VP-KFE. Now flying as SE-BUF
2071	G-AGBS*	10. 2.41	'Lichfield', later 'Lake Nyasa', to E.A.A.C. 2.48 as VP-KFB
2076	G-AGBT*	18. 2.41	'Lincoln', later 'Lake Victoria', to E.A.A.C. 2.48 as VP-KFA, now flying as SE-BUU

540

2090	G-AGBU*	21. 3.41	'Lowestoft', sold in Australia 6.49 as VH-FAD. Now flying as ZK-BJM 'Whetu Marama'
2091	G-AGBV*	24. 3.41	'Ludlow', later 'Lake Albert', to E.A.A.C. 2.48 as VP-KFC
2094	G-AGBW*	31. 3.41	'Lyndhurst', crashed in the Aberdare Mts. 29.11.44
2095	G-AGBX*	7. 4.41	'Llandaff', later 'Lake Edward', to E.A.A.C. 4.48 as VP-KFF
2143	G-AGIL*	22.10.43	'Lake Nyasa', formerly HK855
2144	G-AGIM	23.11.43	'Lake Tanganyika', formerly EW977, now flying as N9926F
2146	G-AGIN*	22.12.43	'Lake Timsah', formerly EW976
2147	G-AGEH*	2. 6.42	'Lake Baringo', formerly HK851 and 41-29635, now flying as N9927F
2148	G-AGIG*	26. 7.43	'Lake Karoun', formerly EW980, now flying as N9928F
2153	G-AGJH*	28. 1.44	'Lake Tana' (2), formerly EW982

* Later converted to Lockheed Model 18-56 Lodestar.

LOCKHEED MODEL 18-08 LODESTAR

(Impressed American aircraft. Previous identities and allotted R.A.F. serials given in Columns 4 and 5)

Not given	G-AGCL	nil	not given	not given	Delivered to the Free French Air Force
2093	G-AGCM*	20.10.41	NC33617	not given	'Lake Mariut', to the R.A.F. 10.46 as VR955
2020	G-AGCN*	20.10.41	NC25630	AX756	'Lake Victoria', now flying as ZK-BVE
2021	G-AGCO*	25.11.41	NC25631	AX758	'Lake Albert'
2022	G-AGCP*	9. 8.41	NC25632	AX721	'Lake Edward'
2072	G-AGCR	30. 7.41	NC3138	AX718	'Lake Rudolf'
2031	G-AGCS	nil	NC25640	AX723	Not delivered to B.O.A.C.
2001	G-AGCT	13. 8.41	NC25604	AX722	'Lake Timsah', to R.A.F. 10.43
2068	G-AGCU*	2. 8.41	NC34900	AX720	'Lake Kivu', now flying as N9932F
2042	G-AGCV*	23. 7.41	NC6175	AX717	'Lake Chad'
1956	G-AGCW	30. 8.41	NC18993	AX719	'Lake Tana' (1), to R.A.F. 9.43 as HK975
2012	G-AGCX	31. 1.42	NC3030	not given	'Lake Mweru', to R.A.F. 9.43 as HK981
2077	G-AGCY	25.11.41	NC1611	AX765	'Lake Rukwa'
2023	G-AGCZ	28.11.41	NC25633	not given	'Lake Stephanie' crashed in Western Desert 22.12.41
2087	G-AGDD	30. 7.41	NX34901	not given	'Loch Losna', to Norwegian Air Force 7.45 as '2087'
2086	G-AGDE	11. 8.41	not given	not given	'Loch Lesja', crashed at sea, 15 miles off Leuchars 17.12.43

* Later converted to Lockheed Model 18-56 Lodestar.

LOCKHEED MODEL 18-56 LODESTAR

(Lend-Lease aircraft, previous U.S.A.A.F. serials given in Column 4)

2084	G-AGEI	20. 8.42	*nil*	'Loch Loen'. To Norwegian Air Force 7.45 as '2084' thence to OH-VKO and SE-BZK
2085	G-AGEJ	12. 9.42	*nil*	'Loch Lange', ditched in North Sea 4.4.43
2491	G-AGIH	26. 5.44	42-56018	Crashed at Kinnekulle 29.8.44
2492	G-AGII	30. 6.44	42-56019	To Norwegian Air Force 7.45 as '2492', thence to SE-BTI
2593	G-AGIJ	28. 3.44	43-16433	To Norwegian Air Force 7.45 as '2593' thence to OH-VKP and SE-BZE
2594	G-AGIK	28. 3.44	43-16434	To Norwegian Air Force 7.45 as '2594' thence to SE-BTG
2615	G-AGLG	15.11.44	43-16455	To Norwegian Air Force 7.45 as '2615' thence to SE-BTH
2616	G-AGLH	4.12.44	43-16456	To Norwegian Air Force 7.45 as '2616' thence to SE-BTK
2620	G-AGLI	30.10.44	43-16460	Lost in Gulf of Bothnia 2.5.45

LOCKHEED MODEL 049E CONSTELLATION

(B.O.A.C. names given in Column 4)

1975	G-AHEJ	21. 5.46	'Bristol'	To Capital Airlines 6.55 as N2740A
1976	G-AHEK	21. 5.46	'Berwick'	To Capital Airlines 6.55 as N2737A
1977	G-AHEL	24. 6.46	'Bangor'	To Capital Airlines 6.55 as N2736A
1978	G-AHEM	24. 6.46	'Balmoral'	To Capital Airlines 6.55 as N2735A, crashed at Charleston 12.5.59
1980	G-AHEN	1. 7.46	'Baltimore'	Sold in U.S.A. 2.51 as N74192, sold in Israel 10.53 as 4X-AKD
1971	G-AKCE	31. 3.48	'Bedford'	Formerly NX54212. To Capital Airlines 6.55 as N2741A
2051	G-AMUP	9. 3.53	'Boston'	Formerly N90921 'Clipper Jupiter'. To Capital Airlines 4.55 as N2738A

2065   G-AMUR   26. 3.53   'Barnstaple' Formerly N90922 'Clipper
                                    Wings of the Morning'.
                                    To Capital Airlines 5.55
                                    as N2739A

LOCKHEED MODEL 749A CONSTELLATION

(Former identities given in Columns 5 and 6)

2548	G-ALAK	30. 6.48	'Brentford'	EI-ACR	'St. Brendan'. Currently operated by Skyways Ltd.
2549	G-ALAL	30. 6.48	'Banbury'	EI-ACS	'St. Patrick'. Currently operated by Skyways Ltd.
2554	G-ALAM	30. 6.48	'Belfast'	EI-ADA	'St. Bridget'. Crashed at Singapore 13.3.54
2555	G-ALAN	30. 6.48	'Beaufort'	EI-ADD	'St. Kevin'
2566	G-ALAO	21. 7.48	'Braemar'	EI-ADE	'St. Finbarr'. To Capitol Airlines 9.58 as N4902C
2671	G-ANNT	25. 9.54	'Buckingham'	N6025C	'Star of Colorado'. To Capitol Airlines 4.58 as N4901C
2504	G-ANTF	15. 9.54	'Berkeley'	VT-CQS VH-EAF	'Mogul Princess' 'Horace Brinsmead'. To Transocean Airlines 3.58 as N9816F
2505	G-ANTG	15.10.54	'Bournemouth'	VT-CQR VH-EAE	'Rajput Princess' 'Bert Hinkler'. To Pacific Northern Airlines 12.58
2562	G-ANUP	9. 2.55	'Branksome'	VH-EAA	'Ross Smith'. Currently operated by Skyways Ltd.
2565	G-ANUR	18. 2.55	'Basildon'	VH-EAB	'Lawrence Hargrave' Currently operated by Skyways Ltd.
2551	G-ANUV	1. 7.55	'Blantyre'	PH-TDC N90607	'Curaçao' Capital Airlines. To Transocean Airlines 1.58 as N9830F
2556	G-ANUX	8.12.54	'Bala'	PH-TDD N90623	'Delft' Capital Airlines. To Pacific Northern Airlines 4.57 as N1593V
2557	G-ANUY	31. 1.55	'Beaulieu'	PH-TDE N90625	'Eindhoven' Capital Airlines. To AVIANCA, Colombia, 5.59

LOCKHEED MODEL 749A CONSTELLATION (*contd.*)

2559	G-ANUZ	30. 5.55	'Belvedere'	PH-TDG	'Goude'
				N90621	Capital Airlines.
					To Transocean Airlines 4.58 as N9812F
2564	G-ANVA	17. 5.55	'Blakeney'	PH-TDH	'Holland'
				N90608	Capital Airlines.
					To AVIANCA, Colombia, 5.59
2589	G-ANVB	31. 3.55	'Blackrod'	PH-TDI	'Enschede'
				N90624	Capital Airlines.
					To Transocean Airlines 4.58 as N9813F
2544	G-ANVD	30. 4.55	'Beverley'	PH-TDB	'Walcheren'
				N90622	Capital Airlines.
					To AVIANCA, Colombia, 5.59

MARTINSYDE F.4 (Hispano-Suiza)

(Former R.A.F. serial given in lieu of constructor's number)

Not given	G-EANM	22.10.19	Sold in Portugal 12.19
D4267	G-EATD	*nil*	Written off 11.22
D4352	G-EAUR	*nil*	Written off 1.23
H7786	G-EAUX	6. 9.20	First flown 20.5.20
H7780	G-EAWE	*nil*	Left for Warsaw 29.1.21
D4279	G-EAXB	*nil*	Crashed at Croydon 5.5.22
Not given	G-EAYK	6.10.21	Scrapped in 1923
D4275	G-EAYP	14.10.21	First flown 4.10.21
H7692	G-EBDM	*nil*	Written off 6.23
H7688	G-EBFA	16. 4.25	Written off 1.27
D4295	G-EBMI	15. 4.26	Crashed at Woodley 24.8.30

MARTINSYDE F.4A

nil	G-EAPP	*nil*	1920 Aerial Derby
nil	G-EAQH	3. 5.20	Crashed 12.20
310	G-EATX	3.11.20	Written off 8.22
A.V.1	G-ABKH	16. 3.31	Crashed at Bekesbourne 5.2.33

MARTINSYDE F.6

nil	G-EAPI	25. 8.20	Withdrawn from use 11.20
61/3	G-EATQ	*nil*	Sold abroad 1920
nil	G-EBDK	11. 7.23	Viper engine, scrapped 1930

MARTINSYDE TYPE A

nil	G-EAMR	*nil*	Lost at sea off Corfu 9.12.19
nil	G-EAPN	*nil*	Sold abroad 1921
218	G-EATY*	6.10.20	Sold abroad 1921

* Type A Mk. II

MARTINSYDE A.D.C.I AND NIMBUS

K.501	G-EBKL	1. 1.25	Burned at Croydon 1930
K.502	G-EBMH	11. 6.26	To the Latvian Air Force 7.26
K.1001	G-EBOJ	2. 7.26	Burned at Croydon 1930
K.1002	G-EBOL	2. 7.26	,, ,,

MIGNET H.M.14 POU DU CIEL

Permits to Fly issued to: G-ADDW*, 'ME, 'MH, 'OU, 'OV, 'PP, 'PV–'PZ, 'SC–'SE, 'UB, 'VI, 'VM, 'VS, 'WR, 'XF, 'XS, 'XY, 'YO, 'ZP, 'ZV; G-AEAD, 'BA, 'BB, 'BR, 'BS, 'CD, 'CE, 'CM, 'CV, 'DF, 'DM, 'DN, 'DP, 'EC, 'EF, 'EH–'EJ, 'EW, 'EY, 'FC–'FE, 'FG, 'FK, 'FP, 'FV, 'FW, 'GD, 'GU, 'GV, 'HD, 'HG, 'IA, 'II, 'IO, 'IP, 'JC, 'JD, 'JO, 'JU, 'JX, 'JZ, 'KH, 'KR, 'LM, 'LN, 'ME, 'ND, 'NV†, 'OH, 'OJ, 'RJ; G-AFBU, 'UL.

Other allocations: G-ADPU, 'VL, 'VU, 'VW, 'WS, 'WX, 'YV, 'ZG, 'ZS, 'ZT, 'ZW, 'ZY; G-AEBT, 'CK, 'CL, 'CN‡, 'DO, 'DR, 'DS, 'ED, 'EE, 'EX, 'FF, 'FI, 'FJ, 'FL, 'FO, 'GT, 'HH, 'HM, 'IE, 'IX, 'IZ, 'JA, 'JE–'JG, 'KA, 'MY, 'NI, 'NJ.

* Originally reserved for Short Scion, issued to Pou du Ciel 19.3.36.
† Mignet H.M.18.
‡ Registration used unofficially on the Burgoyne-Stirling Dicer in 1948.

MILES M.2 HAWK

Allocation: Cumulative c/n 1–92 included M.2 aircraft G-ACGH, 'HJ–'HL, 'HZ, 'IZ, 'JC, 'JD, 'JY, 'KI, 'KX, 'LA, 'LB, 'MH, 'MM, 'MX, 'NX, 'OC, 'NW, 'RB, 'SD, 'SL, 'RT, 'PW, 'TO, 'TI, 'UD, 'VN, 'OP, 'TN, 'XZ, 'YA, 'VO, 'VP, 'ZD–'ZW; G-ADBK, 'DM, 'VR, 'GI, 'GR.

MILES M.2A, M.2B, M.2C AND M.2D HAWK

14	G-ACLI	1.12.33	M.2A	Cabin; burned in hangar fire Brooklands 24.10.36
12	G-ACKW	21.12.33	M.2B	Long range; flown as VT-AES
19	G-ACOB	29. 3.34	M.2C	Gipsy III; sold in France 5.34 as F-AMZW
20	G-ACPC	3. 4.34	M.2D	Three seat; scrapped 5.37
30	G-ACPD	7. 4.34	M.2D	Three seat; scrapped 4.37
32	G-ACSX	15. 5.34	M.2D	Crashed at Bilsdale, Yorks, 5.6.34
35	G-ACSC	18. 5.34	M.2D	Aircraft Distributors Ltd., Skegness
108	G-ACVR	18. 7.34	M.2D	,, ,, ,,

MILES M.2F HAWK MAJOR

36	G-ACTD	5. 7.34	K. Crawford, Macmerry; crashed 31.8.36
109	G-ACVM	28. 7.34	Sir John Carden; crashed 3.37
110	G-ACWV	28. 8.34	Used for skywriting, scrapped during war
111	G-ACWW	6.10.34	L. R. Hiscock, Brooklands; sold abroad 4.40
112	G-ACWX	5.10.34	Crashed 6.36
113	G-ACWY	30. 8.34	F. W. Griffiths, impressed as NF748
114	G-ACXL	17. 9.34	Aircraft Distributors Ltd., Skegness

MILES M.2F HAWK MAJOR (contd.)

115	G-ACXM	2.10.34	Sold in India 11.35 as VT-AGX
116	G-ACXN	19.10.34	Sold in Kenya 9.34 as VP-KBL
117	G-ACYW	10.11.34	Sold in Spain 5.35 as EC-ZZA
118	G-ACXT	8.11.34	North Staffs. Aero Club impressed 1.41 as DG577
119	G-ACXU	12.10.34	Sold in New Zealand 9.34 as ZK-ADJ
120	G-ACYB	12.10.34	Sold in Switzerland 9.34 as HB-OAS
121	G-ACYO	9.11.34	Impressed 9.43 as NF752, crashed at Elstree 28.11.54
134	G-ADAC	2. 1.35	R. K. Dundas Ltd., sold abroad 9.35
147	G-ADCI	9. 2.35	T. A. K. Aga, Brooklands; sold in New Zealand 9.37 as ZK-AFM
166	G-ADGL	24. 5.35	J. P. W. Topham, destroyed by enemy action Lympne 1940
169	G-ADGA	3. 5.35	Used for skywriting, sold abroad 5.41

MILES M.2H HAWK MAJOR

Allocation: Cumulative c/n 122–328 included M2H aircraft G-ACZJ, 'YZ; G-AEFS, G-ACYX, 'ZI, G-ADGE, 'AB, 'AS, 'AW, 'BG, 'BT, 'CW, 'CF, 'CJ, 'CY, 'EN, 'CU, 'DC, 'GD, 'GL, 'FC, 'IT, 'HF, 'LA, 'MW, G-AEEZ, G-ADDU, G-AEFA, G-ADZU, G-AEKJ, 'GP, 'GR, 'NS, G-ADIG, G-AEOX, G-ADLB, G-AFKL, G-AEGE, 'NT

MILES HAWK MAJOR (Other Variants)

156	G-ADCV	6. 4.35	M.2M	Damaged beyond repair 4.2.50
190	G-ADDK	13. 6.35	M.2P	Impressed 8.40 as BD180
194	G-ADLH	21. 8.35	M.2S	Crashed near Rouen 28.10.37
203	G-ADNJ	30. 8.35	M.2T	Crashed in Irish Sea 6.9.35
211	G-ADLN	16. 8.35	M.2R	Impressed 2.41 as DG664
220	G-ADLO	23. 7.35	M.2P	Airwork Ltd., sold in New Zealand 5.37 as ZK-AFL
222	G-ADNK	30. 8.35	M.2T	F. D. Bradbrooke, sold abroad 10.35

MILES HAWK SPEED SIX

43	G-ACTE	5. 7.34	M.2E	W. Humble, sold abroad 9.37
160	G-ADGP	13. 6.35	M.2L	Currently owned by R. R. Paine, Wolverhampton
195	G-ADOD	27. 8.35	M.2U	A. E. Clouston, crashed 1.10.36

MILES M.2W HAWK TRAINER

215	G-ADWT	23.11.35	Impressed 4.43 as NF750. Currently owned by L. D. Blyth
217	G-ADVF	10.10.35	No. 8 E.R.F.T.S., impressed 3.41
224	G-ADWU	23.11.35	,, ,, ,,
228	G-ADWV	23.11.35	,, ,, ,,

MILES M.2X HAWK TRAINER

235	G-ADYZ	2. 7.36	No. 8 E.R.F.T.S., impressed 3.41
241	G-ADZA	31.12.35	No. 8 E.R.F.T.S., impressed 3.41 as DG665
242	G-ADZB	22. 1.36	No. 8 E.R.F.T.S., impressed 3.41
246	G-AEAW	14. 4.36	Withdrawn after accident 1936
249	G-ADZC	13. 1.36	Reading Aero Club, dismantled 1940
254	G-ADZE	4. 2.36	Withdrawn after accident 1936
260	G-AEAX	25. 2.36	Reading Aero Club, impressed 3.41 as DG666
270	G-AEAZ	13. 3.36	Withdrawn after accident 1937
271	G-AEEL	26. 3.36	No. 8 E.R.F.T.S., impressed 3.41

MILES M.2Y HAWK TRAINER

253	G-ADZD	4. 2.36	No. 8 E.R.F.T.S., impressed 3.41
261	G-AEAY	18. 2.36	,, ,, ,,
258	G-AEHP	12. 6.36	Sold to the Rumanian Government 12.36
237	G-AEHR	12. 6.36	,, ,, ,,
245	G-AEHS	12. 6.36	,, ,, ,,
265	G-AEHT	12. 6.36	,, ,, ,,
292	G-AEHU	10. 7.36	,, ,, ,,
293	G-AEHV	15. 6.36	,, ,, ,,
294	G-AEHW	2. 7.36	,, ,, ,,
295	G-AEHX	26. 6.36	,, ,, ,,
296	G-AEHY	10. 7.36	,, ,, ,,
297	G-AEHZ	10. 7.36	,, ,, ,,

MILES M.3 AND M.3A FALCON MAJOR

102	G-ACTM	9.10.34	M.3, H. L. Brooke, crashed 11.36
131	G-ADBF	26. 2.35	Sold as I-ZENA 1935 and as HB-USU 1938
140	G-ADBI	29. 4.35	Air Hire Ltd., sold abroad 3.37
157	G-ADER	18. 4.35	Sold in France 2.37 as F-AQER
163	G-ADHC	21. 2.35	Sold in Italy 3.36 as I-ZENA
181	G-ADHH	28. 5.35	Sold in Palestine 3.40 as VQ-PAO
189	G-ADHI	29. 5.35	Impressed 3.40 as X9300
193	G-ADHG	13. 6.35	Sold in Australia 5.37 as VH-AAT
196	G-ADFH	28. 6.35	Impressed 1.42 as HM496, flown post-war
202	G-ADIU	11. 7.35	Leicestershire Aero Club, sold abroad 1.37
206	G-ADLI	12. 7.35	Crashed at Elstree 10.9.52
209	G-ADZR	7.10.35	Sold in Australia 6.36 as VH-AAS
216	G-AEEG	25. 3.36	Formerly U-20, sold in Sweden 10.36 as SE-AFN
226	G-AETN	22. 4.37	Crashed at Starcross, Devon 17.5.37
229	G-AEFB	8. 6.36	Impressed 3.40 as X9301
234	G-AENG	28. 9.36	Crashed at Scarborough 10.9.37

Constructor's No. and Registration	C. of A. Issued		Remarks

MILES M.3B FALCON SIX

213	G-ADLC	27. 7.35	Owner E. D. Spratt 1938, withdrawn 1940
233	G-AFAY	26.10.35	Formerly OE-DBB, Hawker Aircraft Ltd.'s communications aircraft during war
248	G-AEKK	27. 7.36	Dunlop Rubber Co. Ltd., Castle Bromwich, impressed 2.40
255	G-ADTD	4. 2.36	Currently owned by G. C. Marler, Thruxton
256	G-AFBF	29.11.35	Formerly D-EGYV impressed 5.40 as AV973, sold in France 2.54
259	G-AEDL	26. 5.36	E. G. H. Forsyth, withdrawn 1939
262	G-ADZL	8. 5.36	Fairey Aviation Co. Ltd., crashed during war
269	G-AEAO	18. 1.36	Sold to K. van den Hennel 3.36 as PH-EAO

MILES M.3C, M.3D AND M.3E FALCON SIX

231	G-ADLS	28. 8.35	M.3C	Withdrawn at Abbotsinch 9.40
266	G-AEAG	21. 3.36	M.3D	Sold in Australia 9.40 as VH-ABT
280	G-AECC	27. 4.36	M.3D	Impressed 1.41 as DG576, lost off the Dorset coast 8.5.59
289	G-AFCP	*nil*	M.3E	Registered 11.37, withdrawn 4.38
R4071*	G-AGZX	*nil*	*not given*	To Belgium 12.46 as OO-FLY

* Former R.A.F. serial.

MILES M.5 AND M.5A SPARROWHAWK

239	G-ADNL	21. 8.35	Converted into Sparrowjet 1951–54 with c/n F.G.M.77/1006.
264	G-ADWW	24. 6.36	To Perry Boswell, Hyattsville, Maryland, U.S.A., 11.36 as NC191M
275	G-AELT	16. 9.36	Sold in South Africa 10.37 as ZS-ANO
273	G-AFGA	20. 5.38	Withdrawn from use 1939
276	G-AGDL	3.12.41	Crashed at Tollerton 19.6.48
1006	G-ADNL	17. 6.54	Sparrowjet conversion, currently stored at Barton

MILES M.11A WHITNEY STRAIGHT AND VARIANTS

Allocation: c/n 290 G-AECT; c/n 303–326 including G-AENH, 'RS, 'RC, G-AFJJ, G-AERV, 'RY, 'TB, 'TS, 'UJ, 'UX, 'UY, 'UZ, 'VF, 'VA, 'VG, 'WA, 'VH, 'VL, 'VM, 'WK, 'WT; c/n 341–347 including G-AEYI, 'YA, 'YJ, G-AFAB, G-AEZO; c/n 497–509 including G-AFBV, 'CC, G-AEYB, 'XJ, G-AFCN, 'ZY, 'JX, 'GK. Also G-AITM.

MILES M.14 AND M.14A HAWK TRAINER MK.III (Pre-war Production)

331	G-AETJ	23. 7.37	Sold in New Zealand 4.37 as ZK-AEX
332	G-AETL	23. 7.37	Sold in New Zealand 4.37 as ZK-AEY
495	G-AEZR	31. 7.37	J. M. Barwick, Leeming
538	G-AEZS	21. 7.37	No. 8 E.R.F.T.S., impressed 3.41
539	G-AFBS	6.10.37	Impressed 3.41 as BB661, currently owned by the Denham Flying Club
542	G-AFDB	1.12.37	No. 8 E.R.F.T.S., impressed 3.41 as BB662
556	G-AFET	4. 2.38	Straight Clubs, impressed 5.40 as AV978
557	G-AFEU	17. 2.38	Crashed off Cliftonville, Kent 17.7.38
558	G-AFEV	23. 2.38	Straight Clubs, impressed 8.41
559	G-AFEW	23. 2.38	Plymouth Aero Club, crashed 1938
1080	G-AFWY	3. 8.39	No. 8 E.R.F.T.S., impressed 3.41 as BB665
1081	G-AFXA	10. 8.39	Impressed 3.41 as BB666, restored by R. A. Short 4.49
1082	G-AFXB	17. 8.39	No. 8 E.R.F.T.S., impressed 3.41 as BB667
1083–6	G-AFYV–YY	*nil*	Application for registration cancelled

MILES M.14B HAWK TRAINER MK.II

494	G-AEZP	6. 9.37	Blackburn Aircraft Ltd.
1078	G-AFTR	10. 5.39	No. 8 E.R.F.T.S., impressed 3.41 as BB663
1079	G-AFTS	18. 5.39	No. 8 E.R.F.T.S., impressed 3.41 as BB664

MILES M.14A HAWK TRAINER 3 (Post-war Conversions)

Allocation: c/n 333 erratically to 2255 including former R.A.F. aircraft between L5912 and V1102 civilianised as G-AGEO*, 'VW, 'ZR; G-AHKP, 'NE, 'NU–'NW, 'UJ–'UL, 'YK–'YM; G-AIAI, 'CD, 'CE, 'DF, 'OJ, 'OK, 'TN, 'TO, 'TR–'UG, 'YB–'YD, 'YL, 'ZJ–'ZL; G-AJCM, 'DR, 'GK–'GN, 'GP, 'HA–'HH, 'JI, 'RS–'RV, 'SF, 'ZH; G-AKAS–'AU, 'GR, 'GS, 'JV–'JX, 'KR–'KZ, 'MJ–'MU, 'MY–'NA, 'OL, 'PE–'PG, 'PL, 'PM, 'RH–'RM, 'RT–'RW, 'UA, 'XM, 'XN; G-ALFE, 'FH, 'FI, 'GJ, 'GK, 'GZ–'HB, 'IM–'IP, 'NX–'OC, 'OE–'OH, 'UW, 'UX; G-AMBM–'BP, 'MC, 'MD; G-ANLT, 'WO.

* Never flown as a civil aeroplane, broken up for spares at Thruxton 1949.

MILES M.17 MONARCH

638	G-AFCR	1. 6.38	Impressed as W6461, damaged beyond repair, Este, Venice, 2.7.57
786	G-AFGL	30. 6.38	Airwork Ltd., sold in France 3.39 as F-ARPE
787	G-AGFW	18. 8.38	Formerly and subsequently OO-UMK
789	G-AFJU	2. 9.38	Impressed as X9306, currently owned by D. Jackson, Cambridge
790	G-AFJZ	15. 9.38	Impressed 2.40 as W6462

MILES M.17 MONARCH (contd.)

792	G-AFLW	18.11.38	Currently owned by the Blackpool and Fylde Aero Club Ltd.
793	G-AFRZ	22. 4.39	Impressed as W6463, currently registered G-AIDE owned by C. M. T. Smith-Ryland, Baginton
795	G-AFTX	31. 5.39	Sold abroad 7.39

MILES M.25 MARTINET
(Former R.A.F. serial given in lieu of constructor's number)

HP145	G-AJJK	nil	Sold in Sweden 5.47 as SE-BCP
EM646	G-AJJL	nil	Sold in Sweden 5.47 as SE-BCO
HN913	G-AJJO	nil	Sold in Sweden 5.47 as SE-BCN
MS836	G-AJZB	nil	To spares at Bovingdon 3.48
MS871	G-AJZC	nil	,, ,,

MILES M.38 MESSENGER 2A
Allocation: c/n 6331–6379 including G-AHZS, 'ZT, 'UI; G-AIBD; G-AHZU; G-AIAJ, 'EK, 'DH, 'LL, 'SL; G-AJDM, 'FC; G-AIDK; G-AJKL, 'EY, 'EZ; G-AILI; G-AJFF, 'FG, 'FH, 'KK, 'OE; G-AKKC; G-AJOC, 'VC, 'VL, 'KG; G-AKAV, 'AH, 'AI, 'BN, 'BO; G-AJKT; c/n 6698–6729 including G-AJOD, 'WB; G-AKBL, 'AN, 'AO, 'BM, 'CN, 'DF, 'EZ, 'KN, 'KK, 'KI, 'KM, 'KO, 'KL, 'IM, 'IS, 'IR, 'IP, 'IN, 'IO; c/n H.P.R.146 G-AJYZ.

MILES M.38 MESSENGER 4A
(Former R.A.F. serial given in lieu of constructor's number)

6332*	G-AHFP	25.11.46	Sold in Eire 10.52 as EI-AGB
RG327	G-ALBE	6. 8.48	c/n 4691; owner B. P. Castagnoli
RH368	G-ALAP	25. 5.50	Currently owned by Finch and Knight Ltd.
RH369	G-AKZU	12.11.48	Sold in France 8.52 as F-BGOM
RH370	G-AJDF	5. 5.49	Currently owned by A. W. Ogston, Perth
RH371	G-ALAR	30. 6.49	Sold in Kenya 2.52 as VP-KJL
RH372	G-AKZC	25. 4.49	Withdrawn from use 5.59
RH376	G-ALBP	13. 4.51	Sold in Australia 11.55 as VH-WYN
RH377	G-ALAH	6. 9.48	Currently owned by D. C. Jemmett
RH378	G-ALBR	17. 9.48	Crashed at Elstree 2.7.49
RH421	G-ALAE	10. 2.49	Withdrawn from use 7.59
RH422	G-ALAG	1. 5.50	Sold in France 3.53 as F-BGQZ
RH423	G-ALAI	18. 2.49	Currently owned by the Sky Flying Group
RH424	G-AKZX	31.12.48	Currently owned by Neville Browning
RH425	G-ALAF	26.11.48	Sold in New Zealand 2.54 as ZK-BED
RH426	G-ALAW	20. 8.48	c/n 6351; currently owned by C. A. Taylor, Tollerton
RH427	G-AKVZ	8. 2.49	Currently owned by R. W. Diggens

| RH428 | G-ALAV | 26.10.48 | Currently owned by John Sutcliffe & Sons (Grimsby) Ltd. |
| RH429 | G-ALAJ | 15.10.48 | Wrecked in gale, Christchurch 29.7.56 |

* True c/n, R.A.F. serial not known.

MILES M.38 MESSENGER (Other Variants)

6266	G-AGPX	6.11.45	2B	Currently owned by P. J. Butterfield, Stapleford
6333	G-AHXR	12. 8.46	2B	Currently owned by Mrs. B. Weininger, Sywell
6267	G-AGUW	28. 2.46	2C	Sold in the Belgian Congo 8.46 as OO-CCM
4690	G-AGOY	24.10.45	3	Sold in Eire 6.53 as EI-AGE
6330	G-AHGE	13. 5.46	4	Crashed at Tugela, S. Africa, 25.10.46
6343	G-AIRY	28. 5.47	4	Sold in New Zealand 4.50 as ZK-ATT
6700	G-AKKG	12. 9.47	4	Built as HB-EEC, currently owned by B. G. Heron, Christchurch
RH420*	G-ALAC	20. 9.51	5	Written off in forced landing, Faversham 22.9.51

* Former R.A.F. serial, c/n not recorded.

MILES M.57 AEROVAN 1 and 2

(Class B markings used for test flying given in Column 4)

| 4700 | G-AGOZ | 1. 2.46 | U-0248 | Scrapped at Woodley 11.49 |
| 6432 | G-AGWO | 27. 6.46 | U-8 | Crashed 2.7.47 |

MILES M.57 AEROVAN 3

6380	G-AHTX	28. 6.46	Scrapped in the Lebanon 2.52
6382	G-AHXH	10. 9.46	To Aerovan 4; to N. V. Nastra 2.59 as PH-EAB
6383	G-AIDI	13. 9.46	Scrapped in the Lebanon 2.51
6384	G-AIHK	31.10.46	,, ,, ,,
6385	G-AIHL	28.10.46	Crashed near Kastrup 29.10.46
6386	G-AIIG	23. 1.47	Sold in Italy 11.53 as I-VALF

MILES M.57 AEROVAN 4

Allocation: c/n 6387–6389 G-AIDJ, 'HJ, 'KV; c/n 6391–6398 including G-AILB–'LE, 'SE, 'SF, 'SI, 'LM; c/n 6400–6418 including G-AILF, G-AJKP, 'KM, 'OF, G-AISG, G-AJKJ, 'KU, 'KO, 'OB, 'OG, 'OI, 'WD, 'ZG, 'TC, 'TD, 'TK, 'WK, 'WI; c/n 6420–6425, G-AJZN, 'ZP, 'ZR, G-AKKJ, 'HG, 'HD; c/n H.P.R. 144 G-AJXK; c/n 29 and 47 G-AMYA and 'YC.

MILES M.57 AEROVAN 5, 6 and H.D.M.105

6404	G-AISJ	*nil*	Crashed at Woodley 15.7.47
6399	G-AKHF	24. 1.48	Sold in Italy 5.54 as I-VALK
105/1009	G-AHDM	20. 5.57	Formerly G-AJOF, c/n 6403

MILES M.65 GEMINI 1 to 8

Allocation: c/n 4701 G-AGUS; c/n 6280–6329 including G-AJOJ, 'OK, 'OM; G-AIHI; G-AKDD; G-AISD; G-AJKN, 'FA, 'FB, 'KS, 'WA, 'WF–'WH; G-AKDB; G-AJWC; G-AKDA; G-AJZS; G-AKDE, 'EG, 'DL, 'TE, 'TF, 'TH; G-AHKL; G-AIDO, 'HM, 'DG, 'KW, 'IE, 'LG, 'IF; G-AMRG; G-AIRS; G-AKKE, G-AISK; G-ALUG; G-AJOL; G-AISN; G-AJEX, 'FD; G-AISO, 'WS, G-AJKV, 'TA: c/n 6444–6537 including G-AJTI, 'TJ, 'ZO, G-AKES, 'DJ, 'DH, 'DG, 'DI; G-AJWE; G-AILK, 'SM; G-AJKR, 'OH, 'TB, 'TG, 'WL, 'TL, 'ZI–'ZM; G-AKDK, 'EI, 'EH, 'GA, 'FZ, 'HR; G-AOXW; G-AKKH, 'EJ–'EO, 'GE, 'GG, 'HC, 'ER, 'GD, 'EP, 'FU, 'FV, 'DC. 'FW–'FY, 'GB, 'HA, 'HB, 'HE, 'HS, 'HH–'HP; G-AFLT; G-AKHT, 'HZ, 'KA, 'KD, 'KF; G-ALCS; G-AKKB; c/n H.P.R.141 G-ALZG, 145 G-AMEJ; c/n WAL/C.1002–1006 G-AMDE, 'GF; G-ALMU; G-AMKZ, 'ME; c/n 65/1001 G-AMBH.

MILES M.75 ARIES

75/1002	G-AMDJ	13. 6.52	Sold in Australia 5.54 as VH-FAV
105/1009	G-AOGA	9. 3.56	Currently owned by Pasolds Ltd.

PARNALL HECK

341	G-ACTC	18. 3.35	Scrapped before the war
J.10	G-AEGH	23.12.36	Impressed 1942 as NF749
J.11	G-AEGI	30.11.37	Scrapped at Wolverhampton 1953
J.12	G-AEGJ	6. 9.38	Cannibalised during war
J.13	G-AEGK	*nil*	Flown as G-AEMR
J.14	G-AEGL	*nil*	Experimental
J.13	G-AEMR	23. 8.39	Scrapped at Cardiff 1948
T.20	G-AFKF	29. 9.39	Scrapped during war

PERCIVAL P.1 GULL FOUR

(Individual designations given in Column 4)

D.20	G-ABUR	3. 7.32	P.1	Damaged at Luwinga, Northern Rhodesia 26.8.35
D.21	G-ACAL	10.11.32	P.1B	Crashed at Sandhurst, Kent 1.10.33
D.22	G-ABUV	24. 3.33	P.1A	Crashed 2.11.36
D.23	G-ACFJ	21. 3.33	P.1C	To Guy de Chateaubrun 1.36 as F-AOZS
D.24	G-ACAT	20. 3.33	P.1A	Sold in Australia 4.33 as VH-UQW
D.25	G-ACGC	8. 4.33	P.1C	Sold in Brazil 1.37 as PP-BAA
D.26	G-ACFY	8. 4.33	P.1A	Sold abroad 6.37
D.27	G-ACLG	8. 5.33	P.1C	Sold in India 11.34 as VT-AFV
D.28	G-ACGP	11. 5.33	P.1B	Scrapped at Thame 1946
D.29	G-ACGR	12. 5.33	P.1B	Crashed 12.34
D.30	G-ACHA	17. 6.33	P.1B	Converted to Gull Six
D.31	G-ACHM	24. 5.33	P.1C	To Melle Spitzer 5.36 as F-AQLZ

D.32	G-ACHT	14. 6.33	P.1C	Sold abroad 12.36
D.33	G-ACIP	20. 7.33	P.1B	Sold in the Netherlands 12.35 as PH-HCA
D.34	G-ACIR	26.10.33	P.1B	Crashed at Heston 20.2.35
D.35	G-ACIS	25. 7.33	P.1C	Sold in India 11.34 as VT-AFU
D.36	G-ACJP	1.11.33	P.1C	Sold in Japan 3.34 as J-BASC
D.37	G-ACJR	7.11.33	P.1C	Crashed in the English Channel 2.5.34
D.38	G-ACJW	18. 9.33	P.1C	Sold in Australia 11.34 as VH-UTC
D.39	G-ACJV	2.10.33	P.1C	Registered in Australia 1934 as VH-CKS
D.40	G-ACLJ	18.11.33	P.1B	Henlys Ltd., sold abroad 6.35
D.42	G-ACXY	22.10.34	P.1C	Converted to Gull Six
D.44	G-ACPA	16. 4.34	P.1B	,, ,,
D.45	G-ACUL	18. 8.34	P.1D	,, ,,
D.51	G-ADGK	27. 5.35	P.1D	Crashed 11.35
D.53	G-ADOE	29. 8.35	P.1E	Crashed off Ferring, Sussex 7.10.47

PERCIVAL P.3 GULL SIX

D.30	G-ACHA	17. 6.33	Sold in Australia 12.35 as VH-UTF
D.42	G-ACXY	22.10.34	Sold in France 2.36 as F-AOXY
D.44	G-ACPA	16. 4.34	Crashed at Avignon 2.10.35
D.45	G-ACUL	18. 8.34	Sold in New Zealand 9.36 as ZK-AES
D.46	G-ACUP	7. 7.34	Sold in Australia 5.39 as VH-ACM
D.47	G-ACYS	24.10.34	Sold in India 11.35 as VT-AGY, impressed as HX794
D.48	G-ADEU	26. 3.35	To M. de Suares, Rheims, 2.38 as F-AQNA
D.49	G-ADEP	20. 3.35	Brian Allen Aviation Ltd., sold abroad 8.36
D.50	G-ADFA	17. 4.35	Scrapped during the war
D.52	G-ADKX	17. 7.35	Impressed in Egypt 1940
D.54	G-ADMI	19. 8.35	To M. Lejeune Esbly 8.36 as F-APEI
D.55	G-ADPR	12. 9.35	Impressed as AX866, preserved at Luton
D.58	G-ADSG	3.10.35	Sold in India 5.8.39
D.59	G-ADSM	21.10.35	Asiatic Petroleum Co. Ltd., impressed 9.40
D.63	G-ADZO	17.12.35	H. L. Brook, scrapped during war

PERCIVAL P.2 and P.6 MEW GULL

E.20	G-ACND	11. 7.34	Prototype, scrapped at Gravesend 1934
E.20A	G-ACND	18. 7.35	Remains burned at Luton 7.7.45
E.21	G-AEKL	30. 6.36	Destroyed by bombing, Lympne 1940
E.22	G-AEXF	11. 9.36	Originally ZS-AHM, currently owned by Fred Dunkerley
E.23	G-AEMO	15. 9.36	Crashed as ZS-AHO at Bomboshawa, Southern Rhodesia 31.9.36
E.24	G-AFAA	2. 9.37	Burned at Luton 7.7.45

PERCIVAL P.10, P.10A, P.10B and P10C VEGA GULL

Allocation: c/n K.20–K.109 including G-AEAB, 'CF, 'EM, 'AS, 'HA, 'IF, 'LE, 'JJ, 'KD, 'KE, 'LF, 'LS, 'LW, 'MB, 'RH, 'RL, 'PS, 'TD–'TF, 'WO, 'WP, 'WS, 'XU, 'XV, 'YC, 'YD, 'ZJ–'ZL, G-AFAU, 'BO, 'WG, 'BC, 'AV, 'BR, 'BW, 'EA, 'EK, 'IT, 'EM, 'GU, 'IM, 'IE, 'EH, G-AHET, G-AFVI, 'BD.
Royal Air Force serials allotted to Vega Gulls impressed during World War 2:

W6464	G-AEYC	X9332	G-AFAU	X9391	G-AEXV
W9377	G-AFBW	X9339	G-AEZK	X9392	G-AFEK
X1032	G-AEXU	X9340	G-AFBC	X9435	G-AEWS
X1033	G-AERL	X9349	G-AELW	X9436	G-AEZL
X1034	G-AFAV	X9368	G-AFEM	X9455	G-AEJJ
X9315	G-AFEH	X9371	G-AEMB	BK873	G-AETF

PERCIVAL P.16, P.16A, P.16D and P.16E Q.6
(*R.A.F. impressment serial given in Column 4 where applicable*)

Q.20	G-AEYE	27. 1.38	X9328	Currently owned by J. B. Peak, Cambridge
Q.21	G-AFFD	6. 4.38	X9407	Currently owned by Walter Instruments Ltd.
Q.23	G-AFFE	13. 4.38	X9410	H. B. Legge & Sons Ltd.
Q.24	G-AFVC	15. 6.38	AX860	Formerly F-AQOK
Q.25	G-AFMT	13.12.38	X9454	Formerly VH-ABL
Q.26	G-AFHG	29. 6.38	X9329	Lord Londonderry
Q.27	G-AFGX	13. 7.38	X9336	Intava Ltd.
Q.30	G-AFIW	16. 9.38		Reduced to spares at Luton 9.49
Q.31	G-AFIX	13.12.38	X9406	Crashed at Broomhall 6.5.49
Q.32	G-AFKG	14.10.38	X9363	L. A. Hordern
Q.33	G-AFKC	30. 9.38		Last heard of in Egypt 2.40
Q.37	G-AFMV	5. 4.39	HK838	Viscount Forbes
Q.39	G-AHTB	25. 4.47		Damaged beyond repair, Almaza, 2.11.47
Q.42	G-AHOM	13. 7.46		Currently owned by Central Newbury Garages Ltd.
Q.46	G-AHTA	27. 7.46		Sold in Belgium 11.46 as OO-PQA

PERCIVAL P.28 PROCTOR I

Allocation: Luton built, ex R.A.F. P5998–P6200, c/n K.110–K.259 including G-AHDK, 'BS, 'VJ, 'LW, 'AZ, G-AIKJ, 'IP, 'EX, G-AHDH, G-AIKI, G-AGYC, G-AHVH, 'UX, G-AIHH, G-AHFU, G-AGYA, G-AHMS, 'FX, G-AILP, G-AHTC, 'DI, 'UY, G-AIKG, G-AGWV, G-AHFY; P6226–P6275, c/n K.260–K.309 including G-AHMX, G-AIEY, 'LN, G-AGYB, G-AKVV, G-AJGO, G-AHVI, G-AJLS, G-AIYH, G-AHTN, G-AIEE, 'HE, G-AGZL, G-AIIK, G-AHVB, G-AGZM, G-AHUW, 'FW, 'DJ, 'AB, 'UZ, 'MG, 'TV, 'MR; P6301–P6322, c/n K.310–K.331 including G-AHMW, G-AIEC, 'IW, G-AHVC, G-AIEF, 'IJ, 'ED.

Manchester built, ex R.A.F. R7485–R7529 including G-AHMU, 'NA, G-AIHG, 'KK, G-AHES, 'VD, 'FZ, G-AIEB, G-AHVA, G-AIHF, G-AHNF, 'VE, G-AIXP, G-AHEU, G-AIWA, G-AHKW, 'MT, 'EV; G-AIIR.

PERCIVAL P.30 PROCTOR II

Allocation: Luton built, ex R.A.F. Z7193–Z7222, c/n K.382–K.411 including G-ALMS, G-AKZN, G-ALIS, G-ANWY, G-AOGD, G-AKXI, G-AJDB; Z7237–Z7252, c/n K.412–K.427 including G-ALTG, G-AIRF, G-ALJF.
Manchester built, ex R.A.F. BV535–BV573 including G-AJTS, G-AKWO, G-AHVK, G-AIEH, G-AHMY; BV625–BV658 including G-AIHB, G-AHMP, G-ALGG, G-AJCX, G-AHNB, G-AIEI, G-AHRY, 'VF, G-AIEG, G-AHEE, G-AKAE; G-AOGE; G-AHVL, G-AJCV, G-ALUY, G-AHVG.

PERCIVAL P.34 PROCTOR III

Allocation: *Manchester built*, ex R.A.F. R7530–R7539 including G-AIKJ, G-AKWP, 'WJ; R7559–R7573 including G-AMAL, G-AOAK, G-ALFF; DX181–DX201 including G-ALES, 'FK, G-AJTT, G-ALJH, 'UJ, 'CI, G-AIFE; DX215–DX243 including G-AKWF, G-ALYC, 'CR, G-AKXZ, G-ALTF, G-AKZR, G-ALUK, 'IT, G-AIHD; HM279–HM324 including G-ALFY, G-AJWN, G-AKXJ, G-AJCN, G-ALFV, 'GP, 'JI, G-AMBS; HM337–HM373 including G-AKZD, 'XK, G-ALWR, G-AKZS, G-ALGR, G-AKWV, G-AJCU, G-ANPP, G-ALCE, G-AOEJ, G-AKAF; HM390–HM433 including G-ALCL, G-AKYG, 'WE, 'XL, 'WB, G-ANPR; HM451–HM485 including G-AGOG; LZ556–LZ603 including G-ALCG, G-AKWC, G-AMGE, G-AKWD, G-ALVA, 'CN, 'CJ, 'OK, G-AGTH, G-AHBR, G-ANGB, G-AKZE, G-AGLJ, G-AOCD; LZ621–LZ663 including G-ALFW, G-AMPL, G-ALOJ, G-AJCW, G-ALJG, G-AKWN, 'WM, 'ZF, G-ALCH; LZ672–LZ717 including G-ALER, 'OL, G-AMCO, G-ALCO, 'SM, 'CF, 'CP, G-AKWW, G-ALFC, G-AOBF, G-ALFX, 'FS, 'VE, G-AHGA, G-ALGY, G-AKWR; LZ730–LZ771 including G-AGWB, G-AHVM, G-AJVJ, G-ALJK, 'UI, G-AGVE, G-AJCY, G-AKZG, G-AMAN, G-AJCZ, G-ALCK, G-AKWU, G-AHFK, G-ALFB, G-AIWB; LZ784–LZ804 including G-AHMV, G-AIIL, G-AKEX, G-AIYF, G-ALGS, G-AHTU, G-AHGB, G-AIII, G-ANGC.

PERCIVAL P.31 PROCTOR 4

Allocation: Luton built, ex R.A.F. LA589 became G-ANXI; MX451 became G-ANWP.
Manchester built, ex R.A.F. NP156–NP198 including G-ANWR, 'WS, G-ALGL, G-AJMR, G-ANGM, G-ALEX, G-AOAP, G-ANGN, G-AOAR, G-ANYP, 'YR, G-AOAS, G-ANVW, G-AJMM, 'MI, G-ANZI, G-AJMO, G-AKLB; NP210–NP254 including G-AJMJ, G-ANXD, 'ZA, 'VK, G-AOAU, G-ANWT, G-AJMW, 'MH, G-ANWC, 'WU, G-AJMK, G-ANYS, G-AJMT; NP267–NP309 including G-ANXE, G-AOAW, G-ANWD, G-AOAX, G-AKLD, G-AJTP, G-AKLC, 'EF, G-ALEO, G-AOAY, G-ANZB, G-ANGI, G-AKWL, G-ANGO, 'ZJ, 'GP, 'WE, 'YV, 'ZC; NP323–NP369 including G-ANYT, 'WV, G-AOAZ, 'BA, G-ANWF, 'YU, 'XF, 'VJ, G-AOBW, 'BB, G-AKYI, G-ANXG, G-AJMU, G-ANWA, 'YW, G-AOBI, G-ANZD, G-AOBC, G-ANYY, 'GH; NP382–NP403 including G-AJMP, G-AOBD, G-AJMN, 'MS, 'ZA, 'MV, G-AOBE; RM160–RM197 including G-AJML, G-AGPA, G-ANVX, 'VY, G-AJMX, G-ANXH, 'YD, G-AKYJ, G-ANYZ, 'VZ; RM219–RM230 including G-ANXR, 'YC, G-AKYK, G-AOAT, 'AV. G-AHFR previous identity not known.

PERCIVAL P.44 PROCTOR 5

Allocation: c/n As. 1–3, G-AGSW, 'SX, 'SZ; c/n Ae.1, 1a, 2–150, including
G-AGSY, 'TC, 'TA, 'TB, 'TD–'TF, G-AHBA, 'BB, G-AIAA, G-AHGO,
G-AIAD, G-AHGT, 'BC–'BG, 'WU, 'BH–'BJ, 'GJ, 'GP, G-AIAB, G-AHGN,
'GK–'GM, G-AIZB, 'AC, 'EW, G-AHGR, 'GS, 'TE, 'TF, 'TD, 'TG–'TK, 'WP,
'TL, 'TM, 'WO, 'WR–'WT, 'WV–'WZ, 'ZX–'ZZ, G-AIAE–'AG, 'EM,
G-ANAT, 'MD, 'GG, G-AIEN–'ER, G-AKEB, G-AIZD, 'ES, 'ET, 'ZC, 'EU,
'EV, 'YZ, G-AKYA, 'DY, 'YC, G-AMED, G-AKYB, 'DZ, 'YD, 'CY, G-AIZA,
G-AKIH, 'EA, 'IT, 'IU, 'IX, 'IW, G-AMKM, G-AKIV, G-AMCP, 'TI, 'TJ.

PERCIVAL P.40 PRENTICE I (In order of civil conversion)

(Former R.A.F. serial given in lieu of constructor's number)

VR209	G-AKLF	1. 3.48	To the R.A.F. 1949 as VR209
VR210	G-AKLG	1. 3.48	To the R.A.F. 1949 as VR210
VS382	G-AOKT	*nil*	Test vehicle, broken up 1958
VS397	G-AOWT	19.12.58	To the Lebanon 11.58 as OD-ACQ
VS609	G-AOPL	9. 9.57	Currently owned by W. G. Pritchard, Rhoose
VR249	G-APIY	30. 7.58	Six seater with banner towing yoke
VS687	G-AONS	5. 3.58	To Australia 1958 as VH-BAO
VS613	G-AOPO	28. 3.58	To Belgium 9.58 as OO-OPO
VR200	G-APIU	12. 5.58	Currently used by Surrey Flying Club
VR192	G-APIT	13. 8.58	Currently owned by Airwork Ltd., Perth
VS282	G-APJE	6. 7.59	Prototype seven seater
VS385	G-AOLP	23.10.58	'Fonmon Castle'. Currently owned by Hubbard & Kinnear, Rhoose
VS383	G-AOLO	17.10.58	To the Belgian Congo 12.58 as OO-CIM
VR189	G-APPL	2.12.58	Currently owned by F. J. Ibbotson, Jersey
VR244	G-AONB	5. 3.59	Currently operated by No. 600 Sqn. Flying Group, Biggin Hill
VS374	G-AOLR	*nil*	Currently owned by Aviation Traders Ltd.
VR284	G-AOKF	22. 4.59	Currently operated by Maitland Air Charter Ltd., Biggin Hill
VS628	G-AOPW	8. 5.59	Crashed at Barton 9.8.59
VS621	G-AOKO	4. 6.59	Currently owned by E. F. Allchin, Elmdon
VS374	G-AOMK	24. 7.59	Currently owned by T. D. Keegan Ltd., Lulsgate
VS356	G-AOLU	27. 8.59	Currently operated by Maitland Air Charter Ltd., Biggin Hill
VR313	G-APGT	21. 9.59	Sold in the Belgian Congo 9.59 as OO-CDR

Excepting the above, the following Prentices are in long-term storage awaiting conversion:

G-AOKA–'KZ G-AOPA–'PY G-APGN–'GZ
G-AOLA–'LZ G-AOWA–'WZ G-APHA–'HS
G-AOMA–'MZ G-AOXA–'XE G-APIT–'IY
G-AONA–'NZ G-APBS–'BV G-APJA–'JI
G-AOOA–'OZ G-APGA–'GK

PERCIVAL P.48 MERGANSER, P.50 PRINCE and VARIANTS

Au.1	G-AHMH	*nil*	P.48 reduced to produce 8.48
P.50/1	G-ALCM	18. 8.48	Dismantled at Luton 7.56
P.50/2	G-ALFZ	18. 1.49	To Brazil as PP-XEG, later PP-NBA
P.50/3	G-ALJA	31. 3.49	To Borneo 7.50 as VR-SDB, later VR-UDB
P.50/7	G-ALWG	23. 3.50	To Venezuela 4.50 as YV-P-AEO
P.54/8	G-ALRY	23. 1.50	P.54, to Kenya 5.56 as VP-KNN, to France 3.59 as F-BJAJ
P.50/9	*nil*	*nil*	Test fuselage
P.50/10	G-ALWH	23. 3.50	To Venezuela 4.50 as YV-P-AEQ
P.50/11	G-AKYE	30. 4.51	To Brazil 5.51 as PP-BNF
P.50/13	G-AMMB	*nil*	To South Africa 11.52 as ZS-DGX
P.50/34	G-AMKW	16. 7.52	Currently owned by the Ministry of Aviation
P.50/35	G-AMKX	12.12.52	
P.50/36	G-AMKY	3.11.52	
P.50/37	G-AMKK	28. 3.52	To Borneo 6.52 as VR-SDR, later VR-UDR
P.50/41	G-AMNT	26. 3.52	To the Thai Air Force 4.52 as Q1-1/98
P.50/43	G-AMLW	26. 5.52	To Venezuela 8.52 as YV-P-AEB, to Australia 8.57 as VH-AGF, to France 3.59 as F-BJAI
P.50/44	G-AMLX	8.10.52	To Borneo 3.55 as VR-UDA
P.50/45	G-AMLY	22.10.52	To Venezuela 12.52 as YV-P-AEC, to Borneo 8.58 as VR-UDC
P.50/46	G-AMLZ	14.11.52	Currently owned by Stewart Smith and Co. Ltd.
P.50/47	G-AMOT	16. 7.52	Crashed in Kenya 6.6.58
P.50/48	G-AMPR	30. 9.52	To Tanganyika 2.56 as VR-TBN
P.66/13	G-APNL	*nil*	Formerly WV710, E.T.P.S. No. 25

PIPER J-2 CUB

556	G-AEIK*	5. 5.36	Scrapped during the war
957	G-AESK*	25. 3.37	Withdrawn from use 5.38
971	G-AEXY*	31. 7.37	To Spain 3.53 as EC-ALB
997	G-AEXZ	21. 1.38	Currently owned by K. W. Riley, Farnborough
1166	G-AFFH	25. 4.38	To Spain 3.53 as EC-ALA

* Built as Taylor J-2 Cubs by the Taylor Aircraft Company.

PIPER J-3 CUB

1165	G-AFFJ	6. 4.38	Sold in Germany 1.56
2348	G-AFIO	13. 3.39	Scrapped during the war
2425	G-AFIY	25. 3.39	Dismantled 7.41
2424	G-AFIZ	6.10.38	Sold in Eire 11.47 as EI-ADR

PIPER J-4A CUB COUPÉ

4-441	G-AFPP	21. 2.39	Sold in Germany 6.56 as D-EDED
4-510	G-AFSY	19. 5.39	Dismantled 5.42
4-538	G-AFSZ	31. 5.39	Impressed 11.40 as BT441, currently owned by E. R. Barker
4-541	G-AFTB	15. 6.39	Impressed 12.40 as BV989
4-525	G-AFTC	31. 5.39	Impressed 12.40 as BV990, sold in France 11.49 as F-BFQS
4-542	G-AFTD	15. 6.39	Impressed 10.41 as HL531
4-537	G-AFTE	16. 6.39	Crashed prior to outbreak of war
	G-AFVD		} Reservations for A. J. Walter, aircraft
	G-AFVE		} not imported
4-586	G-AFVF	14. 7.39	Impressed 1.41 as BV991, crashed at Gatwick 24.6.48
4-588	G-AFVG	20. 7.39	Impressed 12.40 as BV987
4-543	G-AFVL	26. 6.39	Impressed 11.40
4-554	G-AFVM	29. 6.39	Impressed 12.40
4-558	G-AFWA	7. 7.39	Impressed 3.41 as BV980
4-559	G-AFWB	13. 7.39	Impressed 3.41 as BV981
4-589	G-AFWR	24. 8.39	Impressed 11.40
4-612	G-AFWS	1. 8.39	Impressed 5.41 as ES923, sold in Finland 7.51 as OH-CPB
4-619	G-AFWU	11. 8.39	Scrapped during the war
4-622	G-AFWV	11. 8.39	Impressed 5.41
4-618	G-AFWW	11. 8.39	,, ,,
4-647	G-AFXS	28. 8.39	Impressed 2.41 as DG667, sold in Finland 5.53 as OH-CPF
4-653	G-AFXT	24. 8.39	Impressed 3.41 as DP852
NC24731*	G-AFXU	nil	Impressed 12.40 as BV984
NC24741*	G-AFXV	nil	Impressed 12.40 as BV986
NC24751*	G-AFXW	nil	Impressed 12.40
NC24761*	G-AFXX	nil	Impressed 12.40 as BV985
NC24771*	G-AFXY	nil	Impressed 12.40

* Previous American licence number.

PIPER L-4H CUB

| 11945 | G-AIIH | 19. 3.47 | Currently owned by W. T. Knapton |
| 11691 | G-AISP | 23.12.46 | Sold in the Canary Islands 11.52 as EC-AKD |

PIPER L-4H CUB (contd.)

11810	G-AISV	23.12.46	Sold in Eire 10.47 as NC74137
11780	G-AISW	23.12.46	Crashed in the North Sea 16.2.48
11663	G-AISX	4. 6.47	Withdrawn from use 2.51
10710	G-AIYU	4. 6.47	To the Netherlands 11.57 as PH-NIL
11295	G-AIYV	12. 9.47	To the Mildenhall Aero Club 7.58 as N9829F
10993	G-AIYX	12. 9.47	To West Germany 1.56 as D-EHAL
12109	G-AJBE	nil	Re-registered 5.48 as G-AKNC
11658	G-AJDS	9. 7.48	To West Germany 8.58 as D-EJYD
10780	G-AKAA	22. 8.47	Currently owned by the Skyways Flying Group, Stansted
12109	G-AKNC	nil	To the American Embassy Flying Club 5.48 as NC6400N
12156	G-ALGH	29. 4.49	To Iceland 7.52 as TF-KAP
12042	G-ALMA	3. 6.49	To West Germany 2.57
11535	G-ALVR	26. 5.50	To West Germany 9.57 as D-EKYR
12192	G-ANXP	13.10.55	To West Germany 10.55 as D-EGUL

PIPER J3C-65 CUB

21967	G-AKBS	6. 1.48	To Eire 8.48 as EI-AEB
21984	G-AKBT	25.11.47	To Portugal 11.48 as CS-AAP
22021	G-AKBU	25.11.47	To Portugal 12.48 as CS-AAQ
21962	G-AKBV	25.11.47	To Spain 1.49 as EC-AJI

PIPER PA-18A SUPER CUB

18-5503	G-AOZT	17. 4.57	Fison-Airwork Ltd., based in West Indies
18-6250	G-APKB	22. 2.58	Farmair Ltd., crashed at Nuthampstead 25.5.59
18-6459	G-APLY	23. 5.58	Currently owned by Farmair Ltd., Kidlington
18-6575	G-APPI	31.10.58	Currently owned by Farmair Ltd., Kidlington
18-6670	G-APUI	25. 5.59	Formerly EI-AKS; currently owned by Flying Farmers Ltd.
18-6644	G-APUJ	25. 6.59	Formerly N9377D; currently owned by A.D.S. (Aerial) Ltd., Stapleford
18-7062	G-APVR	8. 9.59	Currently owned by T. A. Vigors, Kidlington

PIPER PA-22 TRI-PACER

22-2098	G-AORO	4. 7.57	Formerly VP-KMY; currently owned by Waterhead-of-Dryfe Ltd., Kidlington.
22-1025	G-APTJ	3. 4.59	Formerly N1207C; sold in Rhodesia 8.59 as VP-YRE
22-5009	G-APTP	10. 4.59	Formerly EI-AJN; currently owned by County Air Charter Ltd., Yeadon
22-6711	G-APUR	27. 7.59	Currently owned by Whitbread and Co.
22-6673	G-APUT	7. 8.59	Currently owned by the Pressed Steel Co. Ltd., Kidlington

Constructor's No. and Registration		C. of A. Issued		Remarks

PIPER PA-22 TRI-PACER (contd.)

22-6741	G-APVA	23. 9.59	Currently owned by F. Scragg, Barton
22-6666	G-APWR	18. 9.59	Formerly EI-AKP; currently owned by J. J. Sledmore, Doncaster

ROBINSON REDWING

1	G-AAUO	26. 6.30	Crashed at Scarborough 5.33
2	G-ABDO	6.12.30	Last owner Miss E. R. Gerrans, Abridge
3	G-ABLA	4. 5.31	Crashed at Great Durnford, Wilts, 12.10.32
4	G-ABMJ	22. 5.31	Sold in Eire 12.34 as EI-ABC
5	G-ABMF	6. 6.31	Last owner W. H. Sparrow, Christchurch
6	G-ABMU	1. 7.31	Crashed at Ipswich 5.1.33
7	G-ABMV	22. 7.31	Sold in New Zealand 4.33 as ZK-ADD
8	G-ABNP	20. 8.31	Rebuilt as G-ABRM
9	G-ABNX	12. 3.32	Currently at Panshanger
10	G-ABOK	19.10.31	Last owner G. J. Dawson, Croydon
11	G-ABRL	21.12.34	Crashed in Dahomey 3.2.35
12	G-ABRM	22. 2.33	Crashed at Ipswich 1934

SARO A.17 CUTTY SARK

A.17/1	G-AAIP	13. 9.29	Scrapped 1935
A.17/4	G-AAVX	5. 5.30	Sold in Singapore 10.34 as VR-SAA
A.17/5	G-ABBC	2. 7.30	Scrapped during the war
A.17/8	G-AETI	28. 4.32	Originally exported to China
A.17/9	G-ABVF	30. 3.32	Sold in Japan 12.32
A.17/10	G-ACDP	11. 4.33	Scrapped during the war
A.17/11	G-ACDR	24. 4.33	Withdrawn from use 1938
A.17/12	G-ADAF	4. 2.35	Sold in San Domingo 12.35

SCOTTISH AVIATION PRESTWICK PIONEER 1

(Date of first flight given in Column 4)

101	G-AKBF	29. 5.52	5. 5.50	To R.A.F. 9.53 as XE512
103	G-ANAZ	*nil*	3. 9.53	To R.A.F. 9.53 as XE514
105	G-ANRG	26. 6.54	24. 6.54	} Demonstration aircraft
115	G-AODZ	2. 9.55	31. 8.55	
118	G-AOGF	19.12.55	18.12.55	To Iran 3.58 as EP-AHD
119	G-AOUE	26. 7.56	24. 7.56	Sold for scrap 12.56
120	G-AOXP	25. 7.57	21. 2.57	To Iran 3.58 as EP-AHE
125	G-AOGK	1. 2.58	29. 1.56	To R.A.F. 5.56 as XL517
149	G-APNW	*nil*	31. 7.58	To Ceylon 9.58 as CC603
150	G-APNX	*nil*	22. 8.58	To Ceylon 9.58 as CC604

S.878	G-AFBL	30. 3.38	'Cooee', to QANTAS 3.38 as VH-ABF, broken up 1947

SHORT S.26

S.871	G-AFCI	11. 1.42	'Golden Hind', impressed 8.40 as X8275, sank at Harty Ferry 4.54
S.872	G-AFCJ	*nil*	'Golden Fleece', impressed 8.40 as X8274, crashed in Bay of Biscay 8.41
S.873	G-AFCK	23. 3.42	'Golden Horn', impressed 8.40 as X8273, crashed at Lisbon 9.1.43

SHORT S.30 EMPIRE FLYING-BOAT

(Aircraft were broken up at Hythe unless otherwise stated)

S.879	G-AFCT	27.10.38	'Champion', broken up 4.47
S.880	G-AFCU	8. 3.39	'Cabot', impressed 10.39 as V3137, destroyed at Bodo, Norway 5.5.40
S.881	G-AFCV	7. 7.39	'Caribou', impressed 10.39 as V3138, destroyed at Bodo, Norway 6.5.40
S.882	G-AFCW	25. 3.39	'Connemara', burned out at Hythe 19.6.39
S.883	G-AFCX	29. 3.39	'Clyde', sunk in gale at Lisbon 15.2.41
S.884	G-AFCY	24. 4.39	'Awarua', to T.E.A.L. 3.40 as ZK-AMC
S.885	G-AFCZ	6. 4.39	'Australia', renamed 'Clare', lost at sea off West Africa 24.9.42
S.886	G-AFDA	12. 5.39	'Aotearoa', to T.E.A.L. 3.40 as ZK-AMA
S.1003	G-AFKZ	26. 2.40	'Cathay', broken up 3.47

SHORT S.33 EMPIRE FLYING-BOAT

S.1025	G-AFPZ	20. 4.40	'Clifton', to QANTAS 7.42 as VH-ACD, crashed at Rose Bay 18.11.44
S.1026	G-AFRA	8. 5.40	'Cleopatra', broken up 11.46
S.1027	G-AFRB	*nil*	Construction abandoned in 1940

SHORT S.25 SUNDERLAND 3

(Former R.A.F. serial given in lieu of constructor's number. Aircraft were broken up at Hamble unless otherwise stated)

JM660	G-AGER	26. 1.43	'Hadfield', broken up 7.56
JM661	G-AGES	19. 1.43	Unnamed, crashed near Brandon 28.7.43
JM662	G-AGET	5. 2.43	Unnamed, burned out at Calcutta 15.2.46
JM663	G-AGEU	15. 2.43	'Hampshire', broken up 8.53
JM664	G-AGEV	10. 2.43	'Hailsham', crashed at Poole 4.3.46
JM665	G-AGEW	8. 3.43	'Hanwell', sank at Sourabaya 5.9.48
JM722	G-AGHV	31. 8.43	'Hamble', capsized at Rod-el-Farag 9-10.3.46
ML725	G-AGHW	4. 9.43	'Hamilton', crashed at Newport, I.O.W., 19.11.47
ML726	G-AGHX	11. 9.43	'Harlequin', broken up at Hythe 10.48

SHORT S.25 SUNDERLAND 3 (contd.)

ML727	G-AGHZ	14. 9.43	'Hawkesbury', broken up 1.52
ML728	G-AGIA	17. 9.43	'Hazlemere', cannibalised 2.51
ML729	G-AGIB	23. 9.43	Unnamed, crashed near Sollum 5–6.11.43
ML751	G-AGJJ	21. 1.44	'Henley', broken up 1.52
ML752	G-AGJK	5. 2.44	'Howard', broken up 1.52
ML753	G-AGJL	19. 4.44	'Hobart', broken up 1.52
ML754	G-AGJM	16. 2.44	'Hythe', broken up 1.52
ML755	G-AGJN	10. 3.44	'Hudson', damaged at Madeira 21.1.53
ML756	G-AGJO	21. 2.44	'Honduras', damaged at Hythe 21.2.49
ML786	G-AGKV	31.10.44	'Huntingdon', withdrawn from use 5.51
ML787	G-AGKW	28. 7.44	'Hotspur', withdrawn from use 5.51
ML788	G-AGKX*	23. 8.44	'Himalaya', broken up 8.53
ML789	G-AGKY	17. 8.44	'Hungerford', sank at Calshot 28.1.53
ML790	G-AGKZ	1. 9.44	'Harwich', broken up at Hythe 5.49
ML791	G-AGLA	7. 9.44	'Hunter', broken up 8.49
EJ156	G-AGWW	14. 3.46	To Uruguay 5.46 as CX-AFA
ML876	G-AGWX	29. 3.46	To Argentine 3.46 as LV-AAS
JM716	G-AHEO	24. 2.47	'Halstead', broken up 11.49
DD860	G-AHEP	nil	'Hanbury', broken up 9.52
PP142	G-AHER	17. 4.46	'Helmsdale', broken up 1.52

* Converted to Sandringham 1.

SHORT S.25/V SANDRINGHAM 2

(Former R.A.F. serial given in Column 4)

SH.1C	G-AGPZ	17.11.45	DD864	'Argentina', sold as LV-AAO
SH.2C	G-AGPT	5.12.45	DD834	'Uruguay', sold as LV-AAP
Not given	G-AHRE	12.11.46	ML843	'Paraguay', sold as LV-ACT

SHORT S.25/V SANDRINGHAM 3

(Former R.A.F. serial given in Column 4)

SH.3C	G-AGPY	21. 1.46	DD841	'Brazil', sold as LV-AAR
SH.4C	G-AGTZ	26. 2.46	EJ170	'Inglaterra', sold as LV-AAQ

SHORT S.25/V SANDRINGHAM 5

(Former R.A.F. serial given in Column 4)

SH.31C	G-AHYY	4. 3.47	ML838	'Portsmouth', broken up at Hamworthy 3.59
SH.35C	G-AHYZ	nil	ML784	Burned out at Belfast 18.1.47
SH.34C	G-AHZA	22. 4.47	ML783	'Penzance', broken up at Hamworthy 3.59
SH.38C	G-AHZB	25. 4.47	NJ171	'Portland', crashed at Bahrein 22.8.47

SH.39C	G-AHZC	17. 5.47	NJ253	'Pembroke', broken up at Hamworthy 3.59
SH.40C	G-AHZD	28. 5.47	NJ257	'Portmarnock', to QANTAS 7.51 as VH-EBV
SH.36C	G-AHZE	16. 6.47	ML818	'Portsea', broken up at Hamworthy 3.59
SH.41C	G-AHZF	11. 7.47	NJ188	'Poole', to QANTAS 7.51 as VH-EBY
SH.37C	G-AHZG	23. 9.47	ML828	'Pevensey', to QANTAS 7.51 as VH-EBZ
Not given	G-AJMZ	18.12.47	JM681	'Perth', broken up at Hamworthy 3.59

SHORT S.25/V SANDRINGHAM 7

(Former R.A.F. serial given in lieu of constructor's number)

JM719	G-AKCO	18. 3.48	'St. George', to Australia 10.54 as VH-APG, to Tahiti 1958 as F-OBIP
EJ172	G-AKCP	15. 4.48	'St. David', to C.A.U.S.A. 3.51 as CX-ANI
ML840	G-AKCR	1. 5.48	'St. Andrew', to C.A.U.S.A. 12.50 as CX-ANA

SHORT S.45 SOLENT 2

S.1300	G-AHIL	16. 6.48	'Salisbury', converted to Solent 3 in 1950 as 'City of Salisbury'
S.1301	G-AHIM	24. 5.48	'Scarborough'
S.1302	G-AHIN	22. 4.48	'Southampton', converted to Solent 3 in 1950 as 'City of Southampton', sold in Portugal 10.58
S.1303	G-AHIO	27. 1.49	'Somerset', to Australia 10.51 as VH-TOD
S.1304	G-AHIR	4. 5.48	'Sark'
S.1305	G-AHIS	8. 7.48	'Scapa', converted to Solent 3 in 1950 as 'City of York'
S.1306	G-AHIT	10.11.47	'Severn'
S.1307	G-AHIU	2. 3.48	'Solway'
S.1308	G-AHIV	18. 2.48	'Salcombe', to Australia 1.51 as VH-TOC
S.1309	G-AHIW	25. 3.48	'Stornoway'
S.1310	G-AHIX	20.10.48	'Sussex', converted to Solent 3 in 1949 as 'City of Edinburgh', sank in Southampton Water 1.2.50
S.1311	G-AHIY	25.11.48	'Southsea', converted to Solent 3 in 1950

SHORT S.45 SOLENT 3

(Former R.A.F. serial given in Column 4)

| S.1293 | G-ANAJ | 30. 4.54 | NJ201 * | 'City of Funchal', wrecked at Santa Margherita 26.9.56 |
| S.1294 | G-AKNO | 1. 4.49 | NJ202 | 'City of London', sank at Marsaxlokk Bay, Malta 28.1.51 |

Constructor's No. and Registration	C. of A. Issued		Remarks

SHORT S.45 SOLENT 3 (contd.)

S.1295	G-AKNP	19. 3.49	NJ203	'City of Cardiff', to Australia 1.51 as VH-TOB
S.1296	G-AKNR	27. 4.49	NJ204	'City of Belfast', to New Zealand 11.51 as ZK-AMQ
S.1297	G-AKNS	24. 6.49	NJ205	'City of Liverpool'
S.1298	G-AKNT	nil	NJ206	'Singapore', to the U.S.A. 11.55 as N9947F
S.1299	G-AKNU	12.12.51	NJ207	'Sydney' crashed at Chessell Down, Isle of Wight 15.11.57

* Temporarily registered G-AGWU 12.45–2.46

SHORT S.45 SOLENT 4

SH.1556	G-AOBL	5. 5.55	'Aotearoa II', sold in Portugal 10.58
SH.1558	G-ANYI	16. 1.55	'Awateri', sold in Portugal 10.58

SHORT S.A.6 SEALAND 1

SH.1555	G-AIVX	6. 6.52	Broken up at Belfast 4.55
SH.1562	G-AKLM	28. 7.49	Crashed near Lindesnes, Norway 15.10.49
SH.1563	G-AKLN	nil	To Norway 5.52 as LN-SUF
SH.1564	G-AKLO	5. 5.50	To Borneo 10.52 as VR-SDS, later VR-UDS
SH.1565	G-AKLP	11.11.49	To Borneo 9.54 as VR-SDV, later VR-UDV
SH.1566	G-AKLR	nil	To Jugoslavia 9.51 as YU-CFJ
SH.1567	G-AKLS	nil	To Jugoslavia 9.51 as YU-CFK
SH.1568	G-AKLT	nil	To Indonesia 1.51 as PK-CMA
SH.1569	G-AKLU	6. 6.50	To Norway 5.51 as LN-SUH
SH.1570	G-AKLV	16. 4.52	Currently owned by Ralli Bros. Ltd.
SH.1571	G-AKLW	nil	To Egypt 2.52 as SU-AHY
SH.1572	G-AKLX	nil	To Pakistan 12.52 as AP-AGB
SH.1573	G-AKLY	nil	To Pakistan 12.52 as AP-AGC
SH.1574	G-AKLZ	nil	To the Indian Navy 1.53 as INS-101
SH.1575	G-AKMA	nil	To the Indian Navy 1.53 as INS-102

SIKORSKY S-51

5117	G-AJHW	24. 4.47	To Canada 6.57 as CF-JTO
5121	G-AJOO	4. 6.47	Wrecked at Fawar, Sudan 16.10.49
5126	G-AJOP	nil	To the R.A.F. 8.47 as VW209
5132	G-AJOR*	19. 8.47	To Canada 6.57 as CF-JTP
5135	G-AJOV	13.10.47	To Canada 6.57 as CF-JTQ
5128	G-AKCU	28.11.47	Crashed at the Croesor Dam 24.5.49

* Initially flown as G-28-1.

SIMMONDS SPARTAN (Two Seater)

I	G-EBYU	18. 7.28	Prototype, crashed 3.29
10	G-AAWM	8. 4.29	Crashed 12.30
11	G-AAFP	17. 4.29	Crashed 3.30
12	G-AAFR	27. 4.29	Crashed at Bursledon, Hants 27.3.30
14	G-AAGN	27. 4.29	Crashed 12.30
15	G-AAGY	7. 5.29	Scrapped at South Nutfield 8.47
17	G-AAMA	15. 7.29	Withdrawn from use 12.32
20	G-AAMC	28. 6.29	Crashed at Hanworth 28.7.29
21	G-AAMB	31. 7.29	Crashed in sea, Southend, 26.2.39
22	G-AAMH	19. 8.29	Withdrawn from use 10.29
23	G-AAHA	27. 6.29	Sold abroad 3.32
24	G-AAMD	16.12.30	Became G-ABHH 12.30, sold abroad 3.32
25	G-ABNU	21. 9.31	Scrapped at Brooklands 1948
26	G-AAME	3. 8.29	Withdrawn from use 12.31
29	G-AAGO	26. 6.30	Withdrawn from use 12.33
33	G-AAMF	*nil*	Withdrawn from use 12.30
34	G-AAMG	20. 2.30	Crashed near Leicester 19.6.30
35	G-AAMI	13. 2.30	To Norway 4.30 as N-43, later LN-ABG
36	G-AAMJ	*nil*	Withdrawn from use 12.30
37	G-AAMK	*nil*	,, ,,
38	G-AAML	11. 4.30	Crashed at Croydon 3.6.31

SIMMONDS SPARTAN (Three Seater)

19	G-AAJB	25. 6.29	Sold abroad 11.29
27	G-AAGV	17. 5.29	Crashed 9.30, rebuilt as G-ABXO
44	G-AAHV	15. 8.29	Currently at Denham

SOPWITH PUP

(Previous R.A.F. serial given in lieu of constructor's numbers for first eight aircraft)

Not given	G-EAVF	*nil*	M. E. Tanner, scrapped 1921
C440	G-EAVV	*nil*	A.D.C. Ltd., scrapped 1921
C312	G-EAVW	*nil*	F/Lt. T. Gran, Andover
B1807	G-EAVX	*nil*	A. R. M. Rickards, written off Hendon, 21.7.21
C438	G-EAVY	*nil*	A.D.C. Ltd., scrapped 1921
C540	G-EAVZ	*nil*	,, ,, ,,
C1524	G-EBAZ*	*nil*	Last owner P. T. Capon, 1923
C242	G-EBFJ	*nil*	J. T. Norquay, scrapped 1924
W/O 3004/14	G-EBKY †	*nil*	Stored at Old Warden, Beds
nil	G-APUP	*nil*	Replica under construction serialled B5292

All built by the Standard Motor Co. Ltd. 1918 except * Whitehead and † Sopwith.

SOPWITH DOVE

(Subsequent registration given in Column 4 where applicable)

W/O 2714	K-122	11. 6.19	G-EACM, sold abroad 5.20
W/O 2769/1	K-133	7. 8.19	G-EACU, sold abroad 1.23
W/O 2769/2	K-148	30. 6.19	G-EAFI, sold in Norway 7.21

SOPWITH DOVE (contd.)

W/O 3004/1	K-157	14. 8.19	G-EAGA, sold abroad 9.19
W/O 3004/2	K-168	11. 9.19	G-EAHP, sold abroad 9.19
W/O 3004/3	G-EAJI	30. 9.19	Sold in Australia 8.20 as G-AUDN*
W/O 3004/4	G-EAJJ	26. 4.20	To Australia 3.20 as G-AUJJ
W/O 3004/5	G-EAKH	17. 4.20	To Australia 3.20 as G-AUKH
W/O 3004/6	G-EAKT	17. 4.20	To Australia 3.20 as G-AUDP*
W/O 3004/14	G-EBKY	12. 4.27	Converted to Sopwith Pup

* Unconfirmed.

SOPWITH GNU

(Subsequent civil registration given in Column 4 where applicable)

A.16	K-101	*nil*	G-EAAH, crashed 7.19
W/O 2976/1	K-136	7. 7.19	G-EADB, crashed at Horley 2.3.26
W/O 2976/2	K-140	7. 7.19	G-EAEP, withdrawn 1920
W/O 3005/1	K-156	3.10.19	G-EAFR, withdrawn 10.19
W/O 2976/3	K-163	7. 8.19	G-EAGP, crashed at King's Lynn 2.5.26
W/O 2976/4	K-164	7. 8.19	G-EAGQ, withdrawn 1920
W/O 2976/5	K-169	27. 4.20	G-EAHQ, to Australia 5.20 as G-AUBX
W/O 2976/6	G-EAIL	27. 4.20	To Australia 3.20 as G-AUBY
W/O 3005/2	G-EAIM	27.10.19	To Australia 11.19
W/O 3005/4	G-EAME	*nil*	Registration cancelled 8.9.21
W/O 3005/6	G-EAMF	*nil*	,, ,, ,,
W/O 3005/5	G-EAMG	15. 1.21	,, ,, ,,
W/O 3005/3	G-E AMH	*nil*	,, ,, ,,

SOUTHERN MARTLET

2SH	G-AAII	3.10.29	To Eire 12.35 as EI-ABG
201	G-AAVD	23. 6.30	Derelict at Turnhouse 8.44
202	G-AAYX	14. 7.31	Currently at Old Warden
203	G-AAYZ	27. 6.30	Scrapped 1937
204	G-ABBN	8. 8.30	Scrapped 1935
205	G-ABIF	30. 5.31	Given to the A.T.C. 1940
31/1	G-ABJW	*nil*	Metal Martlet, scrapped 11.32
31/2	G-ABMM	*nil*	Metal Martlet, not completed

SPARTAN ARROW

51	G-AAWY	26. 6.30	Isle of Wight Flying Club, dismantled 1940
52	G-AAWZ	27. 6.30	Yapton Aero Club, scrapped during war
75	G-ABBE	27. 6.30	Sold abroad 12.31
76	G-ABKL	4. 4.31	Burned out, Hooton, 11.7.40
77	G-ABGW	10.12.30	Crashed 10.34
78	G-ABWP*	23. 7.32	Currently owned by the Spartan Group
79	G-ABWR*	24. 9.32	Sold in Denmark 8.38 as OY-DOO
80	G-ABHD	19. 1.31	Sold in Australia 2.32 as VH-UQD

81	G-ABHR	7. 1.31	Withdrawn from use 3.39
82	G-ABMK	26. 6.31	Sold in Norway 7.35 as LN-BAS
83	G-ABOB	28. 7.31	Crashed 26.8.41
84	G-ACHE*	16. 6.33	Withdrawn from use 8.38
85	G-ACHF*	7. 7.33	Burned out, Maylands, 6.2.40
86	G-ACHG*	19. 6.33	Sold in Denmark 10.35 as OY-DOK
87	G-ABST*	21. 4.32	Javelin test bed, dismantled 1936

* Ailerons on lower mainplane only.

SPARTAN THREE SEATER I

(*Last owner given in Column 4, all scrapped during the war unless otherwise stated*)

53	G-ABAZ*	26. 6.30	Isle of Wight Flying Club
54	G-ABET*	7.11.30	Lawn Parks (Skegness) Ltd.
55	G-ABKJ*	24. 4.31	,, ,, ,,
56	G-ABJS	31. 3.31	Sold in Australia 12.35 as VH-UUU
57	G-ABKT	10. 4.31	J. W. Stapleton, Peterborough
58	G-ABKK	1. 5.31	Crashed at Coventry 10.5.36
59	G-ABLJ*	22. 7.31	C. J. Rice, Leicester
60	G-ABPZ	7.10.31	Sold in South Africa 11.32
61	G-ABRA	6.10.31	E. A. Rance, Stag Lane; to Eire 1933 as EI-AAT
62	G-ABRB	9.10.31	Sold in Tanganyika 11.32 as VR-TAJ
64	G-ABTT*	20. 2.32	Crashed at Stanton, Suffolk 21.5.32
65	G-ABTU	13. 5.32	B.A.T. Ltd., scrapped 1936
66	G-ABWO	26. 5.32	Burned out, Maylands, 6.2.40
67	G-ABWU	3. 6.32	H. V. Armstrong, Hooton
68	G-ABWV	15. 6.32	Crashed and burned, Grantham 28.9.33
69	G-ABWX	25. 6.32	Crashed at Dumfries 12.9.32
70	G-ABYG	27. 7.32	W. Catton, Abridge
71	G-ABYH	19.11.32	Crashed at Hayling Island 20.7.35

* Gipsy II engine, all others Hermes II.

SPARTAN THREE SEATER II

101	G-ABTR*	2. 6.32	Burned at Gatwick 1947
102	G-ABYN	14. 9.32	Sold in Ireland 10.38 as EI-ABU
103	G-ABZH	4.10.32	Withdrawn from use 10.33
104	G-ABZI	31.12.32	Crashed at Farnborough 7.8.36
105	G-ACAD	10. 2.33	D. B. Prentice, Ford, scrapped during war
106	G-ACAF	31. 3.33	L. C. G. M. Le Champion, scrapped 1938
107	G-ACEF	27.10.36	Malling Aviation Ltd., scrapped during war

* Hermes IIB, all others Hermes IV.

SPARTAN A.24 MAILPLANE and CRUISER I

| A.24/1 | G-ABLI | 24. 2.32 | Mailplane, scrapped 2.33 |
| 24M | G-ABTY | 16. 8.32 | Lost in the English Channel 11.5.35 |

571

Constructor's No. and Registration	C. of A. Issued	Remarks

SPARTAN CRUISER II

2	G-ACBM*	21. 2.33	Sold abroad by Straight Corp'n 7.37
3	G-ACDW	12. 5.33	Sold in Egypt 4.34 as SU-ABL
4	G-ACDX	19. 6.33	Crashed at Gosport 9.10.35
5	G-ACJO	7. 9.33	Sold to Aeroput 9.33 as YU-SAN
6	G-ACMW	28. 3.34	Sold to Aeroput 5.34 as YU-SAO
7	G-ACKG*	14.11.33	Sold in India 9.35 as VT-AER
8	G-ACNO	26. 2.34	Sold to Bata 5.34 as OK-ATQ
9	G-ACOU†	14. 7.34	Sold to Bata 7.34
10	G-ACSM	13. 6.34	Impressed 4.40 as X9433
11	G-ACVT	2. 8.34	Crashed at Ronaldsway 23.3.36
12	G-ACYL	24.10.34	Impressed 4.40 as X9431
13	Not used		
14	G-ACZM	13.12.34	Destroyed 5.42

* Hermes IV. † Walter Major 4.

SPARTAN CRUISER III

101	G-ACYK	16. 4.35	Crashed at Lasas, Ayr 14.1.38
102	G-ADEL	18. 4.35	Impressed 4.40 as X9432
103	G-ADEM	3. 6.35	Crashed at Blackpool 20.11.36

STINSON SR-9 RELIANT

(Variant designation given in Column 4)

5156	G-AEVX	13. 5.37	9B H. Constant, impressed 2.40 as W7980
5253	G-AEVY	13. 5.37	9D J. R. Bryans, impressed 2.40 as W7984
5262	G-AEXW	6. 7.37	9D J. C. Knowles, impressed 2.40 as W7982
5265	G-AEYZ	11. 8.37	9D Hon. C. J. Winn, impressed 3.40 as X8521
5400	G-AFBI	9.11.37	9D Robert Blackburn, impressed 1.40 as W5791
5160	G-AFTM*	26. 7.39	9C E. O. Liebert, impressed 2.40 as W7983

* Formerly NC2217.

STINSON SR-10 RELIANT

5819	G-AFHB	28. 7.38	A. Ellison, Castle Bromwich, impressed 2.40 as W7981, converted to SR-10J, to Kenya 1.47 as VP-KDK
5904	G-AFRS	14. 7.39	Marshalls Flying School, impressed 2.40 as W7978
5911	G-AFVT	25. 1.40	Currently owned by the Fairey Aviation Co. Ltd. as SR-10J
5902	G-AGZV*	6. 5.46	To Kenya 10.47 as VP-KDV and New Zealand 6.54 as ZK-BDV

* Formerly NC21133 impressed 9.40 as BS803.

572

SUPERMARINE CHANNEL Mk.I

(Former R.A.F. serial given in Column 4)

Not given	G-EAED	23. 7.19	N1529	Written off 6.21
Not given	G-EAEE	23. 7.19	N1710	Crashed 8.19
Not given	G-EAEF	7. 8.19	N2452	To Bermuda 11.20
975	G-EAEG	28. 5.20	N2451	To Bermuda 5.20
974	G-EAEH	5. 6.20	N1716	Sold in Norway 5.20 as N-9
973	G-EAEI	28. 5.20	N1715	Sold in Norway 5.20 as N-10
972	G-EAEJ	14. 8.19	N1714	To Bermuda 5.20
971	G-EAEK	23. 7.19	N1711	Dismantled 2.21
970	G-EAEL	28. 5.20	N1528	Sold in Norway 5.20 as N-11
969	G-EAEM	17. 7.20	N1526	Sold in Norway 5.20

SUPERMARINE CHANNEL Mk.II

(No record of former R.A.F. serials now exists)

1141	G-EAWC	29.12.20	Sold in British Guiana 3.21
1142	nil	17.12.20	,, ,,
1146	G-EAWP	25. 7.21	Withdrawn in Fiji 1922

TAYLORCRAFT MODEL A and B

406	G-AFDN	14. 3.38	Impressed as instructional airframe 9.41
nil	G-AFEX	nil	Reserved for Malcolm and Farquharson Ltd.
458	G-AFHF	9. 5.38	Withdrawn from use 5.39
568	G-AFJO	10. 9.38	Crashed at Staverton 15.6.52
585	G-AFJP	10. 9.38	Crashed at Woodbridge 3.10.53
619	G-AFJW	10. 9.38	Crashed at Rearsby in 1939
628	G-AFKN	31.10.38	Crashed at Bury St. Edmunds 11.3.39
1091	G-AFKO*	5. 1.39	Scrapped during the war

* Model B.

TAYLORCRAFT PLUS C

(Impressment serials given in Column 4; ES, HH, HL and HM serials effective from 7.41, 8.41, 9.41 and 10.41 respectively)

100	G-AFNW	9. 5.39	ES956	
101	G-AFTT	16. 5.39		Impressed 7.41
102	G-AFTN	17. 5.39	HL535	Currently stored at Exeter
103	G-AFTO	22. 5.39	HL533	
104	G-AFTP	26. 5.39		Impressed 7.41
105	G-AFTY	7. 6.39		Impressed 9.41
106	G-AFTZ	15. 6.39	HH987	Currently flying as G-AHLJ
107	G-AFUA	20. 6.39		Crashed at Northaw, Mx. 18.10.48
108	G-AFUB	24. 6.39	HL534	To Eire 6.53 as EI-AGD
109	G-AFUD	29. 6.39	HH986	Became G-AHBO post-war
110	T9120	19. 6.46		Became G-AHAF post-war
111	G-AFUX	30. 6.39	HH988	
112	G-AFUY	5. 7.39	ES957	

Constructor's No. and Registration	C. of A. Issued	Remarks

TAYLORCRAFT PLUS C (contd.)

113	G-AFUZ	10. 7.39	ES960
114	G-AFVA	13. 7.39	HH982 Became G-AHAE post-war
115	G-AFVB	14. 7.39	HH985
116	G-AFVU	22. 7.39	Burned at Maylands 6.2.40
117	G-AFVW	22. 7.39	HL532
118	G-AFVX	1. 8.39	HM501
119	G-AFVY	4. 8.39	HH984
120	G-AFVZ	5. 8.39	HH983
121	G-AFWK	22. 8.39	ES958
122	G-AFWL	31. 8.39	Dismantled 5.40
123	G-AFWM	25. 8.39	ES959 Scrapped at Portsmouth 8.56

TAYLORCRAFT PLUS D (Pre-war Production)

124	G-AFWN	31. 8.39	Crashed 1942, rebuilt as Autocrat 1945
125	G-AFWO	17. 4.40	Impressed 2.41 as X7534, currently owned by Stapleford Flying Group
126	G-AFZH	15. 7.40	Impressed 2.40 as W5740, became G-AHEI post-war
127	G-AFZI	15. 7.40	Impressed 3.40 as W5741, currently owned by D. R. White
128	G-AFZJ	18. 7.40	Impressed 2.41 as X7533
129	G-AFZK	nil	⎫ Registration not taken up
130	G-AFZL	nil	⎭
131	G-AGBF	17. 7.40	Believed sold abroad 8.40
132	G-AGDB	nil	Scrapped during the war

TAYLORCRAFT PLUS D (Post-war Conversions)

Allocation: Ex R.A.F. LB263–LB299, c/n 123–169 including G-AIXA, G-AHHC, 'VP, 'UH, 'UG, 'AD, 'HB, 'CI, 'HA, 'GX, 'CH, 'WJ, 'WI; LB311–LB352, c/n 170–211 including G-AHVR, 'XE, 'SJ, 'HX, 'SB, 'AK, G-AGZN, G-AHKN, 'XG, 'SD, 'XF, 'UM, 'SL, 'SC, 'UA, 'SE, G-AIIU, G-AHAH, 'NG, 'VS, 'AI, 'GY, 'CG, 'NZ, 'CR; LB365–LB385, c/n 212–232 including G-AHSK, 'GZ, 'HY, 'SG, 'WK, 'AJ, 'GW, G-AIRE, G-AHSF, G-AIXB, G-AHKO, 'HZ, 'WD.

THRUXTON JACKAROO

(Former R.A.F. Tiger Moth serials given in lieu of constructor's number)

NL906	G-ANFY	13. 2.58	Currently operated by the Wiltshire School of Flying Ltd., Thruxton
T7798	G-ANZT	22.11.57	Currently owned by N. H. Jones, Redhill
NM175	G-AOEX	11. 7.57	Currently owned by the Wiltshire School of Flying Ltd., Thruxton
DF150	G-AOEY	11. 7.57	Sold in Nigeria 9.58 as VR-NCY
N6907	G-AOIO	15. 7.58	Currently owned by the Blackpool & Fylde Aero Club Ltd.

R4972	G-AOIR	12.12.57	Wiltshire School of Flying Ltd.
T5465	G-AOIT	14.11.58	Caledonian Flying Services Ltd.
T6917	G-AOIV	27.10.58	Sold in the Argentine 8.59
T6918	G-AOIW	23. 4.59 ⎫	
T7087	G-AOIX	20. 3.58 ⎪	Operated by the Wiltshire School of
DE978	G-APAI	30.12.57 ⎬	Flying Ltd., Thruxton
T5616	G-APAJ	5. 6.58 ⎭	
T7922	G-APAK	*nil*	Under conversion at Thruxton
N6847	G-APAL	15. 5.59	Wiltshire School of Flying Ltd.
N6850	G-APAM	29.10.59	Miss S. Scott, Thruxton
R4922	G-APAO	1. 5.59	J. S. Read, Thruxton
R5136	G-APAP	11. 9.59	Wiltshire School of Flying Ltd.
N6924	G-APHZ	8. 7.58	Currently owned by Airspray (Colchester) Ltd., Boxted
N7446	G-APJV	30. 1.59	Currently owned by Glamorgan Aviation Ltd., Rhoose
R5130	G-APOV	*nil*	Currently owned by Rollason Aircraft and Engines Ltd., Redhill
N6667	G-APRB	*nil* ⎫	
T8197	G-APRC	*nil* ⎪	Under conversion at Thruxton by
N6585	G-APSU	*nil* ⎬	Jackaroo Aircraft Ltd.
DE636	G-APSV	*nil* ⎭	

TIPSY S.2 (British Built)

T.51*	G-AEOB	14. 1.37	Scrapped at Hanworth 12.37
102	G-AESU	22. 4.37	Crashed 9.37
103	G-AEWJ	*nil*	Crashed at Broadstairs 6.6.37
104	G-AEXK	*nil*	Scrapped at Hooton 8.37
105	G-AEXL	*nil*	Withdrawn from use 1937
106	G-AEYG	*nil*	,, ,,
107	G-AEYH	*nil* ⎫	
108	G-AEZV	*nil* ⎬ Undelivered	
109	G-AEZW	*nil* ⎭	

* Later 101.

TIPSY S.2 (Belgian Built)

20	OO-TIP*	3. 6.36	E. O. Tips, c/o The Fairey Aviation Co. Ltd.
28	G-AENF	29.10.36	Formerly OO-ASA, burned 1948
29	G-AFVH	8. 7.39	Formerly OO-ASB, to Belgium 7.49
36	G-AFFN	9. 3.38	Formerly OO-ASJ, broken up at Blackbushe 2.53

* Tipsy S.1 prototype.

TIPSY B AND BC (Belgian Built)

(Previous registrations given in Column 4)

502	G-AGBM	*nil*	OO-DOP	Sold in Belgium 1.47 as OO-DOP
503	G-AFCM	1. 5.38	OO-DOS	Burned at Slough 1952
506	G-AFEI	18. 1.38	OO-DOV	Burned at Hooton 11.7.40

Constructor's No. and Registration	C. of A. Issued		Remarks

TIPSY TRAINER 1

1	G-AFGF	26. 8.38	Burned at Slough 1952
2	G-AFJR	6.10.38	Converted to Belfair, currently flying
3	G-AFJS	22.10.38	Crashed at St. Mellons, S. Wales, 3.7.55
4	G-AFJT	21.11.38	Sold in Finland 8.50 as OH-SVA
5	G-AFKP	9.12.38	Crashed at Gedaref, Sudan, 4.6.52
6	G-AFMN	27. 1.39	Burned at Hooton 11.7.40
8	G-AFRT	1. 5.39	Burned at Slough 1952
9	G-AFRU	17. 7.39	Broken up at Redhill 3.54
10	G-AFRV	22. 7.39	Currently owned by J. H. Reed, Woolsington
11	G-AFSC	18. 7.39	Currently owned by the A.S. Flying Club, Baginton
12	G-AFVN	21. 7.39	Currently owned by the Montgomeryshire Ultra Light Flying Club
13	G-AFWT	5. 8.39	Currently owned by J. O. Hodgson
14	G-AFVP	29. 8.39	Broken up during the war
15	G-AFVO	29. 6.39	Sold in Belgium 9.46 as OO-DAU
17	G-AISA	27. 6.47	Currently owned by the Cardiff Ultra Light Aeroplane Club
18	G-AISB	29. 9.47	Currently owned by R. F. Wright
19	G-AISC	16. 4.48	Currently owned by the Fairey Aviation Ltd.

TIPSY BELFAIR

(Intended Belgian registration given in Column 4, current owner in Column 5)

2	G-AFJR	27. 1.58	Conversion	G. A. and T. L. Southerland
535	G-APIE	25. 7.58	OO-TIE	Mrs. E. S. Walters, Yeadon
536	G-APOD	*	OO-TIF	D. A. Taylor, Yeadon
537	G-AOXO	21.11.58	OO-TIG	J. C. Riddell, Yeadon

* Not yet certificated.

VICKERS F.B.27A VIMY IV

(Former R.A.F. serial given for the 2nd and 3rd aircraft)

C-105	G-EAAR	*nil*	Registration cancelled 5.20
F8625	G-EAOL	*nil*	Believed sold in Spain 1920
F8630	G-EAOU	3.11.19	Currently stored in Australia

VICKERS F.B.28 VIMY COMMERCIAL

nil	K-107*	20. 7.19	Crashed as G-EAAV, Tabora, 27.2.20
41	G-EASI	13. 5.20	Instone 'City of London'
40	G-EAUL	18. 8.20	Sold in France 8.21
39	G-EAUY	*nil*	Registration cancelled 2.21

* Initially F.B.27B.

VICKERS TYPE 61 VULCAN

1	G-EBBL	23. 6.22	Instone 'City of Antwerp'
2	G-EBDH	28. 8.22	Crashed at Oxted, Surrey 1922
3	G-EBEA	28. 8.22	Sold to Vickers Ltd. 6.23
4	G-EBEK	6.11.22	Air Council, scrapped 1926
5	G-EBEM	15. 9.22	Lost at sea 5.7.26
6	G-EBES	nil	Rejected by QANTAS 4.23
7	G-EBET	27.11.22	,, ,,
8	G-EBFC	23.12.24	Broken up at Croydon 1926
9	G-EBLB	11. 5.25	Crashed at Purley 13.7.28

VICKERS-SUPERMARINE TYPE 236 WALRUS I

(Built at Woolston by Supermarine 1939, metal hulls, R.A.F. serial given in lieu of constructor's number)

L2246	G-AHFL	2. 8.46	'Boojum', United Whalers Ltd., to Norway 7.48
W3070	G-AHFM	25. 7.46	'Moby Dick', scrapped at Cowes 7.50
L2336	G-AHFN	27. 8.46	Wrecked in Loch Ryan 3.7.55
L2282	G-AHFO	8. 7.46	'Snark', scrapped at Cowes 7.50
W2688	G-AHTO	nil	United Whalers Ltd., scrapped at Cowes 7.50
Z1763	G-AHTP	nil	,, ,, ,,
X9467	G-AIIB	nil	Wrecked at Weston-super-Mare 1947
N-18*	G-AIZG	nil	Formerly EI-ACC, scrapped at Thame 1947
'4501'	G-AMCS	nil	F. C. Bettison, not taken up

* Originally built for the Irish Air Corps.

VICKERS-SUPERMARINE TYPE 236 WALRUS II

(Built at Cowes by Saunders-Roe 1942–44, wooden hulls, R.A.F. serial given in lieu of constructor's number)

S2/10761*	G-AIEJ	6.11.47	Western Airways Ltd., scrapped 12.48
HD915	G-AIKL	nil	Western Airways Ltd., scrapped 10.47
HD867	G-AIWU	15. 8.47	Used in Tangier, scrapped 7.50
S2/8474*	G-AJJC	25. 5.48	Essex Aero Ltd., sold in Norway 9.49 as LN-SUK
HD916	G-AJJD	nil	Essex Aero Ltd., scrapped 3.49
S2/23642*	G-AJNO	nil	Scottish Airlines, broken up 1959
S2/8757*	G-AJNP	nil	Scottish Airlines, not taken up
HD925	G-AKJE	nil	Ciro's Aviation Ltd., scrapped at Redhill 1952

* Constructor's number given where R.A.F. serial not recorded.

VICKERS-SUPERMARINE TYPE 309 SEA OTTER

(*Former R.A.F. serial given in lieu of constructor's number*)

014352*	G-AIDM	23. 4.47	Sold in Venezuela 11.47
JM747	G-AJFU	nil	British Aviation Services Ltd., scrapped at Blackbushe 1950
JM959	G-AJFV	21. 4.49	Sold in Burma 4.49 as XY-ABT
JM957	G-AJFW	nil	As G-AJFU above
181716*	G-AJLT	nil	} British South American Airways,
129893*	G-AJLU	nil	} scrapped at Langley 1949
JM966	G-AJVR	nil	J. M. McEwan Gibb, not used
JM826	G-AKIC	nil	} Ciro's Aviation Ltd., scrapped at
JM764	G-AKID	nil	} Redhill 1950
—	G-AKPN–'PV	nil	Sold in Egypt by J. Patient 2.49 (JN139, JN114, JM989, JN197, JN187, JN138, JN137, JN194 respectively)
JM977	G-AKRF	nil	Left Gravesend for Holland 6.49
JN134	G-AKRG	nil	Scrapped at Burnaston 1957
JM968	G-AKRX	nil	As G-AJLT above
JM739	G-AKWA	nil	,, ,,
JM966	G-AKYH	nil	Converted at Squires Gate, sold abroad 10.49
JM827	G-ALTX	nil	Autocars (Worc.) Ltd., sold abroad 3.50
JM818	G-ALVB	nil	Essex Aero Ltd., sold abroad 10.49

* Constructor's number given where R.A.F. serial not recorded.

VICKERS VIKING 1A (Prototypes)

1	G-AGOK	nil	Broken up at Shoebury, Essex 1.47
2	G-AGOL	nil	To the R.A.F. 2.50 as VX238
3	G-AGOM	24. 4.46	To the R.A.F. 12.47 as VX141

VICKERS TYPE 498 VIKING 1A

Allocation: c/n 4–9, 110–112, 114–119 and 121–124 including G-AGON, 'RM– 'RW, G-AHON, 'OP–'OW

British European Airways Fleet 1946

G-AGRU	Vagrant	G-AHOP	Valerie	G-AHOU	Valley
G-AGRV	Value	G-AHOR	Valet	G-AHOV	Valour
G-AGRW	Vagabond	G-AHOS	Valiant	G-AHOW	Vanessa
G-AHON	Valentine	G-AHOT	Valkyrie		

VICKERS TYPE 614 VIKING 1

Allocation: c/n 125, 127–134, 137–139, 141, 142 and 147, including G-AHOX, G-AIJE, G-AHOY–'PA, G-AIKN, G-AHPB–'PJ

British European Airways Fleet 1947

G-AHOX	Vanguard	G-AHPB	Variety	G-AHPF	Vedette
G-AHOY	Vanity	G-AHPC	Vassal	G-AHPG	Velocity
G-AHOZ	Vantage	G-AHPD	Vampire	G-AHPJ	Vengeance
G-AHPA	Varlet	G-AHPE	Vandal		

VICKERS TYPE 610 VIKING 1B

Allocation: c/n 146, 148–167, including G-AIHA, G-AHPK–'PS; c/n 215–229
G-AIVB–'VP; c/n 239–250 G-AJBM–'BY; c/n 252 G-AJCA; c/n 256–260
G-AJCD, 'CE, 'DI–'DK; c/n 262–264 G-AJDL, G-AKBG, 'BH; c/n 289–297
G-AJJN, G-AMGG, 'NR, 'NX, 'GH, 'NS, 'GJ, 'NJ, 'GI

British European Airways Fleet 1947

G-AHPK	Veracity	G-AIVI	Victor	G-AJBU	Virtue
G-AHPL	Verdant	G-AIVJ	Victoria	G-AJBV	Viscount
G-AHPM	Verderer	G-AIVK	Victory	G-AJBW	Vista
G-AHPN	Ventnor	G-AIVL	Vigilant	G-AJBX	Vital
G-AHPO	Venture	G-AIVM	Vigorous	G-AJBY	Vitality
G-AHPP	Venus	G-AIVN	Violet	G-AJCA	Vixen
G-AHPR	Verily	G-AIVO	Villain	G-AJCD	Vizor
G-AHPS	Verity	G-AIVP	Vimy	G-AJCE	Vivacious
G-AIVB	Vernal	G-AJBM	Vincent	G-AJDI	Volatile
G-AIVC	Vernon	G-AJBN	Vindictive	G-AJDJ	Volley
G-AIVD	Veteran	G-AJBO	Vintage	G-AJDK	Volunteer
G-AIVE	Vestal	G-AJBP	Vintner	G-AJDL	Votrex
G-AIVF	Vibrant	G-AJBR	Virginia	G-AKBG	Votary
G-AIVG	Viceroy	G-AJBS	Virgo	G-AKBH	Voyager
G-AIVH	Vicinity	G-AJBT	Viper		

(G-AHPK crashed at Ruislip 6.1.48; G-AHPN at London Airport 31.10.50;
G-AIVE at Largs, Ayrshire 21.4.48; G-AIVP at Berlin 5.4.48)

British European Airways Admiral Class 1951

G-AHPL	Lord Anson	G-AJBT	Sir Thomas Troubridge
G-AHPM	Lord Rodney	G-AJBU	Lord Bridport
G-AHPO	Lord Dundonald	G-AJBV	Sir Henry Morgan
G-AHPP	Sir Charles Saunders	G-AJBW	Sir William Cornwallis
G-AHPR	Prince Rupert	G-AJBX	Sir Edward Hughes
G-AHPS	Sir Doveton Sturdee	G-AJBY	Lord Torrington
G-AIVB	Robert Blake	G-AJCA	Sir John Leake
G-AIVC	Lord Collingwood	G-AJCD	Lord Barham
G-AIVD	Lord Duncan	G-AJCE	Lord Exmouth
G-AIVF	Sir James Somerville	G-AJDI	Lord Keith
G-AIVG	Sir George Rooke	G-AJDJ	Lord Beatty
G-AIVH	Lord Howe	G-AJDK	Richard Kempenfelt
G-AIVI	Viking	G-AJDL	Lord St. Vincent
G-AIVJ	Lord Jellicoe	G-AJJN	Sir Charles Napier
G-AIVK	Lord Keyes	G-AKBG	Sir Thomas Hardy
G-AIVL	Lord Hawke	G-AKBH	Lord Hood
G-AIVM	George Monck	G-AMGG	Sir Robert Calder
G-AIVN	Edward Boscawen	G-AMGH	Sir John Duckworth
G-AIVO	Edward Vernon	G-AMGI	Sir Henry Harwood
G-AJBM	Charles Watson	G-AMGJ	Sir John Warren
G-AJBN	Lord Nelson	G-AMNJ	Lord Fisher
G-AJBO	John Benbow	G-AMNR	Lord Charles Beresford
G-AJBP	Sir Edward Spragge	G-AMNS	Sir Dudley Pound
G-AJBR	Sir Bertram Ramsey	G-AMNX	Sir Philip Broke
G-AJBS	Sir Cloudesley Shovel		

VICKERS VISCOUNT 701

British European Airways Corporation Fleet

G-ALWE	Discovery	G-AMOK	Sir Humphrey Gilbert
G-ALWF	Sir John Franklin	G-AMOL	David Livingstone
G-AMNY	Sir Ernest Shackleton	G-AMOM	James Bruce
G-AMNZ	James Cook	G-AMON	Thomas Cavendish
G-AMOA	George Vancouver	G-AMOO	John Oxenham
G-AMOB	William Baffin	G-AMOP	Mungo Park
G-AMOC	Richard Chancellor	G-ANHA	Anthony Jenkinson
G-AMOD	John Davis	G-ANHB	Sir Henry Stanley
G-AMOE	Sir Edward Parry	G-ANHC	Sir Leopold McClintock
G-AMOF	Sir Martin Frobisher	G-ANHD	William Dampier
G-AMOG	Robert Falcon Scott	G-ANHE	Gino Watkins
G-AMOH	Henry Hudson	G-ANHF	Matthew Flinders
G-AMOI	Sir Hugh Willoughby	G-AOFX	Sir Joseph Banks
G-AMOJ	Sir James Ross		

(G-ALWE crashed at Ringway 14.3.57; G-AMNY destroyed at Malta 5.1.60;
G-AMOM crashed at Blackbushe 20.1.56; G-ANHC at Anzio, Italy 22.10.58)

VICKERS VISCOUNT 802

British European Airways Corporation Fleet

G-AOJA	Sir Samuel White Baker	G-AOHM	Robert Machin
G-AOJB	Stephen Borough	G-AOHN	Alexander Gordon Laing
G-AOJC	Robert O'Hara Burke	G-AOHO	Samuel Wallis
G-AOJD	Sebastian Cabot	G-AOHP	James Weddell
G-AOJE	Sir Alexander Mackenzie	G-AOHR	Sir Richard Burton
G-AOJF	Sir George Somers	G-AOHS	Robert Thorne
G-AOHG	Richard Hakluyt	G-AOHT	Ralph Fitch
G-AOHH	Sir Robert McClure	G-AOHU	Sir George Strong Nares
G-AOHI	Sir Robert Montague	G-AOHV	Sir John Barrow
	Doughty	G-AOHW	Sir Francis Younghusband
G-AOHJ	Sir John Mandeville	G-AORC	Richard Lauder
G-AOHK	John Hanning Speke	G-AORD	Arthur Phillip
G-AOHL	Charles Sturt		

(G-AOJA crashed at Nutts Corner 32.10.57; G-AOHP at Copenhagen 17.11.57;
G-AOHU burned out at London Airport 7.1.60; G-AORC crashed at Craigie,
Ayrshire 28.4.58)

VICKERS VISCOUNT 806

British European Airways Corporation Fleet

G-AOYG	Charles Darwin	G-AOYP	John Napier
G-AOYH	William Harvey	G-AOYR	Sir Richard Arkwright
G-AOYI	Sir Humphry Davy	G-AOYS	George Stephenson
G-AOYJ	Edward Jenner	G-AOYT	James Watt
G-AOYK	Edmund Cartwright	G-APEX	John Harrison
G-AOYL	Lord Joseph Lister	G-APEY	William Murdock
G-AOYM	John Loudon McAdam	G-APIM	Robert Boyle
G-AOYN	Sir Isaac Newton	G-APJU	Sir Gilbert Blane
G-AOYO	Adam Smith	G-APKF	Michael Faraday

VICKERS TYPE 951 and 953 VANGUARD

British European Airways Corporation Fleet

G-APEA Vanguard	G-APEH Audacious	
G-APEB Bellerophon	G-APEI Indefatigable	G-APEO Orion
G-APEC Sirius	G-APEJ Ajax	G-APEP Superb
G-APED Defiance	G-APEK Dreadnought	G-APER Amethyst
G-APEE Euryalus	G-APEL Leander	G-APES Swiftsure
G-APEF Victory	G-APEM Agamemnon	G-APET Temeraire
G-APEG Arethusa	G-APEN Valiant	G-APEU Undaunted

WESTLAND LIMOUSINE I and II

W.A.C.1	K-126*	21. 8.19	Later G-EAFO, wrecked at Netheravon 3.9.25
W.A.C.2	G-EAJL	16.10.19	Sold in Newfoundland 8.22
W.A.C.3	G-EAMV	27. 4.20	,, ,, ,,
W.A.C.4	G-EARE	7.10.20†	Instone Air Line, scrapped 1923
W.A.C.5	G-EARF	21.10.20†	,, ,, ,,
W.A.C.6	G-EARG	29. 9.22	Sold in Newfoundland 11.22
W.A.C.7	G-EARH	*nil*	Believed not constructed

* Limousine I.   † With 300 h.p. Hispano-Suiza.

WESTLAND LIMOUSINE III

W.A.C.8	G-EARV	7. 8.20	Sold in Newfoundland 1.21
W.A.C.9	G-EAWF	13. 4.21	Air Council, scrapped 11.25

WESTLAND WIDGEON I to III

WA.1671	G-EBJT*	16. 9.26	Crashed near Detling 10.10.30
WA.1677	G-EBPW	12. 4.27	Burned out, Bournemouth 6.6.27
WA.1679	G-EBRL	14. 7.27	Crashed at Yeovil 3.6.31
WA.1682	G-EBRO	27. 8.27	Scrapped during the war
WA.1684	G-EBRQ	26. 7.27	Withdrawn from use 5.36
WA.1694	G-EBRP	20. 1.28	Sold in India 1.28 as G-IAAW
WA.1695	G-EBUB	19. 3.28	Sold in Australia 8.28 as G-AUHU
WA.1696	G-EBUC		⎫
WA.1697	G-EBUD		⎬ Not taken up
WA.1698	G-EBUE		⎭
WA.1724	G-EBRN	28. 3.28	Burned at Stranraer 1951
WA.1778	G-AADE	6. 3.29	C. S. Napier, crashed 9.32

* Widgeon II, initially Widgeon I, c/n W.1.

WESTLAND WIDGEON IIIA

WA.1680	G-EBRM	13. 9.27	Scrapped at Brooklands 12.31
WA.1776	G-AAJF	2. 7.29	Miss C. Leathart, crashed 7.31
WA.1779	G-AAFN	26. 3.29	Westland Aircraft Works, crashed 1.30
WA.1782	G-AAFD	25. 3.29	'Miss Ethyl', crashed 6.6.33
WA.1783	G-AALB	1. 8.29	Sold in Canada 1.30 as CF-AIQ
WA.1866	G-AAGH	18. 9.30	Burned out at Merryfield, 27.7.48

Constructor's No. and Registration		C. of A. Issued	Remarks

WESTLAND WESSEX

WA.1771	G-EBXK	21. 3.29	Converted Westland IV, crashed 5.36
WA.1876	G-AAGW	21.10.29	Converted Westland IV, scrapped 1940
WA.1897	G-AAJI	nil	Converted to Wessex G-ABAJ
WA.1897	G-ABAJ	27. 5.30	SABENA OO-AGC; scrapped 1938
WA.1899	G-ADEW	6. 8.30	OO-AGE; lost in the Channel 3.7.35
WA.1900	G-ADFZ	30. 8.30	OO-AGF; scrapped 1936
WA.1901	G-ABEG	2.10.30	Crashed in Northern Rhodesia 1936
WA.2151	G-ACHI	23. 6.33	Scrapped at Hamble 1940
WA.2152	G-ACIJ	27. 9.33	To the Egyptian Air Force 5.34 as W202
WA.2156	G-ABVB	6. 5.32	Crashed at Ryde 30.5.36

WESTLAND SIKORSKY S-51 Mk.1A

WA/H/1	G-AKTW	24. 7.51	Temporarily XD649, to Widgeon 1956
WA/H/2	G-ALEG	26. 4.49	To the R.A.F. 1951 as WZ749
WA/H/3	G-ALIK	25. 4.49	Converted to Widgeon 1955
WA/H/4	G-ALEI	12. 5.49	Crashed at Sion, Switzerland 4.5.50
WA/H/5	G-ALIL	nil	To the R.A.F. 3.49 as WB810
WA/H/6	G-ALMB	31. 3.50	Sold in Italy 4.51 as I-MCOM
WA/H/7	G-ALMC	nil	To the R.A.F. 11.50 as WF308
WA/H/20	G-AMAK	nil	Crashed at Yeovil 7.6.50
WA/H/26	G-AMAS	nil	Sold in Thailand 6.50
WA/H/27	G-AMAT	nil	,, ,,
WA/H/120	G-AMJW	22. 5.53	Sold in Thailand 5.53
WA/H/122	G-AMOW	nil	Sold in Italy 1.53 as MM80038
WA/H/123	G-AMOX	nil	Sold in Italy 1.53 as MM80040
WA/H/121	G-AMRE	26. 9.52	Temporarily LN-ORG, crashed at Yeovil 29.4.57
WA/H/90	G-ANAL	3. 7.53	Currently flying as G-ANZL
WA/H/91	G-ANAM	nil	Sold in Japan 6.53 as JA-7014
WA/H/130	G-ANGR	18. 1.54	Sold in Japan
WA/H/131	G-ANGS	18. 1.54	,, ,,
WA/H/132	G-ANLV	8. 7.54	Crashed at Montfort L'Armory, France 14.6.57
WA/H/133	G-ANLW	6. 7.54	Converted to Widgeon 1957
WA/H/134	G-AOAJ	22. 4.55	Crashed at Yeovil 25.10.56
WA/H/139	G-AOHX	nil	Sold in Japan 5.56 as JA-7025

WESTLAND SIKORSKY S-51 Mk.1B

WA/H/11	G-ALKL	nil	To the Egyptian Air Force 11.49
WA/H/12	G-ALMD	nil	,, ,, ,,
WA/H/29	G-AMHC	16.10.51	To the Congo 1.52 as OO-CWB
WA/H/30	G-AMHB	15. 3.51	To the Congo 5.51 as OO-CWA
WA/H/48	G-AMHD	19.10.51	To the Congo 2.52 as OO-CWC

WESTLAND SIKORSKY S-51 SERIES 2 WIDGEON

WA/H/1	G-AKTW	30. 8.56	Currently flying as G-APPR
WA/H/3	G-ALIK	7. 1.57	Currently flying as G-APPS
WA/H/133	G-ANLW		Current Westland demonstrator
WA/H/140	G-AOZD	12. 8.57⎱	Currently operated by Bristow Heli-
WA/H/141	G-AOZE	12. 8.57⎰	copters Ltd.
WA/H/145	G-APBK	11.12.57	Sold in Hong Kong 10.57 as VR-HFL
WA/H/146	G-APBL	13.12.57	Sold in Hong Kong 10.57 as VR-HFM
WA/H/149	G-APTE	22. 4.59	Operated by Bristow Helicopters Ltd.
WA/H/150	G-APTW	1. 6.59	Operated by Executair Ltd., Elstree
WA/H/151	G-APVD	9. 7.59	Westland Aircraft Ltd., Yeovil
WA/H/152	G-APWK	8. 9.59	,, ,, ,,

WESTLAND SIKORSKY S-55 SERIES 1

55016	G-AMHK*	nil	Evaluated as WW339, sold in Norway 9.53 as LN-ORK
WA/A/1	G-AMJT	nil	To the R.A.F. 3.53 as XA862
WA/A/4	G-AMYN	nil	To the Aeronavale, France 4.54
WA.15	G-ANFH	2.11.54	Currently B.E.A.C. 'Sir Ector'
WA.18	G-ANJS	15. 7.54	Lost off the Brazilian coast 5.11.55
WA.19	G-ANJT	16. 7.54	Lost in Antarctic waters 29.1.58
WA.23	G-ANJU	17. 9.54	Lost in the Atlantic 20.12.56
WA.24	G-ANJV	30. 9.54⎱	Currently owned by the South
WA.39	G-ANUK	4. 5.55⎰	Georgia Co. Ltd.
WA.54	G-ANZN	9. 6.55	To the Bahamas 7.55 as VP-BAF
WA.55	G-ANZO	9. 6.55	To the Bahamas 7.55 as VP-BAG
WA.56	G-AOCF	29. 8.55	Currently owned by B.E.A.C.
WA.113	G-AODA	9. 9.55⎱	Currently operated by the Shell Refin-
WA.114	G-AODB	13. 9.55⎰	ing Co. Ltd. in Bahrein
WA.116	G-AODO	20. 2.56⎱	Currently owned by Fison-Airwork
WA.117	G-AODP	30. 4.56⎰	Ltd.
WA.126	G-AOHE	5.10.56	Currently owned by the South Georgia Co. Ltd.
WA.173	G-AORT	20.11.56	To Saudi Arabian Airlines 12.56 as HZ-ABE
WA.191	G-AOYB	11. 4.57⎱	Currently owned by Fison-Airwork
WA.240	G-AOZK	10. 1.58⎬	Ltd.
WA.250	G-APKC	7. 2.58⎰	
WA.295	G-APRV	7. 4.59	Sold in Bermuda 3.59 as VR-BBE
WA.296	G-APRW	7. 4.59	Sold in Bermuda 3.59 as VR-BBF
WA.297	G-APWM	23.10.59	H. H. Shaikh Abdullah Mubarak al Sabah C.I.E., Kuwait
WA.298	G-APWN	20.10.59	Westland Aircraft Ltd., Yeovil
WA.299	G-APWO	20.10.59	,, ,, ,,
WA.318	G-APXA	12.12.59⎱	H. H. Shaikh Abdullah Mubarak al
WA.319	G-APXB	1. 1.60⎬	Sabah C.I.E., Kuwait
WA.320	G-APXC	20. 2.60⎰	

* American built.

583

Constructor's No. and Registration	C. of A. Issued		Remarks

WESTLAND-SIKORSKY S-55 SERIES 2

WA.115	G-AOCZ	28. 6.55	Current demonstrator
WA.192	G-AOYY	16. 7.57	Sold in Canada 7.57 as CF-KAD
WA.193	G-AOYZ	16. 7.57	Sold in Canada 7.57 as CF-KAE
WA.241	G-APDY	13.11.57	Current demonstrator
WA.268	G-APPY	22. 4.59	Sold in Iran 4.59 as EP-BSK
WA.269	G-APPZ	16. 7.59	Sold in Iran 4.59 as EP-CSK

INDEX OF AEROPLANES

All aircraft mentioned in this book are listed in the index, including those outside the British civil E to Z range. Listing is arranged alphabetically by manufacturers and then in order of type numbers. Where these were not allotted, an alphabetical or chronological list of type names is used. Where aircraft are mentioned in the main narrative, only the first page of that narrative is listed. Pages allotted to each manufacturer in the main narrative and appendixes will be found on pages 7 to 10.

589

591

INDEX OF ENGINES

Note: Where engines are mentioned in the main narrative, only the first page of that narrative is listed.

There are no bits in the beehive. No dust,
no dirt. Before getting down to production
the bees set about the complete
elimination of impurities. As
with bees, so with AIR BP.

BP devotes much time and technical skill in laboratory and field
to perfect fuel cleanliness.
New equipment developed or
adapted by BP engineers already
achieves standards far higher
than are demanded. Great strides
have been made in micro-filtration
(rating 5 microns) and free water separation
(30 parts per million limit) to ensure the delivery
of the cleanest fuel at the maximum rate
to aircraft on busy international routes.

Clean sweep

AIR BP work on these lines continues,
aiming at a clean sweep of the minutest contaminants
in the service of aviation.

WEAVER

AIR BP